Introduction to
Computer Security

Introduction to
Computer Security

Matt Bishop

✦✦Addison-Wesley

Boston • San Francisco • New York • Toronto • Montreal
London • Munich • Paris • Madrid
Capetown • Sydney • Tokyo • Singapore • Mexico City

The publisher offers discounts on this book when ordered in quantity for bulk purchases and special sales. For more information, please contact:

U.S. Corporate and Government Sales
(800) 382-3419
corpsales@pearsontechgroup.com

For sales outside of the U.S., please contact:

International Sales
international@pearsoned.com

Visit Addison-Wesley on the Web: www.awprofessional.com

Library of Congress Cataloging-in-Publication Data
Bishop, Matt (Matthew A.)
  Introduction to computer security / Matt Bishop.
     p. cm.
  Includes bibliographical references and index.
  ISBN 0-321-24744-2 (hardcover : alk. paper)
  1. Computer security. I. Title.

  QA76.9.A25B563 2004
  005.8—dc22   2004019195

ISBN: 0-321-24744-2
Text printed in the United States on recycled paper at Courier in Westford, Massachusetts.
  3 4 5 6 7 8 9 10 11—CRW—080706
Third Printing   October 2006

To my dear Holly; our children Heidi, Steven, David, and Caroline; our grandson Skyler; our son-in-law Mike; and our friends Seaview, Tinker Belle, Stripe, Baby Windsor, Fuzzy, Scout, Fur, Puff, and the rest of the menagerie.

Contents

Preface

On September 11, 2001, terrorists seized control of four airplanes. Three were flown into buildings, and a fourth crashed, with catastrophic loss of life. In the aftermath, the security and reliability of many aspects of society drew renewed scrutiny. One of these aspects was the widespread use of computers and their interconnecting networks.

The issue is not new. In 1988, approximately 5,000 computers throughout the Internet were rendered unusable within 4 hours by a program called a *worm* [386].[1] While the spread, and the effects, of this program alarmed computer scientists, most people were not worried because the worm did not affect their lives or their ability to do their jobs. In 1993, more users of computer systems were alerted to such dangers when a set of programs called *sniffers* were placed on many computers run by network service providers and recorded login names and passwords [339].

After an attack on Tsutomu Shimomura's computer system, and the fascinating way Shimomura followed the attacker's trail, which led to his arrest [821], the public's interest and apprehension were finally aroused. Computers were now vulnerable. Their once reassuring protections were now viewed as flimsy.

Several films explored these concerns. Movies such as *War Games* and *Hackers* provided images of people who can, at will, wander throughout computers and networks, maliciously or frivolously corrupting or destroying information it may have taken millions of dollars to amass. (Reality intruded on *Hackers* when the World Wide Web page set up by MGM/United Artists was quickly altered to present

---

[1] Section 19.4 discusses computer worms.

an irreverent commentary on the movie and to suggest that viewers see *The Net* instead. Paramount Pictures denied doing this [399].) Another film, *Sneakers*, presented a picture of those who test the security of computer (and other) systems for their owners and for the government.

Goals

This book has three goals. The first is to show the importance of theory to practice and of practice to theory. All too often, practitioners regard theory as irrelevant and theoreticians think of practice as trivial. In reality, theory and practice are symbiotic. For example, the theory of covert channels, in which the goal is to limit the ability of processes to communicate through shared resources, provides a mechanism for evaluating the effectiveness of mechanisms that confine processes, such as sandboxes and firewalls. Similarly, business practices in the commercial world led to the development of several security policy models such as the Clark-Wilson model and the Chinese Wall model. These models in turn help the designers of security policies better understand and evaluate the mechanisms and procedures needed to secure their sites.

The second goal is to emphasize that computer security and cryptography are different. Although cryptography is an essential component of computer security, it is by no means the only component. Cryptography provides a mechanism for performing specific functions, such as preventing unauthorized people from reading and altering messages on a network. However, unless developers understand the context in which they are using cryptography, and unless the assumptions underlying the protocol and the cryptographic mechanisms apply to the context, the cryptography may not add to the security of the system. The canonical example is the use of cryptography to secure communications between two low-security systems. If only trusted users can access the two systems, cryptography protects messages in transit. But if untrusted users can access either system (through authorized accounts or, more likely, by breaking in), the cryptography is not sufficient to protect the messages. The attackers can read the messages at either endpoint.

The third goal is to demonstrate that computer security is not just a science but also an art. It is an art because no system can be considered secure without an examination of how it is to be used. The definition of a "secure computer" necessitates a statement of requirements and an expression of those requirements in the form of authorized actions and authorized users. (A computer engaged in work at a university may be considered "secure" for the purposes of the work done at the university. When moved to a military installation, that same system may not provide sufficient control to be deemed "secure" for the purposes of the work done at that installation.) How will people, as well as other computers, interact with the computer system? How clear and restrictive an interface can a designer create without rendering the system unusable while trying to prevent unauthorized use or access to the data or resources on the system?

Just as an artist paints his view of the world onto canvas, so does a designer of security features articulate his view of the world of human/machine interaction in the security policy and mechanisms of the system. Two designers may use entirely different designs to achieve the same creation, just as two artists may use different subjects to achieve the same concept.

Computer security is also a science. Its theory is based on mathematical constructions, analyses, and proofs. Its systems are built in accordance with the accepted practices of engineering. It uses inductive and deductive reasoning to examine the security of systems from key axioms and to discover underlying principles. These scientific principles can then be applied to untraditional situations and new theories, policies, and mechanisms.

Philosophy

Key to understanding the problems that exist in computer security is a recognition that the problems are not new. They are old problems, dating from the beginning of computer security (and, in fact, arising from parallel problems in the noncomputer world). But the locus has changed as the field of computing has changed. Before the mid-1980s, mainframe and mid-level computers dominated the market, and computer security problems and solutions were phrased in terms of securing files or processes on a single system. With the rise of networking and the Internet, the arena has changed. Workstations and servers, and the networking infrastructure that connects them, now dominate the market. Computer security problems and solutions now focus on a networked environment. However, if the workstations and servers, and the supporting network infrastructure, are viewed as a single system, the models, theories, and problem statements developed for systems before the mid-1980s apply equally well to current systems.

As an example, consider the issue of assurance. In the early period, assurance arose in several ways: formal methods and proofs of correctness, validation of policy to requirements, and acquisition of data and programs from trusted sources, to name a few. Those providing assurance analyzed a single system, the code on it, and the sources (vendors and users) from which the code could be acquired to ensure that either the sources could be trusted or the programs could be confined adequately to do minimal damage. In the later period, the same basic principles and techniques apply, except that the scope of some has been greatly expanded (from a single system and a small set of vendors to the world-wide Internet). The work on proof-carrying code, an exciting development in which the proof that a downloadable program module satisfies a stated policy is incorporated into the program itself,[2] is an example of this expansion. It extends the notion of a proof of consistency with a stated policy. It

---

[2] Section 19.6.5.1 discusses proof-carrying code.

advances the technology of the earlier period into the later period. But in order to understand it properly, one must understand the ideas underlying the concept of proof-carrying code, and these ideas lie in the earlier period.

As another example, consider Saltzer and Schroeder's principles of secure design.[3] Enunciated in 1975, they promote simplicity, confinement, and understanding. When security mechanisms grow too complex, attackers can evade or bypass them. Many programmers and vendors are learning this when attackers break into their systems and servers. The argument that the principles are old, and somehow outdated, rings hollow when the result of their violation is a nonsecure system.

The work from the earlier period is sometimes cast in terms of systems that no longer exist and that differ in many ways from modern systems. This does not vitiate the ideas and concepts, which also underlie the work done today. Once these ideas and concepts are properly understood, applying them in a multiplicity of environments becomes possible. Furthermore, the current mechanisms and technologies will become obsolete and of historical interest themselves as new forms of computing arise, but the underlying principles will live on, to underlie the next generation—indeed the next era—of computing.

The philosophy of this book is that certain key concepts underlie all of computer security, and that the study of all parts of computer security enriches the understanding of all parts. Moreover, critical to an understanding of the applications of security-related technologies and methodologies is an understanding of the theory underlying those applications.

Advances in the theory of computer protection have illuminated the foundations of security systems. Issues of abstract modeling, and modeling to meet specific environments, lead to systems designed to achieve a specific and rewarding goal. Theorems about the undecidability of the general security question[4] have indicated the limits of what can be done.

Application of these results has improved the quality of the security of the systems being protected. However, the issue is how compatibly the assumptions of the model (and theory) conform to the environment to which the theory is applied. Although our knowledge of how to apply these abstractions is continually increasing, we still have difficulty correctly transposing the relevant information from a realistic setting to one in which analyses can then proceed. Such abstraction often eliminates vital information. The omitted data may pertain to security in nonobvious ways. Without this information, the analysis is flawed.

Unfortunately, no single work can cover all aspects of computer security, so this book focuses on those parts that are, in the author's opinion, most fundamental and most pervasive. The mechanisms exemplify the applications of these principles.

---

[3] Chapter 12 discusses these principles.

[4] See Section 3.2, "Basic Results."

Organization

The organization of this book reflects its philosophy. It begins with fundamentals and principles that provide boundaries within which security can be modeled and analyzed effectively. This provides a framework for expressing and analyzing the requirements of the security of a system. These policies constrain what is allowed and what is not allowed. Mechanisms provide the ability to implement these policies. The degree to which the mechanisms correctly implement the policies, and indeed the degree to which the policies themselves meet the requirements of the organizations using the system, are questions of assurance. Exploiting failures in policy, in implementation, and in assurance comes next, as well as mechanisms for providing information on the attack. The book concludes with the applications of both theory and policy focused on realistic situations. This natural progression emphasizes the development and application of the principles existent in computer security.

The first chapter describes what computer security is all about and explores the problems and challenges to be faced. It sets the context for the remainder of the book.

Chapters 2 and 3 deal with basic questions such as how "security" can be clearly and functionally defined, whether or not it is realistic, and whether or not it is decidable.

Chapters 4 through 7 probe the relationship between policy and security. The definition of "security" depends on policy. We examine several types of policies, including the ever-present fundamental questions of trust, analysis of policies, and the use of policies to constrain operations and transitions.

Chapters 9 through 12 discuss cryptography and its role in security, focusing on applications and issues such as key management, key distribution, and how cryptosystems are used in networks. A quick study of authentication completes this part.

Chapters 13 through 16 consider how to implement the requirements imposed by policies using system-oriented techniques. Certain design principles are fundamental to effective security mechanisms. Policies define who can act and how they can act, and so identity is a critical aspect of implementation. Mechanisms implementing access control and flow control enforce various aspects of policies.

Chapters 17 and 18 present concepts and standards used to ascertain how well a system, or a product, meets its goals.

Chapters 19 through 22 discuss some miscellaneous aspects of computer security. Malicious logic thwarts many mechanisms. Despite our best efforts at high assurance, systems today are replete with vulnerabilities. Why? How can a system be analyzed to detect vulnerabilities? What models might help us improve the state of the art? Given these security holes, how can we detect attackers who exploit them? A discussion of auditing flows naturally into a discussion of intrusion detection—a detection method for such attacks.

Chapters 23 through 26 present examples of how to apply the principles discussed throughout the book. They begin with networks and proceed to systems, users, and programs. Each chapter states a desired policy and shows how to translate that policy into a set of mechanisms and procedures that support the policy. This part tries to demonstrate that the material covered elsewhere can be, and should be, used in practice.

Each chapter in this book ends with a summary and some suggestions for further reading. The summary highlights the important ideas in the chapter. Interested readers who wish to pursue the topics in any chapter in more depth can go to some of the suggested readings. They expand on the material in the chapter or present other interesting avenues.

Differences Between this Book and *Computer Security: Art and Science*

The differences between this book and *Computer Security: Art and Science* result from the different intended audiences. This book is a shorter version of the latter, omitting much of the mathematical formalism. It is suited for computer security professionals, students, and prospective readers who have a less formal mathematical background, or who are not interested in the mathematical formalisms and would only be distracted by them, or for courses with a more practical than theoretical focus.

The foundations and policy sections of this book do not present results involving formal modeling or derivations of limits on the decidability of security (although it does present the central result, that the generic safety problem is undecidable). Some policies, significant in the history of the development of policy models but no longer used widely, have been omitted, as has discussion of the notions of nondeducibility and noninterference. Further, the section on assurance omits the presentation of formal methods and the detailed discussion of designing and building secure systems. It preserves the exposition of the basic concepts and ideas, especially those related to reference monitors, and discusses commonly encountered evaluation criteria.

The reasons for these differences come from the different backgrounds expected of readers. This book is intended for readers who may not be familiar with highly mathematical concepts, or for classes in which the instructor does not intend to expound upon formalisms, such as those required for the development of high assurance systems, but wants students to be exposed to the ideas underlying a "high assurance system." These situations most often arise in classes in which students' backgrounds may not include classes that provide the understanding needed to assimilate the mathematical details of the work. As a consequence, students are often intimidated by the formalism even if the instructor skips it. The original version of this book is intended for classes where the instructor wishes to explain, or allow the students to explore on their own, the rich mathematical background and formalisms of computer security.

Some students learn best by an informal description of a subject. What is the intuition underlying the ideas and principles of the field? How does the practitioner apply these to improve the state of the art? For these students, this version of the book is more appropriate. Other students are most comfortable with intuition augmented by a formal mathematical exposition of the underlying concepts. How does one make the intuition formal? How does one apply the ideas rigorously to assure a secure system (for an appropriate definition of security)? For these students, the original book, *Computer Security: Art and Science*, would be more appropriate.

Practitioners who are less interested in mathematical expositions of the theories underlying computer security will find this version more to their liking. This version keeps the intuitive, non-mathematical exposition of the underlying principles, but does so using a small amount of formal mathematics. Practitioners will find this version shorter and, most likely, easier to read because they will not be distracted by material they would find irrelevant.

Special Acknowledgment

Elisabeth Sullivan contributed the assurance part of this book. She wrote several drafts, all of which reflect her extensive knowledge and experience in that aspect of computer security. I am particularly grateful to her for contributing her real-world knowledge of how assurance is managed. Too often, books recount the mathematics of assurance without recognizing that other aspects are equally important and more widely used. These other aspects shine through in the assurance section, thanks to Liz. As if that were not enough, she made several suggestions that improved the policy part of this book. I will always be grateful for her contribution, her humor, and especially her friendship.

Acknowledgments

Many people have contributed to this book. Peter Salus' suggestion first got me thinking about writing it, and Peter put me in touch with Addison-Wesley. Midway through the writing, Blaine Burnham reviewed the completed portions and the proposed topics, and suggested that they be reorganized in several ways. The current organization of the book grew from his suggestions. Marvin Schaefer reviewed parts of the book with a keen eye, made suggestions that improved many parts, and encouraged me at the end. I thank these three for their contributions.

Many others contributed to this book in various ways. Special thanks to Steven Alexander, Jim Alves-Foss, Bill Arbaugh, Andrew Arcilla, Alex Aris, Rebecca Bace, Belinda Bashore, Vladimir Berman, Ziad El Bizri, Logan Browne, Terry Brugger,

Serdar Cabuk, Raymond Centeno, Lisa Clark, Michael Clifford, Christopher Clifton, Dan Coming, Kay Connelly, Crispin Cowan, Tom Daniels, Dimitri DeFigueiredo, Joseph-Patrick Dib, Jeremy Frank, Robert Fourney, Martin Gagne, Ron Gove, James Hinde, Xuxian Jiang, Jesper Johansson, Mark Jones, Calvin Ko, Mark-Neil Ledesma, Ken Levine, Karl Levitt, Yunhua Lu, Gary McGraw, Alexander Meau, Nasir Memon, Mark Morrissey, Ather Nawaz, Iulian Neamtiu, Kimberly Nico, Stephen Northcutt, Rafael Obelheiro, Josko Orsulic, Holly Pang, Ryan Poling, Sung Park, Ashwini Raina, Jorge Ramos, Brennen Reynolds, Peter Rozental, Christoph Schuba, David Shambroom, Jonathan Shapiro, Clay Shields, Sriram Srinivasan, Mahesh V. Tripunitara, Tom Walcott, James Walden, Dan Watson, Guido Wedig, Chris Wee, Patrick Wheeler, Paul Williams, Bonnie Xu, Xiaoduan Ye, Lara Whelan, John Zachary, Aleksandr Zingorenko, and to everyone in my computer security classes, who (knowingly or unknowingly) helped me develop and test this material.

The Addison-Wesley folks, Kathleen Billus, Susannah Buzard, Bernie Gaffney, Amy Fleischer, Helen Goldstein, Tom Stone, Asdis Thorsteinsson, and most especially my editor, Peter Gordon, were incredibly patient and helpful, despite fears that this book would never materialize. The fact that it did so is in great measure attributable to their hard work and encouragement. I also thank Rob Mauhar and Elizabeth Ryan for their wonderful work.

Dorothy Denning, my advisor in graduate school, guided me through the maze of computer security when I was just beginning. Peter Denning, Barry Leiner, Karl Levitt, Peter Neumann, Marvin Schaefer, Larry Snyder, and several others influenced my approach to the subject. I hope this work reflects in some small way what they gave to me and passes a modicum of it along to my readers.

I also thank my parents, Leonard Bishop and Linda Allen. My father, a writer, gave me some useful tips on writing, which I tried to follow. My mother, a literary agent, helped me understand the process of getting the book published, and supported me throughout.

Finally, I would like to thank my family for their support throughout the writing. Sometimes they wondered if I would ever finish. My wife Holly and our children Steven, David, and Caroline were very patient and understanding and made sure I had time to work on the book. Our oldest daughter Heidi and her husband Mike also provided much love and encouragement and the most wonderful distraction: our grandson—Skyler. To all, my love and gratitude.

Chapter 1

An Overview of Computer Security

ANTONIO: Whereof what's past is prologue, what to come
In yours and my discharge.
—*The Tempest*, II, i, 257–258.

This chapter presents the basic concepts of computer security. The remainder of the book will elaborate on these concepts in order to reveal the logic underlying the principles of these concepts.

We begin with basic security-related services that protect against threats to the security of the system. The next section discusses security policies that identify the threats and define the requirements for ensuring a secure system. Security mechanisms detect and prevent attacks and recover from those that succeed. Analyzing the security of a system requires an understanding of the mechanisms that enforce the security policy. It also requires a knowledge of the related assumptions and trust, which lead to the threats and the degree to which they may be realized. Such knowledge allows one to design better mechanisms and policies to neutralize these threats. This process leads to risk analysis. Human beings are the weakest link in the security mechanisms of any system. Therefore, policies and procedures must take people into account. This chapter discusses each of these topics.

1.1 The Basic Components

Computer security rests on confidentiality, integrity, and availability. The interpretations of these three aspects vary, as do the contexts in which they arise. The interpretation of an aspect in a given environment is dictated by the needs of the individuals, customs, and laws of the particular organization.

1.1.1   Confidentiality

Confidentiality is the concealment of information or resources. The need for keeping information secret arises from the use of computers in sensitive fields such as government and industry. For example, military and civilian institutions in the government often restrict access to information to those who need that information. The first formal work in computer security was motivated by the military's attempt to implement controls to enforce a "need to know" principle. This principle also applies to industrial firms, which keep their proprietary designs secure lest their competitors try to steal the designs. As a further example, all types of institutions keep personnel records secret.

Access control mechanisms support confidentiality. One access control mechanism for preserving confidentiality is cryptography, which scrambles data to make it incomprehensible. A *cryptographic key* controls access to the unscrambled data, but then the cryptographic key itself becomes another datum to be protected.

EXAMPLE: Enciphering an income tax return will prevent anyone from reading it. If the owner needs to see the return, it must be deciphered. Only the possessor of the cryptographic key can enter it into a deciphering program. However, if someone else can read the key when it is entered into the program, the confidentiality of the tax return has been compromised.

Other system-dependent mechanisms can prevent processes from illicitly accessing information. Unlike enciphered data, however, data protected only by these controls can be read when the controls fail or are bypassed. Then their advantage is offset by a corresponding disadvantage. They can protect the secrecy of data more completely than cryptography, but if they fail or are evaded, the data becomes visible.

Confidentiality also applies to the existence of data, which is sometimes more revealing than the data itself. The precise number of people who distrust a politician may be less important than knowing that such a poll was taken by the politician's staff. How a particular government agency harassed citizens in its country may be less important than knowing that such harassment occurred. Access control mechanisms sometimes conceal the mere existence of data, lest the existence itself reveal information that should be protected.

Resource hiding is another important aspect of confidentiality. Sites often wish to conceal their configuration as well as what systems they are using; organizations may not wish others to know about specific equipment (because it could be used without authorization or in inappropriate ways), and a company renting time from a service provider may not want others to know what resources it is using. Access control mechanisms provide these capabilities as well.

All the mechanisms that enforce confidentiality require supporting services from the system. The assumption is that the security services can rely on the kernel, and other agents, to supply correct data. Thus, assumptions and trust underlie confidentiality mechanisms.

1.1.2   Integrity

Integrity refers to the trustworthiness of data or resources, and it is usually phrased in terms of preventing improper or unauthorized change. Integrity includes data integrity (the content of the information) and origin integrity (the source of the data, often called *authentication*). The source of the information may bear on its accuracy and credibility and on the trust that people place in the information. This dichotomy illustrates the principle that the aspect of integrity known as credibility is central to the proper functioning of a system. We will return to this issue when discussing malicious logic.

EXAMPLE: A newspaper may print information obtained from a leak at the White House but attribute it to the wrong source. The information is printed as received (preserving data integrity), but its source is incorrect (corrupting origin integrity).

Integrity mechanisms fall into two classes: *prevention* mechanisms and *detection* mechanisms.

Prevention mechanisms seek to maintain the integrity of the data by blocking any unauthorized attempts to change the data or any attempts to change the data in unauthorized ways. The distinction between these two types of attempts is important. The former occurs when a user tries to change data which she has no authority to change. The latter occurs when a user authorized to make certain changes in the data tries to change the data in other ways. For example, suppose an accounting system is on a computer. Someone breaks into the system and tries to modify the accounting data. Then an unauthorized user has tried to violate the integrity of the accounting database. But if an accountant hired by the firm to maintain its books tries to embezzle money by sending it overseas and hiding the transactions, a user (the accountant) has tried to change data (the accounting data) in unauthorized ways (by moving it to a Swiss bank account). Adequate authentication and access controls will generally stop the break-in from the outside, but preventing the second type of attempt requires very different controls.

Detection mechanisms do not try to prevent violations of integrity; they simply report that the data's integrity is no longer trustworthy. Detection mechanisms may analyze system events (user or system actions) to detect problems or (more commonly) may analyze the data itself to see if required or expected constraints still hold. The mechanisms may report the actual cause of the integrity violation (a specific part of a file was altered), or they may simply report that the file is now corrupt.

Working with integrity is very different from working with confidentiality. With confidentiality, the data is either compromised or it is not, but integrity includes both the correctness and the trustworthiness of the data. The origin of the data (how and from whom it was obtained), how well the data was protected before it arrived at the current machine, and how well the data is protected on the current machine all affect the integrity of the data. Thus, evaluating integrity is often very difficult, because it relies on assumptions about the source of the data and about trust in that source—two underpinnings of security that are often overlooked.

1.1.3   Availability

Availability refers to the ability to use the information or resource desired. Availability is an important aspect of reliability as well as of system design because an unavailable system is at least as bad as no system at all. The aspect of availability that is relevant to security is that someone may deliberately arrange to deny access to data or to a service by making it unavailable. System designs usually assume a statistical model to analyze expected patterns of use, and mechanisms ensure availability when that statistical model holds. Someone may be able to manipulate use (or parameters that control use, such as network traffic) so that the assumptions of the statistical model are no longer valid. This means that the mechanisms for keeping the resource or data available are working in an environment for which they were not designed. As a result, they will often fail.

EXAMPLE: Suppose Anne has compromised a bank's secondary system server, which supplies bank account balances. When anyone else asks that server for information, Anne can supply any information she desires. Merchants validate checks by contacting the bank's primary balance server. If a merchant gets no response, the secondary server will be asked to supply the data. Anne's colleague prevents merchants from contacting the primary balance server, so all merchant queries go to the secondary server. Anne will never have a check turned down, regardless of her actual account balance. Notice that if the bank had only one server (the primary one), this scheme would not work. The merchant would be unable to validate the check.

Attempts to block availability, called *denial of service attacks*, can be the most difficult to detect, because the analyst must determine if the unusual access patterns are attributable to deliberate manipulation of resources or of environment. Complicating this determination is the nature of statistical models. Even if the model accurately describes the environment, atypical events simply contribute to the nature of the statistics. A deliberate attempt to make a resource unavailable may simply look like, or be, an atypical event. In some environments, it may not even appear atypical.

1.2   Threats

A *threat* is a potential violation of security. The violation need not actually occur for there to be a threat. The fact that the violation *might* occur means that those actions that could cause it to occur must be guarded against (or prepared for). Those actions are called *attacks*. Those who execute such actions, or cause them to be executed, are called *attackers*.

The three security services—confidentiality, integrity, and availability—counter threats to the security of a system. Shirey [823] divides threats into four broad classes: *disclosure*, or unauthorized access to information; *deception*, or acceptance of false data; *disruption*, or interruption or prevention of correct operation; and *usurpation*, or unauthorized control of some part of a system. These four broad classes encompass many common threats. Because the threats are ubiquitous, an introductory discussion of each one will present issues that recur throughout the study of computer security.

Snooping, the unauthorized interception of information, is a form of disclosure. It is passive, suggesting simply that some entity is listening to (or reading) communications or browsing through files or system information. *Wiretapping*, or *passive wiretapping*, is a form of snooping in which a network is monitored. (It is called "wiretapping" because of the "wires" that compose the network, although the term is used even if no physical wiring is involved.) Confidentiality services counter this threat.

Modification or *alteration*, an unauthorized change of information, covers three classes of threats. The goal may be deception, in which some entity relies on the modified data to determine which action to take, or in which incorrect information is accepted as correct and is released. If the modified data controls the operation of the system, the threats of disruption and usurpation arise. Unlike snooping, modification is active; it results from an entity changing information. *Active wiretapping* is a form of modification in which data moving across a network is altered; the term "active" distinguishes it from snooping ("passive" wiretapping). An example is the *man-in-the-middle* attack, in which an intruder reads messages from the sender and sends (possibly modified) versions to the recipient, in hopes that the recipient and sender will not realize the presence of the intermediary. Integrity services counter this threat.

Masquerading or *spoofing*, an impersonation of one entity by another, is a form of both deception and usurpation. It lures a victim into believing that the entity with which it is communicating is a different entity. For example, if a user tries to log into a computer across the Internet but instead reaches another computer that claims to be the desired one, the user has been spoofed. Similarly, if a user tries to read a file, but an attacker has arranged for the user to be given a different file, another spoof has taken place. This may be a passive attack (in which the user does not attempt to authenticate the recipient, but merely accesses it), but it is usually an active attack (in which the masquerader issues responses to mislead the user about its identity). Although primarily deception, it is often used to usurp control of a system by an attacker impersonating an authorized manager or controller. Integrity services (called "authentication services" in this context) counter this threat.

Some forms of masquerading may be allowed. *Delegation* occurs when one entity authorizes a second entity to perform functions on its behalf. The distinctions between delegation and masquerading are important. If Susan delegates to Thomas the authority to act on her behalf, she is giving permission for him to perform specific actions as though she were performing them herself. All parties are aware of the delegation. Thomas will not pretend to be Susan; rather, he will say, "I am Thomas and I have authority to do this on Susan's behalf." If asked, Susan will verify this. On the other hand, in a masquerade, Thomas will pretend to be Susan. No other parties (including Susan) will be aware of the masquerade, and Thomas will say, "I am Susan." Should anyone discover that he or she is dealing with Thomas and ask Susan about it, she will deny that she authorized Thomas to act on her behalf. In terms of security, masquerading is a violation of security, whereas delegation is not.

Repudiation of origin, a false denial that an entity sent (or created) something, is a form of deception. For example, suppose a customer sends a letter to a vendor agreeing to pay a large amount of money for a product. The vendor ships the product and then demands payment. The customer denies having ordered the product and by law is therefore entitled to keep the unsolicited shipment without payment. The customer has repudiated the origin of the letter. If the vendor cannot prove that the letter came from the customer, the attack succeeds. A variant of this is denial by a user that he created specific information or entities such as files. Integrity mechanisms cope with this threat.

Denial of receipt, a false denial that an entity received some information or message, is a form of deception. Suppose a customer orders an expensive product, but the vendor demands payment before shipment. The customer pays, and the vendor ships the product. The customer then asks the vendor when he will receive the product. If the customer has already received the product, the question constitutes a denial of receipt attack. The vendor can defend against this attack only by proving that the customer did, despite his denials, receive the product. Integrity and availability mechanisms guard against these attacks.

Delay, a temporary inhibition of a service, is a form of usurpation, although it can play a supporting role in deception. Typically, delivery of a message or service requires some time t; if an attacker can force the delivery to take more than time t, the attacker has successfully delayed delivery. This requires manipulation of system control structures, such as network components or server components, and hence is a form of usurpation. If an entity is waiting for an authorization message that is delayed, it may query a secondary server for the authorization. Even though the attacker may be unable to masquerade as the primary server, she might be able to masquerade as that secondary server and supply incorrect information. Availability mechanisms can thwart this threat.

Denial of service, a long-term inhibition of service, is a form of usurpation, although it is often used with other mechanisms to deceive. The attacker prevents a server from providing a service. The denial may occur at the source (by preventing the server from obtaining the resources needed to perform its function), at the destination (by blocking the communications from the server), or along the intermediate path (by discarding messages from either the client or the server, or both). Denial of service poses the same threat as an infinite delay. Availability mechanisms counter this threat.

Denial of service or delay may result from direct attacks or from nonsecurity-related problems. From our point of view, the cause and result are important; the intention underlying them is not. If delay or denial of service compromises system security, or is part of a sequence of events leading to the compromise of a system, then we view it as an attempt to breach system security. But the attempt may not be deliberate; indeed, it may be the product of environmental characteristics rather than specific actions of an attacker.

1.3   Policy and Mechanism

Critical to our study of security is the distinction between policy and mechanism.

> **Definition 1–1.** A *security policy* is a statement of what is, and what is not, allowed.

> **Definition 1–2.** A *security mechanism* is a method, tool, or procedure for enforcing a security policy.

Mechanisms can be nontechnical, such as requiring proof of identity before changing a password; in fact, policies often require some procedural mechanisms that technology cannot enforce.

As an example, suppose a university's computer science laboratory has a policy that prohibits any student from copying another student's homework files. The computer system provides mechanisms for preventing others from reading a user's files. Anna fails to use these mechanisms to protect her homework files, and Bill copies them. A breach of security has occurred, because Bill has violated the security policy. Anna's failure to protect her files does not authorize Bill to copy them.

In this example, Anna could easily have protected her files. In other environments, such protection may not be easy. For example, the Internet provides only the most rudimentary security mechanisms, which are not adequate to protect information sent over that network. Nevertheless, acts such as the recording of passwords and other sensitive information violate an implicit security policy of most sites (specifically, that passwords are a user's confidential property and cannot be recorded by anyone).

Policies may be presented mathematically, as a list of allowed (secure) and disallowed (nonsecure) states. For our purposes, we will assume that any given policy provides an axiomatic description of secure states and nonsecure states. In practice, policies are rarely so precise; they normally describe in English what users and staff are allowed to do. The ambiguity inherent in such a description leads to states that are not classified as "allowed" or "disallowed." For example, consider the homework policy discussed above. If someone looks through another user's directory without copying homework files, is that a violation of security? The answer depends on site custom, rules, regulations, and laws, all of which are outside our focus and may change over time.

When two different sites communicate or cooperate, the entity they compose has a security policy based on the security policies of the two entities. If those policies are inconsistent, either or both sites must decide what the security policy for the combined site should be. The inconsistency often manifests itself as a security breach. For example, if proprietary documents were given to a university, the policy of confidentiality in the corporation would conflict with the more open policies of most universities. The university and the company must develop a mutual security policy that meets both their needs in order to produce a consistent policy. When the two sites communicate through an independent third party, such as an Internet service provider, the complexity of the situation grows rapidly.

1.3.1   Goals of Security

Given a security policy's specification of "secure" and "nonsecure" actions, these security mechanisms can prevent the attack, detect the attack, or recover from the attack. The strategies may be used together or separately.

Prevention means that an attack will fail. For example, if one attempts to break into a host over the Internet and that host is not connected to the Internet, the attack has been prevented. Typically, prevention involves implementation of mechanisms that users cannot override and that are trusted to be implemented in a correct, unalterable way, so that the attacker cannot defeat the mechanism by changing it. Preventative mechanisms often are very cumbersome and interfere with system use to the point that they hinder normal use of the system. But some simple preventative mechanisms, such as passwords (which aim to prevent unauthorized users from accessing the system), have become widely accepted. Prevention mechanisms can prevent compromise of parts of the system; once in place, the resource protected by the mechanism need not be monitored for security problems, at least in theory.

Detection is most useful when an attack cannot be prevented, but it can also indicate the effectiveness of preventative measures. Detection mechanisms accept that an attack will occur; the goal is to determine that an attack is under way, or has occurred, and report it. The attack may be monitored, however, to provide data about its nature, severity, and results. Typical detection mechanisms monitor various aspects of the system, looking for actions or information indicating an attack. A good example of such a mechanism is one that gives a warning when a user enters an incorrect password three times. The login may continue, but an error message in a system log reports the unusually high number of mistyped passwords. Detection mechanisms do not prevent compromise of parts of the system, which is a serious drawback. The resource protected by the detection mechanism is continuously or periodically monitored for security problems.

Recovery has two forms. The first is to stop an attack and to assess and repair any damage caused by that attack. As an example, if the attacker deletes a file, one recovery mechanism would be to restore the file from backup tapes. In practice, recovery is far more complex, because the nature of each attack is unique. Thus, the type and extent of any damage can be difficult to characterize completely. Moreover, the attacker may return, so recovery involves identification and fixing of the vulnerabilities used by the attacker to enter the system. In some cases, retaliation (by attacking the attacker's system or taking legal steps to hold the attacker accountable) is part of recovery. In all these cases, the system's functioning is inhibited by the attack. By definition, recovery requires resumption of correct operation.

In a second form of recovery, the system continues to function correctly while an attack is under way. This type of recovery is quite difficult to implement because of the complexity of computer systems. It draws on techniques of fault tolerance as well as techniques of security and is typically used in safety-critical systems. It differs from the first form of recovery, because at no point does the system function incorrectly. However, the system may disable nonessential functionality. Of course, this type of recovery is often implemented in a weaker form whereby the system detects incorrect functioning automatically and then corrects (or attempts to correct) the error.

1.4   Assumptions and Trust

How do we determine if the policy correctly describes the required level and type of security for the site? This question lies at the heart of all security, computer and otherwise. Security rests on assumptions specific to the type of security required and the environment in which it is to be employed.

EXAMPLE: Opening a door lock requires a key. The assumption is that the lock is secure against lock picking. This assumption is treated as an axiom and is made because most people would require a key to open a door lock. A good lock picker, however, can open a lock without a key. Hence, in an environment with a skilled, untrustworthy lock picker, the assumption is wrong and the consequence invalid.

If the lock picker is trustworthy, the assumption is valid. The term "trustworthy" implies that the lock picker will not pick a lock unless the owner of the lock authorizes the lock picking. This is another example of the role of trust. A well-defined exception to the rules provides a "back door" through which the security mechanism (the locks) can be bypassed. The trust resides in the belief that this back door will not be used except as specified by the policy. If it is used, the trust has been misplaced and the security mechanism (the lock) provides no security.

Like the lock example, a policy consists of a set of axioms that the policy makers believe can be enforced. Designers of policies always make two assumptions. First, the policy correctly and unambiguously partitions the set of system states into "secure" and "nonsecure" states. Second, the security mechanisms prevent the system from entering a "nonsecure" state. If either assumption is erroneous, the system will be nonsecure.

These two assumptions are fundamentally different. The first assumption asserts that the policy is a correct description of what constitutes a "secure" system. For example, a bank's policy may state that officers of the bank are authorized to shift money among accounts. If a bank officer puts $100,000 in his account, has the bank's security been violated? Given the aforementioned policy statement, no, because the officer was authorized to move the money. In the "real world," that action would constitute embezzlement, something any bank would consider a security violation.

The second assumption says that the security policy can be enforced by security mechanisms. These mechanisms are either *secure*, *precise*, or *broad*. Let P be the set of all possible states. Let Q be the set of secure states (as specified by the security policy). Let the security mechanisms restrict the system to some set of states R (thus, $R \subseteq P$). Then we have the following definition.

> **Definition 1–3.** A security mechanism is *secure* if $R \subseteq Q$; it is *precise* if $R = Q$; and it is *broad* if there are states r such that $r \in R$ and $r \notin Q$.

Ideally, the union of all security mechanisms active on a system would produce a single precise mechanism (that is, $R = Q$). In practice, security mechanisms are broad; they allow the system to enter nonsecure states. We will revisit this topic when we explore policy formulation in more detail.

Trusting that mechanisms work requires several assumptions.

1. Each mechanism is designed to implement one or more parts of the security policy.
2. The union of the mechanisms implements all aspects of the security policy.
3. The mechanisms are implemented correctly.
4. The mechanisms are installed and administered correctly.

Because of the importance and complexity of trust and of assumptions, we will revisit this topic repeatedly and in various guises throughout this book.

1.5   Assurance

Trust cannot be quantified precisely. System specification, design, and implementation can provide a basis for determining "how much" to trust a system. This aspect of trust is called *assurance*. It is an attempt to provide a basis for bolstering (or substantiating or specifying) how much one can trust a system.

EXAMPLE: In the United States, aspirin from a nationally known and reputable manufacturer, delivered to the drugstore in a safety-sealed container, and sold with the seal still in place, is considered trustworthy by most people. The bases for that trust are as follows.

- The testing and certification of the drug (aspirin) by the Food and Drug Administration. The FDA has jurisdiction over many types of medicines and allows medicines to be marketed only if they meet certain clinical standards of usefulness.

- The manufacturing standards of the company and the precautions it takes to ensure that the drug is not contaminated. National and state regulatory commissions and groups ensure that the manufacture of the drug meets specific acceptable standards.
- The safety seal on the bottle. To insert dangerous chemicals into a safety-sealed bottle without damaging the seal is very difficult.

The three technologies (certification, manufacturing standards, and preventative sealing) provide some degree of assurance that the aspirin is not contaminated. The degree of trust the purchaser has in the purity of the aspirin is a result of these three processes.

In the 1980s, drug manufacturers met two of the criteria above, but none used safety seals.[1] A series of "drug scares" arose when a well-known manufacturer's medicines were contaminated after manufacture but before purchase. The manufacturer promptly introduced safety seals to assure its customers that the medicine in the container was the same as when it was shipped from the manufacturing plants.

Assurance in the computer world is similar. It requires specific steps to ensure that the computer will function properly. The sequence of steps includes detailed specifications of the desired (or undesirable) behavior; an analysis of the design of the hardware, software, and other components to show that the system will not violate the specifications; and arguments or proofs that the implementation, operating procedures, and maintenance procedures will produce the desired behavior.

Definition 1–4. A system is said to *satisfy* a specification if the specification correctly states how the system will function.

This definition also applies to design and implementation satisfying a specification.

1.5.1   Specification

A *specification* is a (formal or informal) statement of the desired functioning of the system. It can be highly mathematical, using any of several languages defined for that purpose. It can also be informal, using, for example, English to describe what the system should do under certain conditions. The specification can be low-level, combining program code with logical and temporal relationships to specify ordering of events. The defining quality is a statement of what the system is allowed to do or what it is not allowed to do.

---

[1] Many used childproof caps, but they prevented only young children (and some adults) from opening the bottles. They were not designed to protect the medicine from malicious adults.

EXAMPLE: A company is purchasing a new computer for internal use. They need to trust the system to be invulnerable to attack over the Internet. One of their (English) specifications would read "The system cannot be attacked over the Internet."

Specifications are used not merely in security but also in systems designed for safety, such as medical technology. They constrain such systems from performing acts that could cause harm. A system that regulates traffic lights must ensure that pairs of lights facing the same way turn red, green, and yellow at the same time and that at most one set of lights facing cross streets at an intersection is green.

A major part of the derivation of specifications is determination of the set of requirements relevant to the system's planned use. Section 1.6 discusses the relationship of requirements to security.

1.5.2   Design

The *design* of a system translates the specifications into components that will implement them. The design is said to *satisfy* the specifications if, under all relevant circumstances, the design will not permit the system to violate those specifications.

EXAMPLE: A design of the computer system for the company mentioned above had no network interface cards, no modem cards, and no network drivers in the kernel. This design satisfied the specification because the system would not connect to the Internet. Hence it could not be attacked over the Internet.

An analyst can determine whether a design satisfies a set of specifications in several ways. If the specifications and designs are expressed in terms of mathematics, the analyst must show that the design formulations are consistent with the specifications. Although much of the work can be done mechanically, a human must still perform some analyses and modify components of the design that violate specifications (or, in some cases, components that cannot be shown to satisfy the specifications). If the specifications and design do not use mathematics, then a convincing and compelling argument should be made. Most often, the specifications are nebulous and the arguments are half-hearted and unconvincing or provide only partial coverage. The design depends on assumptions about what the specifications mean. This leads to vulnerabilities, as we will see.

1.5.3   Implementation

Given a design, the *implementation* creates a system that satisfies that design. If the design also satisfies the specifications, then by transitivity the implementation will also satisfy the specifications.

The difficulty at this step is the complexity of proving that a program correctly implements the design and, in turn, the specifications.

Definition 1–5. A program is *correct* if its implementation performs as specified.

Proofs of correctness require each line of source code to be checked for mathematical correctness. Each line is seen as a function, transforming the input (constrained by preconditions) into some output (constrained by postconditions derived from the function and the preconditions). Each routine is represented by the composition of the functions derived from the lines of code making up the routine. Like those functions, the function corresponding to the routine has inputs and outputs, constrained by preconditions and postconditions, respectively. From the combination of routines, programs can be built and formally verified. One can apply the same techniques to sets of programs and thus verify the correctness of a system.

There are three difficulties in this process. First, the complexity of programs makes their mathematical verification difficult. Aside from the intrinsic difficulties, the program itself has preconditions derived from the environment of the system. These preconditions are often subtle and difficult to specify, but unless the mathematical formalism captures them, the program verification may not be valid because critical assumptions may be wrong. Second, program verification assumes that the programs are compiled correctly, linked and loaded correctly, and executed correctly. Hardware failure, buggy code, and failures in other tools may invalidate the preconditions. A compiler that incorrectly compiles

```
x := x + 1
```

to

```
move x to regA
subtract 1 from contents of regA
move contents of regA to x
```

would invalidate the proof statement that the value of *x* after the line of code is 1 more than the value of *x* before the line of code. This would invalidate the proof of correctness. Third, if the verification relies on conditions on the input, the program must reject any inputs that do not meet those conditions. Otherwise, the program is only partially verified.

Because formal proofs of correctness are so time-consuming, *a posteriori* verification techniques known as *testing* have become widespread. During testing, the tester executes the program (or portions of it) on data to determine if the output is what it should be and to understand how likely the program is to contain an error. Testing techniques range from supplying input to ensure that all execution paths are exercised to introducing errors into the program and determining how they affect the output to stating specifications and testing the program to see if it satisfies the specifications. Although these techniques are considerably simpler than the more formal methods, they do not provide the same degree of assurance that formal methods do.

Furthermore, testing relies on test procedures and documentation, errors in either of which could invalidate the testing results.

Although assurance techniques do not guarantee correctness or security, they provide a firm basis for assessing what one must trust in order to believe that a system is secure. Their value is in eliminating possible, and common, sources of error and forcing designers to define precisely what the system is to do.

1.6   Operational Issues

Any useful policy and mechanism must balance the benefits of the protection against the cost of designing, implementing, and using the mechanism. This balance can be determined by analyzing the risks of a security breach and the likelihood of it occurring. Such an analysis is, to a degree, subjective, because in very few situations can risks be rigorously quantified. Complicating the analysis are the constraints that laws, customs, and society in general place on the acceptability of security procedures and mechanisms; indeed, as these factors change, so do security mechanisms and, possibly, security policies.

1.6.1   Cost-Benefit Analysis

Like any factor in a complex system, the benefits of computer security are weighed against their total cost (including the additional costs incurred if the system is compromised). If the data or resources cost less, or are of less value, than their protection, adding security mechanisms and procedures is not cost-effective because the data or resources can be reconstructed more cheaply than the protections themselves. Unfortunately, this is rarely the case.

EXAMPLE: A database provides salary information to a second system that prints checks. If the data in the database is altered, the company could suffer grievous financial loss; hence, even a cursory cost-benefit analysis would show that the strongest possible integrity mechanisms should protect the data in the database.

Now suppose the company has several branch offices, and every day the database downloads a copy of the data to each branch office. The branch offices use the data to recommend salaries for new employees. However, the main office makes the final decision using the original database (not one of the copies). In this case, guarding the integrity of the copies is not particularly important, because branch offices cannot make any financial decisions based on the data in their copies. Hence, the company cannot suffer any financial loss.

Both of these situations are extreme situations in which the analysis is clear-cut. As an example of a situation in which the analysis is less clear, consider the need for confidentiality of the salaries in the database. The officers of the company must decide the financial cost to the company should the salaries be disclosed, including potential loss from lawsuits (if any); changes in policies, procedures, and personnel; and the effect on future business. These are all business-related judgments, and determining their value is part of what company officers are paid to do.

Overlapping benefits are also a consideration. Suppose the integrity protection mechanism can be augmented very quickly and cheaply to provide confidentiality. Then the cost of providing confidentiality is much lower. This shows that evaluating the cost of a particular security service depends on the mechanism chosen to implement it and on the mechanisms chosen to implement other security services. The cost-benefit analysis should take into account as many mechanisms as possible. Adding security mechanisms to an existing system is often more expensive (and, incidentally, less effective) than designing them into the system in the first place.

1.6.2   Risk Analysis

To determine whether an asset should be protected, and to what level, requires analysis of the potential threats against that asset and the likelihood that they will materialize. The level of protection is a function of the probability of an attack occurring and the effects of the attack should it succeed. If an attack is unlikely, protecting against it has a lower priority than protecting against a likely one. If the unlikely attack would cause long delays in the company's production of widgets but the likely attack would be only a nuisance, then more effort should be put into preventing the unlikely attack. The situations between these extreme cases are far more subjective.

Let's revisit our company with the salary database that transmits salary information over a network to a second computer that prints employees' checks. The data is stored on the database system and then moved over the network to the second system. Hence, the risk of unauthorized changes in the data occurs in three places: on the database system, on the network, and on the printing system. If the network is a local (company-wide) one and no wide area networks are accessible, the threat of attackers entering the systems is confined to untrustworthy internal personnel. If, however, the network is connected to the Internet, the risk of geographically distant attackers attempting to intrude is substantial enough to warrant consideration.

This example illustrates some finer points of risk analysis. First, risk is a function of environment. Attackers from a foreign country are not a threat to the company when the computer is not connected to the Internet. If foreign attackers wanted to break into the system, they would need physically to enter the company (and would cease to be "foreign" because they would then be "local"). But if the computer is connected to the Internet, foreign attackers become a threat because they can attack over the Internet. An additional, less tangible issue is the faith in the company. If the company is not able to meet its payroll because it does not know *whom* it is to pay, the company will lose the faith of its employees. It may be unable to hire anyone, because the people hired would not be sure they would get paid. Investors would not fund the company because of the likelihood of lawsuits by unpaid employees. The risk arises from the environments in which the company functions.

Second, the risks change with time. If a company's network is not connected to the Internet, there seems to be no risk of attacks from other hosts on the Internet. However, despite any policies to the contrary, someone could connect a modem to one of the company computers and connect to the Internet through the modem. Should this happen, any risk analysis predicated on isolation from the Internet would no longer be accurate. Although policies can forbid the connection of such a modem and procedures can be put in place to make such connection difficult, unless the responsible parties can guarantee that no such modem will ever be installed, the risks can change.

Third, many risks are quite remote but still exist. In the modem example, the company has sought to minimize the risk of an Internet connection. Hence, this risk is "acceptable" but not nonexistent. As a practical matter, one does not worry about acceptable risks; instead, one worries that the risk will become unacceptable.

Finally, the problem of "analysis paralysis" refers to making risk analyses with no effort to act on those analyses. To change the example slightly, suppose the company performs a risk analysis. The executives decide that they are not sure if all risks have been found, so they order a second study to verify the first. They reconcile the studies then wait for some time to act on these analyses. At that point, the security officers raise the objection that the conditions in the workplace are no longer those that held when the original risk analyses were done. The analysis is repeated. But the company cannot decide how to ameliorate the risks, so it waits until a plan of action can be developed, and the process continues. The point is that the company is paralyzed and cannot act on the risks it faces.

1.6.3   Laws and Customs

Laws restrict the availability and use of technology and affect procedural controls. Hence, any policy and any selection of mechanisms must take into account legal considerations.

EXAMPLE: Until the year 2000, the United States controlled the export of cryptographic hardware and software (considered munitions under United States law). If a U.S. software company worked with a computer manufacturer in London, the U.S. company could not send cryptographic software to the manufacturer. The U.S. company first would have to obtain a license to export the software from the United States. Any security policy that depended on the London manufacturer using that cryptographic software would need to take this into account.

EXAMPLE: Suppose the law makes it illegal to read a user's file without the user's permission. An attacker breaks into the system and begins to download users' files. If the system administrators notice this and observe what the attacker is reading, they will be reading the victim's files without his permission and therefore will be violating the law themselves. For this reason, most sites require users to give (implicit or explicit) permission for system administrators to read their files. In some jurisdictions, an explicit exception allows system administrators to access information on their systems without permission in order to protect the quality of service provided or to prevent damage to their systems.

Complicating this issue are situations involving the laws of multiple jurisdictions—especially foreign ones.

EXAMPLE: In the 1990s, the laws involving the use of cryptography in France were very different from those in the United States. The laws of France required companies sending enciphered data out of the country to register their cryptographic keys with the government. Security procedures involving the transmission of enciphered data from a company in the United States to a branch office in France had to take these differences into account.

EXAMPLE: If a policy called for prosecution of attackers and intruders came from Russia to a system in the United States, prosecution would involve asking the United States authorities to extradite the alleged attackers from Russia. This undoubtedly would involve court testimony from company personnel involved in handling the intrusion, possibly trips to Russia, and more court time once the extradition was completed. The cost of prosecuting the attackers might be considerably higher than the company would be willing (or able) to pay.

Laws are not the only constraints on policies and selection of mechanisms. Society distinguishes between *legal* and *acceptable* practices. It may be legal for a company to require all its employees to provide DNA samples for authentication purposes, but it is not socially acceptable. Requiring the use of Social Security numbers as passwords is legal (unless the computer is one owned by the U.S. government) but also unacceptable. These practices provide security but at an unacceptable cost, and they encourage users to evade or otherwise overcome the security mechanisms.

The issue that laws and customs raise is the issue of psychological acceptability. A security mechanism that would put users and administrators at legal risk would place a burden on these people that few would be willing to bear; thus, such a mechanism would not be used. An unused mechanism is worse than a nonexistent one, because it gives a false impression that a security service is available. Hence, users may rely on that service to protect their data, when in reality their data is unprotected.

1.7   Human Issues

Implementing computer security controls is complex, and in a large organization procedural controls often become vague or cumbersome. Regardless of the strength of the technical controls, if nontechnical considerations affect their implementation and use, the effect on security can be severe. Moreover, if configured or used incorrectly, even the best security control is useless at best and dangerous at worst. Thus, the designers, implementers, and maintainers of security controls are essential to the correct operation of those controls.

1.7.1   Organizational Problems

Security provides no direct financial rewards to the user. It limits losses, but it also requires the expenditure of resources that could be used elsewhere. Unless losses occur, organizations often believe they are wasting effort related to security. After a loss, the value of these controls suddenly becomes appreciated. Furthermore, security controls often add complexity to otherwise simple operations. For example, if concluding a stock trade takes two minutes without security controls and three minutes with security controls, adding those controls results in a 50% loss of productivity.

Losses occur when security protections are in place, but such losses are expected to be less than they would have been without the security mechanisms. The key question is whether such a loss, combined with the resulting loss in productivity, would be greater than a financial loss or loss of confidence should one of the nonsecured transactions suffer a breach of security.

Compounding this problem is the question of who is responsible for the security of the company's computers. The power to implement appropriate controls must reside with those who are responsible; the consequence of not doing so is that the people who can most clearly see the need for security measures, and who are responsible for implementing them, will be unable to do so. This is simply sound business practice; responsibility without power causes problems in any organization, just as does power without responsibility.

Once clear chains of responsibility and power have been established, the need for security can compete on an equal footing with other needs of the organization. The most common problem a security manager faces is the lack of people trained in the area of computer security. Another common problem is that knowledgeable people are overloaded with work. At many organizations, the "security administrator" is also involved in system administration, development, or some other secondary function. In fact, the security aspect of the job is often secondary. The problem is that indications of security problems often are not obvious and require time and skill to spot. Preparation for an attack makes dealing with it less chaotic, but such preparation takes enough time and requires enough attention so that treating it as a secondary aspect of a job means that it will not be performed well, with the expected consequences.

Lack of resources is another common problem. Securing a system requires resources as well as people. It requires time to design a configuration that will provide an adequate level of security, to implement the configuration, and to administer the system. It requires money to purchase products that are needed to build an adequate security system or to pay someone else to design and implement security measures. It requires computer resources to implement and execute the security mechanisms and procedures. It requires training to ensure that employees understand how to use the security tools, how to interpret the results, and how to implement the nontechnical aspects of the security policy.

1.7.2   People Problems

The heart of any security system is people. This is particularly true in computer security, which deals mainly with technological controls that can usually be bypassed by human intervention. For example, a computer system authenticates a user by asking that user for a secret code; if the correct secret code is supplied, the computer assumes that the user is authorized to use the system. If an authorized user tells another person his secret code, the unauthorized user can masquerade as the authorized user with significantly less likelihood of detection.

People who have some motive to attack an organization and are not authorized to use that organization's systems are called *outsiders* and can pose a serious threat. Experts agree, however, that a far more dangerous threat comes from disgruntled employees and other *insiders* who are authorized to use the computers. Insiders typically know the organization of the company's systems and what procedures the operators and users follow and often know enough passwords to bypass many security controls that would detect an attack launched by an outsider. Insider *misuse* of authorized privileges is a very difficult problem to solve.

Untrained personnel also pose a threat to system security. As an example, one operator did not realize that the contents of backup tapes needed to be verified before the tapes were stored. When attackers deleted several critical system files, she discovered that none of the backup tapes could be read.

System administrators who misread the output of security mechanisms, or do not analyze that output, contribute to the probability of successful attacks against their systems. Similarly, administrators who misconfigure security-related features of a system can weaken the site security. Users can also weaken site security by misusing security mechanisms (such as selecting passwords that are easy to guess).

Lack of training need not be in the technical arena. Many successful break-ins have arisen from the art of *social engineering*. If operators will change passwords based on telephone requests, all an attacker needs to do is to determine the name of someone who uses the computer. A common tactic is to pick someone fairly far above the operator (such as a vice president of the company) and to feign an emergency (such as calling at night and saying that a report to the president of the company is due the next morning) so that the operator will be reluctant to refuse the request. Once the password has been changed to one that the attacker knows, he can simply log in as a normal user. Social engineering attacks are remarkably successful and often devastating.

The problem of misconfiguration is aggravated by the complexity of many security-related configuration files. For instance, a typographical error can disable key protection features. Even worse, software does not always work as advertised.

One widely used system had a vulnerability that arose when an administrator made too long a list that named systems with access to certain files. Because the list was too long, the system simply assumed that the administrator meant to allow those files to be accessed without restriction on who could access them—exactly the opposite of what was intended.

1.8   Tying It All Together

The considerations discussed above appear to flow linearly from one to the next (see Figure 1–1). Human issues pervade each stage of the cycle. In addition, each stage of the cycle feeds back to the preceding stage, and through that stage to all earlier stages. The operation and maintenance stage is critical to the life cycle. Figure 1–1 breaks it out so as to emphasize the impact it has on all stages. The following example shows the importance of feedback.

EXAMPLE: A major corporation decided to improve its security. It hired consultants, determined the threats, and created a policy. From the policy, the consultants derived several specifications that the security mechanisms had to meet. They then developed a design that would meet the specifications.

    During the implementation phase, the company discovered that employees could connect modems to the telephones without being detected. The design required

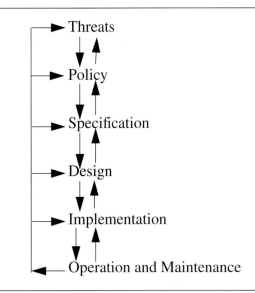

Figure 1–1   The security life cycle.

all incoming connections to go through a firewall. The design had to be modified to divide systems into two classes: systems connected to "the outside," which were put outside the firewall; and all other systems, which were put behind the firewall. The design needed other modifications as well.

When the system was deployed, the operation and maintenance phase revealed several unexpected threats. The most serious was that systems were repeatedly misconfigured to allow sensitive data to be sent across the Internet in the clear. The implementation made use of cryptographic software very difficult. Once this problem had been remedied, the company discovered that several "trusted" hosts (those allowed to log in without authentication) were physically outside the control of the company. This violated policy, but for commercial reasons the company needed to continue to use these hosts. The policy element that designated these systems as "trusted" was modified. Finally, the company detected proprietary material being sent to a competitor over electronic mail. This added a threat that the company had earlier discounted. The company did not realize that it needed to worry about insider attacks.

Feedback from operation is critical. Whether or not a program is tested or proved to be secure, operational environments always introduce unexpected problems or difficulties. If the assurance (specification, design, implementation, and testing/proof) phase is done properly, the extra problems and difficulties are minimal. The analysts can handle them, usually easily and quickly. If the assurance phase has been omitted or done poorly, the problems may require a complete reevaluation of the system. The tools used for the feedback include auditing, in which the operation of the system is recorded and analyzed so that the analyst can determine what the problems are.

1.9   Summary

Computer security depends on many aspects of a computer system. The threats that a site faces, and the level and quality of the countermeasures, depend on the quality of the security services and supporting procedures. The specific mix of these attributes is governed by the site security policy, which is created after careful analysis of the value of the resources on the system or controlled by the system and of the risks involved.

Underlying all this are key assumptions describing what the site and the system accept as true or trustworthy; understanding these assumptions is the key to analyzing the strength of the system's security. This notion of "trust" is the central notion for computer security. If trust is well placed, any system can be made acceptably secure. If it is misplaced, the system cannot be secure in any sense of the word.

Once this is understood, the reason that people consider security to be a relative attribute is plain. Given enough resources, an attacker can often evade the security procedures and mechanisms that are in place. Such a desire is tempered by the cost of the attack, which in some cases can be very expensive. If it is less expensive to regenerate the data than to launch the attack, most attackers will simply regenerate the data.

This chapter has laid the foundation for what follows. All aspects of computer security begin with the nature of threats and countering security services. In future chapters, we will build on these basic concepts.

1.10   Further Reading

Risk analysis arises in a variety of contexts. Molak [646] presents essays on risk management and analysis in a variety of fields. Laudan [552] provides an enjoyable introduction to the subject. Neumann [688] discusses the risks of technology and recent problems. Software safety (Leveson [557]) requires an understanding of the risks posed in the environment. Peterson [717] discusses many programming errors in a readable way. All provide insights into the problems that arise in a variety of environments.

Many authors recount stories of security incidents. The earliest, Parker's wonderful book [713], discusses motives and personalities as well as technical details. Stoll recounts the technical details of uncovering an espionage ring that began as the result of a 75¢ accounting error [878, 880]. Hafner and Markoff describe the same episode in a study of "cyberpunks" [386]. The Internet worm [292, 386, 757, 858] brought the problem of computer security into popular view. Numerous other incidents [339, 386, 577, 821, 838, 873] have heightened public awareness of the problem.

Several books [55, 57, 737, 799] discuss computer security for the layperson. These works tend to focus on attacks that are visible or affect the end user (such as pornography, theft of credit card information, and deception). They are worth reading for those who wish to understand the results of failures in computer security.

1.11   Exercises

1. Classify each of the following as a violation of confidentiality, of integrity, of availability, or of some combination thereof.

   a. John copies Mary's homework.

   b. Paul crashes Linda's system.

   c. Carol changes the amount of Angelo's check from $100 to $1,000.

   d. Gina forges Roger's signature on a deed.

   e. Rhonda registers the domain name "AddisonWesley.com" and refuses to let the publishing house buy or use that domain name.

   f. Jonah obtains Peter's credit card number and has the credit card company cancel the card and replace it with another card bearing a different account number.

> g. Henry spoofs Julie's IP address to gain access to her computer.

2. Identify mechanisms for implementing the following. State what policy or policies they might be enforcing.

   a. A password-changing program will reject passwords that are less than five characters long or that are found in the dictionary.
   b. Only students in a computer science class will be given accounts on the department's computer system.
   c. The login program will disallow logins of any students who enter their passwords incorrectly three times.
   d. The permissions of the file containing Carol's homework will prevent Robert from cheating and copying it.
   e. When World Wide Web traffic climbs to more than 80% of the network's capacity, systems will disallow any further communications to or from Web servers.
   f. Annie, a systems analyst, will be able to detect a student using a program to scan her system for vulnerabilities.
   g. A program used to submit homework will turn itself off just after the due date.

3. The aphorism "security through obscurity" suggests that hiding information provides some level of security. Give an example of a situation in which hiding information does not add appreciably to the security of a system. Then give an example of a situation in which it does.

4. Give an example of a situation in which a compromise of confidentiality leads to a compromise in integrity.

5. Show that the three security services—confidentiality, integrity, and availability—are sufficient to deal with the threats of disclosure, disruption, deception, and usurpation.

6. In addition to mathematical and informal statements of policy, policies can be implicit (not stated). Why might this be done? Might it occur with informally stated policies? What problems can this cause?

7. For each of the following statements, give an example of a situation in which the statement is true.

   a. Prevention is more important than detection and recovery.
   b. Detection is more important than prevention and recovery.
   c. Recovery is more important than prevention and detection.

8. Is it possible to design and implement a system in which *no* assumptions about trust are made? Why or why not?

9. Policy restricts the use of electronic mail on a particular system to faculty and staff. Students cannot send or receive electronic mail on that host. Classify the following mechanisms as secure, precise, or broad.

     a. The electronic mail sending and receiving programs are disabled.

     b. As each letter is sent or received, the system looks up the sender (or recipient) in a database. If that party is listed as faculty or staff, the mail is processed. Otherwise, it is rejected. (Assume that the database entries are correct.)

     c. The electronic mail sending programs ask the user if he or she is a student. If so, the mail is refused. The electronic mail receiving programs are disabled.

10. Consider a very high-assurance system developed for the military. The system has a set of specifications, and both the design and implementation have been proven to satisfy the specifications. What questions should school administrators ask when deciding whether to purchase such a system for their school's use?

11. How do laws protecting privacy impact the ability of system administrators to monitor user activity?

12. Computer viruses are programs that, among other actions, can delete files without a user's permission. A U.S. legislator wrote a law banning the deletion of any files from computer disks. What was the problem with this law from a computer security point of view? Specifically, state which security service would have been affected if the law had been passed.

13. Users often bring in programs or download programs from the Internet. Give an example of a site for which the benefits of allowing users to do this outweigh the dangers. Then give an example of a site for which the dangers of allowing users to do this outweigh the benefits.

14. A respected computer scientist has said that no computer can ever be made perfectly secure. Why might she have said this?

15. An organization makes each lead system administrator responsible for the security of the system he or she runs. However, the management determines what programs are to be on the system and how they are to be configured.

     a. Describe the security problem(s) that this division of power would create.

     b. How would you fix them?

16. The president of a large software development company has become concerned about competitors learning proprietary information. He is determined to stop them. Part of his security mechanism is to require all employees to report any contact with employees of the company's competitors, even if it is purely social. Do you believe this will have the desired effect? Why or why not?

17. The police and the public defender share a computer. What security problems does this present? Do you feel it is a reasonable cost-saving measure to have all public agencies share the same (set of) computers?

18. Companies usually restrict the use of electronic mail to company business but do allow minimal use for personal reasons.

    a. How might a company detect excessive personal use of electronic mail, other than by reading it? (*Hint*: Think about the personal use of a company telephone.)
    b. Intuitively, it seems reasonable to ban *all* personal use of electronic mail on company computers. Explain why most companies do not do this.

19. Argue for or against the following proposition. Ciphers that the government cannot cryptanalyze should be outlawed. How would your argument change if such ciphers could be used provided that the users registered the keys with the government?

20. For many years, industries and financial institutions hired people who broke into their systems once those people were released from prison. Now, such a conviction tends to prevent such people from being hired. Why you think attitudes on this issue changed? Do you think they changed for the better or for the worse?

21. A graduate student accidentally releases a program that spreads from computer system to computer system. It deletes no files but requires much time to implement the necessary defenses. The graduate student is convicted. Despite demands that he be sent to prison for the maximum time possible (to make an example of him), the judge sentences him to pay a fine and perform community service. What factors do you believe caused the judge to hand down the sentence he did? What would you have done were you the judge, and what extra information would you have needed to make your decision?

Chapter 2
Access Control Matrix

GRANDPRÉ: Description cannot suit itself in words
To demonstrate the life of such a battle
In life so lifeless as it shows itself.
—*The Life of Henry the Fifth*, IV, ii, 53–55.

A *protection system* describes the conditions under which a system is secure. In this chapter, we present a classical formulation of a protection system. The *access control matrix model* arose both in operating systems research and in database research; it describes allowed accesses using a matrix.

2.1   Protection State

The *state* of a system is the collection of the current values of all memory locations, all secondary storage, and all registers and other components of the system. The subset of this collection that deals with protection is the *protection state* of the system. An *access control matrix* is one tool that can describe the current protection state.

Consider the set of possible protection states P. Some subset Q of P consists of exactly those states in which the system is authorized to reside. So, whenever the system state is in Q, the system is secure. When the current state is in $P - Q$,[1] the system is not secure. Our interest in representing the state is to characterize those states in Q, and our interest in enforcing security is to ensure that the system state is always an element of Q. Characterizing the states in Q is the function of a *security policy*; preventing the system from entering a state in $P - Q$ is the function of a *security mechanism*. Recall from Definition 1–3 that a mechanism that enforces this restriction is *precise*.

The *access control matrix model* is the most precise model used to describe a protection state. It characterizes the rights of each *subject* (active entity, such as a process) with respect to every other entity. The description of elements of A form a *specification* against which the current state can be compared. Specifications

---

[1] The notation $P - Q$ means all elements of set P not in set Q.

take many forms, and different specification languages have been created to describe the characteristics of allowable states.

As the system changes, the protection state changes. When a command changes the state of the system, a *state transition* occurs. Very often, constraints on the set of allowed states use these transitions inductively; a set of authorized states is defined, and then a set of operations is allowed on the elements of that set. The result of transforming an authorized state with an operation allowed in that state is an authorized state. By induction, the system will always be in an authorized state. Hence, both states and state transitions are often constrained.

In practice, *any* operation on a real system causes multiple state transitions; the reading, loading, altering, and execution of any datum or instruction causes a transition. We are concerned only with those state transitions that affect the protection state of the system, so only transitions that alter the actions a subject is authorized to take are relevant. For example, a program that changes a variable to 0 does not (usually) alter the protection state. However, if the variable altered is one that affects the privileges of a process, then the program does alter the protection state and needs to be accounted for in the set of transitions.

2.2   Access Control Matrix Model

The simplest framework for describing a protection system is the *access control matrix model*, which describes the rights of users over files in a matrix. Butler Lampson first proposed this model in 1971 [543]; Graham and Denning [252, 370] refined it, and we will use their version.

The set of all protected entities (that is, entities that are relevant to the protection state of the system) is called the set of *objects O*. The set of *subjects S* is the set of active objects, such as processes and users. In the access control matrix model, the relationship between these entities is captured by a matrix A with *rights* drawn from a set of rights R in each entry $a[s, o]$, where $s \in S$, $o \in O$, and $a[s, o] \subseteq R$. The subject s has the set of rights $a[s, o]$ over the object o. The set of protection *states* of the system is represented by the triple (S, O, A). For example, Figure 2–1 shows the protection state of a system. Here, process 1 can read or write file 1 and can read file 2; process 2 can append to file 1 and read file 2. Process 1 can communicate with process 2 by writing to it, and process 2 can read from process 1. Each process owns itself and the file with the same number. Note that the processes themselves are treated as both subjects (rows) and objects (columns). This enables a process to be the target of operations as well as the operator.

Interpretation of the meaning of these rights varies from system to system. Reading from, writing to, and appending to files is usually clear enough, but what does "reading from" a process mean? Depending on the instantiation of the model, it could mean that the reader accepts messages from the process being read, or it could mean that the reader simply looks at the state of the process being read (as a debugger does,

	file 1	file 2	process 1	process 2
process 1	read, write, own	read	read, write, execute, own	write
process 2	append	read, own	read	read, write, execute, own

Figure 2–1   An access control matrix. The system has two processes and two files. The set of rights is {read, write, execute, append, own}.

for example). The meaning of the right may vary depending on the object involved. The point is that the access control matrix model is an *abstract* model of the protection state, and when one talks about the meaning of some particular access control matrix, one must always talk with respect to a particular implementation or system.

The *own* right is a distinguished right. In most systems, the creator of an object has special privileges: the ability to add and delete rights for other users (and for the owner). In the system shown in Figure 2–1, for example, process 1 could alter the contents of $A[x,$ file 1$]$, where x is any subject.

EXAMPLE: The UNIX system defines the rights "read," "write," and "execute." When a process accesses a file, these terms mean what one would expect. When a process accesses a directory, "read" means to be able to list the contents of the directory; "write" means to be able to create, rename, or delete files or subdirectories in that directory; and "execute" means to be able to access files or subdirectories in that directory. When a process accesses another process, "read" means to be able to receive signals, "write" means to be able to send signals, and "execute" means to be able to execute the process as a subprocess.

Moreover, the superuser can access any (local) file regardless of the permissions the owner has granted. In effect, the superuser "owns" all objects on the system. Even in this case however, the interpretation of the rights is constrained. For example, the superuser cannot alter a directory using the system calls and commands that alter files. The superuser must use specific system calls and commands to create, rename, and delete files.

Although the "objects" involved in the access control matrix are normally thought of as files, devices, and processes, they could just as easily be messages sent between processes, or indeed systems themselves. Figure 2–2 shows an example access control matrix for three systems on a local area network (LAN). The rights correspond to various network protocols: *own* (the ability to add servers), *ftp* (the ability to access the system using the File Transfer Protocol, or FTP [728]), *nfs* (the ability to access file systems using the Network File System, or NFS, protocol [149, 886]), and *mail* (the ability to send and receive mail using the Simple Mail Transfer

host names	telegraph	nob	toadflax
telegraph	own	ftp	ftp
nob		ftp, nfs, mail, own	ftp, nfs, mail
toadflax		ftp, mail	ftp, nfs, mail, own

Figure 2–2   Rights on a LAN. The set of rights is {ftp, mail, nfs, own}.

Protocol, or SMTP [727]). The subject *telegraph* is a personal computer with an *ftp* client but no servers, so neither of the other systems can access it, but it can *ftp* to them. The subject *nob* is configured to provide NFS service to a set of clients that does not include the host toadflax, and both systems will exchange mail with any host and allow any host to use *ftp*.

   At the micro level, access control matrices can model programming language accesses; in this case, the objects are the variables and the subjects are the procedures (or modules). Consider a program in which events must be synchronized. A module provides functions for incrementing (*inc_ctr*) and decrementing (*dec_ctr*) a counter private to that module. The routine *manager* calls these functions. The access control matrix is shown in Figure 2–3. Note that "+" and "–" are the rights, representing the ability to add and subtract, respectively, and *call* is the ability to invoke a procedure. The routine *manager* can call itself; presumably, it is recursive.

   In the examples above, entries in the access control matrix are rights. However, they could as easily have been functions that determined the set of rights at any particular state based on other data, such as a history of prior accesses, the time of day, the rights another subject has over the object, and so forth. A common form of such a function is a locking function used to enforce the Bernstein conditions,[2] so when a process is writing to a file, other processes cannot access the file; but once the writing is done, the processes can access the file once again.

	counter	inc_ctr	dec_ctr	manager
inc_ctr	+			
dec_ctr	–			
manager		call	call	call

Figure 2–3   Rights in a program. The set of rights is {+, –, call}.

---

[2] The Bernstein conditions ensure that data is consistent. They state that any number of readers may access a datum simultaneously, but if a writer is accessing the datum, no other writers or any reader can access the datum until the current writing is complete [718].

2.3   Protection State Transitions

As processes execute operations, the state of the protection system changes. Let the initial state of the system be $X_0 = (S_0, O_0, A_0)$. The set of state transitions is represented as a set of operations $\tau_1, \tau_2, \ldots$. Successive states are represented as $X_1, X_2, \ldots$, where the notation $\lambda \vdash$, and the expression

$$X_i \vdash_{\tau_{i+1}} X_{i+1}$$

means that state transition τ_{i+1} moves the system from state X_i to state X_{i+1}. When a system starts at some state X and, after a series of state transitions, enters state Y, we can write

$$X \vdash^* Y.$$

The representation of the protection system as an access control matrix must also be updated. In the model, sequences of state transitions are represented as single commands, or *transformation procedures*, that update the access control matrix. The commands state which entry in the matrix is to be changed, and how; hence, the commands require parameters. Formally, let c_k be the kth command with formal parameters $p_{k,1}, \ldots, p_{k,m}$. Then the ith transition would be written as

$$X_i \vdash_{c_{i+1}(p_{i+1,1}, \ldots, p_{i+1,m})} X_{i+1}.$$

Note the similarity in notation between the use of the command and the state transition operations. This is deliberate. For every command, there is a sequence of state transition operations that takes the initial state X_i to the resulting state X_{i+1}. Using the command notation allows us to shorten the description of the transformation as well as list the parameters (subjects, objects, and entries) that affect the transformation operations.

We now focus on the commands themselves. Following Harrison, Ruzzo, and Ullman [401], we define a set of *primitive commands* that alter the access control matrix. In the following list, the protection state is (S, O, A) before the execution of each command and (S', O', A') after each command.

1. Primitive command: **create subject** s

    This primitive command creates a new subject s. Note that s must not exist as a subject *or an object* before this command is executed. This operation does not add any rights. It merely modifies the matrix.

2. Primitive command: **create object** o

    This primitive command creates a new object o. Note that o must not exist before this command is executed. Like **create subject**, this operation does not add any rights. It merely modifies the matrix.

3. Primitive command: **enter** r **into** a[s, o]

   This primitive command adds the right r to the cell a[s, o]. Note that a[s, o] may already contain the right, in which case the effect of this primitive depends on the instantiation of the model (it may add another copy of the right or may do nothing).

4. Primitive command: **delete** r **from** a[s, o]

   This primitive command deletes the right r from the cell a[s, o]. Note that a[s, o] need not contain the right, in which case this operation has no effect.

5. Primitive command: **destroy subject** s

   This primitive command deletes the subject s. The column and row for s in A are deleted also.

6. Primitive command: **destroy object** o

   This primitive command deletes the object o. The column for o in A is deleted also.

These primitive operations can be combined into commands, during which multiple primitive operations may be executed.

EXAMPLE: In the UNIX system, if process p created a file f with owner read (r) and write (w) permission, the command capturing the resulting changes in the access control matrix would be

> **command** create•file(p, f)
>   **create object** f;
>   **enter** own **into** a[p, f];
>   **enter** r **into** a[p, f];
>   **enter** w **into** a[p, f];
> **end**

Suppose the process p wishes to create a new process q. The following command would capture the resulting changes in the access control matrix.

> **command** spawn•process(p, q)
>   **create subject** q;
>   **enter** own **into** a[p, q];
>   **enter** r **into** a[p, q];
>   **enter** w **into** a[p, q];
>   **enter** r **into** a[q, p];
>   **enter** w **into** a[q, p];
> **end**

The r and w rights enable the parent and child to signal each other.

The system can update the matrix only by using defined commands; it cannot use the primitive commands directly. Of course, a command may invoke only a single primitive; such a command is called *mono-operational*.

EXAMPLE: The command

> **command** *make•owner(p, f)*
>   **enter** *own* **into** *a[p, f]*;
> **end**

is a mono-operational command. It does not delete any existing owner rights. It merely adds p to the set of owners of f. Hence, f may have multiple owners after this command is executed.

2.3.1   Conditional Commands

The execution of some primitives requires that specific preconditions be satisfied. For example, suppose a process p wishes to give another process q the right to read a file f. In some systems, p must own f. The abstract command would be

> **command** *grant•read•file•1(p, f, q)*
>   **if** *own* **in** *a[p, f]*
>   **then**
>   **enter** *r* **into** *a[q, f]*;
> **end**

Any number of conditions may be placed together using **and**. For example, suppose a system has the distinguished right c. If a subject has the rights r and c over an object, it may give any other subject r rights over that object. Then

> **command** *grant•read•file•2(p, f, q)*
>   **if** *r* **in** *a[p, f]* **and** *c* **in** *a[p, f]*
>   **then**
>   **enter** *r* **into** *a[q, f]*;
> **end**

Commands with one condition are called *monoconditional*. Commands with two conditions are called *biconditional*. The command *grant•read•file•1* is monoconditional, and the command *grant•read•file•2* is biconditional. Because both have one primitive command, both are mono-operational.

Note that all conditions are joined by **and**, and never by **or**. Because joining conditions with **or** is equivalent to two commands each with one of the conditions, the disjunction is unnecessary and thus is omitted. For example, suppose the right a

enables one to grant the right r to another subject. To achieve the effect of a command equivalent to

> **if** *own* **in** $a[p, f]$ **or** a **in** $a[p, f]$
> **then**
>   **enter** r **into** $a[q, f]$;

define the following two commands:

> **command** *grant•write•file•1*(p, f, q)
>   **if** *own* **in** $a[p, f]$
>   **then**
>   **enter** r **into** $a[q, f]$;
> **end**
> **command** *grant•write•file•2*(p, f, q)
>   **if** a **in** $a[p, f]$
>   **then**
>   **enter** r **into** $a[q, f]$;
> **end**

and then say

> *grant•write•file•1*(p, f, q); *grant•write•file•2*(p, f, q);

Also, the negation of a condition is not permitted—that is, one cannot test for the *absence* of a right within a command by the condition

> **if** r **not in** $A[\mathbf{p}, \mathbf{f}]$.

This has some interesting consequences, which we will explore in the next chapter.

2.4   Summary

The access control matrix is the primary abstraction mechanism in computer security. In its purest form, it can express any expressible security policy. In practice, it is not used directly because of space requirements; most systems have (at least) thousands of objects and could have thousands of subjects, and the storage requirements would simply be too much. However, its simplicity makes it ideal for theoretical analyses of security problems.

Transitions change the state of the system. Transitions are expressed in terms of commands. A command consists of a possible condition followed by one or more primitive operations. Conditions may involve ownership or the ability to copy a right.

2.5   Further Reading

The access control matrix is sometimes called an *authorization matrix* in older literature [426].

In 1972, Conway, Maxwell, and Morgan [205], in parallel with Graham and Denning, proposed a protection method for databases equivalent to the access control model. Hartson and Hsiao [404] point out that databases in particular use functions as described above to control access to records and fields; for this reason, entries in the access control matrix for a database are called *decision procedures* or *decision rules*. These entries are very similar to the earlier formulary model [425], in which access procedures determine whether to grant access and, if so, provide a mapping to virtual addresses and any required encryption and decryption.

Miller and Baldwin [637] use an access control matrix with entries determined by the evaluation of boolean expressions to control access to fields in a database. The *query-set-overlap control* [275] is a prevention mechanism that answers queries only when the size of the intersection of the query set and each previous query set is smaller than some parameter r, and can be represented as an access control matrix with entries determined by the history of queries.

2.6   Exercises

1. Consider a computer system with three users: Alice, Bob, and Cyndy. Alice owns the file *alicerc*, and Bob and Cyndy can read it. Cyndy can read and write the file *bobrc*, which Bob owns, but Alice can only read it. Only Cyndy can read and write the file *cyndyrc*, which she owns. Assume that the owner of each of these files can execute it.

    a. Create the corresponding access control matrix.
    b. Cyndy gives Alice permission to read *cyndyrc*, and Alice removes Bob's ability to read *alicerc*. Show the new access control matrix.

2. Consider the set of rights {*read, write, execute, append, list, modify, own*}.

    a. Using the syntax in Section 2.3, write a command *delete_all_rights* (p, q, s). This command causes p to delete all rights the subject q has over an object s.
    b. Modify your command so that the deletion can occur only if p has *modify* rights over s.
    c. Modify your command so that the deletion can occur only if p has *modify* rights over s and q does *not* have *own* rights over s.

Chapter 3
Foundational Results

In 1976, Harrison, Ruzzo, and Ullman [401] proved that in the most general abstract case, the security of computer systems was undecidable and explored some of the limits of this result.

Models explore the most basic question of the art and science of computer security: under what conditions can a generic algorithm determine whether a system is secure? Understanding models and the results derived from them lays the foundations for coping with limits in policy and policy composition as well as applying the theoretical work.

3.1   The General Question

Given a computer system, how can we determine if it is secure? More simply, is there a generic algorithm that allows us to determine whether a computer system is secure? If so, we could simply apply that algorithm to any system; although the algorithm might not tell us where the security problems were, it would tell us whether any existed.

The first question is the definition of "secure." What policy shall define "secure"? For a general result, the definition should be as broad as possible. We use the access control matrix to express our policy. However, we do not provide any special rights such as *copy* or *own*, and the principle of attenuation of privilege does not apply.

Let R be the set of generic (primitive) rights of the system.

Definition 3–1. When a generic right r is added to an element of the access control matrix not already containing r, that right is said to be *leaked*.

Our policy defines the authorized set of states A to be the set of states in which no command $c(x_1, ..., x_n)$ can leak r. This means that no generic rights can be added to the matrix.

We do not distinguish between the *leaking* of rights and an *authorized* transfer of rights. In our model, there is *no* authorized transfer of rights. (If we wish to allow such a transfer, we designate the subjects involved as "trusted." We then eliminate all trusted subjects from the matrix, because the security mechanisms no longer apply to them.)

Let a computer system begin in protection state s_0.

Definition 3–2. If a system can never leak the right r, the system (including the initial state s_0) is called *safe with respect to the right r*. If the system can leak the right r (enter an unauthorized state), it is called *unsafe with respect to the right r*.

We use these terms rather than *secure* and *nonsecure* because safety refers to the abstract model and security refers to the actual implementation. Thus, a secure system corresponds to a model safe with respect to all rights, but a model safe with respect to all rights does not ensure a secure system.

EXAMPLE: A computer system allows the network administrator to read all network traffic. It disallows all other users from reading this traffic. The system is designed in such a way that the network administrator cannot communicate with other users. Thus, there is no way for the right r of the network administrator over the network device to leak. This system is safe.

Unfortunately, the operating system has a flaw. If a user specifies a certain file name in a file deletion system call, that user can obtain access to any file on the system (bypassing all file system access controls). This is an implementation flaw, not a theoretical one. It also allows the user to read data from the network. So this system is not secure.

Our question (called the *safety question*) is: Does there exist an algorithm for determining whether a given protection system with initial state s_0 is safe with respect to a generic right r?

3.2   Basic Results

The simplest case is a system in which the commands are mono-operational (each consisting of a single primitive command). In such a system, the following theorem holds.

Theorem 3–1. [401] There exists an algorithm that will determine whether a given mono-operational protection system with initial state s_0 is safe with respect to a generic right r.

Proof Because all commands are mono-operational, we can identify each command by the type of primitive operation it invokes. Consider the minimal sequence of commands $c_1, ..., c_k$ needed to leak the right r from the system with initial state s_0.

Because no commands can test for the absence of rights in an access control matrix entry, we can omit the **delete** and **destroy** commands from the analysis. They do not affect the ability of a right to leak.

Now suppose that multiple **create** commands occurred during the sequence of commands, causing a leak. Subsequent commands check only for the presence of rights in an access control matrix element. They distinguish between different elements only by the presence (or lack of presence) of a particular right. Suppose that two subjects s_1 and s_2 are created and the rights in $A[s_1, o_1]$ and $A[s_2, o_2]$ are tested. The same test for $A[s_1, o_1]$ and $A[s_1, o_2] = A[s_1, o_2] \cup A[s_2, o_2]$ will produce the same result. Hence, all **create**s are unnecessary except possibly the first (and that only if there are no subjects initially), and any commands **enter**ing rights into the new subjects are rewritten to enter the new right into the lone created subject. Similarly, any tests for the presence of rights in the new subjects are rewritten to test for the presence of that right in an existing subject (or, if none initially, the first subject created).

Let $|S_0|$ be the number of subjects and $|O_0|$ the number of objects in the initial state. Let n be the number of generic rights. Then, in the worst case, one new subject must be created (one command), and the sequence of commands will enter every right into every element of the access control matrix. After the creation, there are $|S_0| + 1$ subjects and $|O_0| + 1$ objects, and $(|S_0| + 1)(|O_0| + 1)$ elements. Because there are n generic rights, this leads to $n(|S_0| + 1)(|O_0| + 1)$ commands. Hence, $k \le n(|S_0| + 1)(|O_0| + 1) + 1$.

By enumerating all possible states we can determine whether the system is safe. Clearly, this may be computationally infeasible, especially if many subjects, objects, and rights are involved, but it is computable. (See Exercise 2.) Unfortunately, this result does not generalize to all protection systems.

Before proving this, let us review the notation for a *Turing machine*. A Turing machine T consists of a head and an infinite tape divided into cells numbered 1, 2, ..., from left to right. The machine also has a finite set of states K and a finite set of tape symbols M. The distinguished symbol $b \in M$ is a blank and appears on all the cells of the tape at the start of all computations; also, at that time T is in the initial state q_0.

The tape head occupies one square of the tape, and can read and write symbols on that cell of the tape, and can move into the cell to the left or right of the cell it currently occupies. The function $\delta: K \times M \to K \times M \times \{L, R\}$ describes the action of T. For example, let $p, q \in K$ and $A, B \in M$. Then, if $\delta(p, A) = (q, B, R)$, when T is in state p and the head rests on a cell with symbol A, the tape head changes the symbol in the cell to B, moves right to the next cell (that is, if the head is in cell i, it moves to cell $i + 1$), and the Turing machine enters state q. If $\delta(p, A) = (q, B, L)$, then the actions would be the same except the head would move to the left unless it were already in the leftmost square (because the head may never move off the tape).

Let the final state be q_f, if T enters this state, it halts. The *halting problem* is to determine whether an arbitrary Turing machine will enter the state q_f, and is known to be undecidable [299].

Given this, we can now present the following theorem.

Theorem 3–2. [401] It is undecidable whether a given state of a given protection system is safe for a given generic right.

Proof Proof by contradiction. We show that an arbitrary Turing machine can be reduced to the safety problem, with the Turing machine entering a final state corresponding to the leaking of a given generic right. Then, if the safety problem is decidable, we can determine when the Turing machine halts, showing that the halting problem is decidable, which (as we said above) is false.

First, we construct a map from the states and symbols of T to rights in the access control matrix model. Let the set of generic rights be the symbols in M and a set of distinct symbols each representing an element in K; in other words, the set of tape symbols and states are represented by generic rights, one right for each symbol and one for each state.

The cells of the Turing machine tape are sequentially ordered. We consider only the cells that the head has visited, so suppose T has scanned cells 1, 2, ..., n. To simulate this, we represent each cell as a subject and define a distinguished right called *own* such that s_i owns s_{i+1} for $1 \le i < k$. If cell i contains the symbol A, then subject s_i has A rights over itself. Furthermore, the subject s_k, which corresponds to the rightmost cell visited, has *end* rights over itself; notice that s_{k+1} has not been created in this case. Finally, if the head is in cell j and T is in state p, then subject s_j has p rights over itself also. (To keep the meanings of the rights unambiguous, we require the rights corresponding to the symbols for the tape to be distinct from the rights corresponding to the states.) Figure 3–1 shows an example of this mapping, when the head has visited four cells.

Next, we must translate the Turing machine function δ into access control matrix commands. Suppose that $\delta(p, A) = (q, B, L)$ and the head is not in

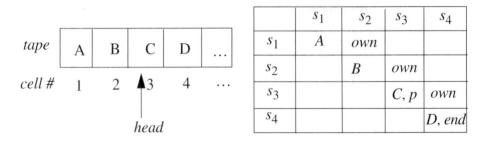

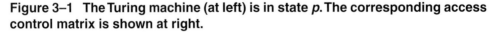

Figure 3–1 The Turing machine (at left) is in state *p*. The corresponding access control matrix is shown at right.

the leftmost cell. Then, in terms of the access control matrix, the rights A and p must be replaced by B in the entry $a[s_i, s_i]$ and the right q must be added to $a[s_{i-1}, s_{i-1}]$. The following access control matrix command, in which s_i represents the subject corresponding to the current cell, captures this.

command $c_{p, A}(s_i, s_{i-1})$
    if *own* **in** $a[s_{i-1}, s_i]$ **and** p **in** $a[s_i, s_i]$ **and** A **in** $a[s_i, s_i]$
    then
        delete p **from** $a[s_i, s_i]$;
        delete A **from** $a[s_i, s_i]$;
        enter B **into** $a[s_i, s_i]$;
        enter q **into** $a[s_{i-1}, s_{i-1}]$;
end

If the head is in the leftmost cell of the tape, both s_i and s_{i-1} are s_1.

Now consider motion to the right, such as $\delta(p, A) = (q, B, R)$. If the head is not in the rightmost cell k, by the same reasoning as for the left motion, we have

command $c_{p, A}(s_i, s_{i+1})$
    if *own* **in** $a[s_i, s_{i+1}]$ **and** p **in** $a[s_i, s_i]$ **and** A **in** $a[s_i, s_i]$
    then
        delete p **from** $a[s_i, s_i]$;
        delete A **from** $a[s_i, s_i]$;
        enter B **into** $a[s_i, s_i]$;
        enter q **into** $a[s_{i+1}, s_{i+1}]$;
end

However, if the head is in the rightmost cell k, the command must create a new subject s_{k+1}. Then, to maintain the consistency of the access control matrix, s_k is given *own* rights over the new subject s_{k+1}, s_{k+1} is given *end* rights over itself, and s_k's *end* rights over itself must be removed. At that point, the problem is reduced to the problem of regular right motion. So:

command $crightmost_{p, A}(s_k, s_{k+1})$
    if *end* **in** $a[s_i, s_i]$ **and** p **in** $a[s_i, s_i]$ **and** A **in** $a[s_i, s_i]$
    then
        delete *end* **from** $a[s_k, s_k]$;
        create new subject s_{k+1};
        enter *own* **into** $a[s_k, s_{k+1}]$;
        enter *end* **into** $a[s_{k+1}, s_{k+1}]$;
        delete p **from** $a[s_i, s_i]$;
        delete A **from** $a[s_i, s_i]$;
        enter B **into** $a[s_i, s_i]$;

enter q **into** $a[s_{i+1}, s_{i+1}]$;
end

Clearly, only one right in any of the access control matrices corresponds to a state, and there will be exactly one *end* right in the matrix (by the nature of the commands simulating Turing machine actions). Hence, in each configuration of the Turing machine, there is at most one applicable command. Thus, the protection system exactly simulates the Turing machine, given the representation above. Now, if the Turing machine enters state q_f, then the protection system has leaked the right q_f; otherwise, the protection system is safe for the generic right q_f. But whether the Turing machine will enter the (halting) state q_f is undecidable, so whether the protection system is safe must be undecidable also.

However, we can generate a list of all unsafe systems.

Theorem 3–3. [242] The set of unsafe systems is recursively enumerable.

Proof See Exercise 3.

Assume that the **create** primitive is disallowed. Clearly, the safety question is decidable (simply enumerate all possible sequences of commands from the given state; as no new subjects or objects are created, at some point no new rights can be added to any element of the access control matrix, so if the leak has not yet occurred, it cannot occur). Hence, we have the following theorem.

Theorem 3–4. [401] For protection systems without the **create** primitives, the question of safety is complete in **P-SPACE**.

Proof Consider a Turing machine bounded in polynomial space. A construction similar to that of Theorem 3–2 reduces that Turing machine in polynomial time to an access control matrix whose size is polynomial in the length of the Turing machine input.

If deleting the **create** primitives makes the safety question decidable, would deleting the **delete** and **destroy** primitives but not the **create** primitive also make the safety question decidable? Such systems are called *monotonic* because they only increase in size and complexity; they cannot decrease. But:

Theorem 3–5. [402] It is undecidable whether a given configuration of a given monotonic protection system is safe for a given generic right.

Restricting the number of conditions in the commands to two does not help:

Theorem 3–6. [402] The safety question for biconditional monotonic protection systems is undecidable.

But if at most one condition per command is allowed:

Theorem 3–7. [402] The safety question for monoconditional monotonic protection systems is decidable.

This can be made somewhat stronger:

Theorem 3–8. [402] The safety question for monoconditional protection systems with **create**, **enter**, and **delete** primitives (but no **destroy** primitive) is decidable.

Thus, the safety question is undecidable for generic protection models but is decidable if the protection system is restricted in some way. Two questions arise. First, given a *particular* system with specific rules for transformation, can we show that the safety question is decidable? Second, what are the weakest restrictions on a protection system that will make the safety question decidable in that system?

3.3   Summary

The safety problem is a rich problem that has led to the development of several models and analysis techniques. The key result is that the general problem of safety is undecidable. But in specific cases, or in systems with limited sets of rules and entities, safety may well be decidable. Ultimately, however, security (the analogue of safety) is analyzed for a system or for a class of systems.

3.4   Further Reading

In that same year as the HRU result, Jones, Lipton, and Snyder [473] presented a specific model, called the Take-Grant Protection Model, in which security was not only decidable, but decidable in time linear with the size of the system. Several papers [112,576,848,849,850] have explored this system and its applications. Budd [141] analyzes safety properties of *grammatical protection schemes*, which he and Lipton defined earlier [575]. Minsky [639] suggested another model to examine what made the general, abstract case undecidable but at least one specific case decidable. Sandhu and others [777,778,779] extended this model, which he called the Schematic Protection Model or SPM, to examine the boundary even more closely. Sandhu has also presented interesting work on the representation of models, and has unified many of them with his *transform* model [781, 782, 786].

Some interesting work [18,19,20,780,783] has characterized the expressive power of these, and other, models.

Sandhu and Ganta [785] have explored the effects of allowing testing for the *absence* of rights in an access control matrix (as opposed to testing for the *presence* of rights, which all the models described in this chapter do).

3.5   Exercises

1. The proof of Theorem 3–1 states the following: Suppose two subjects s_1 and s_2 are created and the rights in $A[s_1, o_1]$ and $A[s_2, o_2]$ are tested. The same test for $A[s_1, o_1]$ and $A[s_1, o_2] = A[s_1, o_2] \cup A[s_2, o_2]$ will produce the same result. Justify this statement. Would it be true if one could test for the absence of rights as well as for the presence of rights?

2. Devise an algorithm that determines whether or not a system is safe by enumerating all possible states. Is this problem *NP*-complete? Justify your answer.

3. Prove Theorem 3–3. (*Hint*: Use a diagonalization argument to test each system as the set of protection systems is enumerated. Whenever a protection system leaks a right, add it to the list of unsafe protection systems.)

Chapter 4
Security Policies

> PORTIA: Of a strange nature is the suit you follow;
> Yet in such rule that the Venetian law
> Cannot impugn you as you do proceed.
> [*To Antonio.*] You stand within his danger, do you not?
> —*The Merchant of Venice*, IV, i, 177–180.

A security policy defines "secure" for a system or a set of systems. Security policies can be informal or highly mathematical in nature. After defining a security policy precisely, we expand on the nature of "trust" and its relationship to security policies. We also discuss different types of policy models.

4.1   Security Policies

Consider a computer system to be a finite-state automaton with a set of transition functions that change state. Then:

> **Definition 4–1.** A *security policy* is a statement that partitions the states of the system into a set of *authorized*, or *secure*, states and a set of *unauthorized*, or *nonsecure*, states.

A security policy sets the context in which we can define a secure system. What is secure under one policy may not be secure under a different policy. More precisely:

> **Definition 4–2.** A *secure system* is a system that starts in an authorized state and cannot enter an unauthorized state.

Consider the finite-state machine in Figure 4–1. It consists of four states and five transitions. The security policy partitions the states into a set of authorized states $A = \{ s_1, s_2 \}$ and a set of unauthorized states $UA = \{ s_3, s_4 \}$. This system is not

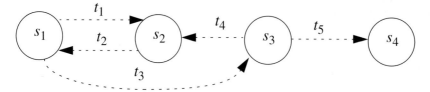

Figure 4–1   A simple finite-state machine. In this example, the authorized states are s_1 and s_2.

secure, because regardless of which authorized state it starts in, it can enter an unauthorized state. However, if the edge from s_1 to s_3 were not present, the system would be secure, because it could not enter an unauthorized state from an authorized state.

> **Definition 4–3.** A *breach of security* occurs when a system enters an unauthorized state.

We informally discussed the three basic properties relevant to security in Section 1.1. We now define them precisely.

> **Definition 4–4.** Let X be a set of entities and let I be some information. Then I has the property of *confidentiality* with respect to X if no member of X can obtain information about I.

Confidentiality implies that information must not be disclosed to some set of entities. It may be disclosed to others. The membership of set X is often implicit—for example, when we speak of a document that is confidential. Some entity has access to the document. All entities not authorized to have such access make up the set X.

> **Definition 4–5.** Let X be a set of entities and let I be some information or a resource. Then I has the property of *integrity* with respect to X if all members of X trust I.

This definition is deceptively simple. In addition to trusting the information itself, the members of X also trust that the conveyance and storage of I do not change the information or its trustworthiness (this aspect is sometimes called *data integrity*). If I is information about the origin of something, or about an identity, the members of X trust that the information is correct and unchanged (this aspect is sometimes called *origin integrity* or, more commonly, *authentication*). Also, I may be a resource rather than information. In that case, integrity means that the resource functions correctly (meeting its specifications). This aspect is called *assurance* and will be discussed in Part 6, "Assurance." As with confidentiality, the membership of X is often implicit.

> **Definition 4–6.** Let X be a set of entities and let I be a resource. Then I has the property of *availability* with respect to X if all members of X can access I.

The exact definition of "access" in Definition 4–6 varies depending on the needs of the members of X, the nature of the resource, and the use to which the resource is put. If a book-selling server takes up to 1 hour to service a request to purchase a book, that may meet the client's requirements for "availability." If a server of medical information takes up to 1 hour to service a request for information regarding an allergy to an anesthetic, that will not meet an emergency room's requirements for "availability."

A security policy considers all relevant aspects of confidentiality, integrity, and availability. With respect to confidentiality, it identifies those states in which information leaks to those not authorized to receive it. This includes not only the leakage of rights but also the illicit transmission of information without leakage of rights, called *information flow*. Also, the policy must handle dynamic changes of authorization, so it includes a temporal element. For example, a contractor working for a company may be authorized to access proprietary information during the lifetime of a nondisclosure agreement, but when that nondisclosure agreement expires, the contractor can no longer access that information. This aspect of the security policy is often called a *confidentiality policy*.

With respect to integrity, a security policy identifies authorized ways in which information may be altered and entities authorized to alter it. Authorization may derive from a variety of relationships, and external influences may constrain it; for example, in many transactions, a principle called *separation of duties* forbids an entity from completing the transaction on its own. Those parts of the security policy that describe the conditions and manner in which data can be altered are called the *integrity policy*.

With respect to availability, a security policy describes what services must be provided. It may present parameters within which the services will be accessible—for example, that a browser may download Web pages but not Java applets. It may require a level of service—for example, that a server will provide authentication data within 1 minute of the request being made. This relates directly to issues of quality of service.

The statement of a security policy may formally state the desired properties of the system. If the system is to be provably secure, the formal statement will allow the designers and implementers to prove that those desired properties hold. If a formal proof is unnecessary or infeasible, analysts can test that the desired properties hold for some set of inputs. Later chapters will discuss both these topics in detail.

In practice, a less formal type of security policy defines the set of authorized states. Typically, the security policy assumes that the reader understands the context in which the policy is issued—in particular, the laws, organizational policies, and other environmental factors. The security policy then describes conduct, actions, and authorizations defining "authorized users" and "authorized use."

EXAMPLE: A university disallows cheating, which is defined to include copying another student's homework assignment (with or without permission). A computer science class requires the students to do their homework on the department's computer. One student notices that a second student has not read protected the file containing her homework and copies it. Has either student (or have both students) breached security?

The second student has not, despite her failure to protect her homework. The security policy requires no action to prevent files from being read. Although she may have been too trusting, the policy does not ban this; hence, the second student has not breached security.

The first student has breached security. The security policy disallows the copying of homework, and the student has done exactly that. Whether the security policy specifically states that "files containing homework shall not be copied" or simply says that "users are bound by the rules of the university" is irrelevant; in the latter case, one of those rules bans cheating. If the security policy is silent on such matters, the most reasonable interpretation is that the policy disallows actions that the university disallows, because the computer science department is part of the university.

The retort that the first user could copy the files, and therefore the action is allowed, confuses *mechanism* with *policy*. The distinction is sharp:

Definition 4–7. A *security mechanism* is an entity or procedure that enforces some part of the security policy.

EXAMPLE: In the preceding example, the policy is the statement that no student may copy another student's homework. One mechanism is the file access controls; if the second student had set permissions to prevent the first student from reading the file containing her homework, the first student could not have copied that file.

EXAMPLE: Another site's security policy states that information relating to a particular product is proprietary and is not to leave the control of the company. The company stores its backup tapes in a vault in the town's bank (this is common practice in case the computer installation is completely destroyed). The company must ensure that only authorized employees have access to the backup tapes even when the tapes are stored off-site; hence, the bank's controls on access to the vault, and the procedures used to transport the tapes to and from the bank, are considered security mechanisms. Note that these mechanisms are not technical controls built into the computer. Procedural, or operational, controls also can be security mechanisms.

Security policies are often implicit rather than explicit. This causes confusion, especially when the policy is defined in terms of the mechanisms. This definition may be ambiguous—for example, if some mechanisms prevent a specific action and others allow it. Such policies lead to confusion, and sites should avoid them.

EXAMPLE: The UNIX operating system, initially developed for a small research group, had mechanisms sufficient to prevent users from accidentally damaging one another's files; for example, the user *ken* could not delete the user *dmr*'s files (unless *dmr* had set the files and the containing directories appropriately). The implied security policy for this friendly environment was "do not delete or corrupt another's files, and any file not protected may be read."

When the UNIX operating system moved into academic institutions and commercial and government environments, the previous security policy became inadequate; for example, some files had to be protected from individual users (rather than from groups of users). Not surprisingly, the security mechanisms were inadequate for those environments.

The difference between a policy and an abstract description of that policy is crucial to the analysis that follows.

Definition 4–8. A *security model* is a model that represents a particular policy or set of policies.

A model abstracts details relevant for analysis. Analyses rarely discuss particular policies; they usually focus on *specific characteristics* of policies, because many policies exhibit these characteristics; and the more policies with those characteristics, the more useful the analysis. By the HRU result (see Theorem 3–2), no single nontrivial analysis can cover all policies, but restricting the class of security policies sufficiently allows meaningful analysis of that class of policies.

4.2   Types of Security Policies

Each site has its own requirements for the levels of confidentiality, integrity, and availability, and the site policy states these needs for that particular site.

Definition 4–9. A *military security policy* (also called a *governmental security policy*) is a security policy developed primarily to provide confidentiality.

The name comes from the military's need to keep information, such as the date that a troop ship will sail, secret. Although integrity and availability are important, organizations using this class of policies can overcome the loss of either—for example, by using orders not sent through a computer network. But the compromise of confidentiality would be catastrophic, because an opponent would be able to plan countermeasures (and the organization may not know of the compromise).

Confidentiality is one of the factors of privacy, an issue recognized in the laws of many government entities (such as the Privacy Act of the United States and similar legislation in Sweden). Aside from constraining what information a government entity can legally obtain from individuals, such acts place constraints on the disclosure and use of that information. Unauthorized disclosure can result in penalties that include jail or fines; also, such disclosure undermines the authority and respect that individuals have for the government and inhibits them from disclosing that type of information to the agencies so compromised.

Definition 4–10. A *commercial security policy* is a security policy developed primarily to provide integrity.

The name comes from the need of commercial firms to prevent tampering with their data, because they could not survive such compromises. For example, if the confidentiality of a bank's computer is compromised, a customer's account balance may be revealed. This would certainly embarrass the bank and possibly cause the customer to take her business elsewhere. But the loss to the bank's "bottom line" would be minor. However, if the integrity of the computer holding the accounts were compromised, the balances in the customers' accounts could be altered, with financially ruinous effects.

Some integrity policies use the notion of a transaction; like database specifications, they require that actions occur in such a way as to leave the database in a consistent state. These policies, called *transaction-oriented integrity security policies*, are critical to organizations that require consistency of databases.

EXAMPLE: When a customer moves money from one account to another, the bank uses a well-formed transaction. This transaction has two distinct parts: money is first debited to the original account and then credited to the second account. Unless both parts of the transaction are completed, the customer will lose the money. With a well-formed transaction, if the transaction is interrupted, the state of the database is still consistent—either as it was before the transaction began or as it would have been when the transaction ended. Hence, part of the bank's security policy is that all transactions must be well-formed.

The role of trust in these policies highlights their difference. Confidentiality policies place no trust in objects; so far as the policy is concerned, the object could be a factually correct report or a tale taken from *Aesop's Fables*. The policy statement dictates whether that object can be disclosed. It says nothing about whether the object should be believed.

Integrity policies, to the contrary, indicate how much the object can be trusted. Given that this level of trust is correct, the policy dictates what a subject can do with that object. But the crucial question is how the level of trust is assigned. For example, if a site obtains a new version of a program, should that program have high integrity (that is, the site trusts the new version of that program) or low integrity (that is, the site does not yet trust the new program), or should the level of trust be somewhere in between (because the vendor supplied the program, but it has not been tested at the local site as thoroughly as the old version)? This makes integrity policies considerably more nebulous than confidentiality policies. The assignment of a level of confidentiality is based on what the classifier wants others to know, but the assignment of a level of integrity is based on what the classifier subjectively believes to be true about the trustworthiness of the information.

Two other terms describe policies related to security needs; because they appear elsewhere, we define them now.

Definition 4–11. A *confidentiality policy* is a security policy dealing only with confidentiality.

Definition 4–12. An *integrity policy* is a security policy dealing only with integrity.

Both confidentiality policies and military policies deal with confidentiality; however, a confidentiality policy does not deal with integrity at all, whereas a military policy may. A similar distinction holds for integrity policies and commercial policies.

4.3   The Role of Trust

The role of trust is crucial to understanding the nature of computer security. This book presents theories and mechanisms for analyzing and enhancing computer security, but any theories or mechanisms rest on certain assumptions. When someone understands the assumptions her security policies, mechanisms, and procedures rest on, she will have a very good understanding of how effective those policies, mechanisms, and procedures are. Let us examine the consequences of this maxim.

A system administrator receives a security patch for her computer's operating system. She installs it. Has she improved the security of her system? She has indeed, given the correctness of certain assumptions:

1. She is assuming that the patch came from the vendor and was not tampered with in transit, rather than from an attacker trying to trick her into installing a bogus patch that would actually open security holes. Winkler [947] describes a penetration test in which this technique enabled attackers to gain direct access to the computer systems of the target.

2. She is assuming that the vendor tested the patch thoroughly. Vendors are often under considerable pressure to issue patches quickly and sometimes test them only against a particular attack. The vulnerability may be deeper, however, and other attacks may succeed. When someone released an exploit of one vendor's operating system code, the vendor released a correcting patch in 24 hours. Unfortunately, the patch opened a second hole, one that was far easier to exploit. The next patch (released 48 hours later) fixed both problems correctly.

3. She is assuming that the vendor's test environment corresponds to her environment. Otherwise, the patch may not work as expected. As an example, a vendor's patch once reset ownerships of executables to the user *root*. At some installations, maintenance procedures required that these executables be owned by the user *bin*. The vendor's patch had to be

undone and fixed for the local configuration. This assumption also covers possible conflicts between different patches, as well as patches that conflict with one another (such as patches from different vendors of software that the system is using).

4. She is assuming that the patch is installed correctly. Some patches are simple to install, because they are simply executable files. Others are complex, requiring the system administrator to reconfigure network-oriented properties, add a user, modify the contents of a registry, give rights to some set of users, and then reboot the system. An error in any of these steps could prevent the patch from correcting the problems, as could an inconsistency between the environments in which the patch was developed and in which the patch is applied. Furthermore, the patch may claim to require specific privileges, when in reality the privileges are unnecessary and in fact dangerous.

These assumptions are fairly high-level, but invalidating any of them makes the patch a potential security problem.

Assumptions arise also at a much lower level. Consider formal verification, an oft-touted panacea for security problems. The important aspect is that formal verification provides a formal mathematical proof that a given program P is correct—that is, given any set of inputs i, j, k, the program P will produce the output x that its specification requires. This level of assurance is greater than most existing programs provide, and hence makes P a desirable program. Suppose a security-related program S has been formally verified for the operating system O. What assumptions would be made when it was installed?

1. The formal verification of S is correct—that is, the proof has no errors. Because formal verification relies on automated theorem provers as well as human analysis, the theorem provers must be programmed correctly.

2. The assumptions made in the formal verification of S are correct; specifically, the preconditions hold in the environment in which the program is to be executed. These preconditions are typically fed to the theorem provers as well as the program S. An implicit aspect of this assumption is that the version of O in the environment in which the program is to be executed is the same as the version of O used to verify S.

3. The program will be transformed into an executable whose actions correspond to those indicated by the source code; in other words, the compiler, linker, loader, and any libraries are correct. An experiment with one version of the UNIX operating system demonstrated how devastating a rigged compiler could be, and attackers have replaced libraries with others that performed additional functions, thereby increasing security risks.

4. The hardware will execute the program as intended. A program that relies on floating point calculations would yield incorrect results on some computer CPU chips, regardless of any formal verification of the program, owing to a flaw in these chips [178]. Similarly, a program that relies on inputs from hardware assumes that specific conditions cause those inputs.

The point is that *any* security policy, mechanism, or procedure is based on assumptions that, if incorrect, destroy the superstructure on which it is built. Analysts and designers (and users) must bear this in mind, because unless they understand what the security policy, mechanism, or procedure is based on, they jump from an unwarranted assumption to an erroneous conclusion.

4.4   Types of Access Control

A security policy may use two types of access controls, alone or in combination. In one, access control is left to the discretion of the owner. In the other, the operating system controls access, and the owner cannot override the controls.

The first type is based on user identity and is the most widely known:

Definition 4–13. If an individual user can set an access control mechanism to allow or deny access to an object, that mechanism is a *discretionary access control* (DAC), also called an *identity-based access control* (IBAC).

Discretionary access controls base access rights on the identity of the subject and the identity of the object involved. Identity is the key; the owner of the object constrains who can access it by allowing only particular subjects to have access. The owner states the constraint in terms of the identity of the subject, or the owner of the subject.

EXAMPLE: Suppose a child keeps a diary. The child controls access to the diary, because she can allow someone to read it (grant read access) or not allow someone to read it (deny read access). The child allows her mother to read it, but no one else. This is a discretionary access control because access to the diary is based on the identity of the subject (mom) requesting read access to the object (the diary).

The second type of access control is based on fiat, and identity is irrelevant:

Definition 4–14. When a system mechanism controls access to an object and an individual user cannot alter that access, the control is a *mandatory access control* (MAC), occasionally called a *rule-based access control*.

The operating system enforces mandatory access controls. Neither the subject nor the owner of the object can determine whether access is granted. Typically, the system mechanism will check information associated with both the subject and the object to determine whether the subject should access the object. Rules describe the conditions under which access is allowed.

EXAMPLE: The law allows a court to access driving records without the owners' permission. This is a mandatory control, because the owner of the record has no control over the court's accessing the information.

> **Definition 4–15.** An *originator controlled access control* (ORCON or ORG-CON) bases access on the creator of an object (or the information it contains).

The goal of this control is to allow the originator of the file (or of the information it contains) to control the dissemination of the information. The owner of the file has no control over who may access the file. Section 7.3 discusses this type of control in detail.

EXAMPLE: Bit Twiddlers, Inc., a company famous for its embedded systems, contracts with Microhackers Ltd., a company equally famous for its microcoding abilities. The contract requires Microhackers to develop a new microcode language for a particular processor designed to be used in high-performance embedded systems. Bit Twiddlers gives Microhackers a copy of its specifications for the processor. The terms of the contract require Microhackers to obtain permission before it gives any information about the processor to its subcontractors. This is an originator controlled access mechanism because, even though Microhackers owns the file containing the specifications, it may not allow anyone to access that information unless the creator, Bit Twiddlers, gives permission.

4.5   Example: Academic Computer Security Policy

Security policies can have few details, or many. The explicitness of a security policy depends on the environment in which it exists. A research lab or office environment may have an unwritten policy. A bank needs a very explicit policy. In practice, policies begin as generic statements of constraints on the members of the organization. These statements are derived from an analysis of threats, as described in Chapter 1, "An Overview of Computer Security." As questions (or incidents) arise, the policy is refined to cover specifics. As an example, we present an academic security policy.

4.5.1   General University Policy

This policy is an "Acceptable Use Policy" (AUP) for the Davis campus of the University of California. Because computing services vary from campus unit to campus unit, the policy does not dictate how the specific resources can be used. Instead, it presents generic constraints that the individual units can tighten.

The policy first presents the goals of campus computing: to provide access to resources and to allow the users to communicate with others throughout the world. It then states the responsibilities associated with the privilege of using campus computers. All users must "respect the rights of other users, respect the integrity of the systems and related physical resources, and observe all relevant laws, regulations, and contractual obligations."[1]

The policy states the intent underlying the rules, and notes that the system managers and users must abide by the law (for example, "Since electronic information is volatile and easily reproduced, users must exercise care in acknowledging and respecting the work of others through strict adherence to software licensing agreements and copyright laws").[2]

The enforcement mechanisms in this policy are procedural. For minor violations, either the unit itself resolves the problem (for example, by asking the offender not to do it again) or formal warnings are given. For more serious infractions, the administration may take stronger action such as denying access to campus computer systems. In very serious cases, the university may invoke disciplinary action. The Office of Student Judicial Affairs hears such cases and determines appropriate consequences.

The policy then enumerates specific examples of actions that are considered to be irresponsible use. Among these are illicitly monitoring others, spamming, and locating and exploiting security vulnerabilities. These are examples; they are not exhaustive. The policy concludes with references to other documents of interest.

This is a typical AUP. It is written informally and is aimed at the user community that is to abide by it. The electronic mail policy presents an interesting contrast to the AUP, probably because the AUP is for UC Davis only, and the electronic mail policy applies to all nine University of California campuses.

4.5.2   Electronic Mail Policy

The university has several auxiliary policies, which are subordinate to the general university policy. The electronic mail policy describes the constraints imposed on access to, and use of, electronic mail. It conforms to the general university policy but details additional constraints on both users and system administrators.

The electronic mail policy consists of three parts. The first is a short summary intended for the general user community, much as the AUP for UC Davis is intended

---

[1] From Part 1, Section 2 of the AUP for the University of California, Davis.
[2] From Part 1, Section 2 of the AUP for the University of California, Davis.

for the general user community. The second part is the full policy for all university campuses and is written as precisely as possible. The last document describes how the Davis campus implements the general university electronic mail policy.

4.5.2.1   The Electronic Mail Policy Summary

The summary first warns users that their electronic mail is not private. It may be read accidentally, in the course of normal system maintenance, or in other ways stated in the full policy. It also warns users that electronic mail can be forged or altered as well as forwarded (and that forwarded messages may be altered). This section is interesting because policies rarely alert users to the threats they face; policies usually focus on the remedial techniques.

The next two sections are lists of what users should, and should not, do. They may be summarized as "think before you send; be courteous and respectful of others; and don't interfere with others' use of electronic mail." They emphasize that supervisors have the right to examine employees' electronic mail that relates to the job. Surprisingly, the university does not ban personal use of electronic mail, probably in the recognition that enforcement would demoralize people and that the overhead of carrying personal mail is minimal in a university environment. The policy does require that users not use personal mail to such an extent that it interferes with their work or causes the university to incur extra expense.

Finally, the policy concludes with a statement about its application. In a private company, this would be unnecessary, but the University of California is a quasi-governmental institution and as such is bound to respect parts of the United States Constitution and the California Constitution that private companies are not bound to respect. Also, as an educational institution, the university takes the issues surrounding freedom of expression and inquiry very seriously. Would a visitor to campus be bound by these policies? The final section says yes. Would an employee of Lawrence Livermore National Laboratories, run for the Department of Energy by the University of California, also be bound by these policies? Here, the summary suggests that they would be, but whether the employees of the lab are Department of Energy employees or University of California employees could affect this. So we turn to the full policy.

4.5.2.2   The Full Policy

The full policy also begins with a description of the context of the policy, as well as its purpose and scope. The scope here is far more explicit than that in the summary. For example, the full policy does not apply to e-mail services of the Department of Energy laboratories run by the university, such as Lawrence Livermore National Laboratories. Moreover, this policy does not apply to printed copies of e-mail, because other university policies apply to such copies.

The general provisions follow. They state that e-mail services and infrastructure are university property, and that all who use them are expected to abide by the law and by university policies. Failure to do so may result in access to e-mail being revoked. The policy reiterates that the university will apply principles of academic freedom and freedom of speech in its handling of e-mail, and so will seek access to e-mail without the holder's permission only under extreme circumstances, which are enumerated, and only with the approval of a campus vice chancellor or a university vice president (essentially, the second ranking officer of a campus or of the university system). If this is infeasible, the e-mail may be read only as is needed to resolve the emergency, and then authorization must be secured after the fact.

The next section discusses legitimate and illegitimate use of the university's e-mail. The policy allows anonymity to senders provided that it does not violate laws or other policies. It disallows using mail to interfere with others, such as by sending spam or letter bombs. It also expressly permits the use of university facilities for sending personal e-mail, provided that doing so does not interfere with university business; and it cautions that such personal e-mail may be treated as a "University record" subject to disclosure.

The discussion of security and confidentiality emphasizes that, although the university will not go out of its way to read e-mail, it can do so for legitimate business purposes and to keep e-mail service robust and reliable. The section on archiving and retention says that people may be able to recover e-mail from end systems where it may be archived as part of a regular backup.

The last three sections discuss the consequences of violations and direct the chancellor of each campus to develop procedures to implement the policy.

An interesting sidelight occurs in Appendix A, "Definitions." The definition of "E-mail" includes any computer records viewed with e-mail systems or services, and the "transactional information associated with such records [E-mail], such as headers, summaries, addresses, and addressees." This appears to encompass the network packets used to carry the e-mail from one host to another. This ambiguity illustrates the problem with policies. The language is imprecise. This motivates the use of more mathematical languages, such as DTEL, for specifying policies.

4.5.2.3 Implementation at UC Davis

This interpretation of the policy simply specifies those points delegated to the campus. Specifically, "incidental personal use" is not allowed if that personal use benefits a non-university organization, with a few specific exceptions enumerated in the policy. Then procedures for inspecting, monitoring, and disclosing the contents of e-mail are given, as are appeal procedures. The section on backups states that the campus does not archive all e-mail, and even if e-mail is backed up incidental to usual backup practices, it need not be made available to the employee.

This interpretation adds campus-specific requirements and procedures to the university's policy. The local augmentation amplifies the system policy; it does not contradict it or limit it. Indeed, what would happen if the campus policy conflicted with the system's policy? In general, the higher (system-wide) policy would prevail. The advantage of leaving implementation to the campuses is that they can take into account local variations and customs, as well as any peculiarities in the way the administration and the Academic Senate govern that campus.

4.6   Summary

Security policies define "security" for a system or site. They may be implied policies defined by the common consensus of the community, or they may be informal policies whose interpretations are defined by the community. Both of these types of policies are usually ambiguous and do not precisely define "security." A policy may be formal, in which case ambiguities arise either from the use of natural languages such as English or from the failure to cover specific areas.

Formal mathematical models of policies enable analysts to deduce a rigorous definition of "security" but do little to improve the average user's understanding of what "security" means for a site. The average user is not mathematically sophisticated enough to read and interpret the mathematics.

Trust underlies all policies and enforcement mechanisms. Policies themselves make assumptions about the way systems, software, hardware, and people behave. At a lower level, security mechanisms and procedures also make such assumptions. Even when rigorous methodologies (such as formal mathematical models or formal verification) are applied, the methodologies themselves simply push the assumptions, and therefore the trust, to a lower level. Understanding the assumptions and the trust involved in any policies and mechanisms deepens one's understanding of the security of a system.

This brief overview of policy, and of policy expression, lays the foundation for understanding the more detailed policy models used in practice.

4.7   Further Reading

Much of security analysis involves definition and refinement of security policies. Wood [954] has published a book of templates for specific parts of policies. That book justifies each part and allows readers to develop policies by selecting the appropriate parts from a large set of possibilities. Essays by Bailey [51] and Abrams and Bailey [4] discuss management of security issues and explain why different members of an organization interpret the same policy differently. Sterne's wonderful paper [875] discusses the nature of policy in general.

Jajodia and his colleagues [467] present a "little language" for expressing authorization policies. They show that their language can express many aspects of existing policies and argue that it allows elements of these policies to be combined into authorization schemes. Other little languages include DTEL [50,336], a constraint language for Java programs [708]. File system state analysis programs use low-level policy languages to describe the current file system state; two examples are the programs tripwire [510] and the RIACS auditing and checking system [98].

Boebert and Kain [119] observed that type checking provides a form of access control. Some policy languages (such as DTEL) are based on this observation. At least one firewall [900] has security mechanisms also based on type checking.

Cholvy and Cuppens [173] describe a method of checking policies for consistency and determining how they apply to given situations.

Son, Chaney, and Thomlinson [856] discuss enforcement of partial security policies in real-time databases to balance real-time requirements with security. Their idea of "partial security policies" has applications in other environments. Zurko and Simon [966] present an alternative focus for policies.

Jones and Lipton [472] explored the balancing of security and precision for confidentiality policies.

4.8   Exercises

1. In Figure 4–1, suppose that edge t_3 went from s_1 to s_4. Would the resulting system be secure?

2. Revisit the example of one student copying another student's homework assignment. Describe three other ways the first student could copy the second student's homework assignment, even assuming that the file access control mechanisms are set to deny him permission to read the file.

3. A noted computer security expert has said that without integrity, no system can provide confidentiality.

   a. Do you agree? Justify your answer.
   b. Can a system provide integrity without confidentiality? Again, justify your answer.

4. A cryptographer once claimed that security mechanisms other than cryptography were unnecessary because cryptography could provide any desired level of confidentiality and integrity. Ignoring availability, either justify or refute the cryptographer's claim.

5. Classify each of the following as an example of a mandatory, discretionary, or originator controlled policy, or a combination thereof. Justify your answers.

   a. The file access control mechanisms of the UNIX operating system
   b. A system in which no memorandum can be distributed without the author's consent
   c. A military facility in which only generals can enter a particular room

     d. A university registrar's office, in which a faculty member can see the grades of a particular student provided that the student has given written permission for the faculty member to see them.

6. Consider the UC Davis policy on reading electronic mail. A research group wants to obtain raw data from a network that carries all network traffic to the Department of Political Science.

     a. Discuss the impact of the electronic mail policy on the collection of such data.

     b. How would you change the policy to allow the collection of this data without abandoning the principle that electronic mail should be protected?

Chapter 5
Confidentiality Policies

> SHEPHERD: Sir, there lies such secrets in this fardel
> and box which none must know but the king;
> and which he shall know within this hour, if I
> may come to the speech of him.
> —*The Winter's Tale*, IV, iv, 785–788.

Confidentiality policies emphasize the protection of confidentiality. The importance of these policies lies in part in what they provide, and in part in their role in the development of the concept of security. This chapter explores one such policy—the Bell-LaPadula Model—and the controversy it engendered.

5.1 Goals of Confidentiality Policies

A confidentiality policy, also called an *information flow policy*, prevents the unauthorized disclosure of information. Unauthorized alteration of information is secondary. For example, the navy must keep confidential the date on which a troop ship will sail. If the date is changed, the redundancy in the systems and paperwork should catch that change. But if the enemy knows the date of sailing, the ship could be sunk. Because of extensive redundancy in military communications channels, availability is also less of a problem.

The term "governmental" covers several requirements that protect citizens' privacy. In the United States, the Privacy Act requires that certain personal data be kept confidential. Income tax returns are legally confidential and are available only to the Internal Revenue Service or to legal authorities with a court order. The principle of "executive privilege" and the system of nonmilitary classifications suggest that the people working in the government need to limit the distribution of certain documents and information. Governmental models represent the policies that satisfy these requirements.

5.2   The Bell-LaPadula Model

The Bell-LaPadula Model [63, 64] corresponds to military-style classifications. It has influenced the development of many other models and indeed much of the development of computer security technologies.[1]

5.2.1   Informal Description

The simplest type of confidentiality classification is a set of *security clearances* arranged in a linear (total) ordering (see Figure 5–1). These clearances represent sensitivity levels. The higher the security clearance, the more sensitive the information (and the greater the need to keep it confidential). A subject has a *security clearance*. In the figure, Claire's security clearance is C (for CONFIDENTIAL), and Thomas' is TS (for TOP SECRET). An object has a *security classification*; the security classification of the electronic mail files is S (for SECRET), and that of the telephone list files is UC (for UNCLASSIFIED). (When we refer to both subject clearances and object classifications, we use the term "classification.") The goal of the Bell-LaPadula security model is to prevent read access to objects at a security classification higher than the subject's clearance.

The Bell-LaPadula security model combines mandatory and discretionary access controls. In what follows, "*S* has discretionary read (write) access to *O*" means that the access control matrix entry for *S* and *O* corresponding to the discretionary access control component contains a read (write) right. In other words, were the mandatory controls not present, *S* would be able to read (write) *O*.

TOP SECRET (TS)	Tamara, Thomas	Personnel Files
|	|	|
SECRET (S)	Sally, Samuel	Electronic Mail Files
|	|	|
CONFIDENTIAL (C)	Claire, Clarence	Activity Log Files
|	|	|
UNCLASSIFIED (UC)	Ulaley, Ursula	Telephone List Files

Figure 5–1   At the left is the basic confidentiality classification system. The four security levels are arranged with the most sensitive at the top and the least sensitive at the bottom. In the middle are individuals grouped by their security clearances, and at the right is a set of documents grouped by their security levels.

---

[1] The terminology in this section follows that of the unified exposition of the Bell-LaPadula Model [64].

Let $L(S) = l_s$ be the security clearance of subject S, and let $L(O) = l_o$ be the security classification of object O. For all security classifications l_i, $i = 0, ..., k-1$, $l_i < l_{i+1}$.

- **Simple Security Condition, Preliminary Version:** S can read O if and only if $l_o \le l_s$ and S has discretionary read access to O.

In Figure 5–1, for example, Claire and Clarence cannot read personnel files, but Tamara and Sally can read the activity log files (and, in fact, Tamara can read any of the files, given her clearance), assuming that the discretionary access controls allow it.

Should Tamara decide to copy the contents of the personnel files into the activity log files and set the discretionary access permissions appropriately, Claire could then read the personnel files. Thus, for all practical purposes, Claire could read the files at a higher level of security. A second property prevents this:

- ***-Property (Star Property), Preliminary Version:** S can write O if and only if $l_s \le l_o$ and S has discretionary write access to O.

Because the activity log files are classified C and Tamara has a clearance of TS, she cannot write to the activity log files.

Define a *secure system* as one in which both the simple security condition, preliminary version, and the *-property, preliminary version, hold. A straightforward induction establishes the following theorem.

Theorem 5–1. Basic Security Theorem, Preliminary Version: Let Σ be a system with a secure initial state σ_0, and let T be a set of state transformations. If every element of T preserves the simple security condition, preliminary version, and the *-property, preliminary version, then every state σ_i, $i \ge 0$, is secure.

Expand the model by adding a set of *categories* to each security classification. Each category describes a kind of information. Objects placed in multiple categories have the kinds of information in all of those categories. These categories arise from the "need to know" principle, which states that no subject should be able to read objects unless reading them is necessary for that subject to perform its functions. The sets of categories to which a person may have access is simply the power set of the set of categories. For example, if the categories are NUC, EUR, and US, someone can have access to any of the following sets of categories: $\varnothing$ (none), { NUC }, { EUR }, { US }, { NUC, EUR }, {NUC, US }, { EUR, US }, and { NUC, EUR, US }. These sets of categories form a lattice under the operation $\subseteq$ (subset of); see Figure 5–2. (Chapter 27, "Lattices," discusses the mathematical nature of lattices.)

Each security level and category form a *security level*.[2] As before, we say that subjects *have clearance at* (or *are cleared into*, or *are in*) a security level and that

---

[2] There is less than full agreement on this terminology. Some call security levels "compartments." However, others use this term as a synonym for "categories." We follow the terminology of the unified exposition [64].

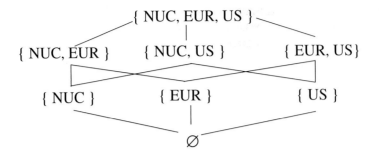

Figure 5–2   Lattice generated by the categories NUC, EUR, and US. The lines represent the ordering relation induced by ⊆.

objects *are at the level of* (or *are in*) a security level. For example, William may be cleared into the level (SECRET, { EUR }) and George into the level (TOP SECRET, { NUC, US }). A document may be classified as (CONFIDENTIAL, {EUR }).

Security levels change access. Because categories are based on a "need to know," someone with access to the category set { NUC, US } presumably has no need to access items in the category EUR. Hence, read access should be denied, even if the security clearance of the subject is higher than the security classification of the object. But if the desired object is in any of the security levels ∅, { NUC }, { US }, or { NUC, US } and the subject's security clearance is no less than the document's security classification, access should be granted because the subject is cleared into the same category set as the object.

This suggests a new relation for capturing the combination of security classification and category set. Define the relation *dom* (dominates) as follows.

> **Definition 5–1.** The security level (L, C) *dominates* the security level (L′, C′) if and only if $L′ \leq L$ and $C′ \subseteq C$.

We write (L, C) ¬*dom* (L′, C′) when (L, C) *dom* (L′, C′) is false. This relation also induces a lattice on the set of security levels [240].

EXAMPLE: George is cleared into security level (SECRET, { NUC, EUR}), DocA is classified as (CONFIDENTIAL, { NUC }), DocB is classified as (SECRET, { EUR, US}), and DocC is classified as (SECRET, { EUR }). Then:

George *dom* DocA as CONFIDENTIAL ≤ SECRET and { NUC } ⊆ { NUC, EUR }

George ¬*dom* DocB as { EUR, US } ⊄ { NUC, EUR }
George *dom* DocC as SECRET ≤ SECRET and { EUR } ⊆ { NUC, EUR }

Let C(S) be the category set of subject S, and let C(O) be the category set of object O. The simple security condition, preliminary version, is modified in the obvious way:

- *Simple Security Condition:* S can read O if and only if S *dom* O and S has discretionary read access to O.

In the example above, George can read DocA and DocC but not DocB (again, assuming that the discretionary access controls allow such access).

Suppose Paul is cleared into security level (SECRET, { EUR, US, NUC }) and has discretionary read access to DocB. Paul can read DocB; were he to copy its contents to DocA and set its access permissions accordingly, George could then read DocB. The modified *-property prevents this:

- ***-Property:*** S can write to O if and only if O *dom* S and S has discretionary write access to O.

Because DocA *dom* Paul is false (because $C(\text{Paul}) \not\subseteq C(\text{DocA})$), Paul cannot write to DocA.

The simple security condition is often described as "no reads up" and the *-property as "no writes down."

Redefine a *secure system* as one in which both the simple security property and the *-property hold. The analogue to the Basic Security Theorem, preliminary version, can also be established by induction.

Theorem 5–2. *Basic Security Theorem:* Let Σ be a system with a secure initial state σ_0, and let T be a set of state transformations. If every element of T preserves the simple security condition and the *-property, then every σ_i, $i \geq 0$, is secure.

At times, a subject must communicate with another subject at a lower level. This requires the higher-level subject to write into a lower-level object that the lower-level subject can read.

EXAMPLE: A colonel with (SECRET, { NUC, EUR }) clearance needs to send a message to a major with (SECRET, { EUR }) clearance. The colonel must write a document that has at most the (SECRET, { EUR }) classification. But this violates the *-property, because (SECRET, { NUC, EUR }) *dom* (SECRET, { EUR }).

The model provides a mechanism for allowing this type of communication. A subject has a *maximum security level* and a *current security level*. The maximum security level must dominate the current security level. A subject may (effectively) decrease its security level from the maximum in order to communicate with entities at lower security levels.

EXAMPLE: The colonel's maximum security level is (SECRET, { NUC, EUR }). She changes her current security level to (SECRET, { EUR }). This is valid, because the maximum security level dominates the current security level. She can then create the document at the major's clearance level and send it to him.

How this policy is instantiated in different environments depends on the requirements of each environment. The conventional use is to define "read" as "allowing information to flow from the object being read to the subject reading," and "write" as "allowing information to flow from the subject writing to the object being written." Thus, "read" usually includes "execute" (because by monitoring the instructions executed, one can determine the contents of portions of the file) and "write" includes "append" (as the information is placed in the file, it does not overwrite what is already in the file, however). Other actions may be included as appropriate; however, those who instantiate the model must understand exactly what those actions are.

5.2.2   Example: The Data General B2 UNIX System

The Data General B2 UNIX (DG/UX) system provides mandatory access controls (MACs). The MAC label is a label identifying a particular compartment. This section describes only the default labels; the system enables other labels to be created.

5.2.2.1   Assigning MAC Labels

When a process (subject) begins, it is assigned the MAC label of its parent. The initial label (assigned at login time) is the label assigned to the user in a database called the *Authorization and Authentication (A&A) Database*. Objects are assigned labels at creation, but the labels may be either *explicit* or *implicit*. The system stores explicit labels as parts of the object's attributes. It determines implicit labels from the parent directory of the object.

The least upper bound of all compartments in the DG/UX lattice has the label IMPL_HI (for "implementation high"); the greatest lower bound has the label IMPL_LO (for "implementation low"). The lattice is divided into three regions, which are summarized in Figure 5–3.[3]

The highest region (administrative region) is reserved for data that users cannot access, such as logs, MAC label definitions, and so forth. Because reading up and writing up are disallowed (the latter is a DG/UX extension to the multilevel security model; see Section 5.2.2.2), users can neither read nor alter data in this region. Administrative processes such as servers execute with MAC labels in this region; however, they sanitize data sent to user processes with MAC labels in the user region.

System programs are in the lowest region (virus prevention region). No user process can write to them, so no user process can alter them. Because execution requires read access, users can execute the programs. The name of this region comes

---

[3] The terminology used here corresponds to that of the DG/UX system. Note that "hierarchy level" corresponds to "clearance" or "classification" in the preceding section.

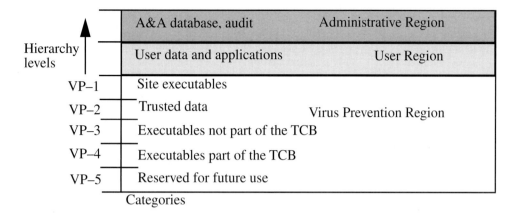

Figure 5–3   The three MAC regions in the MAC lattice (modified from the DG/UX Security Manual [230], p. 4–7, Figure 4–4). TCB stands for "trusted computing base."

from the fact that viruses and other forms of malicious logic involve alterations of trusted executables.[4]

Problems arise when programs of different levels access the same directory. If a program with MAC label *MAC_A* tries to create a file, and a file of that name but with MAC label *MAC_B* (*MAC_B dom MAC_A*) exists, the create will fail. To prevent this leakage of information, only programs with the same MAC label as the directory can create files in that directory. For the */tmp* directory, and the mail spool directory */var/mail*, this restriction will prevent standard operations such as compiling and delivering mail. DG/UX introduces a "multilevel directory" to solve this problem.

A *multilevel directory* is a directory with a set of subdirectories, one for each label. These "hidden directories" normally are not visible to the user, but if a process with MAC label *MAC_A* tries to create a file in */tmp*, it actually creates a file in the hidden directory under */tmp* with MAC label *MAC_A*. The file can have the same name as one in the hidden directory corresponding to label *MAC_A*. The parent directory of a file in */tmp* is the hidden directory. Furthermore, a reference to the parent directory goes to the hidden directory.

EXAMPLE: A process with label *MAC_A* creates a directory */tmp/a*. Another process with label *MAC_B* creates a directory */tmp/a*. The processes then change the correct working directory to */tmp/a* and then to .. (the parent directory). Both processes will appear to have */tmp* as the current working directory. However, the system call

```
stat(".", &stat_buffer)
```

---

[4] The TCB, or trusted computing base, is that part of the system that enforces security.

returns a different inode number for each process, because it returns the inode number of the current working directory—the hidden directory. The system call

```
dg_mstat(".", &stat_buffer)
```

translates the notion of "current working directory" to the multilevel directory when the current working directory is a hidden directory.

Mounting unlabeled file systems requires the files to be labeled. Symbolic links aggravate this problem. Does the MAC label the target of the link control, or does the MAC label the link itself? DG/UX uses a notion of inherited labels (called *implicit labels*) to solve this problem. The following rules control the way objects are labeled.

1. Roots of file systems have explicit MAC labels. If a file system without labels is mounted on a labeled file system, the root directory of the mounted file system receives an explicit label equal to that of the mount point. However, the label of the mount point, and of the underlying tree, is no longer visible, and so its label is unchanged (and will become visible again when the file system is unmounted).
2. An object with an implicit MAC label inherits the label of its parent.
3. When a hard link to an object is created, that object must have an explicit label; if it does not, the object's implicit label is converted to an explicit label. A corollary is that moving a file to a different directory makes its label explicit.
4. If the label of a directory changes, any immediate children with implicit labels have those labels converted to explicit labels before the parent directory's label is changed.
5. When the system resolves a symbolic link, the label of the object is the label of the target of the symbolic link. However, to resolve the link, the process needs access to the symbolic link itself.

Rules 1 and 2 ensure that every file system object has a MAC label, either implicit or explicit. But when a file object has an implicit label, and two hard links from different directories, it may have two labels. Let */x/y/z* and */x/a/b* be hard links to the same object. Suppose *y* has an explicit label IMPL_HI and *a* an explicit label *IMPL_B*. Then the file object can be accessed by a process at IMPL_HI as */x/y/z* and by a process at *IMPL_B* as */x/a/b*. Which label is correct? Two cases arise.

Suppose the hard link is created while the file system is on a DG/UX B2 system. Then the DG/UX system converts the target's implicit label to an explicit one (rule 3). Thus, regardless of the path used to refer to the object, the label of the object will be the same.

Suppose the hard link exists when the file system is mounted on the DG/UX B2 system. In this case, the target had no file label when it was created, and one must be added. If no objects on the paths to the target have explicit labels, the target will have the same (implicit) label regardless of the path being used. But if any object on any path to the target of the link acquires an explicit label, the target's label may depend on which path is taken. To avoid this, the implicit labels of a directory's children must be preserved when the directory's label is made explicit. Rule 4 does this.

Because symbolic links interpolate path names of files, rather than store inode numbers, computing the label of symbolic links is straightforward. If */x/y/z* is a symbolic link to */a/b/c*, then the MAC label of *c* is computed in the usual way. However, the symbolic link itself is a file, and so the process must also have access to the link file *z*.

5.2.2.2 Using MAC Labels

The DG/UX B2 system uses the Bell-LaPadula notion of dominance, with one change. The system obeys the simple security condition (reading down is permitted), but the implementation of the *-property requires that the process MAC label and the object MAC label be equal, so writing up is not permitted, but writing is permitted in the same compartment.

Because of this restriction on writing, the DG/UX system provides processes and objects with a range of labels called a *MAC tuple*. A *range* is a set of labels expressed by a *lower bound* and an *upper bound*. A MAC tuple consists of up to three ranges (one for each of the regions in Figure 5–3).

EXAMPLE: A system has two security levels, TS and S, the former dominating the latter. The categories are COMP, NUC, and ASIA. Examples of ranges are

[(S, { COMP }), (TS, { COMP })]
[(S, ∅), (TS, { COMP, NUC, ASIA })]
[(S, { ASIA }), (TS, { ASIA, NUC })]

The label (TS, {COMP}) is in the first two ranges. The label (S, {NUC, ASIA}) is in the last two ranges. However,

[(S, {ASIA}), (TS, { COMP, NUC})]

is not a valid range because *not* (TS, { COMP, NUC }) *dom* (S, { ASIA }).

An object can have a MAC tuple as well as the required MAC label. If both are present, the tuple overrides the label. A process has read access when its MAC label grants read access to the upper bound of the range. A process has write access when its MAC label grants write access to any label in the MAC tuple range.

EXAMPLE: Suppose an object's MAC tuple is the single range

[(S, { ASIA }), (TS, { ASIA, COMP})]

A subject with MAC label (S, { ASIA }) cannot read the object, because

(TS, { ASIA, COMP}) *dom* (S, { ASIA })

It can write to the object, because (S, { ASIA }) dominates the lower bound and is dominated by the upper bound. A subject with MAC label (TS, { ASIA, COMP, NUC }) can read the object but cannot write the object. A subject with MAC label (TS, { ASIA, COMP }) can both read and write the object. A subject with MAC label (TS, {EUR}) can neither read nor write the object, because its label is incomparable to that of the object, and the *dom* relation does not hold.

A process has both a MAC label and a MAC tuple. The label always lies within the range for the region in which the process is executing. Initially, the subject's accesses are restricted by its MAC label. However, the process may extend its read and write capabilities to within the bounds of the MAC tuple.

5.3   Summary

The influence of the Bell-LaPadula Model permeates all policy modeling in computer security. It was the first mathematical model to capture attributes of a real system in its rules. It formed the basis for several standards, including the Department of Defense's Trusted Computer System Evaluation Criteria (the TCSEC or the "Orange Book" discussed in Chapter 18) [257].

5.4   Further Reading

The developers of the ADEPT-50 system presented a formal model of the security controls that predated the Bell-LaPadula Model [568, 934]. Landwehr and colleagues [545] explored aspects of formal models for computer security. Multics implemented the Bell-LaPadula Model [703]. Denning used the Bell-LaPadula Model in SeaView [245, 248], a database designed with security features. The model forms the basis for several other models, including the database model of Jajodia and Sandhu [468] and the military message system model of Landwehr [548]. The latter is an excellent example of how models are applied in practice.

Dion [271] extended the Bell-LaPadula Model to allow system designers and implementers to use that model more easily. Sidhu and Gasser [828] designed a local area network to handle multiple security levels.

McLean challenged some of the assumptions of the Bell-LaPadula Model [610,611]. Bell [60] and LaPadula [551] responded, discussing the different types of modeling in physical science [560] and mathematics [690].

Feiertag, Levitt, and Robinson [310] developed a multilevel model that has several differences from the Bell-LaPadula Model. Taylor [896] elegantly compares them. Smith and Winslett [843] use a mandatory model to model databases that differ from the Bell-LaPadula Model.

Gambel [344] discusses efforts to apply a confidentiality policy similar to Bell-LaPadula to a system developed from off-the-shelf components, none of which implemented the policy precisely.

Irvine and Volpano [461] cast multilevel security in terms of a type subsystem for a polymorphic programming language.

5.5   Exercises

1. Why is it meaningless to have compartments at the UNCLASSIFIED level (such as (UNCLASSIFIED, { NUC }) and (UNCLASSIFIED, { EUR }))?

2. Given the security levels TOP SECRET, SECRET, CONFIDENTIAL, and UNCLASSIFIED (ordered from highest to lowest), and the categories A, B, and C, specify what type of access (read, write, both, or neither) is allowed in each of the following situations. Assume that discretionary access controls allow anyone access unless otherwise specified.

   a. Paul, cleared for (TOP SECRET, { A, C }), wants to access a document classified (SECRET, { B, C }).

   b. Anna, cleared for (CONFIDENTIAL, { C }), wants to access a document classified (CONFIDENTIAL, { B }).

   c. Jesse, cleared for (SECRET, { C }), wants to access a document classified (CONFIDENTIAL, { C }).

   d. Sammi, cleared for (TOP SECRET, { A, C }), wants to access a document classified (CONFIDENTIAL, { A }).

   e. Robin, who has no clearances (and so works at the UNCLASSIFIED level), wants to access a document classified (CONFIDENTIAL, { B }).

3. Prove that any file in the DG/UX system with a link count greater than 1 must have an explicit MAC label.

4. In the DG/UX system, why is the virus prevention region *below* the user region?

5. In the DG/UX system, why is the administrative region *above* the user region?

6. Declassification effectively violates the *-property of the Bell-LaPadula Model. Would raising the classification of an object violate any properties of the model? Why or why not?

Chapter 6
Integrity Policies

ISABELLA: Some one with child by him? My cousin Juliet?
LUCIO: Is she your cousin?
ISABELLA: Adoptedly; as school-maids change their names
By vain, though apt affection.
—*Measure for Measure*, I, iv, 45–48.

An inventory control system may function correctly if the data it manages is released; but it cannot function correctly if the data can be randomly changed. So integrity, rather than confidentiality, is key. Integrity policies focus on integrity rather than confidentiality, because most commercial and industrial firms are more concerned with accuracy than disclosure. In this chapter we discuss the major integrity security policies and explore their design.

6.1 Goals

Commercial requirements differ from military requirements in their emphasis on preserving data integrity. Lipner [571] identifies five requirements:

1. Users will not write their own programs, but will use existing production programs and databases.
2. Programmers will develop and test programs on a nonproduction system; if they need access to actual data, they will be given production data via a special process, but will use it on their development system.
3. A special process must be followed to install a program from the development system onto the production system.
4. The special process in requirement 3 must be controlled and audited.
5. The managers and auditors must have access to both the system state and the system logs that are generated.

These requirements suggest several principles of operation.

First comes *separation of duty*. The principle of separation of duty states that if two or more steps are required to perform a critical function, at least two different people should perform the steps. Moving a program from the development system to the production system is an example of a critical function. Suppose one of the application programmers made an invalid assumption while developing the program. Part of the installation procedure is for the installer to certify that the program works "correctly," that is, as required. The error is more likely to be caught if the installer is a different person (or set of people) than the developer. Similarly, if the developer wishes to subvert the production data with a corrupt program, the certifier either must not detect the code to do the corruption, or must be in league with the developer.

Next comes *separation of function*. Developers do not develop new programs on production systems because of the potential threat to production data. Similarly, the developers do not process production data on the development systems. Depending on the sensitivity of the data, the developers and testers may receive sanitized production data. Further, the development environment must be as similar as possible to the actual production environment.

Last comes *auditing*. Commercial systems emphasize recovery and accountability. Auditing is the process of analyzing systems to determine what actions took place and who performed them. Hence, commercial systems must allow extensive auditing and thus have extensive logging (the basis for most auditing). Logging and auditing are especially important when programs move from the development system to the production system, since the integrity mechanisms typically do not constrain the certifier. Auditing is, in many senses, external to the model.

Even when disclosure is at issue, the needs of a commercial environment differ from those of a military environment. In a military environment, clearance to access specific categories and security levels brings the ability to access information in those compartments. Commercial firms rarely grant access on the basis of "clearance"; if a particular individual needs to know specific information, he or she will be given it. While this can be modeled using the Bell-LaPadula Model, it requires a large number of categories and security levels, increasing the complexity of the modeling. More difficult is the issue of controlling this proliferation of categories and security levels. In a military environment, creation of security levels and categories is centralized. In commercial firms, this creation would usually be decentralized. The former allows tight control on the number of compartments, whereas the latter allows no such control.

More insidious is the problem of information aggregation. Commercial firms usually allow a limited amount of (innocuous) information to become public, but keep a large amount of (sensitive) information confidential. By aggregating the innocuous information, one can often deduce much sensitive information. Preventing this requires the model to track what questions have been asked, and this complicates the model enormously. Certainly the Bell-LaPadula Model lacks this ability.

6.2   Biba Integrity Model

In 1977, Biba [88] studied the nature of the integrity of systems. In his model, a system consists of a set S of subjects, a set O of objects, and a set I of integrity levels.[1] The levels are ordered. The relation $\leq \subseteq I \times I$ holds when the second integrity level either dominates or is the same as the first. The function $i:S \cup O \rightarrow I$ returns the integrity level of an object or a subject.

Some comments on the meaning of "integrity level" will provide intuition behind the constructions to follow. The higher the level, the more confidence one has that a program will execute correctly (or detect problems with its inputs and stop executing). Data at a higher level is more accurate and/or reliable (with respect to some metric) than data at a lower level. Again, this model implicitly incorporates the notion of "trust"; in fact, the term "trustworthiness" is used as a measure of integrity level. For example, a process at a level higher than that of an object is considered more "trustworthy" than that object.

Integrity labels, in general, are not also security labels. They are assigned and maintained separately, because the reasons behind the labels are different. Security labels primarily limit the flow of information; integrity labels primarily inhibit the modification of information. They may overlap, however, with surprising results (see Exercise 1).

Biba's model is the dual of the Bell-LaPadula Model. Its rules are as follows.

1. $s \in S$ can read $o \in O$ if and only if $i(s) \leq i(o)$.
2. $s \in S$ can write to $o \in O$ if and only if $i(o) \leq i(s)$.
3. $s_1 \in S$ can execute $s_2 \in S$ if and only if $i(s_2) \leq i(s_1)$.

Note that rules 1 and 2 imply that if both read and write are allowed, $i(s) = i(o)$. Also, by replacing the notion of "integrity level" with "integrity compartments," and adding the notion of discretionary controls, one obtains the full dual of Bell-LaPadula.

EXAMPLE: Pozzo and Gray [730, 731] implemented Biba's strict integrity model on the distributed operating system LOCUS [724]. Their goal was to limit execution domains for each program to prevent untrusted software from altering data or other software. Their approach was to make the level of trust in software and data explicit. They have different classes of executable programs. Their *credibility ratings* (Biba's integrity levels) assign a measure of trustworthiness on a scale from 0 (untrusted) to n (highly trusted), depending on the source of the software. Trusted file systems contain only executable files with the same credibility level. Associated with each user (process) is a *risk level* that starts out set to the highest credibility level at which that user can execute. Users may execute programs with credibility levels at least as great

---

[1] The original model did not include categories and compartments. The changes required to add them are straightforward.

as the user's risk level. To execute programs at a lower credibility level, a user must use the *run-untrusted* command. This acknowledges the risk that the user is taking.

6.3   Clark-Wilson Integrity Model

In 1987, David Clark and David Wilson developed an integrity model [177] radically different from previous models. This model uses transactions as the basic operation, which models many commercial systems more realistically than previous models.

One main concern of a commercial environment, as discussed above, is the integrity of the data in the system and of the actions performed on that data. The data is said to be *in a consistent state* (or *consistent*) if it satisfies given properties. For example, let D be the amount of money deposited so far today, W the amount of money withdrawn so far today, YB the amount of money in all accounts at the end of yesterday, and TB the amount of money in all accounts so far today. Then the consistency property is

$$D + YB - W = TB$$

Before and after each action, the consistency conditions must hold. A *well-formed transaction* is a series of operations that transition the system from one consistent state to another consistent state. For example, if a depositor transfers money from one account to another, the transaction is the transfer; two operations, the deduction from the first account and the addition to the second account, make up this transaction. Each operation may leave the data in an inconsistent state, but the well-formed transaction must preserve consistency.

The second feature of a commercial environment relevant to an integrity policy is the integrity of the transactions themselves. Who examines and certifies that the transactions are performed correctly? For example, when a company receives an invoice, the purchasing office requires several steps to pay for it. First, someone must have requested a service, and determined the account that would pay for the service. Next, someone must validate the invoice (was the service being billed for actually performed?). The account authorized to pay for the service must be debited, and the check must be written and signed. If one person performs all these steps, that person could easily pay phony invoices; however, if at least two different people perform these steps, both must conspire to defraud the company. Requiring more than one person to handle this process is an example of the principle of separation of duty.

Computer-based transactions are no different. Someone must certify that the transactions are implemented correctly. The principle of separation of duty requires that the certifier and the implementors be different people. In order for the transaction to corrupt the data (either by illicitly changing the data or by leaving the data in an inconsistent state), two different people must either make similar mistakes or collude to certify the well-formed transaction as correct.

6.3.1   The Model

The Clark-Wilson model defines data subject to its integrity controls as *constrained data items,* or CDIs. Data not subject to the integrity controls are called *unconstrained data items*, or UDIs. For example, in a bank, the balances of accounts are CDIs since their integrity is crucial to the operation of the bank, whereas the gifts selected by the account holders when their accounts were opened would be UDIs, because their integrity is not crucial to the operation of the bank. The set of CDIs and the set of UDIs partition the set of all data in the system being modeled.

A set of *integrity constraints* (similar in spirit to the consistency constraints discussed above) constrain the values of the CDIs. In the bank example, the consistency constraint presented earlier would also be an integrity constraint.

The model also defines two sets of procedures. *Integrity verification procedures*, or IVPs, test that the CDIs conform to the integrity constraints at the time the IVPs are run. In this case, the system is said to be in a *valid state*. *Transformation procedures*, or TPs, change the state of the data in the system from one valid state to another; TPs implement well-formed transactions.

Return to the example of bank accounts. The balances in the accounts are CDIs; checking that the accounts are balanced, as described above, is an IVP. Depositing money, withdrawing money, and transferring money between accounts are TPs. To ensure that the accounts are managed correctly, a bank examiner must certify that the bank is using proper procedures to check that the accounts are balanced, to deposit money, to withdraw money, and to transfer money. Furthermore, those procedures may apply only to deposit and checking accounts; they might not apply to other types of accounts—for example, to petty cash. The Clark-Wilson model captures these requirements in two *certification rules*:

Certification rule 1 (CR1): When any IVP is run, it must ensure that all CDIs are in a valid state.

Certification rule 2 (CR2): For some associated set of CDIs, a TP must transform those CDIs in a valid state into a (possibly different) valid state.

CR2 defines as *certified* a relation that associates a set of CDIs with a particular TP. Let C be the certified relation. Then, in the bank example,

$$(\text{balance, account}_1), (\text{balance, account}_2), \ldots, (\text{balance, account}_n) \in C.$$

CR2 implies that a TP may corrupt a CDI if it is not certified to work on that CDI. For example, the TP that invests money in the bank's stock portfolio would corrupt account balances even if the TP were certified to work on the portfolio, because the actions of the TP make no sense on the bank accounts. Hence, the system must prevent TPs from operating on CDIs for which they have not been certified. This leads to the following *enforcement rule*:

Enforcement rule 1 (ER1): The system must maintain the *certified* relations, and must ensure that only TPs certified to run on a CDI manipulate that CDI.

Specifically, ER1 says that if a TP f operates on a CDI o, then $(f, o) \in C$. However, in a bank, a janitor is not allowed to balance customer accounts. This restriction implies that the model must account for the person performing the TP, or user. The Clark-Wilson model uses an enforcement rule for this:

Enforcement rule 2 (ER2): The system must associate a user with each TP and set of CDIs. The TP may access those CDIs on behalf of the associated user. If the user is not associated with a particular TP and CDI, then the TP cannot access that CDI on behalf of that user.

This defines a set of triples (*user, TP,* { *CDI set* }) to capture the association of users, TPs, and CDIs. Call this relation *allowed A*. Of course, these relations must be certified:

Certification rule 3 (CR3): The *allowed* relations must meet the requirements imposed by the principle of separation of duty.

Because the model represents users, it must ensure that the identification of a user with the system's corresponding user identification code is correct. This suggests:

Enforcement rule 3 (ER3): The system must authenticate each user attempting to execute a TP.

An interesting observation is that the model does not require authentication when a user logs into the system, because the user may manipulate only UDIs. But if the user tries to manipulate a CDI, the user can do so only through a TP; this requires the user to be certified as allowed (per ER2), which requires authentication of the user (per ER3).

Most transaction-based systems log each transaction so that an auditor can review the transactions. The Clark-Wilson model considers the log simply as a CDI, and every TP appends to the log; no TP can overwrite the log. This leads to:

Certification rule 4 (CR4): All TPs must append enough information to reconstruct the operation to an append-only CDI.

When information enters a system, it need not be trusted or constrained. For example, when one deposits money into an automated teller machine (ATM), one need not enter the correct amount. However, when the ATM is opened and the cash or checks counted, the bank personnel will detect the discrepancy and fix it before they enter the deposit amount into one's account. This is an example of a UDI (the stated deposit amount) being checked, fixed if necessary, and certified as correct before being transformed into a CDI (the deposit amount added to one's account). The Clark-Wilson model covers this situation with certification rule 5:

Certification rule 5 (CR5): Any TP that takes as input a UDI may perform only valid transformations, or no transformations, for all possible values of the UDI. The transformation either rejects the UDI or transforms it into a CDI.

The final rule enforces the separation of duty needed to maintain the integrity of the relations in rules ER2 and ER3. If a user could create a TP and associate some set of entities and herself with that TP (as in ER3), she could have the TP perform unauthorized acts that violated integrity constraints. The final enforcement rule prevents this:

Enforcement rule 4 (ER4): Only the certifier of a TP may change the list of entities associated with that TP. No certifier of a TP, or of an entity associated with that TP, may ever have execute permission with respect to that entity.

This rule requires that all possible values of the UDI be known, and that the TP be implemented so as to be able to handle them. This issue arises again in both vulnerabilities analysis and secure programming.

This model contributed two new ideas to integrity models. First, it captured the way most commercial firms work with data. The firms do not classify data using a multilevel scheme, and they enforce separation of duty. Second, the notion of certification is distinct from the notion of enforcement, and each has its own set of rules. Assuming correct design and implementation, a system with a policy following the Clark-Wilson model will ensure that the enforcement rules are obeyed. But the certification rules require outside intervention, and the process of certification is typically complex and prone to error or to incompleteness (because the certifiers make assumptions about what can be trusted). This is a weakness in some sense, but it makes explicit assumptions that other models do not.

6.3.2   Comparison with the Requirements

We now consider whether the Clark-Wilson model meets the five requirements in Section 6.1. We assume that production programs correspond to TPs and that production data (and databases) are CDIs.

Requirement 1. If users are not allowed to perform certifications of TPs, but instead only "trusted personnel" are, then CR5 and ER4 enforce this requirement. Because ordinary users cannot create certified TPs, they cannot write programs to access production databases. They must use existing TPs and CDIs—that is, production programs and production databases.

Requirement 2. This requirement is largely procedural, because no set of technical controls can prevent a programmer from developing and testing programs on production systems. (The standard procedural control is to omit interpreters and compilers from production systems.) However, the notion of providing production data via a special process corresponds to using a TP to sanitize, or simply provide, production data to a test system.

Requirement 3. Installing a program from a development system onto a production system requires a TP to do the installation and "trusted personnel" to do the certification.

Requirement 4. CR4 provides the auditing (logging) of program installation. ER3 authenticates the "trusted personnel" doing the installation. CR5 and ER4 control the installation procedure (the new program being a UDI before certification and a CDI, as well as a TP in the context of other rules, after certification).

Requirement 5. Finally, because the log is simply a CDI, management and auditors can have access to the system logs through appropriate TPs. Similarly, they also have access to the system state.

Thus, the Clark-Wilson model meets Lipner's requirements.

6.3.3   Comparison with Other Models

The contributions of the Clark-Wilson model are many. We compare it with the Biba model to highlight these new features.

Recall that the Biba model attaches integrity levels to objects and subjects. In the broadest sense, so does the Clark-Wilson model, but unlike the Biba model, each object has two levels: constrained or high (the CDIs) and unconstrained or low (the UDIs). Similarly, subjects have two levels: certified (the TPs) and uncertified (all other procedures). Given this similarity, can the Clark-Wilson model be expressed fully using the Biba model?

The critical distinction between the two models lies in the certification rules. The Biba model has none; it asserts that "trusted" subjects exist to ensure that the actions of a system obey the rules of the model. No mechanism or procedure is provided to verify the trusted entities *or their actions*. But the Clark-Wilson model provides explicit requirements that entities and actions must meet; in other words, the *method* of upgrading an entity is itself a TP that a security officer has certified. This underlies the assumptions being made and allows for the upgrading of entities within the constructs of the model (see ER4 and CR5). As with the Bell-LaPadula Model, if the Biba model does not have tranquility, trusted entities must change the objects' integrity levels, and the method of upgrading need not be certified.

Handling changes in integrity levels is critical in systems that receive input from uncontrolled sources. For example, the Biba model requires that a trusted entity, such as a security officer, pass on every input sent to a process running at an integrity level higher than that of the input. This is not practical. However, the Clark-Wilson model requires that a trusted entity (again, perhaps a security officer) certify the method of upgrading data to a higher integrity level. Thus, the trusted entity would not certify each data item being upgraded; it would only need to certify the method for upgrading data, and the data items could be upgraded. This is quite practical.

Can the Clark-Wilson model emulate the Biba model? The relations described in ER2 capture the ability of subjects to act on objects. By choosing TPs appropriately, the emulation succeeds (although the certification rules constrain trusted subjects in the emulation, whereas the Biba model imposes no such constraints). The details of the construction are left as an exercise for the reader (see Exercise 6).

6.4   Summary

Integrity models are gaining in variety and popularity. The problems they address arise from industries in which environments vary wildly. They take into account concepts (such as separation of privilege) from beyond the scope of confidentiality security policies. This area will continue to increase in importance as more and more commercial firms develop models or policies to help them protect their data.

6.5   Further Reading

Nash and Poland discuss realistic situations in which mechanisms are unable to enforce the principle of separation of duty [661]. Other studies of this principle include its use in role-based access control [537, 835], databases [697], and multi-level security [328]. Notargiacomo, Blaustein, and McCollum [696] present a generalization of Clark-Wilson suitable for trusted database management systems that includes dynamic separation of duty. Polk describes an implementation of Clark-Wilson under the UNIX operating system [722].

Integrity requirements arise in many contexts. Saltman [771] provides an informative survey of the requirements for secure electronic voting. Chaum's classic paper on electronic payment [165] raises issues of confidentiality and shows that integrity and anonymity can coexist. Integrity in databases is crucial to their correctness [42, 304, 374]. The analysis of trust in software is also an issue of integrity [22, 650].

Chalmers compares commercial policies with governmental ones [157]. Lee [554] discusses an alternative to Lipner's use of mandatory access controls for implementing commercial policies.

6.6   Exercises

1. Suppose a system implementing Biba's model used the same labels for integrity levels and categories as for security levels and categories. Under what conditions could one subject read an object? Write to an object?

2. In Pozzo and Gray's modification of LOCUS, what would be the effect of omitting the *run-untrusted* command? Do you think this enhances or degrades security?

3. In the Clark-Wilson model, must the TPs be executed serially, or can they be executed in parallel? If the former, why; if the latter, what constraints must be placed on their execution?

4. Prove that applying a sequence of transformation procedures to a system in a valid state results in the system being in a (possibly different) valid state.

5. The relations *certified* (see ER1) and *allowed* (see ER2) can be collapsed into a single relation. Please do so and state the new relation. Why doesn't the Clark-Wilson model do this?

6. Show that the enforcement rules of the Clark-Wilson model can emulate the Biba model.

Chapter 7
Hybrid Policies

JULIET: Come, vial.
What if this mixture do not work at all?
Shall I be marry'd then tomorrow morning?
No, no! this shall forbid it, lie thou there.
— *The Tragedy of Romeo and Juliet*, IV, iii, 20–22.

Few organizations limit their security objectives to confidentiality or integrity only; most desire both, in some mixture. This chapter presents two such models. The Chinese Wall model is derived from the British laws concerning conflict of interest. The Clinical Information Systems security model is derived from medical ethics and laws about dissemination of patient data. Two other models present alternative views of information management. Originator controlled access control lets the creator determine (or assign) who should access the data and how. Role-based access control formalizes the more common notion of "groups" of users.

7.1   Chinese Wall Model

The Chinese Wall model [133] is a model of a security policy that refers equally to confidentiality and integrity. It describes policies that involve a conflict of interest in business, and is as important to those situations as the Bell-LaPadula Model is to the military. For example, British law requires the use of a policy similar to this, and correct implementation of portions of the model provides a defense in cases involving certain criminal charges [586, 587]. The environment of a stock exchange or investment house is the most natural environment for this model. In this context, the goal of the model is to prevent a conflict of interest in which a trader represents two clients, and the best interests of the clients conflict, so the trader could help one gain at the expense of the other.

Consider the database of an investment house. It consists of companies' records about investment and other data that investors are likely to request. Analysts use these records to guide the companies' investments, as well as those of individuals. Suppose Anthony counsels Bank of America in its investments. If he also counsels Citibank, he has a potential conflict of interest, because the two banks' investments may come into conflict. Hence, Anthony cannot counsel both banks.

The following definitions capture this:

Definition 7–1. The *objects* of the database are items of information related to a company.

Definition 7–2. A *company dataset* (CD) contains objects related to a single company.

Definition 7–3. A *conflict of interest* (COI) class contains the datasets of companies in competition.

Let *COI(O)* represent the COI class that contains object *O*, and let *CD(O)* be the company dataset that contains object *O*. The model assumes that each object belongs to exactly one COI class.

Anthony has access to the objects in the CD of Bank of America. Because the CD of Citibank is in the same COI class as that of Bank of America, Anthony cannot gain access to the objects in Citibank's CD. Thus, this structure of the database provides the required ability. (See Figure 7–1.)

This implies a temporal element. Suppose Anthony first worked on Bank of America's portfolio and was then transferred to Citibank's portfolio. Even though he is working only on one CD in the bank COI class at a time, much of the information he learned from Bank of America's portfolio will be current. Hence, he can guide

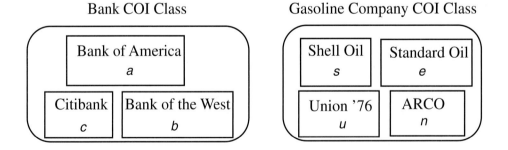

Figure 7–1   The Chinese Wall model database. It has two COI classes. The one for banks contains three CDs. The other one, for gasoline companies, contains four CDs. Each (COI, CD) pair is represented by a lowercase letter (for example, (Bank COI, Citibank) is *c*). Susan may have access to no more than one CD in each COI, so she could access Citibank's CD and ARCO's CD, but not Citibank's CD and Bank of America's CD.

Citibank's investments using information about Bank of America—a conflict of interest. This leads to the following rule, where $PR(S)$ is the set of objects that S has read.

- **CW-Simple Security Condition, Preliminary Version:** S can read O if and only if either of the following is true.
  1. There is an object O' such that S has accessed O' and $CD(O') = CD(O)$.
  2. For all objects O', $O' \in PR(S) \Rightarrow COI(O') \neq COI(O)$.

Initially, $PR(S) = \varnothing$, and the initial read request is assumed to be granted. Given these assumptions, in the situation above, Bank of America's COI class and Citibank's COI class are the same, so the second part of the CW-simple security condition applies, and Anthony cannot access an object in the former, having already accessed an object in the latter.

Two immediate consequences of this rule affect subject rights. First, once a subject reads any object in a COI class, the only other objects in that COI class that the subject can read are in the same CD as the read object. So, if Susan accesses some information in Citibank's CD, she cannot later access information in Bank of America's CD.

Second, the minimum number of subjects needed to access every object in a COI class is the same as the number of CDs in that COI class. If the gasoline company COI class has four CDs, then at least four analysts are needed to access all information in the COI class. Thus, any trading house must have at least four analysts to access all information in that COI class without creating a conflict of interest.

In practice, companies have information they can release publicly, such as annual stockholders' reports and filings before government commissions. The Chinese Wall model should not consider this information restricted, because it is available to all. Hence, the model distinguishes between sanitized data and unsanitized data; the latter falls under the CW-simple security condition, preliminary version, whereas the former does not. The CW-simple security condition can be reformulated to include this notion.

- **CW-Simple Security Condition:** S can read O if and only if any of the following holds.
  1. There is an object O' such that S has accessed O' and $CD(O') = CD(O)$.
  2. For all objects O', $O' \in PR(S) \Rightarrow COI(O') \neq COI(O)$.
  3. O is a sanitized object.

Suppose Anthony and Susan work in the same trading house. Anthony can read objects in Bank of America's CD, and Susan can read objects in Citibank's CD. Both can read objects in ARCO's CD. If Anthony can also write to objects in ARCO's CD, then he can read information from objects in Bank of America's CD and write to objects in ARCO's CD, and then Susan can read that information; so, Susan can indirectly obtain information from Bank of America's CD, causing a conflict of interest. The CW-simple security condition must be augmented to prevent this.

- *CW-*-Property:* A subject S may write to an object O if and only if both of the following conditions hold.

    1. The CW-simple security condition permits S to read O.
    2. For all unsanitized objects O', S can read $O' \Rightarrow CD(O') = CD(O)$.

In the example above, Anthony can read objects in both Bank of America's CD and ARCO's CD. Thus, condition 1 is met. However, assuming that Bank of America's CD contains unsanitized objects (a reasonable assumption), then because Anthony can read those objects, condition 2 is false. Hence, Anthony cannot write to objects in ARCO's CD.

7.1.1   Bell-LaPadula and Chinese Wall Models

The Bell-LaPadula Model and the Chinese Wall model are fundamentally different. Subjects in the Chinese Wall model have no associated security labels, whereas subjects in the Bell-LaPadula Model do have such labels. Furthermore, the Bell-LaPadula Model has no notion of "past accesses," but this notion is central to the Chinese Wall model's controls.

To emulate the Chinese Wall model using Bell-LaPadula, we assign a security category to each (COI, CD) pair. We define two security levels, S (for *sanitized*) and U (for *unsanitized*). By assumption, S *dom* U. Figure 7–2 illustrates this mapping for the system in Figure 7–1. Each object is transformed into two objects, one sanitized and one unsanitized.

Each subject in the Chinese Wall model is then assigned clearance for the compartments that do not contain multiple categories corresponding to CDs in the same COI class. For example, if Susan can read the Bank of America and ARCO CDs, her processes would have clearance for compartment $(U, \{a, n\})$. There are three possible clearances from the bank COI class, and four possible clearances from the gasoline company COI class, combining to give 12 possible clearances for subjects. Of course, all subjects can read all sanitized data.

The CW-simple security condition clearly holds. The CW-*-property also holds, because the Bell-LaPadula *-property ensures that the category of input objects is a subset of the category of output objects. Hence, input objects are either sanitized or in the same category (that is, the same CD) as that of the subject.

This construction shows that at any time the Bell-LaPadula Model can capture the state of a system using the Chinese Wall model. But the Bell-LaPadula Model cannot capture changes over time. For example, suppose Susan falls ill, and Anna needs to access one of the datasets to which Susan has access. How can the system know if Anna is allowed to access that dataset? The Chinese Wall model tracks the history of accesses, from which Anna's ability to access the CD can be determined.

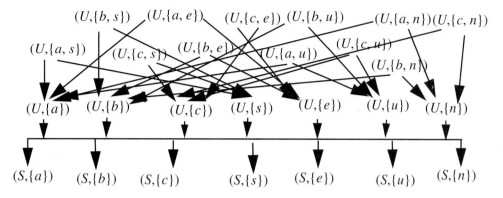

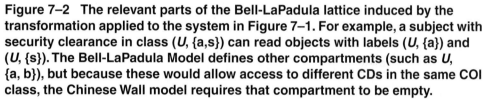

Figure 7–2   The relevant parts of the Bell-LaPadula lattice induced by the transformation applied to the system in Figure 7–1. For example, a subject with security clearance in class (*U*, {a,s}) can read objects with labels (*U*, {a}) and (*U*, {s}). The Bell-LaPadula Model defines other compartments (such as *U*, {a, b}), but because these would allow access to different CDs in the same COI class, the Chinese Wall model requires that compartment to be empty.

But if the corresponding category is not in Anna's clearances, the Bell-LaPadula Model does not retain the history needed to determine whether her accessing the category would violate the Chinese Wall constraints.

A second, more serious problem arises when one considers that subjects in the Chinese Wall model may choose which CDs to access; in other words, initially a subject is free to access *all* objects. The Chinese Wall model's constraints grow as the subject accesses more objects. However, from the initial state, the Bell-LaPadula Model constrains the set of objects that a subject can access. This set cannot change unless a trusted authority (such as a system security officer) changes subject clearances or object classifications. The obvious solution is to clear all subjects for all categories, but this means that any subject can read any object, which violates the CW-simple security condition.

Hence, the Bell-LaPadula Model cannot emulate the Chinese Wall model faithfully. This demonstrates that the two policies are distinct.

However, the Chinese Wall model can emulate the Bell-LaPadula Model; the construction is left as an exercise for the reader. (See Exercise 1.)

7.1.2   Clark-Wilson and Chinese Wall Models

The Clark-Wilson model deals with many aspects of integrity, such as validation and verification, as well as access control. Because the Chinese Wall model deals exclusively with access control, it cannot emulate the Clark-Wilson model fully. So, consider only the access control aspects of the Clark-Wilson model.

The representation of access control in the Clark-Wilson model is the second enforcement rule, ER2. That rule associates users with transformation procedures and CDIs on which they can operate. If one takes the usual view that "subject" and "process" are interchangeable, then a single person could use multiple processes to access objects in multiple CDs in the same COI class. Because the Chinese Wall model would view processes independently of who was executing them, no constraints would be violated. However, by requiring that a "subject" be a specific individual and including all processes executing on that subject's behalf, the Chinese Wall model is consistent with the Clark-Wilson model.

7.2   Clinical Information Systems Security Policy

Medical records require policies that combine confidentiality and integrity, but in a very different way than for brokerage firms. Conflict of interest is not a critical problem. Patient confidentiality, authentication of both records and the personnel making entries in those records, and assurance that the records have not been changed erroneously are critical. Anderson [29] presents a model for such policies that illuminates the combination of confidentiality and integrity to protect patient privacy and record integrity.

Anderson defines three types of entities in the policy.

Definition 7–4. A *patient* is the subject of medical records, or an agent for that person who can give consent for the person to be treated.

Definition 7–5. *Personal health information* is information about a patient's health or treatment enabling that patient to be identified.

In more common parlance, the "personal health information" is contained in a medical record. We will refer to "medical records" throughout, under the assumption that all personal health information is kept in the medical records.

Definition 7–6. A *clinician* is a health-care professional who has access to personal health information while performing his or her job.

The policy also assumes that personal health information concerns one individual at a time. Strictly speaking, this is not true. For example, obstetrics/gynecology records contain information about both the father and the mother. In these cases, special rules come into play, and the policy does not cover them.

The policy is guided by principles similar to the certification and enforcement rules of the Clark-Wilson model. These principles are derived from the medical ethics of several medical societies, and from the experience and advice of practicing clinicians.[1]

---

[1] The principles are numbered differently in Anderson's paper.

The first set of principles deals with access to the medical records themselves. It requires a list of those who can read the records, and a list of those who can append to the records. Auditors are given access to copies of the records, so the auditors cannot alter the original records in any way. Clinicians by whom the patient has consented to be treated can also read and append to the medical records. Because clinicians often work in medical groups, consent may apply to a set of clinicians. The notion of groups abstracts this set well. Thus:

Access Principle 1: Each medical record has an access control list naming the individuals or groups who may read and append information to the record. The system must restrict access to those identified on the access control list.

Medical ethics require that only clinicians and the patient have access to the patient's medical record. Hence:

Access Principle 2: One of the clinicians on the access control list (called the *responsible clinician*) must have the right to add other clinicians to the access control list.

Because the patient must consent to treatment, the patient has the right to know when his or her medical record is accessed or altered. Furthermore, if a clinician who is unfamiliar to the patient accesses the record, the patient should be notified of the leakage of information. This leads to another access principle:

Access Principle 3: The responsible clinician must notify the patient of the names on the access control list whenever the patient's medical record is opened. Except for situations given in statutes, or in cases of emergency, the responsible clinician must obtain the patient's consent.

Erroneous information should be corrected, not deleted, to facilitate auditing of the records. Auditing also requires that all accesses be recorded, along with the date and time of each access and the name of each person accessing the record.

Access Principle 4: The name of the clinician, the date, and the time of the access of a medical record must be recorded. Similar information must be kept for deletions.

The next set of principles concern record creation and information deletion. When a new medical record is created, the clinician creating the record should have access, as should the patient. Typically, the record is created as a result of a referral. The referring clinician needs access to obtain the results of the referral, and so is included on the new record's access control list.

Creation Principle: A clinician may open a record, with the clinician and the patient on the access control list. If the record is opened as a result of a referral, the referring clinician may also be on the access control list.

How long the medical records are kept varies with the circumstances. Normally, medical records can be discarded after 8 years, but in some cases—notably cancer cases—the records are kept longer.

Deletion Principle: Clinical information cannot be deleted from a medical record until the appropriate time has passed.

Containment protects information, so a control must ensure that data copied from one record to another is not available to a new, wider audience. Thus, information from a record can be given only to those on the record's access control list.

Confinement Principle: Information from one medical record may be appended to a different medical record if and only if the access control list of the second record is a subset of the access control list of the first.

A clinician may have access to many records, possibly in the role of an advisor to a medical insurance company or department. If this clinician were corrupt, or could be corrupted or blackmailed, the secrecy of a large number of medical records would be compromised. Patient notification of the addition limits this threat.

Aggregation Principle: Measures for preventing the aggregation of patient data must be effective. In particular, a patient must be notified if anyone is to be added to the access control list for the patients's record and if that person has access to a large number of medical records.

Finally, systems must implement mechanisms for enforcing these principles.

Enforcement Principle: Any computer system that handles medical records must have a subsystem that enforces the preceding principles. The effectiveness of this enforcement must be subject to evaluation by independent auditors.

7.2.1   Bell-LaPadula and Clark-Wilson Models

Anderson notes that the Confinement Principle imposes a lattice structure on the entities in this model, much as the Bell-LaPadula Model imposes a lattice structure on its entities. Hence, the Bell-LaPadula protection model is a subset of the Clinical Information Systems security model. But the Bell-LaPadula Model focuses on the subjects accessing the objects (because there are more subjects than security labels), whereas the Clinical Information Systems model focuses on the objects being accessed by the subjects (because there are more patients, and medical records, than clinicians). This difference does not matter in traditional military applications, but it might aid detection of "insiders" in specific fields such as intelligence.

The Clark-Wilson model provides a framework for the Clinical Information Systems model. Take the CDIs to be the medical records and their associated access control lists. The TPs are the functions that update the medical records and their access control lists. The IVPs certify several items:

- A person identified as a clinician is a clinician (to the level of assurance required by the system).
- A clinician validates, or has validated, information in the medical record.

- When someone (the patient and/or a clinician) is to be notified of an event, such notification occurs.
- When someone (the patient and/or a clinician) must give consent, the operation cannot proceed until the consent is obtained.

Finally, the requirement of auditing (certification rule CR4) is met by making all records append-only, and notifiying the patient whenever the access control list changes.

7.3   Originator Controlled Access Control

Mandatory and discretionary access controls (MACs and DACs) do not handle environments in which the originators of documents retain control over them even after those documents are disseminated. Graubert [375] developed a policy called ORG-CON or ORCON (for "ORiginator CONtrolled") in which a subject can give another subject rights to an object only with the approval of the creator of that object.

EXAMPLE: The Secretary of Defense of the United States drafts a proposed policy document and distributes it to her aides for comment. The aides are not allowed to distribute the document any further without permission from the secretary. The secretary controls dissemination; hence, the policy is ORCON. The trust in this policy is that the aides will not release the document illicitly—that is, without the permission of the secretary.

In practice, a single author does not control dissemination; instead, the organization on whose behalf the document was created does. Hence, objects will be marked as ORCON on behalf of the relevant organization.

Suppose a subject $s \in S$ marks an object $o \in O$ as ORCON on behalf of organization X. Organization X allows o to be disclosed to subjects acting on behalf of a second organization, Y, subject to the following restrictions.

a. The object o cannot be released to subjects acting on behalf of other organizations without X's permission.
b. Any copies of o must have the same restrictions placed on it.

Discretionary access controls are insufficient for this purpose, because the owner of an object can set any permissions desired. Thus, X cannot enforce condition (b).

Mandatory access controls are theoretically sufficient for this purpose, but in practice have a serious drawback. Associate a separate category C containing o, X, and Y and nothing else. If a subject $y \in Y$ wishes to read o, $x \in X$ makes a copy o' of o. The copy o' is in C, so unless $z \in Z$ is also in category C, y cannot give z access to o'. This demonstrates adequacy.

Suppose a member *w* of an organization *W* wants to provide access to a document *d* to members of organization *Y*, but the document is not to be shared with members of organization *X* or *Z*. So, *d* cannot be in category *C* because if it were, members $x \in X$ and $z \in Z$ could access *d*. Another category containing *d*, *W*, and *Y* must be created. Multiplying this by several thousand possible relationships and documents creates an unacceptably large number of categories.

A second problem with mandatory access controls arises from the abstraction. Organizations that use categories grant access to individuals on a "need to know" basis. There is a formal, written policy determining who needs the access based on common characteristics and restrictions. These restrictions are applied at a very high level (national, corporate, organizational, and so forth). This requires a central clearinghouse for categories. The creation of categories to enforce ORCON implies local control of categories rather than central control, and a set of rules dictating who has access to each compartment.

ORCON abstracts none of this. ORCON is a decentralized system of access control in which each originator determines who needs access to the data. No centralized set of rules controls access to data; access is at the complete discretion of the originator. Hence, the MAC representation of ORCON is not suitable.

A solution is to combine features of the MAC and DAC models. The rules are

1. The owner of an object cannot change the access controls of the object.
2. When an object is copied, the access control restrictions of that source are copied and bound to the target of the copy.
3. The creator (originator) can alter the access control restrictions on a per-subject and per-object basis.

The first two rules are from mandatory access controls. They say that the system controls all accesses, and no one may alter the rules governing access to those objects. The third rule is discretionary and gives the originator power to determine who can access the object. Hence, this hybrid scheme is neither MAC nor DAC.

The critical observation here is that the access controls associated with the object are under the control of the *originator* and not the owner of the object. Possession equates to only some control. The owner of the object may determine to whom he or she gives access, but only if the originator allows the access. The owner may not override the originator.

7.4   Role-Based Access Control

The ability, or need, to access information may depend on one's job functions.

EXAMPLE: Allison is the bookkeeper for the Department of Mathematics. She is responsible for balancing the books and keeping track of all accounting for that department. She has access to all departmental accounts. She moves to the university's Office of Admissions to become the head accountant (with a substantial raise). Because she is no longer the bookkeeper for the Department of Mathematics, she no longer has access to those accounts. When that department hires Sally as its new bookkeeper, she will acquire full access to all those accounts. Access to the accounts is a function of the job of bookkeeper, and is not tied to any particular individual.

This suggests associating access with the particular job of the user.

Definition 7–7. A *role* is a collection of job functions. Each role r is authorized to perform one or more transactions (actions in support of a job function). The set of authorized transactions for r is written *trans(r)*.

Definition 7–8. The *active role of a subject s*, written *actr(s)*, is the role that s is currently performing.

Definition 7–9. The *authorized roles of a subject s*, written *authr(s)*, is the set of roles that s is authorized to assume.

Definition 7–10. The predicate *canexec(s, t)* is true if and only if the subject s can execute the transaction t at the current time.

Three rules reflect the ability of a subject to execute a transaction.

Axiom 7–1. Let S be the set of subjects and T the set of transactions. The *rule of role assignment* is $(\forall s \in S)(\forall t \in T)[\ canexec(s, t) \rightarrow actr(s) \neq \varnothing\ ]$.

This axiom simply says that if a subject can execute *any* transaction, then that subject has an active role. This binds the notion of execution of a transaction to the role rather than to the user.

Axiom 7–2. Let S be the set of subjects. Then the *rule of role authorization* is $(\forall s \in S)[\ actr(s) \subseteq authr(s)\ ]$.

This rule means that the subject must be authorized to assume its active role. It cannot assume an unauthorized role. Without this axiom, any subject could assume any role, and hence execute any transaction.

Axiom 7–3. Let S be the set of subjects and T the set of transactions. The *rule of transaction authorization* is $(\forall s \in S)(\forall t \in T)[\ canexec(s, t) \rightarrow t \in trans(actr(s))\ ]$.

This rule says that a subject cannot execute a transaction for which its current role is not authorized.

The forms of these axioms restrict the transactions that can be performed. They do not ensure that the allowed transactions can be executed. This suggests that role-based access control (RBAC) is a form of mandatory access control. The axioms state rules that must be satisfied before a transaction can be executed. Discretionary access control mechanisms may further restrict transactions.

EXAMPLE: Some roles subsume others. For example, a trainer can perform all actions of a trainee, as well as others. One can view this as containment. This suggests a hierarchy of roles, in this case the trainer role containing the trainee role. As another example, many operations are common to a large number of roles. Instead of specifying the operation once for each role, one specifies it for a role containing all other roles. Granting access to a role R implies that access is granted for all roles containing R. This simplifies the use of the RBAC model (and of its implementation).

If role r_i contains role r_j, we write $r_i > r_j$. Using our notation, the implications of containment of roles may be expressed as

$$(\forall s \in S)[\ r_i \in authr(s) \wedge r_i > r_j \rightarrow r_j \in authr(s)\ ]$$

EXAMPLE: RBAC can model the separation of duty rule. Our goal is to specify separation of duty centrally; then it can be imposed on roles through containment, as discussed in the preceding example. The key is to recognize that the users in some roles cannot enter other roles. That is, for two roles r_1 and r_2 bound by separation of duty (so the same individual cannot assume both roles):

$$(\forall s \in S)\ [\ r_1 \in authr(s) \rightarrow r_2 \notin authr(s)\ ]$$

Capturing the notion of mutual exclusion requires a new predicate.

Definition 7–11. Let r be a role, and let s be a subject such that $r \in authr(s)$. Then the predicate *meauth(r)* (for *mutually exclusive authorizations*) is the set of roles that s cannot assume because of the separation of duty requirement.

Putting this definition together with the above example, the principle of separation of duty can be summarized as

$$(\forall r_1, r_2 \in R)\ [\ r_2 \in meauth(r_1) \rightarrow [\ (\forall s \in S)\ [\ r_1 \in authr(s) \rightarrow r_2 \notin authr(s)\ ]\ ]\ ]$$

7.5   Summary

The goal of this chapter was to show that policies typically combine features of both integrity and confidentiality policies. The Chinese Wall model accurately captures requirements of a particular business (brokering) under particular conditions (the

British law). The Clinical Information Systems model does the same thing for medical records. Both models are grounded in current business and clinical practice.

ORCON and RBAC take a different approach, focusing on which entities *will* access the data rather than on which entities *should* access the data. ORCON allows the author (individual or corporate) to control access to the document; RBAC restricts access to individuals performing specific functions. The latter approach can be fruitfully applied to many of the models discussed earlier.

7.6   Further Reading

Meadows [616] discusses moving the Chinese Wall into a multilevel security context. Lin [566] challenges an assumption of the model, leading to a different formulation.

Very little has been written about policy models that are useful for policies in specific fields other than government. Anderson's clinical model is an excellent example of such a policy model, as is the Chinese Wall. Foley and Jacob discuss computer-supported collaborative working confidentiality policies in the guise of specification [329]. Wiemer and Murray discuss policy models in the context of sharing information with foreign governments [941].

McCollum, Messing, and Notargiacomo [603] have suggested an interesting variation of ORCON, called "Owner-Retained Access Control." Unlike ORCON, this model keeps a list of the originators and owners. Like ORCON, the intersection of all sets controls access. Chandramouli [158] provides a framework for implementing many access control policies in CORBA and discusses an RBAC policy as an example. He also presents a little language for describing policies of interest.

7.7   Exercises

1. Develop a construction to show that a system implementing the Chinese Wall model can support the Bell-LaPadula Model.

2. Show that the Clinical Information System model's principles implement the Clark-Wilson enforcement and certification rules.

3. Consider using mandatory access controls and compartments to implement an ORCON control. Assume that there are k different organizations. Organization i will produce $n(i, j)$ documents to be shared with organization j.

   a. How many compartments are needed to allow any organization to share a document with any other organization?

b. Now assume that organization i will need to share $n_m(i, i_1, \ldots, i_m)$ documents with organizations $i_1, \ldots, i_m$. How many compartments will be needed?

4. Someone once observed that "the difference between roles and groups is that a user can shift into and out of roles, whereas that user has a group identity (or identities) that are fixed throughout the session."

   a. Consider a system such as a Berkeley-based UNIX system, in which users have secondary group identities that remain fixed during their login sessions. What are the advantages of roles with the same administrative functions as the groups?

   b. Consider a system such as a System V-based UNIX system, in which a process can have exactly one group identity. To change groups, users must execute the *newgrp* command. Do these groups differ from roles? Why or why not?

5. The models in this chapter do not discuss availability. What unstated assumptions about that service are they making?

6. A physician who is addicted to a pain-killing medicine can prescribe the medication for herself. Please show how RBAC in general, and Definition 7–11 specifically, can be used to govern the dispensing of prescription drugs to prevent a physician from prescribing medicine for herself.

Chapter 8
Basic Cryptography

YORK: Then, York, be still awhile, till time do serve:
Watch thou and wake when others be asleep,
To pry into the secrets of the state;
—*The Second Part of King Henry the Sixth*, I, i, 249–260.

Cryptography is a deep mathematical subject. Because this book focuses on system security, we view cryptography as a supporting tool. Viewed in this context, the reader needs only a brief overview of the major points of cryptography relevant to that use. This chapter provides such an overview.

Cryptographic protocols provide a cornerstone for secure communication. These protocols are built on ideas presented in this chapter and are discussed at length later on.

8.1   What Is Cryptography?

The word *cryptography* comes from two Greek words meaning "secret writing" and is the art and science of concealing meaning. *Cryptanalysis* is the breaking of codes. The basic component of cryptography is a cryptosystem.

> **Definition 8–1.** A *cryptosystem* is a 5-tuple (E, D, M, K, C), where M is the set of *plaintexts*, K the set of *keys*, C is the set of *ciphertexts*, E: $M \times K \rightarrow C$ is the set of *enciphering functions*, and D: $C \times K \rightarrow M$ is the set of *deciphering functions*.

EXAMPLE: The Caesar cipher is the widely known cipher in which letters are shifted. For example, if the key is 3, the letter A becomes D, B becomes E, and so forth, ending with Z becoming C. So the word "HELLO" is enciphered as "KHOOR." Informally, this cipher is a cryptosystem with:

M = { all sequences of Roman letters }

$\mathcal{K} = \{\ i \mid i \text{ an integer such that } 0 \leq i \leq 25\ \}$
$\mathcal{E} = \{\ E_k \mid k \in \mathcal{K} \text{ and for all } m \in \mathcal{M}, E_k(m) = (m + k) \bmod 26\ \}$

Representing each letter by its position in the alphabet (with A in position 0), "HELLO" is 7 4 11 11 14; if $k = 3$, the ciphertext is 10 7 14 14 17, or "KHOOR."

$\mathcal{D} = \{\ D_k \mid k \in \mathcal{K} \text{ and for all } c \in C, D_k(c) = (26 + c - k) \bmod 26\ \}$

Each D_k simply inverts the corresponding E_k.

$C = \mathcal{M}$

because $\mathcal{E}$ is clearly a set of onto functions.

The goal of cryptography is to keep enciphered information secret. Assume that an *adversary* wishes to break a ciphertext. Standard cryptographic practice is to assume that she knows the algorithm used to encipher the plaintext, but not the specific cryptographic key (in other words, she knows $\mathcal{D}$ and $\mathcal{E}$). She may use three types of attacks:

1. In a *ciphertext only* attack, the adversary has only the ciphertext. Her goal is to find the corresponding plaintext. If possible, she may try to find the key, too.
2. In a *known plaintext* attack, the adversary has the ciphertext and the plaintext that was enciphered. Her goal is to find the key that was used.
3. In a *chosen plaintext* attack, the adversary may ask that specific plaintexts be enciphered. She is given the corresponding ciphertexts. Her goal is to find the key that was used.

A good cryptosystem protects against all three types of attacks.

Attacks use both mathematics and statistics. The statistical methods make assumptions about the statistics of the plaintext language and examine the ciphertext to correlate its properties with those assumptions. Those assumptions are collectively called a *model* of the language. Figure 8–1 presents a character-based, or 1-gram, model of English text; others are 2-gram models (reflecting frequencies of pairs of letters), Markov models, and word models. In what follows, we use the 1-gram model and assume that the characters are chosen independently of one another.

8.2   Classical Cryptosystems

Classical cryptosystems (also called *single-key* or *symmetric* cryptosystems) are cryptosystems that use the same key for encipherment and decipherment. In these systems, for all $E_k \in C$ and $k \in \mathcal{K}$, there is a $D_k \in \mathcal{D}$ such that $D_k = E_k^{-1}$.

a	0.080	h	0.060	n	0.070	t	0.090
b	0.015	i	0.065	o	0.080	u	0.030
c	0.030	j	0.005	p	0.020	v	0.010
d	0.040	k	0.005	q	0.002	w	0.015
e	0.130	l	0.035	r	0.065	x	0.005
f	0.020	m	0.030	s	0.060	y	0.020
g	0.015					z	0.002

Figure 8–1   Table of character frequencies in the English language, from Denning [242], Figure 2.3, p. 65.

EXAMPLE: The Caesar cipher discussed earlier had a key of 3, so the enciphering function was E_3. To decipher "KHOOR," we used the same key in the decipherment function D_3. Hence, the Caesar cipher is a classical cipher.

There are two basic types of classical ciphers: *transposition* ciphers and *substitution* ciphers.

8.2.1   Transposition Ciphers

A *transposition cipher* rearranges the characters in the plaintext to form the ciphertext. The letters are not changed.

EXAMPLE: The *rail fence* cipher is composed by writing the plaintext in two rows, proceeding down, then across, and reading the ciphertext across, then down. For example, the plaintext "HELLO, WORLD" would be written as:

HLOOL
ELWRD

resulting in the ciphertext "HLOOLELWRD."

Mathematically, the key to a transposition cipher is a permutation function. Because the permutation does not alter the frequency of plaintext characters, a transposition cipher can be detected by comparing character frequencies with a model of the language. If, for example, character frequencies for 1-grams match those of a model of English, but 2-gram frequencies do not match the model, then the text is probably a transposition cipher.

Attacking a transposition cipher requires rearrangement of the letters of the ciphertext. This process, called *anagramming*, uses tables of *n*-gram frequencies to identify common *n*-grams. The cryptanalyst arranges the letters in such a way that the characters in the ciphertext form some *n*-grams with highest frequency. This process is repeated, using different *n*-grams, until the transposition pattern is found.

EXAMPLE: Consider the ciphertext "HLOOLELWRD." According to a Konheim's digram table [527], the digram "HE" occurs with frequency 0.0305[1] in English. Of the other possible digrams beginning with "H," the frequency of "HO" is the next highest, at 0.0043, and the digrams "HL," "HW," "HR," and "HD" have frequencies of less than 0.0010. Furthermore, the frequency of "WH" is 0.0026, and the digrams "EH," "LH," "OH," "RH," and "DH" occur with frequencies of 0.0002 or less. This suggests that "E" follows "H." We arrange the letters so that each letter in the first block of five letters (from "H" up to but not including the "E") is adjacent to the corresponding letter in the second block of five letters, as follows.

    HE
    LL
    OW
    OR
    LD

Reading the letters across and down produces "HELLOWORLD." Note that the shape of the arrangement is different from that in the previous example. However, the two arrangements are equivalent, leading to the correct solution.

8.2.2   Substitution Ciphers

A *substitution cipher* changes characters in the plaintext to produce the ciphertext.

EXAMPLE: The Caesar cipher discussed earlier had a key of 3, altering each letter in the plaintext by mapping it into the letter three characters later in the alphabet (and circling back to the beginning of the alphabet if needed). This is a substitution cipher.

A Caesar cipher is susceptible to a statistical ciphertext-only attack.

EXAMPLE: Consider the ciphertext "KHOOR ZRUOG." We first compute the frequency of each letter in the ciphertext:

    G 0.1   H 0.1   K 0.1   O 0.3   R 0.2   U 0.1   Z 0.1

---

[1] This means that in Konheim's sample, 3.05% of the digrams were "HE."

i	$\phi(i)$	i	$\phi(i)$	i	$\phi(i)$	i	$\phi(i)$
0	0.0482	7	0.0442	13	0.0520	19	0.0315
1	0.0364	8	0.0202	**14**	**0.0535**	20	0.0302
2	0.0410	9	0.0267	15	0.0226	21	0.0517
3	**0.0575**	**10**	**0.0635**	16	0.0322	22	0.0380
4	0.0252	11	0.0262	17	0.0392	23	0.0370
5	0.0190	12	0.0325	18	0.0299	24	0.0316
6	**0.0660**					25	0.0430

Figure 8–2   The value of $\phi(i)$ for $0 \leq i \leq 25$ using the model in Figure 8–1.

We now apply the character-based model. Let $\phi(i)$ be the correlation of the frequency of each letter in the ciphertext with the character frequencies in English (see Figure 8–1). Let $f(c)$ be the frequency of character c (expressed as a fraction). The formula for this correlation for this ciphertext (with all arithmetic being mod 26) is

$$\phi(i) = \sum_{0 \leq c \leq 25} f(c)p(c - i) = 0.1p(6 - i) + 0.1p(7 - i) + 0.1p(10 - i) + 0.3p(14 - i) + 0.2p(17 - i) + 0.1p(20 - i) + 0.1p(25 - i)$$

This correlation should be a maximum when the key k translates the ciphertext into English. Figure 8–2 shows the values of this function for the values of i. Trying the most likely key first, we obtain as plaintext "EBIIL TLOIA" when $i = 6$, "AXEEH PHKEW" when $i = 10$, "HELLO WORLD" when $i = 3$, and "WTAAD LDGAS" when $i = 14$.

The example above emphasizes the statistical nature of this attack. The statistics indicated that the key was most likely 6, when in fact the correct key was 3. So the attacker must test the results. The statistics simply reduce the number of trials in most cases. Only three trials were needed, as opposed to 13 (the expected number of trials if the keys were simply tried in order).

EXAMPLE: Using Konheim's model of single-character frequencies [527], the most likely keys (in order) are $i = 6$, $i = 10$, $i = 14$, and $i = 3$. Konheim's frequencies are different than Denning's, and this accounts for the change in the third most probable key.

8.2.2.1   Vigenère Cipher

A longer key might obscure the statistics. The Vigenère cipher chooses a sequence of keys, represented by a string. The key letters are applied to successive plaintext

```
  A B C D E F G H I J K L M N O P Q R S T U V W X Y Z
A A B C D E F G H I J K L M N O P Q R S T U V W X Y Z
B B C D E F G H I J K L M N O P Q R S T U V W X Y Z A
C C D E F G H I J K L M N O P Q R S T U V W X Y Z A B
D D E F G H I J K L M N O P Q R S T U V W X Y Z A B C
E E F G H I J K L M N O P Q R S T U V W X Y Z A B C D
F F G H I J K L M N O P Q R S T U V W X Y Z A B C D E
G G H I J K L M N O P Q R S T U V W X Y Z A B C D E F
H H I J K L M N O P Q R S T U V W X Y Z A B C D E F G
I I J K L M N O P Q R S T U V W X Y Z A B C D E F G H
J J K L M N O P Q R S T U V W X Y Z A B C D E F G H I
K K L M N O P Q R S T U V W X Y Z A B C D E F G H I J
L L M N O P Q R S T U V W X Y Z A B C D E F G H I J K
M M N O P Q R S T U V W X Y Z A B C D E F G H I J K L
N N O P Q R S T U V W X Y Z A B C D E F G H I J K L M
O O P Q R S T U V W X Y Z A B C D E F G H I J K L M N
P P Q R S T U V W X Y Z A B C D E F G H I J K L M N O
Q Q R S T U V W X Y Z A B C D E F G H I J K L M N O P
R R S T U V W X Y Z A B C D E F G H I J K L M N O P Q
S S T U V W X Y Z A B C D E F G H I J K L M N O P Q R
T T U V W X Y Z A B C D E F G H I J K L M N O P Q R S
U U V W X Y Z A B C D E F G H I J K L M N O P Q R S T
V V W X Y Z A B C D E F G H I J K L M N O P Q R S T U
W W X Y Z A B C D E F G H I J K L M N O P Q R S T U V
X X Y Z A B C D E F G H I J K L M N O P Q R S T U V W
Y Y Z A B C D E F G H I J K L M N O P Q R S T U V W X
Z Z A B C D E F G H I J K L M N O P Q R S T U V W X Y
```

Figure 8–3 The Vigenère tableau.

characters, and when the end of the key is reached, the key starts over. The length of the key is called the *period* of the cipher. Figure 8–3 shows a *tableau*, or table, to implement this cipher efficiently. Because this requires several different key letters, this type of cipher is called *polyalphabetic*.

EXAMPLE: The first line of a limerick is enciphered using the key "BENCH," as follows.

Key	B	ENCHBENC	HBENC	HBENCH	BENCHBENCH
Plaintext	A	LIMERICK	PACKS	LAUGHS	ANATOMICAL
Ciphertext	B	PVOLSMPM	WBGXU	SBYTJZ	BRNVVNMPCS

The *index of coincidence* measures the differences in the frequencies of the letters in the ciphertext. It is defined as the probability that two randomly chosen letters from the ciphertext will be the same. Let F_c be the frequency of cipher character c, and let N be the length of the ciphertext. It can be shown (see Exercise 7) that the index of coincidence *IC* is $IC = \dfrac{1}{N(N-1)} \sum_{i=0}^{25} F_i(F_i - 1)$. Figure 8–4 shows the expected values of *IC* for several periods. The lower the index of coincidence, the less variation in the characters of the ciphertext and (from our model of English) the longer the period of the cipher.

For many years, the Vigenère cipher was considered unbreakable. Then a Prussian cavalry officer named Kasiski noticed that repetitions occur when characters of the key appear over the same characters in the ciphertext. The number of characters between the repetitions is a multiple of the period.

EXAMPLE: Let the message be THE BOY HAS THE BAG and let the key be VIG. Then:

Key	VIGVIGVIGVIGVIG
Plaintext	THEBOYHASTHEBAG
Ciphertext	OPKWWECIYOPKWIM

In the ciphertext, the string OPK appears twice. Both are caused by the key sequence VIG enciphering the same ciphertext, THE. The ciphertext repetitions are nine characters apart. Hence, 9 is a multiple of the period (which is 3 here).

We examine the ciphertext for multiple repetitions and tabulate their length and the number of characters between successive repetitions. The period is likely to

Period	1	2	3	4	5	10	Large
Expected IC	0.066	0.052	0.047	0.045	0.044	0.041	0.038

Figure 8–4   Indices of coincidences for different periods. From Denning [242], Table 2.2, p. 78.

be a factor of the number of characters between these repetitions. From the repetitions, we establish the probable period, using the index of coincidence to check our deduction. We then tabulate the characters for each key letter separately and solve each as a Caesar cipher.

EXAMPLE: Consider the Vigenère cipher

```
ADQYS   MIUSB   OXKKT   MIBHK   IZOOO   EQOOG   IFBAG   KAUMF
VVTAA   CIDTW   MOCIO   EQOOG   BMBFV   ZGGWP   CIEKQ   HSNEW
VECNE   DLAAV   RWKXS   VNSVP   HCEUT   QOIOF   MEGJS   WTPCH
AJMOC   HIUIX
```

Could this be a Caesar cipher (which is a Vigenère cipher with a key length of 1)? We find that the index of coincidence is 0.043, which indicates a key of length 5 or more. So we assume that the key is of length greater than 1, and apply the Kasiski method. Repetitions of two letters or more are as follows.

Letters	Start	End	Gap length	Factors of gap length
MI	5	15	10	2, 5
OO	22	27	5	5
OEQOOG	24	54	30	2, 3, 5
FV	39	63	24	2, 2, 2, 3
AA	43	87	44	2, 2, 11
MOC	50	122	72	2, 2, 2, 3, 3
QO	56	105	49	7, 7
PC	69	117	48	2, 2, 2, 2, 3
NE	77	83	6	2, 3
SV	94	97	3	3
CH	118	124	6	2, 3

The longest repetition is six characters long; this is unlikely to be a coincidence. The gap between the repetitions is 30. The next longest repetition, MOC, is three characters long and has a gap of 72. The greatest common divisor of 30 and 72 is 6. Of the 11 repetitions, six have gaps with a factor of 6. The only factors that occur more in the gaps are 2 (in eight gaps) and 3 (in seven gaps). As a first guess, let us try 6.

To verify that this is reasonable, we compute the index of coincidence for each alphabet. We first arrange the message into six columns.

```
A   D   Q   Y   S   M
I   U   S   B   O   X
K   K   T   M   I   B
H   K   I   Z   O   O
O   E   Q   O   O   G
I   F   B   A   G   K
A   U   M   F   V   V
T   A   A   C   I   D
T   W   M   O   C   I
O   E   Q   O   O   G
B   M   B   F   V   Z
G   G   W   P   C   I
E   K   Q   H   S   N
E   W   V   E   C   N
E   D   L   A   A   V
R   W   K   X   S   V
N   S   V   P   H   C
E   U   T   Q   O   I
O   F   M   E   G   J
S   W   T   P   C   H
A   J   M   O   C   H
I   U   I   X
```

Each column represents one alphabet. The indices of coincidence are as follows.

Alphabet #1:	IC = 0.069	Alphabet #4:	IC = 0.056
Alphabet #2:	IC = 0.078	Alphabet #5:	IC = 0.124
Alphabet #3:	IC = 0.078	Alphabet #6:	IC = 0.043

All indices of coincidence indicate a single alphabet except for the ICs associated with alphabets #4 (period between 1 and 2) and #6 (period between 5 and 10). Given the statistical nature of the measure, we will assume that these are skewed by the distribution of characters and proceed on the assumption that there are six alphabets, and hence a key of length 6.

Counting characters in each column (alphabet) yields:

Column	A	B	C	D	E	F	G	H	I	J	K	L	M	N	O	P	Q	R	S	T	U	V	W	X	Y	Z
#1	3	1	0	0	4	0	1	1	3	0	1	0	0	1	3	0	0	1	1	2	0	0	0	0	0	0
#2	1	0	0	2	2	2	1	0	0	1	3	0	1	0	0	0	0	1	0	4	0	4	0	0	0	0
#3	1	2	0	0	0	0	0	0	2	0	1	1	4	0	0	0	4	0	1	3	0	2	1	0	0	0
#4	2	1	1	0	2	2	0	1	0	0	0	0	1	0	4	3	1	0	0	0	0	0	0	2	1	1
#5	1	0	5	0	0	0	2	1	2	0	0	0	0	0	5	0	0	0	3	0	0	2	0	0	0	0
#6	0	1	1	1	0	0	2	2	3	1	1	0	1	2	1	0	0	0	0	0	3	0	1	0	1	1

An unshifted alphabet has the following characteristics (L meaning low frequency, M meaning moderate frequency, and H meaning high frequency).

```
H M M M H M M H H M M M M H H M L H H H M L L L L L
```

We now compare the frequency counts in the six alphabets above with the frequency count of the unshifted alphabet. The first alphabet matches the characteristics of the unshifted alphabet (note the values for A, E, and I in particular). Given the gap between B and I, the third alphabet seems to be shifted with I mapping to A. A similar gap occurs in the sixth alphabet between O and V, suggesting that V maps to A. Substituting into the ciphertext (bold letters are plaintext) produces

```
ADIYS   RIUKB   OCKKL   MIGHK   AZOTO   EIOOL   IFTAG   PAUEF

VATAS   CIITW   EOCNO   EIOOL   BMTFV   EGGOP   CNEKI   HSSEW

NECSE   DDAAA   RWCXS   ANSNP   HHEUL   QONOF   EEGOS   WLPCM

AJEOC   MIUAX
```

In the last line, the group **AJE** suggests the word **ARE**. Taking this as a hypothesis, the second alphabet maps A into S. Substituting back produces

```
ALIYS   RICKB   OCKSL   MIGHS   AZOTO   MIOOL   INTAG   PACEF

VATIS   CIITE   EOCNO   MIOOL   BUTFV   EGOOP   CNESI   HSSEE

NECSE   LDAAA   RECXS   ANANP   HHECL   QONON   EEGOS   ELPCM

AREOC   MICAX
```

The last block suggests **MICAL**, because AL is a common ending for adjectives. This means that the fourth alphabet maps O into A, and the cipher becomes

```
ALIMS   RICKP   OCKSL   AIGHS   ANOTO   MICOL   INTOG   PACET

VATIS   QIITE   ECCNO   MICOL   BUTTV   EGOOD   CNESI   VSSEE

NSCSE   LDOAA   RECLS   ANAND   HHECL   EONON   ESGOS   ELDCM

ARECC   MICAL
```

In English, a Q is always followed by a U, so the I in the second group of the second line must map to U. The fifth alphabet maps M to A. The cipher is solved:

```
ALIME   RICKP   ACKSL   AUGHS   ANATO   MICAL   INTOS   PACET

HATIS   QUITE   ECONO   MICAL   BUTTH   EGOOD   ONESI   VESEE

NSOSE   LDOMA   RECLE   ANAND   THECL   EANON   ESSOS   ELDOM

ARECO   MICAL
```

With proper spacing and punctuation, we have

```
A LIMERICK PACKS LAUGHS ANATOMICAL
INTO SPACE THAT IS QUITE ECONOMICAL
   BUT THE GOOD ONES I'VE SEEN
   SO SELDOM ARE CLEAN,
AND THE CLEAN ONES SO SELDOM ARE COMICAL.
```

The key is ASIMOV.

It is worth noting that the Vigenère cipher is easy to break by hand. However, the principles of attack hold for more complex ciphers that can be implemented only by computer. A good example is the encipherments that several older versions of WordPerfect used [75, 78]. These allowed a user to encipher a file with a password. Unfortunately, certain fields in the enciphered file contained information internal to WordPerfect, and these fields could be predicted. This allowed an attacker to derive the password used to encipher the file, and from that the plaintext file itself.

8.2.2.2   One-Time Pad

The one-time pad is a variant of the Vigenère cipher. The technique is the same. The key string is chosen at random, and is at least as long as the message, so it does not repeat. Technically, it is a threshold scheme [815], and is provably impossible to break [115]. The implementation issues of the pad, including random generation of the key and key distribution, do not concern us here (although a later chapter will touch on them).

8.2.3   Data Encryption Standard

The Data Encryption Standard (DES) [662] was designed to encipher sensitive but nonclassified data. It is bit-oriented, unlike the other ciphers we have seen. It uses both transposition and substitution and for that reason is sometimes referred to as a *product cipher.* Its input, output, and key are each 64 bits long. The sets of 64 bits are referred to as *blocks.*

The cipher consists of 16 *rounds*, or iterations. Each round uses a separate key of 48 bits. These *round keys* are generated from the key block by dropping the parity bits (reducing the effective key size to 56 bits), permuting the bits, and extracting 48 bits. A different set of 48 bits is extracted for each of the 16 rounds (see Figure 8–5). If the order in which the round keys is used is reversed, the input is deciphered.

The rounds are executed sequentially, the input of one round being the output of the previous round. The right half of the input, and the round key, are run through a function f that produces 32 bits of output; that output is then xor'ed into the left half, and the resulting left and right halves are swapped (see Figure 8–6).

The function f provides the strength of the DES. The right half of the input (32 bits) is expanded to 48 bits, and this is xor'ed with the round key. The resulting 48 bits are split into eight sets of six bits each, and each set is put through a substitution

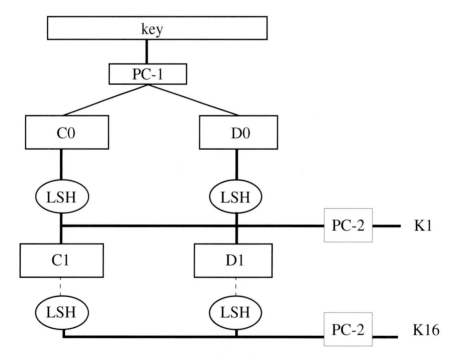

Figure 8–5   DES key schedule generation. PC-1 and PC-2 are permutation tables; LSH is a table of left shifts (rotations).

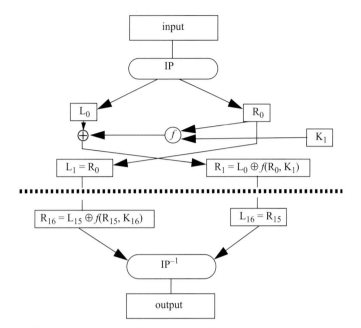

Figure 8–6   DES message encipherment and decipherment.

table called the *S-box*. Each S-box produces four bits of output. They are catenated into a single 32-bit quantity, which is permuted. The resulting 32 bits constitute the output of the *f* function (see Figure 8–7).

When the DES was first announced, it was criticized as too weak. First, Diffie and Hellman [268] argued that a key length of 56 bits was simply too short, and they designed a machine that could break a DES-enciphered message in a matter of days. Although their machine was beyond the technology of the time, they estimated that it could soon be built for about $20,000,000. Second, the reasons for many of the decisions in the design of the DES—most notably, those involving the S-boxes—were classified. Many speculated that the classification hid "trapdoors," or ways to invert the cipher without knowing the key.

Some properties of the DES were worrisome. First, it had four weak keys (keys that were their own inverses) and 12 semiweak keys (keys whose inverses were other keys). Second, let $\bar{k}$, $\bar{m}$, and $\bar{c}$ be the complement of the key k, the plaintext m, and the ciphertext c, respectively. Let $DES_k(m)$ be the encipherment of plaintext m under key k. Then the *complementation property* states that

$$DES_k(m) = c \Rightarrow DES_{\bar{k}}(\bar{m}) = \bar{c}$$

Third, some of the S-boxes exhibited irregular properties. The distribution of odd and even numbers was nonrandom, raising concerns that the DES did not randomize the input sufficiently. Several output bits of the fourth S-box seemed to depend on some

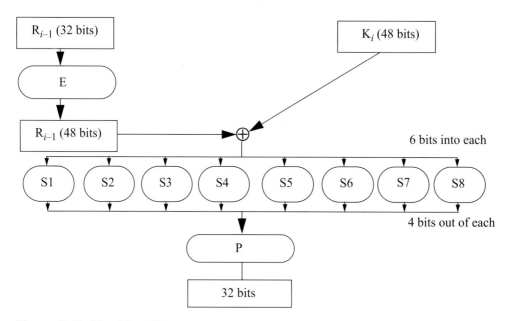

Figure 8–7 The *f* function.

of the output bits of the third S-box. This again suggested that there was a structure to the S-boxes, and because some of the design decisions underlying the S-boxes were unknown, the reasons for the structure were unknown. The structure made hardware implementation of the DES simpler [907]. It distributed the dependence of each output bit on each input bit rapidly, so that after five rounds each output bit depended on every key and input bit [625]. It could have been needed to prevent the cipher from being broken easily. It also could enable a trapdoor to allow the cipher to be broken easily. There was considerable speculation that the NSA had weakened the algorithm, although a congressional investigation did not reflect this [59].

In 1990, a breakthrough in cryptanalysis answered many of these questions. Biham and Shamir applied a technique called *differential cryptanalysis* to the DES [90, 91, 92]. This technique required them to generate 2^{47} pairs of chosen plaintext and ciphertext, considerably fewer than the trial-and-error approach others had used. During the development of this technique, they found several properties of the DES that appeared to answer some of the questions that had been raised.

First, for a known plaintext attack, differential cryptanalysis requires 2^{56} plaintext and ciphertext pairs for a 15-round version of the DES. For the full 16 rounds, 2^{58} known plaintext and ciphertext pairs are needed, which is more than sufficient for a trial-and-error approach. (Matsui subsequently improved this using a variant attack called linear cryptanalysis [596]; this attack requires 2^{43} known plaintext and ciphertext pairs on the average.) Second, small changes in the S-boxes weakened the cipher (so that the required number of chosen plaintext and ciphertext pairs was reduced). Third, making every bit of the round keys independent (for an effective key length of $16 \times 48 = 768$ bits) did not make the DES resistant to differential cryptanalysis, which suggests that the designers of the DES knew about differential analysis. Coppersmith later confirmed this [209].

The DES is used in several modes [663]. Using it directly is called electronic code book (ECB) mode, and is very rare. Modes in which it can be used to generate a pseudo-one-time pad are cipher feed back (CFB) mode (see Section 10.2.1.2) and output feed back (OFB) mode (see Section 10.2.1.1). Its most common modes of use are cipher block chaining (CBC) mode (see Section 10.2.2), encrypt-decrypt-encrypt (EDE) mode, and triple DES mode (the EDE and triple DES modes are described in Section 10.2.2.1).

The CBC mode is an iterative mode in which a block of ciphertext depends not only on its input but also on the preceding ciphertext block. In addition to a 64-bit key, it requires a 64-bit initialization vector. Figure 8–8 shows this mode. It has the *self-healing property*. This property says that if one block of ciphertext is altered, the error propagates for at most two blocks. Figure 8–9 shows how a corrupted block affects others.

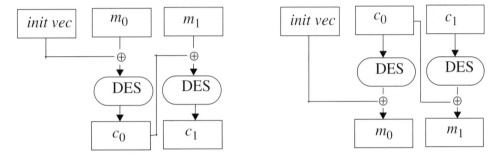

Figure 8–8   Cipher block chaining mode. The left diagram shows encipherment; each ciphertext is "fed back" into the cipher stream. The right diagram shows decipherment.

Incorrect ciphertext:	ef7c4cb2b4ce6f3b	f6266e3a97af0e2c
	746ab9a6308f4256	33e60b451b09603d
Corresponding plaintext:	*efca61e19f4836f1*	3231333336353837
	3231343336353837	3231343336353837
The real plaintext:	3231343336353837	3231343336353837
	3231343336353837	3231343336353837

Figure 8–9   Example of the self-healing property. The ciphertext at the top was stored incorrectly (the italicized 4c should be 4b). Its decipherment is shown next, with the incorrect octets italicized. The plaintext used to create the ciphertext is shown at the bottom.

The EDE mode is used by many financial institutions. It requires two 64-bit keys k and k'. The ciphertext c corresponding to some data m is $c = DES_k$ $(DES_k^{-1}(DES_k(m)))$. Triple DES uses three keys k, k', and k'', and the second step is an encipherment, not a decipherment: $c = DES_k(DES_{k'}(DES_{k''}(m)))$.

In 1998, a design for a computer system and software that could break any DES-enciphered message in a few days was published [358]. This design complemented several challenges to break specific DES messages. Those challenges had been solved using computers distributed throughout the Internet. By 1999, it was clear that the DES no longer provided the same level of security as it had 10 years earlier, and the search was on for a new, stronger cipher (to be called the Advanced Encryption Standard, or AES) to fill the needs that the DES no longer filled.

The DES is one of the most important classical cryptosystems in the history of cryptography. It provided the impetus for many advances in the field and laid the theoretical and practical groundwork for many other ciphers. While analyzing it, researchers developed differential and linear cryptanalysis. Cryptographers developed other ciphers to avoid real, or perceived, weaknesses; cryptanalysts broke many of these ciphers and found weaknesses in others. Many of the features of the DES are used in other ciphers. Hence, even though it is nearing the end of its useful lifetime, it is well worth understanding.

In late 2001, the National Institute of Standards and Technology announced the selection of Rijndael as the Advanced Encryption Standard [672], the successor to the DES. Like the DES, the AES is a product cipher. Unlike the DES, the AES can use keys of 128, 192, or 256 bits and operates on blocks of 128 bits. It was specifically designed to withstand the attacks to which the DES showed weaknesses [228]. Time will show how rapidly it supplants the DES, but the lessons learned from the DES have borne fruit.

8.2.4   Other Classical Ciphers

Several algorithms have been proposed to overcome the weaknesses in the DES. NewDES (which, despite its name, is not a variant of DES but a new algorithm) has a block size of 64 bits and a key length of 120 bits [803]. However, it can be broken using an attack similar to differential cryptanalysis [796]. FEAL is another block cipher, with a block size of 64 bits and a key size of 64 bits [642, 822]. FEAL-4 (FEAL with four rounds) and FEAL-8 (FEAL with eight rounds) fell to differential cryptanalysis with 20 [658] and 10,000 [357] chosen plaintexts, respectively. Biham and Shamir broke FEAL-N, which uses N rounds, for $N < 32$ by differential cryptanalysis more quickly than by trial-and-error [91]. It was proposed that the key be lengthened to 128 bits, but the 128-bit key proved as easy to break as FEAL-N with the original 64-bit key. REDOC-II [226] has an 80-bit block and a 160-bit key. It has 10 rounds, and although a single round was successfully cryptanalyzed [89], the use of 10 rounds appears to withstand differential cryptanalysis.

LOKI89 [137], proposed as an alternative to the DES, was vulnerable to differential cryptanalysis [89]. Its successor, LOKI91 [138], uses a 64-bit key and a 64-bit block size. Differential cryptanalysis fails to break this cipher [516]. Khufu [623] has a block size of 64 bits and a key size of 512 bits. When used with 24 or 32 rounds, it resists chosen plaintext attacks. Its S-boxes are computed from the keys. Khafre [623], similar in design to Khufu, uses fixed S-boxes, but it has been broken [89].

IDEA is an eight-round cipher that uses 64-bit blocks and 128-bit keys [541]. It uses three operations: exclusive or's, addition modulo 2^{16}, and multiplication modulo $2^{16} + 1$. It appears to withstand known attacks but is too new for any definitive statement to be made about its security [796]. It is used in noncommercial software—notably, in the electronic mail program PGP [965]—but is patented and requires licensing for use in commercial software.

8.3   Public Key Cryptography

In 1976, Diffie and Hellman [267] proposed a new type of cryptography that distinguished between encipherment and decipherment keys.[2] One of the keys would be publicly known; the other would be kept private by its owner. Classical cryptography requires the sender and recipient to share a common key. Public key cryptography does not. If the encipherment key is public, to send a secret message simply encipher the message with the recipient's public key. Then send it. The recipient can decipher it using his private key. (Chapter 9, "Key Management," discusses how to make public keys available to others.)

Because one key is public, and its complementary key must remain secret, a public key cryptosystem must meet the following three conditions.

1. It must be computationally easy to encipher or decipher a message given the appropriate key.
2. It must be computationally infeasible to derive the private key from the public key.
3. It must be computationally infeasible to determine the private key from a chosen plaintext attack.

The RSA cipher provides both secrecy and authentication.

---

[2] James Ellis, a cryptographer working for the British government's Communications-Electronics Security Group, said "he showed proof of concept in a January 1970 CESG report titled 'The Possibility of Secure Non-Secret Digital Encryption.'" Two of his colleagues found practical implementations. This work remained classified until 1997 ([244], p. 299).

8.3.1   RSA

RSA [756] is an exponentiation cipher. Choose two large prime numbers p and q, and let $n = pq$. The *totient* $\phi(n)$ of n is the number of numbers less than n with no factors in common with n.[3]

EXAMPLE: Let $n = 10$. The numbers that are less than 10 and are relatively prime to (have no factors in common with) n are 1, 3, 7, and 9. Hence, $\phi(10) = 4$. Similarly, if $n = 21$, the numbers that are relatively prime to n are 1, 2, 4, 5, 8, 10, 11, 13, 16, 17, 19, and 20. So $\phi(21) = 12$.

Choose an integer $e < n$ that is relatively prime to $\phi(n)$. Find a second integer d such that $ed \bmod \phi(n) = 1$. The public key is (e, n), and the private key is d.

Let m be a message. Then:

$$c = m^e \bmod n$$

and

$$m = c^d \bmod n$$

EXAMPLE: Let $p = 7$ and $q = 11$. Then $n = 77$ and $\phi(n) = 60$. Alice chooses $e = 17$, so her private key is $d = 53$. In this cryptosystem, each plaintext character is represented by a number between 00 (A) and 25 (Z); 26 represents a blank. Bob wants to send Alice the message "HELLO WORLD." Using the representation above, the plaintext is 07 04 11 11 14 26 22 14 17 11 03. Using Alice's public key, the ciphertext is

$$07^{17} \bmod 77 = 28$$
$$04^{17} \bmod 77 = 16$$
$$11^{17} \bmod 77 = 44$$

...

$$03^{17} \bmod 77 = 75$$

or 28 16 44 44 42 38 22 42 19 44 75.

In addition to confidentiality, RSA can provide data and origin authentication. If Alice enciphers her message using her private key, anyone can read it, but if anyone alters it, the (altered) ciphertext cannot be deciphered correctly.

---

[3] Our examples will use small numbers for pedagogical purposes. Actual RSA primes should be at least 512 bits each, giving a modulus of at least 1,024 bits. In practice, RSA is combined with cryptographic hash functions to prevent rearrangement of blocks (see Section 10.1.2).

EXAMPLE: Suppose Alice wishes to send Bob the message "HELLO WORLD" in such a way that Bob will be sure that Alice sent it. She enciphers the message with her private key and sends it to Bob. As indicated above, the plaintext is represented as 07 04 11 11 14 26 22 14 17 11 03. Using Alice's private key, the ciphertext is

$$07^{53} \bmod 77 = 35$$
$$04^{53} \bmod 77 = 09$$
$$11^{53} \bmod 77 = 44$$

...

$$03^{53} \bmod 77 = 05$$

or 35 09 44 44 93 12 24 94 04 05. In addition to origin authenticity, Bob can be sure that no letters were altered.

Providing both confidentiality and authentication requires enciphering with the sender's private key and the recipient's public key.

EXAMPLE: Suppose Alice wishes to send Bob the message "HELLO WORLD" in confidence and authenticated. Again, assume that Alice's private key is 53. Take Bob's public key to be 37 (making his private key 13). The plaintext is represented as 07 04 11 11 14 26 22 14 17 11 03. The encipherment is

$$(07^{53} \bmod 77)^{37} \bmod 77 = 07$$
$$(04^{53} \bmod 77)^{37} \bmod 77 = 37$$
$$(11^{53} \bmod 77)^{37} \bmod 77 = 44$$

...

$$(03^{53} \bmod 77)^{37} \bmod 77 = 47$$

or 07 37 44 44 14 59 22 14 61 44 47.

The recipient uses the recipient's private key to decipher the message and the sender's public key to authenticate it.

EXAMPLE: Bob receives the ciphertext above, 07 37 44 44 14 59 22 14 61 44 47. The decipherment is

$$(07^{13} \bmod 77)^{17} \bmod 77 = 07$$
$$(37^{13} \bmod 77)^{17} \bmod 77 = 04$$
$$(44^{13} \bmod 77)^{17} \bmod 77 = 11$$

...

$$(47^{13} \bmod 77)^{17} \bmod 77 = 03$$

or 07 04 11 11 14 26 22 14 17 11 03. This corresponds to the message "HELLO WORLD" from the preceding example.

The use of a public key system provides a technical type of nonrepudiation of origin. The message is deciphered using Alice's public key. Because the public key is the inverse of the private key, only the private key could have enciphered the message. Because Alice is the only one who knows this private key, only she could have enciphered the message. The underlying assumption is that Alice's private key has not been compromised, and that the public key bearing her name really does belong to her.

In practice, no one would use blocks of the size presented here. The issue is that, even if n is very large, if one character per block is enciphered, RSA can be broken using the techniques used to break classical substitution ciphers (see Sections 8.2.2 and 10.1.3). Furthermore, although no individual block can be altered without detection (because the attacker presumably does not have access to the private key), an attacker can rearrange blocks and change the meaning of the message.

EXAMPLE: A general sends a message to headquarters asking if the attack is on. Headquarters replies with the message "ON" enciphered using an RSA cipher with a 1,024-bit modulus, but each letter is enciphered separately. An attacker intercepts the message and swaps the order of the blocks. When the general deciphers the message, it will read "NO," the opposite of the original plaintext.

Moreover, if the attacker knows that headquarters will send one of two messages (here, "NO" or "ON"), the attacker can use a technique called "forward search" or "precomputation" to break the cipher (see Section 10.1.1). For this reason, plaintext is usually padded with random data to make up a block. This can eliminate the problem of forward searching, because the set of possible plaintexts becomes too large to precompute feasibly.

A different general sends the same request as in the example above. Again, headquarters replies with the message "ON" enciphered using an RSA cipher with a 1,024-bit modulus. Each letter is enciphered separately, but the first six bits of each block contain the number of the block, the next eight bits contain the character, and the remaining 1,010 bits contain random data. If the attacker rearranges the blocks, the general will detect that block 2 arrived before block 1 (as a result of the number in the first six bits) and rearrange them. The attacker also cannot precompute the blocks to determine which contains "O," because she would have to compute 2^{1010} blocks, which is computationally infeasible.

8.4   Cryptographic Checksums

Alice wants to send Bob a message of n bits. She wants Bob to be able to verify that the message he receives is the same one that was sent. So she applies a mathematical function, called a checksum function, to generate a smaller set of k bits from the original n bits. This smaller set is called the *checksum* or *message digest*. Alice then sends Bob both the message and the checksum. When Bob gets the message, he recomputes the checksum and compares it with the one Alice sent. If they match, he assumes that the message has not been changed.

EXAMPLE: The parity bit in the ASCII representation is often used as a single-bit checksum. If *odd parity* is used, the sum of the 1-bits in the ASCII representation of the character, and the parity bit, is odd. Assume that Alice sends Bob the letter "A." In ASCII, the representation of "A" using odd parity is $p0111101$ in binary, where p represents the parity bit. Because five bits are set, the parity bit is 0 for odd parity.

When Bob gets the message 00111101, he counts the 1-bits in the message. Because this number is odd, Bob knows that the message has arrived unchanged.

Definition 8–2. A *cryptographic checksum function* (also called a *strong hash function* or a *strong one-way function*) $h: A \rightarrow B$ is a function that has the following properties.

1. For any $x \in A$, $h(x)$ is easy to compute.
2. For any $y \in B$, it is computationally infeasible to find $x \in A$ such that $h(x) = y$.
3. It is computationally infeasible to find x, $x' \in A$, such that $x \neq x'$ and $h(x) = h(x')$. (Such a pair is called a *collision*.)

The third requirement is often stated as:

4. Given any $x \in A$, it is computationally infeasible to find another $x' \in A$ such that $x \neq x'$ and $h(x') = h(x)$.

However, properties 3 and 4 are subtlely different. It is considerably harder to find an x' meeting the conditions in property 4 than it is to find a pair x and x' meeting the conditions in property 3. To explain why, we need to examine some basics of cryptographic checksum functions.

Given that the checksum contains fewer bits than the message, several messages must produce the same checksum. The best checksum functions have the same number of messages produce each checksum. Furthermore, given any message, the checksum it produces can be determined only by computing the checksum. Such a checksum function acts as a random function.

The size of the output of the cryptographic checksum is an important consideration owing to a mathematical principle called the *pigeonhole principle*.

Definition 8–3. The *pigeonhole principle* states that if there are n containers for $n + 1$ objects, at least one container will hold two objects. To understand its application here, consider a cryptographic checksum function that computes hashes of three bits and a set of files each of which contains five bits. This yields $2^3 = 8$ possible hashes for $2^5 = 32$ files. Hence, at least four different files correspond to the same hash.

Now assume that a cryptographic checksum function computes hashes of 128 bits. The probability of finding a message corresponding to a given hash is 2^{-128}, but the probability of finding two messages with the same hash (that is, with the value of neither message being constrained) is 2^{-64} (see Exercise 20).

Definition 8–4. A *keyed* cryptographic checksum function requires a cryptographic key as part of the computation. A *keyless* cryptographic checksum does not.

EXAMPLE: The DES in CBC mode can be used as a message authentication code if 64 bits or fewer are required. The message is enciphered, and the last n bits of the last output are the cryptographic hash. Because the DES requires a cryptographic key, this checksum function (called DES-MAC) is a keyed cryptographic checksum function. Because the DES is vulnerable to attack, so is this checksum technique. Furthermore, because the hash is at most 64 bits, finding two inputs that produce the same output would require 2^{32} messages.

Examples of keyless hash functions include MD2 [489]; MD4 [753]; MD5 [754]; the Secure Hash Algorithm (SHA-1) which produces 160-bit checksums [664, 663]; Snefru (either 128-bit or 256-bit checksums) [622]; and HAVAL, which produces checksums of 128, 160, 192, 224, and 256 bits [963]. Of these, Snefru is vulnerable to differential cryptanalysis if four rounds or fewer are used [92], so Merkle recommends using at least eight passes. Dobbertin devised a method of generating collisions in MD4 [274]; a similar method also works against MD5 but is slower [273].

8.4.1   HMAC

HMAC is a generic term for an algorithm that uses a keyless hash function and a cryptographic key to produce a keyed hash function [531]. This mechanism enables Alice to validate that data Bob sent to her is unchanged in transit. Without the key, anyone could change the data and recompute the message authentication code, and Alice would be none the wiser.

The need for HMAC arose because keyed hash functions are derived from cryptographic algorithms. Many countries restrict the import and export of software that implements such algorithms. They do not restrict software implementing keyless hash functions, because such functions cannot be used to conceal information. Hence, HMAC builds on a keyless hash function using a cryptographic key to create a keyed hash function.

Let h be a keyless hash function that hashes data in blocks of b bytes to produce a hash l bytes long. Let k be a cryptographic key. We assume that the length of k is no greater than b; if it is, use h to hash it to produce a new key of length b. Let k' be the key k padded with bytes containing 0 to make b bytes. Let *ipad* be a sequence of bytes containing the bits 00110110 and repeated b times; let *opad* be a similar sequence with the bits 01011100. The HMAC-h function with key k for message m is

$$\text{HMAC-}h(k, m) = h(k' \oplus opad \parallel h(k' \oplus ipad \parallel m))$$

where $\oplus$ is exclusive or and $\parallel$ is concatenation.

Bellare, Canetti, and Krawczyk [65] analyze the security of HMAC and conclude that the strength of HMAC depends on the strength of the hash function h. Various HMAC functions are used in Internet security protocols (see Chapter 10).

8.5   Summary

For our purposes, three aspects of cryptography require study. Classical cryptography uses a single key shared by all involved. Public key cryptography uses two keys, one shared and the other private. Both types of cryptosystems can provide secrecy and origin authentication (although classical cryptography requires a trusted third party to provide both). Cryptographic hash functions may or may not use a secret key and provide data authentication.

All cryptosystems are based on substitution (of some quantity for another) and permutation (scrambling of some quantity). Cryptanalysis, the breaking of ciphers, uses statistical approaches (such as the Kasiski method and differential cryptanalysis) and mathematical approaches (such as attacks on the RSA method). As techniques of cryptanalysis improve, our understanding of encipherment methods also improves and ciphers become harder to break. The same holds for cryptographic checksum functions. However, as computing power increases, key length must also increase. A 56-bit key was deemed secure by many in 1976; it is clearly not secure now.

8.6   Further Reading

Cryptography is a vast, rich subject. Kahn's book *The Codebreakers* [482, 485] is required reading for anyone interested in this field. Kahn has written other excellent historical books on codebreaking during World War II [483, 484]. Helen Fouché Gaines presents techniques for cryptanalysis of many classical ciphers using traditional, pencil-and-paper analysis [343]. Sinkov applies basic mathematics to many of these classical ciphers [836]. Schneier describes many old, and new, algorithms in a clear, easy-to-understand manner [796]; his book is excellent for implementers. The underpinnings of these algorithms, and others, lie in statistics and mathematics. For classical cryptography, Konheim's book [527] is superb once the reader has mastered his notation. Unlike other books, it focuses on cryptanalysis of classical ciphers using statistical attacks. Meyer and Matyas [626] and Biham and Shamir [92] discuss the strengths and weaknesses of the DES. Seberry and Pieprzyk [805] and Simmons [834] discuss modern cryptography and its applications. Koblitz [521], Coutinho [215], and Goldreich [365] discuss modern mathematics, cryptographic theory, and cryptosystems. Menezes, Van Oorschot, and Vanstone's book [619] is a valuable reference. Trapp and Washington [902] present a good overview of AES-128, the version of the AES that uses 128-bit keys.

The Diffie-Hellman scheme [267] was the first public key cryptosystem proposed, and it is still in use today.

8.7   Exercises

1. A cryptographer once stated that cryptography could provide complete security, and that any other computer security controls were unnecessary. Why is he wrong? (*Hint:* Think of an implementation of a cryptosystem, and ask yourself what aspect(s) of the implementation can cryptography not protect.)

2. Decipher the following ciphertext, which was enciphered using the Caesar cipher: TEBKFKQEBZLROPBLCERJXKBSBKQP.

3. If one-time pads are provably secure, why are they so rarely used in practice?

4. Prove that the DES key consisting of all 0-bits and the DES key consisting of all 1-bits are both weak keys. What are the other two weak keys? (*Note:* Differences in the parity bits, which the PC-1 permutation drops, do not count; the keys must differ in the 56 bits that are used to generate the key schedule.)

5. Prove that the DES cipher satisfies the complementation property (see page 109).

6. Let k be the encipherment key for a Caesar cipher. The decipherment key differs; it is $26 - k$. One of the characteristics of a public key system is that the encipherment and decipherment keys are different. Why then is the Caesar cipher a classical cryptosystem, not a public key cryptosystem? Be specific.

7. The index of coincidence was defined as "the probability that two randomly chosen letters from the ciphertext will be the same." Derive the formula in Section 8.2.2.1 for the index of coincidence from this definition.

8. The following message was enciphered with a Vigenère cipher. Find the key and decipher it.

   TSMVM MPPCW CZUGX HPECP RFAUE IOBQW PPIMS FXIPC TSQPK
   SZNUL OPACR DDPKT SLVFW ELTKR GHIZS FNIDF ARMUE NOSKR
   GDIPH WSGVL EDMCM SMWKP IYOJS TLVFA HPBJI RAQIW HLDGA
   IYOUX

9. In the example enciphering HELLO WORLD using the RSA cipher (the second example in Section 8.3.1), the modulus was chosen as 77, even though the magnitude of the cleartext blocks is at most 25. What problems in transmission and/or representation might this cause?

10. Prove the following:

    a. If p is a prime, $\phi(p) = p - 1$.
    b. If p and q are two distinct primes, $\phi(pq) = (p - 1)(q - 1)$.

11. Fermat's Little Theorem says that, for integers a and n such that a and n are relatively prime, $a^{\phi(n)} \bmod n = 1$. Use this to show that deciphering of an enciphered message produces the original message with the RSA cryptosystem. Does enciphering of a deciphered message produce the original message also?

12. Consider the RSA cryptosystem. Show that the ciphertexts corresponding to the messages 0, 1 and $n - 1$ are the messages themselves. Are there other messages that produce the same ciphertext as plaintext?

13. It is often said that breaking RSA is equivalent to factoring the modulus, n.

    a. Prove that if n can be factored, one can determine the private key d from the modulus n and the public key e.
    b. Show that it is not necessary to factor n in order to determine the private key d from the modulus n and the public key e. (*Hint:* Look closely at the equation for computing the private key from n and e.)

    c. Show that it is not necessary to factor n in order to determine the plaintext m from a given ciphertext c, the public key e, and the modulus n. (*Hint:* Look closely at the equation for computing the ciphertext c.)

14. Prove the fundamental laws of modular arithmetic:

    a. $(a + b) \bmod n = (a \bmod n + b \bmod n) \bmod n$
    b. $ab \bmod n = ((a \bmod n)(b \bmod n)) \bmod n$

15. How would you use the law $ab \bmod n = ((a \bmod n)(b \bmod n)) \bmod n$ to reduce to 13 the number of multiplications required to compute $35^{77} \bmod 83$ from 76 multiplications? Can you reduce it any further?

16. The section on public key cryptosystems discussed nonrepudiation of origin in the context of public key cryptosystems. Consider a secret key system (in which a shared key is used). Bob has a message that he claims came from Alice, and to prove it he shows both the cleartext message and the ciphertext message. The ciphertext corresponds to the plaintext enciphered under the secret key that Alice and Bob share. Explain why this does *not* satisfy the requirements of nonrepudiation of origin. How might you modify a classical cryptosystem to provide nonrepudiation?

17. Suppose Alice and Bob have RSA public keys in a file on a server. They communicate regularly using authenticated, confidential messages. Eve wants to read the messages but is unable to crack the RSA private keys of Alice and Bob. However, she is able to break into the server and alter the file containing Alice's and Bob's public keys.

    a. How should Eve alter that file so that she can read confidential messages sent between Alice and Bob, and forge messages from either?

    b. How might Alice and/or Bob detect Eve's subversion of the public keys?

18. Is the identity function, which outputs its own input, a good cryptographic checksum function? Why or why not?

19. Is the *sum* program, which exclusive or's all words in its input to generate a one-word output, a good cryptographic checksum function? Why or why not?

20. Assume that a cryptographic checksum function computes hashes of 128 bits. Prove that the probability of finding two messages with the same hash (that is, with the value of neither message being constrained) is 2^{-64}.

21. The example involving the DES-MAC cryptographic hash function stated that a birthday attack would find collisions given 2^{32} messages. Alice wants to take advantage of this to swindle Bob. She draws up two contracts, one that Bob has agreed to sign and the other that Bob would not sign. She needs to generate a version of each that has the same checksum. Suggest how she might do this. (*Hint:* Adding blank spaces, or inserting a character followed by a backspace, will not affect the meaning of either contract.)

Chapter 9
Key Management

VALENTINE: Why then, I would resort to her by night.
DUKE: Ay, but the doors be lock'd and keys kept safe,
That no man hath recourse to her by night.
VALENTINE: What lets but one may enter at her window?
—*The Two Gentlemen of Verona*, III, i, 110–113.

Key management refers to the distribution of cryptographic keys; the mechanisms used to bind an identity to a key; and the generation, maintenance, and revoking of such keys. We assume that identities correctly define principals—that is, a key bound to the identity "Bob" is really Bob's key. Alice did not impersonate Bob's identity to obtain it. Chapter 13, "Representing Identity," discusses the problem of identifiers naming principals; Chapter 11, "Authentication," discusses a principal authenticating herself to a single system. This chapter assumes that authentication has been completed and that identity is assigned. The problem is to propagate that authentication to other principals and systems.

We first discuss authentication and key distribution. Next comes key generation and the binding of an identity to a key using certificates. Next, we discuss key storage and revocation. We conclude with digital signatures.

A word about notation. The statement

$$X \rightarrow Y : \{ Z \} k$$

means that entity X sends entity Y a message Z enciphered with key k. Subscripts to keys indicate to whom the keys belong, and are written where multiple keys are in use. For example, k_{Alice} and k_{Bob} refer to keys belonging to Alice and Bob, respectively. If Alice and Bob share a key, that key will be written as $k_{Alice,Bob}$ when the sharers are not immediately clear from the context. In general, k represents a secret key (for a classical cryptosystem), e a public key, and d a private key (for a public key cryptosystem). If multiple messages are listed sequentially, they are concatenated and sent. The operator $a \parallel b$ means that the bit sequences a and b are concatenated.

9.1   Session and Interchange Keys

We distinguish between a *session key* and an *interchange key* [921].

> **Definition 9–1.** An *interchange key* is a cryptographic key associated with a principal to a communication. A *session key* is a cryptographic key associated with the communication itself.

This distinction reflects the difference between a communication and a user involved in that communication. Alice has a cryptographic key used specifically to exchange information with Bob. This key does not change over interactions with Bob. However, if Alice communicates twice with Bob (and "communication" can be with, for example, an e-mail or a Web browser), she does not want to use the same key to encipher the messages. This limits the amount of data enciphered by a single key and reduces the likelihood of an eavesdropper being able to break the cipher. It also hinders the effectiveness of replay attacks. Instead, she will generate a key for that single session. That key enciphers the data only; it does not authenticate either principal, and it is discarded when the session ends. Hence, the name "session key."

Session keys also prevent forward searches [830]. A forward search attack occurs when the set of plaintext messages is small. The adversary enciphers all plaintexts using the target's public key. When ciphertext is intercepted, it is compared with the precomputed texts. This quickly gives the corresponding plaintext. A randomly generated session key, used once, would prevent this attack. (See Exercise 1 for another approach.)

EXAMPLE: Suppose Alice is a client of Bob's stockbrokering firm. She needs to send Bob one of two messages: BUY or SELL. The attacker, Cathy, enciphers both messages with Bob's public key. When Alice sends her message, Cathy compares it with her messages and sees which one it matches.

An interchange key is associated with a principal. Alice can use the key she shares with Bob to convince Bob that the sender is Alice. She uses this key for all sessions. It changes independently of session initiation and termination.

9.2   Key Exchange

The goal of key exchange is to enable Alice to communicate secretly to Bob, and vice versa, using a shared cryptographic key. Solutions to this problem must meet the following criteria.

1. The key that Alice and Bob are to share cannot be transmitted in the clear. Either it must be enciphered when sent, or Alice and Bob must derive it without an exhange of data from which the key can be derived. (Alice and Bob can exchange data, but a third party cannot derive the key from the data exchanged.)

2. Alice and Bob may decide to trust a third party (called "Cathy" here).

3. The cryptosystems and protocols are publicly known. The only secret data is to be the cryptographic keys involved.

Classical cryptosystems and public key cryptosystems use different protocols.

9.2.1 Classical Cryptographic Key Exchange and Authentication

Suppose Alice and Bob wish to communicate. If they share a common key, they can use a classical cryptosystem. But how do they agree on a common key? If Alice sends one to Bob, Eve the eavesdropper will see it and be able to read the traffic between them.

To avoid this bootstrapping problem, classical protocols rely on a trusted third party, Cathy. Alice and Cathy share a secret key, and Bob and Cathy share a (different) secret key. The goal is to provide a secret key that Alice and Bob share. The following simple protocol provides a starting point [796].

1. Alice $\rightarrow$ Cathy: { request for session key to Bob }k_{Alice}
2. Cathy $\rightarrow$ Alice: { $k_{session}$ }k_{Alice} ‖ { $k_{session}$ }k_{Bob}
3. Alice $\rightarrow$ Bob: { $k_{session}$ }k_{Bob}

Bob now deciphers the message and uses $k_{session}$ to communicate with Alice.

This particular protocol is the basis for many more sophisticated protocols. However, Bob does not know to whom he is talking. Assume that Alice sends Bob a message (such as "Deposit \$500 in Dan's bank account today") enciphered under $k_{session}$. If Eve records the second message in the exchange above, and the message enciphered under $k_{session}$, she can send Bob the message { $k_{session}$ }k_{Bob} followed by the message enciphered under $k_{session}$. Bob will not know who is sending it.

Avoiding problems such as this replay attack adds considerable complexity. Key exchange protocols typically add, at a minimum, some sort of authentication and defense against replay attack. One of the best-known such protocols is the Needham-Schroeder protocol [682].

1. Alice $\rightarrow$ Cathy : { Alice ‖ Bob ‖ $rand_1$ }
2. Cathy $\rightarrow$ Alice : { Alice ‖ Bob ‖ $rand_1$ ‖ $k_{session}$ ‖ {Alice ‖ $k_{session}$} k_{Bob} } k_{Alice}

3. Alice $\rightarrow$ Bob : { Alice $\|$ $k_{session}$ } k_{Bob}

4. Bob $\rightarrow$ Alice : { $rand_2$ } $k_{session}$

5. Alice $\rightarrow$ Bob : { $rand_2 - 1$ } $k_{session}$

In this protocol, $rand_1$ and $rand_2$ are two numbers generated at random, except that they cannot repeat between different protocol exchanges. These numbers are called *nonces*. (If Alice begins the protocol anew, her $rand_1$ in the first exchange will not have been used there before.) The basis for the security of this protocol is that both Alice and Bob trust Cathy.

When Bob receives the third message and deciphers it, he sees that the message names Alice. Since he could decipher the message, the message was enciphered using a key he shares only with Cathy. Because he trusts Cathy not to have shared the key k_{Bob} with anyone else, the message must have been enciphered by Cathy. This means that Cathy is vouching that she generated $k_{session}$ so Bob could communicate with Alice. So Bob trusts that Cathy sent the message to Alice, and that Alice forwarded it to him.

However, if Eve recorded the message, she could have replayed it to Bob. In that case, Eve would not have known the session key, so Bob sets out to verify that his unknown recipient does know it. He sends a random message enciphered by $k_{session}$ to Alice. If Eve intercepts the message, she will not know what to return; should she send anything, the odds of her randomly selecting a message that is correct is very low and Bob will detect the attempted replay. But if Alice is indeed initiating the communication, when she gets the message she can decipher it (because she knows $k_{session}$), apply some fixed function to the random data (here, decrement it by 1), and encipher the result and return it to Bob. Then Bob will be sure he is talking to Alice.

Alice needs to convince herself that she is talking to Bob, also. When she receives the second message from Cathy, she deciphers it and checks that Alice, Bob, and $rand_1$ are present. This tells her that Cathy sent the second message (because it was enciphered with k_{Alice}, which only she and Cathy know) and that it was a response to the first message (because $rand_1$ is in both the first and second messages). She obtains the session key and forwards the rest to Bob. She knows that only Bob has $k_{session}$, because only she and Bob can read the messages containing that key. So when she receives messages enciphered with that key, she will be sure that she is talking to Bob.

The Needham-Schroeder protocol assumes that *all* cryptographic keys are secure. In practice, session keys will be generated pseudorandomly. Depending on the algorithm used, it may be possible to predict such keys. Denning and Sacco [250] assumed that Eve could obtain a session key and subverted the protocol. Assume that the protocol above took place. Then:

1. Eve $\rightarrow$ Bob : { Alice $\|$ $k_{session}$ } k_{Bob}

2. Bob $\rightarrow$ Alice : { $rand_3$ } $k_{session}$ [intercepted by Eve]

3. Eve $\rightarrow$ Bob : { $rand_3 - 1$ } $k_{session}$

Now Bob thinks he is talking to Alice. He is really talking to Eve.

Denning and Sacco suggest using timestamps to enable Bob to detect this replay. Applying their method to the Needham-Schroeder protocol yields

1. Alice $\rightarrow$ Cathy : { Alice || Bob || $rand_1$ }
2. Cathy $\rightarrow$ Alice : { Alice || Bob || $rand_1$ || $k_{session}$ ||

$\quad\quad\quad\quad\quad$ {Alice || T || $k_{session}$} k_{Bob} } k_{Alice}
3. Alice $\rightarrow$ Bob : { Alice || T || $k_{session}$ } k_{Bob}
4. Bob $\rightarrow$ Alice : { $rand_2$ } $k_{session}$
5. Alice $\rightarrow$ Bob : { $rand_2 - 1$ } $k_{session}$

where T is a timestamp. When Bob gets the message in step 3, he rejects it if the timestamp is too old (too old being determined from the system in use). This modification requires synchronized clocks. Denning and Sacco note that a principal with a slow clock is vulnerable to a replay attack. Gong [368] adds that a party with a fast clock is also vulnerable, and simply resetting the clock does not eliminate the vulnerability.

The Otway-Rees protocol [706] corrects these problems[1] by avoiding the use of timestamps.

1. Alice $\rightarrow$ Bob : num || Alice || Bob || { $rand_1$ || num || Alice || Bob } k_{Alice}
2. Bob $\rightarrow$ Cathy : num || Alice || Bob, || { $rand_1$ || num || Alice || Bob } k_{Alice} ||

$\quad\quad\quad\quad\quad$ { $rand_2$ || num || Alice || Bob } k_{Bob}
3. Cathy $\rightarrow$ Bob : num || { $rand_1$ || $k_{session}$ } k_{Alice} || { $rand_2$ || $k_{session}$ } k_{Bob}
4. Bob $\rightarrow$ Alice : num || { $rand_1$ || $k_{session}$ } k_{Alice}

The purpose of the integer num is to associate all messages with a particular exchange. Again, consider the elements of the protocol.

When Alice receives the fourth message from Bob, she checks that the num agrees with the num in the first message that she sent to Bob. If so, she knows that this is part of the exchange. She also trusts that Cathy generated the session key because only Cathy and Alice know k_{Alice}, and the random number $rand_1$ agrees with what Alice put in the enciphered portion of the message. Combining these factors, Alice is now convinced that she is talking to Bob.

When Bob receives the message from Cathy, he determines that the num corresponds to the one he received from Alice and sent to Cathy. He deciphers that portion of the message enciphered with his key, and checks that $rand_2$ is what he sent. He then knows that Cathy sent the reply, and that it applies to the exchange with Alice.

Because no timestamps are used, the synchronization of the system clocks is irrelevant. Now suppose that Eve acquired an old session key and the message in 3.

---

[1] Needham and Schroeder also supply a modification [683]; see Exercise 5.

She forwards that message to Alice. Alice immediately rejects it if she has no ongoing key exchanges with Bob. If she does, and *num* does not match, she rejects Eve's message. The only way Eve could impersonate Bob is if she acquired $k_{session}$ for an ongoing exchange, recorded the third message, and resent the relevant portion to Alice before Bob could do so. In that case, however, Eve could simply listen to the traffic, and no replay would be involved.

9.2.2   Kerberos

Kerberos [526, 872] uses the Needham-Schroeder protocol as modified by Denning and Sacco. A client, Alice, wants to use a server S. Kerberos requires her to use two servers to obtain a credential that will authenticate her to S. First, Alice must authenticate herself to the Kerberos system; then she must obtain a *ticket* to use S (see next paragraph). (This separates authentication of the user to the issuer of tickets and the vouching of identity to S.)

The basis of Kerberos is a credential known as the *ticket*. It contains[2]

$$T_{Alice,Barnum} = \text{Barnum} \| \{ \text{Alice} \| \text{Alice address} \| \text{valid time} \| k_{Alice,Barnum} \} k_{Barnum}$$

In this ticket, k_{Barnum} is the key that Barnum shares with the authentication server, and $k_{Alice,Barnum}$ is the session key that Alice and Barnum will share. The valid time is the time interval during which the ticket is valid, which is typically several hours. The ticket is the issuer's voucher for the identity of the requester of the service.

The *authenticator* contains the identity of the sender of a ticket and is used when Alice wants to show Barnum that the party sending the ticket is the same as the party to whom the ticket was issued. It contains[3]

$$A_{Alice,Barnum} = \{ \text{Alice} \| \text{generation time} \| kt \} k_{Alice,Barnum}$$

where $k_{Alice,Barnum}$ is the session key that Alice and Barnum share, kt is an alternative session key, and the authenticator was created at generation time. Alice generates an authenticator whenever she sends a ticket. She sends both the ticket and the authenticator in the same message.

Alice's goal is to print a file using the service Guttenberg. The authentication server is Cerberus and the ticket-granting server is Barnum. The Kerberos (Version 5) protocol proceeds as follows.

1. Alice $\rightarrow$ Cerberus: Alice $\|$ Barnum
2. Cerberus $\rightarrow$ Alice : $\{ k_{Alice,Barnum} \} k_{Alice} \| T_{Alice,Barnum}$

---

[2] See Kohl and Neuman [526], Section 5.3.1, for a complete description of a ticket. We include only the parts that are relevant to our discussion.
[3] See Kohl and Neuman [526], Section 5.3.2, for a complete description of an authenticator. We include only the parts that are relevant to our discussion.

At this point, Alice deciphers the first part of the message to obtain the key she will use to communicate with Barnum. Kerberos uses the user's password as the key, so if Alice enters her password incorrectly, the decipherment of the session key will fail. These steps occur only at login; once Alice has the ticket for the ticket-granting server Barnum, she caches it and uses it:

3. Alice → Barnum : Guttenberg $\|$ $A_{Alice,Barnum}$ $\|$ $T_{Alice,Barnum}$
4. Barnum → Alice : Alice $\|$ $\{k_{Alice,Guttenberg}\}$ $k_{Alice,Barnum}$ $\|$ $T_{Alice,Guttenberg}$
5. Alice → Guttenberg : $A_{Alice,Guttenberg}$ $\|$ $T_{Alice,Guttenberg}$
6. Guttenberg → Alice : $\{ t + 1 \}$ $k_{Alice,Guttenberg}$

In these steps, Alice first constructs an authenticator and sends it, with the ticket and the name of the server, to Barnum. Barnum validates the request by comparing the data in the authenticator with the data in the ticket. Because the ticket is enciphered using the key Barnum shares with Cerberus, he knows that it came from a trusted source. He then generates an appropriate session key and sends Alice a ticket to pass on to Guttenberg. Step 5 repeats step 3, except that the name of the service is not given (because Guttenberg is the desired service). Step 6 is optional; Alice may ask that Guttenberg send it to confirm the request. If it is sent, t is the timestamp.

Bellovin and Merritt [72] discuss several potential problems with the Kerberos protocol. In particular, Kerberos relies on clocks being synchronized to prevent replay attacks. If the clocks are not synchronized, and if old tickets and authenticators are not cached, replay is possible. In Kerberos 5, authenticators are valid for 5 minutes, so tickets and authenticators can be replayed within that interval. Also, because the tickets have some fixed fields, a dictionary attack can be used to determine keys shared by services or users and the ticket-granting service or the authentication service, much as the WordPerfect cipher was broken (see the end of Section 8.2.2.1). Researchers at Purdue University used this technique to show that the session keys generated by Kerberos 4 were weak; they reported deciphering tickets, and finding session keys, within minutes [277].

9.2.3   Public Key Cryptographic Key Exchange and Authentication

Conceptually, public key cryptography makes exchanging keys very easy.

1. Alice → Bob : $\{ k_{session} \}$ e_{Bob}

where e_{Bob} is Bob's public key. Bob deciphers the message and obtains the session key $k_{session}$. Now he and Alice can communicate securely, using a classical cryptosystem.

As attractive as this protocol is, it has a similar flaw to our original classical key exchange protocol. Eve can forge such a message. Bob does not know who the message comes from.

One obvious fix is to sign the session key.

1. Alice $\rightarrow$ Bob : Alice, { { $k_{session}$ } d_{Alice} } e_{Bob}

where d_{Alice} is Alice's private key. When Bob gets the message, uses his private key to decipher the message. He sees the key is from Alice. Alice uses her public key to obtain the session key. Schneier [796] points out that Alice could also include a message enciphered with $k_{session}$.

These protocols assume that Alice has Bob's public key e_{Bob}. If not, she must get it from a public server, Peter. With a bit of ingenuity, Eve can arrange to read Bob's messages to Alice, and vice versa.

1. Alice $\rightarrow$ Peter : { send me Bob's public key } [intercepted by Eve]
2. Eve $\rightarrow$ Peter : { send me Bob's public key }
3. Peter $\rightarrow$ Eve : e_{Bob}
4. Eve $\rightarrow$ Alice : e_{Eve}
5. Alice $\rightarrow$ Bob : { $k_{session}$ } e_{Eve} [intercepted by Eve]
6. Eve $\rightarrow$ Bob : { $k_{session}$ } e_{Bob}

Eve now has the session key and can read any traffic between Alice and Bob. This is called a *man-in-the-middle attack* and illustrates the importance of identification and authentication in key exchange protocols. The man-in-the-middle attack works because there is no binding of identity to a public key. When presented with a public key purportedly belonging to Bob, Alice has no way to verify that the public key in fact belongs to Bob. This issue extends beyond key exchange and authentication. To resolve it, we need to look at the management of cryptographic keys.

9.3   Cryptographic Key Infrastructures

Because classical cryptosystems use shared keys, it is not possible to bind an identity to a key. Instead, two parties need to agree on a shared key. Section 9.2, "Key Exchange," presents protocols that do this.

Public key cryptosystems use two keys, one of which is to be available to all. The association between the cryptographic key and the principal is critical, because it determines the public key used to encipher messages for secrecy. If the binding is erroneous, someone other than the intended recipient could read the message.

For purposes of this discussion, we assume that the principal is identified by a name of some acceptable sort (Chapter 13, "Representing Identity," discusses this issue in more detail) and has been authenticated to the entity that generates the cryptographic keys. The question is how some (possibly different) principal can bind the public key to the representation of identity.

An obvious idea is for the originator to sign the public key with her private key, but this merely pushes the problem to another level, because the recipient would only know that whoever generated the public key also signed it. No identity is present.

Kohnfelder [517] suggests creating a message containing a representation of identity, the corresponding public key, and a timestamp, and having a trusted authority sign it.

$$C_{Alice} = \{\ e_{Alice} \parallel \text{Alice} \parallel T\ \}\ d_{Cathy}$$

This type of structure is called a *certificate*.

> **Definition 9–2.** A *certificate* is a token that binds an identity to a cryptographic key.

When Bob wants to communicate with Alice, he obtain's Alice's certificate C_{Alice}. Assuming that he knows Cathy's public key, he can decipher the certificate. He first checks the timestamp T to see when the certificate was issued. (From this, he can determine if the certificate is too old to be trusted; see below.) He looks at the subject entity (Alice, to whom the certificate was issued). The public key in the certificate belongs to that subject, so Bob now has Alice's public key. He knows that Cathy signed the certificate and therefore that Cathy is vouching to some degree that the public key belongs to Alice. If he trusts Cathy to make such a determination, he accepts the public key as valid and belonging to Alice.

One immediate problem is that Bob must know Cathy's public key to validate the certificate. Two approaches deal with this problem. The first, by Merkle, eliminates Cathy's signature; the second structures certificates into signature chains.

9.3.1 Certificate Signature Chains

The usual form of certification is for the issuer to encipher a hash of the identity of the subject (to whom the certificate is issued), the public key, and information such as time of issue or expiration using the issuer's private key. To validate the certificate, a user uses the issuer's public key to decipher the hash and check the data in the certificate. The user trying to validate the certificate must obtain the issuer's public key. If the issuer has a certificate, the user can get that key from the issuer's certificate. This pushes the problem to another level: how can the issuer's certificate be validated?

Two approaches to this problem are to construct a tree-like hierarchy, with the public key of the root known out of band, or to allow an arbitrary arrangement of certifiers and rely on each individual's knowledge of the certifiers. First, we examine X.509, which describes certificates and certification in general. We then look at the PGP certification structure.

9.3.1.1   X.509: Certification Signature Chains

X.509—the Directory Authentication Framework [460] is the basis for many other protocols. It defines certificate formats and certification validation in a generic context. Soon after its original issue in 1988, I'Anson and Mitchell [454] found problems with both the protocols and the certificate structure. These problems were corrected in the 1993 version, referred to as X.509v3.

The X.509v3 certificate has the following components [865].

1. *Version*. Each successive version of the X.509 certificate has new fields added. If fields 8, 9, and 10 (see below) are present, this field must be 3; if fields 8 and 9 are present, this field is either 2 or 3; and if none of fields 8, 9, and 10 are present, the version number can be 1, 2, or 3.

2. *Serial number*. This must be unique among the certificates issued by this issuer. In other words, the pair (*issuer's Distinguished Name, serial number*) must be unique.

3. *Signature algorithm identifier*. This identifies the algorithm, and any parameters, used to sign the certificate.

4. *Issuer's Distinguished Name*. This is a name that uniquely identifies the issuer. See Chapter 13, "Representing Identity," for a discussion.

5. *Validity interval*. This gives the times at which the certificate becomes valid and expires.

6. *Subject's Distinguished Name*. This is a name that uniquely identifies the subject to whom the certificate is issued. See Chapter 13, "Representing Identity," for a discussion.

7. *Subject's public key information*. This identifies the algorithm, its parameters, and the subject's public key.

8. *Issuer's unique identifier* (Version 2 and 3 certificates only). Under some circumstances, issuer Distinguished Names may be recycled (for example, when the Distinguished Name refers to a role, or when a company closes and a second company with the same Distinguished Name opens). This field allows the issuer to disambiguate among entities with the same issuer name.

9. *Subject's unique identifier* (Version 2 and 3 certificates only). This field is like field 8, but for the subject.

10. *Extensions* (Version 3 certificates only). X.509v3 defines certain extensions in the areas of key and policy information, certification path constraints, and issuer and subject information. For example, if an issuer has multiple certification keys, the "authority key identifier" allows the certificate to indicate which key should be used. The "basic constraints" extension indicates if the certificate holder can issue certificates.

11. *Signature*. This field identifies the algorithm and parameters used to sign the certificate, followed by the signature (an enciphered hash of fields 1 to 10) itself.

To validate the certificate, the user obtains the issuer's public key for the particular signature algorithm (field 3) and deciphers the signature (field 11). She then uses the information in the signature field (field 11) to recompute the hash value from the other fields. If it matches the deciphered signature, the signature is valid if the issuer's public key is correct. The user then checks the period of validity (field 5) to ensure that the certificate is current.

Definition 9–3. A *certification authority* (CA) is an entity that issues certificates.

If all certificates have a common issuer, then the issuer's public key can be distributed out of band. However, this is infeasible. For example, it is highly unlikely that France and the United States could agree on a single issuer for their organizations' and citizens' certificates. This suggests multiple issuers, which complicates the process of validation.

Suppose Alice has a certificate from her local CA, Cathy. She wants to communicate with Bob, whose local CA is Dan. The problem is for Alice and Bob to validate each other's certificates.

Assume that $X<<Y>>$ represents the certificate that X generated for the subject Y (X is the CA that issued the certificate). Bob's certificate is Dan<<Bob>>. If Cathy has issued a certificate to Dan, Dan has a certificate Cathy<<Dan>>; similarly, if Dan has issued a certificate to Cathy, Cathy has a certificate Dan<<Cathy>>. In this case, Dan and Cathy are said to be cross-certified.

Definition 9–4. Two CAs are *cross-certified* if each has issued a certificate for the other.

Because Alice has Cathy's (trusted) public key, she can obtain Cathy<<Dan>> and form the signature chain

Cathy<<Dan>> Dan<<Bob>>

Because Alice can validate Dan's certificate, she can use the public key in that certificate to validate Bob's certificate. Similarly, Bob can acquire Dan<<Cathy>> and validate Alice's certificate.

Dan<<Cathy>> Cathy<<Alice>>

Signature chains can be of arbitrary length. The only requirement is that each certificate can be validated by the one before it in the chain. (X.509 suggests organizing CAs into a hierarchy to minimize the lengths of certificate signature chains, but this is not a requirement.)

Certificates can be revoked, or canceled. A list of such certificates enables a user to detect, and reject, invalidated certificates. Section 9.4.2 discusses this.

9.3.1.2   PGP Certificate Signature Chains

PGP is an encipherment program widely used to provide privacy for electronic mail throughout the Internet, and to sign files digitally. It uses a certificate-based key management infrastructure for users' public keys. Its certificates and key management structure differ from X.509's in several ways. Here, we describe OpenPGP's structure [150]; but much of this discussion also applies to other versions of PGP.

An OpenPGP certificate is composed of *packets*. A packet is a record with a tag describing its purpose. A certificate contains a public key packet followed by zero or more signature packets. An OpenPGP public key packet has the following structure.

1. *Version*. This is either 3 or 4. Version 3 is compatible with all versions of PGP; Version 4 is not compatible with old (Version 2.6) versions of PGP.
2. *Time of creation*. This specifies when the certificate was created.
3. *Validity period* (Version 3 only). This gives the number of days that the certificate is valid. If it is 0, the certificate does not expire.
4. *Public key algorithm and parameters*. This identifies the algorithm used and gives the parameters for the cryptosystem used. Version 3 packets contain the modulus for RSA (see Section 9.3.2). Version 4 packets contain the parameters appropriate for the cryptosystem used.
5. *Public key*. This gives the public key. Version 3 packets contain the exponent for RSA. Version 4 packets contain the public key for the cryptosystem identified in field 4.

The information in an OpenPGP signature packet is different for the two versions. Version 3 contains the following.

1. *Version*. This is 3.
2. *Signature type*. This describes the specific purpose of the signature and encodes a level of trust (see Section 13.5.2, "Trust"). For example, signature type 0x11 says that the signer has not verified that the public key belongs to the named subject.
3. *Creation time*. This specifies the time at which the fields following were hashed.
4. *Key identifier of the signer*. This specifies the key used to generate the signature.
5. *Public key algorithm*. This identifies the algorithm used to generate the signature.
6. *Hash algorithm*. This identifies the algorithm used to hash the signature before signing.
7. *Part of signed hash value*. After the data is hashed, field 2 is given the time at which the hash was computed, and that field is hashed and appended to the previous hash. The first two bytes are placed into this field. The idea is

that the signature can be rejected immediately if the first two bytes hashed during the validation do not match this field.

8. *Signature*. This contains the encipherment of the hash using the signer's private key.

A Version 4 signature packet is considerably more complex, but as a Version 3 signature packet does, it binds a signature to an identifier and data. The interested reader is referred to the OpenPGP specifications [150].

PGP certificates differ from X.509 certificates in several important ways. Unlike X.509, a single key may have multiple signatures. (All Version 4 PGP keys are signed by the owner; this is called *self-signing*.) Also unlike X.509, a notion of "trust" is embedded in each signature, and the signatures for a single key may have different levels of trust. The users of the certificates can determine the level of trust for each signature and act accordingly.

EXAMPLE: Suppose Alice needs to communicate with Bob. She obtains Bob's public key PGP certificate, Ellen,Fred,Giselle,Bob<<Bob>> (where the X.509 notation is extended in the obvious way). Alice knows none of the signers, so she gets Giselle's PGP certificate, Henry,Irene,Giselle<<Giselle>>, from a certificate server. She knows Henry vaguely, so she obtains his certificate, Ellen,Henry<<Henry>>, and verifies Giselle's certificate. She notes that Henry's signature is at the "casual" trust level, so she decides to look elsewhere for confirmation. She obtains Ellen's certificate, Jack,Ellen<<Ellen>>, and immediately recognizes Jack as her husband. She has his certificate and uses it to validate Ellen's certificate. She notes that his signature is at the "positive" trust level, so she accepts Ellen's certificate as valid and uses it to validate Bob's. She notes that Ellen signed the certificate with "positive" trust also, so she concludes that the certificate, and the public key it contains, are trustworthy.

In the example above, Alice followed two signature chains:

Henry<<Henry>> Henry<<Giselle>> Giselle<<Bob>>

and

Jack<<Ellen>> Ellen<<Bob>>

(where the unchecked signatures have been dropped). The trust levels affected how Alice checked the certificate.

A subtle distinction arises here between X.509 and PGP certificates. X.509 certificates include an element of trust, but the trust is not indicated in the certificate. PGP certificates indicate the level of trust, but the same level of trust may have different meanings to different signers. Chapter 13, "Representing Identity," will examine this issue in considerable detail.

9.3.2   Summary

The deployment and management of public keys is complex because of the different requirements of various protocols. Most protocols use some form of the X.509v3 certificates, although the extensions vary. The infrastructure that manages public keys and certification authorities is called a *public key infrastructure*. Several such infrastructures are in place, such as the PGP Certificate Servers and the commercial certificate issuers for World Wide Web browsers.

9.4   Storing and Revoking Keys

Key storage arises when a user needs to protect a cryptographic key in a way other than by remembering it. If the key is public, of course, any certificate-based mechanism will suffice, because the goal is to protect the key's integrity. But secret keys (for classical cryptosystems) and private keys (for public key cryptosystems) must have their confidentiality protected as well.

9.4.1   Key Storage

Protecting cryptographic keys sounds simple: just put the key into a file, and use operating system access control mechanisms to protect it. Unfortunately, as we will discuss in Chapter 20, operating system access control mechanisms can often be evaded or defeated, or may not apply to some users. On a single-user system, this consideration is irrelevant, because no one else will have access to the system while the key is on the system. On a multiuser system, other users have access to the system. On a networked system, an attacker could trick the owner into downloading a program that would send keystrokes and files to the attacker, thereby revealing the confidential cryptographic key. We consider these systems.

On such systems, enciphering the file containing the keys will not work, either. When the user enters the key to decipher the file, the key and the contents of the file will reside in memory at some point; this is potentially visible to other users on a multiuser system. The keystrokes used to decipher the file could be recorded and replayed at a later date. Either will compromise the key.

A feasible solution is to put the key onto one or more physical devices, such as a special terminal, ROM, or smart card [241, 291, 598]. The key never enters the computer's memory. Instead, to encipher a message, the user inserts the smart card into a special device that can read from, and write to, the computer. The computer sends it the message to be protected, and the device uses the key on the smart card to encipher the message and send it back to the computer. At no point is the cryptographic key exposed.

A variant relies on the observation that if the smart card is stolen, the thief has the cryptographic key. Instead of having it on one card, the key is split over multiple devices (two cards, a card and the physical card reader, and so on.) Now, if a thief steals one of the cards, the stolen card is useless because it does not contain the entire key.

9.4.2   Key Revocation

Certificate formats contain a key expiration date. If a key becomes invalid before that date, it must be revoked. Typically, this means that the key is compromised, or that the binding between the subject and the key has changed.

   We distinguish this from an expired certificate. An expired certificate has reached a predesignated period after which it is no longer valid. That the lifetime has been exceeded is the only reason. A revoked certificate has been canceled at the request of the owner or issuer for some reason other than expiration.

   There are two problems with revoking a public key. The first is to ensure that the revocation is correct—in other words, to ensure that the entity revoking the key is authorized to do so. The second is to ensure timeliness of the revocation throughout the infrastructure. This second problem depends on reliable and highly connected servers and is a function of the infrastructure as well as of the locations of the certificates and the principals who have copies of those certificates. Ideally, notice of the revocation will be sent to all parties when received, but invariably there will be a time lag.

   The X.509 and Internet public key infrastructures (PKIs) use lists of certificates.

Definition 9–5. A *certificate revocation list* is a list of certificates that are no longer valid.

A certificate revocation list contains the serial numbers of the revoked certificates and the dates on which they were revoked. It also contains the name of the issuer, the date on which the list was issued, and when the next list is expected to be issued. The issuer also signs the list [865]. Under X.509, only the issuer of a certificate can revoke it.

   PGP allows signers of certificates to revoke their signatures as well as allowing owners of certificates, and their designees, to revoke the entire certificates. The certificate revocation is placed into a PGP packet and is signed just like a regular PGP certificate. A special flag marks it as a revocation message.

9.5   Digital Signatures

As electronic commerce grows, so does the need for a provably high degree of authentication. Think of Alice's signature on a contract with Bob. Bob not only has to know that Alice is the other signer and is signing it; he also must be able to prove to a disinterested third party (called a *judge*) that Alice signed it and that the contract he presents has not been altered since Alice signed it. Such a construct is called a *digital signature*.

Definition 9–6. A *digital signature* is a construct that authenticates both the origin and contents of a message in a manner that is provable to a disinterested third party.

The "proof" requirement introduces a subtlety. Let m be a message. Suppose Alice and Bob share a secret key k. Alice sends Bob $m \parallel \{\ m\ \}k$ (that is, the message and its encipherment under k). Is this a digital signature?

First, Alice has authenticated the contents of the message, because Bob deciphers $\{\ m\ \}k$ and can check that the message matches the deciphered one. Because only Bob and Alice know k, and Bob knows that he did not send the message, he concludes that it has come from Alice. He has authenticated the message origin and integrity. However, based on the mathematics alone, Bob cannot prove that he did not create the message, because he knows the key used to create it. Hence, this is not a digital signature.

Public key cryptography solves this problem. Let d_{Alice} and e_{Alice} be Alice's private and public keys, respectively. Alice sends Bob the message $m \parallel \{\ m\ \}d_{Alice}$. As before, Bob can authenticate the origin and contents of m, but in this situation a judge must determine that Alice signed the message, because only Alice knows the private key with which the message was signed. The judge merely obtains e_{Alice} and computes $\{\ \{\ m\ \}d_{Alice}\ \}\ e_{Alice}$. If the result is m, Alice signed it. This is in fact a digital signature.

A digital signature provides the service of nonrepudiation. If Alice claims she never sent the message, the judge points out that the originator signed the message with her private key, which only she knew. Alice at that point may claim that her private key was stolen, or that her identity was incorrectly bound in the certificate (see Chapter 13, "Representing Identity"). The notion of "nonrepudiation" provided here is strictly abstract. In fact, Alice's key might have been stolen, and she might not have realized this before seeing the digital signature. Such a claim would require ancillary evidence, and a court or other legal agency would need to handle it. For the purposes of this section, we consider the service of nonrepudiation to be the inability to deny that one's cryptographic key was used to produce the digital signature.

9.5.1   Classical Signatures

All classical digital signature schemes rely on a trusted third party. The judge must trust the third party. Merkle's scheme is typical [621].

Let Cathy be the trusted third party. Alice shares a cryptographic key k_{Alice} with Cathy. Likewise, Bob shares k_{Bob} with Cathy. When Alice wants to send Bob a contract m, she computes $\{\ m\ \}k_{Alice}$ and sends it to Bob. Bob sends it to Cathy, who deciphers m, enciphers it with k_{Bob}, and returns $\{\ m\ \}k_{Bob}$ to Bob. He can now decipher it. To verify that Alice sent the message, the judge takes the disputed messages $\{\ m\ \}k_{Alice}$ and $\{\ m\ \}k_{Bob}$ and has Cathy decipher them using Alice's and Bob's keys. If they match, the sending is verified; if not, one of them is a forgery.

9.5.2   Public Key Signatures

In our earlier example, we had Alice encipher the message with her private key to produce a digital signature. We now examine a specific digital signature scheme based on the RSA system (see Section 8.3.1).

We observe that using RSA to authenticate a message produces a digital signature. However, we also observe that the strength of the system relies on the protocol describing how RSA is used as well as on the RSA cryptosystem itself.

First, suppose that Alice wants to trick Bob into signing a message m. She computes two other messages m_1 and m_2 such that $m_1 m_2 \bmod n_{Bob} = m$. She has Bob sign m_1 and m_2. Alice then multiplies the two signatures together and reduces mod n_{Bob}, and she has Bob's signature on m. (See Exercise 6.) The defense is not to sign random documents and, when signing, never sign the document itself; sign a cryptographic hash of the document [796].

EXAMPLE: Let $n_{Alice} = 95$, $e_{Alice} = 59$, $d_{Alice} = 11$, $n_{Bob} = 77$, $e_{Bob} = 53$, and $d_{Bob} = 17$. Alice and Bob have 26 possible contracts, from which they are to select and sign one. Alice first asks Bob to sign contract F (05):

$$05^{17} \bmod 77 = 3$$

She then asks him to sign contract R (17):

$$17^{17} \bmod 77 = 19$$

Alice now computes $05 \times 17 \bmod 77 = 08$. She then claims that Bob agreed to contract I (08), and as evidence presents the signature $3 \times 19 \bmod 77 = 57$. Judge Janice is called, and she computes

$$57^{53} \bmod 77 = 08$$

Naturally, she concludes that Bob is lying, because his public key deciphers the signature. So Alice has successfully tricked Bob.

A second problem [31] demonstrates that messages that are both enciphered and signed should be signed first, then enciphered. Suppose Alice is sending Bob her signature on a confidential contract m. She enciphers it first, then signs it:

$$c = \left(m^{e_{Bob}} \bmod n_{Bob} \right)^{d_{Alice}} \bmod n_{Alice}$$

and sends the result to Bob. However, Bob wants to claim that Alice sent him the contract M. Bob computes a number r such that $M^r \bmod n_{Bob} = m$. He then republishes his public key as (re_{Bob}, n_{Bob}). Note that the modulus does not change. Now, he claims that Alice sent him M. The judge verifies this using his current public key. The simplest way to fix this is to require all users to use the same exponent but vary the moduli.

EXAMPLE: Smarting from Alice's trick, Bob seeks revenge. He and Alice agree to sign the contract G (06). Alice first enciphers it, then signs it:

$$(06^{53} \bmod 77)^{11} \bmod 95 = 63$$

and sends it to Bob. Bob, however, wants the contract to be N (13). He computes an r such that $13^r \bmod 77 = 6$; one such r is $r = 59$. He then computes a new public key $re_{Bob} \bmod \phi(n_{Bob}) = 59 \times 53 \bmod 60 = 7$. He replaces his current public key with $(7, 77)$, and resets his private key to 43. He now claims that Alice sent him contract N, signed by her.

Judge Janice is called. She takes the message 63 and deciphers it:

$$(63^{59} \bmod 95)^{43} \bmod 77 = 13$$

and concludes that Bob is correct.

This attack will not work if one signs first and then enciphers. The reason is that Bob cannot access the information needed to construct a new public key, because he would need to alter Alice's public key. (See Exercise 7.)

9.6   Summary

Cryptographic infrastructure provides the mechanisms needed to use cryptography. The infrastructure sees to the distribution of keys and the security of the procedures and mechanisms implementing cryptographic algorithms and protocols.

Key exchange and authentication protocols, although distinct in principle, are often combined because the first step in most communications is to prove identity. Exchanging a session key in the process saves another exchange. Both public key and classical cryptosystems can provide authentication and key exchange, provided that the appropriate infrastructure is present.

A key element of such an infrastructure is a mechanism for binding cryptographic keys to identity. This mechanism leads to the distinction between session keys (generated once per session, and associated with that session) and interchange keys (generated once per principal, and associated with that principal). It also leads to certification, in which a representation of identity, along with other information such as expiration time, is cryptographically signed and distributed as a unit. The name of the signer (issuer) is included so that the certificate can be verified.

The mechanism used to sign certificates and other documents is a digital signature. A disinterested third party, called a judge, must be able to confirm or disprove that the (alleged) sender computed the digital signature of the (alleged) signed message.

Session keys require pseudorandom number generation. Of the many algorithms in use, the best are mixing algorithms in which every bit of the output depends on every bit of the input, and no bit can be predicted even if all previous bits are known.

The management of keys involves storing them and revoking them, both of which involve system issues as well as cryptographic ones. Another aspect is the idea of key recovery.

9.7   Further Reading

Ellison explores methods of binding an identity to a public key without using certificates [297].

The Internet Security Association and Key Management Protocol [599] deals with key exchange and authentication on the Internet. Several key exchange protocols are based on classical cryptosystems [146, 686]. Protocols based on public key methods abound (see, for example, [682, 705, 895, 951]).

Key generation is based on random numbers generated from physical phenomena [12, 234, 289, 307, 539, 740]. Generating keys pseudorandomly is tricky [711]; the most common method, using polynomial congruential generators, is not safe [128, 129, 532, 746]. Rabin [738] and Adleman, Pomerance, and Rumley [10] discuss generating large prime numbers for use in RSA; their method relies upon pseudorandom number generation.

Several papers discuss issues in public key infrastructure, including interoperation [451, 452, 761], organization [558, 579], requirements [37, 762], and models [207, 714]. Park and Sandhu [710] have proposed extensions for X.509v3 certificates. Adams and Lloyd [7] discuss many aspects of public key infrastructures.

Merkle [621] notes that certificates can be kept as data in a file. Changing any certificate changes the file. This reduces the problem of substituting faked certificates to a data integrity problem.

Key escrowing allows the recovery of data if the cryptographic key is not accessible. The best known such system is the U.S. government's Escrowed Encryption Standard (EES) [116, 251, 665, 667, 678] Beth, Knobloch, Otten, Simmons, and Wichmann [86] identify five desirable properties of such a system; Ganesan [346] developed Yaksha, which meets all of these. Denning and Branstad [246] discuss the architecture of key escrow systems.

Several key escrow schemes explore different ways to control access. Burmester et al. [145] present a protocol with a limited time span. Several authors discuss the nontechnical aspects of the proposed U.S. key escrow system (for example, see [628, 794, 866]). Clark [176] and Walker et al. [929] discuss the relationship between key recovery and key escrow. Others have proposed enhancements and extensions of various Internet protocols for key recovery [53, 593, 798].

Translucent cryptography [66, 67] allows some fraction of the messages to be read. This is not a key escrow system, because the keys are not available, but it does serve the ends of such a system in that the messages can be read with a specified probability.

Digital signature protocols abound. One standard, the DSS [666], uses a variant of El Gamal [294]; Rivest and others have criticized some of its features [755]. Others, especially those associated with the ITU's X.500 series of recommendations, recommend (but do not require) RSA. Grant's book [372] discusses digital signatures in general and presents many case studies.

The electronic commerce protocol SET [812, 813, 814] uses dual digital signatures to tie components of messages together in such a way that neither the messages nor their association can be repudiated. Ford and Baum [330] discuss SET and the supporting infrastructure. Ghosh [353] provides a balanced view of the dangers of Internet commerce using the Web.

9.8   Exercises

1. Reconsider the case of Alice and her stockbroker, Bob. Suppose they decide not to use a session key. Instead, Alice pads the message (BUY or SELL) with random data. Explain under what conditions this approach would be effective. Discuss how the length of the block affects your answer.

2. Modify Kohnfelder's scheme (see page 131) to allow a principal to issue its own certificate. Identify one or more problems other principals might have in relying on such a certificate. In particular, under what conditions would this solve the problem of an imposter spoofing the sender?

3. An X.509 certificate revocation list contains a field specifying when the next such list is expected to be issued. Why is that field present?

4. Consider the following authentication protocol, which uses a classical cryptosystem. Alice generates a random message r, enciphers it with the key k she shares with Bob, and sends the enciphered message $\{r\}k$ to Bob. Bob deciphers it, adds 1 to r, and sends $\{r + 1\}k$ back to Alice. Alice deciphers the message and compares it with r. If the difference is 1, she knows that her correspondent shares the same key k and is therefore Bob. If not, she assumes that her correspondent does not share the key k and so is not Bob. Does this protocol authenticate Bob to Alice? Why or why not?

5. Needham and Schroeder suggest the following variant of their protocol:

   1. Alice → Bob : Alice

2. Bob →Alice : { Alice, $rand_3$ } k_{Bob}
3. Alice → Cathy : { Alice, Bob, $rand_1$, { Alice, $rand_3$ } k_{Bob} }
4. Cathy → Alice : { Alice, Bob, $rand_1$, $k_{session}$, {Alice, $rand_3$, $k_{session}$} k_{Bob} } k_{Alice}
5. Alice → Bob : { Alice, $rand_3$, $k_{session}$ } k_{Bob}
6. Bob → Alice : { $rand_2$ } $k_{session}$
7. Alice → Bob : { $rand_2 - 1$ }$k_{session}$

Show that this protocol solves the problem of replay as a result of stolen session keys.

6. Consider an RSA digital signature scheme (see Section 9.5.2). Alice tricks Bob into signing messages m_1 and m_2 such that $m = m_1 m_2 \bmod n_{Bob}$. Prove that Alice can forge Bob's signature on m.

7. Return to the example on page 140. Bob and Alice agree to sign the contract G (06). This time, Alice signs the message first and then enciphers the result. Show that the attack Bob used when Alice enciphered the message and then signed it will now fail.

Chapter 10
Cipher Techniques

> IAGO: So will I turn her virtue into pitch,
> And out of her own goodness make the net
> That shall enmesh them all.
> —*The Tragedy of Othello*, II, iii, 361–363.

Cryptographic systems are sensitive to environment. Using cryptosystems over a network introduces many problems. This chapter presents examples of these problems and discusses techniques for dealing with them. First comes a description of stream and block ciphers, followed by a review of the organization of the network layers. We then present several network protocols to show how these techniques are used in practice.

The key point of this chapter is that the strength of a cryptosystem depends in part on how it is used. A mathematically strong cryptosystem is vulnerable when used incorrectly.

10.1   Problems

The use of a cipher without consideration of the environment in which it is to be used may not provide the security that the user expects. Three examples will make this point clear.

10.1.1   Precomputing the Possible Messages

Simmons discusses the use of a "forward search" to decipher messages enciphered for confidentiality using a public key cryptosystem [830]. His approach is to focus on the entropy (uncertainty) in the message. To use an example from Section 9.1 (page 124), Cathy knows that Alice will send one of two messages—BUY or SELL—to Bob. The uncertainty is which one Alice will send. So Cathy enciphers both messages with Bob's public key. When Alice sends the message, Cathy intercepts it and compares the ciphertext with the two he computed. From this, she knows which message Alice sent.

Simmons' point is that if the plaintext corresponding to intercepted ciphertext is drawn from a (relatively) small set of possible plaintexts, the cryptanalyst can encipher the set of possible plaintexts and simply search that set for the intercepted ciphertext. Simmons demonstrates that the size of the set of possible plaintexts may not be obvious. As an example, he uses digitized sound. The initial calculations suggest that the number of possible plaintexts for each block is 2^{32}. Using forward search on such a set is clearly impractical, but after some analysis of the redundancy in human speech, Simmons reduces the number of potential plaintexts to about 100,000. This number is small enough so that forward searches become a threat.

This attack is similar to attacks to derive the cryptographic key of symmetric ciphers based on chosen plaintext (see, for example, Hellman's time-memory tradeoff attack [416]). However, Simmons' attack is for public key cryptosystems and does not reveal the private key. It only reveals the plaintext message.

10.1.2 Misordered Blocks

Denning [242] points out that in certain cases, parts of a ciphertext message can be deleted, replayed, or reordered.

EXAMPLE: Consider RSA. As in the example on page 114, take $p = 7$ and $q = 11$. Then $n = 77$ and $\phi(n) = 60$. Bob chooses $e = 17$, so his private key $d = 53$. In this cryptosystem, each plaintext character is represented by a number from 00 (A) to 25 (Z), and 26 represents a blank.

Alice wants to send Bob the message LIVE (11 08 21 04). She enciphers this message using his public key, obtaining 44 57 21 16, and sends the message. Cathy intercepts it and rearranges the ciphertext: 16 21 57 44. When Bob receives it, he deciphers the message and obtains EVIL.

Even if Alice digitally signed each part, Bob could not detect this attack. The problem is that the parts are not bound to one another. Because each part is independent, there is no way to tell when one part is replaced or added, or when parts are rearranged.

One solution is to generate a cryptographic checksum of the entire message (see Section 8.4) and sign that value.

10.1.3 Statistical Regularities

The independence of parts of ciphertext can give information relating to the structure of the enciphered message, even if the message itself is unintelligible. The regularity arises because each part is enciphered separately, so the same plaintext always produces the same ciphertext. This type of encipherment is called *code book mode*, because each part is effectively looked up in a list of plaintext-ciphertext pairs.

10.1.4   Summary

Despite the use of sophisticated cryptosystems and random keys, cipher systems may provide inadequate security if not used carefully. The protocols directing how these cipher systems are used, and the ancillary information that the protocols add to messages and sessions, overcome these problems. This emphasizes that ciphers and codes are not enough. The methods, or protocols, for their use also affect the security of systems.

10.2   Stream and Block Ciphers

Some ciphers divide a message into a sequence of parts, or blocks, and encipher each block with the same key.

Definition 10–1. Let E be an encipherment algorithm, and let $E_k(b)$ be the encipherment of message b with key k. Let a message $m = b_1b_2 \dots$, where each b_i is of a fixed length. Then a *block cipher* is a cipher for which $E_k(m) = E_k(b_1)E_k(b_2) \dots$.

EXAMPLE: The DES is a block cipher. It breaks the message into 64-bit blocks and uses the same 56-bit key to encipher each block.

Other ciphers use a nonrepeating stream of key elements to encipher characters of a message.

Definition 10–2. Let E be an encipherment algorithm, and let $E_k(b)$ be the encipherment of message b with key k. Let a message $m = b_1b_2 \dots$, where each b_i is of a fixed length, and let $k = k_1k_2\dots$. Then a *stream cipher* is a cipher for which $E_k(m) = E_{k1}(b_1)E_{k2}(b_2) \dots$.

If the key stream k of a stream cipher repeats itself, it is a *periodic* cipher.

EXAMPLE: The Vigenère cipher (see Section 8.2.2.1) is a stream cipher. Take b_i to be a character of the message and k_i to be a character of the key. This cipher is periodic, because the key is of finite length, and should the key be shorter than the message, the key is repeated.

The one-time pad is also a stream cipher but is not periodic, because the key stream never repeats.

10.2.1   Stream Ciphers

The one-time pad is a cipher that can be proven secure (see Section 8.2.2.2, "One-Time Pad"). Bit-oriented ciphers implement the one-time pad by exclusive-oring each bit of the key with one bit of the message. For example, if the message is 00101 and the key is 10010, the ciphertext is $0 \oplus 1 \| 0 \oplus 0 \| 1 \oplus 0 \| 0 \oplus 1 \| 1 \oplus 0$ or 10111. But how can one generate a random, infinitely long key?

10.2.1.1   Synchronous Stream Ciphers

To simulate a random, infinitely long key, synchronous stream ciphers generate bits from a source other than the message itself. The simplest such cipher extracts bits from a register to use as the key. The contents of the register change on the basis of the current contents of the register.

> **Definition 10–3.** An *n-stage linear feedback shift register (LFSR)* consists of an *n*-bit register $r = r_0 \ldots r_{n-1}$ and an *n*-bit *tap sequence* $t = t_0 \ldots t_{n-1}$. To obtain a key bit, r_{n-1} is used, the register is shifted one bit to the right, and the new bit $r_0 t_0 \oplus \ldots \oplus r_{n-1} t_{n-1}$ is inserted.

EXAMPLE: Let the tap sequence for a four-stage LFSR be 1001, and let the initial value of the register be 0010. The key bits extracted, and the values in the register, are

Current register	Key	New bit	New register
0010	0	$01 \oplus 00 \oplus 10 \oplus 01 = 0 \oplus 0 \oplus 0 \oplus 0 = 0$	0001
0001	1	$01 \oplus 00 \oplus 00 \oplus 11 = 0 \oplus 0 \oplus 0 \oplus 1 = 1$	1000
1000	0	$11 \oplus 00 \oplus 00 \oplus 01 = 1 \oplus 0 \oplus 0 \oplus 0 = 1$	1100
1100	0	$11 \oplus 10 \oplus 00 \oplus 01 = 1 \oplus 0 \oplus 0 \oplus 0 = 1$	1110
1110	0	$11 \oplus 10 \oplus 10 \oplus 01 = 1 \oplus 0 \oplus 0 \oplus 0 = 1$	1111
1111	1	$11 \oplus 10 \oplus 10 \oplus 11 = 1 \oplus 0 \oplus 0 \oplus 1 = 0$	0111
0111	1	$01 \oplus 10 \oplus 10 \oplus 11 = 0 \oplus 0 \oplus 0 \oplus 1 = 1$	1011
1011	1	$11 \oplus 00 \oplus 10 \oplus 11 = 1 \oplus 0 \oplus 0 \oplus 1 = 0$	0101
0101	1	$01 \oplus 10 \oplus 00 \oplus 11 = 0 \oplus 0 \oplus 0 \oplus 1 = 1$	1010
1010	0	$11 \oplus 00 \oplus 10 \oplus 01 = 1 \oplus 0 \oplus 0 \oplus 0 = 1$	1101
1101	1	$11 \oplus 10 \oplus 00 \oplus 11 = 1 \oplus 0 \oplus 0 \oplus 1 = 0$	0110
0110	0	$01 \oplus 10 \oplus 10 \oplus 01 = 0 \oplus 0 \oplus 0 \oplus 0 = 0$	0011
0011	1	$01 \oplus 00 \oplus 10 \oplus 11 = 0 \oplus 0 \oplus 0 \oplus 1 = 1$	1001
1001	1	$11 \oplus 00 \oplus 00 \oplus 11 = 1 \oplus 0 \oplus 0 \oplus 1 = 0$	0100
0100	0	$01 \oplus 10 \oplus 00 \oplus 01 = 0 \oplus 0 \oplus 0 \oplus 0 = 0$	0010
0010	0	$01 \oplus 00 \oplus 10 \oplus 01 = 0 \oplus 0 \oplus 0 \oplus 0 = 0$	0001

and the cycle repeats. The key stream that this LFSR produces has a period of 15 and is 010001111010110.

The LFSR method is an attempt to simulate a one-time pad by generating a long key sequence from a little information. As with any such attempt, if the key is shorter than the message, breaking part of the ciphertext gives the cryptanalyst information about other parts of the ciphertext. For an LFSR, a known plaintext attack can reveal parts of the key sequence. If the known plaintext is of length $2n$, the tap sequence for an n-stage LFSR can be determined completely.

Nonlinear feedback shift registers do not use tap sequences; instead, the new bit is any function of the current register bits.

Definition 10–4. An *n-stage nonlinear feedback shift register (NLFSR)* consists of an n-bit register $r = r_0...r_{n-1}$. To obtain a key bit, r_{n-1} is used, the register is shifted one bit to the right, and the new bit is set to $f(r_0...r_{n-1})$, where f is any function of n inputs.

EXAMPLE: Let the function f for a four-stage NLFSR be $f(r_0...r_{n-1}) = (r_0$ and $r_2)$ or r_3, and let the initial value of the register be 1100. The key bits extracted, and the values in the register, are

Current register	Key	New bit	New register
1100	0	$f(1, 1, 0, 0) = (1$ and $0)$ or $0 = 0$	0110
0110	0	$f(0, 1, 1, 0) = (0$ and $1)$ or $0 = 0$	0011
0011	1	$f(0, 0, 1, 1) = (0$ and $1)$ or $1 = 1$	1001
1001	1	$f(1, 0, 0, 1) = (1$ and $0)$ or $1 = 1$	1100
1100	0	$f(1, 1, 0, 0) = (1$ and $0)$ or $0 = 0$	0110
0110	0	$f(0, 1, 1, 0) = (0$ and $1)$ or $0 = 0$	0011
0011	1	$f(0, 0, 1, 1) = (0$ and $1)$ or $1 = 1$	1001
1001	1	$f(1, 0, 0, 1) = (1$ and $0)$ or $1 = 1$	1100
1100	0	$f(1, 1, 0, 0) = (1$ and $0)$ or $0 = 0$	0110
0110	0	$f(0, 1, 1, 0) = (0$ and $1)$ or $0 = 0$	0011

and the cycle repeats. The key stream that this NLFSR produces has a period of 4 and is 0011.

NLFSRs are not common because there is no body of theory about how to build NLFSRs with long periods. By contrast, it is known how to design n-stage LFSRs with a period of $2^n - 1$, and that period is maximal.

A second technique for eliminating linearity is called *output feedback mode*. Let E be an encipherment function. Define k as a cryptographic key, and define r as a register. To obtain a bit for the key, compute $E_k(r)$ and put that value into the register. The rightmost bit of the result is exclusive-or'ed with one bit of the message. The process is repeated until the message is enciphered. The key k and the initial value in r are the keys for this method. This method differs from the NLFSR in that the register is never shifted. It is repeatedly enciphered.

A variant of output feedback mode is called the *counter method*. Instead of using a register r, simply use a counter that is incremented for every encipherment. The initial value of the counter replaces r as part of the key. This method enables one to generate the ith bit of the key without generating the bits $0...i-1$. If the initial counter value is i_0, set the register to $i + i_0$. In output feedback mode, one must generate all the preceding key bits.

10.2.1.2 Self-Synchronous Stream Ciphers

Self-synchronous ciphers obtain the key from the message itself. The simplest self-synchronous cipher is called an *autokey* cipher and uses the message itself for the key.

EXAMPLE: The following is an autokey version of the Vigenère cipher, with the key drawn from the plaintext.

key	XTHEBOYHASTHEBA
plaintext	THEBOYHASTHEBAG
ciphertext	QALFPNFHSLALFCT

Contrast this with the example on page 103. The key there is VIG, and the resulting ciphertext contains two three-character repetitions.

The problem with this cipher is the selection of the key. Unlike a one-time pad, any statistical regularities in the plaintext show up in the key. For example, the last two letters of the ciphertext associated with the plaintext word THE are always AL, because H is enciphered with the key letter T and E is enciphered with the key letter H. Furthermore, if the analyst can guess any letter of the plaintext, she can determine all successive plaintext letters.

An alternative is to use the ciphertext as the key stream. A good cipher will produce pseudorandom ciphertext, which approximates a random one-time pad better than a message with nonrandom characteristics (such as a meaningful English sentence).

EXAMPLE: The following is an autokey version of the Vigenère cipher, with the key drawn from the ciphertext.

key	XQXBCQOVVNGNRTT
plaintext	THEBOYHASTHECAT
ciphertext	QXBCQOVVNGNRTTM

This eliminates the repetition (ALF) in the preceding example.

This type of autokey cipher is weak, because plaintext can be deduced from the ciphertext. For example, consider the first two characters of the ciphertext, QX. The X is the ciphertext resulting from enciphering some letter with the key Q. Deciphering, the unknown letter is H. Continuing in this fashion, the analyst can reconstruct all of the plaintext except for the first letter.

A variant of the autokey method, *cipher feedback mode*, uses a shift register. Let E be an encipherment function. Define k as a cryptographic key and r as a register. To obtain a bit for the key, compute $E_k(r)$. The rightmost bit of the result is exclusive-or'ed with one bit of the message, and the other bits of the result are discarded. The resulting ciphertext is fed back into the leftmost bit of the register, which is right shifted one bit. (See Figure 10–1.)

Cipher feedback mode has a *self-healing property*. If a bit is corrupted in transmission of the ciphertext, the next n bits will be deciphered incorrectly. But after n uncorrupted bits have been received, the shift register will be reinitialized to the value used for encipherment and the ciphertext will decipher properly from that point on.

As in the counter method, one can decipher parts of messages enciphered in cipher feedback mode without deciphering the entire message. Let the shift register contain n bits. The analyst obtains the previous n bits of ciphertext. This is the value in the shift register before the bit under consideration was enciphered. The decipherment can then continue from that bit on.

10.2.2   Block Ciphers

Block ciphers encipher and decipher multiple bits at once, rather than one bit at a time. For this reason, software implementations of block ciphers run faster than software implementations of stream ciphers. Errors in transmitting one block generally do not affect other blocks, but as each block is enciphered independently, using the same key, identical plaintext blocks produce identical ciphertext blocks. This allows the analyst to search for data by determining what the encipherment of a specific

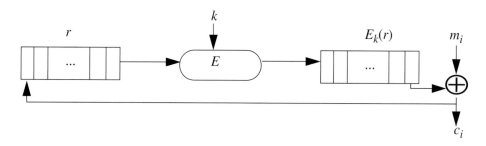

Figure 10–1   Diagram of cipher feedback mode. The register *r* is enciphered with key *k* and algorithm *E*. The rightmost bit of the result is exclusive-or'ed with one bit of the plaintext m_i to produce the ciphertext bit c_i. The register *r* is right shifted one bit, and c_i is fed back into the leftmost bit of *r*.

plaintext block is. For example, if the word INCOME is enciphered as one block, all occurrences of the word produce the same ciphertext.

EXAMPLE: Consider a banking database with two records:

```
MEMBER: HOLLY INCOME $100,000
MEMBER: HEIDI INCOME $100,000
```

Suppose the encipherment of this data under a block cipher is

```
ABCQZRME GHQMRSIB CTXUVYSS RMGRPFQN
ABCQZRME ORMPABRZ CTXUVYSS RMGRPFQN
```

If an attacker determines who these records refer to, and that CTXUVYSS is the encipherment of the INCOME keyword, he will know that Holly and Heidi have the same income.

To prevent this type of attack, some information related to the block's position is inserted into the plaintext block before it is enciphered. The information can be bits from the preceding ciphertext block [311] or a sequence number [502]. The disadvantage is that the effective block size is reduced, because fewer message bits are present in a block.

Cipher block chaining does not require the extra information to occupy bit spaces, so every bit in the block is part of the message. Before a plaintext block is enciphered, that block is exclusive-or'ed with the preceding ciphertext block. In addition to the key, this technique requires an *initialization vector* with which to exclusive-or the initial plaintext block. Taking E_k to be the encipherment algorithm with key k, and I to be the initialization vector, the cipher block chaining technique is

$$c_0 = E_k(m_0 \oplus I)$$
$$c_i = E_k(m_i \oplus c_{i-1}) \text{ for } i > 0$$

10.2.2.1   Multiple Encryption

Other approaches involve multiple encryption. Using two keys k and k' to encipher a message as $c = E_{k'}(E_k(m))$ looks attractive because it has an effective key length of $2n$, whereas the keys to E are of length n. However, Merkle and Hellman [624] have shown that this encryption technique can be broken using 2^{n+1} encryptions, rather than the expected 2^{2n} (see Exercise 3).

Using three encipherments improves the strength of the cipher. There are several ways to do this. Tuchman [908] suggested using two keys k and k':

$$c = E_k(D_{k'}(E_k(m)))$$

This mode, called *Encrypt-Decrypt-Encrypt* (EDE) mode, collapses to a single encipherment when $k = k'$. The DES in EDE mode is widely used in the financial community and is a standard (ANSI X9.17 and ISO 8732). It is not vulnerable to the attack outlined earlier. However, it is vulnerable to a chosen plaintext and a known plaintext attack. If b is the block size in bits, and n is the key length, the chosen plaintext attack takes $O(2^n)$ time, $O(2^n)$ space, and requires 2^n chosen plaintexts. The known plaintext attack requires p known plaintexts, and takes $O(2^{n+b}/p)$ time and $O(p)$ memory.

A second version of triple encipherment is the *triple encryption* mode [624]. In this mode, three keys are used in a chain of encipherments.

$$c = E_k(E_{k'}(E_{k''}(m)))$$

The best attack against this scheme is similar to the attack on double encipherment, but requires $O(2^{2n})$ time and $O(2^n)$ memory. If the key length is 56 bits, this attack is computationally infeasible.

10.3   Networks and Cryptography

Before we discuss Internet protocols, a review of the relevant properties of networks is in order. The ISO/OSI model [894] provides an abstract representation of networks suitable for our purposes. Recall that the ISO/OSI model is composed of a series of layers (see Figure 10–2). Each host, conceptually, has a principal at each layer that communicates with a peer on other hosts. These principals communicate with principals at the same layer on other hosts. Layer 1, 2, and 3 principals interact only with similar principals at neighboring (directly connected) hosts. Principals at layers 4, 5, 6, and 7 interact only with similar principals at the other end of the communication. (For convenience, "host" refers to the appropriate principal in the following discussion.)

Each host in the network is connected to some set of other hosts. They exchange messages with those hosts. If host *nob* wants to send a message to host *windsor*, *nob* determines which of its immediate neighbors is closest to *windsor* (using an appropriate routing protocol) and forwards the message to it. That host, *baton*, determines which of its neighbors is closest to *windsor* and forwards the message to it. This process continues until a host, *sunapee*, receives the message and determines that *windsor* is an immediate neighbor. The message is forwarded to *windsor*, its endpoint.

> **Definition 10–5.** Let hosts C_0, …, C_n be such that C_i and C_{i+1} are directly connected, for $0 \le i < n$. A communications protocol that has C_0 and C_n as its endpoints is called an *end-to-end protocol*. A communications protocol that has C_j and C_{j+1} as its endpoints is called a *link protocol*.

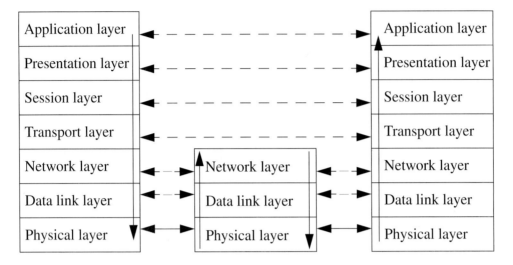

Figure 10–2   The ISO/OSI model. The dashed arrows indicate peer-to-peer communication. For example, the transport layers are communicating with each other. The solid arrows indicate the actual flow of bits. For example, the transport layer invokes network layer routines on the local host, which invoke data link layer routines, which put the bits onto the network. The physical layer passes the bits to the next "hop," or host, on the path. When the message reaches the destination, it is passed up to the appropriate level.

The difference between an end-to-end protocol and a link protocol is that the intermediate hosts play no part in an end-to-end protocol other than forwarding messages. On the other hand, a link protocol describes how each pair of intermediate hosts processes each message.

EXAMPLE: The *telnet* protocol is an applications layer protocol that allows users to obtain a virtual terminal on a remote host. Thus, it is an end-to-end protocol. IP is a network layer protocol that guides messages from a host to one of its immediate neighbors. Thus, it is a link protocol.

The protocols involved can be cryptographic protocols. If the cryptographic processing is done only at the source and at the destination, the protocol is an end-to-end protocol. If cryptographic processing occurs at each host along the path from source to destination, the protocol is a link protocol. When encryption is used with either protocol, we use the terms *end-to-end encryption* and *link encryption*, respectively.

EXAMPLE: If the messages between the *telnet* client and server are enciphered [915], the encipherment and decipherment occur at the client and the server only. The protocol uses end-to-end encryption. The PPP Encryption Control Protocol [627] enciphers messages between intermediate hosts. When a host gets the message, it deciphers the message, determines which neighbor to send it to, reenciphers the message using the key appropriate for that neighbor, and sends it to that neighbor. This protocol uses link encryption.

In link encryption, each host shares a cryptographic key with its neighbor. (If public key cryptography is used, each host has its neighbor's public key. Link encryption based on public keys is rare.) The keys may be set on a per-host basis or a per-host-pair basis. Consider a network with four hosts called *windsor*, *stripe*, *facer*, and *seaview*. Each host is directly connected to the other three. With keys distributed on a per-host basis, each host has its own key, making four keys in all. Each host has the keys for the other three neighbors, as well as its own. All hosts use the same key to communicate with *windsor*. With keys distributed on a per-host-pair basis, each host has one key per possible connection, making six keys in all. Unlike the per-host situation, in the per-host-pair case, each host uses a different key to communicate with *windsor*. The message is deciphered at each intermediate host, reenciphered for the next hop, and forwarded. Attackers monitoring the network medium will not be able to read the messages, but attackers at the intermediate hosts will be able to do so.

In end-to-end encryption, each host shares a cryptographic key with each destination. (Again, if the encryption is based on public key cryptography, each host has—or can obtain—the public key of each destination.) As with link encryption, the keys may be selected on a per-host or per-host-pair basis. The sending host enciphers the message and forwards it to the first intermediate host. The intermediate host forwards it to the next host, and the process continues until the message reaches its destination. The destination host then deciphers it. The message is enciphered throughout its journey. Neither attackers monitoring the network nor attackers on the intermediate hosts can read the message. However, attackers can read the routing information used to forward the message.

These differences affect a form of cryptanalysis known as *traffic analysis*. A cryptanalyst can sometimes deduce information not from the content of the message but from the sender and recipient. For example, during the Allied invasion of Normandy in World War II, the Germans deduced which vessels were the command ships by observing which ships were sending and receiving the most signals. The content of the signals was not relevant; their source and destination were. Similar deductions can reveal information in the electronic world.

EXAMPLE: ARS&C is an engineering firm developing the next generation of network protocols. Each employee of ARS&C has his or her own workstation. All network traffic is enciphered using end-to-end encryption. A competitor of the company appears to be obtaining proprietary data. ARS&C has hired Alice to figure out who is leaking the information.

Alice begins by monitoring all network traffic. She notices that the workstations are grouped into three different divisions: corporate management, sales, and engineering. The leaks are coming from the engineering systems. She looks at the sources and destinations of all connections to and from the engineering systems and notices that the connections from corporate management center on three systems: *curly*, *larry*, and *moe*. The connections from *larry* always occur between midnight and four in the morning; those from the other two occur during the day. Alice then looks at the events of the days on which the connections take place. The connections from *curly* and *moe* occur on the days of management reviews and are invariably to the *ftp* or *www* port. The connections from *larry* are more infrequent and are to the *telnet* port. A few days after each connection, the competitor seems to have acquired new proprietary information.

From this analysis, Alice suggests that the host *larry* is somehow involved in the problem. She needs to check the systems that *larry* connects to and see if the proprietary data is on those systems. At no time has Alice read any of the traffic, because it is encrypted; but from the traffic analysis, she has determined the system involved in the compromise.

10.4   Example Protocols

Several widely used Internet protocols illustrate different facets of cryptographic techniques. This section examines three such protocols, each at a different layer. PEM is a privacy-enhanced electronic mail protocol at the applications layer and demonstrates the considerations needed when designing such a protocol. Its techniques are similar to those of PGP, another widely used security-enhanced electronic mail protocol. SSL provides transport layer security. Application layer protocols such as HTTP can use SSL to ensure secure connections. IPsec provides security mechanisms at the network, or IP, layer.

10.4.1   Secure Electronic Mail: PEM

Electronic mail is a widely used mechanism for communication over the Internet. It is also a good example of how practical considerations affect the design of security-related protocols. We begin by describing the state of electronic mail and then show how security services can be added.

Figure 10–3 shows a typical network mail service. The UA (*user agent*) interacts directly with the sender. When the message is composed, the UA hands it to the MTA (*message transport, or transfer, agent*). The MTA transfers the message to its destination host, or to another MTA, which in turn transfers the message further. At the destination host, the MTA invokes a user agent to deliver the message.

An attacker can read electronic mail at any of the computers on which MTAs handling the message reside, as well as on the network itself. An attacker could also modify the message without the recipient detecting the change. Because authentication mechanisms are minimal and easily evaded, a sender could forge a letter from another and inject it into the message handling system at any MTA, from which it

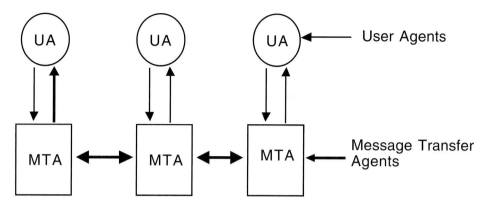

Figure 10–3   Message handling system. The user composes mail on the UA (user agent). When she sends it, the message is passed to the MTA (message transport, or transfer, agent). The MTA passes the message to other MTAs, until it reaches the MTA associated with the destination host. That host transfers it to the appropriate UA for delivery.

would be forwarded to the destination. Finally, a sender could deny having sent a letter, and the recipient could not prove otherwise to a disinterested party. These four types of attacks (violation of confidentiality, authentication, message integrity, and nonrepudiation) make electronic mail nonsecure.

In 1985, the Internet Research Task Force on Privacy (also called the Privacy Research Group) began studying the problem of enhancing the privacy of electronic mail. The goal of this study was to develop electronic mail protocols that would provide the following services.

1. Confidentiality, by making the message unreadable except to the sender and recipient(s)
2. Origin authentication, by identifying the sender precisely
3. Data integrity, by ensuring that any changes in the message are easy to detect
4. Nonrepudiation of origin (if possible)

The protocols were christened Privacy-enhanced Electronic Mail (or PEM).

10.4.1.1   Design Principles

Creating a viable protocol requires the developers to consider several design aspects. Otherwise, acceptance and use of the protocol will be very limited.

Related protocols should not be changed. A protocol is designed to provide specific services (in this case, the privacy enhancements discussed in the preceding section). It should not require alteration of other protocols (such as those that transmit electronic mail). The Privacy Research Group developed new protocols rather than modifying the mail transfer protocols. This also requires development of new software rather than modification of existing software to implement the protocol (although existing software can be modified to support it).

A corollary is compatibility. A general protocol (such as PEM) must be compatible with as many other protocols and programs as possible. The protocols must work with a wide range of software, including software in all environments that connect to the Internet.

Another important principle is independence. The privacy enhancements should be available if desired but should not be mandatory. If a new protocol provides specific services, the user should be able to use the services desired, which may (or may not) be all the ones that the protocol provides. For example, a sender might care about sender authentication but not confidentiality. This also enables some users to send privacy-enhanced electronic mail, and others to send unprotected electronic mail, on the same system. Recipients can also read either type of mail.

Finally, two parties should be able to use the protocol to communicate without prearrangement. Arranging a communications key out of band (such as in person or over the telephone) can be time-consuming and prone to error. Furthermore, callers must authenticate themselves to the recipients. This is difficult and is another error-prone operation.

To summarize, the design goals of PEM were as follows.

1. Not to redesign existing mail system or protocols
2. To be compatible with a range of MTAs, UAs, and other computers
3. To make privacy enhancements available separately, so they are not required
4. To enable two parties to use the protocol to communicate without prearrangement

10.4.1.2   Basic Design

PEM defines two types of keys. The message to be sent is enciphered with a *data encipherment key* (DEK), corresponding to a session key. This key is generated randomly and is used only once. It must be sent to the recipient, so it is enciphered with an *interchange key*. The interchange keys of the sender and recipient must be obtained in some way other than through the message.

This requires several assumptions. First, the interchange key must be available to the respective parties. If symmetric ciphers are used, the keys must be exchanged out of bands—for example, by telephone or courier. If public keys are used, the sender needs to obtain the certificate of the recipient.

If Alice wants to send a confidential message to Bob, she obtains Bob's interchange key k_{Bob}. She generates a random DEK $k_{session}$ and enciphers the message m. She then enciphers the DEK using the interchange key. She sends both to Bob.

$$\text{Alice} \rightarrow \text{Bob:} \ \{ \ m \ \}k_{session}\{ \ k_{session} \ \}k_{Bob}$$

Bob can then decipher the session key and from it obtain the message.

If Alice wants to send an authenticated, integrity-checked message to Bob, she first computes a cryptographic hash $h(m)$ of the message, possibly using a random session key (if the hash function requires one). The value that the hash function computes is called a *message integrity check* (MIC). She then enciphers the MIC (and the session key, if one was used) with her interchange key k_{Alice} and sends it to Bob:

Alice → Bob: $m \{ h(m) \}k_{Alice}$

Bob uses Alice's interchange key to decipher the MIC, recomputes it from m, and compares the two. If they do not match, either the message or the value of the hash has been changed. In either case, the message cannot be trusted.

To send an enciphered, authenticated, integrity-checked message, combine the operations discussed above, as follows.

Alice → Bob: $\{ m \}k_{session}\{ h(m) \}k_{Alice}\{ k_{session} \}k_{Bob}$

The nonrepudiation service comes from the use of public key cryptography. If Alice's interchange key is her private key, a third party can verify that she signed the message by deciphering it with her public key. Alice cannot refute that her private key was used to sign the message. (She can dispute that she signed it by claiming her private key was compromised. Preventing this is beyond the scope of technical protocols. In this context, "nonrepudiation" refers only to the inability to deny that the private key was used to sign the message.)

10.4.1.3   Other Considerations

When the interchange keys are for public key cryptosystems, PEM suggests the use of a certificate-based key management scheme (see Section 13.5, "Naming and Certificates"). However, it is not a requirement.

A major problem is the specification of Internet electronic mail. Among the restrictions placed on it, the requirements that the letter contain only ASCII characters and that the lines be of limited length are the most onerous. Related to this is the difference among character sets. A letter typed on an ASCII-based system will be unreadable on an EBCDIC-based system.

A three-step encoding procedure overcomes these problems.

1. The local representations of the characters making up the letter are changed into a canonical format. This format satisfies the requirements of RFC 822–compliant mailers (specifically, all characters are seven-bit ASCII characters, lines are less than 1,000 characters long, and lines end with a carriage return followed by a newline [221][1]).

---

[1] The dot stuffing convention (so that a line containing a single "." is not seen as a message terminator) is *not* used (see Section 4.3.2.2 of RFC 1421 [569]).

2. The message integrity check is computed and enciphered with the sender's interchange key. If confidentiality is required, the message is enciphered as described above.

3. The message is treated as a stream of bits. Every set of six bits is mapped into a character,[2] and after every 64 characters, a newline is inserted.

The resulting ASCII message has PEM headers (indicating algorithms and key) prepended. PEM headers and body are surrounded by lines indicating the start and end of the PEM message.

If the recipient has PEM-compliant software, she can read the message. Otherwise, she cannot. If the message is authenticated and integrity-checked (but not encrypted), she should be able to read the message even if she does not have PEM-compliant software (remember that one of the design components is compatibility with existing mail programs). The special mode MIC-CLEAR handles this case. In this mode, the message check is computed and added, but the message is not transformed into the representation of step 3. On receipt, the authentication and message integrity check may fail because some MTAs add blank lines, change the end-of-line character, or delete terminating white space from lines. Although this does not alter the *meaning* of the message, it does change the *content*. Hence, PEM-compliant software will report that the message has been altered in transit. But people can use normal mail reading programs to read the letter. (Whether they should trust it is another matter. Given that the PEM software has reported changes, the recipients should at least verify the contents in some way before trusting the letter.)

10.4.1.4   Conclusion

PEM demonstrates how system factors influence the use of cryptographic protocols. While central to the design and implementation of PEM systems, the cryptographic protocols require a supporting infrastructure. The need for compatibility guides many design choices for this infrastructure. The environment of development also affects the infrastructure.

Comparing PGP and PEM illustrates this. Both use the same cryptographic protocols, but by default, PGP uses the IDEA cipher instead of the DES. PGP also uses a different, nonhierarchical certificate management scheme described in Sections 9.3.1.2 and 13.5. Finally, PGP handles line termination characters differently. Messages are labeled *binary* or *text*. If binary, line terminators are untransformed. If text, they are canonicalized (if enciphering) or mapped into the end-of-line character sequence for the current host (if deciphering).

---

[2] The character set is drawn from parts of the international alphabet IA5 common to most other alphabets.

10.4.2   Security at the Network Layer: IPsec

IPsec is a collection of protocols and mechanisms that provide confidentiality, authentication, message integrity, and replay detection at the IP layer. Because cryptography forms the basis for these services, the protocols also include a key management scheme, which we will not discuss here.

Conceptually, think of messages being sent between two hosts as following a path between the hosts. The path also passes through other intermediate hosts. IPsec mechanisms protect all messages sent along a path. If the IPsec mechanisms reside on an intermediate host (for example, a firewall or gateway), that host is called a *security gateway*.

IPsec has two modes. *Transport mode* encapsulates the IP packet data area (which is the upper layer packet) in an IPsec envelope, and then uses IP to send the IPsec-wrapped packet. The IP header is not protected. *Tunnel mode* encapsulates an entire IP packet in an IPsec envelope and then forwards it using IP. Here, the IP header of the encapsulated packet is protected. (Figure 10–4 illustrates these modes.) Transport mode is used when both endpoints support IPsec. Tunnel mode is used when either or both endpoints do not support IPsec but two intermediate hosts do.

EXAMPLE: Secure Corp. and Guards Inc. wish to exchange confidential information about a pending fraud case. The hosts *main.secure.com* and *fraud.guards.com* both support IPsec. The messages between the systems are encapsulated using transport mode at the sender and processed into cleartext at the receiver.

Red Dog LLC is a third corporation that needs access to the data. The data is to be sent to *gotcha.reddog.com*. Red Dog's systems do not support IPsec, with one exception. That exception is the host, *firewall.reddog.com*, that is connected to both Red Dog's internal network and the Internet. Because none of Red Dog's other hosts is connected to the Internet, all traffic to *gotcha* from Secure Corp. must pass through *firewall.reddog.com*. So *main.secure.com* uses tunnel mode to send its IPsec packets to Red Dog. When the packets arrive at *firewall*, the IPsec information is removed and validated, and the enclosed IP packet is forwarded to *gotcha*. In this context, *firewall.reddog.com* is a security gateway.

Figure 10–4   The packet on the left is in transport mode, because the body of the packet is encrypted but its header is not. The packet on the right is in tunnel mode, because the packet header and the packet body are both encrypted. The unencrypted IP header is used to deliver the encrypted packet to a system on which it can be decrypted and forwarded.

Two protocols provide message security. The authentication header (AH) protocol provides message integrity and origin authentication and can provide antireplay services. The encapsulating security payload (ESP) protocol provides confidentiality and can provide the same services as those provided by the AH protocol. Both protocols are based on cryptography, with key management supplied by the Internet Key Exchange (IKE) protocol (although other key exchange protocols, including manual keying, may be used).

10.4.2.1   IPsec Architecture

IPsec mechanisms use a security policy database (SPD) to determine how to handle messages. Legal actions are discarding the message, applying security services to the message, and forwarding the message with no change. The action taken depends on information in the IP and transport layer headers.

IPsec mechanisms determine the security services needed on the basis of the SPD and the path that the packet takes.

When a packet arrives, the IPsec mechanism consults the SPD for the relevant network interface. The SPD determines which entry applies on the basis of the attributes of the packet. These attributes include the source and destination port and address, the transport layer protocol involved, and other data.

EXAMPLE: An SPD has two entries for destination addresses 10.1.2.3 to 10.1.2.103. The first applies to packets with destination port 25. The second applies to packets transporting the protocol HTTP. If a packet arrives with destination address 10.1.2.50, and its destination port is 25, the first entry applies; if its destination port is 80, the second entry applies.

Entries are checked in order. If one has a different policy for securing electronic mail depending on its destination, the more specific entries are placed where they will be searched first. If no entry matches the incoming packet, it is discarded.

EXAMPLE: In the example above, the administrator wants to discard SMTP packets coming from host 192.168.2.9 and forward packets from host 192.168.19.7 without applying IPsec services. Assuming that the SPD entries are searched from first to last, the SPD would have these three entries:

> source 192.168.2.9, destination 10.1.2.3 to 10.1.2.103, port 25, discard
> source 192.168.19.7, destination 10.1.2.3 to 10.1.2.103, port 25, bypass
> destination 10.1.2.3 to 10.1.2.103, port 25, apply IPsec

The heart of applying IPsec is the security association.

Definition 10–6. A *security association* (SA) is an association between peers for security services. The security association is unidirectional.

A security association is a set of security enhancements to a channel along which packets are sent. It is defined uniquely by the destination address, the security protocol (AH or ESP), and a unique 32-bit security parameter index (SPI). It defines the security protocol that is to be applied to packets sent over that association.

Each SA uses either ESP or AH, but not both. If both are required, two SAs are created. Similarly, if IPsec is to provide security between two peers in both directions, two SAs are needed.

When IPsec services are to be applied, the SPD entry identifies one or more security associations and parameters. The parameters describe how to determine which security association(s) to use to process the packet. This leads to the security association database (SAD), which consists of a set of selectors and corresponding security associations.

EXAMPLE: Continuing the example above, focus on the case in which IPsec is to be applied. The SPD entry for 10.1.2.101 could take the selector for the SAD from the packet (so the selector might be the SA with the destination address 10.1.2.101) or from the SPD entry (so the selector might be the SA with the destination addresses in the range 10.1.2.3 to 10.1.2.103).

Each SAD entry contains information about the SA. Key fields are as follows.

- The AH algorithm identifier and keys are used when the SA uses the AH protocol.
- The ESP encipherment algorithm identifier and keys are used when the SA uses the confidentiality service of the ESP protocol.
- The ESP authentication algorithm identifier and keys are used when the SA uses the authentication and data integrity services of the ESP protocol.
- The lifetime of the SA is either the time at which the SA must be deleted and a new one formed or a count of the maximum number of bytes allowed over this SA.
- The IPsec protocol mode is tunnel mode, transport mode, or a wildcard. If it is a wildcard, either protocol mode is acceptable. Security gateways need to support only tunnel mode, but host implementations must support both modes.

An additional field checks for replay in inbound packets.

- The antireplay window field is used to detect replay (see Section 10.4.2.2). If the SA does not use the antireplay feature, this field is not used.

Outbound packets have sequence numbers.

- The sequence number counter generates the AH or ESP sequence number.

- The sequence counter overflow field stops further traffic over the SA if the sequence counter overflows.
- Path Maximum Transmission Unit and aging variables detect time-outs.

When inbound traffic arrives, the destination address, security protocol, and SPI are used to find the associated SA in the SAD. This verifies the properties that the packet should have and enables the replay check (if desired). If the packet is to be forwarded, the SPD determines the relevant services, the appropriate services are supplied, and the packet is forwarded.

In some situations, multiple SAs may protect packets.

Definition 10–7. A *security association bundle* (*SA bundle*) is a sequence of security associations that the IPsec mechanisms apply to packets.

Tunnel mode SAs can be nested. This is called *iterated tunneling* and occurs when multiple hosts build tunnels through which they send traffic. The endpoints may be the same, although support for iterated tunneling is required only when at least one endpoint of the two tunnels is different. The tunnels may be entirely nested.

EXAMPLE: Return to Secure Corp. and Red Dog LLC. The fraud group within Secure has a host, *frauds*, that has IPsec mechanisms. The Red Dog fraud group has a new system, *equity*, that also has IPsec mechanisms. Both Secure's gateway to the internet, *gateway*, and Red Dog's gateway to the Internet, *firewall*, have IPsec mechanisms. Because the data is so sensitive, the fraud groups decide that they need to protect their data within each company. The SA between the gateways is not enough.

The data transfer now has two SAs. The first goes from *gateway.secure.com* to *firewall.reddog.com* and is in tunnel mode. The second, also in tunnel mode, begins at *frauds.secure.com*, tunnels through the SA from *gateway.secure.com* to *firewall.reddog.com*, and terminates at *equity.reddog.com*.

Iteration of transport mode SAs occurs when both the AH and ESP protocols are used. This is called *transport adjacency*, and when it is used, application of the ESP protocol should *precede* application of the AH protocol. The idea is that the ESP protocol protects the higher-layer (transport) protocol and the AH protocol protects the IP packet. Were the AH protocol to be applied first, the ESP protocol would not protect the IP packet headers.

It is instructive to examine the appearance of the packets in the example above. Figure 10–5 shows the packet layout as it travels between the two companies. Notice that the packet generated by *frauds* is encapsulated in another IP packet with the IPsec services applied to the inner packet. Both headers identify *equity* as the destination. When the packet arrives at *gateway*, the original IP header is (probably) not visible to *gateway*. In this case, the SAD and SPD use a special identifier to indicate that the source is obscured. (See Exercise 8.) The appropriate SA directs the packet to be

Figure 10–5 An IPsec-protected packet going through nested tunnels. The filled rectangles represent headers. The rightmost IP header and the following data constitute the original packet. The IPsec mechanisms add the ESP, AH, and IP headers of *frauds* and forward the packet to *gateway*. This is the first SA and is in tunnel mode. The host *gateway* adds the ESP, AH, and IP headers shown, putting the packet into the second tunnel mode SA.

encapsulated and forwarded to *firewall*, so the added IP header identifies *firewall* as the destination IP address. When the packet arrives at *firewall*, it uses the incoming packet's destination IP address (*firewall*), security protocol, and SPI to locate the SA. This bundle tells *firewall* to authenticate and decrypt the contents of the packet. The inner IP packet is then used to look up the appropriate action in the SPD, which (in this case) is to bypass IPsec. The packet is then forwarded to *equity*, which repeats the processing. The innermost IP packet is then forwarded to *equity* and processed.

We now examine the AH and ESP protocols.

10.4.2.2 Authentication Header Protocol

The goal of the authentication header (AH) protocol is to provide origin authentication, message integrity, and protection against replay, if desired. It protects static fields of the IP packet header as well as the contents of the packet.

The important parameters included in the AH header are an indication of the length of the header, the SPI of the SA under which this protocol is applied, a sequence number used to prevent replay, and an Integrity Value Check (IVC)[3] padded to a multiple of 32 bits (for IPv4) or 64 bits (for IPv6).

The AH protocol has two steps. The first checks that replay is not occurring. The second checks the authentication data.

When a packet is sent, the sender assumes that antireplay is used unless it is told otherwise. The sender first checks that the sequence number will not cycle. (If it will, a new SA must be created; see the discussion above.) It adds 1 to the current sequence number. The sender then calculates the IVC of the packet. The IVC includes all fields in the IP header that will not change in transit or that can be predicted (such

---

[3] This is another term for a message integrity check (MIC); we use the AH protocol specification term here for consistency.

as the destination field), the AH header (with the authentication data field set to 0 for this computation), and any encapsulated or higher-layer data. Mutable fields in the IP header (such as the type of service, flags, fragment offset, time to live, and header checksum fields) are set to 0 for this computation.

When a packet arrives, the IPsec mechanism determines if the packet contains an authentication header. If so, it uses the SPI and destination address to find the associated SA in the SAD. If no such SA exists, the packet is discarded. Otherwise, the key, IVC algorithm, and antireplay settings are obtained from the SAD entry.

If the antireplay service is desired, a "sliding window" mechanism checks that the packet is new. Think of the SA as operating on a stream of packets. Conceptually, the window contains slots for at least 32 packets. Each slot has the sequence number of the packet for that slot. When a packet arrives, the mechanism checks that the packet's sequence number is at least that of the leftmost slot in the window. If the packet's sequence number is to the left of the window, the packet is discarded. The IVC of the packet is then verified, and if it is incorrect, the packet is discarded. Otherwise, if the packet's sequence number lies within the window, but the slot with that sequence number is occupied, the packet is discarded. If the slot is empty, the packet is inserted into the slot. Finally, if the packet lies to the right of the window, the window is advanced to create a slot for the packet. The packet is then placed in that slot, which is the rightmost slot in the window.

If the antireplay service is not used, the IVC is verified. The IVC is computed in the same way as the sender (that is, appropriate fields are replaced by zeros) and is compared with the IVC in the AH. If the two differ, the packet is discarded.

All implementations of the AH protocol must support HMAC_MD5 and HMAC_SHA-1. They may support others as well.

10.4.2.3   Encapsulating Security Payload Protocol

The goal of the encapsulating security payload (ESP) protocol is to provide confidentiality, origin authentication, message integrity, protection against replay if desired, and a limited form of traffic flow confidentiality. It protects only the transport data or encapsulated IP data; it does not protect the IP header.

The important parameters included in the ESP header are the SPI of the SA under which this protocol is applied, a sequence number used to prevent replay, a generic "payload data" field, padding, the length of the padding, and an optional authentication data field.

The data in the payload data field depends on the ESP services enabled. For example, if an SA needs to resynchronize a cryptographic algorithm used in chaining mode, the sender could include an initialization vector here. As more algorithms for the ESP are defined, they may specify data to be included in this field.

Because the ESP protocol begins enciphering with the payload data field and protects both header fields and data, the IPsec mechanism may need to pad the packet in order to have the number of bits or bytes required by the cryptographic algorithm. The padding field allows for this adjustment. The padding length field contains the number of padding bytes; no more than 255 bytes of padding are allowed.

At least one of the confidentiality and authentication services must be selected. Furthermore, because packets may not arrive in order, any synchronization material must be carried in the payload field. Otherwise, the packets that follow a missing packet may be unintelligible.

When a packet is sent, the sender adds an ESP header, including any required padding, to the payload (either the transport data or an encapsulated IP packet). The sender enciphers the result (except for the SPI and sequence numbers). If authentication is desired, the authentication is computed as for the AH protocol, except that it is over the ESP header and payload. It does not include the IP header that encapsulates the ESP header and payload. The relevant SA dictates the cryptographic keys and algorithms that are used.

When a packet arrives, the IPsec mechanism determines if the packet contains an ESP header. If so, it uses the SPI and destination address to find the associated SA in the SAD. If no such SA exists, the packet is discarded. Otherwise, the SA parameters are obtained from the SAD entry.

If the authentication service is used, the antireplay feature and the MAC verification proceed as for the AH, again except that only the ESP and the payload are used. Because the authentication data is inserted *after* encipherment, it is not enciphered and so can be used directly.

If the confidentiality service is used, the IPsec mechanisms decipher the enciphered portion of the ESP header. Any padding is processed, and the payload is deciphered. If the SA specifies transport mode, the IP header and payload are treated as the original IP packet. If the SA specifies tunnel mode, the encapsulated IP packet is treated as the original IP packet.

Typical implementations of public key cryptosystems are far slower than implementations of classical cryptosystems. Hence, implementations of ESP assume a classical cryptosystem, although this is not required.

All implementations of ESP must support DES in CBC mode and the NULL encipherment algorithms, as well as the HMAC_MD5, HMAC_SHA-1, and NULL MACs. (The NULL encipherment algorithm and MAC mean that those algorithms are not used. Both should never be NULL at the same time.) Implementations may support other algorithms.

10.4.3   Conclusion

Each of the three protocols adds security to network communications. The "best" protocol to use depends on a variety of factors.

To what do the requisite security services apply? If they are specific to one particular application, such as remote logins, then using a program with application layer security is appropriate. When a program that requires security services is used in an environment that does not supply those services, or that the user does not trust to supply the requisite services, the application should supply its own security.

If more generic services are needed, lower-layer security protocols can supply security services to multiple applications and can do so whether or not the application has its own mechanisms for security services. Transport layer protocols such as SSL are end-to-end security mechanisms. They are appropriate when the intermediate hosts are not trusted, when the end hosts support the transport protocol, and when the application uses a connection-oriented (transport) protocol. Network layer mechanisms such as IPsec may provide security services on either an end-to-end or a link basis. They are appropriate when securing connectionless channels or when the infrastructure supports the network layer security mechanisms.

The application layer security protocol PEM provides security services for electronic mail messages. Consider using SSL for this goal. SSL does not authenticate the message *to the recipient*; it merely authenticates the transport connection. Specifically, if Alice sends Bob a message, PEM will authenticate that Alice composed the message and that Bob received it unaltered (and possibly that the message was kept confidential). SSL can authenticate that Alice sent the message to Bob, that it arrived as sent, and possibly that it was confidential in transit. SSL does *not* verify that Alice composed the message or that the message was confidential and unchanged on Alice's system or Bob's system. In other words, SSL secures the connection; PEM secures the electronic mail (the contents of the connection). Similarly, IPsec protects the packets and their contents in transit, but authentication is of the hosts and not of Alice or Bob.

10.5   Summary

If one uses a cryptosystem without considering the protocols directing its use, the security service that the cryptosystem is to provide can be deficient. Precomputation attacks, assumptions about message sizes, and statistical attacks can all compromise messages.

Stream and block ciphers have different orientations (bits and blocks, respectively) that affect solutions to these problems. Stream ciphers emulate a one-time pad either through an externally keyed source (such as an LFSR, which generates a stream of key bits from an initial seed) or internally (such as the autokey ciphers or through feedback modes). Block ciphers emulate "code books" in which a set of bits maps to a different set of bits. (In practice, the mapping is algorithmic.)

Over a network, cryptographic protocols and cryptosystems are the basis for many security services, including confidentiality, authentication, integrity, and non-repudiation. These services can be provided at different layers, depending on the assumptions about the network and the needs of the servers and clients.

10.6   Further Reading

Seberry and Pieprzyk [805] and Denning [242] discuss the theory of linear feedback shift registers. Schneier [796] presents a variant called Feedback Carry Shift Registers.

Beker and Piper [62] discuss stream ciphers. Rueppel analyzes design criteria for stream ciphers [766]. Several papers discuss the RC4 keystream generator's strength [326, 366, 640].

Bellovin [68] discusses security problems in many Internet protocols; Kent [503] provides a different perspective. Two groups use different techniques to analyze the security of SSL [641, 924]. Oppliger [702], Stallings [865], and Doraswamy and Harkins [279] present overviews of IPsec. Bellovin [70] discusses the cryptographic security of IPsec. Bishop [105] examines the Network Time Protocol NTPv2. Netscape Corporation's SSL protocol [340] and the TLS protocol [265] provide security at the transport layer using a variety of cryptographic mechanisms including Fortezza [676, 677]. Ylönen presents SSH, a protocol for secure remote logins [959]. Vincenzetti, Taino, and Bolognesi add security mechanisms to Telnet [915]. Vixie [917] and Bellovin [69] discuss issues related to the Directory Name Services.

10.7   Exercises

1. Let the function f for a four-stage NLFSR be $f(r_0...r_{n-1}) = (r_0$ and $r_1)$ or r_3, and let the initial value of the register be 1001. Derive the initial sequence and cycle.

2. An n-stage LFSR produces a sequence with a period of length at most $2^n - 1$, but the register has n bits and thus may assume 2^n values. Why can the length of the period never be 2^n? Which register value is excluded from the cycle, and why?

3. Consider double encryption, where $c = E_{k'}(E_k(m))$ and the keys k and k' are each n bits long. Assume that each encipherment takes one time unit. A cryptanalyst will use a known plaintext attack to determine the key from two messages m_0 and m_1 and their corresponding ciphertexts c_0 and c_1.

   a. The cryptanalyst computes $E_x(m_0)$ for each possible key x and stores each in a table. How many bits of memory does the table require? How many time units does it take to compute the entry?

   b. The cryptanalyst computes $y = D_{x'}(c_0)$, where D is the decipherment function corresponding to E, for each possible key x', and then checks the table to see if y is in it. If so, (x, x') is a candidate for the key pair. How should the table be organized to allow the cryptographer to find a match for y in time $O(1)$? How many time units will pass before a match must occur?

   c. How can the cryptographer confirm that (x, x') is in fact the desired key pair?

   d. What are the maximum amounts of time and memory needed for the attack? What are the expected amounts of time and memory?

4. A network consists of n hosts. Assuming that cryptographic keys are distributed on a per-host-pair basis, compute how many different keys are required.

5. One cryptographic checksum is computed by applying the DES in CBC mode to the message or file and using the last n bits of the final enciphered block as the checksum. (This is a keyed hash; the parties must agree on the key and the initalization vector used.) Analyze this hash function. In particular, how difficult is it to find two different messages that hash to the same value? How difficult is it to generate a second message that produces the same hash value as the first message?

6. A variant of the autokey cipher is to pick a well-known book and use its text, starting at some agreed-upon location. For example, the plaintext THEBO YHAST HECAT might be enciphered as the phrase AVARI ANTOF THEAU, with the sender and recipient agreeing that the first sentence in Exercise 6 in Chapter 10 in this book is the initial key. Describe a problem with this approach that could lead to a successful decipherment.

7. Unlike PEM, PGP requires the user to set a flag to indicate whether the file being protected is text or binary data. Explain why such a flag is necessary. Why does PEM not require such a flag?

8. Redraw Figure 10–5 assuming that the SA between *frauds* and *equity* is a transport mode SA rather than a tunnel mode SA.

9. When the IVC for the AH protocol is computed, why are mutable fields set to 0 rather than omitted?

Chapter 11
Authentication

> ANTIPHOLUS OF SYRACUSE: To me she speaks; she moves me for her theme!
> What, was I married to her in my dream?
> Or sleep I now and think I hear all this?
> What error drives our eyes and ears amiss?
> Until I know this sure uncertainty,
> I'll entertain the offer'd fallacy
> —*The Comedy of Errors*, II, ii, 185–190.

Authentication is the binding of an identity to a principal. Network-based authentication mechanisms require a principal to authenticate to a single system, either local or remote. The authentication is then propagated. This chapter explores the question of authentication to a single system.

11.1   Authentication Basics

Subjects act on behalf of some other, external entity. The identity of that entity controls the actions that its associated subjects may take. Hence, the subjects must bind to the identity of that external entity.

Definition 11–1. *Authentication* is the binding of an identity to a subject.

The external entity must provide information to enable the system to confirm its identity. This information comes from one (or more) of the following.

1. What the entity knows (such as passwords or secret information)
2. What the entity has (such as a badge or card)
3. What the entity is (such as fingerprints or retinal characteristics)
4. Where the entity is (such as in front of a particular terminal)

The authentication process consists of obtaining the authentication information from an entity, analyzing the data, and determining if it is associated with that entity. This means that the computer must store some information about the entity. It also suggests that mechanisms for managing the data are required. We represent these requirements in an *authentication system* [106] consisting of five components.

1. The set *A* of *authentication information* is the set of specific information with which entities prove their identities.
2. The set *C* of *complementary information* is the set of information that the system stores and uses to validate the authentication information.
3. The set *F* of *complementation functions* that generate the complementary information from the authentication information. That is, for $f \in F$, $f: A \rightarrow C$.
4. The set *L* of *authentication functions* that verify identity. That is, for $l \in L$, $l: A \times C \rightarrow \{$ **true**, **false** $\}$.
5. The set *S* of *selection functions* that enable an entity to create or alter the authentication and complementary information.

EXAMPLE: A user authenticates himself by entering a password, which the system compares with the cleartext passwords stored online. Here, *A* is the set of strings making up acceptable passwords, $C = A$, $F = \{ I \}$, and $L = \{ $ **eq** $ \}$, where *I* is the identity function and **eq** is **true** if its arguments are the same and **false** if they are not.

11.2   Passwords

Passwords are an example of an authentication mechanism based on what people know: the user supplies a password, and the computer validates it. If the password is the one associated with the user, that user's identity is authenticated. If not, the password is rejected and the authentication fails.

Definition 11–2. A *password* is information associated with an entity that confirms the entity's identity.

The simplest password is some sequence of characters. In this case, the *password space* is the set of all sequences of characters that can be passwords.

EXAMPLE: One installation requires each user to choose a sequence of 10 digits as a password. Then *A* has 10^{10} elements (from "0000000000" to "9999999999").

The set of complementary information may contain more, or fewer, elements than *A*, depending on the nature of the complementation function. Originally, most systems stored passwords in protected files. However, the contents of such files might be accidentally exposed. Morris and Thompson [651] recount an amusing example in which a Multics system editor swapped pointers to the temporary files being used to edit the password file and the message of the day file (printed whenever a user logged in); the result was that whenever a user logged in, the cleartext password file was printed.

The solution is to use a one-way hash function to hash the password into a complement [943].

EXAMPLE: The original UNIX password mechanism does not store the passwords online in the clear. Instead, one of 4,096 functions hashes the password into an 11-character string, and two characters identifying the function used are prepended [651]. The 13-character string is then stored in a file.

A UNIX password is composed of up to eight ASCII characters; for implementation reasons, the ASCII NUL (0) character is disallowed. Hence, A is the set of strings of up to eight characters, each chosen from a set of 127 possible characters.[1] A contains approximately 6.9×10^{16} passwords. However, the set C contains strings of exactly 13 characters chosen from an alphabet of 64 characters. C contains approximately 3.0×10^{23} strings. The subset of C corresponding to selected passwords may or may not be readable. Many UNIX systems store these strings in the file */etc/passwd*, which all users can read. Many other versions of the UNIX system, however, store these strings in *shadow password files* that only the superuser can read [347, 406].

The UNIX hashing functions $f \in F$ are based upon a permutation of the Data Encryption Standard. F consists of 4,096 such functions f_i, $0 \le i < 4{,}096$.

The UNIX authentication functions are *login*, *su*, and other programs that confirm a user's password during execution. This system supplies the proper element of C; that information may not be available to the user. Some of these functions may be accessible over a network—for example, through the telnet or FTP protocols.

Finally, the selection functions are programs such as *passwd* and *nispasswd*, which change the password associated with an entity.

The goal of an authentication system is to ensure that entities are correctly identified. If one entity can guess another's password, then the guesser can impersonate the other. The authentication model provides a systematic way to analyze this problem. The goal is to find an $a \in A$ such that, for $f \in F$, $f(a) = c \in C$ and c is associated with a particular entity (or any entity). Because one can determine whether a is associated with an entity only by computing $f(a)$ or by authenticating via $l(a)$, we have two approaches for protecting the passwords, used simultaneously.

---

[1] In practice, some characters (such as the erase character) have special meanings and are rarely used.

1. Hide enough information so that one of *a*, *c*, or *f* cannot be found.

EXAMPLE: Many UNIX systems make the files containing complementation information readable only by *root*. These schemes, which use *shadow password files*, make the set of complements *c* in actual use unknown. Hence, there is insufficient information to determine whether or not *f(a)* is associated with a user. Similarly, other systems make the set of complementation functions *F* unknown; again, the computation of the value *f(a)* is not possible.

2. Prevent access to the authentication functions *L*.

EXAMPLE: One site does not allow the *root* user to log in from a network. The login functions exist but always fail. Hence, one cannot test authentication of *root* with access to these functions over a network.

Each of these approaches leads to different types of attacks and defenses.

11.2.1 Attacking a Password System

The simplest attack against a password-based system is to guess passwords.

Definition 11–3. A *dictionary attack* is the guessing of a password by repeated trial and error.

The name of this attack comes from the list of words (a "dictionary") used for guesses. The dictionary may be a set of strings in random order or (more usually) a set of strings in decreasing order of probability of selection.

If the complementary information and complementation functions are available, the dictionary attack takes each guess g and computes $f(g)$ for each $f \in F$. If $f(g)$ corresponds to the complementary information for entity E, then g authenticates E under f. This is a *dictionary attack type 1*. If either the complementary information or the complementation functions are unavailable, the authentication functions $l \in L$ may be used. If the guess g results in l returning **true**, g is the correct password. This is a *dictionary attack type 2*.

EXAMPLE: Attackers often obtain a UNIX system's password file and use the (known) complementation function to test guesses. (Many programs such as *crack* automate this process.) This is a type 1 attack. But the attackers need access to the system to obtain the complementation data in the password file. To gain access, they may try to guess a password using the authentication function. They use a known account name (such as *root*) and guess possible passwords by trying to log in. This is a type 2 attack.

The issue of efficiency controls how well an authentication system withstands dictionary attacks.

11.2.2   Countering Password Guessing

Password guessing requires either the set of complementation functions and complementary information or access to the authentication functions. In both approaches, the goal of the defenders is to maximize the time needed to guess the password. A generalization of Anderson's Formula [24] provides the fundamental basis.

Let P be the probability that an attacker guesses a password in a specified period of time. Let G be the number of guesses that can be tested in one time unit. Let T be the number of time units during which guessing occurs. Let N be the number of possible passwords. Then $P \geq \dfrac{TG}{N}$.

EXAMPLE: Let R be the number of bytes per minute that can be sent over a communication line, let E be the number of characters exchanged when logging in, let S be the length of the password, and let A be the number of characters in the alphabet from which the characters of the password are drawn. The number of possible passwords is $N = A^S$, and the number of guesses per minute is $G = R/E$. If the period of guessing extends M months, this time in minutes is $T = 4.32 \times 10^4 M$. Then

$$P \geq \frac{4.32 \times 10^4 M \left(\dfrac{R}{E} \right)}{A^S}, \text{ or } A^S \geq \frac{4.32 \times 10^4 MR}{PE},$$ the original statement of Anderson's Formula.

EXAMPLE: Let passwords be composed of characters drawn from an alphabet of 96 characters. Assume that 10^4 guesses can be tested each second. We wish the probability of a successful guess to be 0.5 over a 365-day period. What is the minimum password length that will give us this probability?

From the formulas above, we want $N \geq \dfrac{TG}{P} = \dfrac{(365 \times 24 \times 60 \times 60)10^4}{0.5} =$

6.31×10^{11}. Thus, we must choose an integer S such that $\displaystyle\sum_{i=0}^{S} 96^i \geq N = 6.31 \times 10^{11}$. This holds when $S \geq 6$. So, to meet the desired conditions, passwords of at least length 6 must be required.

Several assumptions underlie these examples. First, the time required to test a password is constant. Second, all passwords are equally likely to be selected. The first assumption is reasonable, because the algorithms used to validate passwords are fixed, and either the algorithms are independent of the password's length or the variation is negligible. The second assumption is a function of the password selection mechanism. We will now elaborate on these mechanisms.

11.2.2.1   Random Selection of Passwords

The following theorem from probability theory states a maximum on the expected time to guess a password.

> **Theorem 11–1.** Let the expected time required to guess a password be T. Then T is a maximum when the selection of any of a set of possible passwords is equiprobable.

> **Proof** See Exercise 1.

Theorem 11–1 guides selection of passwords in the abstract. In practice, several other factors mediate the result. For example, passwords selected at random include very short passwords. Attackers try short passwords as initial guesses (because there are few enough of them so that all can be tried). This suggests that certain classes of passwords should be eliminated from the space of legal passwords P. The danger, of course, is that by eliminating those classes, the size of P becomes small enough for an exhaustive search.

Complicating these considerations is the quality of the random (or pseudorandom) number generator. If the period of the password generator is too small, the size of P allows every potential password to be tested. This situation can be obvious, although more often it is not.

EXAMPLE: Morris and Thompson [651] tell about a PDP-11 system that randomly generated passwords composed of eight capital letters and digits, so to all appearances, $|P| = (26 + 10)^8 = 36^8$. Taking 0.00156 second per encryption meant that trying all possible passwords would require 140 years. The attacker noticed that the pseudorandom number generator was run on the PDP-11, and it had a period of $2^{16} - 1$ (because the PDP-11 is a 16-bit machine). This meant that there were $2^{16} - 1$, or 65,535, possible passwords, requiring 102 seconds to try them all. It actually took less than 41 seconds to find all the passwords.

Human factors also play a role in this problem. Psychological studies have shown that humans can repeat with perfect accuracy about eight meaningful items, such as digits, letters, or words [206]. If random passwords are eight characters long, humans can remember one such password. So a person who is assigned two random passwords must write them down. Although most authorities consider this to be poor practice, the vulnerabilities of written passwords depend on where a written password is kept. If it is kept in a visible or easily accessed place (such as taped to a terminal or a keyboard or pinned to a bulletin board), writing down the password indeed compromises system security. However, if wallets and purses are rarely stolen by thieves with access to the computer systems, writing a password down and keeping it in a wallet or purse is often acceptable.

Michele Crabb describes a clever method of obscuring the written password [218]. Let X be the set of all strings over some alphabet. A site chooses some simple transformation algorithm $t: X \rightarrow A$. Elements of X are distributed on pieces of paper. Before being used as passwords, they must be transformed by applying t. Typically, t is very simple; it must be memorized, and it must be changed periodically.

EXAMPLE: The transformation algorithm is: "Capitalize the third letter in the word, and append the digit 2." The word on the paper is "Swqgle3". The password will be "SwQgle32".

This scheme is most often used when system administrators need to remember many different passwords to access many different systems. Then, even if the paper is lost, the systems will not be compromised.

11.2.2.2 Pronounceable and Other Computer-Generated Passwords

A compromise between using random, unmemorizable passwords and writing passwords down is to use pronounceable passwords. Gasser [350] did a detailed study of such passwords for the Multics system and concluded that they were viable on that system.

Pronounceable passwords are based on the unit of sound called a *phoneme*. In English, phonemes for constructing passwords are represented by the character sequences *cv*, *vc*, *cvc*, or *vcv*, where *v* is a vowel and *c* a consonant.

EXAMPLE: The passwords "helgoret" and "juttelon" are pronounceable passwords; "przbqxdf" and "zxrptglfn" are not.

The advantage of pronounceable passwords is that fewer phonemes need to be used to reach some limit, so that the user must memorize "chunks" of characters rather than the individual characters themselves. In effect, each phoneme is mapped into a distinct character, and the number of such characters is the number of legal phonemes. In general, this means that the number of pronounceable passwords of length n is considerably lower than the number of random passwords of length n. Hence, a type 1 dictionary attack is expected to take less time for pronounceable passwords than for random passwords.

Assume that passwords are to be at most eight characters long. Were these passwords generated at random from a set of 96 printable characters, there would be 7.3×10^{15} possible passwords. But if there are 440 possible phonemes, generating passwords with up to six phonemes produces approximately the same number of possible passwords. One can easily generalize this from phonemes to words, with similar results.

One way to alleviate this problem is through *key crunching* [373].

Definition 11–4. Let n and k be two integers, with $n \geq k$. *Key crunching* is the hashing of a string of length n or less to another string of length k or less.

Conventional hash functions, such as MD5 and SHA-1, are used for key crunching.

11.2.2.3   User Selection of Passwords

Rather than selecting passwords for users, one can constrain what passwords users are allowed to select. This technique, called *proactive password selection* [107], enables users to propose passwords they can remember, but rejects any that are deemed too easy to guess.

The set of passwords that are easy to guess is derived from experience coupled with specific site information and prior studies [423, 651, 656, 859]. Klein's study [512] is very comprehensive. He took 15,000 password hashes and used a set of dictionaries to guess passwords. Figure 11–1 summarizes his results. Some categories of passwords that researchers have found easy to guess are as follows.

1. Passwords based on account names

    a. Account name followed by a number
    b. Account name surrounded by delimiters

2. Passwords based on user names

    a. Initials repeated 0 or more times
    b. All letters lower- or uppercase
    c. Name reversed
    d. First initial followed by last name reversed

3. Passwords based on computer names
4. Dictionary words
5. Reversed dictionary words
6. Dictionary words with some or all letters capitalized

Type of password	Percent	Length	Percent
Dictionary words	8%		
Common names	4%	1	0.03%
User/account names	3%	2	0.03%
Phrases, patterns	2%	3	0.48%
Male names	1%	4	1.36%
Female names	1%	5	2.30%
Uncommon names	1%	6	8.41%
Machine names	1%	7	5.89%
Place names	1%	8	5.65%
King James Bible	1%		

Figure 11–1   Results of Klein's password guessing experiments. The percentages are from 15,000 potential passwords selected from approximately 50 different sites.

7. Reversed dictionary words with some or all letters capitalized

8. Dictionary words with arbitrary letters turned into control characters

9. Dictionary words with any of the following changes: a → 2 or 4, e → 3, h → 4, i → 1, l → 1, o → 0, s → 5 or $, z → 5.

10. Conjugations or declensions of dictionary words

11. Patterns from the keyboard

12. Passwords shorter than six characters

13. Passwords containing only digits

14. Passwords containing only uppercase or lowercase letters, or letters and numbers, or letters and punctuation

15. Passwords that look like license plate numbers

16. Acronyms (such as "DPMA," "IFIPTC11," "ACM," "IEEE," "USA," and so on)

17. Passwords used in the past

18. Concatenations of dictionary words

19. Dictionary words preceded or followed by digits, punctuation marks, or spaces

20. Dictionary words with all vowels deleted

21. Dictionary words with white spaces deleted

22. Passwords with too many characters in common with the previous (current) password

EXAMPLE: The strings "hello" and "mycomputer" are poor passwords because they violate criteria 4 and 18, respectively. The strings "1PLK107" and "311t3$p32k" are also poor (the first is a California licence plate number and violates criterion 15, and the second is the word "elitespeak" modified as in criterion 9).

Good passwords can be constructed in several ways. A password containing at least one digit, one letter, one punctuation symbol, and one control character is usually quite strong. A second technique is to pick a verse from an obscure poem (or an obscure verse from a well-known poem) and pick the characters for the string from its letters.

EXAMPLE: The string "LlMm*2^Ap" (where ^A represents control-a) is a good password. The letters are chosen from the names of various members of two families, and the combination of characters is unlikely to be guessed even by those who know the families. As a more complex example, few people can recite the third verse of "The Star-Spangled Banner" (the national anthem of the United States of America):

And where is that band who so vauntingly swore
That the havoc of war and the battle's confusion

A home and a country should leave us no more?
Their blood has wiped out their foul footsteps' pollution.
No refuge could save the hireling and slave
From the terror of flight, or the gloom of the grave:
And the star-spangled banner in triumph doth wave
O'er the land of the free and the home of the brave

Choose the second letter of each word of length 4 or greater in the third line, alternating case, and add a "/" followed by the initials of the author of the poem: "OoHeO/FSK." This is also a password that is hard to guess. But see Exercise 5.

Definition 11–5. A *proactive password checker* is software that enforces specific restrictions on the selection of new passwords.

Proactive password checkers must meet several criteria [111]:

1. It must always be invoked. Otherwise, users could bypass the proactive mechanism.
2. It must be able to reject any password in a set of easily guessed passwords (such as in the list above).
3. It must discriminate on a per-user basis. For example, "^AHeidiu'" (^A being control-a) is a reasonable password (modulo Exercise 5) for most people, but not for the author, whose oldest daughter is named "Heidi Tinúviel."
4. It must discriminate on a per-site basis. For example, "^DHMC^DCNH" is a reasonable password at most places, but not at the Dartmouth Hitchcock Medical Center at Dartmouth College, New Hampshire.
5. It should have a pattern-matching facility. Many common passwords, such as "aaaaa," are not in dictionaries but are easily guessed. A pattern-matching language makes detecting these patterns simple. For example, in one pattern-matching language, the pattern "^\(.\)\1*$" will detect all strings composed of a single character repeated one or more times.
6. It should be able to execute subprograms and accept or reject passwords based on the results. This allows the program to handle spellings that are not in dictionaries. For example, most computer dictionaries do not contain the word "waters" (because it is the plural of a word, "water," in that dictionary). A spelling checker would recognize "waters" as a word. Hence, the program should be able to run a spelling checker on proposed passwords, to detect conjugations and declensions of words in the dictionary.
7. The tests should be easy to set up, so administrators do not erroneously allow easily guessed passwords to be accepted.

EXAMPLE: The proactive password checker OPUS [860] addresses the sizes of dictionaries. Its goal is to find a compact representation for very large dictionaries. Bloom filters provide the mechanism. Each word in the dictionary is run through a hash function that produces an integer h_i of size less than some parameter n. This is repeated for k different hash functions, producing k integers $h_1, ..., h_k$. The OPUS dictionary is represented as a bit vector of length n. To put the word into the OPUS dictionary, bits $h_1, ..., h_k$ are set.

When a user proposes a new password, that word is run through the same hash functions. Call the output $h_1', ..., h_k'$. If any of the bits $h_1', ..., h_k'$ are not set in the OPUS dictionary, the word is not in the OPUS dictionary and is accepted. If all are set, then to some degree of probability the word is in a dictionary fed to OPUS and should be rejected.

EXAMPLE: Ganesan and Davies [345] propose a similar approach. They generate a Markov model of the dictionary, extract information about trigrams, and normalize the results. Given a proposed password, they test to see if the word was generated by the Markov model extracted from the dictionary. If so, it is deemed too easy to guess and is rejected.

Both these methods are excellent techniques for reducing the space required to represent a dictionary. However, they do not meet all the requirements of a proactive password checker and should be seen as part of such a program rather than as sufficient on their own.

EXAMPLE: A "little language" designed for proactive password checking [108] was based on these requirements. The language includes functions for checking whether or not words are in a dictionary (a task that could easily use the techniques of OPUS or Ganesan and Davies). It also included pattern matching and the ability to run subprograms, as well as the ability to compare passwords against previously chosen passwords.

The keyword **set** sets the values of variables. For example,

```
set gecos "Matt Bishop, 3085 EU-II"
```

assigns the variable *gecos* to the value `Matt Bishop, 3085 EU-II`. Pattern assignment is available through **setpat**:

```
setpat "$gecos" "^\([^,]\), \(.*\)$" name office
```

This matches the pattern with the value of *gecos* (obtained by prefixing a "$" to the variable name). The strings matched by the subpatterns in "\(" and "\)" are assigned to the variables *name* and *office* (so *name* is `Matt Bishop` and *office* is `3085 EU-II`). Equality and inequality operators work as string operators. All integers are translated to strings before any operations take place. Other functions are available; see Figure 11–2 for some examples.

Function	Action	Example
length($p)	Length of value	length("gueSS/This1!") = 12
alpha($p)	Number of letters	alpha("gueSS/This1!") = 9
substr($p,2,3)	Return substring	substr("gueSS/This1!",2,3) = "ue"
lcase($p)	Make all letters lowercase	lcase("gueSS/This1!") = "guess/this1!"
rev($p)	Reverse the string	rev("gueSS/This1!") = "!1sihT/SSeug"
reflect($p)	Reflect the string	reflect("hello") = "hellolleh"
trans($p, a, b)	Change all a's to b's	trans("ax-ya") = "bx-yb"

Figure 11–2 Examples of functions.

The basic component of the little language is the *password test block*:

```
test length("$p") < 6
true "Your password contains fewer than 6 characters."
endtest
```

This block says to compare the length of the proposed password, stored in the variable *p* earlier, and compare it with 6 (the *test*). If the test is true (that is, if the password is less than six characters long), the message in the second line is printed and the password is rejected. As another example, the test

```
infile("/usr/dict/words", "$p")
```

is true if the value of *p* is a string in the file "/usr/dict/words." The test

```
!inprog("spell", "$p", "$p")
```

is true if the output of the program *spell*, given the value of *p* as input, produces that same value as output. Because *spell* prints all misspelled input words, if the input and output match, then the value of *p* is not a correctly spelled word.

The language contains many other functions, including one for testing for catenated words and another for hashing passwords using the UNIX password hashing function.

11.2.2.4   Reusable Passwords and Dictionary Attacks

As discussed earlier, reusable passwords are quite susceptible to dictionary attacks of type 1. The goal of random passwords, pronounceable passwords, and proactive password checking is to maximize the time needed to guess passwords.

If a type 1 dictionary attack is aimed at finding *any* user's password (as opposed to a *particular* user's password), a technique known as *salting* increases the amount of work required [651]. Salting makes the choice of complementation function a function of randomly selected data. Ideally, the random data is different for each user. Then, to determine if the string s is the password for any of a set of n users, the attacker must perform n complementations, each of which generates a different complement. Thus, salting increases the work by the order of the number of users.

EXAMPLE: Most versions of the UNIX system use salts. The salt is chosen randomly, when the password is set, and is an integer from 0 to 4,095, inclusive. The specific complementation function depends on the salt. Specifically, the E table in the DES is perturbed in one of 4,096 possible ways,[2] and the message of all 0 bits is enciphered using the password as a key. The resulting 64 bits are mapped into 11 characters chosen from a set of 64 characters. The salt is split into two sets of six bits, and those sets are mapped to printable characters using the same alphabet. The 11-character representation of output is appended to the two-character representation of the salt. The authentication function is chosen on the basis of the salt also; hence, the salt must be available to all programs that need to verify passwords.

11.2.2.5   Guessing Through Authentication Functions

If the actual complements, or the complementation functions, are not publicly available, the only way to try to guess a password is to use the authentication function systems provide for authorized users to log in. Although this sounds difficult, the patience of some attackers is amazing. One group of attackers guessed passwords in this manner for more than two weeks before gaining access to one target system.

Unlike a type 1 dictionary attack, this attack cannot be prevented, because the authentication functions must be available to enable legitimate users to access the system. The computer has no way of distinguishing between authorized and unauthorized users except by knowledge of the password.

Defending against such attacks requires that the authentication functions be made difficult for attackers to use, or that the authentication functions be made to react in unusual ways. Four types of techniques are common.

Techniques of the first type are collectively called *backoff* techniques. The most common, *exponential backoff*, begins when a user attempts to authenticate and fails. Let x be a parameter selected by the system administrator. The system waits $x^0 = 1$ second before reprompting for the name and authentication data. If the user fails again, the system reprompts after $x^1 = x$ seconds. After n failures, the system waits x^{n-1} seconds. Other backoff techniques use arithmetic series rather than geometric series (reprompting immediately, then waiting x seconds, then waiting $2x$ seconds, and so forth).

Techniques of the second type involve *disconnection*. After some number of failed authentication attempts, the connection is broken and the user must reestablish it. This technique is most effective when connection setup requires a substantial amount of time, such as redialing a telephone number. It is less effective when connections are quick, such as over a network.

---

[2] Specifically, if bit i in the salt is set, table entries i and $i + 24$ are exchanged [651].

EXAMPLE: If a user fails to supply a valid name and the corresponding password in three tries, FreeBSD (a variant of the UNIX operating system) breaks the connection.

Techniques of the third type use *disabling*. If *n* consecutive attempts to log in to an account fail, the account is disabled until a security manager can reenable it. This prevents an attacker from trying too many passwords. It also alerts security personnel to an attempted attack. They can take appropriate action to counter the threat.

One should consider carefully whether to disable accounts and which accounts to disable. A (possibly apocryphal) story concerns one of the first UNIX vendors to implement account disabling. No accounts were exempt. An attacker broke into a user account, and then attempted to log in as *root* three times. The system disabled that account. The system administrators had to reboot the system to regain *root* access.

EXAMPLE: Both UNIX systems and Windows NT systems have the ability to disable accounts after failed logins. Typically, the UNIX *root* account cannot be disabled. The Windows *administrator* account can be locked out (the equivalent of "disabled" in this context) from network logins, but not from local logins.

The final, fourth type of technique is called *jailing*. The unauthenticated user is given access to a limited part of the system and is gulled into believing that he or she has full access. The jail then records the attacker's actions. This technique is used to determine what the attacker wants or simply to waste the attacker's time.

EXAMPLE: An attacker was breaking into the computers of AT&T Bell Laboratories. Bill Cheswick detected the attack and simulated a slow computer system. He fed the attacker bogus files and watched what the attacker did. He concluded that keeping the jail was not an effective way to discover the attacker's goals [171].

One form of the jailing technique is to plant bogus data on a running system, so that after breaking in the attacker will grab the data. (This technique, called *honeypots*, is often used in intrusion detection. See Section 22.6.2.1, "Containment Phase.") Clifford Stoll used this technique to help trap an attacker who penetrated computers at the Lawrence Berkeley Laboratory. The time required to download the bogus file was sufficient to allow an international team to trace the attacker through the international telephone system [878, 880].

11.2.3 Password Aging

Guessing of passwords requires that access to the complement, the complementation functions, and the authentication functions be obtained. If none of these have changed by the time the password is guessed, then the attacker can use the password to access the system.

Consider the last sentence's conditional clause. The techniques discussed in Section 11.2 attempt to negate the part saying "the password is guessed" by making that task difficult. The other part of the conditional clause, "if none of these have changed," provides a different approach: ensure that, by the time a password is guessed, it is no longer valid.

Definition 11–6. *Password aging* is the requirement that a password be changed after some period of time has passed or after some event has occurred.

Assume that the expected time to guess a password is 180 days. Then changing the password more frequently than every 180 days will, in theory, reduce the probability that an attacker can guess a password that is still being used. In practice, aging by itself ensures little, because the estimated time to guess a password is an average; it balances those passwords that can be easily guessed against those that cannot. If users can choose passwords that are easy to guess, the estimation of the expected time must look for a *minimum*, not an average. Hence, password aging works best in conjunction with other mechanisms such as the ones discussed in this chapter.

There are problems involved in implementing password aging. The first is forcing users to change to a different password. The second is providing notice of the need to change and a user-friendly method of changing passwords.

Password aging is useless if a user can simply change the current password to the same thing. One technique to prevent this is to record the *n* previous passwords. When a user changes a password, the proposed password is compared with these *n* previous ones. If there is a match, the proposed password is rejected. The problem with this mechanism is that users can change passwords *n* times very quickly, and then change them back to the original passwords. This defeats the goal of password aging.

An alternative approach is based on time. In this implementation, the user must change the password to one other than the current password. The password cannot be changed for a minimum period of time. This prevents the rapid cycling of passwords. However, it also prevents the user from changing the password should it be compromised within that time period.

EXAMPLE: UNIX systems use the time period method to age passwords (when password aging is turned on). They record the time of the last change, the minimum time before which the password can be changed again, and the time by which the password must be changed. Different systems use different formats. System V UNIX systems record the information in terms of weeks since January 1, 1970; HP/UX systems running in trusted mode record it in terms of seconds since midnight of that epoch.

If passwords are selected by users, the manner in which users are reminded to change their passwords is crucial. Users must be given time to think of good passwords or must have their password choices checked. Grampp and Morris [371] point out that, although there is no formal statistical evidence to support it, they have found that the easiest passwords to guess are on systems that do not give adequate notice of upcoming password expirations.

EXAMPLE: Most System V–based UNIX systems give no warnings or reminders before passwords expire. Instead, when users try to log in, they are told that their passwords have expired. Before they can complete the logins, they must change their passwords as part of the login process. Trusted HP/UX, on the other hand, gives warning messages every time a user logs in within some period of time before the password expires. The specific period of time is set by the system administrator.

11.3   Challenge-Response

Passwords have the fundamental problem that they are *reusable*. If an attacker sees a password, she can later *replay* the password. The system cannot distinguish between the attacker and the legitimate user, and allows access. An alternative is to authenticate in such a way that the transmitted password changes each time. Then, if an attacker replays a previously used password, the system will reject it.

Definition 11–7. Let user U desire to authenticate himself to system S. Let U and S have an agreed-on secret function f. A *challenge-response* authentication system is one in which S sends a random message m (the challenge) to U, and U replies with the transformation $r = f(m)$ (the response). S validates r by computing it separately.

Challenge-response algorithms are similar to the IFF (identification—friend or foe) techniques that military airplanes use to identify allies and enemies.

11.3.1   Pass Algorithms

Definition 11–8. Let there be a challenge-response authentication system in which the function f is the secret. Then f is called a *pass algorithm*.

Under this definition, no cryptographic keys or other secret information may be input to f. The algorithm computing f is itself the secret.

EXAMPLE: Haskett [405] suggests using this scheme in combination with a standard password scheme. After the user supplies a reusable password, a second prompt is given (Haskett points out that this could be the same as the system's standard prompt, to confuse attackers). At this point, the user must enter some string based on an algorithm. For example, if the prompt "abcdefg" were given, the appropriate response could be "bdf"; if the prompt were "ageksido," the appropriate response could be "gkio" (the algorithm is every other letter beginning with the second). Or, to use Haskett's example, the pass algorithm can alter a fixed password. In this case, at the prompt, the user would enter "wucsmfxymap" if the terminal were on a dial-in line, "acdflmq" if it were in a semisecure area, and "cfm" if it were in a secure area. Here, "cfm" is the expected password; the location dictates how many random characters surround each of the letters.

11.3.2   One-Time Passwords

The ultimate form of password aging occurs when a password is valid for exactly one use. In some sense, challenge-response mechanisms use one-time passwords. Think of the response as the password. As the challenges for successive authentications differ, the responses differ. Hence, the acceptability of each response (password) is invalidated after each use.

> **Definition 11–9.** A *one-time* password is a password that is invalidated as soon as it is used.

A mechanism that uses one-time passwords is also a challenge-response mechanism. The challenge is the number of the authentication attempt; the response is the one-time password.

The problems in any one-time password scheme are the generation of random passwords and the synchronization of the user and the system. The former problem is solved by using a cryptographic hash function or enciphering function such as the DES, and the latter by having the system inform the user which password it expects—for example, by having all the user's passwords numbered and the system providing the number of the one-time password it expects.

EXAMPLE: S/Key [390] implements a one-time password scheme. It uses a technique first suggested by Lamport [542] to generate the passwords. Let h be a one-way hash function (S/Key uses MD4 or MD5, depending on the version). Then the user chooses an initial seed k, and the key generator calculates

$$h(k) = k_1, h(k_1) = k_2, ..., h(k_{n-1}) = k_n$$

The passwords, in the order they are used, are

$$p_1 = k_n, p_2 = k_{n-1}, ..., p_{n-1} = k_2, p_n = k_1$$

Suppose an attacker intercepts p_i. Because $p_i = k_{n-i+1}$, $p_{i+1} = k_{n-i}$, and $h(k_{n-i}) = k_{n-i+1}$, the attacker would need to invert h, or launch a dictionary attack on h, in order to determine the next password. Because h is a one-way function, it cannot be inverted.

Furthermore, for MD4 and MD5, dictionary attacks are not a threat provided the seeds are chosen randomly, an assumption we (and the authors of S/Key) make implicitly.

The S/Key system takes the seed the user enters and generates a list of n passwords. The implementation presents each password as a sequence of six short words (but the internal representation is an integer). The user can generate a numbered list of these sequences. S/Key initializes a database, called the *skeykeys* file, with the number of the next password to be supplied and the hexadecimal representation of the last password correctly supplied.

The protocol proceeds as follows.

1. User Matt supplies his name to the server.
2. The server replies with the number i stored in the *skeykeys* file.
3. Matt supplies the corresponding password p_i.
4. The server computes $h(p_i) = h(k_{n-i+1}) = k_{n-i+2} = p_{i-1}$ and compares the result with the stored password. If they match, the authentication succeeds. S/Key updates the number in the *skeykeys* file to $i - 1$ and stores p_i in the file. If the authentication fails, the *skeykeys* file is left unchanged.

When a user has used all passwords of a particular sequence of passwords, that user's entry in the *skeykeys* file must be reinitialized. This requires the user to reregister with the S/Key program.

One-time passwords are considerably simpler with hardware support because the passwords need not be printed on paper or some other medium.

11.3.3   Hardware-Supported Challenge-Response Procedures

Hardware support comes in two forms: a program for a general-purpose computer and special-purpose hardware support. Both perform the same functions.

The first type of hardware device, informally called a *token*, provides mechanisms for hashing or enciphering information. With this type of device, the system sends a challenge. The user enters it into the device. The device returns the appropriate response. Some devices require the user to enter a personal identification number or password, which is used as a cryptographic key or is combined with the challenge to produce the response.

The second type of hardware device is temporally based. Every 60 seconds, it displays a different number. The numbers range from 0 to $10^n - 1$, inclusive. A similar device is attached to the computer. It knows what number the device for each registered user should display. To authenticate, the user provides his login name. The system requests a password. The user then enters the number shown on the hardware device, followed by a fixed (reusable) password. The system validates that the number is the one expected for the user at that time and that the reusable portion of the password is correct.

EXAMPLE: The RSA SecureID card uses a system based on time. In addition to the features described above, the password is invalidated once a login succeeds. (See Exercise 12.)

11.3.4   Challenge-Response and Dictionary Attacks

Whether or not a challenge-response technique is vulnerable to a dictionary attack of type 1 depends on the nature of the challenge and the response. In general, if the attacker knows the challenge and the response, a dictionary attack proceeds as for a reusable password system.

EXAMPLE: Suppose a user is authenticating herself using a challenge-response system. The system generates a random challenge r, and the user returns the value $E_k(r)$ of r enciphered using the key k. Then the attacker knows both r and $E_k(r)$ and can try different values of k until the encipherment of r matches $E_k(r)$.

In practice, it is not necessary to know the value of r. Most challenges are composed of random data combined with public data that an attacker can determine.

EXAMPLE: In the authentication system Kerberos [872], an authentication server enciphers data consisting of a name, a timestamp, some random data, and a cryptographic key. An attacker does not see the original data sent to the server. By knowing the form and contents of part of the data sent back, the attacker can try cryptographic keys until the known parts of the enciphered data decipher correctly. From this, she can derive the cryptographic key to be used in future communications. Researchers at Purdue University combined this with a weakness in key generation to compromise Kerberos Version 4 [277].

Bellovin and Merritt [73] propose a technique, called *encrypted key exchange*, that defeats dictionary attacks of type 1. Basically, it ensures that random challenges are never sent in the clear. Because the challenges are random, and unknown to the attacker, the attacker cannot verify when she has correctly deciphered them. Hence, the dictionary attack is infeasible.

The protocol assumes that Alice shares a secret password with Bob.

1. Alice uses the shared password s to encipher a randomly selected public key p for a public key system. Alice then forwards this key, along with her name, to Bob.

2. Bob determines the public key using the shared password, generates a random secret key k, enciphers it with p, enciphers the result with s, and sends it to Alice.

3. Alice deciphers the message to get k. Now both Bob and Alice share a randomly generated secret key. At this point, the challenge-response phase of the protocol begins.

Alice generates a random challenge R_A, enciphers it using k, and sends $E_k(R_A)$ to Bob.

4. Bob uses k to decipher R_A. He then generates a random challenge R_B and enciphers both with k to produce $E_k(R_AR_B)$. He sends this to Alice.

5. Alice deciphers the message, validates R_A, and determines R_B. She enciphers it using k and sends the message $E_k(R_B)$ back to Bob.

6. Bob deciphers the message and verifies R_B.

At this point, both Alice and Bob know that they are sharing the same random key k. To see that this system is immune to dictionary attacks of type 1, look at each exchange. Because the data sent in each exchange is randomly selected and never visible to the attacker in plaintext form, the attacker cannot know when she has correctly deciphered the message.

11.4   Biometrics

Identification by physical characteristics is as old as humanity. Recognizing people by their voices or appearance, and impersonating people by assuming their appearance, was widely known in classical times. Efforts to find physical characteristics that uniquely identify people include the Bertillion cranial maps, fingerprints, and DNA sampling. Using such a feature to identify people for a computer would ideally eliminate errors in authentication.

Biometrics is the automated measurement of biological or behavioral features that identify a person [635]. When a user is given an account, the system administration takes a set of measurements that identify that user to an acceptable degree of error. Whenever the user accesses the system, the biometric authentication mechanism verifies the identity. Lawton [553] points out that this is considerably easier than identifying the user because no searching is required. A comparison to the known data for the claimed user's identity will either verify or reject the claim. Common characteristics are fingerprints, voice characteristics, eyes, facial features, and keystroke dynamics.

11.4.1   Fingerprints

Fingerprints can be scanned optically, but the cameras needed are bulky. A capacitive technique uses the differences in electrical charges of the whorls on the finger to detect those parts of the finger touching a chip and those raised. The data is converted into a graph in which ridges are represented by vertices and vertices corresponding to adjacent ridges are connected. Each vertex has a number approximating the length of the corresponding ridge. At this point, determining matches becomes a problem of graph matching [463]. This problem is similar to the classical graph isomorphism problem, but because of imprecision in measurements, the graph generated from the fingerprint may have different numbers of edges and vertices. Thus, the matching algorithm is an approximation.

11.4.2   Voices

Authentication by voice, also called *speaker verification* or *speaker recognition*, involves recognition of a speaker's voice characteristics [151] or verbal information verification [561, 562]. The former uses statistical techniques to test the hypothesis that the speaker's identity is as claimed. The system is first trained on fixed pass-phrases or phonemes that can be combined. To authenticate, either the speaker says the pass-phrase or repeats a word (or set of words) composed of the learned phonemes. Verbal information verification deals with the contents of utterances. The system asks a set of questions such as "What is your mother's maiden name?" and "In which city were you born?" It then checks that the answers spoken are the same as the answers recorded in its database. The key difference is that speaker verification techniques are speaker-dependent, but verbal information verification techniques are speaker-independent, relying only on the content of the answers [563].

11.4.3   Eyes

Authentication by eye characteristics uses the iris and the retina. Patterns within the iris are unique for each person. Hence, one verification approach is to compare the patterns statistically and ask whether the differences are random [231]. A second approach is to correlate the images using statistical tests to see if they match [942]. Retinal scans rely on the uniqueness of the patterns made by blood vessels at the back of the eye. This requires a laser beaming onto the retina, which is highly intrusive. This method is typically used only in the most secure facilities [553].

11.4.4   Faces

Face recognition consists of several steps. First, the face is located. If the user places her face in a predetermined position (for example, by resting her chin on a support), the problem becomes somewhat easier. However, facial features such as hair and glasses may make the recognition harder. Techniques for doing this include the use of neural networks [716] and templates [962]. The resulting image is then compared with the relevant image in the database. The correlation is affected by the differences in the lighting between the current image and the reference image, by distortion, by "noise," and by the view of the face. The correlation mechanism must be "trained." Several different methods of correlation have been used, with varying degrees of success [647]. An alternative approach is to focus on the facial features such as the distance between the nose and the chin, and the angle of the line drawn from one to the other [775].

11.4.5   Keystrokes

Keystroke dynamics requires a signature based on keystroke intervals, keystroke pressure, keystroke duration, and where the key is struck (on the edge or in the middle). This signature is believed to be unique in the same way that written signatures are unique [477]. Keystroke recognition can be both static and dynamic. Static recognition is done once, at authentication time, and usually involves typing of a fixed or known string [139, 648]. Once authentication has been completed, an attacker can capture the connection (or take over the terminal) without detection. Dynamic recognition is done throughout the session, so the aforementioned attack is not feasible. However, the signature must be chosen so that variations within an individual's session do not cause the authentication to fail. For example, keystroke intervals may vary widely, and the dynamic recognition mechanism must take this into account. The statistics gathered from a user's typing are then run through statistical tests (which may discard some data as invalid, depending on the technique used) that account for acceptable variance in the data.

11.4.6   Combinations

Several researchers have combined some of the techniques decribed above to improve the accuracy of biometric authentication. Dieckmann, Plankensteiner, and Wagner [264] combined voice sounds and lip motion with the facial image. Duc, Bigun, Bigun, Maire, and Fischer [281] describe a "supervisor module" for melding voice and face recognition with a success rate of 99.5%. The results indicate that a higher degree of accuracy can be attained than when only a single characteristic is used.

11.4.7   Caution

Because biometrics measures characteristics of the individual, people are tempted to believe that attackers cannot pose as authorized users on systems that use biometrics. Two assumptions underlie this belief. The first is that the biometric device is accurate in the environment in which it is used. For example, if a fingerprint scanner is under observation, having it scan a mask of another person's finger would be detected. But if it is not under observation, such a trick might not be detected and the unauthorized user might gain access. The second assumption is that the transmission from the biometric device to the computer's analysis process is tamperproof. Otherwise, one could record a legitimate authentication and replay it later to gain access. Exercise 13 explores this in more detail.

11.5   Location

Denning and MacDoran [249] suggest an innovative approach to authentication. They reason that if a user claims to be Anna, who is at that moment working in a bank in California but is also logging in from Russia at the same time, the user is impersonating Anna. Their scheme is based on the Global Positioning System (GPS), which can pinpoint a location to within a few meters. The physical location of an entity is described by a location signature derived from the GPS satellites. Each location (to within a few meters) and time (to within a few milliseconds) is unique, and hence form a location signature. This signature is transmitted to authenticate the user. The host also has a location signature sensor (LSS) and obtains a similar signature for the user. If the signatures disagree, the authentication fails.

This technique relies on special-purpose hardware. If the LSS is stolen, the thief would have to log in from an authorized geographic location. Because the signature is generated from GPS data, which changes with respect to time, location, and a variety of vagaries resulting from the nature of the electromagnetic waves used to establish position, any such signature would be unique and could not be forged. Moreover, if intercepted, it could not be replayed except within the window of temporal uniqueness.

This technique can also restrict the locations from which an authorized user can access the system.

EXAMPLE: Suppose Anna is an employee of a bank in California. The bank uses location-based authentication to verify logins. Anna's LSS is stolen, and the thief takes it to New York. From there, the thief tries to access the bank's computer.

Anna's LSS generates a signature and transmits it to the bank. The bank's LSS determines that Anna's LSS is in New York and is supplying a correct signature. However, Anna is not authorized to access the bank's computer from New York, so the authentication is rejected. If the thief tries to forge a message indicating that Anna is connecting from inside California, the host's LSS would report that Anna was at a different location and would reject the connection.

An interesting point is that the authentication can be done continuously. The LSS simply intermingles signature data with the transmitted data, and the host checks it. If the connection were hijacked, the data from the LSS would be lost.

11.6   Multiple Methods

Authentication methods can be combined, or multiple methods can be used.

EXAMPLE: Authenticating by location generally uses special-purpose hardware. Although the key feature of this technique is physical *location*, without the LSS it will not work. It combines location with a token or with what one possesses.

EXAMPLE: Most challenge-response schemes require the use of a computer or smart card as well as a key or password. They combine what you know (password) with what you have (computer or smart card).

Techniques using multiple methods assign one or more authentication methods to each entity. The entity must authenticate using the specific method, or methods, chosen. The specific authentication methods vary from system to system, but in all cases the multiple layers of authentication require an attacker to know more, or possess more, than is required to spoof a single layer.

EXAMPLE: Some versions of the UNIX operating system provide a mechanism called *pluggable authentication modules* (PAM) [776]. When a program authenticates a user, it invokes a library routine, *pam_authenticate*, that accesses a set of configuration files. These files are in the directory */etc/pam.d*. Each file in that directory has the same name as the program to which it applies. For example, the library routine will access the file */etc/pam.d/ftpd* when called from the program *ftpd*. That file contains a sequence of lines describing the authentication modules to be invoked and how their results are to be handled.

```
auth    sufficient  /usr/lib/security/pam_ftp.so
auth    required    /usr/lib/security/pam_unix_auth.so \
                    use_first_pass
auth    required    /usr/lib/security/pam_listfile.so \
                    onerr=succeed item=user sense=deny \
                    file=/etc/ftpusers
```

The first field describes the nature of the line. All checks that the PAM library function will make relate to authentication of a user. The first entry invokes the module */usr/lib/security/pam_ftp.so*. This module obtains the user's name and password. If the name is "anonymous," the password is assumed to be the user's e-mail address. In this case, the module succeeds. If the user's name is not "anonymous," the variable PAM_AUTHTOK is set to the entered password, the variable PAM_RUSER is set to the entered user name, and the module fails.

If the module succeeds, the library returns to the caller, indicating success (because of the "sufficient" in the second field). If it fails, the next two entries will be used (because of the "required" in their second fields). The second entry invokes a module that performs the standard UNIX password authentication. The argument "use_first_pass" means that the password is in the variable PAM_AUTHTOK. If the module fails, the failure is recorded, but the next line is invoked anyway. Then the third entry is invoked. Its module looks in the file */etc/ftpusers* for the user name in the variable PAM_RUSER (because of "item=user"). If found, the module fails ("sense=deny"). If an error occurs (for example, because the file does not exist), the module succeeds ("onerr=succeed"). If both of the modules in the last two lines succeed, the user is authenticated. If not, the user's authentication fails.

The second field controls the calling of the modules. The entries are processed in the order in which they appear. If the second field is "sufficient" and the module succeeds, authentication is completed. If the second field is "required," failure of the module makes authentication fail, but *all* required modules are invoked before the failure is reported. To make the PAM library routine return immediately after the failure of a module, the second field must be set to "requisite." Finally, an "optional" field indicates that if all other modules fail (whether they precede or follow this entry), the module in this entry is invoked.

The idea of invoking successive modules is called *stacking*. The interval variables PAM_AUTHTOK and PAM_RUSER (and some others) enable stacked modules to communicate with one another. (The option "use_first_pass" in entry 2 is an example of this.) The caller need know nothing about how the administrator has set up authentication. Because the order in which the PAM modules are called can change, the caller can make no assumptions about how the modules work. The authentication is in effect hidden from the program.

Modules can control access to resources on the basis of factors other than authentication. The following file, */etc/pam.d/login*, corresponds to standard UNIX authentication and resource checking at login time.

```
auth      required  /usr/lib/security/pam_unix_auth.so
account   required  /usr/lib/security/pam_unix_acct.so
password  required  /usr/lib/security/pam_unix_passwd.so
session   required  /usr/lib/security/pam_unix_session.so
```

The first entry performs the standard password authentication. The second line controls access on the basis of such factors as time of day, and the fourth line does so on the basis of the resources available for the session. The third entry is invoked when the user changes the password.

11.7 Summary

Authentication consists of an entity, the *user*, trying to convince a different entity, the *verifier*, of the user's identity. The user does so by claiming to know some information, to possess something, to have some particular set of physical characteristics, or to be in a specific location. The verifier has some method of validating the claim, possibly with auxiliary equipment.

Passwords are the most basic authentication mechanism. They are vulnerable to guessing unless precautions ensure that there is a large enough set of possible passwords and that each potential password in the set is equally likely to be selected. Challenge-response techniques allow the system to vary the password and are less vulnerable to compromise because the password is never transmitted in the clear.

One-time passwords, an example of this technique, are particularly effective against guessing attacks because even if a password is guessed, it may not be reused.

Some forms of authentication require hardware support. A cryptographic key is embedded in the device. The verifier transmits a challenge. The user computes a response using the hardware device and transmits it to the verifier. The verifier then validates the signature.

Biometrics measures physical characteristics of the user. These characteristics are sent to the verifier, which validates them. Critical to the successful use of biometric measurements is the understanding that they are simply passwords (although very complex ones) and must be protected in the same way that passwords must be protected.

Location requires the verifier to determine the location of the user. If the location is not as it should be, the verifier rejects the claim.

In practice, some combination of these methods is used. The specific methods, and their ordering, depend on the resources available to the verifier and the user, the strength of the authentication required, and external factors such as laws and customs.

11.8   Further Reading

Discussions of the strength of the UNIX password scheme provide insight into how gracefully authentication schemes age. Bishop [102] and Feldmeier and Karn [312] discuss attacks on the UNIX scheme. Su and Bishop use a Connection Machine in a dictionary attack [884]; Kedem and Ishihara use a PixelFlow SIMD computer [499]. Leong and Tham [556] discuss specific password-cracking hardware. Manber [589] discusses a salting scheme. Bergadano, Crispo, and Ruffo discuss techniques for compressing dictionaries for use with proactive password checkers [76, 77].

The U.S. Department of Defense has issued specific guidelines for password selection and management [256]. Jermyn, Mayer, Monrose, Reiter, and Rubin use the graphical capabilities of many systems to generate passwords [470]. Rubin presents an alternative one-time password scheme [763].

Many network-oriented protocols are challenge-response protocols. Seberry and Pieprzyk [805] and Schneier [796] discuss network-oriented authentication in depth. Chapter 10, "Key Management," discusses some of these protocols.

Itoi and Honeyman [465] have developed a version of PAM for Windows NT.

11.9   Exercises

1. Prove Theorem 11–1.
2. A system allows the user to choose a password with a length of one to eight characters, inclusive. Assume that 10,000 passwords can be tested

per second. The system administrators want to expire passwords once they have a probability of 0.10 of having been guessed. Determine the expected time to meet this probability under each of the following conditions.

   a. Password characters may be any ASCII characters from 1 to 127, inclusive.

   b. Password characters may be any alphanumeric characters ("A" through "Z," "a" through "z," and "0" through "9").

   c. Password characters must be digits.

3. Anderson's Formula assumes that all passwords are equally likely to be chosen. Generalize the formula to handle cases in which the probability of the ith string in a set of possible passwords is p_i.

4. Classify the following proposed passwords as good choices or poor choices, and justify your reasoning.

   a. Mary

   b. go2work

   c. cat&dog

   d. 3.1515pi

5. The strings used as examples of good passwords are constructed to make them difficult to guess. Yet the particular good passwords in this chapter should not be used as passwords. Why not?

6. If password aging is based on previous passwords, why should those previous passwords not be stored in the clear on disk?

7. Why should salts be chosen at random?

8. Does using passwords with salts make attacking a specific account more difficult than using passwords without salts? Explain why or why not.

9. Show that a system using an EKE scheme is vulnerable to a dictionary attack of type 2.

10. The designers of the UNIX password algorithm used a 12-bit salt to perturb the first and third sets of 12 entries in the E-table of the UNIX hashing function (the DES). Consider a system with 2^{24} users. Assume that each user is assigned a salt from a uniform random distribution and that anyone can read the password hashes and salts for the users.

   a. What is the expected time to find all users' passwords using a dictionary attack?

   b. Assume that eight more characters were added to the password and that the DES algorithm was changed so as to use all 16 password characters. What would be the expected time to find all users' passwords using a dictionary attack?

    c. Assume that the passwords were eight characters long but that the salt length was increased to 24 bits. Again, the salts (and the corresponding algorithms) are known to all users. What would be the expected time to find all users' passwords using a dictionary attack?

11. The example describing S/Key stated that "for MD4 and MD5, dictionary attacks are not a threat provided the seeds are chosen randomly." Why? How realistic is this assumption?

12. Why should a time-based authentication system invalidate the current password on a successful authentication?

13. A computer system uses biometrics to authenticate users. Discuss ways in which an attacker might try to spoof the system under each of the following conditions.

    a. The biometric hardware is directly connected to the system, and the authentication software is loaded onto the system.

    b. The biometric hardware is on a stand-alone computer connected to the system, and the authentication software on the stand-alone computer sends a "yes" or "no" to the system indicating whether or not the user has been authenticated.

14. What complications arise in dynamic keystroke monitoring as a biometric authentication mechanism when the user's keystrokes are sent over the Internet? In particular, what characteristics of the keystroke sequences are valid, and which ones are distorted by the network?

15. PAM can be used to provide authorization as well as authentication. Design a set of modules for the PAM scheme that implements the Chinese Wall model.

Chapter 12
Design Principles

> FALSTAFF: If I had a thousand sons, the
> first human principle I would teach them should
> be, to forswear thin potations and to addict
> themselves to sack.
> —*The Second Part of King Henry the Fourth*, IV, iii, 133–136.

Specific design principles underlie the design and implementation of mechanisms for supporting security policies. These principles build on the ideas of simplicity and restriction. This chapter discusses those basic ideas and eight design principles.

12.1   Overview

Saltzer and Schroeder [773] describe eight principles for the design and implementation of security mechanisms. The principles draw on the ideas of simplicity and restriction.

Simplicity makes designs and mechanisms easy to understand. More importantly, less can go wrong with simple designs. Minimizing the interaction of system components minimizes the number of sanity checks on data being transmitted from one component to another.

EXAMPLE: The program *sendmail* reads configuration data from a binary file. System administrators generated the binary file by "freezing," or compiling, a text version of the configuration file. This created three interfaces: the mechanism used to edit the text file, the mechanism used to freeze the file, and the mechanism *sendmail* used to read the frozen file. The second interface required manual intervention and was often overlooked. To minimize this problem, *sendmail* checked that the frozen file was newer than the text file. If not, it warned the user to update the frozen configuration file.

The security problem lies in the assumptions that *sendmail* made. For example, the compiler would check that a particular option had an integer value. However, *sendmail* would not recheck; it assumed that the compiler had done the checking.

Errors in the compiler checks, or *sendmail*'s assumptions being inconsistent with those of the compiler, could produce security problems. If the compiler allowed the default UID to be a user name (say, *daemon* with a UID of 1), but *sendmail* assumed that it was an integer UID, then *sendmail* would scan the string "daemon" as though it were an integer. Most input routines would recognize that this string is not an integer and would default the return value to 0. Thus, *sendmail* would deliver mail with the *root* UID rather than with the desired *daemon* UID.

Simplicity also reduces the potential for inconsistencies within a policy or set of policies.

EXAMPLE: A college rule requires any teaching assistant who becomes aware of cheating to report it. A different rule ensures the privacy of student files. A TA contacts a student, pointing out that some files for a program were not submitted. The student tells the TA that the files are in the student's directory, and asks the TA to get the files. The TA does so, and while looking for the files notices two sets, one with names beginning with "x" and the other set not. Unsure of which set to use, the TA takes the first set. The comments show that they were written by a second student. The TA gets the second set, and the comments show that they were written by the first student. On comparing the two sets, the TA notes that they are identical except for the names in the comments. Although concerned about a possible countercharge for violation of privacy, the TA reports the student for cheating. As expected, the student charges the TA with violating his privacy by reading the first set of files. The rules conflict. Which charge or charges should be sustained?

Restriction minimizes the power of an entity. The entity can access only information it needs.

EXAMPLE: Government officials are denied access to information for which they have no need (the "need to know" policy). They cannot communicate that which they do not know.

Entities can communicate with other entities only when necessary, and in as few (and narrow) ways as possible.

EXAMPLE: All communications with prisoners are monitored. Prisoners can communicate with people on a list (given to the prison warden) through personal visits or mail, both of which are monitored to prevent the prisoners from receiving contraband such as files for cutting through prison bars or weapons to help them break out. The only exception to the monitoring policy is when prisoners meet with their attorneys. Such communications are privileged and so cannot be monitored.

"Communication" is used in its widest possible sense, including that of imparting information by not communicating.

EXAMPLE: Bernstein and Woodward, the reporters who broke the Watergate scandal, describe an attempt to receive information from a source without the source's directly answering the question. They suggested a scheme in which the source would hang up if the information was inaccurate and remain on the line if the information was accurate. The source remained on the line, confirming the information [80].

12.2 Design Principles

The principles of secure design discussed in this section express common-sense applications of simplicity and restriction in terms of computing. We will discuss detailed applications of these principles throughout the remainder of Part 5, and in Part 8, "Practicum." However, we will mention examples here.

12.2.1 Principle of Least Privilege

This principle restricts how privileges are granted.

> **Definition 12–1.** The *principle of least privilege* states that a subject should be given only those privileges that it needs in order to complete its task.

If a subject does not need an access right, the subject should not have that right. Furthermore, the *function* of the subject (as opposed to its identity) should control the assignment of rights. If a specific action requires that a subject's access rights be augmented, those extra rights should be relinquished *immediately* on completion of the action. This is the analogue of the "need to know" rule: if the subject does not need access to an object to perform its task, it should not have the right to access that object. More precisely, if a subject needs to append to an object, but not to alter the information already contained in the object, it should be given append rights and not write rights.

In practice, most systems do not have the granularity of privileges and permissions required to apply this principle precisely. The designers of security mechanisms then apply this principle as best they can. In such systems, the consequences of security problems are often more severe than the consequences for systems that adhere to this principle.

EXAMPLE: The UNIX operating system does not apply access controls to the user *root*. That user can terminate any process and read, write, or delete any file. Thus, users who create backups can also delete files. The *administrator* account on Windows has the same powers.

This principle requires that processes should be confined to as small a protection domain as possible.

EXAMPLE: A mail server accepts mail from the Internet and copies the messages into a spool directory; a local server will complete delivery. The mail server needs the rights to access the appropriate network port, to create files in the spool directory, and to alter those files (so it can copy the message into the file, rewrite the delivery address if needed, and add the appropriate "Received" lines). It should surrender the right to access the file as soon as it has finished writing the file into the spool directory, because it does not need to access that file again. The server should not be able to access any user's files, or any files other than its own configuration files.

12.2.2   Principle of Fail-Safe Defaults

This principle restricts how privileges are initialized when a subject or object is created.

> **Definition 12–2.** The *principle of fail-safe defaults* states that, unless a subject is given explicit access to an object, it should be denied access to that object.

> This principle requires that the default access to an object is *none*. Whenever access, privileges, or some security-related attribute is not *explicitly* granted, it should be denied. Moreover, if the subject is unable to complete its action or task, it should undo those changes it made in the security state of the system before it terminates. This way, even if the program fails, the system is still safe.

EXAMPLE: If the mail server is unable to create a file in the spool directory, it should close the network connection, issue an error message, and stop. It should *not* try to store the message elsewhere or to expand its privileges to save the message in another location, because an attacker could use that ability to overwrite other files or fill up other disks (a denial of service attack). The protections on the mail spool directory itself should allow create and write access only to the mail server and read and delete access only to the local server. No other user should have access to the directory.

In practice, most systems will allow an administrator access to the mail spool directory. By the principle of least privilege, that administrator should be able to access *only* the subjects and objects involved in mail queueing and delivery. As we have seen, this constraint minimizes the threats if that administrator's account is compromised. The mail system can be damaged or destroyed, but nothing else can be.

12.2.3   Principle of Economy of Mechanism

This principle simplifies the design and implementation of security mechanisms.

> **Definition 12–3.** The *principle of economy of mechanism* states that security mechanisms should be as simple as possible.

If a design and implementation are simple, fewer possibilities exist for errors. The checking and testing process is less complex, because fewer components and cases need to be tested. Complex mechanisms often make assumptions about the system and environment in which they run. If these assumptions are incorrect, security problems may result.

EXAMPLE: The *ident* protocol [769] sends the user name associated with a process that has a TCP connection to a remote host. A mechanism on host *A* that allows access based on the results of an ident protocol result makes the assumption that the originating host is trustworthy. If host *B* decides to attack host *A*, it can connect and then send any identity it chooses in response to the ident request. This is an example of a mechanism making an incorrect assumption about the environment (specifically, that host *B* can be trusted).

Interfaces to other modules are particularly suspect, because modules often make implicit assumptions about input or output parameters or the current system state; should any of these assumptions be wrong, the module's actions may produce unexpected, and erroneous, results. Interaction with external entities, such as other programs, systems, or humans, amplifies this problem.

EXAMPLE: The *finger* protocol transmits information about a user or system [964]. Many client implementations assume that the server's response is well-formed. However, if an attacker were to create a server that generated an infinite stream of characters, and a finger client were to connect to it, the client would print all the characters. As a result, log files and disks could be filled up, resulting in a denial of service attack on the querying host. This is an example of incorrect assumptions about the input to the client.

12.2.4   Principle of Complete Mediation

This principle restricts the caching of information, which often leads to simpler implementations of mechanisms.

Definition 12–4. The *principle of complete mediation* requires that all accesses to objects be checked to ensure that they are allowed.

Whenever a subject attempts to read an object, the operating system should mediate the action. First, it determines if the subject is allowed to read the object. If so, it provides the resources for the read to occur. If the subject tries to read the object again, the system should check that the subject is still allowed to read the object. Most systems would not make the second check. They would cache the results of the first check and base the second access on the cached results.

EXAMPLE: When a UNIX process tries to read a file, the operating system determines if the process is allowed to read the file. If so, the process receives a file descriptor encoding the allowed access. Whenever the process wants to read the file, it presents the file descriptor to the kernel. The kernel then allows the access.

    If the owner of the file disallows the process permission to read the file after the file descriptor is issued, the kernel still allows access. This scheme violates the principle of complete mediation, because the second access is not checked. The cached value is used, resulting in the denial of access being ineffective.

EXAMPLE: The Domain Name Service (DNS) caches information mapping host names into IP addresses. If an attacker is able to "poison" the cache by implanting records associating a bogus IP address with a name, one host will route connections to another host incorrectly. Section 13.6.1.2 discusses this in more detail.

12.2.5   Principle of Open Design

This principle suggests that complexity does not add security.

> **Definition 12–5.** The *principle of open design* states that the security of a mechanism should not depend on the secrecy of its design or implementation.

    Designers and implementers of a program must not depend on secrecy of the details of their design and implementation to ensure security. Others can ferret out such details either through technical means, such as disassembly and analysis, or through nontechnical means, such as searching through garbage receptacles for source code listings (called "dumpster-diving"). If the strength of the program's security depends on the ignorance of the user, a knowledgeable user can defeat that security mechanism. The term "security through obscurity" captures this concept exactly.

    This is especially true of cryptographic software and systems. Because cryptography is a highly mathematical subject, companies that market cryptographic software or use cryptography to protect user data frequently keep their algorithms secret. Experience has shown that such secrecy adds little if anything to the security of the system. Worse, it gives an aura of strength that is all too often lacking in the actual implementation of the system.

    Keeping cryptographic keys and passwords secret does *not* violate this principle, because a key is not an algorithm. However, keeping the enciphering and deciphering algorithms secret would violate it.

    Issues of proprietary software and trade secrets complicate the application of this principle. In some cases, companies may not want their designs made public, lest their competitors use them. The principle then requires that the design and implementation be available to people barred from disclosing it outside the company.

EXAMPLE: The Content Scrambling System (CSS) is a cryptographic algorithm that protects DVD movie disks from unauthorized copying. The DVD disk has an authentication key, a disk key, and a title key. The title key is enciphered with the disk key. A block on the DVD contains several copies of the disk key, each enciphered by a different player key, and a checksum of the disk key. When a DVD is inserted into a DVD player, the algorithm reads the authentication key. It then deciphers the disk keys using the DVD player's unique key. When it finds a deciphered key with the correct hash, it uses that key to decipher the title key, and it uses the title key to decipher the movie [876]. (Figure 12–1 shows the layout of the keys.) The authentication and disk keys are not located in the file containing the movie, so if one copies the file, one still needs the DVD disk in the DVD player to be able to play the movie.

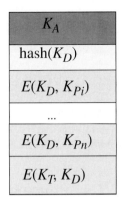

Figure 12–1 DVD key layout. K_A **is the authentication key,** K_T **the title key,** K_D **the disk key, and** K_{Pi} **the key for DVD player** *i*. **The disk key is enciphered once for each player key.**

In 1999, a group in Norway acquired a (software) DVD playing program that had an unenciphered key. They also derived an algorithm completely compatible with the CSS algorithm from the software. This enabled them to decipher any DVD movie file. Software that could perform these functions rapidly became available throughout the Internet, much to the discomfort of the DVD Copyright Control Association, which promptly sued to prevent the code from being made public [698, 712]. As if to emphasize the problems of providing security by concealing algorithms, the plaintiff's lawyers filed a declaration containing the source code of an implementation of the CSS algorithm. When they realized this, they requested that the declaration be sealed from public view. By then, the declaration had been posted on several Internet sites, including one that had more than 21,000 downloads of the declaration before the court sealed it [604].

12.2.6 Principle of Separation of Privilege

This principle is restrictive because it limits access to system entities.

> **Definition 12–6.** The *principle of separation of privilege* states that a system should not grant permission based on a single condition.

This principle is equivalent to the separation of duty principle discussed in Section 6.1. Company checks for more than $75,000 must be signed by two officers of the company. If either does not sign, the check is not valid. The two conditions are the signatures of both officers.

Similarly, systems and programs granting access to resources should do so only when more than one condition is met. This provides a fine-grained control over the resource as well as additional assurance that the access is authorized.

EXAMPLE: On Berkeley-based versions of the UNIX operating system, users are not allowed to change from their accounts to the *root* account unless two conditions are met. The first condition is that the user knows the *root* password. The second condition is that the user is in the *wheel* group (the group with GID 0). Meeting either condition is not sufficient to acquire *root* access; meeting both conditions is required.

12.2.7   Principle of Least Common Mechanism

This principle is restrictive because it limits sharing.

> **Definition 12–7.** The *principle of least common mechanism* states that mechanisms used to access resources should not be shared.

Sharing resources provides a channel along which information can be transmitted, and so such sharing should be minimized. In practice, if the operating system provides support for virtual machines, the operating system will enforce this privilege automatically to some degree (see Chapter 16, "Confinement Problem"). Otherwise, it will provide some support (such as a virtual memory space) but not complete support (because the file system will appear as shared among several processes).

EXAMPLE: A Web site provides electronic commerce services for a major company. Attackers want to deprive the company of the revenue it obtains from that Web site. They flood the site with messages and tie up the electronic commerce services. Legitimate customers are unable to access the Web site and, as a result, take their business elsewhere.

Here, the sharing of the Internet with the attackers' sites caused the attack to succeed. The appropriate countermeasure would be to restrict the attackers' access to the segment of the Internet connected to the Web site. Techniques for doing this include proxy servers such as the Purdue SYN intermediary [801] or traffic throttling (see Section 23.4, "Availability and Network Flooding"). The former targets suspect connections; the latter reduces the load on the relevant segment of the network indiscriminately.

12.2.8   Principle of Psychological Acceptability

This principle recognizes the human element in computer security.

> **Definition 12–8.** The *principle of psychological acceptability* states that security mechanisms should not make the resource more difficult to access than if the security mechanisms were not present.

Configuring and executing a program should be as easy and as intuitive as possible, and any output should be clear, direct, and useful. If security-related software is too complicated to configure, system administrators may unintentionally set up the software in a nonsecure manner. Similarly, security-related user programs must be easy to use and must output understandable messages. If a password is rejected, the password changing program should state why it was rejected rather than giving a cryptic error message. If a configuration file has an incorrect parameter, the error message should describe the proper parameter.

EXAMPLE: The *ssh* program [959] allows a user to set up a public key mechanism for enciphering communications between systems. The installation and configuration mechanisms for the UNIX version allow one to arrange that the public key be stored locally without any password protection. In this case, one need not supply a password to connect to the remote system, but will still obtain the enciphered connection. This mechanism satisfies the principle of psychological acceptability.

On the other hand, security requires that the messages impart no unnecessary information.

EXAMPLE: When a user supplies the wrong password during login, the system should reject the attempt with a message stating that the login failed. If it were to say that the password was incorrect, the user would know that the account name was legitimate. If the "user" were really an unauthorized attacker, she would then know the name of an account for which she could try to guess a password.

In practice, the principle of psychological acceptability is interpreted to mean that the security mechanism may add some extra burden, but that burden must be both minimal and reasonable.

EXAMPLE: A mainframe system allows users to place passwords on files. Accessing the files requires that the program supply the password. Although this mechanism violates the principle as stated, it is considered sufficiently minimal to be acceptable. On an interactive system, where the pattern of file accesses is more frequent and more transient, this requirement would be too great a burden to be acceptable.

12.3   Summary

The design principles discussed in this chapter are fundamental to the design and implementation of security mechanisms. They encompass not only technical details but also human interaction. Several principles come from nontechnical environments, such as the principle of least privilege. Each principle involves the restriction of privilege according to some criterion, or the minimization of complexity to make the mechanisms less likely to fail.

12.4 Further Reading

Many papers discuss the application of these principles to security mechanisms. Succeeding chapters will present references for this aspect of the principles. Other papers present different sets of principles. These papers are generally specializations or alternative views of Saltzer and Schroeder's principles, tailored for particular environments. Abadi and Needham [2] and Anderson and Needham [31] discuss principles for the design of cryptographic protocols; Syverson discusses their limits [890]. Moore [649] and Abadi [1] describe problems in cryptographic protocols. Wood [952, 953] discusses principles for secure systems design with an emphasis on groupware. Bonyun [125] focuses on architectural principles. Landwehr and Goldschlag [547] present principles for Internet security.

12.5 Exercises

1. The PostScript language [11] describes page layout for printers. Among its features is the ability to request that the interpreter execute commands on the host system.

   a. Describe a danger that this feature presents when the language interpreter is running with administrative or *root* privileges.

   b. Explain how the principle of least privilege could be used to ameliorate this danger.

2. A common technique for inhibiting password guessing is to disable an account after three consecutive failed login attempts.

   a. Discuss how this technique might prevent legitimate users from accessing the system. Why is this action a violation of the principle of least common mechanism?

   b. One can argue that this is an example of fail-safe defaults, because by blocking access to an account under attack, the system is defaulting to a known, safe state. Do you agree or disagree with this argument? Justify your answer.

3. Kernighan and Plauger [506] argue a minimalist philosophy of tool building. Their thesis is that each program should perform exactly one task, and more complex programs should be formed by combining simpler programs. Discuss how this philosophy fits in with the principle of

economy of mechanism. In particular, how does the advantage of the simplicity of each component of a software system offset the disadvantage of a multiplicity of interfaces among the various components?

4. Design an experiment to determine the performance impact of checking access permissions for each file *access* (as opposed to once at the file's opening). If you have access to a system on which you can modify the file access mechanism, run your experiment and determine the impact.

5. A company publishes the design of its security software product in a manual that accompanies the executable software.

   a. In what ways does this satisfy the principle of open design? In what ways does it not?
   b. Given that the design is known, what advantages does keeping the source code unavailable give the company and those who purchase the software? What disadvantages does it cause?

6. Assume that processes on a system share no resources. Is it possible for one process to block another process' access to a resource? Why or why not? From your answer, argue that denial of service attacks are possible or impossible.

7. Given that the Internet is a shared network, discuss whether preventing denial of service attacks is inherently possible or not possible. Do systems connected to the Internet violate the principle of least common mechanism?

8. A program called *lsu* [104] gives access to role accounts. The user's access rights are checked, and the user is required to enter her password. If access rules allow the change and the user's password is correct, *lsu* allows the change. Given that Mary uses *lsu* from her account, why does *lsu* require her to enter her password? Name the principles involved, and why they require this.

9. Recall the S/Key one-time password algorithm discussed in Section 12.3.2. When a user prints a list of S/Key passwords for future use, the system encodes each hash value as a set of six short words and prints them. Why does it not merely print out the hash values?

10. The program *su* enables a UNIX user to access another user's account. Unless the first user is the superuser, *su* requires that the password of the second user be given. A (possibly apocryphal) version of *su* would ask for the user's password and, if it could not determine if the password was correct because the password file could not be opened, *immediately* grant superuser access so that the user could fix the problem. Discuss which of the design principles this approach meets, and which ones it violates.

Chapter 13
Representing Identity

AEMELIA: Most mighty duke, behold a man much wrong'd.
All gather to see them.
ADRIANA: I see two husbands, or mine eyes deceive me!
DUKE SOLINUS: One of these men is Genius to the other;
And so of these, which is the natural man,
And which the spirit? Who deciphers them?
DROMIO OF SYRACUSE: I, sir, am Dromio: command him away.
DROMIO OF EPHESUS: I, sir, am Dromio: pray, let me stay.
—*The Comedy of Errors*, V, i, 332–338.

The theme of identity runs throughout humanity's experience, and computers are no exception. In computer science, an identity is the basis for assignment of privileges and is integral in the designation of a protection domain. This chapter discusses the many different types of identity and the contexts in which they arise. It begins with the identity of a principal on a system, first singly and then as defined by function. Designation of identity for certificates follows, as does identity on a network with respect to both individual processes and individual hosts. The chapter concludes with the notion of an anonymous user.

13.1 What Is Identity?

Identity is simply a computer's representation of an entity.

> **Definition 13–1.** A *principal* is a unique entity. An *identity* specifies a principal.

Authentication binds a principal to a representation of identity internal to the computer. Each system has its own way of expressing this representation, but all decisions of access and resource allocation assume that the binding is correct.

Identities are used for several purposes. The two main ones are for accountability and for access control. Accountability requires an identity that tracks principals across actions and changes of other identities, so that the principal taking any action can be unambiguously identified. Access control requires an identity that the access control mechanisms can use to determine if a specific access (or type of access) should be allowed.

Accountability is tied to logging and auditing. It requires an unambiguous identification of the principal involved. On many systems, this is not possible. Instead, the logged identity maps to a user account, to a group, or to a role.

Most systems base access rights on the identity of the principal executing the process. That is, all processes executed by user *bishop* have some set of rights. All processes executed by user *holly* have a set of rights that may differ from those that *bishop*'s processes have. However, a process may have fewer rights than the principal executing it, and in fact there are substantial reasons to reduce privileges. Chapter 14, "Access Control Mechanisms," discusses this topic in more depth.

13.2   Files and Objects

The identity of a file or other entity (here called an "object") depends on the system that contains the object.

Local systems identify objects by assigning names. The name may be intended for human use (such as a file name), for process use (such as a file descriptor or handle), or for kernel use (such as a file allocation table entry). Each name may have different semantics.

EXAMPLE: The UNIX operating system offers four different types of file names. The *inode* uniquely identifies a file. It contains file attribute information such as access control permissions and ownership information, and identifies the specific disk blocks that contain the file's data. Processes read files using a *file descriptor* that abstracts the inode into a representation that the process can read from, write to, and so forth. Once created, the file descriptor cannot be rebound to a different file. Processes (and users) can also use *file names* that identify files by describing their positions in the file hierarchy. UNIX file names may be *absolute path names* that describe the locations of files with respect to the root of the UNIX file hierarchy, or *relative path names* that describe the locations of files with respect to the directory in which the current process is executing.

The semantics of the names differ in important ways. Most critically, when a process or user operates on a file, the kernel maps the file name to an inode using an iterative procedure. It obtains the inode of the first directory in the path,[1] opens it,

---

[1] If the path is an absolute path name, the first directory in the path is the root directory, which has a well-known inode number (typically 0, 1, or 2). If the path is a relative path name, the first directory has the same inode number as the directory in which the process executes.

and within that directory locates the inode number of the next component in the path. This continues until the file's inode number is found. Two references to the same file name will reference different file objects when the file is deleted after the first reference and a new file, with the same name as the deleted file, is created. This can create problems with programs (see Section 26.5.3.3, "Race Conditions in File Accesses").

However, when a file descriptor is created, it refers to a specific object. Regardless of how the file is manipulated, the inode that the file descriptor refers to remains present until the file descriptor is closed, which breaks the association between the descriptor and the inode.

If the object resides on a different system, the name must encode the location of the object.

EXAMPLE: A *uniform resource locator* (URL) identifies an object by specifying its location and the protocol needed to access it. The object with the URL *ftp://abccorp.com/pub/README* specifies that the named object can be accessed by using the FTP protocol to request the object */pub/README* from the host *abccorp.com*. The URL does *not* say that the object is located on that host. Indeed, the host may construct the object to respond to the request, or it may forward the request to another host.

One file may have multiple names. The semantics of the system determine the effects of each name. For example, some systems define "deleting a file" to mean removing the given file name. The file object itself will not be deleted until all its names (or all names meeting certain conditions) have been deleted. Section 25.3.1.3, "File Deletion," discusses this issue further.

13.3 Users

In general, a *user* is an identity tied to a single entity. Specific systems may add additional constraints. Systems represent user identity in a number of different ways. Indeed, the same system may use different representations of identity in different contexts.

EXAMPLE: Versions of the UNIX operating system usually represent user identity as an integer between 0 and some large integer (usually 65,535). This integer is called the *user identification number*, or UID. Principals (called *users*) may also be assigned *login names*. Each login name corresponds to a single UID (although one UID may have many different login names).

When the kernel deals with user identity, it uses the UID; for example, the superuser is any user whose UID is 0 regardless of that user's name. However, when a user logs in, she provides her identity as her login name. Similarly, all logging uses the login name rather than the numeric UID.

The same principal may have many different identities. Typically each identity serves a particular function.

EXAMPLE: Versions of the UNIX operating system provide several types of user identities [608]. Because a user is a subject, and a process executes on behalf of a user, the various identities are associated with processes. The *real* UID is the user identity at initial login, but it can be changed. The *effective* UID is the user identity used for access control. For example, if only UID 22 can read a particular file, and a process' real UID is 22 and its effective UID is 35, the user will not be able to read the file. If the process' real UID were 35 and its effective UID were 22, access would be granted.

A special class of programs, called *setuid* programs [347], create processes with the effective UID being that of the owner of the program rather than that of the user executing the program. The resulting process has the access rights of the owner of the program rather than those of the user executing the program.

In an effort to limit the need for special privileges, many UNIX systems (such as Solaris and FreeBSD) provide a *saved* UID. Whenever the effective UID changes, the saved UID is set to the value of the effective UID *before* the change. The user can switch among the real, effective, and saved UIDs. This allows the process to be given *root privileges*, use them for a limited time (effective UID of 0), drop them (saved UID of 0, nonzero effective UID), and reacquire them later.

Traditionally, the real UID was used to track the original UID of the process. However, the superuser can change it. To provide an unalterable means of recording the original real UID of the process, many UNIX systems provide an *audit* or *login* UID. This UID is assigned at login and cannot be changed.[2]

13.4   Groups and Roles

The "entity" may be a set of entities referred to by a single identifier. The members of the set must be distinguishable, but the set may have an identity separate from any of its elements.

Principals often need to share access to files. Most systems allow principals to be grouped into sets called, logically enough, *groups*. Groups are essentially a shorthand tool for assigning rights to a set of principals simultaneously.

Two implementations of groups provide different abilities and therefore are based on different models. The first simply uses a group as an alias for a set of principals. Principals are assigned to groups, and they stay in those groups for the lifetimes of their sessions. The second model allows principals to change from one group to another. After each change, the rights belonging to the principal as a member of the previous group are discarded and the rights of the new group are added.

---

[2] Interestingly, some systems allow *root* to change the audit UID after assignment.

The difference lies in the representations of identity. In the former model, the identity assigned to a principal remains static; it is the principal identity and the set of identities of each group that the principal is a part of. This identity does not change throughout the lifetime of the session. In the latter model, the identity of the principal is the identity of the user and the set of identities of each group of which the principal is currently a member. It is dynamic, and should the principal change from one group to another, the identity of that principal also changes.

In practice, one discusses "user identity" and "group identity."

EXAMPLE: UNIX users are assigned membership to a group when they log in [608]. Each process has two identities, a "user identification" and a "group identification." On older UNIX systems, each principal can be in only one group at a time. The command *newgrp*(1) changes this identity. The principal can change to any group of which he is a member. On other UNIX systems, each principal can be in several groups at a time. On login, the user is placed into all groups of which he is a member.

A *role* is a type of group that ties membership to function. When a principal assumes a role, the principal is given certain rights that belong to that role. When the principal leaves the role, those rights are removed. The rights given are consistent with the functionality that the principal needs to perform the tasks expected of members of the role.

EXAMPLE: On the DG/UX system, system administration privileges belong to the *sysadmin* role, not the *root* user [230]. That user's rights are restricted. The *sysuser* user can assume the *sysadmin* role to administer the host, or the *netadmin* role to administer the network. Several such roles are defined.

13.5   Naming and Certificates

Chapter 9 described certificates as a mechanism for binding cryptographic keys to identifiers. The identifier corresponds to a principal. The identifier must uniquely identify the principal to avoid confusion.

Suppose the principals are people. The identifiers cannot be names, because many different people may have the same name. (How many people named "John Smith" or "Pierre LeBlanc" are there?) The identifiers must include ancillary information to distinguish the "Matt Bishop" who teaches at UC Davis from the "Matt Bishop" who works at Microsoft Corporation.

EXAMPLE: The X.509v3 certificates use identifiers called *Distinguished Names*. A Distinguished Name identifies a principal. It consists of a series of fields, each with a *key* and a *value*. When written as strings, the fields are separated by "/" and the key and value by "=".[3] To use our earlier example, the "Matt Bishop" who teaches at the University of California might have the Distinguished Name

```
/O=University of California/OU=Davis campus/OU=Department
of Computer Science/CN=Matt Bishop/
```

(where the key "O" means organization, "OU" means organizational unit, and "CN" means common name) and the "Matt Bishop" who works at Microsoft might have the Distinguished Name

```
/O=Microsoft Corporation/OU=Quality Assurance/CN=Matt
Bishop/
```

Although the names are the same, the individuals, and hence the Distinguished Names, are different.

Certification authorities (CAs) vouch, at some level, for the identity of the principal to which the certificate is issued. Every CA has two policies controlling how it issues certificates.

Definition 13–2. A *CA authentication policy* describes the level of authentication required to identify the principal to whom the certificate is to be issued.

Definition 13–3. A *CA issuance policy* describes the principals to whom the CA will issue certificates.

The difference between these two policies is that the first simply establishes the level of proof of identity needed for the CA to accept the principal's claim of identity whereas the second answers the question, "Given the identity of the principal, will the CA issue a certificate?"

EXAMPLE: In 1996, Verisign Corporation ran several CAs. Each had its own policies of issuance and authentication for certificates [348].

Individuals obtained certificates (called "Digital IDs") from one of three CAs.[4] The class 1 CA authenticated the individual's electronic mail address. This CA provided a certificate for sending and receiving electronic mail securely. The class 2 CA required that the individual supply his real name and address, which was verified through an online database. This CA provided a certificate suitable for online purchasing and was (roughly) equivalent to the level of authentication for a credit card. The class 3 CA required a background check from an investigative service. The certificate

---

[3] When compiled into a binary format, in many cases the key is implied by the data structure.

[4] Actually, a single CA issues multiple types of certificates. Conceptually, the single organization is acting as though it were multiple CAs.

from this CA provided a higher level of assurance of identity than the other two certificates. All three CAs had the same issuance policy: that certificates were issued to individuals. A fourth CA provided certificates to Web servers. This CA had the same issuance policy as the class 3 CA. Consumers who did business with the Web site had a high degree of assurance that the Web site was whom it claimed to be.

CAs can issue certificates to other organizations. The certificate-based key management architecture for the Internet [504] demonstrates how such an organization can lead to a simple hierarchical structure of policies.

EXAMPLE: The infrastructure organizes CAs into a hierarchical, tree-based structure. Each node in the tree corresponds to a CA. Consider a node that is the root of a subtree. The CAs under that root are constrained by the policies of that root; the subordinate nodes may issue certificates with more restrictive policies, but not with more liberal policies.

The root of the tree is the *Internet Policy Registration Authority* (IPRA). It sets policies that all subordinate CAs must follow, and it certifies other CAs called *policy certification authorities* (PCAs). Each PCA has its own issuance and authentication policies, but those policies must not conflict with the policies set by the IPRA. The PCAs issue certificates to ordinary CAs, which can then issue certificates to organizations or individuals. The IPRA and PCAs do not issue certificates to individuals or organizations. All CAs, PCAs, and the IPRA have unique Distinguished Names.

The elegance of this approach is twofold. Because all PCA policies are public, on receiving a certificate one can determine how much trust to place in the identity in the certificate (authentication policy) as well as the requirements that the holder had to meet to have the certificate issued (issuance policy).

To understand how this works, suppose the University of Valmont wished to establish a CA for both students and staff. The requirements for certification for these groups are different. Students must present valid registration cards to obtain certificates. These certificates would be considered low-assurance certificates (because of the nature of the registration process) and so would be signed using the university's low-assurance certificate. This certificate, in turn, is signed by a PCA that requires its subordinate CAs to make a good-faith effort to verify the identities of those to whom it issues certificates. But the university requires staff members to present proof of employment and fingerprints, which are compared with the fingerprints obtained when each employee was hired. This provides a high level of assurance of identity, and so the University of Valmont signs these certificates with its high-assurance certificate, obtained from a different PCA that requires the use of biometrics for verification of identity.

The certificates for student John and professor Marsha are both signed by the same organization, but they are signed using different cryptographic keys. John's certificate is signed by the key corresponding to a low-assurance certificate (because the first PCA signed it), and Marsha's certificate is signed by the key corresponding to a high-assurance certificate (because the second PCA signed it). By checking the policies of each of the PCAs, and (possibly) the CA, the recipient of one of these certificates can tell what the policies of issuance and assurance are. (A potential conflict arises because the CA has the same Distinguished Name for two different types of policies.)

As another example of how the certificates encode policy, note that Marsha's certificate implicitly identifies her as being affiliated with the University of Valmont. This type of certificate is called an *organizational certificate*. The Internet infrastructure defines a second type of certificate, a *residential certificate*, that identifies the principal's residential address. Marsha has one of these, issued by the post office, and identifying her as a citizen residing in the city of Valmont.

```
/C=US/SP=Louisiana/L=Valmont/PA=27 Russell Blvd./
CN=Marsha/
```

(Here, "C" is the country code, "SP" is the province or state name, "L" is the locality (city, town, or village), and "PA" is the street address.

The principals need not be people or organizations; they can be roles.

EXAMPLE: A company wishes to have its comptroller authorized to digitally sign documents. To this end, it issues a certificate to the role.

```
/O=Hodgepodge Corporation/OU=Office of Big Money/
RN=Comptroller/
```

Even if the current comptroller leaves and a new one is hired, the same certificate can be used. Here, "Comptroller" is a role (and the use of the "RN" key, for "Role Name," reflects this).

The identifiers in a certificate need not be formal Distinguished Names. The certificates used with PGP, for example, allow the subject to select any identifier he or she wishes. The convention is to use an electronic mail address, but this permits a high level of ambiguity, especially when mail addresses change frequently. This leads directly to conflicts; how can a CA ensure that the certificate it issues does not conflict with another?

13.5.1   The Meaning of the Identity

The authentication policy defines the way in which principals prove their identities. Each CA has its own requirements (although they may be constrained by contractual requirements, such as with PCAs). All rely on nonelectronic proofs of identity, such as biometrics (fingerprints), documents (driver's license, passports), or personal knowledge. If any of these means can be compromised, the CA may issue the certificate in good faith to the wrong person.

This hearkens back to the issue of trust. Ignoring the trust required for cryptography to work, the certificate is the binding of an *external* identity to a cryptographic key and a Distinguished Name. If the issuer can be fooled, all who rely on that certificate may also be fooled.

With the erosion of privacy in many societies comes the need for anonymity. This conflicts with the notion of a certificate binding an identity to a Distinguished Name and a public key. The conflict arises when the anonymous principal needs to send a set of integrity-checked, confidential electronic messages to a recipient and to ensure that the recipient realizes that all of the messages have come from the same source (but the recipient cannot know what the source is).

EXAMPLE: A government plans to require all citizens with a specific gene to register, because anecdotal evidence suggests that people with that gene commit crimes slightly more often than other people. The government plans to make the law without publicity, because aside from the civil liberties issues, there is no reputable scientific evidence to back up the belief. A government employee decides to alert the media. She realizes that the government will promptly deny the plan and change its approach to getting the law passed. She feels that she will be fired (or charged with a crime) if the government determines who she is, and would therefore be unable to reveal any changes in the plan. So she decides to publicize the plans anonymously.

Anonymous, or *persona*, certificates supply the requisite anonymity. A CA issues a *persona* certificate under a policy that makes the Distinguished Name of the principal meaningless. For example, a *persona* certificate with a principal Distinguished Name of

```
/C=US/O=Microsoft Corp./CN=John Smith/
```

does not imply that the certificate was issued to someone named John Smith. PGP certificates can have any name to identify the principal, and can innately provide anonymity in this sense.

EXAMPLE: Continuing, our heroine obtains a *persona* certificate and sends a copy of the government's plan to the media, using electronic mail, as described above. The government denies the plan and secretly changes its strategy. It has some employees leak verifiably false information so that if the original whistleblower sends another message, it is less likely to be believed. But she does, and she uses the same certificate to authenticate the message. Now the media can check that the two messages came from the same source (or at least were signed with the same certificate), whereas the false messages were signed by different certificates.

13.5.2   Trust

The goal of certificates is to bind the correct identity to the public key. When a user obtains a certificate, the issuer of that certificate is vouching, to some degree of certainty, that the identity corresponds to the principal owning the public key. The critical question is the degree of that assurance.

X.509v3, and the PEM certification hierarchy, define the degree of certainty in the policy of the CA that issues the certificate. If a CA requires a passport as identification, then the degree of certainty is high; if it requires an unsworn statement of identity, the degree of certainty is low. But even high-assurance CAs can be fooled. In the case of the passport, passports can be stolen or forged. So the level of trust in an identity is not quantifiable. Rather, it is an estimate based on the policy of the CA, the rigor with which that policy is followed, and the assumptions that the policy makes.

EXAMPLE: Consider the CA that requires a passport to issue a certificate. The certificate will have as its DN the name in the passport, the name of the country issuing the passport, and the passport number. There are several points of trust in this policy. First, the CA assumes that the passport is not forged and that the name has not been altered. Second, the CA assumes that the country issuing the passport issued it to the person named in the passport. Third, the CA assumes that the individual presenting the passport is the individual to whom the passport was issued.[5] Fourth, the users of the certificate assume that the CA has actually checked the passport and the individual using the passport to obtain a certificate.

PGP certificates include a series of signature fields (see Section 9.3.1.2), each of which contains a level of trust.[6] The OpenPGP specification defines four levels [150].

1. Generic certification of a user name and a public key; this makes no assertions.
2. Persona certification of a user name and a public key; the signer has done no verification that the user name correctly identifies the principal.
3. Casual certification of a user name and a public key; the signer has done some verification that the user name correctly identifies the principal.
4. Positive certification of a user name and a public key; the signer has done substantial verification that the user name correctly identifies the principal.

Even here, though, the trust is not quantifiable. What exactly do "some verification" and "substantial verification" mean? The OpenPGP specification does not

---

[5] Passport photographs are notoriously poor, making visual identification questionable unless conditions are optimal.

[6] This is encoded in the signature type field of the signature.

define them, preferring to leave their definitions to the signer, but the same terms can imply different levels of assurance to different signers.

EXAMPLE: At a university, "substantial verification" may mean having a student identification card and a matching driver's license. The university's CA would sign the student's PGP certificate with level 4 trust. But at a high-security government installation that requires background checks before certificates are signed, the university's "substantial verification" would most likely be considered level 2 trust, "no verification."

The point is that knowing the policy, or the trust level with which the certificate is signed, is not enough to evaluate how likely it is that the identity identifies the correct principal. Other knowledge, about how the CA or signer interprets the policy and enforces its requirements, is needed.

EXAMPLE: On March 22, 2001, Verisign, Inc. and Microsoft Corporation [203] reported that Verisign had issued two certificates to someone claiming to be a representative of Microsoft Corporation. The individual was not. Both companies took steps to cancel the certificates and prevent them from being used.

13.6   Identity on the Web

Certificates are not ubiquitous on the Internet. Several other means attach identity to information, even though the binding may be very transient.

The Internet requires every host to have an address. The address may be fixed or may change, and without cryptography the binding is weak. Many servers send information about the state of the client's interaction, so that when the client reconnects, the server can resume the transaction or glean information about previous transactions.

13.6.1   Host Identity

Host identity is intimately bound to networking. A host not connected to *any* network can have any name, because the name is used only locally. A host connected to a network can have many names or one name, depending on how the interface to the network is structured and the context in which the name is used.

The ISO/OSI model [894] provides a context for the issue of naming. Recall that the ISO/OSI model is composed of a series of layers (see Figure 10–2). Each host, conceptually, has a principal at each layer that communicates with a peer on other hosts. These principals communicate with principals at the same layer on other hosts. Each principal on an individual host can have different names (also called "addresses") at each layer. All names identify the same host, but each one refers to a particular context in which the host functions.

EXAMPLE: A computer has an Ethernet (media access control layer, or MAC) address of 00:05:02:6B:A8:21, an IP address of 192.168.35.89, and a host name of *cherry.orchard.net*. At the data link level, the system is known by its Ethernet address. At the network level, it is known by its IP address. At the application level, it is known by its host name. The system is also on an AppleTalk network, with an AppleTalk address of network 51, node 235. Other systems on the AppleTalk network identify the host by that name.

Shoch [825] suggests that a "name" identifies a principal and an "address" identifies where that principal is located. In the context of host identification, the "address" indicates where on a network (and, sometimes, the specific network) the host is located. A "name" indicates in what domain the host resides, and corresponds to a particular address. Although Shoch's terminology is instructive in many contexts, in this context a location identifies a principal just as well as a name. We do not distinguish between the two in the context of identification.

If an attacker is able to spoof the identity of another host, all protocols that rely on that identity are relying on a faulty premise and are therefore being spoofed. When a host has a sequence of names, each relying on the preceding name, then an attacker spoofing the first identity can compromise all the other identities. For example, the host identity is based on the IP identity. Similarly, the IP identity is based on the Ethernet identity. If an attacker can alter entries in databases containing the mapping of a lower-level identity to a higher-level identity, the attacker can spoof one host by routing traffic to another.

13.6.1.1   Static and Dynamic Identifiers

An identifier can be either static or dynamic. A static identifier does not change over time; a dynamic identifier changes either as a result of an event (such as a connection to a network) or over time.

Databases contain mappings between different names. The best known of these is the Domain Name Service (DNS) [643, 644], which associates host names and IP addresses. In the absence of cryptographic authentication of hosts, the consistency of the DNS is used to provide weak authentication.

EXAMPLE: The DNS contains *forward* records, which map host names into IP addresses, and *reverse* records, which map IP addresses into names. A reverse domain lookup occurs when a process extracts the IP address of its remote peer, determines the associated host name (perhaps using the DNS), and then obtains the set of IP addresses associated with that host name (again, possibly using the DNS). If the IP address obtained from the peer matches any of the IP addresses associated with that host name, then the host name is accepted as the one obtained in the first lookup. Otherwise, the host name is rejected as untrusted.

The belief in the trustworthiness of the host name in this case relies on the integrity of the DNS database. Section 13.6.1.2, "Security Issues with the Domain Name Service," examines this issue.

Floating identifiers are assigned to principals for a limited time. Typically, a server maintains a pool of identifiers. A client contacts the server using an identifier agreed on between the two (the *local identifier*). The server transmits an identifier that the client can use in other contexts (the *global identifier*) and notifies any intermediate hosts (such as gateways) of the association between the local and global identifiers.

EXAMPLE: The Bootless University provides a network to which students can hook up laptops. Rather than assign each student laptop an IP address, the university has created a DHCP server [14] for this network. When a student connects her laptop to the network, the laptop transmits its MAC (media access control) address to the server. The server responds with an unused IP address belonging to the network. The laptop accepts that IP address and uses it to communicate on the Internet.

A gateway can translate between a local address and a global address.

EXAMPLE: The Zerbche company has 500 computers on a local area network, but only 256 Internet addresses. The internal network assigns as (fixed) local addresses the IP addresses 10.1.*x*.*y*, where *x* and *y* reflect internal configuration details not relevant here. A gateway connects the internal network to the Internet.

When a user at (say) host 10.1.3.241 wants to access the Internet, it forwards its packets to the gateway. The gateway assigns a legitimate IP address to the internal, local address; say that IP address is 101.43.21.241. The gateway then rewrites the source address of each packet, changing 10.1.3.241 to 101.43.21.241, and puts the packets out on the Internet. When the gateway receives packets destined for host 101.43.21.241, it checks its internal table, rewrites those addresses as 10.1.3.241, and forwards them to the internal network, and the packets go to their destination. This translation is invisible to either end of the communication, and enables up to some number of hosts on the internal network to communicate with hosts on the Internet. The Network Address protocol (NAT) [864] is used on the Internet to perform this function.

In the absence of cryptography, authentication using dynamic naming is different from authentication using static naming. The primary problem is that the association of the identity with a principal varies over time, so any authentication based on the name must also account for the time. For example, if the DNS record entries corresponding to the dynamic name are not updated whenever the name is reassigned, the reverse domain lookup method of authentication fails.[7]

---

[7] This failure does not necessarily mean that the DNS has been compromised. Some systems store the forward and reverse lookup information in separate files. Updating the forward lookup information file does not change the reverse lookup information file. Unless the latter is updated also, the stated problem occurs.

The contrast between static and dynamic naming in authentication is worth noting in light of the different properties described in Chapter 11, "Authentication." The reverse domain lookup technique of authentication corresponds to checking a property of a principal (what it is) with static naming, because the name is bound permanently to the principal. But that technique corresponds to checking a possession of a principal (what it has) with dynamic naming, because the principal will relinquish that name at some point.

13.6.1.2   Security Issues with the Domain Name Service

Understanding the centrality of trust in the databases that record associations of identity with principals is critical to understanding the accuracy of the identity. The DNS provides an example of this. The belief in the trustworthiness of the host name in this case relies on the integrity of the DNS database. If the association between a host name and an IP address can be corrupted, the identifier in question will be associated with the wrong host.

Bellovin [69] and Schuba [800] discuss several attacks on the DNS. The goal of these attacks is to cause a victim to associate incorrectly a particular IP address with a host name. They assume the attacker is able to control the responses from an authoritative domain name server. "Control" means that the attacker has control over the name server or can intercept queries to that server and return its own responses.

The attacker can change the records associating the IP address with the host name, so that a query for one returns an incorrect answer for the other. A second technique, known as "cache poisoning," relies on the ability of a server to add extra DNS records to the answer to a query. In this case, the extra records added give incorrect association information. Schuba uses this to demonstrate how the reverse name lookup can be compromised. The attacker connects to the victim. The victim queries the DNS for the host name associated with the IP address. The attacker ensures that two records are returned: a record with the bogus host name associated with the IP address, and the reverse record. The DNS protocol allows this piggybacking to enable the client to cache records. The cache is checked before any records are requested from the server, so this may save a network request. The third technique ("ask me") is similar: the attacker prepares a request that the victim must resolve by querying the attacker. When the victim queries the attacker, the attacker returns the answer, along with two records for the mapping that he is trying to spoof (one for the forward mapping, one for the reverse).

Judicious use of cryptographically based techniques coupled with careful administration of DNS servers can effectively limit the ability of attackers to use these attacks. Supporting infrastructure is under design and development (for example, see [284, 285, 286, 287, 288]).

13.6.2   State and Cookies

Many Internet applications require that the client or server maintain state to simplify the transaction process [534].

> **Definition 13–4.** A *cookie* is a token that contains information about the state of a transaction on a network.

Although the transaction can be any client-server interaction, the term "cookie" is most widely used in reference to interactions between Web browsers and clients. These cookies minimize the storage requirements of the servers and put the burden of maintaining required information on the client. The cookies consist of several values.

1. The *name* and *value* are encoded into the cookie and represent the state. The interpretation is that the *name* has an associated *value*.

2. The *expires* field indicates when the cookie is valid. Expired cookies are discarded; they are not to be given out. If this field is not present, the cookie will be deleted at the end of the session.

3. The *domain* states the domain for which the cookie is intended. It consists of the last *n* fields of the domain name of a server. The cookie will be sent to servers in that domain. For example, `domain=.adv.com` specifies that the cookie is to be sent to any requesting server in the *adv.com* domain. A domain field must have at least one embedded "." in it; this prevents a server from sending over a cookie ending in ".com" and then requesting all cookies for the domain ".com."
   There is no requirement that a cookie be sent from a host in the domain. This can be used to track certain types of accesses, as discussed below.

4. The *path* further restricts the dissemination of the cookie. When a Web server requests a cookie, it provides a domain (its own). Cookies that match that domain may be sent to the server. If the server specifies a path, the path must be the leading substring of the path specified in the cookie.

5. If the *secure* field is set, the cookie will be sent only over secured connections (that is, to "https" or "http" over SSL).

EXAMPLE: Caroline logs in to a Web server, *www.books.com*, used to sell books. She selects two books to buy and adds them to her "shopping cart." The Web server sends her a cookie with key "bought" and value "BK=234&BK=8763." The domain for the cookie is ".books.com." The expiration field is omitted. When Caroline goes to the page to pay for the books, the server asks for the cookie "bought" belonging to the domain ".books.com." From the value of the cookie, the server sees that Caroline wants to buy books numbered 234 and 8763. Had Caroline terminated the session (by exiting her browser, for example), the cookie would be deleted and no record would exist of the books she thought about purchasing.

The restriction of sending cookies to hosts in the cookie's domain prevents one Web server from requesting cookies sent by a second Web server. However, a Web server can send cookies marked for the domain of a second server. When the user accesses the second Web server, that server can request the cookies marked for its domain but sent by the first server.

EXAMPLE: When Caroline accesses the Web server to buy books, that server sends her a cookie with key "id," value "books.com," and domain "adv.com." Several advertisements at the *www.books.com* Web site take Caroline to the server *www.adv.com*. When Caroline follows one of those links to that server, the server requests her cookies for that domain. Caroline's browser sends the cookie. From this, *www.adv.com* can determine the Web site from which Caroline obtained the cookie.

Caroline need not even follow the advertisement. Most such advertisements are images, and the *www.books.com* server does not have those images online. Instead, the Web page contains a pointer to some other server, such as *www.adv.com*. When Caroline's browser pulls the *www.books.com* Web page over, it contains an instruction for her browser to contact *www.adv.com* to get the advertising image. At that connection, *www.adv.com* can request the cookie that *www.books.com* had sent over.

Cookies can contain authentication information, both user-related and host-related. Using cookies for authentication treats them as tokens supplied by the browser to validate (or state and validate) an identity. Depending on the sensitivity of the interactions with the server, protecting the confidentiality of these cookies may be critical. Exercise 1 explores this topic in more detail.

13.6.3   Anonymity on the Web

Identification on the Internet arises from associating a particular host with a connection or message. The recipient can determine the origin from the incoming packet. If only one person is using the originating host, and the address is not spoofed, someone could guess the identity of the sender with a high degree of accuracy.

An anonymizer is a site that hides the origins of connections. It functions as a *proxy server*—that is, it operates on behalf of another entity. A user connects to the anonymizer and tells it the destination. The anonymizer makes the connection, so the destination host sees only the anonymizer. The anonymizer forwards traffic in both directions.

The destination believes it is communicating with the anonymizer because all traffic will have the anonymizer's address in it. However, the anonymizer is merely a go-between and merely passes information between the destination and the origin.

Anonymizers work primarily on electronic mail and http traffic, although the same principles apply to any type of network messages. In what follows, we focus on electronic mail, because electronic mail anonymizers are conceptually simple and demonstrate the techniques used and the privacy issues that arise. The story of the Finnish anonymizer *anon.penet.fi* is worth recounting, because it was the first widely used anonymizer. Its demise points out the problems in both using and running anonymizers.

EXAMPLE: The host *anon.penet.fi* offered an anonymous electronic mail service. One would send a letter to it, naming another destination (either an individual or a USENET news group). The anonymizer would strip off the headers, assign an anonymous ID (*anon374*, for example) to the letter, and record the sender and the associated anonymous ID in a database. The letter would then be delivered to its destination, as though user *anon374* at *anon.penet.fi* had sent it. The recipients could not tell the original sender from the letter. They would reply to the letter by sending the reply to *anon374* at *anon.penet.fi*. This letter would be anonymized in the same way the original letter was anonymized, and would then be forwarded to the real electronic mail address corresponding to *anon374*.

This exchange is not truly anonymous. Even though the end parties do not know who each other are, the anonymizer knows who both are.

Definition 13–5. A *pseudo-anonymous* (or *pseudonymous*) *remailer* is a remailer that replaces the originating electronic mail addresses (and associated data) of messages it receives before it forwards them, but keeps mappings of the anonymous identities and the associated origins.

The problem is that the binding between the anonymous address and the real address is known somewhere. If that point can be made to reveal the association, anonymity ceases to exist.

EXAMPLE: The association between the anonymous ID and the electronic mail address of the sender was *anon.penet.fi*'s undoing [418]. Some material, claimed to be copyrighted, was circulated through the site. A Finnish court directed the owner of the site to reveal the database so the plaintiffs could determine the electronic mail address of the sender, thereby ending the anonymity. Although the owner appealed the order, he subsequently shut down the site.

The association can be obscured by using a sequence of pseudo-anonymous remailers. Tracing the origin then requires the trackers to obtain information from several sites. But the chain must exist if replies are to be sent back to the original sender. Eliminating that requirement allows true anonymity.

Definition 13–6. [300] A *Cypherpunk* (or *type 1*) *remailer* is a remailer that deletes the header of an incoming message and forwards the remainder to its destination.

Unlike a pseudo-anonymous remailer, no record of the association between the originating address and the remailer address is kept. Thus, one cannot trace the message by mapping the remailer's user name to an electronic mail address.

Cypherpunk remailers are typically used in a chain, and messages sent through them are always enciphered [382]. Figure 13–1 shows how this works. Bob composes a message to Alice and then uses PGP to encipher it twice. The first encipherment is for the destination "remailer 2." The resulting message is then enciphered for delivery to remailer 1. Bob then mails the message to remailer 1. It deciphers the message, sees that it is to be sent to remailer 2, and forwards it. Remailer 2 receives the message, deciphers it, and forwards the message to Alice. Because there is no record of who sent the message to remailer 1, it cannot be tied back to Bob's electronic mail address. Because remailer 2 received the message from remailer 1, it cannot

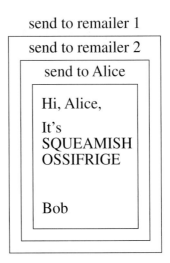

send to remailer 1

send to remailer 2

send to Alice

Hi, Alice,

It's
SQUEAMISH
OSSIFRIGE

Bob

Figure 13–1   A message sent to a Cypherpunk remailer. Remailer 1 forwards the message to remailer 2, and remailer 2 sends it to Alice.

associate any real electronic mail address with the destination address (Alice). This illustrates the reason for using chains of Cypherpunk remailers. Were only one remailer used, it could associate the real sender with the real recipients. Although two remailers, or any number of remailers, could cooperate to do the same thing, in practice such cooperation is very difficult to achieve. Again, the issue of trust in the remailers is central to the success of Cypherpunk remailers.

But there is still a weakness. Suppose an attacker could monitor all traffic between the source and the destination but the remailers themselves remained uncompromised. Then the attacker could view traffic into and out of a remailer but could not see the association of incoming traffic with outgoing traffic. The goal of the attacker would be to reconstruct this association [213, 382].

Obviously, reconstructing this association from cleartext messages is simple: just compare the bodies of incoming messages with those of outgoing messages. The envelope for the current remailer will be deleted; otherwise, the bodies will be the same. This is the reason to encipher all messages going through a Cypherpunk remailer. In the following discussion, we assume that all such messages are enciphered. The attacks all involve traffic analysis.

If a remailer immediately forwards a message after receiving it, and before any other message arrives (or if processing is guaranteed to occur in order of arrival), then the attacker can determine the association. One approach to obscuring this is to hold messages for random intervals of time; however, unless the interval is greater than the average interarrival time, the delay does not help. (Some remailers allow the sender to specify the length of the interval.)

A second approach is to randomize the order of processing of the incoming messages; implicit in this approach is a delay to allow such reordering. Cypherpunk remailers that do this keep a pool of incoming messages. No messages are sent out until the pool contains a fixed number, call it n, of messages. When the nth message arrives, one of the messages in the pool is selected and sent. This protects the associations against passive attacks. However, an active attacker can send enough messages to the remailer so that all $n - 1$ messages in the pool are sent. (See Exercise 2.)

A third approach deals with message size. As a message moves through its chain of remailers, each remailer strips off an outside envelope. Thus, the size of the message decreases. The attacker can use this by recording the sizes of messages entering and leaving the remailer. No outbound message can be associated with an inbound message of lesser or equal size. Furthermore, the size of the envelope can be estimated well enough to estimate how much the message would shrink by, thus eliminating more possible associations. To limit this threat, some remailers allow users to append junk to the message and instruct the remailer to delete it. Again, this reduces message size; it does not increase it.

The final attack is also active. The attacker replays the messages many times to the first remailer, which forwards them. The attacker monitors the outbound traffic and looks for a bump in the amount of traffic from the remailer corresponding to the messages sent into the remailer. This associates the outbound path with the inbound path. To prevent this attack, remailers cannot forward the same message more than once.

A second type of remailer, based on ideas from Chaum's paper [164] (which uses the term "mix" to describe the obscuring of information), does not suffer from these problems.

Definition 13–7. [212] A *Mixmaster* (or *type 2*) *remailer* is a Cypherpunk remailer that handles only enciphered messages and that pads or fragments messages to a fixed size before sending them.

This hinders the attacks described above. The contents of the incoming and outgoing messages cannot be matched, because everything is enciphered. Traffic analysis based on size is not possible, because all messages (incoming and outgoing) are of the same size. All messages are uniquely numbered, so replay attacks are not possible. Message fragments are not reassembled until the message reaches the last remailer in the chain, so reordering attacks are more difficult. Figure 13–2 shows what a Mixmaster message looks like. Special software is used to construct the messages, whereas Cypherpunk remailers can accept messages constructed by hand.

In practice, messages sent through Mixmaster remailers are untraceable unless the remailers themselves are compromised. In that case, one could track packet and message IDs and make associations as desired. The point is that anonymity assumes that the remailers can be trusted not to disclose associations. The Mixmaster technique minimizes the threat of compromised remailers, because all remailers must track origin, packet, and message IDs, and the final remailer must also track destination address, packet, and message IDs for the sender to be associated with a received

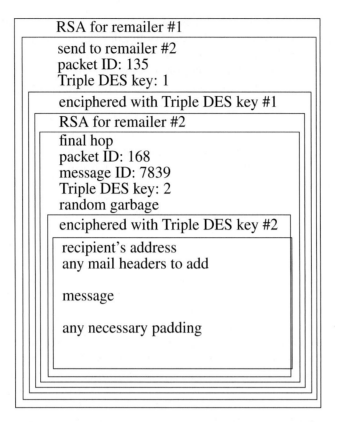

Figure 13–2   A Mixmaster message. This is a fragment of a multipart message sent through two remailers. Messages are enciphered using both RSA and Triple DES, and random garbage is added as well as padding. The recipient's address is visible only to the last remailer.

message. This technique is not foolproof; if only one message is sent over the network, an attacker can easily determine the sender and receiver, for example. But it substantially adds to the difficulty of matching an anonymous letter to a sender.

The Mixmaster remailer BABEL [382] adds the ability to reply without knowing the identity of, or even the actual e-mail address of, the sender (see Exercise 3).

13.6.3.1   Anonymity for Better or Worse

Anonymity provides a shield to protect people from having to associate their identities with some data. Is this desirable?

The easiest way to answer this is to ask what the purpose of anonymity is. Anonymity is power, because it allows one to make statements without fear of reprisals. One can even deny having made the statements when questioned, and with true anonymity, the denial cannot be disproved.

Anonymity allows one to shape the course of debate by implication. Alexander Hamilton, James Madison, and John Jay deliberately used the name "Publius" to hide their authorship of the Federalist Papers. Aside from hiding the authors' identity, the "Publius" pseudonym was chosen because the Roman Publius was seen as a model governor. The pseudonym implied that the authors stood for responsible political philosophy and legislation [392]. The discussion of the Federalist Papers focused on their content, not on the personalities of their authors.

Anonymity allows whistleblowers considerable protection. Those who criticize the powerholders often fall into disfavor, even when their criticism is valid, and the powerholders take action. Galileo promulgated the theory that the earth circles the sun and was brought before the Inquisition [415]. Ernest Fitzgerald exposed cost overruns on the U.S. Air Force C-54 airplane and was removed from his position. After several court victories, he was reinstated [147]. Contrast this with the anonymous sources that spoke with Bernstein and Woodward during the Watergate scandal. The reporters combined those anonymous sources (especially one called "Deep Throat") with public records to uncover a pattern of activity that ultimately led to impeachment charges against President Richard Nixon, his resignation, and criminal indictments and convictions of many government officials. No action could be taken against the sources, because their identities were unknown (and, as of this writing, the identity of "Deep Throat" has not been revealed) [80, 81].

Whether these are benefits or drawbacks depends on whether one is the powerholder under attack or the person attacking the powerholder. In many societies, questioning of authority is considered desirable and beneficial to the society, and in such cases the need for anonymity outweighs the problems, especially when the powerholders will strike back at the critics. In other societies, those who hold power are considered to be more experienced and knowledgeable and are trusted to act in the best interests of the society. In those societies, anonymous criticism would be considered destabilizing and inimical to the best interests of the social order. The reader must decide how anonymity affects the society of which he or she is a part.

Just as anonymity is a tool with which powerholders can be attacked, the powerholders can use it to attack those they consider to be adversaries. Franz Kafka's book *The Trial* [480], which describes a trial in which the accused does not know the (anonymous) judges, is considered a masterpiece of existential literature. However, as dissidents in many countries have found, anonymous judges are not always fictional. In the United States during the period when Martin Dies and Joseph McCarthy held sway, anonymous accusers cost many people their livelihoods, and in some cases their lives (see, for example, Donner [278] and Nizer [693]).

Anonymity also protects privacy. From this perspective, as we move through a society, parts of that society gather information about us. Grocery stores can record what we purchase, bookstores can record what books we buy, and libraries can record what books we read. Individually, each datum seems unimportant, but when the data is correlated, the conclusions that can be drawn are frighteningly complete. Credit bureaus do this to a degree already, by obtaining information from a variety of credit sources and amalgamating them into a single credit report that includes income, loans, and revolving credit accounts such as credit cards.

This poses three risks to individuals. First, incorrect conclusions can come from data interpreted incorrectly. For example, suppose one visits Web sites looking for information on a proscribed narcotic. One conclusion is that the individual is looking for information on making or obtaining such a drug for illicit purposes, but this conclusion could be wrong. The individual could be a high school student assigned to write a report on dangerous drugs. The individual could be a doctor seeking information on the effects of the use of the drug, for treating a patient. Or the individual could simply be curious. There is insufficient information to draw any of these conclusions.

Second, erroneous information can cause great harm. The best examples of this are the increasingly common cases of "identity theft," in which one person impersonates another, using a faked driver's license, Social Security card, or passport to obtain credit in another's name [244]. The credit reporting agencies will amalgamate the information under the real person's records, and when the thief defaults, the victim will have to clear himself.

Third, the right to privacy inherent in many societies includes what Warren and Brandeis called the "right to be let alone—the most comprehensive of rights and the right most valued by civilized men" [931]. Anonymity serves as a shield behind which one can go about one's business and be let alone. No central, or distributed, authority can tie information obtained about an anonymous entity back to an individual. Without the right to anonymity, protecting one's privacy becomes problematic. Stalkers can locate people and harrass them; indeed, in one case a stalker murdered an actress [46]. On the Web, one may have to accept cookies that can be used to construct a profile of the visitor. Organizations that use cookies for this purpose generally adopt an "opt-out" approach, in which a user must request that no information be gathered, rather than an "opt-in" approach, in which a user must expressly give permission for the information to be gathered. If the user is anonymous, no meaningful profile can be constructed. Furthermore, the information gathered cannot be matched with information in credit records and other data banks. The ability to prevent others from gathering information about you without your consent is an example of the right to privacy.

Anonymity for personal protection has its disadvantages, too. Jeremy Bentham's panopticon introduced the notion of perpetual and complete monitoring to prevent crime and protect citizens. The idea that governments should be able to detect crimes as they happen and intervene, or establish that a crime has been committed and act to apprehend the perpetrators, is attractive because of the sense of security it gives citizens. But many, including the Founding Fathers of the United States, regarded this as too high a price to be paid. As Benjamin Franklin wrote, "They that can give up essential liberty to obtain a little temporary safety deserve neither liberty nor safety" [58].

Perhaps the only conclusion one can draw is that, like all freedoms and all powers, anonymity can be used for good or for evil. The right to remain anonymous entails a responsibility to use that right wisely.

13.7   Summary

Every access control mechanism is based on an identity of some sort. An identity may have many different representations (for example, as an integer and as a string). A principal may have many different identities. One certificate may identify the principal by its role, another by its job, and a third by its address. A host on the Internet has multiple addresses, each of which is an identity.

Identities are bound to principals, and the strength and accuracy of that binding determines how systems act when presented with the identity. Unfortunately, trust cannot be measured in absolute terms except for complete trust and no trust. Reality dictates a continuum, not discrete values. Understanding how an identity is bound to a principal provides insight into the trustworthiness of that identity.

Anonymity allows a principal to interact with others without revealing his or her true identity. Anonymity comes in two forms: pseudo-anonymity, in which an intermediary knows the true identity (and can relay messages without revealing that identity); and true anonymity, in which no one knows the true identity. The use of anonymity entails a responsibility to use it wisely.

13.8   Further Reading

Representation of identity varies from system to system. The use of roles is becoming a widely studied topic. Bishop [104] discusses implementation of role accounts using standard UNIX account mechanisms. McNutt [614] presents requirements and procedures for implementing roles to manage UNIX systems. Sandhu and Ahn [784] extend the UNIX group semantics to include hierarchies.

Ellison explores methods of identifying a principal through relationships to others [297] and the meaning of a name [298]. Saltzer [774] lucidly discusses the issues and principles that affect naming on the Internet. Several RFCs discuss schemes for naming hosts and other principals on the Internet [38, 61, 396, 397, 630, 926].

Several cryptographic protocols allow information to be broadcast anonymously. The best-known such algorithm is Chaum's "Dining Cryptographers Problem" [166], in which the goal is to determine if one of the dining cryptographers paid for the meal (without revealing which one), or someone else did. Waidner and Pfitzmann [927] point out that Chaum's solution could be disrupted if one of the cryptographers lies, and present an algorithm (called "The Dining Cryptographers in the Disco") to detect it.

Chaum [165] first described digital cash. Okamoto and Ohta [701] list desirable properties for digital cash systems and present a protocol that meets them. Other protocols include Brands' protocol [131], electronic checks [167, 169], CAFE [122], and NetCash [617]. Smart cards can carry digital cash [28, 168, 170], and some European banks are using this technology [352, 594]. Von Solms and Naccache note that the untraceability of digital cash makes solving certain crimes more difficult [852].

Bacard [47] discusses the basics of remailers. Mazières and Kaashoek [601] describe a type 1 remailer in operation. Cottrell [212] cites the Cypherpunk remailers, and a discussion on the Cypherpunk mailing list, as the inspiration for the development of Mixmaster remailers. His discussion of attacking Mixmaster and remailer sites [213] is perceptive. Engelfriet (also known as "Galactus") [300] presents technical details of anonymity on the Web.

13.9   Exercises

1. The Web site *www.widget.com* requires users to supply a user name and a password. This information is encoded into a cookie and sent back to the browser. Whenever the user connects to the Web server, the cookie is sent. This means that the user need only supply a password at the beginning of the session. Whenever the server requests reauthentication, the client simply sends the cookie. The name of the cookie is "identif."

   a. Assume that the password is kept in the clear in the cookie. What should the settings of the secure and expires fields be, and why?

   b. Assume that the name and password are hashed and that the hash is stored in the cookie. What information must the server store to determine the user name associated with the cookie?

   c. Is the cookie storing state or acting as an authentication token, or both? Justify your answer.

2. Assume that a Cypherpunk remailer reorders messages. It has a pool of $n - 1$ messages at all times. When the nth message arrives, one of the n messages is selected at random and forwarded. An attacker floods the server with enough messages to force the $n - 1$ messages in the original pool to be sent.

   a. Assuming that the message to be sent is chosen according to a uniform random distribution, what is the expected number of messages that the attacker would have to send to achieve this goal?

   b. How can the attacker determine when all the messages originally in the pool have been sent?

3. Consider a scheme that allows a recipient to reply to a message from a chain of Cypherpunk remailers. Assume that encipherment is used throughout the chain.

a. Bob selects a chain of remailers for the return path. He creates a set of keys and enciphers them so that only the key for the current remailer is visible to that remailer. Design a technique by which he could accomplish this. Describe how he would include this data in his message.

b. How should Alice's mailer handle the processing of the return address information?

c. When Bob receives the reply, what does it contain? How can he obtain the cleartext reply?

4. Give reasons why *root* should not be able to change the audit UID on a UNIX system, and give reasons why it should. Which reasons sound more persuasive to you?

Chapter 14
Access Control Mechanisms

Recall the access control matrix discussed in Chapter 2. As in the theoretical model, an implementation of the array and the commands to manipulate it provide a mechanism that the system can use to control access to objects. Unfortunately, there are several problems with a straightforward implementation. On a typical system, the number of subjects and objects will be sufficiently large that the matrix's size will use significant amounts of storage. Second, most entries in the matrix will be either blank (indicating no access) or the same (because implementations often provide a default setting). Third, the creation and deletion of subjects and objects will require the matrix to manage its storage carefully, adding to the complexity of this code.

Instead, several optimizations enable systems to use more convenient, and in some cases simpler, versions of the access control matrix. Access control lists and capabilities are variants based on the access control matrix that eliminate many of the problems mentioned above. Various organizations of these mechanisms lead to powerful controls such as the ring-based mechanism of Multics. A third mechanism, locks and keys, is based on cryptography and provides a powerful alternative. A fourth mechanism uses access control lists to implement an ORCON-like control.

14.1 Access Control Lists

An obvious variant of the access control matrix is to store each column with the object it represents. Thus, each object has associated with it a set of pairs, with each pair containing a subject and a set of rights. The named subject can access the associated object using any of those rights. More formally:

Definition 14–1. Let S be the set of subjects, and R the set of rights, of a system. An *access control list* (ACL) l is a set of pairs $l = \{ (s, r) : s \in S, r \subseteq R \}$. Let *acl* be a function that determines the access control list l associated with a particular object o. The interpretation of the access control list $acl(o) = \{ (s_i, r_i) : 1 \le i \le n \}$ is that subject s_i may access o using any right in r_i.

EXAMPLE: Consider the access control matrix in Figure 2–1, on page 29. The set of subjects is process 1 and process 2, and the set of objects is file 1, file 2, process 1, and process 2. The corresponding access control lists are

acl(file 1) = { (process 1, { read, write, own }), (process 2, { append }) }
acl(file 2) = { (process 1, { read }), (process 2, { read, own }) }
acl(process 1) = { (process 1, { read, write, execute, own }), (process 2, { read }) }
acl(process 2) = { (process 1, { write }), (process 2, { read, write, execute, own }) }

Each subject and object has an associated ACL. Thus, process 1 owns file 1, and can read from or write to it; process 2 can only append to file 1. Similarly, both processes can read file 2, which process 2 owns. Both processes can read from process 1; both processes can write to process 2. The exact meanings of "read" and "write" depend on the instantiation of the rights.

One issue is the matter of default permission. If a subject is not named in the ACL, it has no rights over the associated object. On a system with many subjects, the ACL may be very large. If many subjects have the same right over the file, one could define a "wildcard" to match any unnamed subjects, and give them default rights.

EXAMPLE: UNICOS 7.0 ACLs have entries of the form (*user, group, rights*) [220]. If the *user* is in the named *group*, he or she has those *rights* over the object. For example, the triplet (*holly, maceranch, r*) gives user *holly* read (*r*) access over the object only when *holly* has *maceranch* as her group.

If either *user* or *group* is specified as "*", that character is taken to match all users or all groups. Thus, (*holly, *, r*) gives *holly* read permission over the object regardless of the group she is in; (*, maceranch, r*) gives any user read permission over the object when that user is in the group *maceranch*.

14.1.1   Abbreviations of Access Control Lists

Some systems abbreviate access control lists. The basis for file access control in the UNIX operating system is of this variety. UNIX systems divide the set of users into three classes: the *owner* of the file, the *group owner* of the file, and all other users. Each class has a separate set of rights.

EXAMPLE: UNIX systems provide read (r), write (w), and execute (x) rights. When user *bishop* creates a file, assume that it is in the group *vulner*. Initially, *bishop* requests that he be able to read from and write to the file, that members of the group be allowed to read from the file, and that no one else have access to the file. Then the permissions would be *rw* for owner, *r* for group, and none for other.

UNIX permissions are represented as three triplets. The first is the owner rights; the second, group rights; and the third, other rights. Within each triplet, the first position is *r* if read access is allowed or – if it is not; the second position is *w* if write access is allowed or – if it is not; and the third position is *x* if execute access is allowed or – if it is not. The permissions for *bishop*'s file would be *rw–r–––––*.

An interesting question is how UNIX systems assign group ownership. Traditionally, UNIX systems assign the effective principal group ID of the creating process. But in some cases this is not appropriate. For instance, suppose the line printer program works by using group permissions; say its group is *lpdaemon*. Then, when a user copies a file into the spool directory, *lpdaemon* must own the spool file. The simplest way to enforce this requirement is to make the spool directory group owned by *lpdaemon* and to have the group ownership inherited by all files created in that directory. Some systems—notably, Solaris and SunOS systems—augment the semantics of file protection modes by setting the setgid bit on the directory when any files created in the directory are to inherit the group ownership of the containing directory.

Abbreviations of access control lists, such as those supported by the UNIX operating system, suffer from a loss of granularity. Suppose a UNIX system has five users. Anne wants to allow Beth to read her file, Caroline to write to it, Della to read and write to it, and Elizabeth to execute it. Because there are only three sets of permissions and five desired arrangements of rights (including Alice), three triplets are insufficient to allow all desired modes of access. Hence, Alice must compromise, and either give someone more rights than she desires or give someone fewer rights. Similarly, traditional UNIX access control does not allow one to say "everybody but user Fran"; to do this, one must create groups of all users *except* Fran. Such an arrangement is cumbersome, the more so because only a system administrator can create groups.

Many systems augment abbreviations of ACLs with full-blown ACLs. This scheme uses the abbreviations of ACLs as the default permission controls; the explicit ACL overrides the defaults as needed. The exact method varies.

EXAMPLE: IBM's version of the UNIX operating system, called AIX, uses an ACL (called "extended permissions") to augment the traditional UNIX abbreviations of ACL (called "base permissions") [341]. Unlike traditional ACLs, the AIX ACL allows one to specify permissions to be added or deleted from the user's set. Like UNICOS, AIX bases matches on group and user identity. The specific algorithm (using AIX's terminology, in which "base permissions" are the UNIX abbreviations of ACLs and "extended permissions" are unabbreviated ACL entries) is as follows.

1. Determine what set S of permissions the user has from the base permissions.

2. If extended permissions are disabled, stop. The set S is the user's set of permissions.

3. Get the next entry in the extended permissions. If there are no more, stop. The set S is the user's set of permissions.

4. If the entry has the same user and group as the process requesting access, determine if the entry denies access. If so, stop. Access is denied.

5. Modify S as dictated by the permissions in the entry.

6. Go to 3.

As a specific example, consider the following representation of an AIX system's access control permissions for the file *xyzzy*.

```
attributes:
base permissions
    owner(bishop):     rw-
    group(sys):        r--
    others:            ---
extended permissions  enabled
    specify            rw-        u:holly
    permit             -w-        u:heidi, g=sys
    permit             rw-        u:matt
    deny               -w-        u:holly, g=faculty
```

In the extended permissions lines, the first field determines what the line means ("specify" to override the base permissions, "permit" to add rights, and "deny" to delete rights); the second field states the rights involved, using the traditional UNIX triplet; and the third field defines the user ("u:") and group ("g:") involved.

In this example, *holly* can read *xyzzy* because the first and fourth lines in the extended permissions section override the base permission denial of access to others (the class of which *holly* is a member). If *holly* is working in the faculty group, she cannot write to *xyzzy* (the last line) but can read it (first line). The user *heidi*, working in group *sys*, can read and write to the file (the group line in the base permissions gives *heidi* read permission; the first permit line in the extended permissions section gives her write permission). In this way, the extended permissions augment the base permissions.

14.1.2   Creation and Maintenance of Access Control Lists

Specific implementations of ACLs differ in details. Some of the issues are as follows.

1. Which subjects can modify an object's ACL?

2. If there is a privileged user (such as *root* in the UNIX system or *administrator* in Windows NT), do the ACLs apply to that user?

3. Does the ACL support groups or wildcards (that is, can users be grouped into sets based on a system notion of "group" or on pattern matching)?

4. How are contradictory access control permissions handled? If one entry grants read privileges only and another grants write privileges only, which right does the subject have over the object?

5. If a default setting is allowed, do the ACL permissions modify it, or is the default used only when the subject is not explicitly mentioned in the ACL?

Because these isues are critical to the correct use of ACLs on a system, we will explore them in more detail.

14.1.2.1   Which Subjects Can Modify an Object's ACL?

When an ACL is created, rights are instantiated. Chief among these rights is the one we will call *own*. Possessors of the *own* right can modify the ACL.

Creating an object also creates its ACL, with some initial value (possibly empty, but more usually the creator is initially given all rights, including *own*, over the new object). By convention, the subject with *own* rights is allowed to modify the ACL. However, some systems allow anyone with access to manipulate the rights.

EXAMPLE: The relational database System R [381] contains sets of *n*-tuples making up the records, and each element of each *n*-tuple has attributes. These *n*-tuples are stored as tables, with the records as the rows and the attributes as the columns. Each table defines a relation.

The rights for manipulating a table (relation) include *read* (for reading rows, querying using the relation, or defining views), *update* (for writing to a table), *insert* (for adding rows), *delete* (for deleting rows), and *drop* (for deleting tables). Each right has a modifier, called the *grant* option, which if set allows the possessor to give the right to another. Any user with access to a table can give rights to any other user, provided the right has the *grant* option. Hence, possession of access (and a *grant* option associated with each right), not ownership, controls the transfer of rights.

14.1.2.2   Do the ACLs Apply to a Privileged User?

Many systems have users with extra privileges. The two best known are the *root* super-user on UNIX systems and the *administrator* user on Windows NT and 2000 systems. Typically, ACLs (or their degenerate forms) are applied in a limited fashion to such users.

EXAMPLE: Solaris UNIX systems use both the abbreviations of ACLs standard to UNIX systems and a full-blown ACL. The abbreviations of ACLs are ignored when *root* is the subject, but the full ACLs apply even to *root*.

14.1.2.3   Does the ACL Support Groups and Wildcards?

In its classic form, ACLs do not support groups or wildcards. In practice, systems support one or the other (or both) to limit the size of the ACL and to make manipulation of the lists easier. A group can either refine the characteristics of the processes to be allowed access or be a synonym for a set of users (the members of the group).

EXAMPLE: In the AIX example above, recall that the extended permission lines (corresponding to the full ACL) were

```
extended permissions enabled
    specify            rw-      u:holly
    permit             -w-      u:heidi, g=sys
    permit             rw-      u:matt
    deny               -w-      u:holly, g=faculty
```

Initially, the group *sys* had read permission only on the file. The second line adds write permission for processes with UID *heidi* and GID *sys*. The first line gives processes with UID *holly* read and write access, except when the GID of the process is *faculty*, in which case the process cannot write to the object (see the fourth line).

EXAMPLE: The UNICOS operating system provides ACLs similar to those of AIX, but allows wildcards [220]. For example,

```
holly : maceranch : r
```

means that a process with UID *holly* and GID *maceranch* can read the object with which the ACL is associated. The ACL entry

```
holly : * : r
```

means that a process with UID *holly* can access the object regardless of the group that the process is in. And the entry

```
* : maceranch : r
```

means that any process with GID *maceranch* can read the object.

14.1.2.4   Conflicts

A conflict arises when two access control list entries in the same ACL give different permissions to the subject. The system can allow access if any entry would give access, deny access if any entry would deny access, or apply the first entry that matches the subject.

EXAMPLE: If any entry in an AIX ACL denies access, the subject is denied access regardless of the location of that entry. Otherwise, if any entry has granted access, the subject is granted access. This is an example of denial taking precedence.

EXAMPLE: Cisco routers apply the first access control list entry that matches the incoming packet [414]. If none applies, the incoming packet is discarded. This is an example of the second approach, with a default rule of deny.

14.1.2.5   ACLs and Default Permissions

When ACLs and abbreviations of access control lists or default access rights coexist (as on many UNIX systems), there are two ways to determine access rights. The first is to apply the appropriate ACL entry, if one exists, and to apply the default permissions or abbreviations of access control lists otherwise. The second way is to augment the default permissions or abbreviations of access control lists with those in the appropriate ACL entry.

EXAMPLE: The AIX extended permissions fall into the second category, because they modify the base permissions.

EXAMPLE: If a packet entering a Cisco router is destined for a host on a network behind the router, but the router has no access list entry that allows the packet to be forwarded, the packet is discarded. This is an example of the first method, because the default permission is deny.

14.1.3   Revocation of Rights

Revocation, or the prevention of a subject's accessing an object, requires that the subject's rights be deleted from the object's ACL.

Preventing a subject from accessing an object is simple. The entry for the subject is deleted from the object's ACL. If only specific rights are to be deleted, they are removed from the relevant subject's entry in the ACL.

If ownership does not control the giving of rights, revocation is more complex.

EXAMPLE: Return to System R. Suppose Anna has given Peter *update* rights over a relation *T* but now wishes to revoke them. System R holds that after the revoking, the protection state of the system should be as it was before Anna gave Peter any rights. Specifically, if Peter gave Mary *update* rights, when Anna revokes Peter's *update* rights, Mary's *update* rights should be revoked *unless someone other than Peter has also given her* update *rights*.

To implement this, System R defines a relation called *Sysauth*. The attributes of this relation are (*User, Table, Grantor, Read, Insert, Delete, Drop, Update*). The values of the attributes corresponding to the rights are timestamps indicating when the right was given (except for *Update*, which we will deal with later). For example, if Anna gave Peter *read* rights over the relation *Reports* at time 10, and Peter gave them to Mary at time 20, the table would be as follows.

User	Table	Grantor	Read
Peter	Reports	Anna	10
Mary	Reports	Peter	20

If Anna revokes Peter's *read* rights, and Mary obtained her *read* rights from Peter after Anna gave them to Peter, her *read* rights would also be revoked. However, suppose that Michelle had also given Mary *read* rights over *Reports*. Then deleting the last row in the table leaves an entry for Mary—namely, the one from Michelle:

User	Table	Grantor	Read
Peter	Reports	Anna	10
Mary	Reports	Michelle	5

So Mary can still read *Reports*.

The *update* right has a value of *All*, *Some*, or *None*. These values refer to the set of rows that can be changed. If the value is *Some*, a second relation called *Syscolauth* records the columns that the subject can update. This table also records times, and revocation proceeds as for the other columns.

14.1.4   Example: Windows NT Access Control Lists

Windows NT provides access control lists for those files on NTFS partitions [767]. Windows NT allows a user or group to read, write, execute, delete, change the permissions of, or take ownership of a file or directory. These rights are grouped into commonly assigned sets called *generic rights*. The generic rights for files are as follows.

- *no access*, whereby the subject cannot access the file
- *read*, whereby the subject can read or execute the file
- *change*, whereby the subject can read, execute, write, or delete the file
- *full control*, whereby the subject has all rights to the file

In addition, the generic right *special access* allows the assignment of any of the six permissions.

Windows NT directories also have their own notion of generic rights.

- *no access*, whereby the subject cannot access the directory
- *read*, whereby the subject can read or execute files within the directory
- *list*, whereby the subject can list the contents of the directory and may change to a subdirectory within that directory
- *add*, whereby the subject may create files or subdirectories in the directory
- *add and read*, which combines the generic rights *add* and *read*
- *change*, whereby the subject can create, read, execute, or write files within the directory and can delete subdirectories
- *full control*, whereby the subject has all rights over the files and subdirectories in the directory

As before, the generic *special access* right allows assignment of other combinations of permissions.

When a user accesses a file, Windows NT first examines the file's ACL. If the user is not present in the ACL, and is not a member of any group listed in the ACL, access is denied. Otherwise, if any ACL entry denies the user access, Windows NT denies the access (this is an explicit denial, which is calculated first). If access is not explicitly denied, and the user is named in the ACL (as either a user or a member of a group), the user has the union of the set of rights from each ACL entry in which the user is named.

As an example, suppose Paul, Quentin, and Regina are users of a Windows NT system. Paul and Quentin are in the group *students*. Quentin and Regina are in the group *staff*. The directory *e:\stuff* has its access control list set to (*staff, add*), (*Quentin, change*), (*students, no access*). Under this list, the first entry enables Regina to create subdirectories or files in *e:\stuff*. The third entry disallows all members of the group *students* from accessing the directory. The second entry would allow Quentin to delete subdirectories, except that Quentin is in the *students* group, and in Windows NT an explicit deny (as given in the third entry) overrides any grants of permission. Hence, Quentin cannot access the directory.

Now, let Regina create a subdirectory *plugh* in *e:\stuff*. She then disallows Paul's access, but wants to allow Quentin to have *change* access. She does the following.

- Create *e:\stuff\plugh*; its ACL is (*staff, add*), (*Quentin, change*), (*students, no access*).
- Delete the last entry in ACL; from the second entry, this gives Quentin *change* access.
- Add the entry (Paul, *no access*) to the ACL.

The last step is superfluous, because Windows NT denies access by default, but it is safer to add it anyway, lest the group *students* be given rights. If that should happen, Paul would get those rights unless the (Paul, *no access*) entry were present.

14.2   Capabilities

Conceptually, a capability is like the row of an access control matrix. Each subject has associated with it a set of pairs, with each pair containing an object and a set of rights. The subject associated with this list can access the named object in any of the ways indicated by the named rights. More formally:

> **Definition 14–2.** Let O be the set of objects, and R the set of rights, of a system. A *capability list* c is a set of pairs $c = \{ (o, r) : o \in O, r \subseteq R \}$. Let *cap* be a function that determines the capability list c associated with a particular subject s. The interpretation of the capability list $cap(s) = \{ (o_i, r_i) : 1 \leq i \leq n \}$ is that subject s may access o_i using any right in r_i.

We abbreviate "capability list" as C-List.

EXAMPLE: Again, consider the access control matrix in Figure 2–1 on page 29. The set of subjects is process 1 and process 2. The corresponding capability lists are

cap(process 1) = { (file 1, { read, write, own }), (file 2, { read }),
(process 1, {read, write, execute, own}), (process 2, { write }) }

cap(process 2) = { (file 1, { append }), (file 2, { read, own }),
(process 1, { read }), (process 2, {read, write, execute, own}) }

Each subject has an associated C-List. Thus, process 1 owns file 1, and can read or write to it; process 1 can read file 2; process 1 can read, write to, or execute itself and owns itself; and process 1 can write to process 2. Similarly, process 2 can append to file 1; process 2 owns file 2 and can read it; process 2 can read process 1; and process 2 can read, write to, or execute itself and owns itself.

Capabilities encapsulate object identity. When a process presents a capability on behalf of a user, the operating system examines the capability to determine both the object and the access to which the process is entitled. This reflects how capabilities for memory management work; the location of the object in memory is encapsulated in the capability. Without a capability, the process cannot name the object in a way that will give it the desired access.

EXAMPLE: To open a UNIX file, a process gives the file name to the kernel. The kernel obtains the file's inode number by resolving the name through the file hierarchy. Once the inode is obtained, the system determines if the requested access should be granted using the access control permissions. If the access is granted, the operating system returns a capability called a *file descriptor*. The capability is tightly bound to the file object, so even if the file is deleted and a new file with the same name is created, the file descriptor still refers to the previous file.

The "codewords" of Iliffe [457, 458] are similar to capabilities. Dennis and Van Horn [255] first suggested "capabilities" as a way to control access to objects in memory or secondary storage. Fabry generalized this idea to implement capability-based addressing [306].

The architecture of capabilities is more interesting than that of access control lists. The access control list and the process identity are under the control of the operating system. In the absence of flaws, user processes can change them only by invoking the operating system services. However, a process must identify a capability in order to use it, so the process must have some control over the capabilities. If the process can forge a capability and then use it, access controls fail.

14.2.1   Implementation of Capabilities

Three mechanisms are used to protect capabilities: tags, protected memory, and cryptography.

A *tagged* architecture has a set of bits associated with each hardware word. The tag has two states: *set* and *unset*. If the tag is set, an ordinary process can read but not modify the word. If the tag is unset, an ordinary process can read and modify the word. Further, an ordinary process cannot change the state of the tag; the processor must be in a privileged mode to do so.

EXAMPLE: The B5700 [704] used a tagged architecture (although it did not use capabilities as protection mechanisms). The tag field consisted of three bits and indicated how the architecture was to treat the word (pointer, descriptor, type, and so on).

More common is to use the protection bits associated with paging or segmentation. All capabilities are stored in a page (segment) that the process can read but not alter. This requires no special-purpose hardware other than that used by the memory management scheme. But the process must reference capabilities indirectly, usually through pointers, rather than directly.

EXAMPLE: The CAP system [684] did not allow processes to modify the segment in which instructions lay. It also stored capabilities in this segment. A fence register separated instructions and capabilities.

A third alternative is to use cryptography. The goal of tags and memory protection is to prevent the capabilities from being altered. This is akin to integrity checking. Cryptographic checksums are another mechanism for checking the integrity of information. Each capability has a cryptographic checksum associated with it, and the checksum is digitally enciphered using a cryptosystem whose key is known to the operating system.

When the process presents a capability to the operating system, the system first recomputes the cryptographic checksum associated with the capability. It then either enciphers the checksum using the cryptographic key and compares it with the one stored in the capability, or deciphers the checksum provided with the capability and compares it with the computed checksum. If they match, the capability is unaltered. If not, the capability is rejected.

EXAMPLE: The Amoeba system is a distributed system that uses capabilities to name objects [893]. On creation, a capability corresponding to the object is returned. To use the object, the program presents the corresponding capability. The capability encodes the name of the object (24 bits), the server that created it (48 bits), and the rights (8 bits) in a 128-bit quantity. Initially, all rights are turned on.

The last 48 bits are used as a check field. This is a random number selected at creation time. (Because the capability is given to the owner of the object, the owner can freely modify the rights without danger.) The number is stored in a table corresponding to the server that created the object, so whenever the capability is presented to that server, it verifies that the random number is correct. An attacker would need to know the random number in order to be able to forge a capability. However, as Tanenbaum notes, the system is vulnerable if a capability is disclosed.

14.2.2   Copying and Amplifying Capabilities

The ability to copy capabilities implies the ability to give rights. To prevent processes from indiscriminately giving away rights, a *copy flag* is associated with capabilities. A process cannot copy a capability to another process unless the copy flag is set. If the process does copy the capability, the copy flag may be turned off (at the discretion of either the process or the kernel).

EXAMPLE: Amoeba uses an interesting scheme. It does not control copying rights. However, the uses to which those copied rights can be put are restricted.

Suppose user *matt* wishes to allow user *holly* to read an object he owns. He passes his capability for that object to the server and requests a restricted capability for reading. The server creates a new capability for the object but with only the read right turned on. The rights field now is all 0's except for the read bit, which is a 1. This is xor'ed with the random check and input to a cryptographic hash function. The output is the new random number for this capability. The restricted capability is then passed back to *matt*, who gives it to *holly*.

When *holly* uses the capability, the server notes that at least one bit in the rights field is 0. It takes the rights field, xor's it with the random number of the original capability (stored in its tables), and hashes the result. If the resulting hash matches the random number in the capability, the capability is valid; otherwise, it is not.

Amplification is the increasing of privileges. The idea of modular programming, and especially of abstract data types, requires that the rights a process has over an object be amplified.

To understand why, consider the following abstract data type for a counter.

```
module counter;
    procedure entry increment(var ctr: integer);
    begin
        ctr := ctr + 1;
    end;
    function entry getval(ctr: integer);
    begin
        getval := ctr;
    end;
    procedure entry clear(var ctr: integer);
    begin
        ctr := 0;
    end;
end.
```

Suppose x is declared to be a counter. The rules of abstract data types allow that object to be accessed *only* by the *counter* module. So, initially the capability for x would contain the right to invoke the *counter* module only. But when the object is passed to the *counter* module, the process must now be able to read and write to that object. Hence, the capability must be *amplified* temporarily while the module *counter* is active.

EXAMPLE: The seminal system HYDRA [179, 957] used amplification templates to amplify a process' rights. Associated with each procedure in the module is a template that adds rights to the capabilities as needed. For example, the template for the *getval* procedure would add read rights while the procedure was active. The template for the *increment* procedure would add read and write rights.

EXAMPLE: The Intel iAPX 432 system [486, 909] implements a similar mechanism in hardware. Its "access descriptors" correspond to capabilities. Three bits in the capability control various system functions. One of these bits controls amplification of rights. When an abstract data type module is constructed, the permission bits of the type control object (which defines the data type) are set to the permissions that the procedure needs. When the procedure is called, the system checks the amplification bit. If it is set, the rights in the type control object are or'ed with the rights in the descriptor of the object being passed. This combination defines the rights available to the procedure.

14.2.3   Revocation of Rights

In a capability system, revoking access to an object requires that all the capabilities granting access to that object be revoked. Conceptually, each process could be checked, and the capabilities deleted. The cost of such an operation would be unacceptable, however, so alternative methods are used.

The simplest mechanism is indirection [745]. Define one or more *global object tables*. In this scheme, each object has a corresponding entry in a table. Capabilities do not name the object directly; they name the entry in the table corresponding to the object.

This scheme has several advantages. First, to revoke capabilities, the entry in the global object table is invalidated. Then any references will obtain an invalid table entry and will be rejected. Second, if only some of the capabilities are to be revoked, the object can have multiple entries, each corresponding to a different set of rights or a different group of users.

EXAMPLE: Amoeba uses essentially this scheme. To revoke a capability, the owner of the object requests that the server change the random number and issue a new capability. This invalidates all existing capabilities.

An alternative revocation mechanism uses abstract data type managers. Included with each abstract data type is a revocation procedure. When access is to be revoked, the type manager simpy disallows further accesses by the subject whose rights are being revoked. This does not affect alternative methods of accessing the objects underlying the abstract data types. For example, access to a file may be revoked, but this technique would not block access to the underlying segments through an alternative type manager. The SCP3 system used this technique [949].

14.2.4   Limits of Capabilities

Boebert [117] credits Neumann and his colleagues [689] with a demonstration of the importance of controlling the copying of capabilities. Without such restrictions, a capability system cannot enforce the *-property of the Bell-LaPadula Model (see Chapter 5).

Suppose capabilities can be copied into one's C-List. Let Heidi be cleared for HIGH information, and Lou only for LOW information. The file "lough" has LOW classification. Lou asks for a capability to read and write to the file "lough" and obtains it (call the capability "rw*lough"). Lou stores the capability in the file "lough." Now, Heidi requests a capability to read "lough" (call it "r*lough"); by the simple security condition, this is granted. Heidi uses this to read "lough," thereby obtaining the capability "rw*lough." She can now write to a LOW object, even though she has HIGH clearance. This violates the *-property. (See Figure 14–1.)

Kain and Landwehr [488] present two ways to handle this problem. Their first technique assigns a security classification to the capability itself. When the capability is created, its compartment is the same as the requesting process, and the capability contains read, read and write, or write rights depending on whether its compartment dominates, is the same as, or is dominated by that of the object to which the capability refers. Similar rules apply when a capability is copied. So, in Boebert's example,

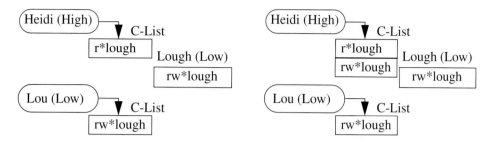

Figure 14–1 Copying and reading capabilities. In the left diagram, Lou has the capability rw*lough, which he copies into the file lough. Heidi obtains the capability r*lough. In the right diagram, Heidi has used her r*lough capability to read the contents of the file lough and has added the capability it contains to her C-List. She can now write to lough, violating the *-property. One solution is to separate the "copy" and "read" rights.

because the capability "rw*lough" is copied to HIGH, and because the destination (HIGH level) dominates the source ("lough," at the LOW level), the resulting capability has only the right to read.

Their second solution uses a technique from Karger and Herbert [495], although in a different context. Before a capability is passed to another process, the kernel evaluates the capability to determine if passing it to the subject violates any security properties. In Boebert's example, the *-property is violated, so Heidi's request to obtain "rw*lough" would be denied.

A simpler approach is to distinguish between the "copy capability" right and the "read" right. The Take-Grant Protection Model uses this difference to resolve Boebert's example. That Heidi could *read* the capability did not mean that she could *acquire* (take or copy) it. Heidi would be able to read the capability but could not add it to her C-List.

14.2.5   Comparison with Access Control Lists

Two questions underlie the use of access controls:

1. Given a subject, what objects can it access, and how?
2. Given an object, what subjects can access it, and how?

In theory, either access control lists or capabilities can answer these questions. For the first question, capabilities are the simplest; just list the elements of the subject's associated C-List. For the second question, ACLs are the simplest; just list the elements of the object's access control list. In an ACL-based system, answering the first question requires all objects to be scanned. The system extracts all ACL entries associated with the subject in question. In a capability-based system, answering the second question requires all subjects to be scanned. The system extracts all capabilities associated with the object in question.

Karger and Herbert [495] speculate that the practical difference in answering the second question is the reason more systems use access control lists than capabilities. This question is asked more often than the first. As the focus of incident response (see Section 22.6, "Intrusion Response") shifts from "who accessed the object" to include "what else did that subject access," capability-based systems may become more common.

14.3   Locks and Keys

The locks and keys technique combines features of access control lists and capabilities. A piece of information (the lock) is associated with the object and a second piece of information (the key) is associated with those subjects authorized to access the object and the manner in which they are allowed to access the object. When a subject tries to access an object, the subject's set of keys is checked. If the subject has a key corresponding to any of the object's locks, access of the appropriate type is granted.

The difference between locks and keys and the other access control mechanisms is the dynamic nature of the former. An access control list is static in the sense that all changes to it are manual; a user or process must interact with the list to make the change. Locks and keys, on the other hand, may change in response to system constraints, general instructions about how entries are to be added, and any factors other than a manual change.

Gifford [356] suggests a cryptographic implementation of locks and keys. The object o is enciphered with a cryptographic key. The subject has a deciphering key. To access the object, the subject deciphers it. Gifford points out that this provides a simple way to allow n subjects to access the data (called *or-access*). Simply encipher n copies of the data using n different keys, one per subject. The object o is then represented as o', where

$$o' = (\, E_1(o), \, \ldots, \, E_n(o))$$

The system can easily deny access except on the request of n subjects (called *and-access*). Simply iterate the cipher using n different keys, one per subject:

$$o' = E_1(\ldots(E_n(o))\ldots)$$

EXAMPLE: The IBM 370 system [487] assigns each process an access key and assigns each page a storage key and a fetch bit. If the fetch bit is cleared, only read accesses are allowed. If the fetch bit is set and the access key is 0 (which occurs in nonuser mode), the process can write to any page. If not, and the access key matches the storage key of a particular page, the process can write to that page. If the access key is neither 0 nor the same as the storage key, the process cannot access the page.

EXAMPLE: CISCO routers have a mechanism called *dynamic access control lists* that is a locks and keys mechanism [414]. Consider a router that transfers packets between the Internet and an internal network. We want to limit external access to the (internal) server with address 10.1.2.3 to weekdays between 9:00 A.M. and 5:00 P.M. Our router's IP address is 10.1.1.1. The following is the relevant portion of the dynamic access control list.

```
access-list 100 permit tcp any host 10.1.1.1 eq telnet
access-list 100 dynamic test timeout 180 permit ip any
host
    10.1.2.3 time-range my-time
time-range my-time
    periodic weekdays 9:00 to 17:00
line vty 0 2
    login local
    autocommand access-enable host timeout 10
```

The first line tells the router to accept packets coming to it over the Internet and going to the *telnet* port. (The binding of the access control list to the Internet connection is not shown.) The user will enter a name and a password, and if they match a pair in the configuration file, the connection will close and the router will add an access control list entry for that remote host to access the server 10.1.2.3 over any IP protocol. After 180 minutes, the access control list entry will be discarded even if there are connections at that time (this effectively terminates the connections). The access control entry is valid only between 9:00 A.M. and 5:00 P.M. on weekdays (the "time-range" block). Furthermore, any host matching this new entry is to be allowed access; if no packets from that host are received within a 10-minute interval, the access control entry is to be deleted (the "line" block).

14.3.1   Type Checking

Type checking restricts access on the basis of the types of the subject and object. It is a form of locks and keys access control, the pieces of information being the type. Systems use type checking in areas other than security.

EXAMPLE: UNIX-like systems use type checking to protect the integrity of their file systems. Under the UNIX model, all file system objects are files, but the kernel disallows the use of *write* to change the directory. Instead, users must call specific system calls to create and delete entities in the directory. This allows the kernel to ensure that all writing to the directory file will create entries of the correct format. The kernel disallows certain operations, such as *write*, to file system objects of type *directory*.

The simplest case of type checking is distinguishing instructions from data. The operation "execute" can be performed only on instructions, and the operations "read" and "write" can be performed only on data. Many systems, such as PDP-11 [269], enforce this distinction.

EXAMPLE: One form of a type of attack called *buffer overflow* (see Section 20.3.1, "Two Security Flaws") involves overwriting of a buffer stored on a memory stack and changing of the return address on the stack to the location of the buffer. When the input routine executes a return to the caller, the return address is popped from the stack and placed in the program counter. The contents of the buffer are then executed as instructions.

Some vendors have tried to eliminate this type of attack by marking the memory in which the stack resides as data. The systems cannot execute data, and therefore the program terminates right after the return address is popped and placed into the program counter.

Like pages, files can be either "executable" or "data."

EXAMPLE: Boebert, Young, Kain, and Hansohn [120] propose labeling of subjects and objects in Logical Coprocessor Kernel or LOCK (formerly Secure Ada Target or SAT) [120, 388, 789, 790], a system designed to meet the highest level of security under the Department of Defense criteria [257]. Once compiled, programs have the label "data" and cannot be executed until a sequence of specific, auditable events changes the label to "executable." After that, the program cannot be modified.

Strictly enforced type checking is a powerful protection mechanism. The DTEL policy language and the supporting domain and type enforcement (DTE) mechanism, are good examples. Walker et al. [928] discuss the implementation of DTE using DTEL at length for the UNIX operating system. The Sidewinder firewall uses a similar approach.

EXAMPLE: Like DTEL, Sidewinder [900] assigns each subject a domain and each object a type. The *domain definition table* defines how domains may interact with types. For instance, packets coming from inside the firewall are assigned one type, and packets from the outside are assigned a second type. This separates the two.

Suppose that an attacker outside the firewall is able to embed in a legal packet a second, fake packet and that this fake packet contains an IP source address that is inside the firewall. The attacker sends the packet to the Sidewinder firewall and then sends a second packet to overwrite the part of the first packet before the fake packet. If there were no typing, the firewall could confuse the fake packet, which came from outside, with a legitimate packet originating from inside the firewall. However, because Sidewinder types outside packets differently than those originating behind the firewall, the fake packet will have the type "outside" even though the source address is from the inside. Thus, it will not be forwarded to the inside.

14.4 Ring-Based Access Control

The Multics system [210, 703] generalizes the notion of a supervisor and user state with a protection mechanism called *ring-based access control*. To understand its simplicity and elegance, one must realize that files and memory are treated the same from the protection point of view. For example, a procedure may occupy a segment of the disk. When invoked, the segment is mapped into memory and executed. Data occupies other segments on disk, and when accessed, they are mapped into memory and accessed. In other words, there is no conceptual difference between a segment of memory and a segment on a disk.

Segments are of two kinds: data and procedure. A segment could have r (read) rights, w (write) rights, e (execute) rights, and a (append) rights associated with it. These rights are contained in access control lists, which constrain access on a per-user basis. So all procedures that user *bishop* executes would have the rights associated with that user, *bishop*.

In addition, the Multics system defines a sequence of *protection rings* (or *rings*, for short) numbered from 0 to 63.[1] The kernel resides in ring 0. The higher the ring number, the lower the privileges of the segments in that ring. We also say that "a procedure executes in ring r" because the ring is associated with the individual *segment*, not with the entire process.

Subject to the access constraints noted below, procedures can "cross" ring boundaries. In some cases, the crossing causes a "ring-crossing fault" that traps to the kernel. At that point, a mechanism called the Gatekeeper checks arguments and access and performs other functions that constrain ring crossings. In other cases, no ring-crossing fault is induced, and access is permitted if the access modes allow.

A *gate* is simply an entry point (like the "public" designators of object-oriented languages). Gates are specially declared within programs, and the compiler and linker generate special code to make these entry points available to other procedures.

Assume that a procedure executing in ring r wants to access a data segment. Associated with each data segment is a pair of ring numbers called an *access bracket* (a_1, a_2), with $a_1 \leq a_2$. Assume that the data segment's permissions allow the desired access. The ring numbering adds an extra constraint:

- $r \leq a_1$: access permitted
- $a_1 < r \leq a_2$: r and e access permitted; w and a access denied
- $a_2 < r$: all accesses denied

Assume that the same procedure, again executing in ring r, wants to access a procedure segment. Each procedure segment has an access bracket, just like a data segment. A procedure segment may also have a *call bracket* (c_1, c_2), with $c_1 \leq c_2$. By

---

[1] In fact, the system as implemented had eight rings ([703], p. 141).

convention, when a call bracket is present, $c_1 = a_2$, leading to an alternative notation of (a_1, a_2, a_3), where (a_1, a_2) is the access bracket and (a_2, a_3) is the call bracket (that is, $c_2 = a_3$). The rules for access differ slightly from those for accessing a data segment:

- $r < a_1$: access permitted, but a ring-crossing fault occurs
- $a_1 \leq r \leq a_2$: all accesses permitted and no fault occurs
- $a_2 < r \leq a_3$: access permitted if made through a valid gate
- $a_3 < r$: all accesses denied

EXAMPLE: Assume that a data segment has the access bracket (2, 4) and *heidi* has *rw* rights over the segment. If *heidi*'s procedure executes in ring 1, and tries to read the process, the read succeeds. If *heidi*'s procedure executes in ring 3, any reads succeed and any writes fail. If *heidi*'s procedure executes in ring 5, all accesses fail.

EXAMPLE: Assume that a procedure segment has the bracket (2, 4, 6)—that is, its access bracket is (2, 4) and its call bracket is (4, 6). *heidi*'s procedure calls that procedure. If *heidi*'s procedure executes in ring 1, a ring-crossing fault occurs, but the call succeeds (unless the Gatekeeper blocks the call). If *heidi*'s procedure executes in ring 3, the call succeeds and no ring-crossing fault occurs. If *heidi*'s procedure executes in ring 5 and calls the procedure segment through a valid gate, the call succeeds; otherwise, it fails. If *heidi*'s procedure executes in ring 7, the call fails.

The reason for the brackets shows how practical details complicate ideal solutions. Conceptually, the access bracket should contain one ring. However, consider a procedure embodying a service routine (such as "access file"). Then procedures in other rings accessing that routine would cause a large number of ring crossings. The operating system would need to handle these crossings, increasing the overhead. But if the procedures were within the service routine's access bracket, no ring-crossing faults would occur. Hence, the access bracket minimizes operating system overhead in this context.

A similar situation arises with different classes of users. Suppose a service routine lies in ring *a*. Some users need to invoke this routine. Others are allowed to invoke it in specific ways—for example, to access some system resource in a particular manner. Still others should not invoke it at all. The access bracket handles the first and third sets of users, but the second set cannot be handled with an access bracket. However, with a call bracket, the second set can access the service routine and be forced to use predefined entry points (the gates). Hence, the need for call brackets.

Variants of the ring mechanism have been used by other systems. The VAX system of Digital Equipment Corporation, for example, provides four levels of privilege: user, monitor, executive, and kernel. Contrast this with the more traditional two levels (user and supervisor) and the influence of the rings of Multics is clear.

14.5   Propagated Access Control Lists

The Propagated Access Control List (PACL) mechanism [940] provides the creator of an object with control over who can access the object. It is an implementation that is ideal for the ORCON policy (see Section 7.3). The creator (originator) is kept with the PACL, and only the creator can change the PACL. When a subject reads an object, the PACL of the object is associated with the subject. When a subject creates an object, the PACL of the subject is associated with the object.

The notation $PACL_{subject}$ means that *subject* is the originator of the PACL. Only *subject* can change that PACL. The notation PACL(*entity*) is the PACL associated with *entity*.

EXAMPLE: Ann creates the file *dates*. Ann wants to control who can read the file. The file's PACL is the PACL associated with Ann: PACL(*dates*) = $PACL_{Ann}$.

Let the PACL of an object o be $PACL_s$. When another subject s' reads o, PACL(o) must augment PACL(s'). Otherwise, s' could create another subject o', and copy the data from o to o'. Then s would have no control over the data in o, defeating the purpose of using PACLs.

Hence, an object can have PACLs associated with two creators. If so, both creators control access to the object. Only subjects common to both PACLs can access the object. Otherwise, one creator would not control access to the data it expects to control. The default is to deny access unless both creators allow it.

EXAMPLE: Ann allows Betty, Dorothy, and Elisabeth access to the file *dates*. Before Betty reads *dates*, PACL(Betty) = $PACL_{Betty}$. After Betty reads *dates*, her PACL changes to PACL(Betty) = $PACL_{Betty} \cap$ PACL(*dates*) = $PACL_{Betty} \cap PACL_{Ann}$. Write this as $PACL_{Betty,Ann}$.

Betty creates the file *datescopy*. The system assigns Betty's PACL to *datescopy*. Hence, PACL(*datescopy*) = PACL(Betty) = $PACL_{Betty,Ann}$.

If $PACL_{Betty}$ allows Cherisse and Dorothy access to objects, Dorothy will be able to access *datescopy* but Cherisse and Elisabeth will not. Because Dorothy is in both $PACL_{Ann}$ and $PACL_{Betty}$, both originators of *datescopy* agree that Dorothy can access the data in that file. So Dorothy is in $PACL_{Betty,Ann}$. Because Cherisse is not in $PACL_{Ann}$, and because Elisabeth is not in $PACL_{Betty}$, one originator of *datescopy* does not want them to have access to the data in *datescopy*. Hence, neither of them is in $PACL_{Betty,Ann}$.

Discretionary access controls can augment PACLs. They restrict access, but they cannot allow access to subjects excluded by the PACL.

EXAMPLE: Betty does not want Dorothy to be able to read the file *datescopy*. However, Dorothy is allowed access by $PACL_{Betty,Ann}$. Betty, being the owner of the file, can change the access control list associated with the file (but not the PACL). So Betty sets the access control list to deny access to Dorothy.

This example illustrates the distinction between the PACL mechanism and the ACL mechanism. A PACL is associated with data, whereas an ACL is associated with an object. The PACL follows the information as it flows around the system, but an ACL stays with each object. In the example, Cherisse cannot access the information in *dates* because of the setting of PACL(*dates*), and cannot access the information in any derivative of *dates* because PACL(*dates*) propagates with the information. The copiers of the information cannot change this.

Were the files protected by ACLs instead of PACLs, the ACL would not be copied with the information. So, Cherisse would not be able to read *dates*, but Betty could copy that file and set the ACL so that Cherisse could read it. Ann would not control the information; she would have to trust those with access to *dates* not to give access to others.

14.6   Summary

Access control mechanisms implement controls on subjects and objects. Access control lists bind the data controlling access to the object. Capability lists bind that data to the subject. Locks and keys distribute the data between the subject and the object. All are particularly well-suited for discretionary access controls, because usually the owners of the objects determine who gets access. If the controller of access is the operating system, then these mechanisms also can implement mandatory access controls.

Ring-based mechanisms generalize the notion of "monitor" and "user" mode. They are particularly well-suited for mandatory access controls, because the operating system enforces the barriers to ring crossings. However, the brackets must be chosen judiciously.

Propagated access control lists are associated with information rather than with the objects that contain the information. This makes them particularly suitable for implementing originator controlled policies.

14.7   Further Reading

Saltzer [772] describes the use of access control lists in Multics. Kramer [530] describes their incorporation into the Linus system. Stiegler [877] describes structures used to implement ACLs. Riechmann and Hauck [750] discuss extensions. In addition to the systems described in this chapter, several others, both abstract and real, use capabilities [367, 403, 919]. Klein [511] describes how to emulate capabilities using setuid programs in traditional UNIX systems. The KeyKOS system implemented capabilities [123, 398, 739], and its descendent, EROS [816, 817, 818], is revisiting the concepts. Ko [520] developed a model of the ring bracket mechanism and demonstrated that it can enforce either the Bell-LaPadula confidentiality policy or the Biba integrity policy, but not both. Lock and key schemes can be implemented using key sharing techniques, such as those proposed by Shamir [815], Blakley [114] and Asmuth and Bloom [41]. Simmons discusses several generalizations [831, 832, 833]. Others discuss several forms of cheating [134, 565, 901].

14.8   Exercises

1. In general, ACLs and C-List entries use "owners" (users) rather than individual processes. Why?

2. Alice can read and write to the file x, can read the file y, and can execute the file z. Bob can read x, can read and write to y, and cannot access z.

   a. Write a set of access control lists for this situation. Which list is associated with which file?
   b. Write a set of capability lists for this situation. With what is each list associated?

3. Revoking an individual's access to a particular file is easy when an access control list is used. How hard is it to revoke a user's access to a particular set of files, but not to all files? Compare and contrast this with the problem of revocation using capabilities.

4. Explain why some UNIX-based systems with access control lists do not allow *root* to alter the ACL. What problems might this raise?

5. It is said that UNIX uses access control lists. Does the UNIX model include capabilities as well as access control lists? (*Hint:* Consider file descriptors. If a file is opened, and its protection mode is changed to exclude access by the opener, can the process still access the file using the file descriptor?)

6. Suppose a user wishes to edit the file *xyzzy* in a capability-based system. How can he be sure that the editor cannot access any other file? Could this be done in an ACL-based system? If so, how? If not, why not?

7. Consider Multics procedures p and q. Procedure p is executing and needs to invoke procedure q. Procedure q's access bracket is (5, 6) and its call bracket is (6, 9). Assume that q's access control list gives p full (read, write, append, and execute) rights to q. In which ring(s) must p execute for the following to happen?

   a. p can invoke q, but a ring-crossing fault occurs.
   b. p can invoke q provided that a valid gate is used as an entry point.
   c. p cannot invoke q.

    d. *p* can invoke *q* without any ring-crossing fault occurring, but not necessarily through a valid gate.

8. Consider Multics procedure *p* and data segment *d*. Procedure *p* is executing and needs to access segment *d*. Segment *d*'s access bracket is (5, 6). Assume that *d*'s access control list gives *p* full (read, write, append, and execute) rights to *d*. In which ring(s) must *p* execute for the following to happen?

    a. *p* can read, write to, and append to *d*.

    b. *p* can read *d* but not write to or append to *d*.

    c. *p* cannot access *q*.

9. Although most systems allow objects to have only one owner, it is possible for an object to have two (or more) owners. Consider ownership as a right that allows the changing of capabilities (or access control lists). How might you implement this right using capabilities? How might you implement it using access control lists? Contrast these implementations of capability lists and access control lists with PACLs.

Chapter 15
Information Flow

BOTTOM: Masters, I am to discourse wonders: but
ask me not what; for if I tell you, I am no true
Athenian. I will tell you every thing, right as it
fell out.
—*A Midsummer Night's Dream*, IV, ii, 30–33.

Although access controls can constrain the rights of a user, they cannot constrain the flow of information about a system. In particular, when a system has a security policy regulating information flow, the system must ensure that the information flows do not violate the constraints of the policy. Both compile-time mechanisms and runtime mechanisms support the checking of information flows. Several systems implementing these mechanisms demonstrate their effectiveness.

15.1 Basics and Background

Information flow policies define the way information moves throughout a system. Typically, these policies are designed to preserve confidentiality of data or integrity of data. In the former, the policy's goal is to prevent information from flowing to a user not authorized to receive it. In the latter, information may flow only to processes that are no more trustworthy than the data.

Any confidentiality and integrity policy embodies an information flow policy.

EXAMPLE: The Bell-LaPadula Model describes a lattice-based information flow policy. Given two compartments A and B, information can flow from an object in A to a subject in B if and only if B dominates A.

Let x be a variable in a program. The notation $\underline{x}$ refers to the information flow class of x.

EXAMPLE: Consider a system that uses the Bell-LaPadula Model. The variable x, which holds data in the compartment (TS, { NUC, EUR }), is set to 3. Then $x = 3$ and $\underline{x} = $ (TS, { NUC, EUR }).

Intuitively, information flows from an object x to an object y if the application of a sequence of commands c causes the information initially in x to affect the information in y.

Definition 15–1. The command sequence c causes a *flow of information from x to y* if, after execution of c, some information about the value of x before c was executed can be deduced from the value of y after c was executed.

This definition views information flow in terms of the information that the value of y allows one to deduce about the value in x. For example, the statement

```
y := x;
```

reveals the value of x in the initial state, so information about the value of x in the initial state can be deduced from the value of y after the statement is executed. The statement

```
y := x / z;
```

reveals some information about x, but not as much as the first statement.

The final result of the sequence c must reveal information about the initial value of x for information to flow. The sequence

```
tmp := x;
y := tmp;
```

has information flowing from x to y because the (unknown) value of x at the beginning of the sequence is revealed when the value of y is determined at the end of the sequence. However, no information flow occurs from *tmp* to x, because the initial value of *tmp* cannot be determined at the end of the sequence.

EXAMPLE: Consider the statement

```
x := y + z;
```

Let y take any of the integer values from 0 to 7, inclusive, with equal probability, and let z take the value 1 with probability 0.5 and the values 2 and 3 with probability 0.25 each. Once the resulting value of x is known, the initial value of y can assume at most three values. Thus, information flows from y to x. Similar results hold for z.

EXAMPLE: Consider a program in which x and y are integers that may be either 0 or 1. The statement

```
if x = 1 then y := 0;
else y := 1;
```

does not explicitly assign the value of x to y.

Assume that x is equally likely to be 0 or 1. Then $H(x_s) = 1$. But $H(x_s \mid y_t) = 0$, because if y is 0, x is 1, and vice versa. Hence, $H(x_s \mid y_t) = 0 < H(x_s \mid y_s) = H(x_s) = 1$. Thus, information flows from x to y.

> **Definition 15–2.** An *implicit flow of information* occurs when information flows from x to y without an explicit assignment of the form $y := f(x)$, where $f(x)$ is an arithmetic expression with the variable x.

The flow of information occurs, not because of an assignment of the value of x, but because of a flow of control based on the value of x. This demonstrates that analyzing programs for assignments to detect information flows is not enough. To detect all flows of information, implicit flows must be examined.

15.1.1   Information Flow Models and Mechanisms

An information flow policy is a security policy that describes the authorized paths along which that information can flow. Each model associates a label, representing a security class, with information and with entities containing that information. Each model has rules about the conditions under which information can move throughout the system.

In this chapter, we use the notation $x \leq y$ to mean that information can flow from an element of class x to an element of class y. Equivalently, this says that information with a label placing it in class x can flow into class y.

Earlier chapters usually assumed that the models of information flow policies were lattices. We first consider nonlattice information flow policies and how their structures affect the analysis of information flow. We then turn to compiler-based information flow mechanisms and runtime mechanisms. We conclude with a look at flow controls in practice.

15.2   Compiler-Based Mechanisms

Compiler-based mechanisms check that information flows throughout a program are authorized. The mechanisms determine if the information flows in a program *could* violate a given information flow policy. This determination is not precise, in that secure paths of information flow may be marked as violating the policy; but it is secure, in that no unauthorized path along which information may flow will be undetected.

> **Definition 15–3.** A set of statements is *certified* with respect to an information flow policy if the information flow within that set of statements does not violate the policy.

EXAMPLE: Consider the program statement

```
if x = 1 then y := a;
else y := b;
```

By the rules discussed earlier, information flows from x and a to y or from x and b to y, so if the policy says that $\underline{a} \leq \underline{y}$, $\underline{b} \leq \underline{y}$, and $\underline{x} \leq \underline{y}$, then the information flow is secure. But if $\underline{a} \leq \underline{y}$ only when some other variable $z = 1$, the compiler-based mechanism must determine whether $z = 1$ before certifying the statement. Typically, this is infeasible. Hence, the compiler-based mechanism would not certify the statement. The mechanisms described here follow those developed by Denning and Denning [247] and Denning [242].

15.2.1   Declarations

For our discussion, we assume that the allowed flows are supplied to the checking mechanisms through some external means, such as from a file. The specifications of allowed flows involve security classes of language constructs. The program involves variables, so some language construct must relate variables to security classes. One way is to assign each variable to exactly one security class. We opt for a more liberal approach, in which the language constructs specify the set of classes from which information may flow into the variable. For example,

```
x: integer class { A, B }
```

states that x is an integer variable and that data from security classes A and B may flow into x. Note that the classes are statically, not dynamically, assigned. Viewing the security classes as a lattice, this means that x's class must be at least the least upper bound of classes A and B—that is, $lub\{A, B\} \leq \underline{x}$.

Two distinguished classes, *Low* and *High*, represent the greatest lower bound and least upper bound, respectively, of the lattice. All constants are of class *Low*.

Information can be passed into or out of a procedure through parameters. We classify parameters as *input parameters* (through which data is passed into the procedure), *output parameters* (through which data is passed out of the procedure), and *input/output parameters* (through which data is passed into and out of the procedure).

```
(* input parameters are named i_s; output parameters, o_s; *)
(* and input/output parameters, io_s, with s a subscript *)
proc something(i_1, ..., i_k; var o_1, ..., o_m, io_1, ..., io_n);
var l_1, ..., l_j;                    (* local variables *)
begin
        S;                            (* body of procedure *)
end;
```

The class of an input parameter is simply the class of the actual argument:

i_s: *type* **class** { i_s }

Let $r_1, ..., r_p$ be the set of input and input/output variables from which information flows to the output variable o_s. The declaration for the type must capture this:

o_s: *type* **class** { $r_1, ..., r_p$ }

(We implicitly assume that any output-only parameter is initialized in the procedure.) The input/output parameters are like output parameters, except that the initial value (as input) affects the allowed security classes. Again, let $r_1, ..., r_p$ be defined as above. Then:

io_s: *type* **class** { $r_1, ..., r_p, io_1, ..., io_k$ }

EXAMPLE: Consider the following procedure for adding two numbers.

```
proc sum(x: int class { x };
            var out: int class { x, out });
begin
        out := out + x;
end;
```

Here, we require that $x \leq out$ and $out \leq out$ (the latter holding because $\leq$ is reflexive).

The declarations presented so far deal only with basic types, such as integers, characters, floating point numbers, and so forth. Nonscalar types, such as arrays, records (structures), and variant records (unions) also contain information. The rules for information flow classes for these data types are built on the scalar types.
Consider the array

```
a: array 1 .. 100 of int;
```

First, look at information flows out of an element $a[i]$ of the array. In this case, information flows from $a[i]$ and from i, the latter by virtue of the index indicating which element of the array to use. Information flows into $a[i]$ affect only the value in $a[i]$, and so do not affect the information in i. Thus, for information flows from $a[i]$, the class involved is $lub\{\ \underline{a[i]},\ \underline{i}\ \}$; for information flows into $a[i]$, the class involved is $\underline{a[i]}$.

15.2.2 Program Statements

A program consists of several types of statements. Typically, they are

1. Assignment statements
2. Compound statements
3. Conditional statements
4. Iterative statements
5. Goto statements
6. Procedure calls
7. Function calls
8. Input/output statements.

We consider each of these types of statements separately, with two exceptions. Function calls can be modeled as procedure calls by treating the return value of the function as an output parameter of the procedure. Input/output statements can be modeled as assignment statements in which the value is assigned to (or assigned from) a file. Hence, we do not consider function calls and input/output statements separately.

15.2.2.1 Assignment Statements

An assignment statement has the form

```
y := f(x₁, ..., xₙ)
```

where y and $x_1, \ldots, x_n$ are variables and f is some function of those variables. Information flows from each of the x_i's to y. Hence, the requirement for the information flow to be secure is

- $lub\{\underline{x_1}, \ldots, \underline{x_n}\} \leq \underline{y}$

EXAMPLE: Consider the statement

```
x := y + z;
```

Then the requirement for the information flow to be secure is $lub\{\ \underline{y}, \underline{z}\ \} \leq \underline{x}$.

15.2.2.2   Compound Statements

A compound statement has the form

```
begin
        S1;
        ...
        Sn;
end;
```

where each of the S_i's is a statement. If the information flow in each of the statements is secure, then the information flow in the compound statement is secure. Hence, the requirements for the information flow to be secure are

- S_1 secure

- ...

- S_n secure

EXAMPLE: Consider the statements

```
begin
        x := y + z;
        a := b * c - x;
end;
```

Then the requirements for the information flow to be secure are $lub\{\ \underline{y}, \underline{z}\ \} \leq \underline{x}$ for S_1 and $lub\{\ \underline{b}, \underline{c}, \underline{x}\ \} \leq \underline{a}$ for S_2. So, the requirements for secure information flow are $lub\{\ \underline{y}, \underline{z}\ \} \leq \underline{x}$ and $lub\{\ \underline{b}, \underline{c}, \underline{x}\ \} \leq \underline{a}$.

15.2.2.3   Conditional Statements

A conditional statement has the form

```
if f(x1, ..., xn) then
        S1;
else
        S2;
end;
```

where $x_1, ..., x_n$ are variables and f is some (boolean) function of those variables. Either S_1 or S_2 may be executed, depending on the value of f, so both must be secure. As discussed earlier, the selection of either S_1 or S_2 imparts information about the values of the variables $x_1, ..., x_n$, so information must be able to flow from those variables to any targets of assignments in S_1 and S_2. This is possible if and only if the *lowest* class of the targets dominates the highest class of the variables $x_1, ..., x_n$. Thus, the requirements for the information flow to be secure are

- S_1 secure
- S_2 secure
- $lub\{\underline{x_1}, ..., \underline{x_n}\} \leq glb\{\underline{y} \mid y$ is the target of an assignment in S_1 and $S_2\ \}$

As a degenerate case, if statement S_2 is empty, it is trivially secure and has no assignments.

EXAMPLE: Consider the statements

```
if x + y < z then
        a := b;
else
        d := b * c - x;
end;
```

Then the requirements for the information flow to be secure are $\underline{b} \leq \underline{a}$ for S_1 and $lub\{\ \underline{b}, \underline{c}, \underline{x}\ \} \leq \underline{d}$ for S_2. But the statement that is executed depends on the values of x, y, and z. Hence, information also flows from x, y, and z to d and a. So, the requirements are $lub\{\ \underline{y}, \underline{z}\ \} \leq \underline{x}$, $\underline{b} \leq \underline{a}$, and $lub\{\ \underline{x}, \underline{y}, \underline{z}\ \} \leq glb\{\ \underline{a}, \underline{d}\ \}$.

15.2.2.4   Iterative Statements

An iterative statement has the form

```
while f(x₁, ..., xₙ) do
        S;
```

where $x_1, ..., x_n$ are variables and f is some (boolean) function of those variables. Aside from the repetition, this is a conditional statement, so the requirements for information flow to be secure for a conditional statement apply here.

To handle the repetition, first note that the number of repetitions causes information to flow only through assignments to variables in S. The number of repetitions is controlled by the values in the variables $x_1, ..., x_n$, so information flows from those variables to the targets of assignments in S—but this is detected by the requirements for information flow of conditional statements.

However, if the program never leaves the iterative statement, statements after the loop will never be executed. In this case, information has flowed from the variables $x_1, ..., x_n$ by the *absence* of execution. Hence, secure information flow also requires that the loop terminate.

Thus, the requirements for the information flow to be secure are

- Iterative statement terminates
- *S* secure
- $lub\{\underline{x_1}, ..., \underline{x_n}\} \leq glb\{\underline{y} \mid y$ is the target of an assignment in $S\ \}$

EXAMPLE: Consider the statements

```
while i < n do
begin
      a[i] := b[i];
      i := i + 1;
end;
```

This loop terminates. If $n \leq i$ initially, the loop is never entered. If $i < n$, i is incremented by a positive integer, 1, and so increases, at each iteration. Hence, after $n - i$ iterations, $n = i$, and the loop terminates.

Now consider the compound statement that makes up the body of the loop. The first statement is secure if $\underline{i} \leq \underline{a[i]}$ and $\underline{b[i]} \leq \underline{a[i]}$; the second statement is secure because $\underline{i} \leq \underline{i}$. Hence, the compound statement is secure if $lub\{\ \underline{i}, \underline{b[i]}\ \} \leq \underline{a[i]}$.

Finally, $a[i]$ and i are targets of assignments in the body of the loop. Hence, information flows into them from the variables in the expression in the *while* statement. So, $lub\{\ \underline{i}, \underline{n}\ \} \leq glb\{\ \underline{a[i]}, \underline{i}\ \}$. Putting these together, the requirement for the information flow to be secure is $lub\{\ \underline{b[i]}, \underline{i}, \underline{n}\ \} \leq glb\{\ \underline{a[i]}, \underline{i}\ \}$ (see Exercise 2).

15.2.2.5 Goto Statements

A goto statement contains no assignments, so no explicit flows of information occur. Implicit flows may occur; analysis detects these flows.

Definition 15–4. A *basic block* is a sequence of statements in a program that has one entry point and one exit point.

EXAMPLE: Consider the following code fragment.

```
proc transmatrix(x: array [1..10][1..10] of int class { x };
          var y: array [1..10][1..10] of int class { y } );
    var i, j: int class { tmp };
    begin
        i := 1;                    (* b₁ *)
    12: if i > 10 goto 17;         (* b₂ *)
        j := 1;                    (* b₃ *)
    14: if j > 10 then goto 16;    (* b₄ *)
```

```
        y[j][i] := x[i][j];              (* b₅ *)
        j := j + 1;
        goto 14;
   16:  i := i + 1;                       (* b₆ *)
        goto 12;
   17:                                    (* b₇ *)
end;
```

There are seven basic blocks, labeled b_1 through b_7 and separated by lines. The second and fourth blocks have two ways to arrive at the entry—either from a jump to the label or from the previous line. They also have two ways to exit—either by the branch or by falling through to the next line. The fifth block has three lines and always ends with a branch. The sixth block has two lines and can be entered either from a jump to the label or from the previous line. The last block is always entered by a jump.

Control within a basic block flows from the first line to the last. Analyzing the flow of control within a program is therefore equivalent to analyzing the flow of control among the program's basic blocks. Figure 15–1 shows the flow of control among the basic blocks of the body of the procedure *transmatrix*.

When a basic block has two exit paths, the block reveals information implicitly by the path along which control flows. When these paths converge later in the program, the (implicit) information flow derived from the exit path from the basic block becomes either explicit (through an assignment) or irrelevant. Hence, the class

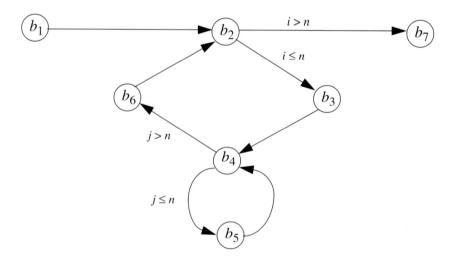

Figure 15–1   The control flow graph of the procedure *transmatrix*. The basic blocks are labeled b_1 through b_7. The conditions under which branches are taken are shown over the edges corresponding to the branches.

of the expression that causes a particular execution path to be selected affects the required classes of the blocks along the path up to the block at which the divergent paths converge.

Definition 15–5. An *immediate forward dominator* of a basic block b (written $IFD(b)$) is the first block that lies on all paths of execution that pass through b.

EXAMPLE: In the procedure *transmatrix*, the immediate forward dominators of each block are $IFD(b_1) = b_2$, $IFD(b_2) = b_7$, $IFD(b_3) = b_4$, $IFD(b_4) = b_6$, $IFD(b_5) = b_4$, and $IFD(b_6) = b_2$.

Computing the information flow requirement for the set of blocks along the path is now simply applying the logic for the conditional statement. Each block along the path is taken because of the value of an expression. Information flows from the variables of the expression into the set of variables assigned in the blocks. Let B_i be the set of blocks along an execution path from b_i to $IFD(b_i)$, but excluding these endpoints. (See Exercise 3.) Let $x_{i1}, \ldots, x_{in}$ be the set of variables in the expression that selects the execution path containing the blocks in B_i. The requirements for the program's information flows to be secure are

- All statements in each basic block secure
- $lub\{x_{i1}, \ldots, x_{in}\} \leq glb\{\ y \mid y$ is the target of an assignment in $B_i\ \}$

EXAMPLE: Consider the body of the procedure *transmatrix*. We first state requirements for information flow within each basic block:

b_1: $Low \leq \underline{i} \Rightarrow$ secure
b_3: $Low \leq \underline{j} \Rightarrow$ secure
b_5: $lub\{\ \underline{x[i][j]}, \underline{i}, \underline{j}\ \} \leq \underline{y[j][i]}; \underline{j} \leq \underline{j} \Rightarrow lub\{\ \underline{x[i][j]}, \underline{i}, \underline{j}\ \} \leq \underline{y[j][i]}$
b_6: $lub\{\ Low, \underline{i}\ \} \leq \underline{i} \Rightarrow$ secure

The requirement for the statements in each basic block to be secure is, for $i = 1, \ldots, n$ and $j = 1, \ldots, n$, $lub\{\ \underline{x[i][j]}, \underline{i}, \underline{j}\ \} \leq \underline{y[j][i]}$. By the declarations, this is true when $lub\{\underline{x}, \underline{i}\} \leq \underline{y}$.

In this procedure, $B_2 = \{\ b_3, b_4, b_5, b_6\ \}$ and $B_4 = \{\ b_5\ \}$. Thus, in B_2, statements assign values to i, j, and $y[j][i]$. In B_4, statements assign values to j and $y[j][i]$. The expression controlling which basic blocks in B_2 are executed is $i \leq 10$; the expression controlling which basic blocks in B_4 are executed is $j \leq 10$. Secure information flow requires that $\underline{i} \leq glb\{\ \underline{i}, \underline{j}, \underline{y[j][i]}\} $ and $\underline{j} \leq glb\{\ \underline{j}, \underline{y[j][i]}\ \}$. In other words, $\underline{i} \leq glb\{\ \underline{i}, \underline{y}\ \}$ and $\underline{i} \leq glb\{\ \underline{i}, \underline{y}\ \}$, or $\underline{i} \leq \underline{y}$.

Combining these requirements, the requirement for the body of the procedure to be secure with respect to information flow is $lub\{\underline{x}, \underline{i}\} \leq \underline{y}$.

15.2.2.6   Procedure Calls

A procedure call has the form

```
proc procname(i₁, ..., iₘ : int; var o₁, ..., oₙ : int);
begin
      S;
end;
```

where each of the i_j's is an input parameter and each of the o_j's is an input/output parameter. The information flow in the body S must be secure. As discussed earlier, information flow relationships may also exist between the input parameters and the output parameters. If so, these relationships are necessary for S to be secure. The actual parameters (those variables supplied in the call to the procedure) must also satisfy these relationships for the call to be secure. Let $x_1, ..., x_m$ and $y_1, ..., y_n$ be the actual input and input/output parameters, respectively. The requirements for the information flow to be secure are

- S secure
- For $j = 1, ..., m$ and $k = 1, ..., n$, if $\underline{i_j} \leq \underline{o_k}$ then $\underline{x_j} \leq \underline{y_k}$
- For $j = 1, ..., n$ and $k = 1, ..., n$, if $\underline{o_j} \leq \underline{o_k}$ then $\underline{y_j} \leq \underline{y_k}$

EXAMPLE: Consider the procedure *transmatrix* from the preceding section. As we showed there, the body of the procedure is secure with respect to information flow when $lub\{\underline{x}, \underline{tmp}\} \leq \underline{y}$. This indicates that the formal parameters x and y have the information flow relationship $\underline{x} \leq \underline{y}$. Now, suppose a program contains the call

```
transmatrix(a, b)
```

The second condition asserts that this call is secure with respect to information flow if and only if $\underline{a} \leq \underline{b}$.

15.2.3   Exceptions and Infinite Loops

Exceptions can cause information to flow.

EXAMPLE: Consider the following procedure, which copies the (approximate) value of x to y.[1]

```
proc copy(x: int class { x }; var y: int class Low);
var   sum: int class { x };
      z: int class Low;
```

---

[1] From Denning [242], p. 306.

```
begin
     z := 0;
     sum := 0;
     y := 0;
     while z = 0 do begin
              sum := sum + x;
              y := y + 1;
     end
end
```

When *sum* overflows, a trap occurs. If the trap is not handled, the procedure exits. The value of *x* is *MAXINT* / *y*, where *MAXINT* is the largest integer representable as an *int* on the system. At no point, however, is the flow relationship $\underline{x} \leq \underline{y}$ checked.

If exceptions are handled explicitly, the compiler can detect problems such as this. Denning again supplies such a solution.

EXAMPLE: Suppose the system ignores all exceptions unless the programmer specifically handles them. Ignoring the exception in the preceding example would cause the program to loop indefinitely. So, the programmer would want the loop to terminate when the exception occurred. The following line does this.

```
on overflowexception sum do z := 1;
```

This line causes information to flow from *sum* to *z*, meaning that $\underline{sum} \leq \underline{z}$. Because $\underline{z}$ is *Low* and $\underline{sum}$ is { *x* }, this is incorrect and the procedure is not secure with respect to information flow.

Denning also notes that infinite loops can cause information to flow in unexpected ways.

EXAMPLE: The following procedure copies data from *x* to *y*. It assumes that *x* and *y* are either 0 or 1.

```
proc copy(x: int 0..1 class { x };
            var y: int 0..1 class Low);
begin
     y := 0;
     while x = 0 do
            (* nothing *);
     y := 1;
end.
```

If *x* is 0 initially, the procedure does not terminate. If *x* is 1, it does terminate, with *y* being 1. At no time is there an explicit flow from *x* to *y*. This is an example of a *covert channel*, which we will discuss in detail in the next chapter.

15.2.4 Concurrency

Of the many concurrency control mechanisms that are available, we choose to study information flow using semaphores [270]. Their operation is simple, and they can be used to express many higher-level constructs [135, 718]. The specific semaphore constructs are

```
wait(x): if x = 0 then block until x > 0; x := x - 1;
signal(x): x := x + 1;
```

where x is a semaphore. As usual, the *wait* and the *signal* are indivisible; once either one has started, no other instruction will execute until the *wait* or *signal* finishes.

Reitman and his colleagues [33, 748] point out that concurrent mechanisms add information flows when values common to multiple processes cause specific actions. For example, in the block

```
begin
      wait(sem);
      x := x + 1;
end;
```

the program blocks at the *wait* if *sem* is 0, and executes the next statement when *sem* is nonzero. The earlier certification requirement for compound statements is not sufficient because of the implied flow between *sem* and x. The certification requirements must take flows among local and shared variables (semaphores) into account.

Let the block be

```
begin
      S₁;
      ...
      Sₙ;
end;
```

Assume that each of the statements $S_1, \ldots, S_n$ is certified. Semaphores in the *signal* do not affect information flow in the program in which the *signal* occurs, because the *signal* statement does not block. But following a *wait* statement, which may block, information implicitly flows from the semaphore in the *wait* to the targets of successive assignments.

Let statement S_i be a *wait* statement, and let *shared*(S_i) be the set of shared variables that are read (so information flows from them). Let $g(S_i)$ be the greatest lower bound of the targets of assignments following S_i. A requirement that the block be secure is that $\underline{shared(S_i)} \leq \underline{g(S_i)}$. Thus, the requirements for certification of a compound statement with concurrent constructs are

- S_1 secure
- ...
- S_n secure
- For $i = 1, ..., n$ [$\underline{shared(S_i)} \leq g(\underline{S_i})$]

EXAMPLE: Consider the statements

```
begin
     x := y + z;
     wait(sem);
     a := b * c - x;
end;
```

The requirements that the information flow be secure are $lub\{\underline{y}, \underline{z}\} \leq \underline{x}$ for S_1 and $lub\{\underline{b}, \underline{c}, \underline{x}\} \leq \underline{a}$ for S_2. Information flows implicitly from *sem* to *a*, so $\underline{sem} \leq \underline{a}$. The requirements for certification are $lub\{\underline{y}, \underline{z}\} \leq \underline{x}$, $lub\{\underline{b}, \underline{c}, \underline{x}\} \leq \underline{a}$, and $\underline{sem} \leq \underline{a}$.

Loops are handled similarly. The only difference is in the last requirement, because after completion of one iteration of the loop, control may return to the beginning of the loop. Hence, a semaphore may affect assignments that precede the *wait* statement in which the semaphore is used. This simplifies the last condition in the compound statement requirement considerably. Information must be able to flow from all shared variables named in the loop to the targets of all assignments. Let $shared(S_i)$ be the set of shared variables read, and let $t_1, ..., t_m$ be the targets of assignments in the loop. Then the certification conditions for the iterative statement

```
while f(x₁, ..., xₙ) do
     S;
```

are

- Iterative statement terminates
- *S* secure
- $lub\{\underline{x_1}, ..., \underline{x_n}\} \leq glb\{\underline{t_1}, ..., \underline{t_m}\}$
- $lub\{\underline{shared(S_1)}, ,,,, \underline{shared(S_n)}\} \leq glb\{\underline{t_1}, ..., \underline{t_m}\}$

EXAMPLE: Consider the statements

```
while i < n do
begin
     a[i] := item;
     wait(sem);
     i := i + 1;
end;
```

This loop terminates. If $n \leq i$ initially, the loop is never entered. If $i < n$, i is incremented by a positive integer, 1, and so increases, at each iteration. Hence, after $n - i$ iterations, $n = i$, and the loop terminates.

Now consider the compound statement that makes up the body of the loop. The first statement is secure if $\underline{i} \leq \underline{a[i]}$ and $\underline{item} \leq \underline{a[i]}$. The third statement is secure because $\underline{i} \leq \underline{i}$. The second statement induces an implicit flow, so $\underline{sem} \leq \underline{a[i]}$ and $\underline{sem} \leq \underline{i}$. The requirements are thus $\underline{i} \leq \underline{a[i]}$, $\underline{item} \leq \underline{a[i]}$, $\underline{sem} \leq \underline{a[i]}$, and $\underline{sem} \leq \underline{i}$.

Finally, concurrent statements have no information flow among them per se. Any such flows occur because of semaphores and involve compound statements (discussed above). The certification conditions for the concurrent statement

```
cobegin
     S₁;
     ...
     Sₙ;
coend;
```

are

- S_1 secure
- ...
- S_n secure

EXAMPLE: Consider the statements

```
cobegin
     x := y + z;
     a := b * c - y;
coend;
```

The requirements that the information flow be secure are $lub\{\, \underline{y}, \underline{z}\,\} \leq \underline{x}$ for S_1 and $lub\{\, \underline{b}, \underline{c}, \underline{y}\,\} \leq \underline{a}$ for S_2. The requirement for certification is simply that both of these requirements hold.

15.2.5   Soundness

Denning and Denning [247], Andrews and Reitman [33], and others build their argument for security on the intuition that combining secure information flows produces a secure information flow, for some security policy. However, they never formally prove this intuition. Volpano, Irvine, and Smith [920] express the semantics of the above-mentioned information on flow analysis as a set of types, and equate certification that a certain flow can occur to the correct use of types. In this context, checking for valid information flows is equivalent to checking that variable and expression types conform to the semantics imposed by the security policy.

Let x and y be two variables in the program. Let x's label dominate y's label. A set of information flow rules is sound if the value in x cannot affect the value in y during the execution of the program. Volpano, Irvine, and Smith use language-based techniques to prove that, given a type system equivalent to the certification rules discussed above, all programs without type errors have the noninterference property described above. Hence, the information flow certification rules of Denning and of Andrews and Reitman are sound.

15.3   Execution-Based Mechanisms

The goal of an execution-based mechanism is to prevent an information flow that violates policy. Checking the flow requirements of explicit flows achieves this result for statements involving explicit flows. Before the assignment

$$y = f(x_1, \ldots, x_n)$$

is executed, the execution-based mechanism verifies that

$$lub(\underline{x}_1, \ldots, \underline{x}_n) \leq \underline{y}$$

If the condition is true, the assignment proceeds. If not, it fails. A naïve approach, then, is to check information flow conditions whenever an explicit flow occurs.

Implicit flows complicate checking.

EXAMPLE: Let x and y be variables. The requirement for certification for a particular statement y op x is that $\underline{x} \leq \underline{y}$. The conditional statement

$$if\ x = 1\ then\ y := a;$$

causes a flow from x to y. Now, suppose that when $x \neq 1$, $\underline{x} = High$ and $\underline{y} = Low$. If flows were verified only when explicit, and $x \neq 1$, the implicit flow would not be checked. The statement may be incorrectly certified as complying with the information flow policy.

Fenton explored this problem using a special abstract machine.

15.3.1   Fenton's Data Mark Machine

Fenton [313] created an abstract machine called the *Data Mark Machine* to study handling of implicit flows at execution time. Each variable in this machine had an associated security class, or tag. Fenton also included a tag for the program counter (PC).

The inclusion of the PC allowed Fenton to treat implicit flows as explicit flows, because branches are merely assignments to the PC. He defined the semantics of the Data Mark Machine. In the following discussion, *skip* means that the instruction is not executed, *push(x, x)* means to push the variable x and its security class $\underline{x}$ onto the program stack, and *pop(x, x)* means to pop the top value and security class off the program stack and assign them to x and $\underline{x}$, respectively.

Fenton defined five instructions. The relationships between execution of the instructions and the classes of the variables are as follows.

1. The increment instruction

   ```
   x := x + 1
   ```

   is equivalent to

   ```
   if PC ≤ x then x := x + 1; else skip
   ```

2. The conditional instruction

   ```
   if x = 0 then goto n else x := x - 1
   ```

   is equivalent to

   ```
   if x = 0 then { push(PC, PC); PC = lub(PC, x); PC := n; }
   else            { if PC ≤ x then { x := x - 1; } else skip }
   ```

   This branches, and pushes the PC and its security class onto the program stack. (As is customary, the PC is incremented so that when it is popped, the instruction following the *if* statement is executed.) This captures the PC containing information from x (specifically, that x is 0) while following the **goto**.

3. The return

   ```
   return
   ```

   is equivalent to

   ```
   pop(PC, PC);
   ```

This returns control to the statement following the last *if* statement. Because the flow of control would have arrived at this statement, the PC no longer contains information about *x*, and the old class can be restored.

4. The branch instruction

```
if' x = 0 then goto n else x := x - 1
```

is equivalent to

```
if x = 0 then { if x ≤ PC then { PC := n; } else skip }
else            { if PC ≤ x then { x := x - 1; } else skip }
```

This branches without saving the PC on the stack. If the branch occurs, the PC is in a higher security class than the conditional variable *x*, so adding information from *x* to the PC does not change the PC's security class.

5. The halt instruction

```
halt
```

is equivalent to

```
if program stack empty then halt execution
```

The program stack being empty ensures that the user cannot obtain information by looking at the program stack after the program has halted (for example, to determine which *if* statement was last taken).

EXAMPLE: Consider the following program, in which *x* initially contains 0 or 1.[2]

```
1.  if x = 0 then goto 4 else x := x - 1
2.  if z = 0 then goto 6 else z := z - 1
3.  halt
4.  z := z + 1
5.  return
6.  y := y + 1
7.  return
```

This program copies the value of *x* to *y*. Suppose that *x* = 1 initially. The following table shows the contents of memory, the security class of the PC at each step, and the corresponding certification check.

---

[2] From Denning [242], Figure 5.7, p. 290.

x	y	z	PC	PC	stack	certification check
1	0	0	1	*Low*	—	
0	0	0	2	*Low*	—	$Low \leq \underline{x}$
0	0	0	6	$\underline{x}$	(3, *Low*)	
0	1	0	7	$\underline{x}$	(3, *Low*)	$\underline{PC} \leq \underline{y}$
0	1	0	3	*Low*	—	

Fenton's machine handles errors by ignoring them. Suppose that, in the program above, $\underline{y} \leq \underline{x}$. Then at the fifth step, the certification check fails (because $\underline{PC} = \underline{x}$). So, the assignment is skipped, and at the end $y = 0$ regardless of the value of x. But if the machine reports errors, the error message informing the user of the failure of the certification check means that the program has attempted to execute step 6. It could do so only if it had taken the branch in step 2, meaning that $z = 0$. If $z = 0$, then the *else* branch of statement 1 could not have been taken, meaning that $x = 0$ initially.

To prevent this type of deduction, Fenton's machine continues executing in the face of errors, but ignores the statement that would cause the violation. This satisfies the requirements. Aborting the program, or creating an exception visible to the user, would also cause information to flow against policy.

The problem with reporting of errors is that a user with lower clearance than the information causing the error can deduce the information from knowing that there has been an error. If the error is logged in such a way that the entries in the log, and the action of logging, are visible only to those who have adequate clearance, then no violation of policy occurs. But if the clearance of the user is sufficiently high, then the user can see the error without a violation of policy. Thus, the error can be logged for the system administrator (or other appropriate user), even if it cannot be displayed to the user who is running the program. Similar comments apply to any exception action, such as abnormal termination.

15.3.2   Variable Classes

The classes of the variables in the examples above are fixed. Fenton's machine alters the class of the PC as the program runs. This suggests a notion of dynamic classes, wherein a variable can change its class. For explicit assignments, the change is straightforward. When the assignment

```
y := f(x₁, ..., xₙ)
```

occurs, y's class is changed to $lub(\underline{x}_1, \ldots, \underline{x}_n)$. Again, implicit flows complicate matters.

EXAMPLE: Consider the following program (which is the same as the program in the example for the Data Mark Machine).[3]

---

[3] From Denning [242], Figure 5.5, p. 285.

```
proc copy(x : integer class { x };
          var y : integer class { y });
var z : integer class variable { Low };
begin
     y := 0;
     z := 0;
     if x = 0 then z := 1;
     if z = 0 then y := 1;
end;
```

In this program, z is variable and initially *Low*. It changes when something is assigned to z. Flows are certified whenever anything is assigned to y. Suppose $y < x$.

If $x = 0$ initially, the first statement checks that $Low \leq y$ (trivially true). The second statement sets z to 0 and z to *Low*. The third statement changes z to 1 and z to $lub(Low, x)$ $= x$. The fourth statement is skipped (because $z = 1$). Hence, y is set to 0 on exit.

If $x = 1$ initially, the first statement checks that $Low \leq y$ (trivially true). The second statement sets z to 0 and z to *Low*. The third statement is skipped (because $x = 1$). The fourth statement assigns 1 to y and checks that $lub(Low, z) = Low \leq y$ (again, trivially true). Hence, y is set to 1 on exit.

Information has therefore flowed from x to y even though $y < x$. The program violates the policy but is nevertheless certified.

Fenton's Data Mark Machine would detect the violation (see Exercise 4).

Denning [239] suggests an alternative approach. She raises the class of the targets of assignments in the conditionals and verifies the information flow requirements, even when the branch is not taken. Her method would raise z to x in the third statement (even when the conditional is false). The certification check at the fourth statement then would fail, because $lub(Low, z) = x \leq y$ is false.

Denning ([242], p. 285) credits Lampson with another mechanism. Lampson suggested changing classes only when explicit flows occur. But all flows force certification checks. For example, when $x = 0$, the third statement sets z to *Low* and then verifies $x \leq z$ (which is true if and only if $x = Low$).

15.4   Example Information Flow Controls

Like the program-based information flow mechanisms discussed above, both special-purpose and general-purpose computer systems have information flow controls at the system level. File access controls, integrity controls, and other types of access controls are mechanisms that attempt to inhibit the flow of information within a system, or between systems.

The first example is a special-purpose computer that checks I/O operations between a host and a secondary storage unit. It can be easily adapted to other purposes.

A mail guard for electronic mail moving between a classified network and an unclassified one follows. The goal of both mechanisms is to prevent the illicit flow of information from one system unit to another.

15.4.1   Security Pipeline Interface

Hoffman and Davis [428] propose adding a processor, called a *security pipeline interface* (SPI), between a host and a destination. Data that the host writes to the destination first goes through the SPI, which can analyze the data, alter it, or delete it. But the SPI does not have access to the host's internal memory; it can only operate on the data being output. Furthermore, the host has no control over the SPI. Hoffman and Davis note that SPIs could be linked into a series of SPIs, or be run in parallel.

They suggest that the SPI could check for corrupted programs. A host requests a file from the main disk. An SPI lies on the path between the disk and the host (see Figure 15–2.) Associated with each file is a cryptographic checksum that is stored on a second disk connected to the first SPI. When the file reaches the first SPI, it computes the cryptographic checksum of the file and compares it with the checksum stored on the second disk. If the two match, it assumes that the file is uncorrupted. If not, the SPI requests a clean copy from the second disk, records the corruption in a log, and notifies the user, who can update the main disk.

The information flow being restricted here is an integrity flow, rather than the confidentiality flow of the other examples. The inhibition is not to prevent the corrupt data from being seen, but to prevent the system from trusting it. This emphasizes that, although information flow is usually seen as a mechanism for maintaining confidentiality, its application in maintaining integrity is equally important.

15.4.2   Secure Network Server Mail Guard

Consider two networks, one of which has data classified SECRET[4] and the other of which is a public network. The authorities controlling the SECRET network need to

Figure 15–2 Use of an SPI to check for corrupted files.

---

[4] For this example, assume that the network has only one category, which we omit.

allow electronic mail to go to the unclassified network. They do not want SECRET information to transit the unclassified network, of course. The Secure Network Server Mail Guard (SNSMG) [844] is a computer that sits between the two networks. It analyzes messages and, when needed, sanitizes or blocks them.

The SNSMG accepts messages from either network to be forwarded to the other. It then applies several filters to the message; the specific filters may depend on the source address, destination address, sender, recipient, and/or contents of the message. Examples of the functions of such filters are as follows.

- Check that the sender of a message from the SECRET network is authorized to send messages to the unclassified network.

- Scan any attachments to messages coming from the unclassified network to locate, and eliminate, any computer viruses.

- Require all messages moving from the SECRET to the unclassified network to have a clearance label, and if the label is anything other than UNCLASS (unclassified), encipher the message before forwarding it to the unclassified network.

The SNSMG is a computer that runs two different message transfer agents (MTAs), one for the SECRET network and one for the unclassified network (see Figure 15–3). It uses an assured pipeline [700] to move messages from the MTA to the filter, and vice versa. In this pipeline, messages output from the SECRET network's MTA have type a, and messages output from the filters have a different type, type b. The unclassified network's MTA will accept as input only messages of type b. If a message somehow goes from the SECRET network's MTA to the unclassified network's MTA, the unclassified network's MTA will reject the message as being of the wrong type.

The SNSMG is an information flow enforcement mechanism. It ensures that information cannot flow from a higher security level to a lower one. It can perform other functions, such as restricting the flow of untrusted information from the unclassified network to the trusted, SECRET network. In this sense, the information flow is an integrity issue, not a confidentiality issue.

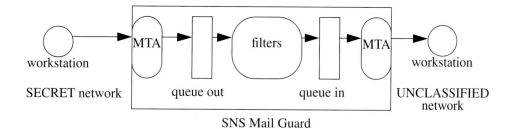

SNS Mail Guard

Figure 15–3   Secure Network Server Mail Guard. The SNSMG is processing a message from the SECRET network. The filters are part of a highly trusted system and perform checking and sanitizing of messages.

15.5   Summary

Two aspects of information flow are the amount of information flowing and the way in which it flows. Given the value of one variable, entropy measures the amount of information that one can deduce about a second variable. The flow can be explicit, as in the assignment of the value of one variable to another, or implicit, as in the antecedent of a conditional statement depending on the conditional expression.

Traditionally, models of information flow policies form lattices. Should the models not form lattices, they can be embedded in lattice structures. Hence, analysis of information flow assumes a lattice model.

A compiler-based mechanism assesses the flow of information in a program with respect to a given information flow policy. The mechanism either certifies that the program meets the policy or shows that it fails to meet the policy. It has been shown that if a set of statements meet the information flow policy, their combination (using higher-level language programming constructs) meets the information flow policy.

Execution-based mechanisms check flows at runtime. Unlike compiler-based mechanisms, execution-based mechanisms either allow the flow to occur (if the flow satisfies the information flow policy) or block it (if the flow violates the policy). Classifications of information may be static or dynamic.

Two example information flow control mechanisms, the Security Pipeline Interface and the Secure Network Server Mail Guard, provide information flow controls at the system level rather than at the program and program statement levels.

15.6   Further Reading

The Decentralized Label Model [660] allows one to specify information flow policies on a per-entity basis. Formal models sometimes lead to reports of flows not present in the system; Eckmann [290] discusses these reports, as well as approaches to eliminating them. Guttmann draws lessons from the failure of an information flow analysis technique [385].

Foley [327] presented a model of confinement flow suitable for nonlattice structures, and models nontransitive systems of infoormation flow. Denning [240] describes how to turn a partially ordered set into a lattice, and presents requirements for information flow policies.

The cascade problem is identified in the Trusted Network Interpretation [258]. Numerous studies of this problem describe analyses and approaches [320, 441, 631]; the problem of correcting it with minimum cost is *NP*-complete [440].

Gendler-Fishman and Gudes [351] examine a compile-time flow control mechanism for object-oriented databases. McHugh and Good describe a flow analysis tool [606] for the language Gypsy. Greenwald et al. [379], Kocher [522], Sands

[787], and Shore [826] discuss guards and other mechanisms for control of information flow.

A multithreaded environment adds to the complexity of constraints on information flow [842]. Some architectural characteristics can be used to enforce these constraints [462].

15.7   Exercises

1. Extend the semantics of the information flow security mechanism in Section 15.2.1 for records (structures).

2. Why can we omit the requirement $lub\{\ i,\ b[i]\ \} \le a[i]$ from the requirements for secure information flow in the example for iterative statements (see Section 15.2.2.4)?

3. In the flow certification requirement for the *goto* statement in Section 15.2.2.5, the set of blocks along an execution path from b_i to IFD(b_i) excludes these endpoints. Why are they excluded?

4. Prove that Fenton's Data Mark Machine described in Section 15.3.1 would detect the violation of policy in the execution time certification of the *copy* procedure.

5. Discuss how the Security Pipeline Interface in Section 15.4.1 can prevent information flows that violate a confidentiality model. (*Hint:* Think of scanning messages for confidential data and sanitizing or blocking that data.)

Chapter 16
Confinement Problem

> TROILUS: This is the monstruosity in love, lady; that
> the will is infinite and the execution confin'd; that
> the desire is boundless and the act a slave to limit.
> —*Troilus and Cressida* III, ii, 82–84.

When a program executes, it interacts with its environment. The security policy allows some interactions and disallows others. The confinement problem deals with prevention of processes from taking disallowed actions. Beginning with Lampson's characterization of this problem, this chapter continues with a discussion of methods for confinement such as virtual machines and sandboxes. It concludes with a discussion of covert channels. This chapter focuses on confinement. Chapter 19, "Malicious Logic," discusses tools and techniques used to breach confinement.

16.1   The Confinement Problem

Consider a client and a server. When the client issues a request to the server, the client sends the server some data. The server then uses the data to perform some function and returns a result (or no result) to the client. Access control affects the function of the server in two ways.

1. The server must ensure that the resources it accesses on behalf of the client include only those resources that the client is authorized to access.
2. The server must ensure that it does not reveal the client's data to any other entity not authorized to see the client's data.

The first requirement represents the goal of the service provider. That goal is to prevent the client from sending messages to the server that cause it to access, alter, transmit, or consume resources that the client is not authorized to access, alter, transmit, or consume. The second requirement represents the goal of the service user. That goal is to prevent the server from transmitting confidential information to the service provider. In both cases, the server must be confined to accessing only a specific set of resources.

EXAMPLE: A server balances accounts for subscribers. The subscribers use a client to transmit the register entries, the current bank balance, and those withdrawals and deposits that have cleared the bank to the server. The server returns the list of outstanding checks and deposits and any discrepancy between the register balance and the bank balance. Subscribers pay a fee for each use.

The service provider requires that the server correctly record who used the service each time it is used. Otherwise, the service provider cannot bill for the use of the service. The threat is that someone may use the service without being detected (and therefore without being charged) or that the user may impersonate another subscriber (resulting in the wrong subscriber being charged). The service provider also does not want the server to transmit billing records or any other unauthorized information to the client. The server should send only the information it derived from the data that the client sent. So the server must be confined to operating only on the data it is sent.

The subscriber expects certain security services from the server. The server must correctly log the user's invocation so that the user is not charged incorrectly. (This matches the need of the service provider.) The server must not record or transmit the data that the subscriber sends to it because the subscriber's data is confidential to the subscriber and is not relevant to the service provider. So the server must be confined to keeping the data to itself and to sending the results only to the subscriber.

Lampson [544] calls this the *confinement problem*.

Definition 16–1. The *confinement problem* is the problem of preventing a server from leaking information that the user of the service considers confidential.

One characteristic of processes that do not leak information comes from the observation that a process must store data for later retrieval (the leaking). A process that does not store information cannot leak it. However, in the extreme, such processes also cannot perform any computations, because an analyst could observe the flow of control (or state of the process) and from that flow deduce information about the inputs. This leads to the observation that a process that cannot be observed and cannot communicate with other processes cannot leak information. Lampson calls this *total isolation*.

In practice, achieving total isolation is difficult. The processes to be confined usually share resources such as CPUs, networks, and disk storage with other, unconfined processes. The unconfined processes can transmit information over those shared resources.

Definition 16–2. A *covert channel* is a path of communication that was not designed to be used for communication.

EXAMPLE: Process *p* is to be confined such that it cannot communicate with process *q*. However, processes *p* and *q* share a file system. In order for process *p* to send a message to process *q*, it creates a file called *send* in a directory that both processes can read. Just before process *q* is to read the information, *q* deletes the *send* file. Process *p* then transmits a bit by creating a file named *0bit* or *1bit*, as appropriate. When *q* detects either file, it records the bit and deletes the file. This continues until *p* creates a file called *end*, at which point the communication ceases.

Confinement is transitive. Assume that a process *p* is confined to prevent leakage. If it invokes a second process *q*, then *q* must be similarly confined or *q* could leak the information that *p* passes.

Definition 16–3. The *rule of transitive confinement* states that if a confined process invokes a second process, the second process must be as confined as the caller.

Confinement is a mechanism for enforcing the principle of least privilege (see Section 12.2.1). A properly confined process cannot transmit data to a second process unless the transmission is needed to complete their task. The problem is that the confined process needs access to the data to be transmitted and so the confinement must be on the transmission, not on the data access. To complicate matters, the process may have to transmit some information to the second process. In this case, the confinement mechanism must distinguish between transmission of authorized data and transmission of unauthorized data.

The combination of these problems illustrates the difficulty of preventing leakage. The dilemma is that modern computers are designed to share resources, and yet by the act of sharing they create channels of communication along which information can be leaked.

Lipner [570] examines the problem from a policy and modeling aspect. He considers two types of covert channels. The first involves the use of storage to transmit information. If a model correctly describes *all* ways in which information can be stored and read, then the model abstracts both legitimate and covert channels along which information can flow. The model constrains *all* accesses to storage. The only accesses allowed are those authorized by the policy, so the flows of information are legitimate. However, if the model does not capture all such flows, then unauthorized flows, or covert channels, arise.

Lipner then notes that all processes can obtain at least a rough idea of time. This makes time a communication channel. A program can "read" time by checking the system clock or (alternatively) by counting the number of instructions it has executed during a period of wall clock time. A program can "write" time by executing a set number of instructions and stopping, allowing another process to execute. This shared channel cannot be made exclusive unless a process does not share the computer with another process, which suggests isolation as a remedy.

Kocher's timing attacks on cryptosystems illustrate this problem [523]. Kocher notes that the instructions executed by implementations of cryptosystems

```
x := 1; atmp := a;
for i := 0 to k-1 do begin
    if z_i = 1 then
        x := (x * atmp) mod n;
    atmp := (atmp * atmp) mod n;
end;
result := x;
```

Figure 16–1   A fast modular exponentiation routine. This routine computes $x = a^z \bmod n$**. The bits of** z **are** $z_{k-1}, \ldots, z_0$**.**

depend on the setting of bits in the key. For example, the algorithm in Figure 16–1 implements a fast modular exponentiation function. If a bit is 1, two multiplications occur; otherwise, one multiplication occurs. The extra multiplication takes extra time. Kocher determines bits of the confidential exponent by measuring computation time.

We explore the mechanism of isolation first. Then we examine covert channels in more detail and discuss other approaches to analyzing them, including techniques for identifying covert channels and isolating them.

16.2   Isolation

Systems isolate processes in two ways. In the first, the process is presented with an environment that appears to be a computer running only that process or those processes to be isolated. In the second, an environment is provided in which process actions are analyzed to determine if they leak information. The first type of environment prevents the process from accessing the underlying computer system and any processes or resources that are not part of that environment. The second type of environment does not emulate a computer. It merely alters the interface between the existing computer and the process(es).

16.2.1   Virtual Machines

The first type of environment is called a *virtual machine*.

> **Definition 16–4.** A *virtual machine* is a program that simulates the hardware of a (possibly abstract) computer system.

A virtual machine uses a special operating system called a *virtual machine monitor* to provide a virtual machine on which conventional operating systems can run. Chapter 29 discusses virtual machines in more detail.

The primary advantage of a virtual machine is that existing operating systems do not need to be modified. They run on the virtual machine monitor. The virtual machine monitor enforces the desired security policy. This is transparent to the user. The virtual machine monitor functions as a security kernel.

In terms of policy, the virtual machine monitor deals with subjects (the subjects being the virtual machines). Even if one virtual machine is running hundreds of processes, the virtual machine monitor knows only about the virtual machine. Thus, it can apply security checks to its subjects, and those controls apply to the processes that those subjects are running. This satisfies the rule of transitive confinement.

EXAMPLE: The KVM/370 was a security-enhanced version of the IBM VM/370 virtual machine monitor [363]. This system provided virtual machines for its users, and one of its goals was to prevent communications between virtual machines of different security classes, so users in different security classes could use the system at the same time. Like VM/370, it provided virtual machines with minidisks and allowed systems to share some areas of disk. Unlike VM/370, it used a security policy to mediate access to shared areas of the disk to limit communications between systems.

EXAMPLE: Karger and colleagues at Digital Equipment Corporation developed a virtual machine monitor (VMM) for the DEC VAX [498]. The monitor is a security kernel and can run either the VMS or the Ultrix operating system. The VMM runs on the native VAX hardware and is invoked whenever the virtual machine executes a privileged instruction. Its structure is typical of virtual machines designed to provide security.

The VAX has four levels of privilege: user, supervisor, executive, and kernel modes. In order to provide a compatible virtual machine, the virtual machines must also have four levels of privilege. However, the kernel mode allows a process to access privileged instructions on the VAX hardware directly. Only the VMM is allowed to do this. The virtual machines cannot access kernel mode. The solution is to provide virtual modes. These modes are VM user (corresponding to user mode), VM supervisor mode, and VM executive and VM kernel modes (both actually executive mode).[1]

The VMM subjects are users and virtual machines. VMM has a basic, flat file system for its own use and partitions the remaining disk space among the virtual machines. Those machines may use any file structure they desire, and each virtual machine has its own set of file systems. Each subject and object has a multilevel security and integrity label, and the security and integrity levels form an *access class*. Two entities have the same access class if and only if their security and integrity labels are the same, and one entity dominates another if and only if both the security and integrity classes dominate.

An integral component of the VMM is an auditing mechanism. This mechanism records actions for later analysis.

---

[1] Chapter 29, "Virtual Machines," discusses this approach in more detail.

Because virtual machines provide the same interface for communication with other virtual machines that computers provide, those channels of communication can be controlled or severed. As mentioned earlier, if a single host runs multiple virtual machines, those virtual machines share the physical resources of the host on which they run. (They may also share logical resources, depending on how the virtualizing kernel is implemented.) This provides a fertile ground for covert channels, a subject explored in Section 16.3.

16.2.2   Sandboxes

A playground sandbox provides a safe environment for children to stay in. If the children leave the sandbox without supervision, they may do things they are not supposed to do. The computer sandbox is similar. It provides a safe environment for programs to execute in. If the programs "leave" the sandbox, they may do things that they are not supposed to do. Both types of sandboxes restrict the actions of their occupants.

> **Definition 16–5.** A *sandbox* is an environment in which the actions of a process are restricted according to a security policy.

Systems may enforce restrictions in two ways. First, the sandbox can limit the execution environment as needed. This is usually done by adding extra security-checking mechanisms to the libraries or kernel. The program itself is not modified. For example, the VMM kernel discussed earlier is a sandbox because it constrains the accesses of the (unmodified) operating systems that run on it. The Java virtual machine is a sandbox because its security manager limits access of downloaded programs to system resources as dictated by a security policy [152].

EXAMPLE: The operational kernel of the Sidewinder firewall [900] uses type enforcement to confine processes (see the example on page 254 in Section 14.3.1). This is an example of a sandbox built into a kernel, and it has the property that the sandbox is defined by the vendor. It is not intended to be altered at the site. Such a design is typical for a turnkey system, which is the intended use for a Sidewinder firewall.

The Java virtual machine, in which downloaded applets are executed, is another example of a sandbox. The sandbox restricts the set of files that the applet can access and the hosts to which the applet can connect. Other security mechanisms enhance the sandbox [369].

DTE, the type enforcement mechanism for DTEL [50, 336], is an example in which kernel modifications enable system administrators to configure their own sandboxes. The kernel enforces the constraints.

The second enforcement method is to modify the program (or process) to be executed. Dynamic debuggers [8, 296, 393, 867] and some profilers [101] use this technique by adding breakpoints to the code and, when the trap occurs, analyzing the state of the running process. A variant, known as *software fault isolation* [841, 925], adds instructions that perform memory access checks or other checks as the program runs, so any attempt to violate the security policy causes an error.

EXAMPLE: Janus [364] implements a sandbox. It is an execution environment in which system calls are trapped and checked. Users execute it to restrict the objects and modes of access of an untrusted program. Janus consists of a *framework*, which does the runtime checking, and *modules*, which determine which accesses are to be allowed.

Janus first reads a configuration file. This file instructs it to load certain modules. Along with the module identification is a list of constraints. The following example configuration file defines the environment variable **IFS** for the child and restricts the child's access to the file system. The child cannot access any files except those that are named below (this meets the principle of fail-safe defaults discussed in Section 12.2.2). The child can read or write to any file in the */usr* file system except for those in the */usr/lib* and */usr/local/lib* directories (which are read only) and in */usr/bin* (read and execute). The child can read any file in the */lib* directory and can read and execute any file in the */sbin* and */bin* directories. In the configuration file below, the first word in each instruction line is the name of the module and the other words are the arguments passed to the modules ("#" begins a comment).

```
# basic module
basic

# define subprocess environment variables
putenv IFS="\t\n " PATH=/sbin:/bin:/usr/bin TZ=PST8PDT

# deny access to everything except files under /usr
path deny read,write *
path allow read,write /usr/*
# allow subprocess to read files in library directories
# needed for dynamic loading
path allow read /lib/* /usr/lib/* /usr/local/lib/*
# needed so child can execute programs
path allow read,exec /sbin/* /bin/* /usr/bin/*
```

Each module constrains system calls. The framework uses the modules to build a linked list for each monitored system call. The list defines allowed and disallowed actions. Once this list has been constructed, the Janus framework invokes the program in such a way that all monitored system calls are trapped.

When the program executes a monitored system call, the program traps and the Janus framework is invoked. It has access to the arguments supplied to the sysem call. It validates that the system call, with these specific parameters, is allowed. If the system call is not allowed, the framework sets the child's environment so that the system call appears to have failed. If the system call is allowed, the framework returns control to the child, which in turn passes control to the kernel. On return, control goes to the framework, which updates any internal state and returns the results to the child.

An example use would be in reading MIME mail. One could have set the mail reading program to pass control to a Postscript display engine. Some such engines have a mechanism for executing system-level commands embedded in the Postscript file. Hence, an attacker could put a file deletion command in the Postscript file. The recipient would run the display engine to read the file, and some of her files would be deleted [191]. However, the user (or system administrator) can set up the Janus configuration file to disallow execution of any subprograms. Then the embedded command will be detected (on the system call to execute it) and rejected.

Like a virtual machine monitor, a sandbox forms part of the trusted computing base. If the sandbox fails, it provides less protection than it is believed to provide. Hence, ensuring that the sandbox correctly implements a desired security policy is critical to the security of the system.

16.3   Covert Channels

Covert channels use shared resources as paths of communication. This requires sharing of space or sharing of time.

> **Definition 16–6.** A *covert storage channel* uses an attribute of the shared resource. A *covert timing channel* uses a temporal or ordering relationship among accesses to a shared resource.

EXAMPLE: The covert channel in the example on page 289 is a covert storage channel. The shared resource is the directory and the names of the files in that directory. The processes communicate by altering characteristics (file names and file existence) of the shared resource.

EXAMPLE: A study of the security of the KVM/370 system [791] found that two virtual machines could establish a covert channel based on the CPU quantum that each virtual machine received. If the sending virtual machine wished to send a "0" bit, it would relinquish the CPU immediately; to send a "1," it would use its full quantum. By determining how quickly it got the CPU, the second virtual machine could deduce whether the first was sending a "1" or a "0." The shared resource is the CPU. The processes communicate by using a real-time clock to measure the intervals between accesses to the shared resource. Hence, this is a covert timing channel.

A covert timing channel is usually defined in terms of a real-time clock or a timer, but temporal relationships sometimes use neither. An ordering of events implies a time-based relationship that involves neither a real-time clock nor a timer.

EXAMPLE: Consider a variant of a channel identified in KVM/370 [363, 956]. Two virtual machines share cylinders 100 through 200 on a disk. The disk uses a SCAN algorithm [718] to schedule disk accesses. One virtual machine has security class *High*, and the other has class *Low*. A process on the *High* machine is written to send information to a process on the *Low* machine.

The process on the *Low* machine issues a read request for data on cylinder 150. When that request completes, it relinquishes the CPU. The process on the *High* machine runs, issues a seek to cylinder 140, and relinquishes the CPU. The process on the *Low* machine runs and issues seek requests to cylinders 139 and 161. Because the disk arm is moving over the cylinders in descending order, the seek issued to cylinder 139 is satisfied first, followed by the seek issued to cylinder 161. This ordering represents a 1 bit.

To send a 0 bit, the process on the *High* machine issues a read request for data on cylinder 160 instead of cylinder 140. Then the process on the *Low* machine's requests will be satisfied first on cylinder 161 and then on cylinder 139.

Is this a covert timing channel or a covert storage channel? Because it does not involve a real-time clock or timer, the usual definition implies that it is a covert storage channel.

Modify the example slightly to postulate a timer. The process on the *Low* machine uses this timer to determine how long it takes for its requests to complete. If the timer shows that the time required to satisfy the request for a seek to cylinder 139 is less than the time required to satisfy the request for a seek to cylinder 161, then a 1 bit is being sent. If the timings indicate the opposite, a 0 bit is being sent. This modification clearly uses a covert timing channel.

The difference between the modified example and the original example is the presence of a timer. The timer changes nothing about the way the channel works. For this reason, we include relative ordering of events as a covert timing channel.

A second property distinguishes between a covert channel that only the sender and receiver have access to and a covert channel that others have access to as well.

Definition 16–7. A *noiseless covert channel* is a covert channel that uses a resource available to the sender and receiver only. A *noisy covert channel* is a covert channel that uses a resource available to subjects other than the sender and receiver, as well as to the sender and receiver.

The difference between these two types of channels lies in the need to filter out extraneous information. Any information that the receiver obtains from a noiseless channel comes from the sender. However, in a noisy channel, the sender's information is mixed with meaningless information, or noise, from other entities using the resource. A noisy covert channel requires a protocol to minimize this interference.

The key properties of covert channels are *existence* and *bandwidth*. Existence tells us that there is a channel along which information can be transmitted. Bandwidth tells us how rapidly information can be sent. Covert channel analysis establishes both properties. Then the channels can be eliminated or their bandwidths can be reduced.

16.3.1   Detection of Covert Channels

Covert channels require sharing. The manner in which the resource is shared controls which subjects can send and receive information using that shared resource. Detection methods begin with this observation.

Porras and Kemmerer have devised an approach to representing security violations that spring from the application of fault trees [725]. They model the flow of information through shared resources with a tree. The paths of flow are identified in this structure. The analyst determines whether each flow is legitimate or covert.

A covert flow tree is a tree-structured representation of the sequence of operations that move information from one process to another. It consists of five types of nodes.

1. *Goal symbols* specify states that must exist for the information to flow. There are several such states:

   a. A *modification goal* is reached when an attribute is modified.

   b. A *recognition goal* is reached when a modification of an attribute is detected.

   c. A *direct recognition goal* is reached when a subject can detect the modification of an attribute by referencing it directly or calling a function that returns it.

   d. An *inferred recognition goal* is reached when a subject can detect the modification of an attribute without referencing it directly and without calling a function that references the attribute directly. For example, the subject may call a function that performs one of two computations depending on the value of the attribute in question.

   e. An *inferred-via goal* is reached when information is passed from one attribute to other attributes using a specified primitive operation (such as a system call).

   f. A *recognize-new-state goal* is reached when an attribute that was modified when information was passed using it is specified by an inferred-via goal. The *value* need not be determined, but the fact that the attribute has been modified must be determined.

2. An *operation symbol* is a symbol that represents a primitive operation. The operation symbols may vary among systems if they have different primitive operations.

3. A *failure symbol* indicates that information cannot be sent along the path on which it lies. It means that the goal to which it is attached cannot be met.

4. An *and symbol* is a goal that is reached when *both* of the following hold for all children:

   a. If the child is a goal, then the goal is reached.

   b. The child is an operation.

5. An *or symbol* is a goal that is reached when *either* of the following holds for any children:

    a. If the child is a goal, then the goal is reached.

    b. The child is an operation.

Constructing the tree is a three-step process. To make the steps concrete, we present a simple set of operations and then ask if they can create a covert channel.

EXAMPLE: Consider a file system in which each file has three attributes. The boolean attributes *locked* and *isopen* are true when the file is locked or opened, respectively, and are false otherwise. The third attribute, *inuse*, is a set that contains the process ID of each process that has the file open. The function *read_access(p, f)* is true if process *p* has read rights over file *f*, and *empty(s)* is true if set *s* has no members. The function *random* returns one of its arguments chosen at random. The following operations are defined.

```
(* lock the file if it is not locked and not opened *)
(* otherwise indicate it is locked by returning false *)
procedure Lockfile(f: file): boolean;
begin
   if not f.locked and empty(f.inuse) then
       f.locked := true;
end;

(* unlock the file *)
procedure Unlockfile(f: file);
begin
   if f.locked then
       f.locked := false;
end;

(* say whether the file is locked *)
function Filelocked(f: file): boolean;
begin
   Filelocked := f.locked;
end;

(* open the file if it isn't locked and the *)
(* process has the right to read the file *)
procedure Openfile(f: file);
begin
   if not f.locked and read_access(process_id, f) then
       (* add the process ID to the inuse set *)
       f.inuse = f.inuse + process_id;
end;
```

```
(* if the process can read the file, say if the *)
(* file is open, otherwise return a value at random *)
function Fileopened(f: file): boolean;
begin
   if not read_access(process_id, f) then
       Fileopened := random(true, false);
   else
       Fileopened := not isempty(f.inuse);
end
```

Assuming that processes are not allowed to communicate with one another, the reader is invited to try to find a covert storage channel.

The first step in constructing a covert flow tree is to determine what attributes (if any) the primitive operations reference, modify, and return.

EXAMPLE: The functions in the preceding example affect file attributes in different ways, as follows.

	Lockfile	Unlockfile	Filelocked	Openfile	Fileopened
reference	locked, inuse	locked	locked	locked, inuse	inuse
modify	locked	∅	∅	inuse	∅
return	∅	∅	locked	∅	inuse

The symbol ∅ means that no attribute is affected in the specified manner.

The second step begins with the goal of locating a covert storage channel that uses some attribute. The analyst constructs the covert flow tree. The type of goal controls the construction, as follows.

1. The *topmost goal* requires that the attribute be modified and that the modification be recognized. Hence, it has one child (an *and* symbol), which in turn has two children (a modification goal symbol and a recognition goal symbol).

2. A *modification goal* requires some primitive operation to modify the attribute. Hence, it has one *or* child, which has one child operation symbol per operation for all operations that modify the attribute.

3. A *recognition goal* requires that a subject either directly recognize or infer a change in an attribute. It has an *or* symbol as its child. The *or* symbol has two children, one a direct recognition goal symbol and the other an inferred recognition goal symbol.

4. A *direct recognition goal* requires that an operation access the attribute. Like the modification goal, it has one *or* child, and that child in turn has

one child operation symbol for each operation that returns the attribute. If no operation returns the attribute, a failure symbol is attached.

5. An *inferred recognition goal* requires that the modification be inferred on the basis of one or more other attributes. Hence, it has one child, an *or* symbol, which has one child inferred-via symbol for each operation that references an attribute and that modifies some attribute (possibly the same one that was referenced).

6. An *inferred-via goal* requires that the value of the attribute be inferred via some operation and a recognition of the new state of the attribute resulting from that operation. Hence, it has one child (an *and* symbol), which has two children (an operation symbol representing the primitive operation used to draw the inference and a recognize-new-state goal symbol).

7. A *recognize-new-state goal* requires that the value of the attribute be inferred via some operation and a recognition of the new state of the attribute resulting from that operation. The latter requires a recognition goal for the attribute. So, the child node of the recognize-new-state goal symbol is an *or* symbol, and for each attribute enabling the inference of the modification of the attribute in question, the *or* symbol has a recognition goal symbol child.

Tree construction ends when all paths through the tree terminate in either an operation symbol or a failure symbol. Because the construction is recursive, the analyst may encounter a loop in the tree construction. Should this happen, a parameter called *repeat* defines the number of times that the path may be traversed. This places an upper bound on the size of the tree.

EXAMPLE: We build the covert flow tree for the attribute *locked* in our previous two examples. The goal state is "covert storage channel via attribute *locked*." The *and* node beneath it has two children, "modification of attribute *locked*" and "recognition of attribute *locked*." At this point, the tree looks like this:

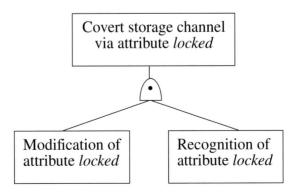

From the table in the preceding example, the operations *Lockfile* and *Unlock-file* modify the attribute *locked*. So that branch of the tree becomes:

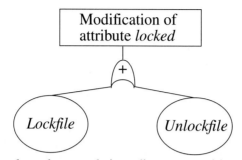

The recognition branch expands into direct recognition and inferred recognition branches. The direct recognition branch has an *and* with one child, *Filelocked*, because *Filelocked* returns the value of the *locked* attribute. The inferred recognition branch has an *or* child with one child, an "inferred-via" node that infers *locked* from *inuse*. This branch comes from comparing the "reference" row of the table in the preceding example with the "modify" row. If an operation references the *locked* attribute and modifies another attribute, inference is possible (assuming that the modification can be detected). At this point, the recognition branch looks like this:

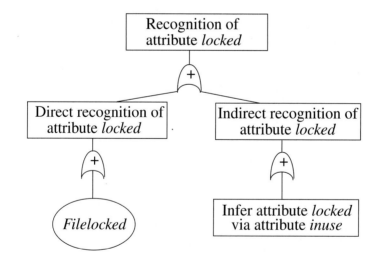

Inferring that the attribute *locked* has changed from the attribute *inuse* requires the operation *Openfile*. After that operation, the recognize-new-state goal represents the change in the attribute *inuse*:

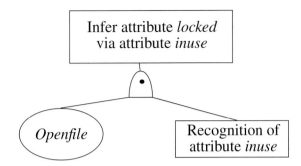

This in turn requires the recognition of modification of the attribute *inuse* (hence, a recognition state). The operation *Fileopened* recognizes this change directly; nothing recognizes it indirectly. The result is:

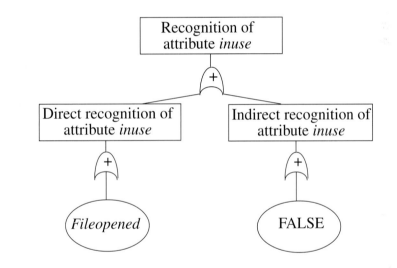

Figure 16–2 shows the full covert flow tree.

The analyst now constructs two lists. The first list contains sequences of operations that modify the attribute, and the second list contains sequences of operations that recognize modifications in the attribute. A sequence from the first list followed by a sequence from the second list is a channel along which information can flow. The analyst examines these channels to determine which are covert.

EXAMPLE: In the covert flow tree presented above, the first list has two sequences:

List 1 = ((*Lockfile*), (*Unlockfile*))

because both operations modify the attribute (and lie on the "modified" branch under the root of the tree). The second list also has two sequences:

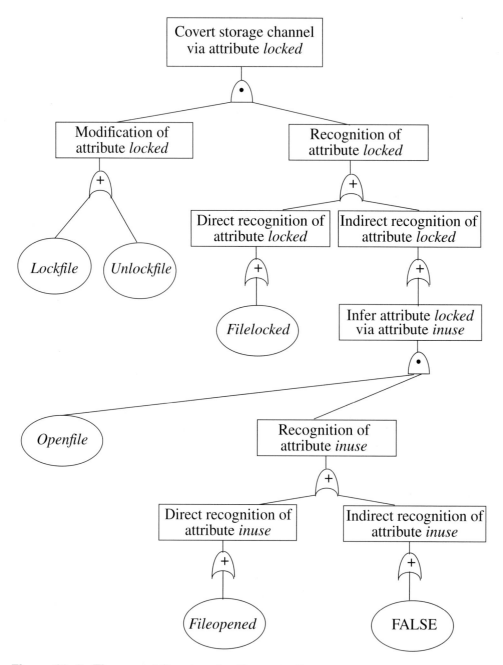

Figure 16–2 The covert flow tree for the operations.

List 2 = ((*Filelocked*), (*Openfile, Fileopened*))

—the first from the direct recognition of the modification of the attribute and the second from the indirect recognition. These sequences result in four channels of communication.

1. *Lockfile* followed by *Filelocked*
2. *Unlockfile* followed by *Filelocked*
3. *Lockfile* followed by *Openfile*, then *Fileopened*
4. *Unlockfile* followed by *Openfile*, then *Fileopened*.

If a *High*-level user transmits information to a *Low*-level user by locking and unlocking a file, the first two channels (in combination) represent a direct covert storage channel. The last two represent an indirect covert storage channel. To use the channel, the *High*-level process locks a file to send a 0 bit and unlocks a file to send a 1 bit. The *Low* process tries to open the locked file. It then uses *Fileopened* to see if it has opened the file. If the file is opened, the *High* process did not lock the file (a 0 bit). If the file is not opened, the *High* process did lock the file (a 1 bit).

The shared resource matrix model and covert flow trees spring from the idea of examining shared resources for modification and reference operations, and both can be used at any point within the software development life cycle. One advantage of covert flow trees over the SRM model is that the former identifies explicit sequences of operations that cause information to flow from one process to another. The latter identifies *channels* rather than sequences of operations. In comparisons involving file system access operations and the Secure Ada Target, the covert flow tree method identified sequences of operations corresponding to the covert storage channels found by the SRM method and the noninterference method, as well as one not found by the other two.

16.3.2   Mitigation of Covert Channels

Covert channels convey information by varying the use of shared resources. An obvious way to eliminate all covert channels is to require processes to state what resources they need before execution and provide these resources in such a manner that only the process can access them. This includes runtime, and when the stated runtime is reached, the process is terminated and the resources are released. The resources remain allocated for the full runtime even if the process terminates earlier. Otherwise, a second process could infer information from the timing of the release of the resources (including access to the CPU). This strategy effectively implements Lampson's idea of total isolation, but it is usually unworkable in practice.

An alternative approach is to obscure the amount of resources that a process uses. A receiving process cannot determine what amount of resource usage is attributable to the sender and what amount is attributable to the obfuscation. This can be done in two ways. First, the resources devoted to each process can be made uniform. This is a variant of isolation, because each process gets the same amount of resources and cannot tell whether a second process is accessing the resource by measuring the timing or amount of resources available. In essence, the system eliminates meaningful irregularities in resource allocation and use. Second, a system can inject randomness into the allocation and use of resources. The goal is to make the covert channel a noisy one and to have the noise dominate the channel. This does not close the covert channel (because it still exists) but renders it useless.

Both these techniques affect efficiency. Assigning fixed allocations and constraining use waste resources. Fixing the time slices on the KVM system means that the CPU will be unused (or will execute an idle process) when another virtual machine could run a non-idle process. Increasing the probability of aborts in the multilevel secure database system will abort some transactions that would normally commit, increasing the expected number of tries to update the database. Whether the closing of the covert channel or the limiting of the bandwidth compensates adequately for the loss in efficiency is a policy decision.

A device known as a *pump* is the basis of several techniques for defeating covert channels.

EXAMPLE: The pump [490] is a (hardware or software) tool for controlling a communication path between a *High* process and a *Low* process. It consists of a buffer for messages to and from the *High* process, a buffer for messages to and from the *Low* process, and a communications buffer of length n that is connected to both of the other buffers (see Figure 16–3). We assume that messages are numbered and that the communications buffer preserves messages if the pump crashes. Under these

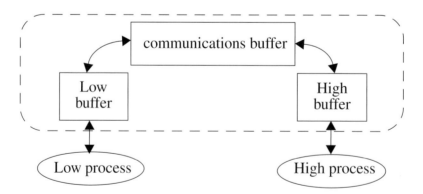

Figure 16–3 The pump. Messages going between the High and Low processes enter the pump (represented by the dashed oval). The pump controls the rate at which the messages flow between the two processes. The pump acknowledges each message as it is moved from the process buffer to the communications buffer.

assumptions, the processes can recover (so that either the messages in the pump are delivered or the sender detects that they are lost and resends the message; see Exercise 5).

A covert timing channel occurs when the *High* process can control the rate at which the pump passes messages to it. The *Low* process fills the communications buffer by sending messages to the pump until it fails to receive an acknowledgment. At that point, the *High* and *Low* processes begin their trials. At the beginning of each trial, if the *High* process wants to send a 1, it allows the pump to send it one of the queued messages. If the *High* process wants to send a 0, it does not accept any messages from the pump. If the *Low* process receives an acknowledgment, it means that a message has moved from the *Low* buffer to the communications buffer. This can happen only if a space in the communications buffer opens. This occurs when the *High* process reads a message. Hence, if the *Low* process gets an acknowledgment, the *High* process is signaling a 1. By a similar argument, if the *Low* process does not get an acknowledgment, the *High* process is signaling a 0. Following the trial, if the *Low* process has received an acknowledgment, it must send another message to the pump to enter the state required for the next trial.

In what follows, we assume that the *Low* process and the pump can process messages more quickly than the *High* process. Three cases arise.

1. The *High* process can process messages in less time than it takes for the *Low* process to get the acknowledgment. Because this contradicts our assumption above, the pump must be artificially delaying acknowledgments. This means that the *Low* process will wait for an acknowledgment regardless of whether the communications buffer is full or not. Although this closes the covert timing channel, it is not optimal because the processes may wait even when they do not need to.

2. The *Low* process is sending messages into the pump faster than the *High* process can remove them. Although it maximizes performance, it opens the covert channel.

3. The pump and the processes handle messages at the same rate. It balances security and performance by decreasing the bandwidth of the covert channel (with respect to time) and increases performance. The covert channel is open, however, and performance is not optimal.

Kang and Moskowitz [490] showed that adding noise to the channel in such a way as to approximate the third case reduced the covert channel capacity to at most $1/nr$, where r is the time between the *Low* process' sending a message to the pump and its receiving an acknowledgment when the communications buffer is not full. They concluded that the pump substantially reduces the capacity of covert channels between *High* and *Low* processes when compared with direct connection of those processes.

16.4   Summary

The confinement problem is the problem of preventing a process from illicitly leaking information. Its solutions lie in some form of separation or isolation. Virtual machines provide a basis for these mechanisms, as do less restrictive sandbox environments. Virtual machines and sandboxes limit the transfer of information by controlling expected paths used to send (or receive) data.

Shared resources provide unexpected paths for transmission of information. Detecting and analyzing these covert channels require deduction of common resources, which processes can manipulate (alter) the resources, which processes can access (read) the resources, and how much information per trial the channel can transmit.

Covert channels are difficult to eliminate. Countermeasures focus on making the channel less useful by decreasing its capacity, usually through the addition of randomness to obscure the regularity that sending and receiving requires.

16.5   Further Reading

Confinement mechanisms are used to limit the actions of downloaded or untrusted programs [23, 54, 160, 217, 588, 618]. McLean [613] raises questions about the effectiveness of sandboxes. Dean, Felten, and Wallach examine the Java security model [235]. Nieh and Leonard [692] discuss VMware, a virtual machine system implemented for Intel hardware, and Sugerman, Venkitachalam, and Lim [885] consider its performance.

Other methods have been used to detect covert channels, such as the Shared Resource Matrix methodology [500, 501], methods based on noninterference [388, 389],and methods based on information flow analysis [905]. Millen [632] models covert channels, and Costich and Moskowitz [211] examined the covert channel created by a multilevel secure database that used replication to ensure data availability.

Millen [634] provides a retrospective of covert channel research, including an amusing view of the disk-arm covert channel. Gold, Linde, and Cudney [362] review the successes and failures of KVM/370. Karger and Wray [497] discuss covert storage channels in disk accesses. Hu [449] discusses a countermeasure against covert channels arising from process scheduling. Kocher, Jaffe, and Jun [524] extend the timing analysis work to analysis of power consumption to obtain cryptographic keys, with remarkable success.

Several studies describe the relationship between noise and the capacity of timing channels [652, 653, 654, 956]. Gray [376] suggests alternating between secure and nonsecure modes to limit bandwidth. Tsai and Gligor [906] examine a Markov model for bandwidth computation in covert storage channels. Browne [140] examines state transitions to place upper bounds on covert channels. Meadows [615] discusses covert channels in integrity lock architectures, in which a trusted component mediates access to databases. Venkatraman and Newman-Wolfe [913] examine the capacity of a covert channel on a network. The "light pink book" [261] looks at covert channels in the context of government security requirements.

Hu [448] describes an interesting approach to limiting covert timing channels on the VAX virtualizing security kernel;Trostle [903] improved on his technique.

Variations of the pump extend its concept to other arenas, including the network [491, 492] and a nozzle for limiting the effectiveness of denial of service attacks [882].

16.6 Exercises

1. Consider the rule of transitive confinement. Suppose a process needs to execute a subprocess in such a way that the child can access exactly two files, one only for reading and one only for writing.

   a. Could capabilities be used to implement this? If so, how?
   b. Could access control lists implement this? If so, how?

2. A company wishes to market a secure version of the Swiss Cheese Operating System (SCOS), known as much for its advanced user and database management features as for its security vulnerabilities. The company plans to build a virtual machine to run SCOS and run that virtual machine on a second system, the Somewhat Secure Operating System (SSOS). The marketing literature claims that the VM running SCOS provides total isolation, thereby eliminating any potential security problems.

   a. Does this arrangement provide total isolation? If your answer is not "yes," discuss what features the VM would need to include to provide total isolation or show why this arrangement cannot provide total isolation.
   b. The literature states that "the VM mediates all accesses to real system resources, providing an impenetrable barrier to any attacker trying to break out of the SCOS and attack other copies of SCOS running on the SSOS." Do you agree or disagree with this statement? Why? (If you would need more information in order to make a decision, state what information you would need and why.)

3. In the Janus system, when the framework disallows a system call, the error code **EINTR** (interrupted system call) is returned.

   a. When some programs have read or write system calls terminated with this error, they retry the calls. What problems might this create?
   b. Why did the developers of Janus not devise a new error code (say, **EJAN**) to indicate an unauthorized system call?

4. In the covert flow tree technique, it is possible for some part of the tree to enter a loop in which recognition of attribute *a* depends on recognition of attribute *b*, which in turn is possible when attribute *a* is recognized.

   a. Give a specific example of such a loop.
   b. Should such a loop occur, the covert flow tree path is labeled with a *repeat* parameter that dictates the maximum number of times that branch may be traversed. Discuss the advantages and drawbacks of this solution.

5. Prove that if the pump crashes, either every message in the pump has been delivered or the sender detects that a message has been lost and resends it.

Chapter 17
Introduction to Assurance

> BOTTOM: Not a whit: I have a device to make all
> well. Write me a prologue; and let the prologue
> seem to say, we will do no harm with our swords,
> and that Pyramus is not killed indeed; and,
> for the more better assurance, tell them that I,
> Pyramus, am not Pyramus, but Bottom the
> weaver: this will put them out of fear.
>
> —*A Midsummer Night's Dream*, III, i, 17–23.

This chapter presents an overview of the concepts of security assurance and trusted systems. Assurance for secure and trusted systems must be an integral part of the development process. The following chapters will elaborate on the concepts and ideas introduced here.

17.1   Assurance and Trust

In previous chapters we have used the terms *trusted system* and *secure system* without defining them precisely. When looked on as an absolute, creating a secure system is an ultimate, albeit unachievable, goal. As soon as we have figured out how to address one type of attack on a system, other types of attacks occur. In reality, we cannot yet build systems that are guaranteed to be secure or to remain secure over time. However, vendors frequently use the term "secure" in product names and product literature to refer to products and systems that have "some" security included in their design and implementation. The amount of security provided can vary from a few mechanisms to specific, well-defined security requirements and well-implemented security mechanisms to meet those requirements. However, providing security requirements and functionality may not be sufficient to engender trust in the system.

Intuitively, *trust* is a belief or desire that a computer entity will do what it should to protect resources and be safe from attack. However, in the realm of computer security, trust has a very specific meaning. We will define trust in terms of a related concept.

Definition 17–1. An entity is *trustworthy* if there is sufficient credible evidence leading one to believe that the system will meet a set of given requirements. *Trust* is a measure of trustworthiness, relying on the evidence provided.

These definitions emphasize that calling something "trusted" or "trustworthy" does not make it so. Trust and trustworthiness in computer systems must be backed by concrete evidence that the system meets its requirements, and any literature using these terms needs to be read with this qualification in mind. To determine trustworthiness, we focus on methodologies and metrics that allow us to measure the degree of confidence that we can place in the entity under consideration. A different term captures this notion.

Definition 17–2. *Security assurance*, or simply *assurance*, is confidence that an entity meets its security requirements, based on specific evidence provided by the application of assurance techniques.

Examples of assurance techniques include the use of a development methodology, formal methods for design analysis, and testing. Evidence specific to a particular technique may be simplistic or may be complex and fine-grained. For example, evidence that measures a development methodology may be a brief description of the methodology to be followed. Alternatively, development processes may be measured against standards under a technique such as the System Security Engineering Capability Maturity Model (SSE-CMM; see Section 18.5).

Assurance techniques can be categorized as informal, semiformal, or formal. Informal methods use natural languages for specifications and justifications of claims. Informal methods impose a minimum of rigor on the processes used. Semiformal methods also use natural languages for specifications and justifications but apply a specific overall method that imposes some rigor on the process. Often these methods mimic formal methods. Formal methods use mathematics and other machine-parsable languages with tools and rigorous techniques such as formal mathematical proofs.

Security assurance is acquired by applying a variety of assurance techniques that provide justification and evidence that the mechanism, as implemented and operated, meets the security requirements described in the security policy for the mechanism (or collection of mechanisms). Figure 17–1 illustrates this process.

A related term, *information assurance*, refers to the ability to access information and preserve the quality and security of that information [679]. It differs from security assurance, because the focus is on the threats to information and the mechanisms used to protect information and not on the correctness, consistency, or completeness of the requirements and implementation of those mechanisms. However, we use the word "assurance" to mean "security assurance" unless explicitly stated otherwise.

We are now in a position to define a trusted system.

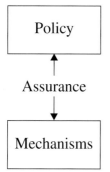

Policy — Statement of requirements that explicitly defines the security expectations of the mechanism(s)

Assurance — Provides justification that the mechanism meets policy through assurance evidence and approvals based on evidence

Mechanisms — Executable entities that are designed and implemented to meet the requirements of the policy

Figure 17–1   Assurance, policy, and mechanisms.

Definition 17–3. A *trusted system* is a system that has been shown to meet well-defined requirements under an evaluation by a credible body of experts who are certified to assign trust ratings to evaluated products and systems.

Specific methodologies aggregate evidence of assurance, and results are interpreted to assign levels of trustworthiness. The Trusted Computer System Evaluation Criteria [257] and the Information Technology Security Evaluation Criteria [186] are two standards that have been replaced by the Common Criteria [668, 669, 670]. These methodologies provide increasing "levels of trust," each level having more stringent assurance requirements than the previous one. When experts evaluate and review the evidence of assurance, they provide a check that the evidence amassed by the vendor is credible to disinterested parties and that the evidence supports the claims of the security requirements. Certification by these experts signifies that they accept the evidence.

17.1.1   The Need for Assurance

Applying assurance techniques is time-consuming and expensive. Operating systems, critical applications, and computer systems are often marketed as "secure," whereas in reality they have serious flaws that undermine their security features, or they are used in environments other than those for which their security features were developed. The marketing creates a false sense of well-being, which in turn encourages the users, system administrators, and organizations to act as though their systems were protected. So they fail to develop the defenses needed to protect critical information.

Accidental or unintentional failures of computer systems, as well as intentional compromises of security mechanisms, can lead to security failures. Neumann [688] describes nine types of problem sources in computer systems.

1. Requirements definitions, omissions, and mistakes
2. System design flaws
3. Hardware implementation flaws, such as wiring and chip flaws
4. Software implementation errors, program bugs, and compiler bugs
5. System use and operation errors and inadvertent mistakes
6. Willful system misuse
7. Hardware, communication, or other equipment malfunction
8. Environmental problems, natural causes, and acts of God
9. Evolution, maintenance, faulty upgrades, and decommissions

Assurance addresses each of these problem sources (except for natural causes and acts of God). Design assurance techniques applied to requirements address items 1, 2, and 6. A specification of requirements must be rigorously analyzed, reviewed, and verified to address completeness, consistency, and correctness. If the security requirements are faulty, the definition of security for that system is faulty, so the system cannot be "secure." Proper identification of threats and appropriate selection of countermeasures reduce the ability to misuse the system. Design assurance techniques can detect security design flaws, allowing their correction prior to costly development and deployment of flawed systems.

Implementation assurance deals with hardware and software implementation errors (items 3, 4, and 7), errors in maintenance and upgrades (item 9), willful misuse (item 6), and environmentally induced problems (item 8). Thorough security testing as well as detailed and significant vulnerabilities assessment find flaws that can be corrected prior to deployment of the system.

Operational assurance can address system use and operational errors (item 5) as well as some willful misuse issues (item 6).

Neumann's list is not exclusive to security problems. It also addresses risks to safety, reliability, and privacy.

EXAMPLE: [688] The space shuttle Challenger exploded on January 28, 1986, killing everyone on board. An essential failure was a decision to take shortcuts to meet an accelerated launch schedule. Among other steps, several sensors were removed from the booster rockets. The sensors might have enabled analysts to detect that the cold weather was affecting the booster rockets adversely and to delay the launch. Better assurance techniques might have detected the possible effects of removing the sensors, as well as other problems in the design of the booster rockets.

EXAMPLE: [688] Three patients died from a radiation overdose attributed to a Therac 25 computer-based electron accelerator radiation therapy system. The flaws in the system resulted from two flaws in the design of the system's software and the removal of a hardware safety interlock. Assurance techniques would have detected the flaws in the software's design, and ongoing assurance techniques would have detected the removal of the interlock.

EXAMPLE: [688] Although the most significant root cause of the Three Mile Island nuclear failure was a hardware problem (nonstandard instruments were used to measure core temperature), design and software problems contributed significantly. When the temperature rose very high, the system printed a string of question marks rather than the measured temperature. In addition, the intended, rather than the actual, valve settings were displayed. Assurance techniques would have detected these software flaws.

Sometimes safety and security measures can backfire. Assurance techniques highlight the consequences of these errors.

EXAMPLE: [688] The Bell V22 Osprey is a high-technology helicopter. After a fifth Osprey had crashed, an analysis traced the cause to a failure to correct for malfunctioning components. The Osprey implemented a majority-voting algorithm, and the cross-wiring of two roll-rate sensors allowed two faulty components to outvote the third, correctly functioning, component. Although assurance techniques might not have prevented the incorrect voting, they would have emphasized the results that could have occurred if faulty components overrode the correctly functioning components.

Other failures have had less serious consequences. When bugs were found in the trigonometric functions of the Intel 486 chip, Intel's public reputation was damaged, and replacing the chips cost Intel time and money. As a result, Intel began using high-assurance methods to verify the correctness of requirements in their chip design [732].

17.1.2   The Role of Requirements in Assurance

Although security policies define security for a particular system, the policies themselves are created to meet needs. These needs are the requirements.

Definition 17–4. A *requirement* is a statement of goals that must be satisfied.

A statement of goals can vary from generic, high-level goals to concrete, detailed design considerations. The term *security objectives* refers to the high-level security issues and business goals, and the term *security requirements* refers to the specific and concrete issues.

A brief review of definitions will prove helpful. Definition 4–1 states that a *security policy* is a statement that partitions the states of the system into a set of authorized or secure states and a set of unauthorized or nonsecure states. Equivalently, we can consider a security policy to be a set of specific statements that, when enforced, result in a secure system. The individual statements are the security requirements for the entity and describe what behavior must take place (or not take place) in order to define the authorized states of the system. Typically, requirements do not contain implementation details, which are the realm of the implementing *mechanism* (see Definition 4–7). On the other hand, a *security model* describes a family of policies, systems, or entities (see Definition 4–8) and is more abstract than a policy, which is specific to a particular entity or set of entities.

EXAMPLE: Suppose a high-level security goal for an entity is to ensure the confidentiality of certain data that the entity must process. A set of individual security requirements that specify an access control mechanism to restrict access to the information would address this objective. Individual requirements might describe the access control policy, the rules it implements, the security attributes associated with the data, and other specific issues. Another group of requirements that could address this objective might require encryption of the information when it is in transit from one part of the entity to another.

Selecting the right security requirements for a computer entity requires an understanding of the intended use of that entity as well as of the environment in which it must function. One can then examine policy models to determine if any are appropriate. Earlier chapters described several types of policies and models that have been used in the past. These models have been subjected to significant analysis and peer review, and most have had corrections during their life spans. This process of acceptance is like the acceptance of mathematical proofs over the centuries. Typically, mathematicians study a mathematical proof to find its flaws and weaknesses. Some proofs have survived this test of time, and others have not.

17.1.3   Assurance Throughout the Life Cycle

The goal of assurance is to show that an implemented and operational system meets its security requirements throughout its life cycle. Because of the difference in the levels of abstraction between high-level security requirements and low-level implementation details, the demonstration is usually done in stages. Different assurance techniques apply to different stages of system development. For this reason, it is convenient to classify assurance into policy assurance, design assurance, implementation assurance, and operational or administrative assurance.

Definition 17–5. *Policy assurance* is the evidence establishing that the set of security requirements in the policy is complete, consistent, and technically sound.

Policy assurance is based on a rigorous evaluation of the requirements. Completeness and consistency are demonstrated by identifying security threats and objectives and by showing that the requirements are sufficient to counter the threats or meet the requirements. If a security policy model is used, the justifications in the model can support the technical soundness of the requirements.

Once the proper requirements have been defined, justified, and approved for the system, the design and development process can begin with confidence. The developers create the system design to implement the security requirements and provide assurance evidence that the design meets the security requirements. The next step is to show that the system implements the design correctly. The design and development approach is illustrated in Figure 17–2. As that figure shows, following every design and implementation refinement step is an assurance justification step that shows that the requirements continue to be met at successive levels of development of the trusted system.

This process is usually iterative, because assurance steps identify flaws that must be corrected. When this happens, the affected steps must be rechecked.

EXAMPLE: If assurance step 4 indicates a flaw in the implementation, the implementation will have to be adjusted and the affected parts of step 4 redone. If this flaw in the implementation in turn indicates a flaw in the design, the design must be adjusted, causing steps 1, 2, 3, and 4 to be revisited. On rare occasions, a flaw in the implementation or design may point to a flaw in the requirements.

Assurance must continue throughout the life of the system. Because maintenance and patching usually affect the system design and implementation, the assurance requirements are similar to those described above.

Definition 17–6. *Design assurance* is the evidence establishing that a design is sufficient to meet the requirements of the security policy.

Design assurance includes the use of good security engineering practices to create an appropriate security design to implement the security requirements. It also includes an assessment of how well the system design meets the security requirements.

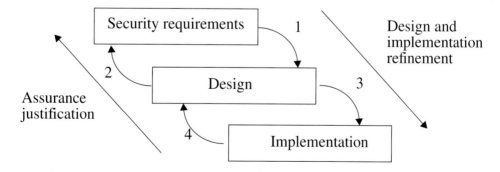

Figure 17–2   Development of a trusted system. There may be multiple levels of design and implementation. Note that the refinement steps alternate with the assurance steps.

Design assessment techniques use a policy or model of the security requirements for the system as well as a description or specification of the system design. Claims are made about the correctness of the design with respect to security requirements. The design assurance techniques provide a justification or proof of such claims.

> **Definition 17–7.** *Implementation assurance* is the evidence establishing that the implementation is consistent with the security requirements of the security policy.

In practice, implementation assurance shows that the implementation is consistent with the design, which design assurance showed was consistent with the security requirements found in the security policy. Implementation assurance includes the use of good security engineering practices to implement the design correctly, both during development and through the maintenance and repair cycles. It also includes an assessment of how well the system as implemented meets its security requirements through testing and proof of correctness techniques, as well as vulnerability assessment.

Design assurance and implementation assurance verify that the security policy requirements are properly designed and built into the system. However, computer systems and applications must be delivered, installed, and operated as assumed during design and implementation. Typically, the vendor provides procedures and processes in the form of supporting automated tools and documentation. The customer is responsible for ensuring their correct use.

> **Definition 17–8.** *Operational* or *administrative assurance* is the evidence establishing that the system sustains the security policy requirements during installation, configuration, and day-to-day operation.

One fundamental operational assurance technique is a thorough review of product or system documentation and procedures, to ensure that the system cannot accidentally be placed into a nonsecure state. This emphasizes the importance of proper and *complete* documentation for computer applications, systems, and other entities.

17.2   Building Secure and Trusted Systems

Building secure and trusted systems depends on standard software engineering techniques augmented with specific technologies and methodologies. Hence, a review of the life cycles of systems will clarify much of what follows.

17.2.1   Life Cycle

The concept of a *life cycle* addresses security-relevant decisions that often are made outside the engineering disciplines in business situations. There is more to building a product or system than just the engineering steps. Security goals may impact both the life cycle and the engineering process used. Such processes establish both discipline and control and provide confidence in the consistency and quality of the resulting system. Assurance requires a life cycle model and engineering process in every situation, although the size and complexity of the project, the project team, and the organization guide selection of the appropriate model and process. In a small operation, where individuals play multiple roles, an informal structure of the life cycle process may work best. In a larger company with complex roles and interactions among several projects and project team members, a more rigorous and formal process might be more appropriate.

A life cycle starts when a system is considered for development and use. The life cycle ends when the system is no longer used. A life cycle includes a set of processes that define how to perform activities, as well as methods for managing activities. Examples of such activities are writing of marketing literature, sales training, and design and development of code. Management activities include planning, configuration management, and selection and use of standards. Both types of activities follow the system from its initial conception through the decision to create the system, the steps required to develop, sell, and deploy the system, the maintenance of the system, and the decommissioning and retirement of the system.

A typical life cycle process is defined in stages. Some stages depend on previous stages, whereas others do not. Each stage describes activities of all the involved disciplines and controls interdiscipline interactions. As work progresses, the project ideally transitions from one stage to the next. In practice, there is often some iteration of the stages—for example, when a more advanced stage uncovers flaws or omissions in the work of the previous stage.

Consider a very general life cycle "metamodel" to illustrate these concepts. This model captures the fundamental areas of system life for any type of project, although the focus is on software engineering projects. An actual, functioning life cycle process may be more detailed, but this metamodel addresses the needs of any business application. It incorporates the four stages of conception, manufacture, deployment, and fielded product life. Engineering processes tend to focus on manufacture and, to a lesser degree, on fielded product life, although engineering function responsibilities may exceed this typical view.

17.2.1.1   Conception

The conception stage starts with an idea. Ideas come from anywhere—for example, from customers, engineers, other disciplines, user groups, or others. The organization decision makers may decide to

- fund the idea and make it a project,
- reject the idea, or
- ask for further information or for a demonstration that the idea has merit.

How decisions are made varies. A decision may be rather spontaneous in a very small and self-contained organization, where communication is ubiquitous and informal. A larger company may have formalized processes for initiation of new projects requiring many layers of approval.

> **Definition 17–9.** A *proof of concept* is a demonstration that an idea has merit.

The decision makers may ask for a proof of concept if they are unsure, or not convinced, that the idea is worth pursuing. Developing proofs of concept typically involves small projects. A request for a proof of concept may result in a rapid prototype, an analysis, or another type of proof. It need not involve the engineering staff, and it need not use steps in the engineering process.

The output of the conception stage must provide sufficient information for all disciplines to begin their tasks in the next stage. This information may be an overview of the project; high-level requirements that the project should meet; or schedule, budget, staffing, or planning information. The planning information could be a detailed project plan or more general high-level plans for each of the disciplines involved in the project. The exact nature of the information depends on the size and complexity of the project.

Security feasibility and high-level requirement analysis should begin during this stage of the life cycle. Before time and resources are invested in development or in proof of concept activities, the following questions should be considered.

- What does "secure" mean for this concept?
- Is it possible for this concept to meet this meaning of security?
- Is the organization willing to support the additional resources required to make this concept meet this meaning of security?

Identification of threats comprises another important set of security issues. It is especially important to determine the threats that are visible at the conception stage. This allows those threats to be addressed in rapid prototypes and proofs of concept. It also helps develop realistic and meaningful requirements at later stages. It provides the basis for a detailed threat analysis that may be required in the manufacturing phase to refine requirements.

Development of assurance considerations is important at this stage. A decision to incorporate assurance, and to evaluate mechanisms and other evidence of assurance, will influence every subsequent step of development. Assurance decisions will affect schedules and time to market.

17.2.1.2   Manufacture

Once a project has been accepted, funded, approved, and staffed, the manufacturing stage begins. Each required discipline has a set of substages or steps determined in part by the size of, complexity of, and market for the system. For most disciplines, the manufacturing stage is the longest.

Manufacturing begins with the development of more detailed plans for each of the involved disciplines, which could include marketing plans, sales training plans, development plans, and test plans. These documents describe the specific tasks for this stage of the life cycle within each discipline. The actual work required by each discipline depends on the nature of the system. For example, a system designed for internal use would not have sales requirements, and marketing requirements might target internal groups who may use the completed entity. Alternatively, a product designed for commercial use could require massive marketing campaigns and significant effort on the part of the sales force.

The software development or engineering process lies in this stage. It includes procedures, tools, and techniques used to develop and maintain the system. Technical work may include design techniques, development standards and guidelines, and testing tools and methods. Management aspects may include planning, scheduling, review processes, documentation guidelines, metrics, and configuration management such as source code control mechanisms and documentation version controls.

The output of this stage from each discipline should be the materials necessary to determine whether to proceed. Marketing groups could complete marketing collateral such as white papers and data sheets. Sales groups could develop documented leads and sales channels, as well as training materials for the sales force. Engineering groups would develop a tested, debugged system that is ready for use. Documentation groups would complete manuals and guides. Service groups would add staffing to handle telephone calls, installation support, bug tracking, and the like. The focus of this book is on the engineering steps of this stage.

17.2.1.3   Deployment

Once the system has passed the acceptance criteria in the manufacturing stage, it is ready for deployment. This stage is the process of getting the system out to the customer. It is divided into two substages.

The first substage is the domain of production, distribution, and shipping. The role of the other disciplines (such as engineering and marketing) is to deliver masters to the production staff. That staff creates and packages the materials that are actually shipped. If there is no assurance that masters have been appropriately protected from modification, and that copies are replicas of the masters, then the painstaking assurance steps taken during manufacture may be for naught.

The distribution organization ships systems to customers and to other sales organizations. In the case of an internal system, this step may be small. Users of the system may require specific types of documentation. Security and assurance issues in this part of deployment include knowing that what was received is actually what was shipped.

The second substage of deployment is proper installation and configuration of the system in its production setting. The developers must ensure that the system will work appropriately in this environment. The developers are also responsible for appropriate assurance measures for functionality, tools, and documentation. Service personnel must know appropriate security procedures as well as all other aspects of the system.

17.2.1.4   Fielded Product Life

The primary tasks of fielded product life are patching or fixing of bugs, maintenance, and customer service. Routine maintenance and emergency patching may be the responsibility of engineering in smaller organizations, or for systems in internal use only. Alternatively, maintenance and patching may the responsibility of an organization entirely separate from the product development organization. Wherever this responsibility lies, an engineering process must track maintenance and patches, and a deployment process must distribute patches and new releases. Modifications and enhancements must meet the same level of assurance rigor as the original development.

Commercial systems often have separate customer service and support organizations and engineering organizations. The support organization tasks could include answering questions, recording bugs, and solving routine customer problems. The engineering organization handles maintenance and patching.

Product retirement, or the decision to take a product out of service, is a critical part of this stage of the life cycle. Vendors need to consider migration plans for customers, routine maintenance for retired products still in use, and other issues.

17.2.2   The Waterfall Life Cycle Model

We have discussed life cycles in terms of stages. The waterfall model captures this.

> **Definition 17–10.** [760] The *waterfall life cycle model* is the model of building in stages, whereby one stage is completed before the next stage begins.

This model is not the only technique for building secure and trusted systems, but it is perhaps the most common. It consists of five stages, pictured in Figure 17–3. The solid arrows show the flow from each stage to the next.

17.2.2.1   Requirements Definition and Analysis

In this phase, the high-level requirements are expanded. Development of the overall architecture of the system may lead to more detailed requirements. It is likely that there will be some iteration between the requirements definition step and the architecture step before either can be completed.

Requirements may be functional requirements or nonfunctional requirements. Functional requirements describe interactions between the system and its environment. Nonfunctional requirements are constraints or restrictions on the system that limit design or implementation choices. Requirements describe *what* and not *how*. They should be implementation-independent.

Often, two sets of requirements are defined. A requirements definition of what the customer can expect the system to do is generally presented in natural language. A technical description of system characteristics, sometimes called a *requirements specification*, may be presented in a more precise form. The analysis of the require-

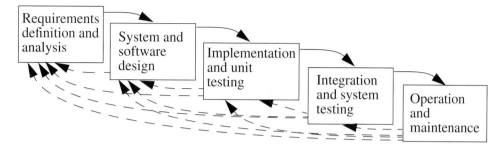

Figure 17–3 The waterfall life cycle model. The solid arrows represent the flow of development in the model. The dashed arrows represent the paths along which information about errors may be sent.

ments may include a feasibility study and may examine whether or not the requirements are correct, consistent, complete, realistic, verifiable, and traceable.

System design includes the development of the overall system architecture by partitioning requirements into hardware and/or software systems. The nature of the overall architecture may place additional constraints or requirements on the system, thus creating the need for iteration between this step and the previous one. An architecture document may or may not be required. In projects that are revisions or new releases of previous products, the basic architecture may be already defined. The architecture and the requirements must be reconciled to be consistent—that is, the architecture must be able to support the requirements.

17.2.2.2   System and Software Design

Software design further partitions the requirements into specific executable programs. Typically, at this stage, external functional specifications and internal design specifications are written. The external functional specifications describe the inputs, outputs, and constraints on functions that are external to the entity being specified, whereas the internal design specifications describe algorithms to be used, data structures, and required internal routines.

This stage is sometimes broken into the two phases *system design*, in which the system as a whole is designed, and *program design*, in which the programs of the system are individually designed.

17.2.2.3   Implementation and Unit Testing[1]

Implementation is the development of software programs based on the software design from the previous step. Typically, the work is divided into a set of programs or

---

[1] Some authors break this phase into two parts: implementation testing and unit testing. In practice, the developer of a program is usually responsible for the unit testing of that program. Because the two are often done concurrently, it seems appropriate to treat them as a single phase.

program units. *Unit testing* is the process of establishing that the unit as implemented meets its specifications. It is in this phase that many of the supporting processes described earlier come into play.

17.2.2.4   Integration and System Testing

Integration is the process of combining all the unit-tested program units into a complete system. Automated tools and guidelines governing the integration process may be in place. *System testing* is the process of ensuring that the system as a whole meets the requirements. System testing is an iterative step because invariably bugs and errors are found that have to be corrected. Typically, the errors are sent back to the development team to be corrected. This requires iteration with the previous step. The corrected code is reintegrated into the system, and system testing is repeated.

17.2.2.5   Operation and Maintenance

Once the system is finished,[2] it is moved into production. This is called *fielding the system*. Maintenance involves correction of errors that have been reported from the field and that have not been corrected at earlier stages. This stage also involves routine maintenance and the release of new versions of the system. Finally, retirement of the system also falls under this phase.

17.2.2.6   Discussion

In reality, there is usually some iteration between the processes at each stage of the waterfall because a later process may uncover deficiencies in a previous stage, causing it to be revisited. For example, implementation errors in the fielded system may not become clear until the operation and maintenance stage. Correction of such a deficiency will "trickle down" through the waterfall of phases. For example, if an error discovered in system testing is found to impact the software design, that change would feed into the system and software design phase, through implementation and unit testing to integration and system testing. An error found in the field may affect any stage from requirements to integration and system testing. Figure 17–3 shows the waterfall model, depicted by the solid arrows, and the potential error paths, represented by the dotted arrows.

Use of good system engineering practices provides discipline and process control during development and maintenance. Security analysis and development of assurance evidence on a regular basis, and as an integral part of the development and maintenance activities, increase confidence that the resulting system meets its security requirements. Use of a life cycle model and reliable supporting tools cannot ensure freedom from flaws or compliance with requirements. However, an appropri-

---

[2] By "finished," we mean that the system meets the criteria established to define when it has been completed.

ate process may help limit the number of flaws, especially those that can lead to security violations. Hence, building security into a product increases its trustworthiness. This demonstrates that the methods used to build a system are critical to the security of that system.

17.2.3   Other Models of Software Development

A few words on other life cycle models will illuminate the differences between those models and the waterfall model with respect to assurance [855].

17.2.3.1   Exploratory Programming

In exploratory programming approaches, a working system is developed quickly and then modified until it performs adequately. This approach is commonly used in artificial intelligence (AI) system development, in which users cannot formulate a detailed requirements specification and in which adequacy rather than correctness is the aim of the system designers. The key to using this approach successfully is to use techniques that allow for rapid system iterations. Using a very high-level programming language may facilitate rapid changes.

In this technique, there are no requirements or design specifications. Hence, assurance becomes difficult. A system subjected to continual modification suffers the same vulnerabilities that plague any add-on system. The focus on adequacy rather than correctness leaves the implementation potentially vulnerable to attack. Therefore, this model is not particularly useful for building secure and trusted systems because such systems need precise requirements and detailed verification that they meet those requirements as implemented.

17.2.3.2   Prototyping

Prototyping is similar to exploratory programming. The first phase of development involves rapid development of a working system. However, in this case, the objective of the rapid development is specifically to establish the system requirements. Then the software is reimplemented to create a production-quality system. The reimplementation can be done using another model that is more conducive to development of secure and trusted systems.

17.2.3.3   Formal Transformation

In the formal transformation model, developers create a formal specification of the software system. They transform this specification into a program using correctness-preserving transformations. The act of formal specification, if tied to well-formed security requirements, is beneficial to security and to design in general. The use of correctness-preserving transformations and automated methods can assist in developing a correct implementation. However, a system developed by such a method should be subjected to the same rigorous implementation testing and vulnerabilities analysis that are applied to any other methodology.

17.2.3.4   System Assembly from Reusable Components

This technique assumes that systems are made up mostly of components that already exist. The system development process becomes one of assembly rather than creation. Developing trusted systems out of trusted components is complex because of the need to reconcile the security models and requirements of each component, and developing trusted systems out of untrusted components is even more complex. However, this is a common approach to building secure and trusted systems.

17.2.3.5   Extreme Programming

Extreme programming is a development methodology based on rapid prototyping and best practices such as separate testing of components, frequent reviewing, frequent integration of components, and simple design. A project is driven by business decisions, not by project stakeholders, and requirements are open until the project is complete. The design evolves as needed to remove complexity and add flexibility. Programmers work in teams or pairs. Component testing procedures and mechanisms are developed before the components are developed. The components are integrated and tested several times a day. One objective of this model is to put a minimal system into production as quickly as possible and then enhance it as appropriate.

Use of this technique for security has several benefits and several drawbacks. The nature of an evolving design leaves the product vulnerable to the problems of an add-on product. Leaving requirements open does not ensure that security requirements will be properly implemented into the system. However, if threats were analyzed and appropriate security requirements developed before the system was designed, a secure or trusted system could result. However, evidence of trustworthiness would need to be adduced *after* the system was developed and implemented.

17.3   Building Security In or Adding Security Later

Like performance, security is an integral part of a computer system. It should be integrated into the system from the beginning, rather than added on later.

Imagine trying to create a high-performance product out of one that has poor performance. If the poor performance is attributable to specific functions, those functions must be redesigned. However, the fundamental structure, design, and style of the system are probably at the heart of the performance problem. Fixing the underlying structure and system design is a much harder problem. It might be better to start over, redesigning the system to address performance as a primary goal. Creating a high-security system from one that previously did not address security is similar to creating a high-performance system. Products claiming security that are created from previous versions without security cannot achieve high trust because they lack the fundamental and structural concepts required for high assurance.

A basic concept in the design and development of secure computer systems is the concept of a reference monitor and its implementation—the reference validation mechanism.

> **Definition 17–11.** [25] A *reference monitor* is an access control concept of an abstract machine that mediates all accesses to objects by subjects.

> **Definition 17–12.** [25] A *reference validation mechanism* (RVM) is an implementation of the reference monitor concept. An RVM must be tamper-proof, must always be invoked (and can never be bypassed), and must be small enough to be subject to analysis and testing, the completeness of which can be assured.

Any secure or trusted system must obviously meet the first two requirements. The "analysis and testing" of the reference monitor provides evidence of assurance. The third requirement engenders trust by providing assurance that the operational system meets its requirements.

> **Definition 17–13.** [25] A *security kernel* is a combination of hardware and software that implements a reference monitor.

Security kernels were early examples of reference validation mechanisms. The idea of a security kernel was later generalized by the definition of a trusted computing base, which applies the reference validation mechanism rules to additional security enforcement mechanisms.

> **Definition 17–14.** [257] A *trusted computing base* (TCB) consists of all protection mechanisms within a computer system—including hardware, firmware, and software—that are responsible for enforcing a security policy.

A TCB consists of one or more components that together enforce the security policy of a system. The ability of a TCB to enforce a security policy depends solely on the mechanisms within the TCB and on the correct input of parameters (such as a user's clearance) related to the security policy.

If a system is designed and implemented so as to be "small enough to be subject to analysis and testing, the completeness of which can be assured," it will be more amenable to assurance than a system that is not so designed and implemented. Design analysis is possible using a variety of formal and informal methods. More thorough testing is possible because what must be tested is clear from the structured, analyzed design. More and deeper assurance leads to a higher level of trust in the resulting system. However, trade-offs may occur between features and simplicity.

Inclusion of many features often leads to complexity, which limits the ability to analyze the system, which in turn lowers the potential level of assurance.

Systems in which security mechanisms are added to a previous product are not as amenable to extensive analysis as those that are specifically built for security. Often the functions are spread throughout the system in such a way that a thorough design analysis must analyze the entire system. Rigorous analysis of large and complex designs is difficult. So, it may not be feasible to determine how well the design implements the requirements. Assurance may be limited to test results. Testing of conformance to a flawed design is similar to designing a system to meet inappropriate requirements. The gap in abstraction between security requirements and implementation code may prohibit complete requirements testing. Hence, systems with security mechanisms added after development has been completed are inherently less trustworthy.

Building a system with security as a significant goal may provide the best opportunity to create a truly secure system. In the future, this may be the norm. However, many products today, including many high-assurance products, are developed by rearchitecting existing products and reusing parts as much as possible while addressing fundamental structure as well as adding new security features.

EXAMPLE: Multics [703] was one of the early general-purpose operating systems that was built for secure applications. It borrowed much from the other operating systems of the day. Although it is no longer in use, many security experts consider Multics to be the best example of an operating system built for security.

EXAMPLE: Gemsos [793] is a high-assurance, formally verified operating system that has a minimal UNIX-like kernel and limited functionality. Seaview [583] was a high-assurance database management system that was intended to run on the Gemsos operating system. Seaview was designed for security but was implemented by rearchitecting an existing database product.

EXAMPLE: Information flow control mechanisms, called *guards* (see Section 15.4), are often high-assurance devices. The RECON guard [27] controls the flow of information from a highly classified reconnaissance database to an unclassified network. The Restricted Access Processor [733] controlled the flow of information between two differently classified networks. Firewalls are a form of guards, although they are usually single-purpose applications built on security-hardened versions of existing operating systems rather than systems developed specifically for high assurance.

EXAMPLE: In the late 1980s and early 1990s, AT&T undertook two projects to provide secure versions of UNIX System V that supported mandatory access controls. The first project was market-driven, in response to specific requests from customers. The underlying goals of this project were quick time to market and minimal impact on the user interface and on the look and feel of the resulting UNIX system, called SV/MLS [130, 325]. The chosen approach was to add security functionality to AT&T

UNIX System V Release 3.2. The second project was focused on restructuring and re-creating a UNIX system to provide a medium-to-high level of trust. This version, called SVR4.1ES, involved significant rearchitecting of the UNIX system with security built in [765]. The technical differences between these two products illustrate the superiority of building security in over adding it on.

The SVR4.1ES project involved extensive restructuring of the UNIX kernel to meet high-modularity requirements and to incorporate an implementation of the principle of least privilege that was integral to the UNIX kernel. SV/MLS used the existing UNIX kernel modular structure and did not provide an implementation of least privilege. The basic architecture of SVR4.1ES was new, and the architecture of SV/MLS was essentially unchanged from its parent product.

In UNIX systems, the inode structure contains attribute information about each file or object, such as access permission information and file owner. The inode also has a pointer to the file or object itself. There is insufficient space in the inode to house security labels of any significant size. SV/MLS chose not to disturb the existing inode structure. The designers created a separate table to hold mandatory access control labels and used a free location in the inode structure to point to the table. When an object is created, a code defining both the mandatory access control label and the discretionary security attributes is stored in the table. Security attributes for subjects are stored internally in the same code structure. An access control check becomes a comparison of the codes for the subject and object, effectively doing a mandatory access control check and a discretionary access control check in one operation.

Even if the implementation of this table is correct and the comparison of the codes properly reflects the mandatory and discretionary access control requirements, there are potential weaknesses in this design. The coupling between the table and the file is inherently weaker than the coupling between the inode and the file. Two accesses are required to reach the coded mandatory and discretionary access control attributes of the object (first to the inode, then to the table), potentially weakening the tie between the actual object and its security attributes. Updating of discretionary access control security attributes is done to the inode version of the discretionary access control requirements. An additional step to update the table entry occurs whenever the permissions or owner is changed. This introduces the potential for inconsistency between the inode attributes and the coded interpretation. During a table update, the mandatory access control information for that object may be exposed. Finally, if the table is corrupted, the mandatory and discretionary access permissions for the entire file system may be impacted. Although the SV/MLS implementations addressed these issues satisfactorily, the potential for these vulnerabilities still existed.

The SVR4.1ES implementation simply redefined the inode structure. These new inodes, called *vnodes*, contained the mandatory access control label as well as the discretionary access control attributes in the vnode. Access to the vnode provided access to the mandatory and discretionary attributes. SVR4.1ES reused the UNIX discretionary access control mechanisms and augmented them with access control lists. Checks of mandatory and discretionary access were independent checks.

SVR4.1ES was not constrained by minimal impact requirements, resulting in a stronger set of access control mechanisms. Because of the structural change, SVR4.1ES was able to reuse other parts of the system with little impact.

17.4   Summary

Assurance is the foundation for determining the trustworthiness of a computer system. Assurance techniques test the appropriateness of requirements and the effectiveness of specification, design, implementation, and maintenance. These techniques cannot guarantee system security or safety, but they can significantly increase the likelihood of finding security flaws during requirements definition, design, and implementation. Errors found early can be corrected early. A well-defined life cycle process provides rigorous, well-defined steps with checks and balances that contribute significantly to the quality of the software developed and also increases the credibility of the measures of assurance that are used.

17.5   Further Reading

Any serious student of assurance should read James Anderson's seminal paper [25]. This paper defines many key concepts on which assurance is based.

Assurance techniques have been developed for a variety of environments, including outer space [691, 758], systems that control trains [355, 597], telephone and electronic switching systems [32, 533], and aviation [87, 154].

Metrics have been used to measure assurance with respect to specific properties, such as failure tolerance [918], abnormal system behavior [305], and test coverage [17]. The Visual Network Rating Methodology (VNRM) [709] helps users organize and document assurance arguments.

Pfleeger's book [720] presents an excellent description of software engineering. Berzins and Luqi [85] discuss applications of formal methods to software engineering. Brooks' description of the development of OS/360 [136] focuses on the human practices and problems as well as the technical ones. It is a classic in the field of software engineering.

17.6 Exercises

1. Definition 17–2 defines assurance in terms of "confidence." A vendor advertises that its system was connected to the Internet for three months, and no one was able to break into it. It claims that this means that the system cannot be broken into from any network.

   a. Do you share the vendor's confidence? Why or why not?
   b. If a commercial evaluation service had monitored the testing of this system and confirmed that, despite numerous attempts, no attacker had succeeded in breaking into it, would your confidence in the vendor's claim be increased, decreased, or left unchanged? Justify your answer.

2. A computer security expert contends that most break-ins to computer systems today are attributable to flawed programming or incorrect configuration of systems and products. If this claim is true, do you think design assurance is as important as implementation and operational assurance? Why or why not?

3. Suppose you are the developer of a computer product that can process critical data and will likely run in a hostile environment. You have an outstanding design and development team, and you are very confident in the quality of their work.

   a. Explain why you would add assurance steps to your development environment.
   b. What additional information (if any) would you need in order to decide whether or not the product should be formally evaluated?

4. Requirements are often difficult to derive, especially when the environment in which the system will function, and the specific tasks it will perform, are unknown. Explain the problems that this causes during development of assurance.

5. Why is the waterfall model of software engineering the most commonly used method for development of trusted systems?

6. The goal of a researcher is to develop new ideas and then test them to see if they are feasible. Software developed to test a new idea is usually similar to software developed for proof of concept (see Definition 17–9). A commercial firm trying to market software that uses a new idea decides to use the software that the researchers developed.

   a. What are the problems with this decision from an assurance point of view?
   b. What should the company do to improve the software (and save its reputation)?

7. A company develops a new security product using the extreme programming software development methodology. Programmers code, then test, then add more code, then test, and continue this iteration. Every day, they test the code base as a whole. The programmers work in pairs when writing code to ensure that at least two people review the code. The company does not adduce any additional evidence of assurance. How would you explain to the management of this company why their software is in fact not "high-assurance" software?

Chapter 18
Evaluating Systems

> LEONATO: O, she tore the letter into a thousand
> halfpence; railed at herself, that she should be
> so immodest to write to one that she knew would
> flout her; 'I measure him,' says she, 'by my own
> spirit; for I should flout him, if he writ to me;
> yea, though I love him, I should.'
> —*Much Ado About Nothing*, II, iii, 150–161.

Evaluation is a process in which the evidence for assurance is gathered and analyzed against criteria for functionality and assurance. It can result in a measure of trust that indicates how well a system meets particular criteria. The criteria used depend on the goals of the evaluation and the evaluation technology used. The Trusted Computer System Evaluation Criteria (TCSEC) was the first widely used formal evaluation methodology, and subsequent methodologies built and improved on it over time. This chapter explores several past and present evaluation methodologies, emphasizing the differences among them and the lessons learned from each methodology.

18.1 Goals of Formal Evaluation

Perfect security is an ultimate, but unachievable, goal for computer systems. As the complexity of computer systems increases, it becomes increasingly difficult to address the reference validation mechanism concept of a system being simple enough to analyze. A *trusted* system is one that has been shown to meet specific security requirements under specific conditions. The trust is based on assurance evidence. Although a trusted system cannot guarantee perfect security, it does provide a basis for confidence in the system within the scope of the evaluation.

Formal security evaluation techniques were created to facilitate the development of trusted systems. Typically, an evaluation methodology provides the following features.

- A set of requirements defining the security functionality for the system or product.
- A set of assurance requirements that delineate the steps for establishing that the system or product meets its functional requirements. The requirements usually specify required evidence of assurance.
- A methodology for determining that the product or system meets the functional requirements based on analysis of the assurance evidence.
- A measure of the evaluation result (called a *level of trust*) that indicates how trustworthy the product or system is with respect to the security functional requirements defined for it.

Definition 18–1. A *formal evaluation methodology* is a technique used to provide measurements of trust based on specific security requirements and evidence of assurance.

Several evaluation standards have affected formal evaluation methodologies. Among the major standards have been the Trusted Computer System Evaluation Criteria (TCSEC) [257] and the Information Technology Security Evaluation Criteria (ITSEC) [186]. The Common Criteria (CC) [668, 669, 670] has supplanted these standards as a standard evaluation methodology. This chapter discusses components of each standard.

Even when a system is not formally evaluated, the security functional requirements and assurance requirements provide an excellent overview of the considerations that improve assurance. These considerations are invaluable to any development process.

18.1.1   Deciding to Evaluate

A decision to evaluate a system formally must take into consideration the many trade-offs between security and cost, such as time to market and the number of features. Groups seeking formal evaluation may have to pay the evaluator's charge as well as staffing costs for skilled experts to develop security documentation and assurance evidence. Interaction with the evaluator for training, clarification, or corrections takes development staff time and could affect development and delivery schedules. Unfortunately, security evaluation cannot prove that a system is invulnerable to attack. Most systems today must operate in hostile environments, and the systems must provide their own protections from attacks and inadvertent errors.

Security and trust are no longer the exclusive realm of the government and military, nor are they of concern only to financial institutions and online businesses.

Computers are at the heart of the economy, medical processes and equipment, power infrastructures, and communications infrastructures. Systems having no security are unacceptable in most environments today. Systems providing some security are a step in the right direction, but a trusted system that reliably addresses specifically defined security issues engenders stronger confidence. Evaluation provides an independent assessment by experts and a measure of assurance, which can be used to compare products.

The independent assessment by experts of the effectiveness of security mechanisms and the correctness of their implementation and operation is invaluable in finding vulnerabilities and flaws in a product or system. An evaluated product has been scrutinized by security experts who did not design or implement the product and can bring a fresh eye to the analysis. Hence, the evaluated product is less likely to contain major flaws than a product that has not been evaluated. The analysis of such a system begins with an assessment of requirements. The requirements must be consistent, complete, technically sound, and sufficient to counter the threats to the system. Assessing how well the security features meet the requirements is another part of the evaluation. Evaluation programs require specific types of administrative, user, installation, and other system documentation, which provide the administrators and maintainers the information needed to configure and administer the system properly, so that the security mechanisms will work as intended.

The level of risk in the environment affects the level of trust required in the system. The measure of trust associated with an evaluated product helps find the optimum combination of trust in the product and in the environment to meet the security needs.

18.1.2   Historical Perspective of Evaluation Methodologies

Government and military establishments were the early drivers of computer security research. They also drove the creation of a security evaluation process. Before evaluation methodologies were available for commercial products, government and military establishments developed their own secure software and used internal methodologies to make decisions about their security. With the rapid expansion of technology, government and military establishments wanted to use commercial products for their systems rather than developing them. This drove the development of methodologies to address the security and trustworthiness of commercial products.

Evaluation methodologies provide functional requirements, assurance requirements, and levels of trust in different formats. Some list requirements and use them to build trust categories. Others list the requirements only within the description of a trust category. To help the reader compare the development of the methodologies, we present each methodology in a standard manner. We first present overview information about the methodology. Descriptions of functional requirements (when they exist), assurance requirements, and levels of trust follow. If the methodology was widely used to evaluate systems, we describe the evaluation process. The final discussion for each methodology addresses its strengths, its weaknesses, and the contributions it makes to the evaluation technology. Unfortunately, the methodologies use slightly different terminologies. In the discussion of each methodology, we will describe the terminology specific to that technique and relate it to the specific terminologies of previous methodologies.

18.2   TCSEC: 1983–1999

The Trusted Computer System Evaluation Criteria (TCSEC), also known as the Orange Book, was developed by the U.S. government and was the first major computer security evaluation methodology. It presents a set of criteria for evaluating the security of commercial computer products. The TCSEC defined criteria for six different *evaluation classes* identified by their rating scale of C1, C2, B1, B2, B3, and A1. Each evaluation class contains both functional and assurance requirements, which are cumulative and increasing throughout the evaluation classes. Classes were subdivided into three different "divisions" of lesser importance to our discussion than individual evaluation classes. A fourth division, D, was provided for products that attempted evaluation but failed to meet all the requirements of any of the six classes. The vendor could select the level of trust to pursue by selecting an evaluation class but otherwise had no say in either the functional or assurance requirements to be met.

The reference monitor concept (see Section 17.3) and the Bell-LaPadula security policy model (see Section 5.2) heavily influenced the TCSEC criteria and approach. Recall that a trusted computing base (TCB) is a generalization of the reference validation mechanism (RVM). The TCB is not required to meet the RVM requirements (always invoked, tamperproof, and small enough to analyze) for all classes. In the TCSEC, the TCB need not be a full RVM until class B3.

The TCSEC emphasizes confidentiality, with a bias toward the protection of government classified information. Although there is no specific reference to data integrity in the TCSEC, it is indirectly addressed by the *-property of the embedded Bell-LaPadula Model.[1] However, this is not a complete data integrity solution, because it does not address the integrity of data outside the mandatory access control policy. System availability is not addressed.

During the first few years that the TCSEC was available, the National Computer Security Center published a large collection of documents that expanded on requirement areas from the TCSEC. These "Rainbow Series"[2] documents discussed the requirements in specific contexts such as networks, databases, and audit systems, and some are still applicable today.

The TCSEC provides seven levels of trust measurement called *ratings*, which are represented by the six evaluation classes C1, C2, B1, B2, B3, and A1, plus an

---

[1] Recall that the *-property addresses writing of data, which provides some controls on the unauthorized modification of information. See Section 5.2.1.

[2] Each document had a different color cover.

additional class, D. An evaluated product is a *rated product*. Under the TCSEC, some requirements that this text considers to be functional in nature appear under headings that use the word *assurance*. These requirements are identified in the text below.

18.2.1   TCSEC Requirements

The TCSEC is organized by evaluation class and uses an outline structure to identify named requirement areas. It defines both functional and assurance requirements within the context of the evaluation classes. The actual requirements are embedded in a prose description of each named area. The divisions and subdivisions of the document are of lesser importance than the actual requirement areas found within them.

18.2.1.1   TCSEC Functional Requirements

Discretionary access control (DAC) requirements identify an access control mechanism that allows for controlled sharing of named objects by named individuals and/ or groups. Requirements address propagation of access rights, granularity of control, and access control lists.

Object reuse requirements address the threat of an attacker gathering information from reusable objects such as memory or disk memory. The requirements address the revocation of access rights from a previous owner when the reusable object is released and the inability of a new user to read the previous contents of that reusable object.

Mandatory access control (MAC) requirements, not required until class B1, embody the simple security condition and the *-property from the Bell-LaPadula Model. These requirements include a description of the hierarchy of labels. Labels attached to subjects reflect the authorizations they have and are derived from approvals such as security clearances. Labels attached to objects reflect the protection requirements for objects. For example, a file labeled "secret" must be protected at that level by restricting access to subjects who have authorizations reflecting a secret (or higher) clearance.

Label requirements, also not required until class B1, enable enforcement of mandatory access controls. Both subjects and objects have labels. Other requirements address accurate representation of classifications and clearances, exporting of labeled information, and labeling of human-readable output and devices.

Identification and authentication (I&A) requirements specify that a user identify herself to the system and that the system authenticate that identity before allowing the user to use the system. These requirements also address the granularity of the authentication data (per group, per user, and so on), protecting authentication data, and associating identity with auditable actions.

Trusted path requirements, not required until class B2, provide a communications path that is guaranteed to be between the user and the TCB.

Audit requirements address the existence of an audit mechanism as well as protection of the audit data. They define what audit records must contain and what events the audit mechanism must record. As other requirements increase, the set of auditable events increases, causing the auditing requirements to expand as one moves to higher classes.

The TCSEC presents other requirements that it identifies as system architecture requirements. They are in fact functional requirements, and they include a tamperproof reference validation mechanism, process isolation, the principle of least privilege, and well-defined user interfaces.

TCSEC operational assurance requirements that are functional in nature include the following. Trusted facility management requires the separation of operator and administrator roles and are required starting at class B2. Trusted recovery procedure requirements ensure a secure recovery after a failure (or other discontinuity). These requirements are unique to class A1. Finally, a system integrity requirement mandates hardware diagnostics to validate the on-site hardware and firmware elements of the TCB.

18.2.1.2   TCSEC Assurance Requirements

Configuration management requirements for the TCSEC begin at class B2 and increase for higher classes. They require identification of configuration items, consistent mappings among all documentation and code, and tools for generating the TCB.

The *trusted distribution requirement* addresses the integrity of the mapping between masters and on-site versions as well as acceptance procedures for the customer. This requirement is unique to class A1.

TCSEC system architecture requirements mandate modularity, minimization of complexity, and other techniques for keeping the TCB as small and simple as possible. These requirements begin at class C1 and increase until class B3, where the TCB must be a full reference validation mechanism.

The *design specification and verification requirements* address a large number of individual requirements, which vary dramatically among the evaluation classes. Classes C1 and C2 have no requirements in this area. Class B1 requires an informal security policy model that is shown to be consistent with its axioms. Class B2 requires that the model be formal and be proven consistent with its axioms and that the system have a descriptive top-level specification (DTLS). Class B3 requires that the DTLS be shown to be consistent with the security policy model. Finally, class A1 requires a formal top level specification (FTLS) and that approved formal methods be used to show that the FTLS is consistent with the security policy model. Class A1 also requires a mapping between the FTLS and the source code.

The *testing requirements* address conformance with claims, resistance to penetration, and correction of flaws followed by retesting. A requirement to search for covert channels includes the use of formal methods at higher evaluation classes.

Product documentation requirements are divided into a Security Features User's Guide (SFUG) and an administrator guide called a Trusted Facility Manual (TFM). The SFUG requirements include a description of the protection mechanisms, how they interact, and how to use them. The TFM addresses requirements for running the product securely, including generation, start-up, and other procedures. All classes require this documentation, and as the level of the class increases, the functional and assurance requirements increase.

Internal documentation includes design and test documentation. The design documentation requirements and the design specification and verification requirements overlap somewhat. Other documentation requirements include a statement of the philosophy of protection and a description of interfaces. Test documentation requirements specify test plans, procedures, tests, and test results. As with the user and administrator documentation, requirements for test and design documentation increase as the functional and assurance requirements increase as the classes increase.

18.2.2   The TCSEC Evaluation Classes

Class C1, called *discretionary protection*, has minimal functional requirements only for identification and authentication and for discretionary access controls. The assurance requirements are also minimal, covering testing and documentation only. This class was used only briefly, and no products were evaluated under this class after 1986.

Class C2, called *controlled access protection*, requires object reuse and auditing in addition to the class C1 functional requirements and contains somewhat more stringent security testing requirements. This was the most commonly used class for commercial products. Most operating system developers incorporated class C2 requirements into their primary product by the end of the lifetime of the TCSEC.

Class B1, called *labeled security protection*, requires mandatory access controls, but these controls can be restricted to a specified set of objects. Labeling supports the MAC implementation. Security testing requirements are more stringent. An informal model of the security policy, shown to be consistent with its axioms, completes class B1. Many operating system vendors offered a class B1 product in addition to their primary products. Unfortunately, the B1 products did not always receive the updates in technology that the main line received, and they often fell behind technically.

Class B2, called *structured protection*, is acceptable for some government applications. At class B2, mandatory access control is required for all objects. Labeling is expanded, and a trusted path for login is introduced. Class B2 requires the use of the principle of least privilege to restrict the assignment of privilege to the users least required to perform the specific task. Assurance requirements include covert channel analysis, configuration management, more stringent documentation, and a formal model of the security policy that has been proven to be consistent with its axioms.

Class B3, called *security domains*, implements the full reference validation mechanism. It increases the trusted path requirements and constrains how the code is developed in terms of modularity, simplicity, and use of techniques such as layering and data hiding. It has significant assurance requirements that include all the requirements of class B2 plus more stringent testing, more requirements on the DTLS, an administrator's guide, and design documentation.

Class A1, called *verified protection*, has the same functional requirements as class B3. The difference is in the assurance. Class A1 requires significant use of formal methods in covert channel analysis, design specification, and verification. It also requires trusted distribution and increases both test and design documentation requirements. A correspondence between the code and the FTLS is required.

18.2.3   The TCSEC Evaluation Process

Government-sponsored evaluators staffed and managed TCSEC evaluations at no fee to the vendor. The evaluation had three phases: application, preliminary technical review (PTR), and evaluation. If the government did not need a particular product, the application might be denied. The PTR was essentially a readiness review, including comprehensive discussions of the evaluation process, schedules, the development process, product technical content, requirement discussions, and the like. The PTR determined when an evaluation team would be provided, as well as the fundamental schedule for the evaluation.

The evaluation phase was divided into design analysis, test analysis, and a final review. In each part, the results obtained by the evaluation team were presented to a technical review board (TRB), which approved that part of the evaluation before the evaluation moved to the next step. The TRB consisted of senior evaluators who were not on the evaluation team being reviewed.

The design analysis consisted of a rigorous review of the system design based on the documentation provided. Because TCSEC evaluators did not read the source code, they imposed stringent requirements on the completeness and correctness of the documentation. Evaluators developed the initial product assessment report (IPAR) for this phase. Test analysis included a thorough test coverage assessment as well as an execution of the vendor-supplied tests. The evaluation team produced a final evaluation report (FER) after approval of the initial product assessment report and the test review. Once the technical review board had approved the final evaluation report, and the evaluators and vendor had closed all items, the rating was awarded.

The Ratings Maintenance Program (RAMP) maintained assurance for new versions of an evaluated product. The vendor took the responsibility for updating the assurance evidence to support product changes and enhancements. A technical review board reviewed the vendor's report and, when the report had been approved, the evaluation rating was assigned to the new version of the product. RAMP did not accept all enhancements. For example, structural changes and the addition of some new functions could require a new evaluation.

18.2.4   Impacts

The TCSEC created a new approach to identifying how secure a product is. The approach was based on the analysis of design, implementation, documentation, and procedures. The TCSEC was the first evaluation technology, and it set several precedents for future methodologies. The concepts of evaluation classes, assurance requirements, and assurance-based evaluations are fundamental to evaluation today. The TCSEC set high technical standards for evaluation. The technical depth of the TCSEC evaluation came from the strength of the foundation of requirements and classes, from the rigor of the evaluation process, and from the checks and balances provided by reviews from within the evaluation team and the technical review boards from outside the evaluation team.

However, the TCSEC was far from perfect. Its scope was limited. The evaluation process was difficult and often lacked needed resources. The TCSEC bound assurance and functionality together in the evaluation classes, which troubled some users. Finally, the TCSEC evaluations were recognzed only in the United States, and evaluations from other countries were not valid in the United States.

18.2.4.1   Scope Limitations

The TCSEC was written for operating systems and does not translate well to other types of products or to systems. Also, the TCSEC focused on the security needs of the U.S. government and military establishments, who funded its development. All evaluation classes except C1 and C2 require mandatory access control, which most commercial environments do not use. Furthermore, the TCSEC did not address integrity, availability, or other requirements critical to business applications.

The National Computer Security Center (NCSC) tried to address the scope problems by providing criteria for other types of products. After an attempt to define a criteria document for networks, the NCSC chose to develop the Trusted Network Interpretation (TNI) of the TCSEC [258], released in 1987. The TNI offered two approaches: evaluation of networks and evaluation of network components. The TNI network approach addressed centralized networks with a single accreditation authority, policy, and Network TCB (NTCB). In the first part of the TNI, the TCSEC criteria were interpreted for networks, and one could evaluate a network at the same levels offered by the TCSEC. The second part of the TNI offered evaluation of network components. A network component may be designed to provide a subset of the security functions of the network as a whole. The TNI could provide an evaluation based on the specific functionality that the component offered.

In 1992, a Trusted Database Management System Interpretation (TDI) [260] of the TCSEC was released. In the early 1990s, IBM and Amdahl pushed for a Trusted Virtual Machine Monitor Interpretation [904] of the TCSEC, but this project was eventually dropped. The interpretations had to address issues that were outside the scope of the TCSEC, and each had limitations that restricted their utility. Not many evaluations resulted from the TNI or the TDI.

18.2.4.2   Process Limitations

The TCSEC evaluation methodology had two fundamental problems. The first was "criteria creep," or the gradual expansion of the requirements that defined the TCSEC evaluation classes. Evaluators found that they needed to interpret the criteria to apply them to specific products. Rather than publish frequent revisions of the TCSEC to address these requirement interpretations, the NCSC chose to develop a process for approval of interpretations and to publish them as an informal addendum to the TCSEC. The interpretations were sometimes clearer and more specific than the original requirement. Over time, the list became quite large and expanded the scope of the individual criteria in the TCSEC and its interpretations. The requirements of the classes became the union of the requirements in the TCSEC and the set of applicable interpretations. Thus, a class C2 operating system may have been required to meet stronger requirements than a system evaluated a few years before. This put an additional burden on the newer products under evaluation and meant that the minimum-security enforcement of all C2 operating systems was not the same. Although there were many problems with these differences, it caused the security community to learn more about security and create better security products.

The second problem with the evaluation process was that evaluations took too much time. Three factors contributed to this problem. Many vendors misunderstood the depth of the evaluation and the required interactions with the evaluation teams. The practices of the evaluation management caused misunderstandings and scheduling problems. Finally, the motivation to complete a free evaluation was often lacking. Typically, both vendors and evaluators caused delays in the schedule. Vendors often had to do additional unanticipated work. Evaluators were assigned to multiple evaluations, and the schedule of one evaluation could cause delays for another vendor. Many evaluations took so long to complete that the product was obsolete before the rating was awarded. Toward the end of the life of the TCSEC, commercial labs approved by the government were allowed to do TCSEC evaluations for a fee. Vendors had to be prepared for evaluation, and there was significantly less interaction between evaluators and vendors. This change addressed much of the timeliness problem, with labs completing evaluations in roughly a year.

A related problem was that RAMP cycles were as difficult as full evaluations and suffered from similar delays. Consequently, RAMP was not used very much.

18.2.4.3   Contributions

The TCSEC provided a process for security evaluation of commercial products. Its existence heightened the awareness of the commercial sector to the needs for computer security. This awareness would have arisen later if not for the influence of the TCSEC.

In the 1990s, new varieties of products emerged, including virus checkers, firewalls, virtual private networks, IPsec implementations, and cryptographic modules. The TCSEC remained centered on operating systems, and its interpretations were insufficient to evaluate all types of networks or the new varieties of products. The commercial sector was dissatisfied with the functional requirements of the evaluation classes. These inadequacies of the TCSEC stimulated a wave of new approaches to evaluation that significantly affected evaluation technology. Commercial organizations wrote their own criteria. Other commercial organizations offered a pass-fail "certification" based on testing. The Computer Security Act of 1987 gave the responsibility to the National Security Agency (NSA) for security of computer systems processing classified and national security–relevant information. The National Institute of Standards and Technology (NIST) received a charter for systems processing sensitive and unclassified information. In 1991, NIST and the NSA began working on new evaluation criteria called the Federal Criteria (FC). All these activities sprang from the impact of the TCSEC.

18.3   FIPS 140: 1994–Present

During the time of the TCSEC, the U.S. government had no mechanism for evaluating cryptographic modules. Evaluation of such modules was needed in order to ensure their quality and security enforcement. Evaluation of cryptographic modules outside the United States under the ITSEC or within the United States under the commercial pass-or-fail techniques did not meet these needs. In 1994, U.S. government agencies and the Canadian Security Establishment (CSE) jointly established FIPS 140-1 as an evaluation standard for cryptographic modules for both countries. This standard was updated in 2001 to FIPS 140-2 [671] to address changes in technology and process since 1994. The program is now sponsored jointly by NIST and CSE under the Cryptographic Module Validation (CMV) Program. Certification laboratories are accredited in Canada and the United States to perform the evaluations, which are validated jointly under the CMV Program, sponsored by CSE and NIST. This scheme for evaluating cryptographic products has been highly successful and is actively used today. Currently, the United Kingdom is negotiating to enter the CMV program.

A cryptographic module is a set of hardware, firmware, or software, or some combination thereof, that implements cryptographic logic or processes. If the cryptographic logic is implemented in software, then the processor that executes the software is also a part of the cryptographic module. The evaluation of software cryptographic modules automatically includes the operating system.

18.3.1   FIPS 140 Requirements

FIPS 140-1 and FIPS 140-2 provide the security requirements for a cryptographic module implemented within federal computer systems. Each standard defines four increasing, qualitative levels of security (called *security levels*) intended to cover a wide range of potential environments. The requirements for FIPS 140-1 cover basic design and documentation, module interfaces, roles and services, physical security, software security, operating system security, key management, cryptographic algorithms, electromagnetic interference/electromagnetic compatibility, and self-testing. The requirements for FIPS 140-2 include areas related to the secure design and implementation of cryptographic modules: specification; ports and interfaces; roles, services, and authentication; a finite state model; physical security; the operational environment; cryptographic key management; electromagnetic interference/electromagnetic compatibility; self-testing; design assurance; and mitigation of other attacks.

18.3.2   FIPS 140-2 Security Levels

In this section we present an overview of the security levels of FIPS 140-2. Changes from those of FIPS 140-1 reflect changes in standards (particularly the move from the TCSEC to the Common Criteria), changes in technology, and comments from users of FIPS 140-1.

Security Level 1 provides the lowest level of security. It specifies that the encryption algorithm be a FIPS-approved algorithm but does not require physical security mechanisms in the module beyond the use of production-grade equipment. Security Level 1 allows the software and firmware components of a cryptographic module to be executed on a general-purpose computing system using an unevaluated operating system. An example of a Level 1 cryptographic module is a personal computer board that does encryption.

Security Level 2 dictates greater physical security than Security Level 1 by requiring tamper-evident coatings or seals, or pick-resistant locks. Level 2 provides for role-based authentication, in which a module must authenticate that an operator is authorized to assume a specific role and perform a corresponding set of services. Level 2 also allows software cryptography in multiuser timeshared systems when used in conjunction with an operating system evaluated at EAL2 or better under the Common Criteria (see Section 18.4) using one of a set of specifically identified Common Criteria protection profiles.

Security Level 3 requires enhanced physical security generally available in many existing commercial security products. Level 3 attempts to prevent potential intruders from gaining access to critical security parameters held within the module. It provides for identity-based authentication as well as stronger requirements for entering and outputting critical security parameters. Security Level 3 requirements on the underlying operating system include an EAL3 evaluation under specific Common Criteria protection profiles (see Section 18.4.1), a trusted path, and an informal security policy model. An equivalent evaluated trusted operating system may be used.

Security Level 4 provides the highest level of security. Level 4 physical security provides an envelope of protection around the cryptographic module with the intent of detecting and responding to all unauthorized attempts at physical access. Level 4 also protects a cryptographic module against a security compromise resulting from environmental conditions or fluctuations outside the module's normal operating ranges of voltage and temperature. Level 4 allows the software and firmware components of a cryptographic module to be executed on a general-purpose computing system using an operating system that meets the functional requirements specified for Security Level 3 and that is evaluated at the CC evaluation assurance level EAL4 (or higher). An equivalent evaluated trusted operating system may be used.

18.3.3   Impact

The CMV program has improved the quality and security of cryptographic modules. By 2002, 164 modules and 332 algorithms had been tested. Of the 164 modules, approximately half had security flaws and more than 95% had documentation errors. Of the 332 algorithms, approximately 25% had security flaws and more than 65% had documentation errors. Vendors were able to correct these problems before their modules and algorithms were deployed and used.

18.4   The Common Criteria: 1998–Present

The Common Criteria (CC) approach to security evaluation draws from the strengths of TCSEC, ITSEC, CTCPEC, and FC, as well as from commercial efforts. The original participants in the Common Criteria Project included Canada, NIST and the NSA from the United States, the United Kingdom, France, Germany, and the Netherlands. Although all participants had the common goal of developing a technically strong, easy to use, mutually reciprocal evaluation technology, each of the participants represented previous methodologies. The United Kingdom, France, Germany, and the Netherlands represented the ITSEC community. NIST and the NSA represented the work done for the Federal Criteria Project, and the NSA also represented the TCSEC and the interests of the U.S. military establishment for very high-assurance systems. Canada represented the CTCPEC. In 1998, the first signers of the Arrangement on the Recognition of the Common Criteria Certifications in the Field of Information Technology Security were the United States, the United Kingdom, France, Germany, and Canada. This arrangement is called the Common Criteria Recognition Arrangement (CCRA), and also the Mutual Recognition Arrangement (MRA), in the literature. As of May 2002, Australia, New Zealand, Finland, Greece, Israel, Italy, the Netherlands, Spain, Sweden, and Norway have signed the CCRA. Japan, Russia, India, and South Korea are working on developing appropriate evaluation schemes (see below), which is a requirement for any country signing the CCRA. To date, Canada, the United Kingdom, the United States, and Germany have been the most prolific in producing CC evaluated products. The CC is also Standard 15408 of the International Standards Organization (ISO).

The CC became the de facto security evaluation standard in the United States in 1998. The TCSEC was retired in 2000, when the last TCSEC evaluation was completed. European countries that used the ITSEC similarly retired it, although remnants of the old evaluation programs still exist.

The Common Criteria evaluation methodology has three parts: the CC documents, the CC Evaluation Methodology (CEM), and a country-specific evaluation methodology called an *Evaluation Scheme* or *National Scheme*. The CC provides an overview of the methodology and identifies functional requirements, assurance requirements, and Evaluation Assurance Levels (EALs). The CEM provides detailed guidelines for the evaluation of products and systems at each EAL. This document is useful to developers and invaluable to evaluators. Currently, the CEM is complete for only the first four EALs defined in the CC. The first four EALs address low and medium levels of trust, whereas the higher three levels are specific to what are called high-assurance products and systems. Individual country Evaluation Schemes provide the infrastructure necessary to implement CC evaluation. Each country implements the methodology in its own way. The CC documents and the CEM set the fundamental criteria, EALs, and evaluation strategy, but countries may have different methods of selecting evaluators, awarding certifications, structuring interactions between evaluators and vendors, and the like. In the United States, for example, the Evaluation Scheme is the Common Criteria Evaluation and Validation Scheme (CCEVS), which is implemented within NIST. Under this scheme, NIST accredits commercial evaluation laboratories, which then perform product and system or protection profile evaluations. The sponsoring agencies of NIST then validate the evaluation and award the appropriate EALs.

The CC uses the following terms.

> **Definition 18–2.** A TOE Security Policy (TSP) is a set of rules that regulate how assets are managed, protected, and distributed within a product or system.

> **Definition 18–3.** The TOE Security Functions (TSF) is a set consisting of all hardware, software, and firmware of the product or system that must be relied on for the correct enforcement of the TSP.

Notice that the TSF is a generalization of the TCSEC concept of a trusted computing base (TCB).

The following discussion is based on Version 2.1 of the Common Criteria.

18.4.1   Overview of the Methodology

The CC supports two kinds of evaluations: evaluations of protection profiles and evaluations of products or systems against security targets (STs). Product evaluations are awarded at one of seven predefined EALs or at another, user-defined, EAL. All CC evaluations are reciprocal to the signers of the CCRA.

The concept of a protection profile evolved from the Federal Criteria, the CTCPEC profiles, and the ITSEC functionality classes. The form, structure, and terminology of a CC protection profile differs from that of an FC protection profile, although the concepts are similar.

> **Definition 18–4.** A CC *protection profile* (PP) is an implementation-independent set of security requirements for a category of products or systems that meet specific consumer needs.

The PP provides a thorough description of a family of products in terms of threats, environmental issues and assumptions, security objectives, and CC requirements. The requirements include both functional requirements, chosen from the CC functional requirements by the PP author, and assurance requirements, which include one of the seven EALs and may include additional assurance requirements as well. The final section of the PP provides the assurance evidence in the form of a rationale that the PP is complete, consistent, and technically sound. PPs do not have to be evaluated and validated. PPs that are evaluated must undergo evaluation in accordance with the methodology outlined in the CC assurance class APE: Protection Profile Evaluation.

A PP consists of six sections.

1. *Introduction.* This section contains

   a. the *PP Identification*, which is precise information used to identify, catalogue, register, and cross reference the PP; and

   b. the *PP Overview*, which is a narrative summary of the PP that should be acceptable as a stand-alone abstract for use in catalogues and registries.

2. *Product or System Family Description.* This section includes a description of the type and the general IT features of the product or system. If the primary function of the product or system is security, this section may describe the wider application context into which the product or system will fit.

3. *Product or System Family Security Environment.* This section presents

   a. assumptions about the intended usage and the environment of use;

   b. threats to the assets requiring protection, in terms of threat agents, types of attacks, and assets that are the targets of the attacks; and

   c. organizational security policies by which the product or system must abide.

4. *Security Objectives.* There are two types of security objectives:

   a. the *security objectives for the product or system* must be traced back to aspects of identified threats and/or organizational security policies; and

   b. the *security objectives for the environment* must be traced back to threats not completely countered by the product or system and/or organizational policies or assumptions not completely met by the product or system.

5. *IT Security Requirements.* This section covers functional and assurance requirements.

   a. The *security functional requirements* are drawn from the CC. If no CC requirements are appropriate, the PP author may supply other requirements explicitly without reference to the CC.

   b. The *security assurance requirements* are based on an EAL. The PP author may augment an EAL by adding extra security assurance requirements from the CC or may supply other requirements explicitly without reference to the CC. This includes security requirements for the environment, as applicable.

6. *Rationale*. This section includes both objectives and requirements.

    a. The *security objectives rationale* demonstrates that the stated objectives are traceable to all of the assumptions, threats, and organizational policies.

    b. The *security requirements rationale* demonstrates that the requirements for the product or system and the requirements for the environment are traceable to the objectives and meet them.

The second form of evaluation offered by the CC is the evaluation of a product or system against a security target (ST). The results of the evaluation are recognized by all signatories to the CCRA. This type of evaluation has two parts. The first is the evaluation of the ST in accordance with assurance class ASE: Security Target Evaluation (see Section 18.4.4). The product or system itself is then evaluated against the ST.

Under the CC, the functional requirements for a specific product or system are defined in an ST, just as was done under the ITSEC. The concept of a security target evolved from the ITSEC, and the idea of evaluating a security target against an evaluated protection profile evolved from the FC.

Definition 18–5. A *security target* (ST) is a set of security requirements and specifications to be used as the basis for evaluation of an identified product or system.

There are two approaches to developing an ST. The first approach is to develop an ST based on a PP. The second approach is to develop an ST directly from the CC. If an evaluated PP is used, the ST process is generally simpler because much of the rationale in the ST can reference the PP directly. The ST addresses the same fundamental issues as the PP, with some notable differences. A significant difference is that the ST addresses the issues for the specific product or system, not for a family of potential products or systems.

An ST consists of eight sections.

1. *Introduction*. This section has three parts.

    a. The *ST Identification* gives precise information that is used to control and identify the ST and the product or system to which it refers.

    b. The *ST Overview* is a narrative summary of the ST that should be acceptable as a stand-alone abstract for use in evaluated product lists.

    c. The *CC Conformance Claim* is a statement of conformance to the CC. An ST is *part 2 conformant* if it uses only functional requirements found in part 2 of the CC. If it uses extended requirements defined by the vendor, it is called *part 2 extended*. *Part 3 conformant* and *part 3 extended* are similarly defined. An ST is conformant to a PP only if it is compliant with all parts of the PP.

2. *Product or System Description*. This section includes a description of the TOE as an aid to understanding its security requirements. It addresses the product or system type and the scope and boundaries of the TOE (both physically and logically).

3. *Product or System Family Security Environment*. This section includes

   a. assumptions about the intended usage and about the environment of use;

   b. threats to the assets requiring protection, in terms of threat agents, types of attacks, and assets that are the targets of attacks; and

   c. organizational security policies by which the product or system must abide.

4. *Security Objectives*. There are two types of security objectives:

   a. *the security objectives for the product or system* must be traced back to aspects of identified threats and/or organizational security policies; and

   b. *the security objectives for the environment* must be traced back to threats not completely countered by the product or system and/or organizational policies or assumptions not completely met by the product or system.

5. *IT Security Requirements*. This section covers functional and assurance requirements.

   a. The *security functional requirements* are drawn from the CC. If no CC requirements are appropriate, the ST author may supply other requirements explicitly without reference to the CC.

   b. The *security assurance requirements* are based on an EAL. The ST author may augment an EAL by adding extra security assurance requirements from the CC or may supply other requirements explicitly without reference to the CC. This includes security requirements for the environment, as applicable.

6. *Product or System Summary Specification*. This specification defines the instantiation of the security requirements for the product or system and includes

   a. a statement of security functions and a description of how these functions meet the functional requirements; and

   b. a statement of assurance measures specifying how the assurance requirements are met.

7. *PP Claims.* This section makes claims of conformance with the requirements of one or more protection profiles.

8. *Rationale.* This section explains various aspects of the ST.

    a. The *security objectives rationale* demonstrates that the stated objectives are traceable to all of the assumptions, threats, and organizational policies.

    b. The *security requirements rationale* demonstrates that the requirements for the product or system and the requirements for the environment are traceable to the objectives and meet them.

    c. The *TOE summary specification rationale* demonstrates how the TOE security functions and assurance measures meet the security requirements.

    d. A rationale for not meeting all dependencies.

    e. The *PP claims rationale* explains differences between the ST objectives and requirements and those of any PP to which conformance is claimed.

As shown in the list above, in addition to the PP issues, the ST includes a product or system summary specification that identifies specific security functions and mechanisms. It also describes the strength of the functional requirements and the assurance measures used to analyze those requirements. A PP claims section identifies claims made to PPs that the ST implements. The ST rationale section contains a summary specification rationale that shows how the security functional requirements are met, how any strength-of-function claims are met, and that the assurance measures are sufficient for the assurance requirements. An ST that claims to implement a PP must state those claims and justify them in the rationale.

The CC also has a scheme for assurance maintenance. The goal of such activities is to build confidence that assurance already established for a product or system will be maintained and that the product or system will continue to meet the security requirements through changes in the product or system or its environment.

18.4.2   CC Requirements

The heart of the CC is the requirements themselves. The CC defines both functional and assurance requirements and then builds EALs out of the assurance requirements. The requirements are organized into a somewhat elaborate naming and numbering scheme. However, this scheme is much easier to use than the textual descriptions of multiple requirements in a single section, as is done in other methodologies. Functional and assurance requirements are divided into classes based on common purpose. Classes are broken into smaller groups called families. Families contain components, which contain definitions of detailed requirements as well as dependent requirements and a definition of hierarchy of requirements.

18.4.3   CC Security Functional Requirements

There are 11 classes of security functional requirements, each having one or more families. Two of the security functional requirement classes are auditing and security management. The related requirements are unique in the sense that many requirements in other classes generate auditing and/or management requirements. A management section of each family overview provides specific information about management issues relevant to the subdivisions and requirements of the family. Similarly, the audit section of the family overview identifies relevant auditable events associated with the requirements of the family. Requirements may be hierarchical in nature. Requirement A is hierarchical to requirement B if the functional elements of requirement B contain the functional elements of requirement A along with some additions. Finally, nonhierarchical dependencies, which may cross classes, are also identified with each requirement. These four structural approaches (identification of management requirements, audit requirements, hierarchical issues, and nonhierarchical dependencies) help define a consistent and complete specification using the CC.

Consider the security functional requirements of the CC by class and family. The class is indicated by the title, and the families are identified in the descriptive text. All other requirements are derived from previously discussed methodologies.

Class FAU: *Security Audit*. This class contains six families of requirements that address audit automatic response, audit data generation, audit analysis, audit review, audit event selection, and audit event storage.

Class FCO: *Communication*. This class contains two families that address nonrepudiation of origin and nonrepudiation of receipt. The CC is the first methodology to contain this requirement.

Class FCS: *Cryptographic Support*. This class contains two families that address cryptographic key management and cryptographic operation. Encryption algorithms and other implementation issues can be addressed using FIPS 140-2.

Class FDP: *User Data Protection*. This class has 13 families. It includes two different types of security policies, each with one family for each type of policy and another family that defines the functions for that type of policy. These are access control and information flow policies. The difference between these two types of policies is essentially that an access control policy makes decisions based on discrete sets of information, such as access control lists or access permissions, whereas an information flow control policy addresses the flow of information from one repository to another. A discretionary access control policy is an access control policy and a mandatory access control policy is an information flow control policy. These families are also represented in other methodologies, but they are generalized in the CC, for flexibility.

The residual information protection family addresses the issues called "object reuse" in previous criteria. Other families address data authentication, rollback, stored data integrity, inter-TSF user data confidentiality transfer protection, inter-TSF user data integrity transfer protection, exporting to outside the TSF control, and importing from outside the TSF control.

Class FIA: *Identification and Authentication*. This class has six families that include authentication failures, user attribute definition, specification of secrets, user authentication, user identification, and user/subject binding.

Class FMT: *Security Management*. This class contains six families that include management of security attributes, management of TSF data, management roles, management of functions in TSF, and revocation.

Class FPR: *Privacy*. The CC is the first evaluation methodology to support this class. Its families address anonymity, pseudonymity, unlinkability, and unobservability.

Class FPT: *Protection of Security Functions*. This class has 16 families. TSF physical protection, reference mediation, and domain separation represent the reference monitor requirements. Other families address underlying abstract machine tests, TSF self-tests, trusted recovery, availability of exported TSF data, confidentiality of exported TSF data, integrity of exported TSF data, internal product or system TSF data transfer, replay detection, state synchrony protocol, timestamps, inter-TSF data consistency, internal product or system TSF data relocation consistency, and TSF self-tests.

Class FRU: *Resource Utilization*. The three families in this class deal with fault tolerance, resource allocation, and priority of service (first used in the CC).

Class FTA: *TOE Access*. This class has six families. They include limitations on multiple concurrent sessions, session locking, access history and session establishment, product or system access banners, and limitations on the scope of selectable attributes (system entry constraints).

Class FTP: *Trusted Path*. This class has two families. The inter-TSF trusted channel family is new to the CC, but the trusted path family was in all previous criteria.

EXAMPLE: As indicated above, Class FAU contains six families. The management section for each family identifies potential management functions of class FMT that should be considered relative to the components of that family. The audit section for each family description identifies auditable events that must be addressed if the component FAU_GEN is selected in the PP or ST.

Component FAU_SAA addresses security audit analysis. Within FAU_SAA there are four components, two of which are described here. FAU_SAA.1, potential violation analysis, is a component that is hierarchical to no other components. This means that there is no lesser requirement in this family on this topic. FAU_SAA.1 depends on requirement FAU_GEN.1, a requirement from another FAU family. This means that if FAU_SAA.1 is selected, FAU_GEN.1 must also be selected. Within FAU_SAA.1 there are two functional requirements. The next component is FAU_SAA.2, profile-based anomaly detection. It is hierarchical to FAU_SAA.1, meaning that the requirements of FAU_SAA.2 are more stringent than those of FAU_SAA.1 and subsume the requirements of FAU_SAA.1. FAU_SAA.2 is also dependent on FIA_UID.1, a requirement for a family in another class. FAU_SAA.2 contains two individual requirements.

18.4.4   Assurance Requirements

There are ten security assurance classes. One assurance class relates to protection profiles, one to security targets, and one to the maintenance of assurance. The other seven directly address assurance for the product or system.

Class APE: *Protection Profile Evaluation.* This class has six families, one for each of the first five sections of the PP and one for non-CC requirements.

Class ASE: *Security Target Evaluation.* This class contains eight families, one for each of the eight sections of the ST. They are similar to the PP families and include families for product or system summary specification, PP claims, and non-CC requirements. Like the requirements of class APE, these requirements are unique to the CC.

Class ACM: *Configuration Management (CM).* This class has three families: CM automation, CM capabilities, and CM scope.

Class ADO: *Delivery and Operation.* This class has two families: delivery and installation, and generation and start-up.

Class ADV: *Development.* This class contains seven families: functional specification, low-level design, implementation representation, TSF internals, high-level design, representation correspondence, and security policy modeling.

Class AGD: *Guidance Documentation.* The two families in this class are administrator guidance and user guidance.

Class ALC: *Life Cycle.* There are four families in this class: development security, flaw remediation, tools and techniques, and life cycle definition.

Class ATE: *Tests.* There are four families in this class: test coverage, test depth, functional tests, and independent testing.

Class AVA: *Vulnerabilities Assessment.* There are four families in this class: covert channel analysis, misuse, strength of functions, and vulnerability analysis.

Class AMA: *Maintenance of Assurance.* This class has four families: assurance maintenance plan, product or system component categorization report, evidence of assurance maintenance, and security impact analysis. These were not formal requirements in any of the previous methodologies, but the TCSEC Ratings Maintenance Program (RAMP) addressed all of them. The ITSEC had a similar program that included all these families.

18.4.5   Evaluation Assurance Levels

The CC has seven levels of assurance.

EAL1: *Functionally Tested.* This level is based on an analysis of security functions using functional and interface specifications, examining the guidance documentation provided, and is supported by independent testing. EAL1 is applicable to systems in which some confidence in correct operation is required but security threats are not serious.

EAL2: *Structurally Tested*. This level is based on an analysis of security functions, including the high-level design in the analysis. The analysis is supported by independent testing, as in EAL1, as well as by evidence of developer testing based on the functional specification, independent confirmation of developer test results, strength-of-functions analysis, and a vulnerability search for obvious flaws. EAL2 is applicable to systems for which a low to moderate level of independent assurance is required but the complete developmental record may not be available, such as legacy systems.

EAL3: *Methodically Tested and Checked*. At this level, the analysis of security functions is the same as at EAL2. The analysis is supported as in EAL2, with the addition of high-level design as a basis for developer testing and the use of development environment controls and configuration management.

EAL4: *Methodically Designed, Tested, and Reviewed*. This level adds low-level design, a complete interface description, and a subset of the implementation to the inputs for the security function analysis. An informal model of the product or system security policy is also required. Other assurance measures at EAL4 require additional configuration management including automation. This is the highest EAL that is likely to be feasible for retrofitting of an existing product line. It is applicable to systems for which a moderate to high level of independently assured security is required.

EAL5: *Semiformally Designed and Tested*. This level adds the full implementation to the inputs for the security function analysis for EAL4. A formal model, a semiformal functional specification, a semiformal high-level design, and a semiformal correspondence among the different levels of specification are all required. The product or system design must also be modular. The vulnerability search must address penetration attackers with moderate attack potential and must provide a covert channel analysis. Configuration management must be comprehensive. This level is the highest EAL at which rigorous commercial development practices supported by a moderate amount of specialist computer security engineering will suffice. This EAL is applicable to systems for which a high level of independently assured security is needed.

EAL6: *Semiformally Verified Design and Tested*. This level requires a structured presentation of the implementation in addition to the inputs for the security function analysis for EAL5. A semiformal low-level design must be included in the semiformal correspondence. The design must support layering as well as modularity. The vulnerability search at EAL6 addresses penetration attackers with high attack potential, and the covert channel analysis must be systematic. A structured development process must be used.

EAL7: *Formally Verified Design and Tested*. The final level requires a formal presentation of the functional specification and a high-level design, and formal and semiformal demonstrations must be used in the correspondence, as appropriate. The product or system design must be simple. The analysis requires that the implementation representation be used as a basis for testing. Independent confirmation of the developer test results must be complete. EAL 7 is applicable in extremely high-risk situations and requires substantial security engineering.

The following table gives a rough matching of the levels of trust of various methodologies. Although the correspondences are not exact, they are reasonably close. The table indicates that the CC offers a level that is lower than any previously offered level.

TCSEC	ITSEC	CC	Other
D	E0	No equivalent	
No equivalent	No equivalent	EAL1	Private testing labs
C1	E1	EAL2	OS for FIPS 140-2 L2
C2	E2	EAL3	OS for FIPS 140-2 L3
B1	E3	EAL4	OS for FIPS 140-2 L4
B2	E4	EAL5	
B3	E5	EAL6	
A1	E6	EAL7	

18.4.6   Evaluation Process

The CC evaluation process in the United States is controlled by the CC Evaluation Methodology (CEM) and NIST. Evaluations are performed by NIST-accredited commercial laboratories that do evaluations for a fee. Many of the evaluation laboratories have separate organizations or partner organizations that can support vendors in getting ready for evaluations. Teams of evaluators are provided to evaluate protection profiles as well as systems or products and their respective security targets. Typically the size of the team is close to the size of a TCSEC team (four to six individuals) but this may vary from laboratory to laboratory.

Typically, a vendor selects an accredited laboratory to evaluate a PP or a product or system. The laboratory performs the evaluation on a fee basis. Once negotiations and a baseline schedule have been developed, the laboratory must coordinate with the validating body. Under the U.S. scheme, the evaluation laboratory must develop a work plan and must coordinate on the evaluation project with the validator and with an oversight board. The evaluation of a PP procedes precisely as outlined in the CEM and according to schedules agreed to by the evaluation laboratory and the PP authors. When the PP evaluation is complete, the laboratory presents its findings to the validating agency, which decides whether or not to validate the PP evaluation and award the EAL rating.

Evaluation of a product or system is slightly more complex because there are more steps involved and more evaluation evidence deliverables. A draft of the product or system ST must be provided before the laboratory can coordinate the project with the validating organization. The vendor and the evaluation laboratory must coordinate schedules for deliverables of evaluation evidence, but otherwise the process is the same as described above for a PP. When the laboratory finishes the evaluation, it presents its findings to the validating agency, which decides whether or not to validate the product or system evaluation and award the EAL rating.

18.4.7   Impacts

The CC addresses many issues with which other evaluation criteria and methodologies have struggled. However, the CC is not perfect. At first glance, one might think that the protection profiles and security targets of the CC suffer the same weaknesses as those that plagued the security targets of the ITSEC. In some sense, this is true. A PP or ST may not be as strong as TCSEC classes because fewer security experts have reviewed it and it has not yet faced the test of time. Some of the CC requirements were derived from requirements of the previous methodologies. Such requirements may inherently have more credibility. Mature requirements and the CC process of identifying dependencies, audit requirements, and management requirements can contribute to the completeness, consistency, and technical correctness of a resulting PP or ST. The clarity of presentation of the requirements also helps, but ultimately the correctness of an ST lies in the hands of the vendor and the evaluation team.

The CC is much more complete than the functional requirements of most preceding technologies. However, it is not immune to "criteria creep." A CC project board manages interpretations to support consistent evaluation results. Interpretations can be submitted by any national scheme for international review. The final interpretations agreed on become required on all subsequent evaluations under the CC and form the basis for future CC updates. Although this is a well-managed process, it does not address the fact that a newer evaluation may have more stringent requirements levied on it than an older evaluation of the same type.

Having a team member who is not motivated by financial issues to complete the evaluation quickly lends support to the depth of the evaluation and in some respects addresses the functions of a technical review board by providing impartial review. The evaluation process itself is very well-defined and well-monitored by the validating body. The process itself is less subjective than some of the preceding methodologies because every step is well-defined and carefully applied. Because many U.S. CC evaluators were part of the TCSEC evaluation system, the U.S. CC evaluations are probably close to the TCSEC evaluations in depth.

18.4.8   Future of the Common Criteria

The CC documentation and methodology continue to evolve. A new version of the CC is planned for release in mid-2003. The revision will include approved interpretations as well as other changes currently under consideration.

18.4.8.1   Interpretations

The Common Criteria Interpretation Management Board (CCIMB) is an international body responsible for maintaining the Common Criteria. Each signatory of the CCRA has a representative on the CCIMB. This group has the responsibility of accepting or rejecting interpretations of the CC submitted by national schemes or the general public. The charter of the CCIMB is to facilitate consistent evaluation results under the CCRA. Interpretations begin as Requests for Interpretation (RIs) that national schemes or the general public submit to the CCIMB for consideration. RIs fall into the following categories.

- A perceived error that some content in the CC or CEM requires correction
- An identified need for additional material in the CC or CEM
- A proposed method for applying the CC or CEM in a specific circumstance for which endorsement is sought
- A request for information to assist with understanding the CC or CEM

The CCIMB prioritizes the RIs, responds to each RI, and posts the RI on its Web site for approximately 3 months of public review. The CCIMB then reviews the feedback and finalizes the interpretation. Final interpretations agreed to by the CCIMB are posted and are levied on all subsequent evaluations certified by organizations party to the CCRA.

18.4.8.2   Assurance Class AMA and Family ALC_FLR

Class AMA is Maintenance of Assurance, which allows for assurance ratings to be applied to later releases of an evaluated product in specific cases. Family FLR is flaw remediation, which specifies the requirements for fixing flaws in a certified, released product. The combination of these activities creates a program along the lines of RAMP, which was initiated under the TCSEC. The updates to these areas will be released in a supplement prior to release 3.0 of the CC and will be incorporated in release 3.0 of the CC.

18.4.8.3   Products Versus Systems

Although the CC has been used successfully for many computer products, evaluations of systems are less frequent and less well-defined. The process for systems is being refined, with the intention of having significantly more information available for system evaluation in the next release.

18.4.8.4   Protection Profiles and Security Targets

The requirements and content of a PP or an ST are defined in several locations within the three parts of Common Criteria Version 2.1. These sections are being consolidated into part 3 of the CC. In addition to consolidation, there are some contextual changes in these documents. In addition, low-assurance PP and ST documents are to be substantially simplified. These changes are targeted for CC Version 3.0.

18.4.8.5   Assurance Class AVA

The assurance class AVA, Vulnerability Assessment, is currently under revision to make it better suited to the market and to ensure more consistent application between schemes. This class is the most common area for augmentation. Family AVA_VLI is being revised to address attack methods, vulnerability exploitation determination, and vulnerability identification. These changes are also targeted for CC Version 3.0.

18.4.8.6   EAL5

Currently the CEM defines the steps an evaluator must take for evaluations at levels EAL1 through EAL4. An effort is underway to increase the scope of the CEM to include the detailed evaluation methodology for level EAL5.

18.5   SSE-CMM: 1997–Present

The System Security Engineering Capability Maturity Model (SSE-CMM) [412, 413, 528, 889] is a process-oriented methodology for developing secure systems based on the Software Engineering Capability Maturity Model (SE-CMM). SSE-CMM was developed by a team of security experts from the U.S. government and industries to advance security engineering as a defined, mature, and measurable discipline. It helps engineering organizations define practices and processes and to focus on improvement efforts. The SSE-CMM became ISO Standard 21827 in 2002.

Taking a very abstract view, there is a similarity between evaluation of processes using a capability model and evaluation of security functionality using an assurance model. Capability models define requirements for processes, whereas methodologies such as the CC and its predecessors define requirements for security functionality. Capability models assess how mature a process is, whereas the CC type methodology evaluates how much assurance is provided for the functionality. SSE-CMM provides maturity levels, whereas the other methodologies provide levels of trust. In each case, there are specific requirements for the process or functionality and different levels of maturity or trust that can be applied to each.

The SSE-CMM can be used to assess the capabilities of security engineering processes and provide guidance in designing and improving them, thereby improving an organization's security engineering capability. The SSE-CMM provides an evaluation technique for an organization's security engineering. Applying the SSE-CMM can support assurance evidence and increase confidence in the trustworthiness of a product or system.

18.5.1   The SSE-CMM Model

The SSE-CMM is organized into processes and maturity levels. Generally speaking, the processes define what needs to be accomplished by the security engineering process and the maturity levels categorize how well the process accomplishes its goals.

> **Definition 18–6.** A *process capability* is the range of expected results that can be achieved by following the process. It is a predictor of future project outcomes.

> **Definition 18–7.** *Process performance* is a measure of the actual results achieved.

> **Definition 18–8.** *Process maturity* is the extent to which a process is explicitly defined, managed, measured, controlled, and effective.

The SSE-CMM contains 11 process areas.

- Administer Security Controls
- Assess Impact
- Assess Security Risk
- Assess Threat
- Assess Vulnerability
- Build Assurance Argument
- Coordinate Security
- Monitor System Security Posture
- Provide Security Input
- Specify Security Needs
- Verify and Validate Security

The definition of each process area contains a goal for the process area and a set of base processes that support the process area. The SSE-CMM defines more than 60 base processes within the 11 process areas.

EXAMPLE: The definition of the Assess Threat process area contains the goal that threats to the security of the system be identified and characterized. The base processes are

- Identify Natural Threats
- Identify Human-Made Threats

- Identify Threat Units of Measure
- Assess Threat Agent Capability
- Assess Threat Likelihood
- Monitor Threats and Their Characteristics

Eleven additional process areas related to project and organizational practices adapted from the SE-CMM are

- Ensure Quality
- Manage Configuration
- Manage Project Risk
- Monitor and Control Technical Effort
- Plan Technical Effort
- Define Organization's Systems Engineering Process
- Improve Organization's Systems Engineering Process
- Manage Product Line Evolution
- Manage Systems Engineering Support Environment
- Provide Ongoing Skills and Knowledge
- Coordinate with Suppliers

The five Capability Maturity Levels that represent increasing process maturity are as follows.

1. *Performed Informally.* Base processes are performed.
2. *Planned and Tracked.* Project-level definition, planning, and performance verification issues are addressed.
3. *Well-Defined.* The focus is on defining and refining a standard practice and coordinating it across the organization.
4. *Quantitatively Controlled.* This level focuses on establishing measurable quality goals and objectively managing their performance.
5. *Continuously Improving.* At this level, organizational capability and process effectiveness are improved.

18.5.2   Using the SSE-CMM

Application of the SSE-CMM is a straightforward analysis of existing processes to determine which base processes have been met and the maturity levels they have achieved. The same process can help an organization determine which security engineering processes they may need but do not currently have in practice.

This is accomplished using the well-defined base processes and capability maturity levels that were overviewed in the preceding section. One starts with a process area, identifying the area goals and base processes that SSE-CMM defines for the process area. If all the processes within a process area are present, then the next step of the analysis involves determining how mature the base processes are by assessing them against the Capability Maturity Levels. Such an analysis is not simple and may involve interactions with engineers who actually use the process. The result of the analysis culminates in identification of the current level of maturity for each base process in the process area.

The analysis continues as described above for each process area. Processes within an area may have varying levels of maturity, and the level of maturity for the process area would be the lowest level represented by the set of levels for the base process. A useful way of looking at the result of a complete SSE-CMM analysis is to use a Rating Profile, which is a tabular representation of process areas versus maturity levels. An example of such a profile is provided in Figure 18–1. In a similar fashion, process area rating profiles can be used to show the ratings provided for individual base processes within a process area.

18.6   Summary

Since the early 1980s, the international computer security community has been developing criteria and methodologies for the security evaluation of IT products and systems. The first public and widely used technique was provided by the Trusted Computer System Evaluation Criteria (TCSEC), which was driven by the U.S. Department of Defense. Although the TCSEC was widely used for nearly two decades, criticisms of it inspired research and development of other approaches that addressed many areas of concern, including limitations of scope, problems with the

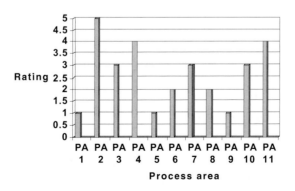

Figure 18–1   Example of a rating profile for the 11 process areas of the SSE-CMM (from [315]) .

evaluation process, binding of assurance and functionality, lack of recognition of evaluations in one country by the authorities of another, and inflexibility in selection of requirements, to name the most significant ones. New methodologies were developed to address these issues. Most notable of these were the Information Technology Security Evaluation Criteria (ITSEC) in Europe, the Canadian Trusted Computer Product Evaluation Criteria (CTCPEC), and the Federal Criteria (FC) in the United States. These foundational methodologies have culminated in the Common Criteria, which today has world-wide support.

Other evaluation techniques include a special-purpose evaluation of cryptographic modules, jointly managed by NIST and the Canadian CSE, and the process-oriented System Security Engineering Capability Maturity Model (SSE-CMM).

18.7   Further Reading

The evaluation process of the TCSEC has been widely discussed and critiqued [35, 74, 172, 471, 687, 729, 811], and changes have been proposed for specific environments such as real-time embedded systems [16]. Several products and systems aimed at levels of the TCSEC have also been analyzed [130, 272, 301, 765, 898, 948]. Pfleeger [719] compares the TCSEC with then-current European evaluation methodologies.

The Canadian Trusted Computer Product Evaluation Criteria (CTCPEC) [153] in 1989 was influenced by the TCSEC. Several nations developed another criterion, the Information Technology Security Evaluation Criteria (ITSEC). The results of ITSEC evaluations have been presented [148, 447]. Straw [881] compares the ITSEC with the Federal Criteria, and Borrett [126] discusses the differences between evaluation under the TCSEC and under the U.K. ITSEC.

Individuals from American Express and Electronic Data Systems (EDS) joined forces to develop the Commercial International Security Requirements (CISR) [227]. The 1992 Federal Criteria [675] attempted to address the shortcomings of the TCSEC and of the ITSEC and to address the concerns of the CISR authors.

The basis for CC requirements arises in several papers, including one that describes the functional criteria for distributed systems [224]. Other papers discuss various aspects of CC ratings [121, 453] and protection profiles, including the use of SSE-CMM processes to develop those profiles [37, 945]. Some evaluations have also been discussed [5, 400].

Hefner [412, 413] and Menk [620] discuss the origins and evaluation partnerships under the SSE-CMM. Some papers [507, 508] discuss the relationships between product-oriented evaluation and process-oriented evaluation. In particular, Ferraiolo [315] discusses the contribution of process capability to assurance and the definition of metrics to support process-based assurance arguments. Ferraiolo's tutorial [316] provides a good introduction to SSE-CMM.

Some systems have demanded their own specialized certification processes [324], as have some environments [163, 295].

Lipner [572] gives a short, interesting historical retrospective on evaluation, and Snow [847] briefly discusses the future.

Many organizations keep the most current information on evaluation standards and processes on the World Wide Web. For example, the FIPS 140-2 Web site [674] gives information about NIST's cryptographic module verification program. The Common Criteria Web site [187] contains copies of the Common Criteria and various national schemes, such as that of the United States [673]. It also offers historical information, information about current projects, registries of evaluated and unevaluated protection profiles, evaluated product and system listings (most of which include the security target for the product or system), products and PPs currently being evaluated, and information on testing laboratories and recognition agreements among the participating countries. Detailed information about SSE-CMM is also on the WWW [806].

18.8 Exercises

1. The issue of binding assurance requirements to functional requirements versus treating them as mutually exclusive sets has been debated over the years. Which approach do you think is preferable, and why?

2. What are the values of doing formal evaluation? What do you see as the drawbacks of evaluation?

3. Recall that "criteria creep" is the process of refining evaluation requirements as the industry gains experience with them, making the evaluation criteria something of a moving target. (See Section 18.2.4.2.) This issue is not confined to the TCSEC, but rather is a problem universal to all evaluation technologies. Discuss the benefits and drawbacks of the CC methodology for handling criteria creep.

4. What are the conceptual differences between a reference validation mechanism, a trusted computing base, and the TOE Security Functions?

5. Choose a Common Criteria protection profile and a security target of a product that implements that profile (see the Common Criteria Web site [187]). Identify the differences between the PP and the ST that implements the PP.

6. Identify the specific requirements in the Common Criteria that describe a reference validation mechanism. *Hint*: Look in both security functional classes and security assurance classes.

7. Use the Common Criteria to write security requirements for identifying the security functional and assurance requirements that define a security policy that implements the Bell-LaPadula Model.

8. Map the assurance requirements of the TCSEC (as defined in this chapter) to the assurance requirements of the CC.

9. Map the security functional requirements of the CC to the functional requirements of the TCSEC (as described in this chapter).

10. Describe a family of security functional requirements that is not covered in the Common Criteria. Using the CC style and format, develop several requirements.

Chapter 19
Malicious Logic

> TITUS ANDRONICUS: Ah!, wherefore dost thou urge the name of hands?
> To bid Aeneas tell the tale twice o'er,
> How Troy was burnt and he made miserable?
> —*The Tragedy of Titus Andronicus*, III, ii, 26–28.

Computer viruses, worms, and Trojan horses are effective tools with which to attack computer systems. They assume an authorized user's identity. This makes most traditional access controls useless. This chapter presents several types of malicious logic, focusing on Trojan horses and computer viruses, and discusses defenses.

19.1   Introduction

Odysseus, of Trojan War fame, found the most effective way to breach a hitherto-impregnable fortress was to have people inside bring him in without knowing they were doing so [432, 916]. The same approach works for computer systems.

Definition 19–1. *Malicious logic* is a set of instructions that cause a site's security policy to be violated.

EXAMPLE: The following UNIX script is named *ls* and is placed in a directory.

```
cp /bin/sh /tmp/.xxsh
chmod u+s,o+x /tmp/.xxsh
rm ./ls
ls $*
```

It creates a copy of the UNIX shell that is setuid to the user executing this program (see Section 13.3). This program is deleted, and then the correct *ls* command is executed. On most systems, it is against policy to trick someone into creating a shell that is setuid to themselves. If someone is tricked into executing this script, a violation of the (implicit) security policy occurs. This script is an example of malicious logic.

19.2   Trojan Horses

A critical observation is the notion of "tricked." Suppose the user *root* executed this script unintentionally (for example, by typing "ls" in the directory containing this file). This would be a violation of the security policy. However, if *root* deliberately typed

```
cp /bin/sh /tmp/.xxsh
chmod o+s,w+x /tmp/.xxsh
```

the security policy would not be violated. This illustrates a crucial component of the problems with malicious logic. The system cannot determine whether the instructions being executed by a process are known to the user or are a set of instructions that the user does not intend to execute. The next definition makes this distinction explicit.

> **Definition 19–2.** A *Trojan horse* is a program with an overt (documented or known) effect and a *covert* (undocumented or unexpected) effect.

EXAMPLE: In the preceding example, the overt purpose is to list the files in a directory. The covert purpose is to create a shell that is setuid to the user executing the script. Hence, this program is a Trojan horse.

Dan Edwards was the first to use this term [25]. Trojan horses are often used in conjunction with other tools to attack systems.

EXAMPLE: The NetBus program allows an attacker to control a Windows NT workstation remotely. The attacker can intercept keystrokes or mouse motions, upload and download files, and act as a system administrator would act. In order for this program to work, the victim Windows NT system must have a server with which the NetBus program can communicate. This requires someone on the victim's system to load and execute a small program that runs the server.

This small program was placed in several small game programs as well as in some other "fun" programs, which could be distributed to Web sites where unsuspecting users would be likely to download them.

Trojan horses can make copies of themselves. One of the earliest Trojan horses was a version of the game *animal*. When this game was played, it created an extra copy of itself. These copies spread, taking up much room. The program was modified to delete one copy of the earlier version and create two copies of the modified program. Because it spread even more rapidly than the earlier version, the modified version of *animal* soon completely supplanted the earlier version. After a preset date, each copy of the later version deleted itself after it was played [262].

Definition 19–3. A *propagating Trojan horse* (also called a *replicating Trojan horse*) is a Trojan horse that creates a copy of itself.

Karger and Schell [496], and later Thompson [899], examined detection of Trojan horses. They constructed a Trojan horse that propagated itself slowly and in a manner that was difficult to detect. The central idea is that the Trojan horse modifies the compiler to insert itself into specific programs, including future versions of the compiler itself.

EXAMPLE: Thompson [899] added a Trojan horse to the *login* program. When a user logged in, the Trojan horse would accept a fixed password as well as the user's normal password. However, anyone reading the source code for the *login* program would instantly detect this Trojan horse. To obscure it, Thompson had the compiler check the program being compiled. If that program was *login*, the compiler added the code to use the fixed password. Now, no code needed to be added to the *login* program. Thus, an analyst inspecting the *login* program source code would see nothing amiss. If the analyst compiled the *login* program from that source, she would believe the executable to be uncorrupted.

The extra code is visible in the compiler source. To eliminate this problem, Thompson modified the compiler. This second version checked to see if the compiler (actually, the C preprocessor) was being recompiled. If so, the code to modify the compiler so as to include both this Trojan horse and the *login* Trojan horse code would be inserted. He compiled the second version of the compiler and installed the executable. He then replaced the corrupted source with the original version of the compiler. As with the *login* program, inspection of the source code would reveal nothing amiss, but compiling and installing the compiler would insert the two Trojan horses.

Thompson took special pains to ensure that the second version of the compiler was never released. It remained on the system for a considerable time before someone overwrote the executable with a new version from a different system [751]. Thompson's point[1] was that "no amount of source-level verification or scrutiny will protect you from using untrusted code," a point to be reiterated later.

19.3   Computer Viruses

This type of Trojan horse propagates itself only as specific programs (in the preceding example, the compiler and the *login* program). When the Trojan horse can propagate freely and insert a copy of itself into another file, it becomes a computer virus.

---

[1] See [899], p. 763.

Definition 19–4. A *computer virus* is a program that inserts itself into one or more files and then performs some (possibly null) action.

The first phase, in which the virus inserts itself into a file, is called the *insertion phase*. The second phase, in which it performs some action, is called the *execution phase*. The following pseudocode fragment shows how a simple computer virus works.

```
beginvirus:
    if spread-condition then begin
        for some set of target files do begin
            if target is not infected then begin
                determine where to place virus instructions
                copy instructions from beginvirus to endvirus
                    into target
                alter target to execute added instructions
            end;
        end;
    end;
    perform some action(s)
    goto beginning of infected program
endvirus:
```

As this code indicates, the insertion phase must be present but need not always be executed. For example, the Lehigh virus [421] would check for an uninfected boot file (the *spread-condition* mentioned in the pseudocode) and, if one was found, would infect that file (the *set of target files*). Then it would increment a counter and test to see if the counter was at 4. If so, it would erase the disk. These operations were the *action(s)*.

Authorities differ on whether or not a computer virus is a type of Trojan horse. Most equate the purpose of the infected program with the overt action and consider the insertion and execution phases to be the covert action. To them, a computer virus is a Trojan horse [280, 464]. However, others argue that a computer virus has *no* covert purpose. Its overt purpose is to infect and execute. To these authorities, it is not a Trojan horse [180, 659]. In some sense this disagreement is semantic. In any case, defenses against a Trojan horse inhibit computer viruses.

According to Ferbrache [314], programmers wrote the first computer viruses on Apple II computers. A virus developed for research purposes in 1980 wrote itself to the disk boot sectors when the catalogue command was executed. Another one infected many copies of the game "Congo," which stopped working. Friends of its author had released it before it was fully debugged. The author rewrote it to replace existing copies of itself with the fully debugged version. Released into the wild, it rapidly supplanted the buggy copies.

In 1983, Fred Cohen was a graduate student at the University of Southern California. During a seminar on computer security, he described a type of Trojan horse that the teacher, Len Adleman, christened a computer virus [181]. To demonstrate the effectiveness of the proposed attack, Cohen designed a computer virus to acquire privileges on a VAX-11/750 running the UNIX operating system. He obtained all system rights within half an hour on the average, the longest time being an hour and the shortest being less than 5 minutes. Because the virus did not degrade response time noticeably, most users never knew the system was under attack.

In 1984, an experiment involving a UNIVAC 1108 showed that viruses could spread throughout that system, too. Unlike the UNIX system, the UNIVAC partially implemented the Bell-LaPadula Model, using mandatory protection mechanisms.[2] Cohen's experiments indicated that the security mechanisms of systems that did not inhibit writing using mandatory access controls did little if anything to inhibit computer virus propagation [180, 181].

The Brain (or Pakistani) virus, written for IBM PCs, is thought to have been created in early 1986 [314] but was first reported in the United States in October 1987. It alters the boot sectors of floppy disks, possibly corrupting files in the process. It also spreads to any uninfected floppy disks inserted into the system. Since then, numerous variations of this virus have been reported [422].

In 1987, computer viruses infected Macintosh, Amiga, and other computers. The MacMag Peace virus would print a "universal message of peace" on March 2, 1988, and then delete itself [321]. This computer virus infected copies of the Aldus FreeHand program, which were recalled by their manufacturer [314].

In 1987, Tom Duff experimented on UNIX systems with a small virus that copied itself into executable files. The virus was not particularly virulent, but when Duff placed 48 infected programs on the most heavily used machine in the computing center, the virus spread to 46 different systems and infected 466 files, including at least one system program on each computer system, within 8 days. Duff did not violate the security mechanisms in any way when he seeded the original 48 programs [282]. He wrote another virus in a Bourne shell script. It could attach itself to any UNIX program. This demonstrated that computer viruses are not intrinsically machine-dependent and can spread to systems of varying architectures.

In 1989, Dr. Harold Joseph Highland developed a virus for Lotus 1-2-3 [422]. This virus, stored as a set of commands for that spreadsheet, was loaded automatically when a file was opened. Because the virus was intended for a demonstration only, it changed the value in a specific row and column and then spread to other files. This demonstrated that macros for office-type programs on personal computers could contain viruses.

Several types of computer viruses have been identified.

19.3.1 Boot Sector Infectors

The *boot sector* is the part of a disk used to bootstrap the system or mount a disk. Code in that sector is executed when the system "sees" the disk for the first time.

---

[2] Specifically, it implemented the simple security condition but not the *-property [464].

When the system boots, or the disk is mounted, any virus in that sector is executed. (The actual boot code is moved to another place, possibly another sector.)

> **Definition 19–5.** A *boot sector infector* is a virus that inserts itself into the boot sector of a disk.

EXAMPLE: The Brain virus for the IBM PC is a boot sector infector. When the system boots from an infected disk, the virus is in the boot sector and is loaded. It moves the disk interrupt vector (location 13H or 19) to an alternative interrupt vector (location 6DH or 109) and sets the disk interrupt vector location to invoke the Brain virus now in memory. It then loads the original boot sector and continues the boot.

Whenever the user reads a floppy, the interrupt at location 13H is invoked. The Brain virus checks for the signature 1234H in the word at location 4. If the signature is present, control is transferred to the interrupt vector at location 6DH so that a normal read can proceed. Otherwise, the virus infects the disk.

To do this, it first allocates to itself three contiguous clusters (of two contiguous sectors each). The virus then copies the original boot sector to the first of the six contiguous sectors and puts copies of itself into the boot sector and the remaining five sectors.

If there are no unused clusters, the virus will not infect the disk. If it finds only one unused cluster, it will simply overwrite the next two. This accounts for the sometimes destructive nature of the Brain virus.

19.3.2   Executable Infectors

> **Definition 19–6.** An *executable infector* is a virus that infects executable programs.

The PC variety of executable infectors are called COM or EXE viruses because they infect programs with those extensions. Figure 19–1 illustrates how infection can

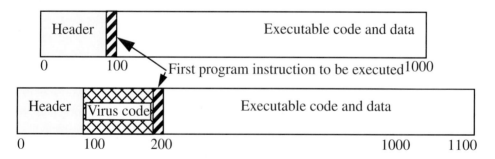

Figure 19–1   How an executable infector works. It inserts itself into the program so that the virus code will be executed before the application code. In this example, the virus is 100 words long and prepends itself to the executable code.

occur. The virus can prepend itself to the executable (as shown in the figure) or append itself.

EXAMPLE: The Jerusalem virus (also called the Israeli virus) is triggered when an infected program is executed. The virus first puts the value 0E0H into register ax and invokes the DOS service interrupt (21H). If on return the high eight bits of register ax contain 03H, the virus is already resident on the system and the executing version quits, invoking the original program. Otherwise, the virus sets itself up to respond to traps to the DOS service interrupt vector.

The Jerusalem virus then checks the date. If the year is 1987, it does nothing. Otherwise, if it is not a Friday and not the 13th (of any month), it sets itself up to respond to clock interrupts (but it will not infect on clock calls). It then loads and executes the file originally executed. When that file finishes, the virus puts itself in memory. It then responds to calls to the DOS service interrupt.

If it is a Friday and the 13th (of any month), and the year is not 1987, the virus sets a flag in memory to be destructive. This flag means that the virus will delete files instead of infecting them.

Once in memory, the virus checks all calls to the DOS service interrupt, looking for those asking that files be executed (function 4B00H). When this happens, the virus checks the name of the file. If it is COMND.COM, the virus does nothing. If the memory flag is set to be destructive, the file is deleted. Otherwise, the virus checks the last five bytes of the file. If they are the string "MsDos," the file is infected.[3] If they are not, the virus checks the last character of the file name. If it is "M," the virus assumes that a .COM file is being executed and infects it; if it is "E," the virus assumes that a .EXE file is being executed and infects it. The file's attributes, especially the date and time of modification, are left unchanged.

19.3.3 Multipartite Viruses

Definition 19–7. A *multipartite virus* is one that can infect either boot sectors or applications.

Such a virus typically has two parts, one for each type. When it infects an executable, it acts as an executable infector; when it infects a boot sector, it works as a boot sector infector.

---

[3] According to Compulit, as cited in [422], "[t]he author of the virus apparently forgot to set the signature during .EXE file infection. This will cause multiple infections of .EXE files" (p. 47). Analysts at the Hebrew University of Jerusalem found that the size of a .COM file increased only one time, but the size of a .EXE file increased every time the file was executed.

19.3.4   TSR Viruses

> **Definition 19–8.** A *terminate and stay resident* (TSR) virus is one that stays active (resident) in memory after the application (or bootstrapping, or disk mounting) has terminated.

TSR viruses can be boot sector infectors or executable infectors. Both the Brain and Jerusalem viruses are TSR viruses.

Viruses that are not TSR execute only when the host application is executed (or the disk containing the infected boot sector is mounted). An example is the Encroacher virus, which appends itself to the ends of executables.

19.3.5   Stealth Viruses

> **Definition 19–9.** *Stealth* viruses are viruses that conceal the infection of files.

These viruses intercept calls to the operating system that access files. If the call is to obtain file attributes, the original attributes of the file are returned. If the call is to read the file, the file is disinfected as its data is returned. But if the call is to execute the file, the infected file is executed.

EXAMPLE: The Stealth virus (also called the IDF virus or the 4096 virus) is an executable infector. It modifies the DOS service interrupt handler (rather than the interrupt vector; this way, checking the values in the interrupt vector will not reveal the presence of the virus). If the request is for the length of the file, the length of the *uninfected* file is returned. If the request is to open the file, the file is temporarily disinfected; it is reinfected on closing. The Stealth virus also changes the time of last modification of the file in the file allocation table to indicate that the file is infected.

19.3.6   Encrypted Viruses

Computer virus detectors often look for known sequences of code to identify computer viruses (see Section 19.6.4). To conceal these sequences, some viruses encipher most of the virus code, leaving only a small decryption routine and a random cryptographic key in the clear. Figure 19–2 summarizes this technique.

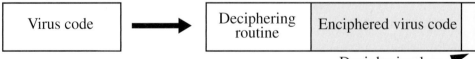

Figure 19–2   An encrypted virus. The ordinary virus code is at the left. The encrypted virus, plus encapsulating decryption information, is at the right.

Definition 19–10. An *encrypted* virus is one that enciphers all of the virus code except for a small decryption routine.

EXAMPLE: Ferbrache[4] cites the following as the decryption code in the 1260 virus. It uses two keys, stored in *k1* and *k2*. The virus code itself begins at the location *sov* and ends at the location *eov*. The pseudocode is as follows.

```
(* initialize the registers with the keys *)
rA ← k1;
rB ← k2;
(* initialize rC with the message *)
rC ← sov;
(* the encipherment loop *)
while (rC != eov) do begin
    (* encipher the byte of the message *)
    (*rC) ← (*rC) xor rA xor rB;
    (* advance all the counters *)
    rC ← rC + 1;
    rA ← rA + 1;
end
```

The dual keys and the shifting of the first key prevent a simple *xor*'ing from uncovering the deciphered virus.

19.3.7   Polymorphic Viruses

Definition 19–11. *A polymorphic virus is a virus that changes its form each time it inserts itself into another program.*

Consider an encrypted virus. The body of the virus varies depending on the key chosen, so detecting known sequences of instructions will not detect the virus. However, the decryption algorithm can be detected. Polymorphic viruses were designed to prevent this. They change the instructions in the virus to something equivalent but different. In particular, the deciphering code is the segment of the virus that is changed. In some sense, they are successors to the encrypting viruses and are often used in conjunction with them.

Consider polymorphism at the instruction level. All of the instructions

```
add 0 to operand
or 1 with operand
no operation
subtract 0 from operand
```

---

[4] See [314], p. 75.

have exactly the same effect, but they are represented as different bit patterns on most architectures. A polymorphic virus would insert these instructions into the deciphering segment of code.

EXAMPLE: A polymorphic version of the 1260 computer virus might look like the following. (The lines marked "random line" do nothing and are changed whenever the virus replicates.)

```
(* initialize the registers with the keys *)
rA ← k1;
rD ← rD + 1;(* random line *)
rB ← k2;
(* initialize rC with the message *)
rC ← sov;
rC ← rC + 1;(* random line *)
(* the encipherment loop *)
while (rC != eov) do begin
    rC ← rC - 1;(* random line X *)
    (* encipher the byte of the message *)
    (*rC) ← (*rC) xor rA xor rB;
    (* advance all the counters *)
    rC ← rC + 2;(* counter incremented ... *)
    (* to handle random line X *)
    rD ← rD + 1;(* random line *)
    rA ← rA + 1;
end
while (rC != sov) do begin(* random line *)
    rD ← rD - 1;(* random line *)
end(* random line *)
```

Examination shows that these instructions have the same effect as the four instructions listed above.

The production of polymorphic viruses at the instruction level has been automated. At least two tool kits, the Mutation Engine (MtE) and the Trident Polymorphic Engine (TPE), were available in 1992 [958].

Polymorphism can exist at many levels. For example, a deciphering algorithm may have two completely different implementations, or two different algorithms may produce the same result. In these cases, the polymorphism is at a higher level and is more difficult to detect.

19.3.8   Macro Viruses

Definition 19–12. A *macro* virus is a virus composed of a sequence of instructions that is interpreted, rather than executed directly.

Conceptually, macro viruses are no different from ordinary computer viruses. Like Duff's *sh* computer virus, they can execute on any system that can interpret the instructions. For example, a spreadsheet virus executes when the spreadsheet interprets these instructions. If the macro language allows the macro to access files or other systems, the virus can access them, too.

EXAMPLE: The Melissa virus infected Word 97 and 98 documents on Windows and Macintosh systems. It is invoked when the program opens an infected file. It installs itself as the "open" macro and copies itself into the Normal template (so any files that are opened are infected). It then invokes a mail program and sends copies of itself to people in the user's address book associated with the program.

A macro virus can infect either executables or data files (the latter leads to the name *data virus*). If it infects executable files, it must arrange to be interpreted at some point. Duff's experiments did this by wrapping the executables with shell scripts. The resulting executables invoked the Bourne shell, which interpreted the virus code before invoking the usual executable.

Macro viruses are not bound by machine architecture. They use specific programs, and so, for example, a macro virus targeted at a Microsoft Word program will work on any system running Microsoft Word. The effects may differ. For example, most Macintosh users do not use the particular mail program that Melissa invoked, so although Macintosh Word files could have been infected, and the infection could have been spread, the virus did not mail itself to other users. On a Windows system, where most users did use that mail program, the infection was spread by mail.

19.4　Computer Worms

A computer virus infects other programs. A variant of the virus is a program that spreads from computer to computer, spawning copies of itself on each one.

Definition 19–13. A *computer worm* is a program that copies itself from one computer to another.

Research into computer worms began in the mid-1970s. Schoch and Hupp [797] developed distributed programs to do computer animations, broadcast messages, and perform other computations. These programs probed workstations. If the workstation was idle, the worm copied a *segment* onto the system. The segment was given data to process and communicated with the worm's controller. When any activity other than the segment's began on the workstation, the segment shut down.

EXAMPLE: On November 2, 1988, a program targeting Berkeley and Sun UNIX-based computers entered the Internet; within hours, it had rendered several thousand computers unusable [292, 293, 757, 808, 809, 857, 858, 879]. Among other techniques, this program used a virus-like attack to spread: it inserted some instructions into a running process on the target machine and arranged for those instructions to be executed. To recover, these machines had to be disconnected from the network and rebooted, and several critical programs had to be changed and recompiled to prevent reinfection. Worse, the only way to determine if the program had suffered other malicious side effects (such as deletion of files) was to disassemble it. Fortunately, the only purpose of this virus turned out to be self-propagation. Infected sites were extremely lucky that the worm[5] did not infect a system program with a virus designed to delete files and did not attempt to damage attacked systems.

Since then, there have been several incidents involving worms. The Father Christmas worm was interesting because it was a form of macro worm.

EXAMPLE: Slightly before the Internet worm, an electronic "Christmas card" passed around several IBM-based networks. This card was an electronic letter instructing the recipient to save the message and run it as a program. The program drew a Christmas tree (complete with blinking lights) and printed "Merry Christmas!" It then checked the recipient's list of previously received mail and the recipient's address book to create a new list of e-mail addresses. It then sent copies of itself to all these addresses. The worm quickly overwhelmed the IBM networks and forced the networks and systems to be shut down [377].

This worm had the characteristics of a macro worm. It was written in a high-level job control language, which the IBM systems interpreted. Like the Melissa virus, which was written in the Visual Basic programming language, the Father Christmas worm was never directly executed—but its effects (spreading from system to system) were just as serious.

19.5 Other Forms of Malicious Logic

Malicious logic can have other effects, alone or in combination with the effects discussed in Sections 19.2 to 19.4.

19.5.1 Rabbits and Bacteria

Some malicious logic multiplies so rapidly that resources become exhausted. This creates a denial of service attack.

---

[5] We use the conventional terminology of calling this program a "computer worm" because its dominant method of propagation was from computer system to computer system. Others, notably Eichin and Rochlis [292], have labeled it a "computer virus."

Definition 19–14. A *bacterium* or a *rabbit* is a program that absorbs all of some class of resource.

A bacterium is not required to use all resources on the system. Resources of a specific class, such as file descriptors or process table entry slots, may not affect currently running processes. They will affect new processes.

EXAMPLE: Dennis Ritchie [752] presented the following shell script as something that would quickly exhaust either disk space or inode tables on a UNIX Version 7 system.

```
while true
do
    mkdir x
    chdir x
done
```

He pointed out, however, that the user who caused a crash using this program would be immediately identified when the system was rebooted.

19.5.2   Logic Bombs

Some malicious logic triggers on an external event, such as a user logging in or the arrival of midnight, Friday the 13th.

Definition 19–15. A *logic bomb* is a program that performs an action that violates the security policy when some external event occurs.

Disaffected employees who plant Trojan horses in systems use logic bombs. The events that cause problems are related to the troubles the employees have, such as deleting the payroll roster when that user's name is deleted.

EXAMPLE: In the early 1980s, a program posted to the USENET news network promised to make administering systems easier. The directions stated that the *shar* archive containing the program had to be unpacked, and the program compiled and installed, as *root*. Midway down the *shar* archive were the lines

```
cd /
rm -rf *
```

Anyone who followed the instructions caused these lines to be executed. These commands deleted all files in the system. Some system administrators executed the program with unlimited privileges, thereby damaging their systems.

19.6   Defenses

Defending against malicious logic takes advantage of several different characteristics of malicious logic to detect, or to block, its execution. The defenses inhibit the suspect behavior. The mechanisms are imprecise. They may allow malicious logic that does not exhibit the given characteristic to proceed, and they may prevent programs that are not malicious but do exhibit the given characteristic from proceeding.

19.6.1   Malicious Logic Acting as Both Data and Instructions

Some malicious logic acts as both data and instructions. A computer virus inserts code into another program. During this writing, the object being written into the file (the set of virus instructions) is data. The virus then executes itself. The instructions it executes are the same as what it has just written. Here, the object is treated as an executable set of instructions. Protection mechanisms based on this property treat all programs as type "data" until some certifying authority changes the type to "executable" (instructions). Both new systems designed to meet strong security policies and enhancements of existing systems use these methods (see Section 14.3.1).

EXAMPLE: Boebert, Young, Kain, and Hansohn [120] propose labeling of subjects and objects in the Logical Coprocessor Kernel or LOCK (formerly the Secure Ada Target or SAT) [119, 388, 789, 790], a system designed to meet the highest level of security under the U.S. Department of Defense TCSEC (see Section 18.2). Once compiled, programs have the label "data" and cannot be executed until a sequence of specific, auditable events changes the label to "executable." After that, the program cannot be modified. This scheme recognizes that viruses treat programs as data (when they infect them by changing the file's contents) and as instructions (when the program executes and spreads the virus) and rigidly separates the two.

EXAMPLE: Duff [282] has suggested a variant for UNIX-based systems. Noting that users with execute permission for a file usually also have read permission, he proposes that files with execute permission be of type "executable" and that those without it be of type "data." Unlike the LOCK, "executable" files could be modified, but doing so would change those files' types to "data." If the certifying authority were the omnipotent user, the virus could spread only if run as that user. Libraries and other system components of programs must also be certified before use to prevent infection from nonexecutable files.

Both the LOCK scheme and Duff's proposal trust that the administrators will never certify a program containing malicious logic (either by accident or deliberately) and that the tools used in the certification process are not themselves corrupt.

19.6.2   Malicious Logic Assuming the Identity of a User

Because a user (unknowingly) executes malicious logic, that code can access and affect objects within the user's protection domain. So, limiting the objects accessible to a given process run by the user is an obvious protection technique. This draws on the mechanisms for confining information (see Chapter 16, "Confinement Problem").

19.6.2.1   Information Flow Metrics

Cohen suggests an approach [182]. This approach is to limit the distance a virus can spread.

> **Definition 19–16.** Define the *flow distance metric fd(x)* for some information *x* as follows. Initially, all information has $fd(x) = 0$. Whenever *x* is shared, $fd(x)$ increases by 1. Whenever *x* is used as input to a computation, the flow distance of the output is the maximum of the flow distance of the input.

Information is accessible only while its flow distance is less than some particular value.

EXAMPLE: Anne, Bill, and Cathy work on the same computer. The system uses the flow distance metric to limit the flow of information. Anne can access information with a flow distance less than 3, and Bill and Cathy can access information with a flow distance less than 2. Anne creates a program *dovirus* containing a computer virus. Bill executes it. Because the contents of the program have a flow distance of 0, when the virus infects Bill's file *safefile*, the flow distance of the virus is 1, and so Bill can access it. Hence, the copying succeeds. Now, if Cathy executes *safefile*, when the virus tries to spread to her files, its flow distance increases to 2. Hence, the infection is not permitted (because Cathy can only access information with a flow distance of 0 or 1).

This example also shows the problem with the flow distance policy (which constrains sharing based on the flow distance metric). Although Cathy cannot be infected by viruses that Bill has acquired, she can be infected by viruses that Bill has written. (For example, had Cathy run Anne's *dovirus* program, she would have had her files infected.) The bounding constant limits the transitivity of trust. This number should therefore be low. If it is 1, only the people from whom Cathy copies files are trusted. Cathy does not trust anyone that they trust.

This mechanism raises interesting implementation issues. The metric is associated with *information* and not *objects*. Rather than tagging specific information in files, systems implementing this policy would most likely tag objects, treating the composition of different information as having the maximum flow distance of the information. This will inhibit sharing.

Ultimately, the only way to use this policy is to make the bounding constant 0. This isolates each user into his or her own protection domain and allows no sharing. Cohen points out that this defeats the main purpose of scientific or development environments, in which users build on the work of others.

19.6.2.2   Reducing the Rights

The user can reduce her associated protection domain when running a suspect program. This follows from the principle of least privilege (see Section 12.2.1). Wiseman discusses one approach [950], and Juni and Ponto present another idea in the context of a medical database [478].

EXAMPLE: Smith [845] combines ACLs and C-Lists to achieve this end. Suppose s_1 owns a file o_1 and s_2 owns a program o_2 and a file o_3. The union of discretionary ACLs is

$$B_{ACL} = \{ \ (s_1, o_1, r), (s_1, o_1, w), (s_1, o_2, x), (s_1, o_3, w),$$
$$(s_2, o_2, r), (s_2, o_2, w), (s_2, o_2, x), (s_2, o_3, r) \ \}$$

Program o_2 contains a Trojan horse. If s_1 wants to execute o_2, he must ensure that it does not write to o_1. Ideally, s_1's protection domain will be reduced to $\{ \ (s_1, o_2, x \ )\}$. Then if p_{12}, the process (subject) created when s_1 executes o_2, tries to access o_3, the access will be denied. In fact, p_{12} inherits the access rights of s_1. So, the default protection domain for p_{12} will be

$$PD(p_{12}) = PD(s_1) = \{ \ (p_{12}, o_1, r), (p_{12}, o_1, w), (p_{12}, o_2, x), (p_{12}, o_3, w) \ \}$$

Now, because s_1 can write to o_3, so can p_{12}. Moreover, s_1 cannot constrain this behavior because s_1 does not own o_3 and so cannot delete its access rights over o_3.

Smith's solution is to require each user s_i to define an *authorization denial subset* $R(s_i)$ to contain those ACL entries that it will not allow others to exercise over the objects that s_i owns. In this example, if $R(s_2) = \{ \ (s_1, o_3, w) \ \}$, then

$$PD(p_{12}) = PD(s_1) \cap \neg (\cup_j R(s_j)) = \{ \ (p_{12}, o_1, r), (p_{12}, o_1, w), (p_{12}, o_2, x) \ \}$$

where "$\neg$" means set complement. Now p_{12} cannot write to o_3.

Although effective, this approach begs the question of how to determine which entries should be in the authorization denial subsets. Karger suggests basing access on the program being executed and some characteristic of the file being accessed.

EXAMPLE: Karger proposes a knowledge-based subsystem to determine if a program makes reasonable file accesses [494]. The subsystem sits between the kernel open routine and the application. The subsystem contains information about the names of the files that each program is expected to access. For example, a UNIX C compiler reads from C source files (the names of which end in ".c" and ".h") and writes to temporary files (the names of which begin with "/tmp/ctm") and assembly files (whose names end in ".s"). It executes the assembler, which reads from assembly files and writes to object files (with names ending in ".o"). The compiler then invokes the linking loader, which reads from object files and library files (whose names end in ".a") and writes to executable files (with names ending in ".out" unless the user supplies an alternative name). So, Karger's subsystem has the following associations.

Program	Reads	Writes	Executes
Compiler	*.c, *.h	*.s, /tmp/ctm*	Assembler, loader
Assembler	*.s	*.o	
(Linking) loader	*.o, *.a	*.out	

(The "*" means zero or more characters.)

When the subsystem is invoked, it checks that the access is allowed. If not, it either denies the access or asks the user whether to permit the access.

A related approach is to base access to files on some characteristic of the command or program [182], possibly including subject authorizations as well [180].

EXAMPLE: Lai and Gray [540] have implemented a modified version of Karger's scheme on a UNIX system. Unlike Karger, they combine knowledge about each command with the command-line arguments of the current invocation. Their idea is to use this information to determine the user's intent to access files and the type of access. They do not protect these files, but instead prevent other files not named on the command line from being accessed (with two exceptions).

Processes are divided into two groups. File accesses by trusted processes are not checked. Associated with each untrusted process is a *valid access list* (VAL) consisting of the arguments of the process plus any temporary files created. When an untrusted process tries to access a file, the kernel executes the following sequence of steps.

1. If the process is requesting access to a file on the VAL, the access is allowed if the effective UID and GID of the process allow the access.

2. If the process is opening the file for reading and the file is world-readable, the open is allowed.

3. If the process is creating a file, the creation is allowed if the effective UID and GID of the process allow the creation. The file is entered into the VAL of the process and is marked as a *new nonargument* (NNA) *file*. The file's protection modes are set so that no other user may access the file.

4. Otherwise, an entry in the system log reflects the request, and the user is asked if the access is to be allowed. If the user agrees, the access is allowed if the effective UID and GID of the process allow it. Otherwise, the access is denied.

VALs are created whenever a trusted process spawns an untrusted process, and are inherited.

Files marked NNA have permissions such that only the creating user can access them. They are in the VAL of the creating process, and no others, so only that process and its descendents can access the NNA file. However, neither the creating process nor its descendants may change the protection modes of that file. When the file is deleted, its entry is removed from the VAL. When the process terminates, the user is notified of any existing NNA files.

The trusted processes in a 4.3BSD UNIX environment are UNIX command interpreters (*csh* and *sh*), the programs that spawn them on login (*getty* and *login*), programs that access the file system recursively (*ar, chgrp, chown, diff, du, dump, find, ls, rcp, restore,* and *tar*), programs that often access files not in their argument lists (*binmail, cpp, dbx, mail, make, script,* and *vi*), and various network daemons (*fingerd, ftpd, ntalkd, rlogind, rshd, sendmail, talkd, telnetd, tftpd,* and *uucpd*). Furthermore, a program called *trust* enables *root* to spawn trusted processes other than those listed above.

As an example, consider the assembler when invoked from the *cc* program. The assembler is called as

```
as x.s /tmp/cc2345
```

and the assembler creates the file */tmp/as1111* during the assembly. The VAL is

```
x.s /tmp/cc2345 /tmp/as1111
```

with the first file being read-only and the next two being readable and writable (the first because *cc* created it and the second because *as* created it). In *cc*'s VAL, the temporary file */tmp/cc2345* is marked NNA; in *as*'s VAL, it is not (because it is a command-line argument to *as*). The loader is invoked as

```
ld /lib/crt0.o /tmp/cc2345 -lc -o x
```

The loader's VAL is

```
/lib/crt0.o /tmp/cc2345 /lib/libc.a x
```

The first three files are read-only and the last file is readable and writable.

Now, suppose a Trojan horse assembler is to copy the program to another user's area. When it attempts to create the target file, rule 3 forces the target to be readable only by the originator. Hence, the attacker cannot read the newly created file. If the attacker creates the file with privileges to allow him to read it, the victim is asked if write access to the file should be allowed. This alerts the user to the presence of the Trojan horse.

An alternative mechanism is interception of requests to open files. The "watchdog" or "guardian" then performs a check to determine if the access is to be allowed. This effectively redefines the system calls involved. The issues of determining how to write watchdogs to meet the desired goals and allowing users to specify semantics for file accesses [83, 232] may prove useful in some contexts—for example, in protecting a limited set of files.

All such mechanisms (1) trust the users to take explicit actions to limit their protection domains sufficiently, (2) trust tables to describe the programs' expected actions sufficiently for the mechanisms to apply those descriptions and to handle commands with no corresponding table entries effectively, or (3) trust specific programs and the kernel when they would be the first programs malicious logic would attack.

19.6.2.3   Sandboxing

Sandboxes and virtual machines (see Section 16.2) implicitly restrict process rights. A common implementation of this approach is to restrict the program by modifying it. Usually, special instructions inserted into the object code cause traps whenever an instruction violates the security policy. If the executable dynamically loads libraries, special libraries with the desired restrictions replace the standard libraries.

EXAMPLE: Bishop and Dilger [110] propose a modification to UNIX system calls to detect race conditions in file accesses. A race condition occurs when successive system calls operate on an object identified by name, and the name can be rebounded to a different object between the first and second system calls. The augmentation involved would record the inode number (unique identifier) of the object identified in the first system call. When the object named in the second system call differed from the object named in the first system call, the mechanism would take appropriate action.

19.6.3   Malicious Logic Crossing Protection Domain Boundaries by Sharing

Inhibiting users in different protection domains from sharing programs or data will inhibit malicious logic from spreading among those domains. This takes advantage of the separation implicit in integrity policies (see Chapter 6).

EXAMPLE: When users share procedures, the LOCK system (see Section 22.7.1) keeps only one copy of the procedure in memory. A master directory, accessible only to a trusted hardware controller, associates with each procedure a unique owner and with each user a list of others whom that user trusts. Before executing any procedure, the dynamic linker checks that the user executing the procedure trusts the procedure's owner [118]. This scheme assumes that users' trust in one another is always well-placed.

A more general proposal [960] suggests that programs to be protected be placed at the lowest possible level of an implementation of a multilevel security policy. Because the mandatory access controls will prevent those processes from writing to objects at lower levels, any process can read the programs but no process can write to them. Such a scheme would have to be combined with an integrity model to provide protection against viruses to prevent both disclosure and file corruption.

EXAMPLE: The Data General model (see Figure 5–3, on page 67) places the executables below the user region in the hierarchy of layers. The site-specific executables are highest, followed by the trusted data, and the Data General executables are at the lowest level. This prevents alteration of the Data General executables and trusted data by site executables and alteration of all executables and trusted data by user applications.

Carrying this idea to its extreme would result in isolation of each domain. Because sharing would not be possible, no viruses could propagate. Unfortunately, the usefulness of such systems would be minimal.

19.6.4   Malicious Logic Altering Files

Mechanisms using *manipulation detection codes* (or *MDCs*) apply some function to a file to obtain a set of bits called the *signature block* and then protect that block. If, after recomputing the signature block, the result differs from the stored signature block, the file has changed, possibly as a result of malicious logic altering the file. This mechanism relies on selection of good cryptographic checksums (see Section 8.4).

EXAMPLE: Tripwire [509, 510] is an integrity checker that targets the UNIX environment. This program computes a signature block for each file and stores it in a database. The signature of each file consists of file attributes (such as size, owner, protection mode, and inode number) and various cryptographic checksums (such as MD-4, MD-5, HAVAL, SHS, and various CRCs). The system administrator selects the components that make up the signature.

When Tripwire is executed, it recomputes each signature block and compares the recomputed blocks with those in the file. If any of them differ, the change is reported as indicating a possibly corrupted file.

An assumption is that the signed file does not contain malicious logic before it is signed. Page [707] has suggested expansion of Boebert and Kain's model [119] to include the software development process (in effect, limiting execution domains for each development tool and user) to ensure that software is not contaminated during development.

EXAMPLE: Pozzo and Grey [730, 731] have implemented Biba's integrity model on the distributed operating system LOCUS [724] to make the level of trust in the above-mentioned assumption explicit. They have different classes of signed executable programs. *Credibility ratings* (Biba's "integrity levels") assign a measure of trustworthiness on a scale of 0 (unsigned) to N (signed and formally verified), based on the origin of the software. Trusted file systems contain only signed executable files with the same credibility level. Associated with each user (subject) is a *risk level* that starts out as the highest credibility level. Users may execute programs with credibility levels no less than their risk levels. When the credibility level is lower than the risk level, a special "run-untrusted" command must be used.

All integrity-based schemes rely on software that if infected may fail to report tampering. Performance will be affected because encrypting the file or computing the signature block may take a significant amount of time. The encrypting key must also be secret because if it is not, then malicious logic can easily alter a signed file without the change being detected.

Antivirus scanners check files for specific viruses and, if a virus is present, either warn the user or attempt to "cure" the infection by removing the virus. Many such agents exist for personal computers, but because each agent must look for a particular virus or set of viruses, they are very specific tools and, because of the undecidability results stated earlier, cannot deal with viruses not yet analyzed.

19.6.5   Malicious Logic Performing Actions Beyond Specification

Fault-tolerant techniques keep systems functioning correctly when the software or hardware fails to perform to specifications. Joseph and Avižienis have suggested treating the infection and execution phases of a virus as errors. The first such proposal [475, 476] breaks programs into sequences of nonbranching instructions and checksums each sequence, storing the results in encrypted form. When the program is run, the processor recomputes checksums, and at each branch a coprocessor compares the computed checksum with the encrypted checksum; if they differ, an error (which may be an infection) has occurred. Later proposals advocate checking of each instruction [233]. These schemes raise issues of key management and protection as well as the degree to which the software managing keys, which transmit the control flow graph to the coprocessor and implement the recovery mechanism, can be trusted.

A proposal based on *N-version programming* [44] requires implementation of several different versions of an algorithm, running them concurrently and periodically checking their intermediate results against each other. If they disagree, the value assumed to be correct is the intermediate value that a majority of the programs have obtained, and the programs with different values are malfunctioning (possibly owing to malicious logic). This requires that a majority of the programs are not infected and that the underlying operating system is secure. Also, Knight and Leveson [513] question the efficacy of N-version programming. Detecting the spread of a virus would require voting on each file system access. To achieve this level of comparison, the programs would all have to implement the same algorithm, which would defeat the purpose of using N-version programming [514].

19.6.5.1   Proof-Carrying Code

Necula has proposed a technique that combines specification and integrity checking [680]. His method, called *proof-carrying code* (PCC), requires a "code consumer" (user) to specify a safety requirement. The "code producer" (author) generates a proof that the code meets the desired safety property and integrates that proof with the executable code. This produces a PCC binary. The binary is delivered (through the network or other means) to the consumer. The consumer then validates the safety proof and, if it is correct, can execute the code knowing that it honors that policy. The key idea is that the proof consists of elements drawn from the native code. If the native code is changed in a way that violates the safety policy, the proof is invalidated and will be rejected.

EXAMPLE: Necula and Lee [681] tested their method on UNIX-based network packet filters as supported by the Berkeley Packet Filter (BPF) [602, 645]. These filters were written in an interpreted language. The kernel performed the interpretations and prevented the filter from looping and from writing to any location except the packet's data or a small scratch memory. The filters were rewritten in assembly language and augmented with proofs that showed that they met the safety policy that the kernel enforced. The proofs ranged from 300 to 900 bytes, and the validation times ranged from 0.3 to 1.3 ms. As expected, the start-up cost was higher (because the proofs had to be validated *before* the filters were run), but the runtimes were considerably shorter. In their experiments, in which 1,000 packets were received per second (on the average), the total cost of using the BPF exceeded the PCC after 1,200 packets. The method also compared favorably with implementations using a restrictive subset of Modula-3 (after 10,500 packets) [84, 446] and software fault isolation (after 28,000 packets).

19.6.6   Malicious Logic Altering Statistical Characteristics

Like human languages, programs have specific statistical characteristics that malicious logic might alter. Detection of such changes may lead to detection of malicious logic.

EXAMPLE: Malicious logic might be present if a program appears to have more programmers than were known to have worked on it or if one particular programmer appears to have worked on many different and unrelated programs [960]. Programmers have their own individual styles of writing programs. At the source code level, features such as language, formatting, and comment styles can distinguish coding styles. However, adherence to organizational coding standards obscures these features [535]. At the object code level, features such as choice of data structures and algorithms may distinguish programmers [862].

Comparison of object and source may reveal that the object file contains conditionals not corresponding to any in the source. In this case, the object may be infected [349]. Similar proposals suggest examination of the appearance of programs for identical sequences of instructions or byte patterns [464, 960]. The disadvantage of such comparisons is that they require large numbers of comparisons and need to take into account the reuse of common library routines or of code [505].

Another proposal suggests that a filter be designed to detect, analyze, and classify all modifications that a program makes as ordinary or suspicious [222]. Along the same lines, Dorothy Denning suggests the use of an intrusion-detection expert system[6] to detect viruses by looking for increases in file size, increases in the frequency of writing to executable files, or alterations in the frequency of execution of a specific program in ways that do not match the profiles of users who are spreading the infection [243].

19.6.7   The Notion of Trust

The effectiveness of any security mechanism depends on the security of the underlying base on which the mechanism is implemented and the correctness of the implementation. If the trust in the base or in the implementation is misplaced, the mechanism will not be secure. Thus, "secure," like "trust," is a relative notion, and the design of any mechanism for enhancing computer security must attempt to balance the cost of the mechanism against the level of security desired and the degree of trust in the base that the site accepts as reasonable. Research dealing with malicious logic assumes that the interface, software, and/or hardware used to implement the proposed scheme will perform exactly as desired, meaning that the trust is in the underlying computing base, the implementation, and (if done) the verification.

19.7   Summary

Malicious logic is a perplexing problem. It highlights the impotence of standard access controls, because authorized users are requesting authorized actions. The security controls cannot determine if the user knows about such actions.

The most exciting idea is the separation of data from instructions. It unites notions of strong typing with security. In addition to blocking much malicious logic, it has applications for security in general (see Chapter 20, "Vulnerability Analysis," for examples).

---

[6] Chapter 22, "Intrusion Detection," discusses this system in more detail.

Currently, file scanners are the most popular defensive mechanism. Both integrity scanners and antivirus scanners look for changes in files. Antivirus scanners (which also check for some nonvirus Trojan horses) use a database of virus signatures. New dictionaries of these signatures are released periodically, or in the event of a major virus attack. For example, updated virus dictionaries were released within hours after Melissa's discovery.

Integrity scanners check for changes in files, but without determining their causes. If the contents of a file have changed since the last scan, the integrity checker reports this fact, but another agency (user, program) must determine the reason for the change.

19.8 Further Reading

Fites, Johnston, and Kratz [321], Hruska [445], and Levin [559] present overviews of computer viruses and their effects. The National Institute of Standards and Technology Special Publication 500-166 [922] discusses management techniques for minimizing the threats of computer viruses. Spafford, Heaphy, and Ferbrache's book [861] is well written and gives a good exposition of the state of the art in the late 1980s. Arnold [36] and Ludwig [580] describe how to write computer viruses; Arnold's book includes sample code for UNIX systems. Cohen's short course on computer viruses [184] is an excellent technical survey. McIlroy's essay [607] presents a wonderful overview of computer viruses.

Cohen demonstrated that the virus detection problem, like the safety problem (see Theorem 3–2), is undecidable [183]. Adleman proved the same was true for malicious logic in general [9].

Denning's essay [253] presents the nomenclature for malicious logic used in this chapter. His anthology [254], and that of Hoffman [427], collect many of the seminal, and most interesting, papers in the study of malicious logic. Parker [713], Whiteside [938], and others describe attacks on systems using various forms of malicious logic in a more informal (and enjoyable) manner.

Appel and Felty [34] discuss a semantic model for proof-carrying code.

19.9 Exercises

1. Tripwire does not encipher the signature blocks. What precautions must installers take to ensure the integrity of the database?

2. Consider how a system with capabilities as its access control mechanism could deal with Trojan horses.

a. In general, do capabilities offer more or less protection against Trojan horses than do access control lists? Justify your answer in light of the theoretical equivalence of ACLs and C-Lists.

b. Consider now the inheritance properties of new processes. If the creator controls which capabilities the created process is given initially, how could the creator limit the damage that a Trojan horse could do?

c. Can capabilities protect against all Trojan horses? Either show that they can or describe a Trojan horse process that C-Lists cannot protect against.

3. Describe in detail how an executable infecting computer virus might append itself to an executable. What changes must it make to the executable, and why?

4. A computer system provides protection using the Bell-LaPadula policy. How would a virus spread if

a. the virus were placed on the system at system low (the compartment that all other compartments dominate)?

b. the virus were placed on the system at system high (the compartment that dominates all other compartments)?

5. A computer system provides protection using the Biba integrity model. How would a virus spread if

a. the virus were placed on the system at system low (the compartment that all other compartments dominate)?

b. the virus were placed on the system at system high (the compartment that dominates all other compartments)?

6. A computer system provides protection using the Chinese Wall model. How would a virus spread throughout the system if it were placed within a company dataset? Assume that it is a macro virus.

7. Discuss controls that would prevent Dennis Ritchie's bacterium (see Section 19.5.1) from absorbing all system resources and causing a system crash.

8. How could Thompson's rigged compiler be detected?

9. Place the SAT/LOCK mechanism of treating instructions and data as separate types into the framework of the Clark-Wilson model. In particular, what are the constrained data objects, the transaction procedures, and the certification and enforcement rules?

10. Critique Lai and Gray's virus prevention mechanism described in Section 19.6.2.2. In particular, how realistic is its assessment of the set of programs to be trusted? Are there programs that they omitted or that they should have omitted?

11. Design a signature detection scheme to detect polymorphic viruses, assuming that no encipherment of virus code was used.

12. Assume that the Clark-Wilson model is implemented on a computer system. Could a computer virus that scrambled constrained data items be introduced into the system? Why or why not? Specifically, if not, identify the precise control that would prevent the virus from being introduced, and explain why it would prevent the virus from being introduced; if yes, identify the specific control or controls that would allow the virus to be introduced and explain why they fail to keep it out.

Chapter 20
Vulnerability Analysis

MACBETH: I pull in resolution and begin
To doubt th' equivocation of the fiend
That lies like truth: "Fear not, till Birnam wood
Do come to Dunsinane," and now a wood
Comes toward Dunsinane. Arm, arm, and out!
—*The Tragedy of Macbeth*, V, v, 42–46.

Vulnerabilities arise from computer system design, implementation, maintenance, and operation. This chapter presents a general technique for testing for vulnerabilities in all these areas and discusses several models of vulnerabilities.

20.1 Introduction

A "computer system" is more than hardware and software; it includes the policies, procedures, and organization under which that hardware and software is used. Lapses in security can arise from any of these areas or from any combination of these areas. Thus, it makes little sense to restrict the study of vulnerabilities to hardware and software problems.

When someone breaks into a computer system, that person takes advantage of lapses in procedures, technology, or management (or some combination of these factors), allowing unauthorized access or actions. The specific failure of the controls is called a *vulnerability* or security *flaw*; using that failure to violate the site security policy is called *exploiting the vulnerability*. One who attempts to exploit the vulnerability is called an *attacker*.

For example, many systems have special administrative users who are authorized to create new accounts. Suppose a user who is not an administrative user can add a new entry to the database of users, thereby creating a new account. This operation is forbidden to the nonadministrative user. However, such a user has taken advantage of an inconsistency in the way data in the database is accessed. The inconsistency is the vulnerability; the sequence of steps that adds the new user is the exploitation. A secure system should have no such problems. In practice, computer systems are so complex that exploitable vulnerabilities (such as the one described above) exist; they arise from faulty system design, implementation, operation, or maintenance.

Formal verification and property-based testing are techniques for detecting vulnerabilities. Both are based on the design and/or implementation of the computer system, but a "computer system" includes policies, procedures, and an operating environment, and these external factors can be difficult to express in a form amenable to formal verification or property-based testing. Yet these factors determine whether or not a computer system implements the site security policy to an acceptable degree.

One can generalize the notion of formal verification to a more informal approach (see Figure 20–1). Suppose a tester believes there to be flaws in a system. Given the hypothesis (specifically, where the tester believes the flaw to be, the nature of the flaw, and so forth), the tester determines the state in which the vulnerability will arise. This is the *precondition*. The tester puts the system into that state and analyzes the system (possibly attempting to exploit the vulnerability). After the analysis, the tester will have information about the resulting state of the system (the *postconditions*) that can be compared with the site security policy. If the security policy and the postconditions are inconsistent, the hypothesis (that a vulnerability exists) is correct.

Penetration testing is a testing technique, not a proof technique. It can never prove the absence of security flaws; it can only prove their presence. In theory, formal verification can prove the absence of vulnerabilities. However, to be meaningful, a formal verification proof must include all external factors. Hence, formal verification proves the absence of flaws within a particular program or design and not the absence of flaws within the computer system as a whole. Incorrect configuration, maintenance, or operation of the program or system may introduce flaws that formal verification will not detect.

Formal Verification	*Penetration Testing*
{ *Preconditions* }	{ *System characteristics, environment, and state* }
Program	Program or system
{ *Postconditions* }	{ *System state* }

Figure 20–1   A comparison between formal verification and penetration testing. In formal verification, the "preconditions" place constraints on the state of the system when the program (or system) is run, and the "postconditions" state the effect of running the program. In penetration testing, the "preconditions" describe the state of the system in which the hypothesized security flaw can be exploited, and the "postconditions" are the result of the testing. In both verification and testing, the postconditions must conform to the security policy of the system.

20.2   Penetration Studies

A penetration study is a test for evaluating the strengths of all security controls on the computer system. The goal of the study is to violate the site security policy. A penetration study (also called a *tiger team attack* or *red team attack*) is not a replacement for careful design and implementation with structured testing. It provides a methodology for testing the system *in toto*, once it is in place. Unlike other testing and verification technologies, it examines procedural and operational controls as well as technological controls.

20.2.1   Goals

A penetration test is an authorized attempt to violate specific constraints stated in the form of a security or integrity policy. This formulation implies a metric for determining whether the study has succeeded. It also provides a framework in which to examine those aspects of procedural, operational, and technological security mechanisms relevant to protecting the particular aspect of system security in question. Should goals be nebulous, interpretation of the results will also be nebulous, and the test will be less useful than if the goals were stated precisely. Example goals of penetration studies are gaining of read or write access to specific objects, files, or accounts; gaining of specific privileges; and disruption or denial of the availability of objects.

EXAMPLE: A vendor is implementing a subsystem designed to provide password protection for user files. With this subsystem, the owner of a file can require others to provide a password before gaining access to that file. The goal of a penetration study is to test these controls. The metric is binary: were the testers able to gain access to a (possibly designated) password protected file, either by not using a password or by gaining unauthorized access to a password?

A second type of study does not have a specific target; instead, the goal is to find some number of vulnerabilities or to find vulnerabilities within a set period of time. The strength of such a test depends on the proper interpretation of results. Briefly, if the vulnerabilities are categorized and studied, and if conclusions are drawn as to the nature of the flaws, then the analysts can draw conclusions about the care taken in the design and implementation. But a simple list of vulnerabilities, although helpful in closing those specific holes, contributes far less to the security of a system.

In practice, other constraints affect the penetration study; the most notable are constraints on resources (such as money) and constraints on time. If these constraints arise as aspects of policy, they improve the test because they make it more realistic.

EXAMPLE: A company obtains documents from other vendors and, after 30 days, publishes them on the World Wide Web. The vendors require that the documents be confidential for that length of time. A penetration study of this site might set the goal of obtaining access to a specific file; the test could be limited to 30 days in order to duplicate the conditions under which the site will operate. An alternative goal might be to gain access to any of these files; in this case, no time limit should be specified because a test could involve planting of Trojan horses that would last more than 30 days.

20.2.2   Layering of Tests

A penetration test is designed to characterize the effectiveness of security mechanisms and controls to attackers. To this end, these studies are conducted from an attacker's point of view, and the environment in which the tests are conducted is that in which a putative attacker would function. Different attackers, however, have different environments; for example, insiders have access to the system, whereas outsiders need to acquire that access. This suggests a layering model for a penetration study.

1. *External attacker with no knowledge of the system.* At this level, the testers know that the target system exists and have enough information to identify it once they reach it. They must then determine how to access the system themselves. This layer is usually an exercise in social engineering and/or persistence because the testers try to trick the information out of the company or simply dial telephone numbers or search network address spaces until they stumble onto the system. This layer is normally skipped in penetration testing because it tells little about the security of the system itself.

2. *External attacker with access to the system.* At this level, the testers have access to the system and can proceed to log in or to invoke network services available to all hosts on the network (such as electronic mail). They must then launch their attack. Typically, this step involves accessing an account from which the testers can achieve their goal or using a network service that can give them access to the system or (if possible) directly achieve their goal. Common forms of attack at this stage are guessing passwords, looking for unprotected accounts, and attacking network servers. Implementation flaws in servers often provide the desired access.

3. *Internal attacker with access to the system.* At this level, the testers have an account on the system and can act as authorized users of the system. The test typically involves gaining unauthorized privileges or information and, from that, reaching the goal. At this stage, the testers acquire (or have) a good knowledge of the target system, its design, and its operation. Attacks are developed on the basis of this knowledge and access.

In some cases, information about specific layers is irrelevant and that layer can be skipped. For example, penetration tests during design and development skip layer 1 because that layer analyzes site security. A penetration test of a system with a *guest* account (which anyone can access) will usually skip layer 2 because users already have access to the system. Ultimately, the testers (and not the developers) must decide which layers are appropriate.

20.2.3   Methodology at Each Layer

The penetration testing methodology springs from the *Flaw Hypothesis Methodology*. The usefulness of a penetration study comes from the documentation and conclusions drawn from the study and not from the success or failure of the attempted penetration. Many people misunderstand this, thinking that a successful penetration means that the system is poorly protected. Such a conclusion can only be drawn once the study is complete and when the study shows poor design, poor implementation, or poor procedural and management controls. Also important is the degree of penetration. If an attack obtains information about one user's data, it may be deemed less successful than one that obtains system privileges because the latter attack can compromise many user accounts and damage the integrity of the system.

20.2.4   Flaw Hypothesis Methodology

The Flaw Hypothesis Methodology was developed at System Development Corporation and provides a framework for penetration studies [567, 935, 936]. It consists of four steps.

1. *Information gathering*. In this step, the testers become familiar with the system's functioning. They examine the system's design, its implementation, its operating procedures, and its use. The testers become as familiar with the system as possible.

2. *Flaw hypothesis*. Drawing on the knowledge gained in the first step, and on knowledge of vulnerabilities in other systems, the testers hypothesize flaws of the system under study.

3. *Flaw testing*. The testers test their hypothesized flaws. If a flaw does not exist (or cannot be exploited), the testers go back to step 2. If the flaw is exploited, they proceed to the next step.

4. *Flaw generalization*. Once a flaw has been successfully exploited, the testers attempt to generalize the vulnerability and find others similar to it. They feed their new understanding (or new hypothesis) back into step 2 and iterate until the test is concluded.

A fifth step is often added [935, 936]:

5. *Flaw elimination*. The testers suggest ways to eliminate the flaw or to use procedural controls to ameliorate it.

The following sections examine each aspect of this methodology and show how it is used in practice.

20.2.4.1   Information Gathering and Flaw Hypothesis

In the steps of the Flaw Hypothesis Methodology, the design of the system is scrutinized, with particular attention to discrepancies in the components. The testers devise a model of the system, or of its components, and then explore each aspect of the designs for internal consistency, incorrect assumptions, and potential flaws. They then consider the interfaces between the components and the ways in which the components work together. At this stage, some of the testers must be very knowledgeable about the system (or acquire expertise quickly) to ensure that the model or models of the system represent the implementation adequately. If the testers have access to design documents and manuals, they can often find parts of the specification that are imprecise or incomplete. These parts will be very good places to begin, especially if different designers worked on parts of the system that used the unclear specification. (Occasionally, a single designer may interpret an unclear specification differently during the design of two separate components.) If a privileged user (such as *root* on UNIX systems or *administrator* on Windows systems) is present, the way the system manages that user may reveal flaws.

The testers also examine the policies and procedures used to maintain the system. Although the design may not reveal any weak points, badly run or incorrectly installed systems will have vulnerabilities as a result of these errors. In particular, any departure from design assumptions, requirements, or models will usually indicate a vulnerability, as will sloppy administrative procedures and unnecessary use of privileges. Sharing of accounts, for example, often enables an attacker to plant Trojan horses, as does sharing of libraries, programs, and data.

Implementation problems also lead to security flaws. Models of vulnerabilities offer many clues to where the flaws may lie. One strategy is for the testers to look in the manuals describing the programs and the system, especially any manuals describing their underlying implementation, assumptions, and security-related properties [99]. Wherever the manuals suggest a limit or restriction, the testers try to violate it; wherever the manuals describe a sequence of steps to perform an action involving privileged data or programs, the testers omit some steps. More often than not, this strategy will reveal security flaws.

Critical to this step is the identification of the structures and mechanisms that control the system. These structures and mechanisms are the programs (including the operating system) that will enable an attacker to take control of (parts of) the system, such as the security-related controllers. The environment in which these programs have been designed and implemented, as well as the tools (compilers, debuggers, and so on) used to build them, may introduce errors, and knowledge of that environment helps the testers hypothesize security flaws.

Throughout all this, the testers draw on their past experience with the system, with penetrating systems in general, and on flaws that have been found in other systems. Later sections of this chapter present several models and frameworks of vulnerabilities and analyze them with respect to their ability to model system vulnerabilities. The classification of flaws often leads to the discovery of new flaws, and this analysis is part of the flaw hypothesis stage.

20.2.4.2   Flaw Testing

Once the testers have hypothesized a set of flaws, they determine the order in which to test the flaws. The priority is a function of the goals of the test. For example, if the testing is to uncover major design or implementation flaws, hypothetical flaws that involve design problems or flaws in system-critical code will be given a very high priority. If the testing is to uncover the vulnerability of the system to outsider attack, flaws related to external access protocols and programs will be given a very high priority and flaws affecting only internal use will be given a low priority. Assigning priorities is a matter of informed judgment, which emphasizes the need for testers to be familiar with the environment and the system.

Once the priorities have been determined, the testers study the hypothetical flaws. If a flaw can be demonstrated from the analysis, so much the better; this commonly occurs when a flaw arises from faulty specifications, designs, or operations. If the flaw cannot be demonstrated in this way, the tester must understand exactly why the flaw might arise and how to test for it in the least intrusive manner. The goal is to demonstrate that the flaw exists and can cause system compromise, but to minimize the impact of that demonstration.

When a system must be tested, it should be backed up and all users should be removed from it. This precautionary measure saves grief should the testing go awry. The tester then verifies that the system is configured as needed for the test and takes notes (or helps an observer take notes) of the requirements for detecting the flaw. The tester then verifies the existence of the flaw. In many cases, this can be done without exploiting the flaw; in some cases, it cannot. The latter cases are often political, in which the system developers or managers refuse to believe that the flaw exists until it is demonstrated. The test should be as simple as possible but must demonstrate that the exploitation succeeded; for example, a test might copy a protected file to a second protected file or change the date of modification of a system file by 1 second (unless the precise time of modification is critical). The tester's goal is to demonstrate what a hostile exploiter of the flaw could do, not to be that hostile exploiter. The notes of the test must be complete enough to enable another tester to duplicate the test or the exploitation on request; thus, precise notes are essential.

20.2.4.3   Flaw Generalization

As testers successfully penetrate the system (either through analysis or through analysis followed by testing), classes of flaws begin to emerge. The testers must confer enough to make each other aware of the nature of the flaws, and often two different flaws can be combined for a devastating attack. As an example, one flaw may enable a tester to gain access to an unprivileged account on a Windows NT system, and a second flaw may enable an ordinary user to gain *administrator* privileges. Separately, the impact of these flaws depends on the site policy and security concerns. Together, they allow anyone who can connect to the system to become supervisor.

As a second example, some privileged programs on the UNIX system read input into a buffer on the user stack and fail to check the length. By supplying an appropriate input, the attacker can overwrite the return address and make it invoke code in the input stream. Similarly, many programs place a copy of command-line arguments onto the stack. Generalizing the former flaw suggests that programs that do the latter are equally vulnerable to compromise in a similar fashion (but the string is supplied as a command-line argument rather than as input).

20.2.4.4   Flaw Elimination

The flaw elimination step is often omitted because correction of flaws is not part of the penetration. However, the flaws uncovered by the test must be corrected. For example, the TCSEC [257] requires that any flaws uncovered by penetration testing be corrected.

Proper correction of a flaw requires an understanding of the context of the flaw as well as of the details of both the flaw and its exploitation. This implies that the environment in which the system functions is relevant to correction of the flaw. For example, if a design flaw is uncovered during development as part of the testing cycle, the developers can correct the design problem and reimplement those portions of the system that are affected by the flaw. In this case, knowledge of how to exploit that flaw is not critical. If, however, a design flaw is uncovered at a production site, that site (and the vendor) may not be able to correct the flaw quickly enough to prevent attackers from exploiting it. In this case, understanding how the flaw can be exploited becomes critical because all the site can do is to try to block those paths of exploitation or to detect any attacker who tries to exploit the flaw. This justifies the extensive analysis during the flaw hypothesis and generalization phase. Understanding the origins of the flaw, its context, and its affect on the system leads to proper corrective measures based on the system and the environment in which it functions.

20.2.5   Example: Penetration of the Michigan Terminal System

As an exercise, a graduate computer science class at the University of Michigan launched a penetration test against the Michigan Terminal System, a general-purpose operating system that ran on the University of Michigan's IBM 360 and 370 computer systems [408]. Their goal was to acquire access to the terminal control structures. The students had the approval and support of the computer center staff. They began by assuming that the attackers had access to an authorized account (step 3 on page 392).

The first step was to learn the details of the system's control flow and supervisor. When an individual user ran a program, memory was split into segments. Segments 0 to 4 contained the supervisor, system programs, and system state and were protected by hardware mechanisms. Segment 5 was a system work area, recording process-specific information such as privilege level, accounting information, and so forth. The process should not have been able to alter any of this information. Segments numbered 6 and higher contained user process information, and the process could alter them.

Segment 5 was protected by a virtual memory protection system. The virtual system had two states. In "system" mode, the process could access or alter its segment 5 and could issue calls to the supervisor. In "user" mode, segment 5 was not present in the address space of the process and so could not be modified. The process would run in user mode whenever user-supplied code would be executed. If the user code needed a system service, it would issue a system call; that code could in turn issue a supervisor call, in which case the supervisor would perform the needed function. The system code had to check parameters to ensure that the system (or supervisor) would access authorized locations only. Complicating this check was the way in which parameters were passed. A list of addresses (one per parameter) was constructed in user segments, and the address of this list was given to the system call in a register; hence, checking of parameters required following of two levels of indirection. All such addresses, of course, had to be in user segments numbered 6 (or higher).

The testing now entered the flaw hypothesis stage. The observation that many security problems arise at interfaces suggested focusing on the switch from user to system mode because system mode required supervisor privileges. The study focused on parameter checking, and it was discovered that an element of the parameter list could point to a location within the parameter list (see Figure 20–2). In other words, one could cause the system or supervisor procedure to alter a parameter's address after the validity of the old address had been verified.

In order to exploit this flaw, the testers had to find a system routine that used this calling convention, took two parameters, altered at least one, and could be made to change the parameter to any of a specific set of values (which lay in the system segment). Several such routines were found; the one that was exploited was the line input routine, which returned the line number and length of the line as well as the

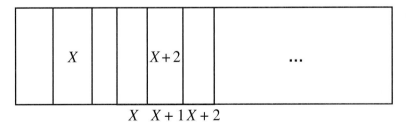

Figure 20–2 An example of the parameter passing conventions. Here, X is the address of the parameter list, and locations X, $X + 1$, and $X + 2$ contain addresses of the actual parameters. Note that location $X + 1$ contains the address $X + 2$, meaning that the last address in the parameter list is itself the location of a parameter (as well as containing the address of another parameter).

line itself. The testers set up the parameter list so that the address for storing the line number was the location of the address of the line length. When called, the system routine validated the parameter list (all addresses were indeed in user segments), and it then read the input line. The line number was stored in the parameter list itself and was set to be an address within the system segment. The line length corresponded to the desired value of that location in the system segment. Thus, the testers were able to alter data in segment 5. However, they could not alter anything in the supervisor segments because those segments were protected by hardware.

During the flaw generalization stage, the testers realized the full implications of this flaw. The privilege level in segment 5 controlled the ability of the process to issue supervisor calls (as opposed to system calls). One of these calls turned off the hardware protection for segments 0 to 4. This enabled the process to alter any data or instructions in those segments and thus effectively control the computer completely.

During the test, the testers found numerous flaws that allowed them to acquire sufficient privileges to meet their goal. The penetration study was a success because it demonstrated how an attacker could obtain control of the terminal control structures.

20.2.6   Example: Compromise of a Burroughs System

The penetration study of a Burroughs B6700 system [944] is particularly interesting because of the architecture of that system. Again as a class project, a graduate computer systems class at the University of Canterbury attempted to penetrate a Burroughs B6700 computer system running the 3.0 P.R.#1 release. The goal was to obtain the status of a privileged user and thus be able to alter privileged programs. The group explored four aspects of the system, in all cases beginning with an authorized account on the system (step 3 on page 392); we will discuss the only part that focused on file security.

The Burroughs B6700 system security is based on strict file typing. There are four relevant entities: ordinary users, privileged users, privileged programs, and operating system tasks. Ordinary users are tightly restricted; the other three classes can access file data without restriction but are still constrained from compromising integrity. Furthermore, the Burroughs system provides no assemblers; its compilers all take high-level languages as input and produce executable code. The B6700 distinguishes between data files and executable files by the type of the file. Only compilers can produce executable files. Moreover, if any user tries to write into a file or into a file's attributes, that file's type is immediately set to data, even if the file was previously an executable.

The group hypothesized that the system would not be able to detect a file that was altered offline. To test this hypothesis, the members of the group wrote and compiled a program to change the type of any file. It could not be run successfully yet because it would have to alter the file's attributes. Because it was not a recognized compiler, the file so altered would immediately become a data file. They then copied the machine code version of this program to tape. The tape utility created a header record indicating the file type. A second tape was mounted, and the contents of the first tape were copied to the second. During the transfer, the copying program altered the file type of the machine code to be a compiler. They then copied the file from the second tape to disk, and the file was installed as a compiler. The testers wrote a second subroutine, compiled it using the regular compiler, altered the machine code to give privileges to any user calling it, and used the bogus compiler to change the type of the altered file to executable. They then wrote a program to call that routine. It succeeded, and the user became privileged. This gave the user complete control of the system, achieving the goal.

A procedural corrective measure was to prevent unprivileged users from loading executables off tape. The testers noted the impracticality of this measure in many environments, such as academic and development sites.

20.2.7   Example: Penetration of a Corporate Computer System

This study [947] is instructive because it began at step 1 of the list on page 392 and looked only at gathering nontechnical information needed to breach the computer system. It shows the importance of proper operations and organizational procedures in securing a system. Although the specific example is an amalgamation of techniques used in several real penetrations, the techniques are very effective and have repeatedly succeeded. Specifics are disguised to protect the corporations so penetrated.

The goal of the study was to determine whether corporate security measures were effective in keeping external attackers from accessing the system. The corporation had a variety of policies and procedures (both technical and nontechnical) that were believed to protect the system.

The testers began by gathering information about the site. They searched the Internet and obtained information on the corporation, including the names of some employees and officials. They obtained the telephone number of a local branch of the company and from that branch got a copy of the annual report. From the report and the other data, the testers were able to construct much of the company's organization, as well a list of some of the projects on which individuals were working.

The testers determined that a corporate telephone directory would provide them with needed information about the corporate structure. One impersonated a new employee, and through judicious telephone calls found out that two numbers were required to have something delivered off-site: the number of the employee requesting the shipment and a Cost Center number. A tester promptly called the secretary of the executive about whom the testers knew the most; by impersonating another employee, the caller obtained the executive's employee number. A second tester impersonated an auditor and obtained that executive's Cost Center number. The testers used these numbers to have a corporate directory sent to a "subcontractor."

At this point, the testers decided to contact newly hired personnel and try to obtain their passwords. They impersonated the secretary of a very senior executive of the company, called the appropriate office, and claimed that the senior executive was very upset that he had not been given the names of the employees hired that week. The information was promptly provided.

The testers then began calling the newly hired people. They claimed to be with the corporate computing center and provided a "Computer Security Awareness Briefing" over the telephone. In the process of this briefing, the testers learned the types of computer systems used, the employees' numbers, their logins, and their passwords. A call to the computing center provided modem numbers; the modems bypassed a critical security system. At this point, the testers had compromised the system sufficiently that the penetration study was deemed successful.

20.2.8   Example: Penetrating a UNIX System

In this example, the first goal is to gain access to the system. Our target is a system connected to the Internet.

We begin by scanning the network ports on the target system. Figure 20–3 shows some of these ports, together with a list of protocols that servers listening on those ports may use. Note that protocols are running on ports 79, 111, 512, 513, 514, and 540; these ports are typically used on UNIX systems. Let us make this assumption.

Many UNIX systems use *sendmail* as their SMTP server. This large program has had many security problems [190, 194, 195, 196, 197, 419, 829, 888]. By connecting to the port, we determine that the target is using *sendmail* Version 3.1. Drawing on previous experience and widely known information [97], we hypothesize that the SMTP agent will recognize the command *shell* and give us a *root*-owned shell on the system. To do this, we need to execute the *wiz* command first. We are successful, as Figure 20–4 shows. On this particular system, we have obtained *root* privileges.

The key to this attack is an understanding of how most UNIX systems are configured and a knowledge of known vulnerabilities. Most UNIX systems use some variant of *sendmail* as their SMTP agent, and that program prints version information when a connection is made. The information enabled the testers to determine

```
ftp                21/tcp File Transfer
telnet             23/tcp Telnet
smtp               25/tcp Simple Mail Transfer
finger             79/tcp Finger
sunrpc            111/tcp SUN Remote Procedure Call
exec              512/tcp remote process execution
(rexecd)
login             513/tcp remote login (rlogind)
shell             514/tcp rlogin style exec (rshd)
printer           515/tcp spooler (lpd)
uucp              540/tcp uucpd
nfs              2049/tcp networked file system
xterm            6000/tcp x-windows server
```

Figure 20–3 **The output of the UNIX port scan. These are the ports that provide**

```
220 zzz.com sendmail 3.1/zzz.3.9, Dallas, Texas, ready at Wed,
        2 Apr 97 22:07:31 CST
helo xxx
250 zzz.com Hello xxx.org, pleased to meet you
wiz
250 Enter, O mighty wizard!
shell
#
```

Figure 20–4   A successful accessing of a UNIX system.

what set of attacks would be likely to be fruitful. Given the wide variation in *send-mail*s (owing to differences in vendors' patches), the flaw had to be tested for. The test succeeded.

Now assume we are at step 3 of the list on page 392. We have an unprivileged account on the system. We determine that this system has a dynamically loaded kernel; the program used to add modules to the kernel is *loadmodule*. Because such a program must be privileged (or else it could not update the kernel tables), an unprivileged user can execute a privileged process. As indicated before, this suggests that the program does some sort of validation or authorization check. Our vulnerabilities models (see Section 20.4) indicate that this is a source of many problems. Let us examine this program more closely.

The program *loadmodule* validates the module as being a dynamically loadable module and then invokes the dynamic loader *ld.so* to perform the actual load. It also needs to determine the architecture of the system, and it uses the program *arch* to obtain this information. A logical question is how it executes these programs. The simplest way is to use a library function *system*. This function does not reset any part of the environment. Hence, if the *system* call is used, the environment in which we execute *loadmodule* is passed to the subprocesses, and these subprocesses are run as *root*. In this case, we can set our environment to look for programs in our local directory first, and then in system directories (by setting the **PATH** variable to have "." as the first directory).

We accept this as a working hypothesis, and we set out to verify that this flaw exists. We write a small program that prints its effective UID, name it *ld.so*, and move it to the current working directory. We then reset our **PATH** variable as indicated above and run *loadmodule*. Unfortunately, our program does not execute; nothing is printed.

Why not? Once we understand this, we may be able to figure out a way to bypass this check, and our understanding of the system will increase. We scan the executable looking for ASCII strings, to see exactly how their dynamic loader invokes those subprograms. We see that the invocations are "/bin/arch" and "/bin/ld.so". So our attempt to change the search path (**PATH** environment variable) was irrelevant; the system never looked at that variable because full path names were given.

Rereading the manual page for the library function *system*, we notice that it invokes the command interpreter *sh*. Looking at *sh*'s manual page, we learn that the **IFS** environment variable has as its value characters used to separate words in commands that *sh* executes. Given that *loadmodule* invokes "/bin/arch", if the character "/" were in the value of the environment variable **IFS**, *sh* would treat this command as "bin arch". Then we could use the idea that just failed, but call the program *bin* rather than *ld.so*.

We could verify this idea without a test, but it would require disassemby of the *loadmodule* executable unless we had source code (we would look for anything that reset the environment within *loadmodule*). Assuming that we do not have source code, we change the value of **IFS** to include "/", reset **PATH** and **IFS** as described above, change the name of our small program from *ld.so* to *bin*, and run *loadmodule*. The process prints that its effective UID is 0 (*root*). Our test has succeeded. (Chapter 26, "Program Security," discusses corrective measures for problems of this type. The vendor fixed the problem [192].)

Incidentally, this example leads to a simple flaw generalization. The problem of subprocesses inheriting environment variables and their values suggests that the privileged program did not adequately sanitize the (untrusted) environment in which that program executes before invoking subprograms that are to be trusted. Hence, *any* privileged program may have this flaw. One could even hypothesize that a standard library routine or system call is invoked. So, a general class of flaws would involve failure to sanitize the environment, and the indicator of such a flaw might be one or more specific function calls. At this point, the testers would look in the programmers' manuals to see if such routines existed; if so, they would analyze programs to see which privileged programs called them. This could lead to a large number of other vulnerabilities.

This penetration test required more study than the first and demonstrates how failure can lead to success. When a test fails, the testers may have not understood the system completely and so need to study why the test failed. In this example, the failure led to a reexamination of the relevant library function, which led to a review of one of the system command interpreters. During this review, one of the testers noticed an obscure but documented control over the way the command interpreter interpreted commands. This led to a successful test. Patience is often said to be a virtue, and this is certainly true in penetration testing.

20.2.9   Example: Penetrating a Windows NT System

As in the preceding example, we begin at step 2 of the list on page 392, and all we know is that the system is connected to the Internet. We begin as before, by probing network ports, and from the results (see Figure 20–5)—especially the service running on port 139—we conclude that the system is a Windows NT server.

We first probe for easy-to-guess passwords. We discover that the system administrator has chosen the password *Admin*, and we obtain access to the system. At this point, we have administrator privilege on the local system. We would like to obtain rights to other systems in the domain.

```
qotd          17/tcp    Quote of the Day
ftp           21/tcp    File Transfer [Control]
loc-srv      135/tcp    Location Service
netbios-ssn 139/tcp    NETBIOS Session Service [JBP]
```

Figure 20–5 The output of the Windows NT port scan. These are the ports that provide network service.

We examine the local system and discover that the domain administrator has installed a service that is running with the privileges of a domain administrator. We then obtain a program that will dump the local security authority database, and load it onto the system. After executing it, we obtain the service account password. Using this password, we acquire domain administrator privileges and can now access any system in the domain.

This penetration test uncovered a serious administrative problem. For some reason, a sensitive account had a password that was easy to guess. This indicates a procedural problem within the company. Perhaps the system administrators were too busy, or forgot, to choose a good password. Two generalizations are appropriate. First, other systems should be checked for weak passwords. Second, the company's security policies should be reviewed, as should its education of its system administrators and its mechanisms for publicizing the policies.

20.2.10   Debate

Considerable debate has arisen about the validity of penetration studies for testing system security. At one end of the spectrum are some vendors who report that "after 1 year of our system being on the Internet, no one has successfully penetrated the system," implying (and in some cases stating) that this shows that their product is quite secure. At the other end is the claim that penetration testing has no validity, and only rigorous design, implementation, and validation comprise an adequate test of security.

The resolution lies somewhere between two these extremes. Penetration testing is no substitute for good, thorough specification, rigorous design, careful and correct implementation, and meticulous testing. It is, however, a very valuable component of the final stage, "testing"; it is simply a form of a posteriori testing. Ideally, it should be unnecessary; but human beings are fallible and make mistakes, and computer systems are so complex that no single individual, or group, understands all aspects of the hardware's construction, the software's design, implementation, and the computer system's interactions with users and environment. Hence, errors will be introduced. Properly done, penetration tests examine the design and implementation of security mechanisms from the point of view of an attacker. The knowledge and understanding gleaned from such a viewpoint is invaluable.

20.2.11   Conclusion

Penetration testing is a very informal, nonrigorous technique for checking the security of a system. Two problems with the Flaw Hypothesis Methodology described in Section 20.2.4 are its dependence on the caliber of the testers and its lack of systematic examination of the system. High-caliber testers will examine the design systematically, but all too often the testing degenerates into a more scattered analysis.

In an attempt to make the process more systematic, and less dependent on the knowledge of the individuals conducting the test, testers often look at flaws that exist on other systems and decide which ones could translate into the tested system's model. Classification schemes can help in this regard; they group similar vulnerabilities together and enable the analyst to extract common features. Hence, such schemes are important in the flaw hypothesis step and are worth exploring.

20.3   Vulnerability Classification

Vulnerability classification frameworks describe security flaws from various perspectives. Some frameworks describe vulnerabilities by classifying the techniques used to exploit them. Others characterize vulnerabilities in terms of the software and hardware components and interfaces that make up the vulnerability. Still others classify vulnerabilities by their nature, in hopes of discovering techniques for finding previously unknown vulnerabilities.

The goal of vulnerability analysis is to develop methodologies that provide the following abilities.

1. The ability to specify, design, and implement a computer system without vulnerabilities.
2. The ability to analyze a computer system to detect vulnerabilities (which feeds into the Flaw Hypothesis Methodology step of penetration testing).
3. The ability to address any vulnerabilities introduced during the operation of the computer system (possibly leading to a redesign or reimplementation of the flawed components).
4. The ability to detect attempted exploitatons of vulnerabilities.

Ideally, one can generalize information about security flaws. From these generalizations, one then looks for underlying principles that lead toward the desired goals. Because the abstraction's purpose is tied to the classifiers' understanding of the goal, and of how best to reach that goal, both of these factors influence the classification system developed. Hence, the vulnerability frameworks covering design often differ from those covering the detection of exploitation of vulnerabilities. Before we present several different frameworks, however, a discussion of two security flaws will provide a basis for understanding several of the problems of these frameworks.

20.3.1   Two Security Flaws

This section presents two widely known security vulnerabilities in some versions of the UNIX operating system. We will use these vulnerabilities as examples when comparing and contrasting the various frameworks.

The program *xterm* is a program that emulates a terminal under the X11 window system. For reasons not relevant to this discussion, it must run as the omnipotent user *root* on UNIX systems. It enables the user to log all input and output to a log file. If the file does not exist, *xterm* creates it and assigns ownership to the user; if the file already exists, *xterm* checks that the user can write to it before opening the file. Because any *root* process can write to any file in the system, the extra check is necessary to prevent a user from directing *xterm* to append log output to (say) the system password file and gaining privileges by altering that file.

Suppose the user wishes to log to an existing file. The following code fragment opens the file for writing.

```
if (access("/usr/tom/X", W_OK) == 0){
    if ((fd = open("/usr/tom/X", O_WRONLY|O_APPEND) )< 0){
        /* handle error: cannot open file */
        }
}
```

The semantics of the UNIX operating system cause the name of the file to be loosely bound to the data object it represents, and the binding is asserted each time the name is used. If the data object corresponding to */usr/tom/X* changes after the *access* but before the *open*, the *open* will not open the file checked by *access*. So if, during that interval, an attacker deletes the file and links a system file (such as the password file) to the name of the deleted file, *xterm* appends logging output to the password file. At this point, the user can create a *root* account without a password and gain *root* privileges. Figure 20–6 shows this graphically.

The Internet worm of 1988 [292, 386, 757, 858] publicized our second flaw. It continues to recur—for example, in implementations of various network servers [200, 201, 202]. The *finger* protocol [964] obtains information about the users of a remote system. The client program, called *finger*, contacts a server, called *fingerd*, on the remote system and sends a name of at most 512 characters. The server reads the name and returns the relevant information, but the server does not check the length of the name that *finger* sends. The storage space for the name is allocated on the stack, directly above the return address for the I/O routine. The attacker writes a small program (in machine code) to obtain a command interpreter and pads it to 512 bytes. She then sets the next 24 bytes to return to the input buffer instead of to the rightful caller (the main routine, in this case). The entire 536-byte buffer is sent to the daemon. The first 512 bytes go into the input storage array, and the excess 24 bytes overwrite the stack locations in which the caller's return address and status word are stored. The input routine returns to the code to spawn the command interpreter. The attacker now has access to the system. Figure 20–7 shows the changes in the user stack.

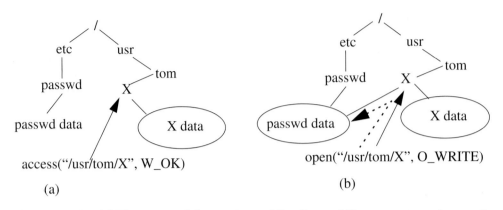

Figure 20–6   (a) The state of the system at the time of the *access* system call; the solid arrow indicates that the *access* refers to */usr/tom/X*. Both */usr/tom/X* and */etc/passwd* name distinct objects. However, before the process makes its *open* system call, */usr/tom/X* is deleted and a direct alias (hard link) for */etc/passwd* is created and is named */usr/tom/X*. Then the *open* accesses the data associated with */etc/passwd* when it opens */usr/tom/X* because */usr/tom/X* and */etc/passwd* now refer to the same file. This is shown in (b); with the dashed arrow indicating which data is actually read and the solid arrow indicating the name given to *open*.

20.4   Frameworks

The goals of a framework dictate the framework's structure. For example, if the framework is to guide the development of an attack detection tool, the focus of the framework will be on the steps needed to exploit vulnerabilities. If the framework is intended to aid the software development process, it will emphasize programming and design errors that cause vulnerabilities. Each of the following classification schemes was designed with a specific goal in mind.

Each of the following frameworks classifies a vulnerability as an *n*-tuple, the elements of the *n*-tuple being the specific classes into which the vulnerability falls. Some have a single set of categories; others are multidimensional ($n > 1$) because they are examining multiple characteristics of the vulnerabilities.

20.4.1   The RISOS Study

The RISOS (Research Into Secure Operating Systems) study [3] was prepared to aid computer and system managers and information processing specialists in understanding security issues in operating systems and to help them determine the level of effort required to enhance their system security. The investigators classified flaws into seven general classes.

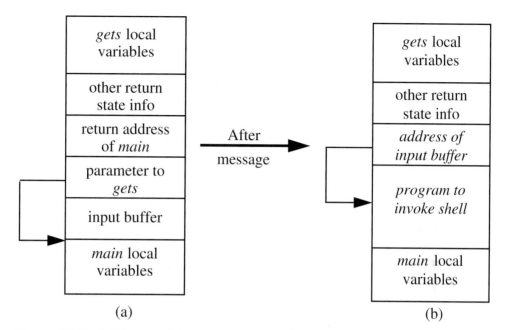

Figure 20–7 (a) The stack frame of *fingerd* when input is to be read. The arrow indicates the location to which the parameter to *gets* refers (it is past the address of the input buffer). (b) The same stack after the bogus input is stored. The input string overwrites the input buffer and parameter to *gets*, allowing a return to the contents of the input buffer. The arrow shows that the return address of *main* was overwritten with the address of the input buffer. When *gets* returns, it will pop its return address (now the address of the input buffer) and resume execution at that address.

1. Incomplete parameter validation
2. Inconsistent parameter validation
3. Implicit sharing of privileged/confidential data
4. Asynchronous validation/inadequate serialization
5. Inadequate identification/authentication/authorization
6. Violable prohibition/limit
7. Exploitable logic error

The investigators discussed techniques for avoiding, or ameliorating, the flaws in each class. They also attempted to develop methodologies and software for detecting incomplete parameter validation flaws. The survey examined several operating systems (MULTICS, BBN's TENEX, DEC's TOPS-10, Honeywell's GECOS, IBM's OS/MVT, SDS's SDS-940, and UNIVAC's EXEC-8) but noted that the flaw classes applied to other systems as well.

20.4.1.1   The Flaw Classes

Incomplete parameter validation occurs when a parameter is not checked before use. The buffer overflows discussed earlier are the classic example of this type of flaw. Another example is a flaw in one computer's software emulator for integer division [188]. The caller provided two addresses as parameters, one for the quotient and one for the remainder. The quotient address was checked to ensure that it lay within the user's protection domain, but the remainder address was not similarly checked. By passing the address of the user identification number for the remainder, the programmer was able to acquire system privileges. Parameters need to be checked for type (and possibly format), ranges of values, access rights, and presence (or absence).

Inconsistent parameter validation is a design flaw in which each individual routine using data checks that the data is in the proper format for that routine, but the routines require different formats. Basically, the inconsistency across interfaces causes this flaw. An example occurs in a database in which each record is one line, with colons separating the fields. If one program accepts colons and newlines as part of data but other programs read the colons so accepted as field separators and the newlines so accepted as record separators, the inconsistency can cause bogus records to be entered into the database.

When an operating system fails to isolate processes and users properly, an *implicit sharing of privileged/confidential data* flaw occurs. The ability to recover a file's password in TENEX is an example of this type of flaw [893]. TENEX allowed the user to determine when paging occurred. Furthermore, when a file access required a password, the password was checked character by character, and the checking stopped at the first incorrect character. So, an attacker would position a guess for the password so that a page boundary lay between the first and second characters. He would then try to access the file. If paging occurred, the first character of the password was correct; if not, it was incorrect. Continuing in this fashion, the attacker could quickly recover the password needed to access the file. Kocher's timing attack against RSA, in which small variations in the speed of encipherment enable an attacker to deduce the private key (see Section 16.1), is another example of this type of flaw [523].

Race conditions and time-of-check to time-of-use flaws such as that shown in Figure 20–6 are members of the *asynchronous validation/inadequate serialization* class of flaws.

Inadequate identification/authorization/authentication flaws arise when a system allows a user to be erroneously identified, when one user can assume another's privilege, or when a user can trick the system (or another user) into executing a program without authorization. Trojan horses are examples of this type of flaw, as are accounts without passwords, because any user can access them freely. The UNIVAC 1100 provides an example related to file naming [3]. On that system, access to the system file SYS$*DLOC$ meant that the process was privileged. The system checked this by seeing if the process could access any file with the first three characters of the qualifier name SYS and the first three characters of the file name DLO. So, any process that could access the file SYSA*DLOC$, which was an ordinary (non-system) file, was also privileged and could access any file without the file access key.

Violable prohibition/limit flaws arise when system designers fail to handle bounds conditions properly. For example, early versions of TENEX kept the operating system in low memory and gave the user process access to all memory cells with addresses above a fixed value (marking the last memory location of the operating system). The limit of memory addressing was the address of the highest memory location; but when a user addressed a location beyond the end of memory, it was reduced modulo the memory size and so accessed a word in the operating system's area. Because the address was a large number, however, it was treated as being in user space—and hence could be altered [893].

Exploitable logic error flaws encompass problems not falling into any of the other classes; examples include incorrect error handling, unexpected side effects of instructions, and incorrect allocation of resources. One such flaw that occurred in early versions of TENEX requires an understanding of how the TENEX monitor implemented a return to the user's program. Basically, the monitor would execute a *skip return* to the address following the one stored in the user's program counter; the system would simply add 1 to the user's return word and return. On the PDP-10, the index field was a bit in the return word. If the return word was set to −1, the addition would overflow into the index field and change its semantics to refer to the contents of register 1, so the return would be to the location stored in that register. The attacker would load a bootstrap program into other registers, manipulate the contents of register 1 through a series of system calls so that it contained the address of the first bootstrap instruction, and then cause the monitor to execute a skip return. The bootstrap program would execute, loading the attacker's program and executing it with system privileges [546].

20.4.1.2 Legacy

The RISOS project created a seminal study of vulnerabilities. It provided valuable insights into the nature of flaws, among them that security is a function of site requirements and threats, that there are a small number of fundamental flaws that recur in different contexts, and that operating system security is not a critical factor in the design of operating systems. It spurred research efforts into detection and/or repair of vulnerabilities in existing systems; the Protection Analysis study was the most influential of these efforts.

20.4.2 Protection Analysis Model

The Protection Analysis (PA) study [95] attempted to break the operating system protection problem into smaller, more manageable pieces. The investigators hoped that this would reduce the expertise required of individuals working on operating systems. The study aimed at development of techniques that would have an impact within 10 years. It developed a general strategy, called *pattern-directed protection evaluation*, and applied it to several operating systems. In one case, the investigators found previously unknown security vulnerabilities. From this approach grew a classification scheme for vulnerabilities. Neumann's presentation [688] of this study organizes the ten classes of flaws in order to show the connections among the major classes and subclasses of flaws (the italicized names in parentheses are the names used in the original study).

1. Improper protection domain initialization and enforcement
    a. Improper choice of initial protection domain (*domain*)
    b. Improper isolation of implementation detail (*exposed representations*)
    c. Improper change (*consistency of data over time*)
    d. Improper naming (*naming*)
    e. Improper deallocation or deletion (*residuals*)
2. Improper validation (*validation of operands, queue management dependencies*)
3. Improper synchronization
    a. Improper indivisibility (*interrupted atomic operations*)
    b. Improper sequencing (*serialization*)
4. Improper choice of operand or operation (*critical operator selection errors*)

20.4.2.1   The Flaw Classes

The investigators identified ten classes of errors and noted that a simple hierarchy could be built; however, the subclasses overlapped. Neumann's reorganization eliminated the overlap and is conceptually simpler than the original.

The first class is *improper protection domain initialization and enforcement*; it includes security flaws arising from initialization of the system or programs and enforcement of the security requirements. For example, when a system boots, the protection modes of the file containing the identifiers of all users logged in can be altered by any user. Under most security policies, the initial assignment of protections is incorrect, and hence a vulnerability exists. The subclass in which this particular flaw lies is *improper choice of initial protection domain*, which includes any flaw related to an initial incorrect assignment of privileges or of security and integrity classes, especially when that flaw allows untrusted users to manipulate security-critical data.

Improper protection flaws often arise when an abstraction is mapped into an implementation. The covert timing channel in the IBM KVM/370 system (see the example that begins on page 294) is an example of an *improper isolation of implementation detail*. This subclass also includes flaws that allow users to bypass the operating system and write directly to absolute I/O locations or to alter data structures in ways that are inconsistent with their functions (for example, altering the rights of a process by writing directly to memory).

Another example of an improper protection flaw can arise when a privileged program needs to open a file after checking that some particular condition holds. The goal of the adversary is to have the privileged program open another file for which the condition does not hold. The attack is an attempt to switch the binding of the name between the check and the open. Figure 20–6 shows an example for the UNIX system [109]. This is an instance of the subclass called *improper change.* Another instance of this subclass is when some object, such as a parameter, a file, or the binding of a process to a network port, changes unexpectedly.

If two different objects have the same name, a user may access or execute the wrong object. The classic example is the venerable Trojan horse (see Section 19.2): an attacker crafts a program that will copy data to a hidden location for later viewing and then invoke an editor, and gives it the same name as the widely used system editor. Now, a user invoking the editor may get the correct program or may get the bogus editor. Other examples of *improper naming* arise in networking. The best example occurs when two hosts have the same IP address. Messages intended for one of the hosts may be routed to the other, without any indication to the sender.

Failing to clear memory before it is reallocated, or to clear the disk blocks used in a file before they are assigned to a new file, causes *improper deallocation or deletion* errors. One example occurs when a program dumps core in a publicly readable file and the core dump contains sensitive information such as passwords.

The second major class of flaws is *improper validation.* These flaws arise from inadequate checking, such as *fingerd*'s lack of bounds checking (with the results shown in Figure 20–7). A second example occurs in some versions of Secure NIS. By default, that protocol maps the *root* user into an untrusted user *nobody* on the theory that the server should not trust any claim to *root* privileges from remote systems unless the credentials asserting those privileges are cryptographic. If the Secure NIS server is misconfigured so that *root* has no private key, however, the remote client can claim to be *root* and supply credentials of the *nobody* user. The flawed system will determine that it cannot validate *root*'s credentials and will promptly check for *nobody*'s private key (because *root* is remapped when needed). Because the credentials will be validated, the remote client will be given *root* privileges [193].

Improper synchronization arises when processes fail to coordinate their activities. These flaws can occur when operations that should be uninterruptable are interrupted (the oxymoron "interrupting atomic operations" is often used to describe this phenomenon), or the flaws can arise when two processes are not synchronized properly. The flaw in the UNIX *mkdir* command in Version 7 is an example of the first case [893]. That command created directories by executing a privileged operation to create the directory and then giving it to the requester by changing the ownership of the directory. This should be done as a single operation, but in Version 7 UNIX systems two distinct system calls were needed.

```
mknod("xxx", directory)
chown("xxx", user, group)
```

If an attacker changed the binding of the name "xxx" to refer to the password file between these calls, the attacker would own that file and so could create and delete accounts with impunity. Thus, such a flaw is an example of *improper indivisibility*. The second subtype, *improper sequencing*, arises in at least one one-time password scheme. If the target system can run multiple copies of the server and two users attempt to access the same account, both may be granted access even though the password should be valid for at most one use. Essentially, accesses to the file need to be paired as a read followed by a write; but if multiple copies of the server run, nothing enforces this ordering of access types. This system suffers from *improper sequencing*.

The last category, *improper choice of operand or operation*, includes calling of inappropriate or erroneous functions. Examples include cryptographic key generation software calling pseudorandom number generation functions that produce predictable sequences of numbers or sequences of numbers with insufficient randomness. The Kerberos authentication system [277], as well as numerous other security-related programs, have suffered from this problem.

20.4.2.2   Legacy

The Protection Analysis project was the first project to explore automatic detection of security flaws in programs and systems. Its methods were not widely used, in part because of the inability to automate part of the procedure, in part because of its complexity, and in part because the procedure for reducing flaws to system-independent patterns was not complete. However, the efficacy of the idea was demonstrated, and the classification scheme of flaws greatly influenced the study of vulnerabilities. The PA project was a milestone in computer security research and was the last published vulnerability study for some time, because efforts were turned toward development of methods that were free of these errors.

20.4.3   The NRL Taxonomy

In 1992, Landwehr, Bull, McDermott, and Choi [546] developed a taxonomy to help designers and operators of systems enforce security. They tried to answer three questions: how did the flaw enter the system, when did it enter the system, and where in the system is it manifest? They built three different classification systems, one to answer each of the three questions, and classified more than 50 vulnerabilities in these schemes.

20.4.3.1   The Flaw Classes

The first classification scheme classified vulnerabilities by genesis. The class of *inadvertent* flaws was broken down using the RISOS categories (except that the incomplete and inconsistent validation classes were merged), and the class of *intentional* flaws was broken into *malicious* and *nonmalicious* flaws. Figure 20–8 summa-

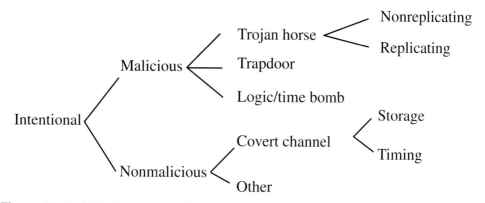
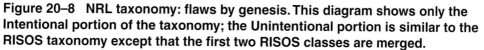

Figure 20–8   NRL taxonomy: flaws by genesis. This diagram shows only the Intentional portion of the taxonomy; the Unintentional portion is similar to the RISOS taxonomy except that the first two RISOS classes are merged.

rizes these classes. The investigators felt that because most security flaws were inadvertent, better design and coding reviews could eliminate many of them; but if the flaws were intentional, measures such as hiring more trustworthy designers and programmers and doing more security-related testing would be more appropriate.

The second scheme classified vulnerabilities by time of introduction; Figure 20–9 summarizes the subclasses. The investigators wanted to know if security errors were more likely to be introduced at any particular point in the software life cycle in order to determine if focusing efforts on security at any specific point would be helpful. They defined the *development* phase to be all activities up to the release of the initial version of the software, the *maintenance* phase to be all activities leading to changes in the software performed under configuration control, and the *operation* phase to be all activities involving patching of the software and not under configuration control (for example, installing a vendor patch).

The third scheme classified by location of the flaw; Figure 20–10 summarizes the classes. The intent is to capture where the flaw manifests itself and to determine

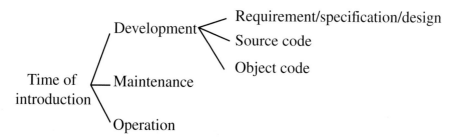
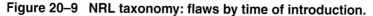

Figure 20–9   NRL taxonomy: flaws by time of introduction.

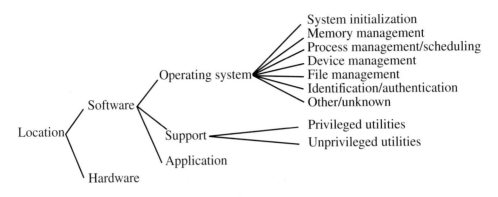

Figure 20–10   NRL taxonomy: flaws by location.

if any one location is more likely to be flawed than any other. If so, focusing resources on that location would improve security.

20.4.3.2   Legacy

The investigators noted that their sample size (50 flaws) was too small to draw any statistically sound conclusions. However, by plotting the classes against one another on scatter plots, they concluded that with a large enough sample size, an analyst could study the relationships between location and genesis, genesis and time of introduction, and location and time of introduction. The knowledge gained from such a study would help developers concentrate on the most likely places, times, and causes of security flaws.

Landwehr's taxonomy differs from the others in that it focuses on social processes as well as technical details of flaws. In order to classify a security flaw correctly on the time of introduction and genesis axes, either the precise history of the particular flaw must be known or the classifier must make assumptions. This ambiguity is unsettling, because this information is not always available. However, when available, this information is quite useful, and the study was the first to approach the problem of reducing vulnerabilities by studying the environments in which they were introduced.

20.4.4   Aslam's Model

Aslam [40] developed a classification scheme for security flaws that categorized faults and grouped similar faults together. It differed from both the PA and RISOS studies in that it drew on software fault studies to develop its categories, and it focused specifically on implementation flaws in the UNIX system. Moreover, the categories and classes in both PA and RISOS had considerable overlap; Aslam presented a decision procedure for classifying faults unambiguously. This made it useful for organizing vulnerability data in a database, one of the goals of his study.

20.4.4.1   The Flaw Classes

Aslam distinguished between *coding faults*, which were introduced during software development, and *emergent faults*, which resulted from incorrect initialization, use, or application. For example, a program that fails to check the length of an input string before storing it in an array has a coding fault, but allowing a message transfer agent to forward mail to an arbitrary file on the system is an emergent fault. The mail agent is performing exactly according to specification, but the results produce a dangerous security hole.

The class of coding faults is subdivided into synchronization errors and condition validation errors. Synchronization errors arise when a timing window between two operations allows a fault to be exploited or when operations are improperly serialized. For example, the *xterm* flaw discussed previously is a classic synchronization error. Condition validation errors arise when bounds are not checked, access rights are ignored, input is not validated, or authentication and identification fails. The *finger* flaw is an example of this.

Emergent faults are either configuration errors or environment faults. The former arise from installing a program in the wrong place, with the wrong initialization or configuration information, or with the wrong permissions. For example, if the *tftp* daemon is installed so that any file in the system can be accessed, the installer has caused a configuration error. Environment faults are those faults introduced by the environment as opposed to those from the code or from the configuration. On older UNIX systems, for example, any shell whose name began with "-" was interactive; so an attacker could link a setuid shell script to the name "-gotcha" and execute it, thereby getting a setuid to *root* shell [96].

Aslam's decision procedure [39] consisted of a set of questions for each class of flaws, the questions being ordered so that each flaw had exactly one classification.

20.4.4.2   Legacy

The contribution of Aslam's taxonomy was to tie security flaws to software faults and to introduce a precise classification scheme. In this scheme, each vulnerability belonged to exactly one class of security flaws. Furthermore, the decision procedure was well-defined and unambiguous, leading to a simple mechanism for representing similar flaws in a database.

20.4.5   Comparison and Analysis

Consider the flaws described in Section 20.3.1. Both depend on the interaction of two processes: the trusted process (*xterm* or *fingerd*) and a second process (the *attacker*). For the *xterm* flaw, the attacker deletes the existing log file and inserts a link to the password file; for the *fingerd* flaw, the attacker writes a name the length of which exceeds the buffer size. Furthermore, the processes use operating system services to communicate. So, three processes are involved: the flawed process, the attacker process, and the operating system service routines. The view of the flaw when considered from the perspective of any of these processes may differ from the view when considered from the perspective of the other two. For example, from the point of view of the flawed process, the flaw may be an incomplete validation of a parameter because the process does not adequately check the parameter it passes to the operating system by means of a system call. From the point of view of the operating system, however, the flaw may be a violable prohibition/limit, because the parameter may refer to an address outside the space of the process. Which classification is appropriate?

Levels of abstraction muddy this issue even more. At the lowest level, the flaw may be, say, an inconsistent parameter validation because successive system calls do not check that the argument refers to the same object. At a higher level, this may be characterized as a race condition or an asynchronous validation/inadequate serialization problem. At an even higher level, it may be seen as an exploitable logic error because a resource (object) can be deleted while in use.

The levels of abstraction are defined differently for every system, and this contributes to the ambiguity. In the following discussion, the "higher" the level, the more abstract it is, without implying precisely where in the abstraction hierarchy either level occurs. Only the relationship, not the distance, of the levels is important in this context.

We now expand on these questions using our two sample flaws.

20.4.5.1   The *xterm* Log File Flaw

We begin with the PA taxonomy. From the point of view of the *xterm* process, the flaw is clearly an *improper change* flaw because the problem is that between the time of check (*access*) and the time of use (*open*), the referent of the name changes. However, with respect to the attacker process, the flaw is an *improper deallocation or deletion* flaw because something (in this case, the binding between the name and the referent) is being deleted improperly. And from the operating system's point of view, the flaw is an *improper indivisibility* flaw because the opening of the file should atomically check that the access is allowed.

Reconsider the problem at a higher level of abstraction from the point of view of the operating system. At this level, a directory object is seen simply as an object; deletion and creation of files in the directory are semantically equivalent to writing in the directory, and obtaining file status and opening a file require that the directory be read. In this case, the flaw may be seen as a violation of the Bernstein conditions [79] (requiring no reading during writing, and a single writer), which means that the flaw is one of *improper sequencing*.

At the abstraction level corresponding to design, the attacking process should not be able to write into the directory in the first place, leading to a characterization of the flaw as one of *improper choice of initial protection domain*. This is not a valid characterization at the implementation level because both the attacking process and the *xterm* are being executed by the same user and the semantics of the implementation of the UNIX operating system require that both processes be able to access the same objects in the same way.

At the implementation level, with respect to the *xterm* process and the RISOS taxonomy, the *xterm* flaw is clearly an *asynchronous validation/inadequate serialization* flaw because the file access is checked and then opened nonatomically. From the point of view of the attacker, the ability to delete the file makes the flaw an *exploitable logic error* as well as a *violable prohibition/limit* flaw because the attacker is manipulating a binding in the system's domain. And from the operating system's point of view, the flaw is an *inconsistent parameter validation* flaw because the access check and open use the same parameters, but the objects they refer to are different, and this is not checked.

Interestingly, moving up in the hierarchy of abstractions, the flaw may once again be characterized as a violation of the Bernstein conditions, or the nonatomicity of an operation that should be atomic; in either case, it is an *asynchronous validation/ inadequate serialization* flaw. So the process view prevails.

At the design level, a write being allowed where it should not be is an *inadequate identification/authentication/authorization* flaw because the resource (the containing directory) is not adequately protected. Again, owing to the nature of the protection model of the UNIX operating system, this would not be a valid characterization at the implementation level.

Hence, this single flaw has several different characterizations. At the implementation level, depending on the classifier's point of view, the *xterm* flaw can be classified in three different ways. Trying to abstract the underlying principles under one taxonomy places the flaw in a fourth class, and under the other taxonomy, one view (the *xterm* process view) prevails. Moving up to the design level, a completely different classification is needed. Clearly, the ambiguity in the PA and RISOS classifications makes it difficult to classify flaws with precision.

The classification under the NRL taxonomy depends on whether this flaw was intentional or not; the history is unclear. If it was intentional, at the lowest level, it is an *inadvertent flaw of serialization/aliasing*; if it was unintentional (because on earlier systems *xterm* need not be privileged), it is a *nonmalicious: other* flaw. In either case, at higher levels of abstraction, the classification would parallel that of the RISOS scheme. Given the history, the time of introduction is clearly *during development*, and the location is in the class *support: privileged utilities*. So, this taxonomy classifies this particular flaw unambiguously on two axes. However, the third classification is ambiguous even when points of view and levels of abstraction are ignored.

The selection criteria for fault classification in Aslam's taxonomy places the flaw in the *object installed with incorrect permissions* class from the point of view of the attacking program (because the attacking program can delete the file), in the *access rights validation error* class from the point of view of the *xterm* program (because *xterm* does not properly validate the file at the time of access), and in the *improper or inadequate serialization error* class from the point of view of the operating system (because the deletion and creation should not be interspersed between the access and open). As an aside, in the absence of the explicit decision procedure, the flaw could also have been placed in a fourth class, *race conditions*. So, although this taxonomy classifies flaws into specific classes, the class into which a flaw is placed is a function of the decision procedure as well as the nature of the flaw itself. The fact that this ambiguity of classification is not a unique characteristic of one flaw is apparent when we study the second flaw—the *fingerd* flaw.

20.4.5.2   *The fingerd* Buffer Overflow Flaw

With respect to the *fingerd* process and the PA taxonomy, the buffer overflow flaw is clearly an *improper validation* flaw because the problem is failure to check parameters, leading to addressing of memory not in its memory space by referencing through an out-of-bounds pointer value. However, with respect to the attacker process (the *finger* program), the flaw is one of *improper choice of operand or operation* because an operand (the data written onto the connection) is improper (specifically, too long, and arguably not what *fingerd* is to be given). And from the operating system's point of view, the flaw is an *improper isolation of implementation detail* flaw because the user is allowed to write directly into what should be in the space of the process (the return address) and to execute what should be treated as data only.

Moving still higher in the layers of abstraction, the storage space of the return address is a variable or an object. From the operating system's point of view, this makes the flaw an *improper change* flaw because a parameter—specifically, the return address—changes unexpectedly. From the *fingerd* point of view, however, the more abstract issue is the execution of data (the input); this is improper validation—specifically, failure to validate the type of the instructions being executed. So, again, the flaw is an *improper validation* flaw.

At the highest level, the system is changing a security-related value in memory and is executing data that should not be executable. Hence, this is again an *improper choice of initial protection domain* flaw. But this is not a valid characterization at the implementation level because the architectural design of the system requires the return address to be stored on the stack, just as the input buffer is allocated on the stack, and, because the hardware supporting most versions of the UNIX operating system cannot protect specific words in memory (instead, protection is provided for all words on a page or segment), the system requires that the process be able to write to, and read from, its stack.

With respect to the *fingerd* process using the RISOS taxonomy, the buffer overflow flaw is clearly an *incomplete parameter validation* flaw because the problem is failure to check parameters, allowing the buffer to overflow. However, with respect to the *fingerd* process, the flaw is a *violable prohibition/limit* flaw because the limit on input data to be sent can be ignored (violated). And from the operating system's point of view, the flaw is an *inadequate identification/authentication/authorization* flaw because the user is allowed to write directly to what should be in the space of the process (the return address) and to execute what should be treated as data only.

Moving still higher, the storage space of the return address is a variable or an object. From the operating system's point of view, this makes the flaw one of *asynchronous validation/inadequate serialization* because a parameter—specifically, the return address—changes unexpectedly. From the *fingerd* point of view, however, the more abstract issue is the execution of data (the input); this is *improper validation*—specifically, failure to validate the type of the instructions being executed. So the flaw is an *inadequate identification/authentication/authorization* flaw.

At the highest level, this is again an *inadequate identification/authentication/authorization* flaw because the system is changing a security-related value in memory and is executing data that should not be executable. Again, owing to the nature of the protection model of the UNIX operating system, this would not be a valid characterization at the implementation level.

The NRL taxonomy suffers from similar problems in its classification by genesis, which—for inadvertent flaws, as this is—uses the RISOS taxonomy. In this case, the time of introduction is clearly *during development*, and the location is in the *support: privileged utilities* class. So, this taxonomy classifies this particular flaw unambiguously on two axes. Note that knowledge of the history of the program is needed to perform the classification. A rogue programmer could easily have inserted this vulnerability into a patch distributed to system administrators, in which case the genesis classification would be as a malicious flaw, falling in the trapdoor category, and the time of introduction would be in the operating class.

Finally, under Aslam's taxonomy, the flaw is a *boundary condition error* from the point of view of the attacking program (because the limit on input data can be ignored) and from the point of view of the *xterm* program (because the process writes beyond a valid address boundary) and an *environment fault* from the point of view of the operating system (because the error occurs when the program is executed on a particular machine—specifically, a stack-based machine). As an aside, in the absence of the explicit decision procedure, the flaw could also have been placed in the class of *access rights validation errors* because the code executed in the input buffer should be data only and because the return address is outside the protection domain of the process and yet is altered by it. So, again, this taxonomy satisfies the decision procedure criterion, but not the uniqueness criterion.

The RISOS classifications are somewhat more consistent among the levels of abstraction because the improper authorization classification runs through the layers of abstraction. However, point of view plays a role here because that classification applies to the operating system's point of view at two levels and to the process view between them. This, again, limits the usefulness of the classification scheme. Because Landwehr's work is based on RISOS, it has similar problems.

20.4.5.3 Summary

Flaw classification is not consistent among different levels of abstraction. Ideally, a flaw should be classified the same at all levels (possibly with more refinement at lower levels). This problem is ameliorated somewhat by the overlap of the flaw classifications because as one refines the flaws, the flaws may shift classes. However, the classes themselves should be distinct; they are not, leading to this problem.

The point of view is also a problem. The point of view should not affect the class into which a flaw falls, but, as the examples show, it clearly does. So, can we use this as a tool for classification—that is, identify flaws on the basis of the three classes into which they fall? The problem is that the classes are not partitions; they overlap, and so it is often not clear which class should be used for a component of the triple.

In short, the *xterm* and *fingerd* examples demonstrate weaknesses of the PA, RISOS, NRL, and Aslam classifications: either the classifications of some flaws are not well defined or they are arbitrary and vary with the levels of abstraction and points of view from which the flaws are considered.

20.5   Summary

As the Internet has grown, so has connectivity, enabling attackers to break into an increasing number of systems. Often very inexperienced attackers appear to have used extremely sophisticated techniques to break into systems, but on investigation it can be seen that they have used attack tools. Indeed, attack tools are becoming very widespread, and most systems cannot resist a determined attack.

In the past, attention was focused on building secure systems. Because of the large number of nonsecure systems in use today, it is unrealistic to expect that new, secure systems will be deployed widely enough to protect the companies and individuals connected to the Internet. Instead, existing systems will be made more secure, and as vulnerabilities are found they will be eliminated or monitored. The vulnerability models discussed in this chapter guide us in improving the software engineering cycle and in reducing the risk of introducing new vulnerabilities, and penetration analyses enable us to test admittedly nonsecure systems to determine whether or not they are sufficiently secure for the uses to which they are put.

20.6   Further Reading

Descriptions of vulnerabilities usually are anecdotal or are found through informal sources (such as the Internet). Papers describing security incident handling, security incident response, and security tools [171, 657, 768, 878] often describe both successful and unsuccessful attacks. Some books and papers [13, 409, 699] describe attack tools in detail. Others [515, 759] describe techniques for attacking systems. Parker [713] outlines several techniques that unsuccessful criminals have used.

Several papers discuss analyses of programs and systems for vulnerabilities. One paper [110] describes a syntactic approach to finding potential race conditions. Others [216, 638, 923] discuss buffer overflows. The use of fault injection to find potential vulnerabilities has also been discussed [354, 918].

Gupta and Gligor developed a formal analysis technique arising from failure to perform adequate checks [383, 384].

The Common Vulnerabilities and Exposures list is discussed in two papers [174, 590].

20.7   Exercises

1. Classify the following vulnerabilities using the RISOS model. Assume that the classification is for the implementation level. Justify your answer.

   a. The presence of the "wiz" command in the *sendmail* program (see Section 20.2.8).

   b. The failure to handle the **IFS** shell variable by *loadmodule* (see Section 20.2.8).

   c. The failure to select an *Administrator* password that was difficult to guess (see Section 20.2.9).

   d. The failure of the Burroughs system to detect offline changes to files (see Section 20.2.6).

2. Classify the vulnerabilities in Exercise 1 using the PA model. Assume that the classification is for the implementation level. Justify your answer.

3. The C shell does not treat the **IFS** variable as a special variable. (That is, the C shell separates arguments to commands by white spaces; this behavior is built in and cannot be changed.) How might this affect the *loadmodule* exploitation?

4. A common error on UNIX systems occurs during the configuration of *bind*, a directory name server. The time-to-expire field is set at 0.5 because the administrator believes that this field's unit is minutes (and wishes to set the time to 30 seconds). However, *bind* expects the field to be in seconds and reads the value as 0—meaning that no data is ever expired.

   a. Classify this vulnerability using the RISOS model, and justify your answer.

   b. Classify this vulnerability using the PA model, and justify your answer.

   c. Classify this vulnerability using Aslam's model, and justify your answer.

5. Can the UNIX Bourne shell variable **HOME**, which identifies the home directory of a user to programs that read start-up files from the user's home directory, be used to compromise a system? If so, how?

6. An attacker breaks into a Web server running on a Windows 2000–based system. Because of the ease with which he broke in, he concludes that Windows 2000 is an operating system with very poor security features. Is his conclusion reasonable? Why or why not?

7. Generalize the vulnerability described in Section 20.2.6 in order to suggest other ways in which the system could be penetrated.

8. Generalize the example in Section 20.2.7 in order to describe other weaknesses that the security of the computer system might have.

9. Why might an analyst care how similar two vulnerabilities are?

10. One expert noted that the PA model and the RISOS model are isomorphic. Show that the PA vulnerability classifications correspond to the RISOS vulnerability classes and vice versa.

11. The NRL classification scheme has three axes: genesis, time of introduction, and location. Name two other axes that would be of interest to an analyst. Justify your answer.

12. In the NRL classification scheme for the "time of introduction" axis, must the development phase precede the maintenance and operation phases, and must the maintenance phase precede the operation phase? Justify your answer.

13. In the NRL classification scheme for the "genesis" axis, how might one determine whether a vulnerability is "malicious" or "nonmalicious"?

14. In the NRL classification scheme for the "genesis" axis, can the classes "Trojan horse" and "covert channel" overlap? Justify your answer. If your answer is yes, describe a Trojan horse that is also a covert channel or vice versa.

15. Aslam's classification scheme classifies each vulnerability into a single category based on a decision tree that requires "yes" or "no" answers to questions about the vulnerability. A researcher has suggested replacing the tree with a vector, the components of which correspond to questions about the vulnerability. A "1" in the vector corresponds to a "yes" answer to the question; a "0" corresponds to a "no" answer. Compare and contrast the two approaches.

16. For the *fingerd* security hole to be exploited, certain conditions must hold. Based on the discussion in Section 20.3.1, enumerate these conditions.

17. For the *xterm* security hole to be exploited, certain conditions must hold. Based on the discussion in Section 20.3.1, enumerate these conditions.

18. Perform a penetration test on a system ***after you obtain authorization to do so.*** Apply the Flaw Hypothesis Methodology to obtain a meaningful assessment of the system's security.

Chapter 21
Auditing

LADY MACBETH: Your servants ever
Have theirs, themselves and what is theirs, in compt,
To make their audit at your highness' pleasure,
Still to return your own.
—*The Tragedy of Macbeth*, I, vi, 27–30.

Auditing is an a posteriori technique for determining security violations. This chapter presents the notions of logging (recording of system events and actions) and auditing (analysis of these records). Auditing plays a major role in detection of security violations and in postmortem analysis to determine precisely what happened and how. This makes an effective auditing subsystem a key security component of any system.

21.1   Definitions

The development of techniques for auditing computer systems sprang from the need to trace access to sensitive or important information stored on computer systems as well as access to the computer systems themselves. Anderson [26] first proposed the use of audit trails to monitor threats. The use of existing audit records suggested the development of simple tools that would check for unauthorized access to systems and files. The premise—that the logging mechanism was in place and active— required that the logs be augmented with additional information, but Anderson did not propose modification of the basic structure of the system's logging design, the implication being that redesign of the security monitoring mechanism was beyond the scope of the study.

> **Definition 21–1.** *Logging* is the recording of events or statistics to provide information about system use and performance.

Definition 21–2. *Auditing* is the analysis of log records to present information about the system in a clear and understandable manner.

With respect to computer security, logs provide a mechanism for analyzing the system security state, either to determine if a requested action will put the system in a nonsecure state or to determine the sequence of events leading to the system being in a nonsecure (compromised) state. If the log records all events that cause state transitions, as well as the previous and new values of the objects that are changed, the system state can be reconstructed at any time. Even if only a subset of this information is recorded, one might be able to eliminate some possible causes of a security problem; what remains provides a valuable starting point for further analysis.

Gligor [360] suggests other uses for the auditing mechanism. It allows systems analysts to review patterns of usage in order to evaluate the effectiveness of protection mechanisms. These patterns can be used to establish expected patterns of resource usage, which are critical for some intrusion detection systems. (See Chapter 25, "Intrusion Detection.") Auditing mechanisms must record any use of privileges. A security control that would restrict an ordinary user may not restrict the empowered user. Finally, audit mechanisms deter attacks because of the record and the analysis, thereby providing assurance that any violation of security policies will be detected.

Two distinct but related problems arise: which information to log and which information to audit. The decision of which events and actions should be audited requires a knowledge of the security policy of the system, what attempts to violate that policy involve, and how such attempts can be detected. The question of how such attempts can be detected raises the question of what should be logged: what commands must an attacker use to (attempt to) violate the security policy, what system calls must be made, who must issue the commands or system calls and in what order, what objects must be altered, and so forth. Logging of all events implicitly provides all this information; the problem is how to discern which parts of the information are relevant, which is the problem of determining what to audit.

21.2   Anatomy of an Auditing System

An auditing system consists of three components: the logger, the analyzer, and the notifier. These components collect data, analyze it, and report the results.

21.2.1   Logger

Logging mechanisms record information. The type and quantity of information are dictated by system or program configuration parameters. The mechanisms may record information in binary or human-readable form or transmit it directly to an analysis mechanism (see Section 21.2.2). A log-viewing tool is usually provided if the logs are recorded in binary form, so a user can examine the raw data or manipulate it using text-processing tools.

EXAMPLE: RACF [303] is a security enhancement package for the IBM MVS operating system and VM environment. It logs failed access attempts and the use of privileges to change security levels, and it can be set to log RACF interactions. The command LISTUSER lists information about RACF users as follows.

```
USER=EW125004   NAME=S.J.TURNER   OWNER=SECADM   CREATED=88.004
  DEFAULT-GROUP=HUMRES     PASSDATE=88.004    PASS-INTERVAL=30
  ATTRIBUTES=ADSP
  REVOKE DATE=NONE     RESUME-DATE=NONE
  LAST-ACCESS=88.020/14:15:10
  CLASS AUTHORIZATIONS=NONE
  NO-INSTALLATION-DATA
  NO-MODEL-NAME
  LOGON ALLOWED      (DAYS)  (TIME)
  -------------------------------
  ANYDAY                  ANYTIME
    GROUP=HUMRES AUTH=JOIN CONNECT-OWNER=SECADM
                                      CONNECT-DATE=88.004
      CONNECTS= 15  UACC=READ LAST-CONNECT=88.018/16:45:06
      CONNECT ATTRIBUTES=NONE
      REVOKE DATE=NONE RESUME DATE=NONE
    GROUP=PERSNL AUTH=JOIN CONNECT-OWNER=SECADM CONNECT-
    DATE:88.004
      CONNECTS= 25 UACC=READ LAST-CONNECT=88.020/14:15:10
      CONNECT ATTRIBUTES=NONE
      REVOKE DATE=NONE RESUME DATE=NONE
    SECURITY-LEVEL=NONE SPECIFIED
    CATEGORY AUTHORIZATION
       NONE SPECIFIED
```

RACF can also log its interactions with users, so that if a user attempts to modify it in any way, a log entry will be made.

EXAMPLE: Microsoft's Windows NT has three different sets of logs. The *system event* log contains records of events that Microsoft has determined warrant recording, such as system crashes, component failures, and other events. The *application event* log contains records that applications have added. These records are under the control of the applications. The *security event* log contains records corresponding to security-critical events such as logging in and out, system resource overuses, and accesses to system files. Only administrators can access the security event log.

The Windows NT logger defines a record as a header followed by a description and possibly an additional data field. The header contains an event identifier, user identity information (a user identifier and, if appropriate, an impersonation identifier), the date and time, the source that caused the record to be generated, the specific policy setting that triggered the record, and the computer involved. All records are kept in binary form. A tool called the *event viewer* translates the records into readable form.

An example security event log record might look like the following (but would be displayed in a graphic format).

```
Date:      2/12/2000        Source:    Security
Time:      13:03            Category:  Detailed Tracking
Type:      Success          EventID:   592
User:      WINDSOR\Administrator
Computer:  WINDSOR

Description:
A new process has been created:
   New Process ID:      2216594592
   Image File Name:
        \Program Files\Internet Explorer\IEXPLORE.EXE
   Creator Process ID: 2217918496
   User Name:          Administrator
   FDomain:            WINDSOR
   Logon ID:           (0x0,0x14B4c4)
```

This system logs process execution and termination in the security log. This event arose from the Administrator successfully executing the Internet Explorer. The Administrator configured the system to log successful process initiations (hence the value of the type field).

The designers of Windows NT allowed the system administrator to specify what should happen if the log should get full. The Administrator can have the system shut down when the log is full, disable logging completely, or cause the oldest entries to be overwritten or discarded.

21.2.2   Analyzer

An analyzer takes a log as input and analyzes it. The results of the analysis may lead to changes in the data being recorded, to detection of some event or problem, or both.

EXAMPLE: Suppose a system administrator wants to list all systems from which users have connected using the *rlogin* or *telnet* program, excluding systems at the site. The following *swatch* patterns [394, 395] match the lines generated by these remote connections.

```
/rlogin/&!/localhost/&!/*.site.com/
/telnet/&!/localhost/&!/*.site.com/
```

This line matches all log file entries containing the word "rlogin" and not containing either "localhost" or any string ending in ".site.com"—the local host's domain.

EXAMPLE: A database query control mechanism that uses prior queries to determine whether to answer contains both a logger and an analyzer. The logger records queries. When a user makes a new query, the analyzer examines the answers to past queries. If there are too many answers in common, the analyzer determines whether the overlap is within acceptable limits.

EXAMPLE: An intrusion detection system (see Chapter 22) detects attacks by analyzing log records for unexpected activity or for activity that is known to be an attempt to compromise the system. The analysis mechanism of the intrusion detection system is an example of an audit analysis mechanism.

21.2.3   Notifier

The analyzer passes the results of the analysis to the notifier. The notifier informs the analyst, and other entities, of the results of the audit. The entities may take some action in response to these results.

EXAMPLE: The *swatch* program mentioned above provides a notification facility. The configuration file to make *swatch* report *rlogin* and *telnet* connections is

```
/rlogin/&!/localhost/&!/*.site.com/mail staff
/telnet/&!/localhost/&!/*.site.com/mail staff
```

EXAMPLE: The notifier in the database query set size control blocks responses to queries that reduce the union of all previous query set sizes to less than r.

EXAMPLE: Consider the login system described on page 184, in which three consecutive failed login attempts disable the user's account. The logging mechanism records each attempt. The audit mechanism checks the number of consecutive failed login attempts. When this number reaches 3, the audit mechanism invokes the notifier, which reports the problem to the system administrator and disables the account.

21.3   Designing an Auditing System

A single, well-unified logging process is an essential component of computer security mechanisms [124]. The design of the logging subsystem is an integral part of the overall system design. The auditing mechanism, which builds on the data from the logging subsystem, analyzes information related to the security state of the system and determines if specific actions have occurred or if certain states have been entered.

The goals of the auditing process determine what information is logged [56]. In general, the auditors desire to detect violations of policy. Let A_i be the set of possible actions on a system. The security policy provides a set of constraints p_i that the design must meet in order for the system to be secure. This implies that the functions that could cause those constraints to fail must be audited.

Represent constraints as "*action* $\Rightarrow$ *condition*." Implication requires that the *action* be true (which means that the action occurred, in this context) before any valid conclusion about the *condition* can be deduced. Although this notation is unusual, it allows us simply to list constraints against which records can be audited. If the record's action is a "read," for example, and the constraint's *action* is a "write," then the constraint clearly holds. Furthermore, the goal of the auditing is to determine if the policy has been violated (causing a breach of security), so the result (success or failure) of the operation should match the satisfaction of the constraint. That is, if the constraint is true, the result is irrelevant, but if the constraint is false and the operation is successful, a security violation has occurred.

EXAMPLE: Recall that the simplest form of the Bell-LaPadula policy model linearly orders the security levels L_i. A subject S has the level $L(S)$, and the object O has the level $L(O)$. Under this policy, a system state is illegal if S reads O when $L(S) < L(O)$ or if S writes to O when $L(S) > L(O)$. The corresponding constraints are

1. S reads $O \Rightarrow L(S) \geq L(O)$
2. S writes $O \Rightarrow L(S) \leq L(O)$

Auditing for security violations merely requires auditing for writes from a subject to a lower-level object or reads from a higher-level object and checking for violations of these constraints. Logs must contain security levels of the subjects and objects involved, the action (to determine which constraint applies), and the result (success or failure). From these logs, testing for the violation of the constraints above is trivial.

Surprisingly, the *names* of the subject and object need not be recorded. However, in practice, the site security policy would require the security analyst to identify both the object of the violation and the user who attempted the violation. With this modification of the policy, the names of the subject and object would also be recorded.

To summarize in this limited case, auditing of reads and writes in a Bell-LaPadula-based systems requires logging the subject's security level, the object's security level, and the result of the action

21.3.1   Implementation Considerations

The example models above showed that analyzing the specific rules and axioms of a model reveal specific requirements for logging enough information to detect security violations. Interestingly enough, one need not assume that the system begins in a secure (or valid) state because all the models assert that the rules above are necessary but not sufficient for secure operation and auditing tests necessity. That is, if the auditing of the logs above shows a security violation, the system is not secure; but if it shows no violation, the system may still not be secure because if the initial state of the system is nonsecure, the result will (most likely) be a nonsecure state. Hence, if one desires to use auditing to detect that the system is not secure rather than detect actions that violate security, one needs also to capture the initial state of the system. In all cases, this means recording at start time the information that would be logged on changes in the state.

The examples above discussed logging requirements quite generically. The discussion of the Bell-LaPadula Model asserted specific types of data to be recorded during a "write." In an implementation, instantiating "write" may embody other system-specific operations ("append," "create directory," and so on). Moreover, the notion of a "write" may be quite subtle—for example, it may include alteration of protection modes, setting the system clock, and so forth. How this affects other entities is less clear, but typically it involves the use of covert channels (see Section 16.3) to write (send) information. These channels also must be modeled.

Naming also affects the implementation of logging criteria. Typically, objects have multiple names by which they can be accessed. However, if the criteria involve the entity, the system must log all constrained actions with that entity regardless of the name used. For example, each UNIX file has at least two representations: first, the usual one (accessed through the file system), and second, the low-level one (composed of disk blocks and an inode and accessed through the raw disk device). Logging all accesses to a particular file requires that the system log accesses through both representations. Systems generally do not provide logging and auditing at the disk block level (owing to performance). However, this means that UNIX systems generally cannot log all accesses to a given file.

21.3.2   Syntactic Issues

One critical issue is *how* to log: what data should be placed in the log file, and how it should be expressed, to allow an audit to draw conclusions that can be justified through reference to the log. This enables the analyst to display the reasoning behind the conclusions of the audit. The problem is that many systems log data ambiguously or do not present enough context to determine to what the elements of the log entry refer.

EXAMPLE: A UNIX system logs the names of files that a user retrieves using *ftp*. The log contains the file name */etc/passwd*. If the associated user is the anonymous user (indicating an anonymous login), then the file *actually* retrieved is the password file in the anonymous *ftp* subtree, not the system's password file. This is an example of the naming issue discussed in the preceding section.

This example demonstrates that a single log entry may not contain all the information about a particular action. The context of the entry conveys information. An analysis engine benefits from analyzing the context as well as the entries.

Flack and Atallah [323] suggest using a grammar-based approach to specifying log content. The grammar, expressed using a notation such as BNF, forces the designer to specify the syntax and semantic content of the log. Because the grammar of the log is completely specified, writing tools to extract information from the log requires development of a parser using the stated grammar. The analyzer can then process log entries using this grammar.

EXAMPLE: Suppose the following grammar describes log entries in a typical UNIX system's log for failed attempts to change user privileges.

```
entry : date host prog [ bad ] user [ "from" host ] "to"
                                user "on" tty
date  : daytime
host  : string
prog  : string ":"
bad   : "FAILED"
user  : string
tty   : "/dev/" string
```

Here, "string" and "daytime" are terminals and the quoted strings are literals. An analyst would check that this log entry format contained all the information needed for analysis. Then all programs that created these login entries would use a format derived from this grammar. This would provide consistency for the entries and would allow a single tool to extract the desired information from the log file.

Flack and Atallah point out that most current log entries are not specified using grammars. They examined BSM's description and entries (see Section 21.5.2) and found some ambiguities. For example, one BSM entry has two optional text fields followed by two mandatory text fields. The documentation does not specify how to interpret a sequence of three text fields in this context, so it is unclear *which* of the two optional text fields is present. They developed a BSM grammar that treats the optional fields as either both present or both absent, so three text fields generate a parse error. Any ambiguous log entries will thereby generate the exception. The analyst can then examine the log entry and best determine how to handle the situation.

21.3.3   Log Sanitization

A site may consider a set of information confidential. Logs may contain some of this information. If the site wishes to make logs available, it must delete the confidential information.

> **Definition 21–3.** Let U be a set of users. The policy P defines a set of information $C(U)$ that members of U are not allowed to see. Then the log L is *sanitized* with respect to P and U when all instances of information in $C(U)$ are deleted from L.

Confidentiality policies may impact logs in two distinct ways. First, P may forbid the information to leave the site. For example, the log may contain file names that give indications of proprietary projects or enable an industrial spy to determine the IP addresses of machines containing sensitive information. In this case, the unsanitized logs are available to the site administrators. Second, P may forbid the information to leave the system. In this case, the goal is to prevent the system administration from spying on the users. For example, if the Crashing Computer Company rents time on Denise's Distributed System, the CCC may not want the administrators of the system to determine what they are doing. Privacy considerations also affect the policy. Laws may allow the system administration to monitor users only when they have reason to believe that users are attacking the system or engaging in illegal activities. When they do look at the logs, the site must protect the privacy of other users so that the investigators cannot determine what activities the unsuspected users are engaged in.

The distinction controls the organization of the logging. Figure 21–1 shows where the sanitizers are applied. The top figure shows a sanitizer that removes information from an existing log file before the analysts examine it. This protects company confidentiality because the external viewers are denied information that the company wishes to keep confidential. It does *not* protect users' privacy because the site administration has access to the unsanitized log. The bottom figure shows a configuration in which users' privacy is protected, because the data is sanitized *before* it is written to the log. The system administrators cannot determine the true value of the sanitized data because it is never written to the log file. If they must be able to recover the data at some future point (to satisfy a court order, for example), the sanitizer can use cryptography to protect the data by encrypting it or by using a cryptographic scheme allowing a *reidentifier* to reassemble the unsanitized data.

This suggests two different types of sanitization.

> **Definition 21–4.** An *anonymizing sanitizer* deletes information in such a way that it cannot be reconstructed by either the recipient or the originator of the data in the log. A *pseudonymizing sanitizer* deletes information in such a way that the originator of the log can reconstruct the deleted information.

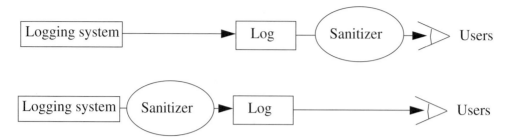

Figure 21–1   The different types of sanitization. The top figure shows logs being sanitized for external viewing. The bottom figure shows logs being sanitized for privacy of users. In this case, the sanitizer may save information in a separate log that enables the reconstruction of the omitted information. Cryptographic techniques enforce separation of privilege, so multiple administrators must agree to view the unsanitized logs.

These issues affect the design of the log. The sanitizer must preserve information and relationships relevant to the analysis of the data in the log. Otherwise, the analyzers may miss information that would enable them to detect attacks.

EXAMPLE: The Humongous Corporation wishes to conceal the IP addresses of a set of hosts containing proprietary data. The actual IP addresses are 10.163.5.10 through 10.163.5.14. The corporation wants to make its logs available to a consultant for analysis. The corporation must replace the IP addresses.

The log shows connections to port 25 (the electronic mail port) of the IP addresses in question. The order of the probing is as follows.

10.163.5.10, 10.163.5.11, 10.163.5.12, 10.163.5.13, 10.163.5.14

If the corporation replaces the IP addresses at random, the log entries will reflect e-mail being sent to a set of random hosts. If the corporation preserves the sequential order of the IP addresses, the log entries will reflect a port scanning probe. This often precedes an attack of some sort.

Biskup and Flegel [113] point out that one need not sanitize data that is not collected. Therefore, if a log is to be sanitized to provide anonymity, the simplest technique is simply not to collect the data. However, pseudonymity requires that the data be collected. Two techniques provide the hiding ability.

Suppose the policy allows site administrative personnel to view the data but others to see only the sanitized log. The first step is to determine a set of *pseudonyms* that preserve the relationships that are relevant to the analysis. The sanitizer replaces the data with the pseudonyms and maintains a table mapping pseudonyms to actual values (similar to a pseudonymous remailer; see Definition 14–5). Because all site administrators have access to this table, any of them could reconstruct the actual log.

The second technique is appropriate when the policy requires that some set of individuals, *not* including the system administrators, be able to see the unsanitized data (for example, law enforcement officers or intrusion analysts at a remote site) [113]. The unsanitized data cannot be stored in the clear on the system because the system security officers could then obtain the unsanitized data. One approach is to use a random enciphering key to encipher each sensitive datum and treat the decryption key as the representation of the datum. Then a secret sharing scheme allows the shadows of the decryption key to be split among as many people (or entities) as desired.

21.3.4   Application and System Logging

Application logs consist of entries made by applications. These entries typically use high-level abstractions, such as

```
su: bishop to root on /dev/ttyp0
smtp: delivery failed; could not connect to abcxy.net:25
```

These entries describe the problems (or results) encountered at the application layer. These logs usually do not include detailed information about the system calls that are made, the results that are returned, or the sequence of events leading up to the log entry.

System logs consist of entries of kernel events. These entries do not include high-level information. They report system calls and events. The first part of a system log corresponding to the *su* line above on a FreeBSD system is as follows.

```
3876 ktrace   CALL   execve(0xbfbff0c0,0xbfbff5cc,0xbfbff5d8)
3876 ktrace   NAMI   "/usr/bin/su"
3876 ktrace   NAMI   "/usr/libexec/ld-elf.so.1"
3876 su       RET    execve 0
3876 su       CALL   __sysctl(0xbfbff47c,0x2,0x2805c928,0xbfbff478,0,0)
3876 su       RET    __sysctl 0
3876 su       CALL   mmap(0,0x8000,0x3,0x1002,0xffffffff,0,0,0)
3876 su       RET    mmap 671473664/0x2805e000
3876 su       CALL   geteuid
3876 su       RET    geteuid 0
3876 su       CALL   getuid
3876 su       RET    getuid 0
3876 su       CALL   getegid
```

The system log consists of 1,879 lines detailing the system calls (the "CALL" lines), their return values ("RET"), file name lookups ("NAMI"), file I/O (including the data read or written), and any other actions requiring the kernel.

The difference in the two logs is their focus. If the audit is to focus on application events, such as failures to provide correct passwords (the *su* entry) or failures to deliver letters (the SMTP entry), an application log provides a simple way of recording the events for analysis. If system events such as file accesses or memory mapping affect the outcome of the auditing, then system logging is appropriate. In some cases, audits using both logs can uncover the system events leading up to an application event.

The advantage of system logs is the completeness of the information recorded. Rather than indicating that a configuration file could not be accessed, the system level log will identify the particular file, the type of access, and the reason for the failure. This leads to large log files that may require special handling. If a log overflows, the system can turn off logging, begin overwriting the least recent log entries, or shut down the system. Many systems allow the auditor to specify the types of information, or the specific system events, to be logged. By a judicious choice of which events to log, the danger of logs overflowing can be minimized.

The advantage of application logs is the level of abstraction. The applications provide the auditor with data that has undergone some interpretation before being entered. For example, rather than identifying a particular file as inaccessible, an application log should indicate the reason for accessing the file:

```
appx: cannot open config file appx.cf for reading: no such file
```

The correlation problem relates system and application logs. Given a system log composed of events from one execution of an application, and the corresponding application log, how can one determine which system log entries correspond to entries in the application log, and vice versa? This issue identifies the need to understand what an application level failure means at a system level and what application failures are caused by system level problems. The point is that the application logs are abstractions of system level events interpreted by the application in view of the previous application level events. By understanding the events at both the system and application levels, the auditor can learn about the causes of failures and determine if they are the results of attempts to breach system security.

21.4   A Posteriori Design

The design of an effective auditing subsystem is straightforward when one is aware of all possible policy violations and can detect them. Unfortunately, this is rarely the case. Most security breaches arise on existing systems that were not designed with security considerations in mind. In this case, auditing may have two different goals. The first goal is to detect *any* violations of a stated policy; the second is to detect actions that are known to be part of an attempt to breach security.

The difference is subtle but important. The first goal focuses on the policy and, as with the a priori design of an auditing subsystem, records (attempted) actions that violate the policy. The set of such actions may not be known in advance. The second goal focuses on *specific* actions that the managers of the system have determined indicate behavior that poses a threat to system security. Thus, one approaches the first goal by examining the desired policy, whereas one approaches the second goal by examining the actions (attacks) that pose the threat.

21.4.1   Auditing to Detect Violations of a Known Policy

Implementation of this type of auditing is similar to the auditing subsystem design discussed in Section 21.3. The idea is to determine whether or not a state violates the policy. Unlike mechanisms designed into the system, the auditing mechanisms must be integrated into the existing system. Analysts must analyze the system to determine what actions and settings are consistent with the policy. They then design mechanisms for checking that the actions and settings are in fact consistent with the policy. There are two ways to proceed: state-based auditing and transition-based auditing.

21.4.1.1   State-Based Auditing

The designer can opt for a state-based approach, in which states of the system are analyzed to determine if a policy violation exists.

> **Definition 21–5.** A *state-based logging mechanism* records information about a system's state. A *state-based auditing mechanism* determines whether or not a state of the system is unauthorized.

Typically, a state-based auditing mechanism is built on a state-based logging system. There is a tacit assumption that a state-based logging mechanism can take a snapshot of the system. More generally, the state-based logging mechanism must obtain a consistent state. Algorithms such as Chandy-Lamport [159] can supply a consistent state for distributed resources, but obtaining a state for nondistributed resources requires the resources to be quiescent while the state is obtained. On most systems in which multiple resources supply components of the state, this is infeasible.

EXAMPLE: File system auditing tools that scan file systems and compare results to a database, looking for changes, are usually discussed under the rubric of "static analysis tools." This implies that they analyze a single state of the system. In fact, unless they are run on quiescent file systems, these tools take slices of different states because the attributes are read while the system transitions as other programs access the resource. The effect of this incremental construction of a union of slices of the states during the tool's run can affect the correctness of the report. If a test that the scanner performs near the end of the tool's run depends on some assumptions derived from a check made near the beginning of its run, the state may change and the test may appear to succeed, when in reality it reveals no (or misleading) information. With consistent static analysis, because the state does not change during the run of the tool, the tool may rely on the assumptions, but with inconsistent static analysis, such reliance leads to a classic "time of check to time of use" flaw. The same observation holds for any inconsistent static tool that relies on assumptions deduced from an earlier part of its current incarnation.

21.4.1.2   Transition-Based Auditing

The designer can opt for a transition-based approach, in which actions that could violate the policy are checked to determine if they do indeed cause violations.

> **Definition 21–6.** A *transition-based logging mechanism* records information about an action on a system. A *transition-based auditing mechanism* examines the current state of the system and the proposed transition (command) to determine if the result will place the system in an unauthorized state.

An important observation is that transition-based logging may not be sufficient to enable a transition-based auditing mechanism to determine if the system will enter an unauthorized state. Specifically, if the system begins in a state that violates policy, a transition-based auditing mechanism will not detect the security problem if the transition alone was analyzed and determined not to move the system from a secure state to a nonsecure state. For this reason, transition-based logging is used only when specific transitions always require an examination (as in the example of changes of privilege) or when some state analysis is also performed.

EXAMPLE: The program *tcp_wrappers* intercepts TCP connections to UNIX-based systems and determines whether or not the connections are to be allowed. The connections that are to be denied are identified in the file *hosts.deny*. The logging mechanism determines where the connection comes from. The auditing mechanism compares that point of origin (the IP address, the destination port, and possibly the user name) with the data in the *hosts.deny* file. If the point of origin matches the data in the *hosts.deny* file, the connection is blocked. This is transition-based auditing because the mechanism analyzes a command (the putative connection) to determine if it will put the system in an unauthorized state (by allowing a connection in the *hosts.deny* file). The current state of the system is not examined.

EXAMPLE: America Online's instant messaging system allows a user to sign on from at most one computer at a time. The mechanism that detects when a user tries to sign on from two computers simultaneously is a mixture of state-based and transition-based auditing. It examines the transition (the sign-on) and the current state (whether or not that user signed on already). If the transition would put the system in an unauthorized state (the user signed on twice), the audit mechanism reports the problem. The system responds by blocking the second sign-on.

21.4.2   Auditing to Detect Known Violations of a Policy

In many cases, the security policy is not stated explicitly. However, certain behaviors are considered to be "nonsecure." For example, an attack that floods a network to the point that it is not usable, or accessing of a computer by an unauthorized person, would violate the implicit security policy. Under these conditions, analysts can determine specific sequences of commands, or properties of states, that indicate a security violation and look for that violation.

EXAMPLE: Daniels and Spafford [229] present an analysis of the Land attack [198], which causes a denial of service by causing the target of the attack to hang or to respond very slowly. This attack is built on an exchange that begins a TCP connection.

When a TCP connection begins, the source sends a SYN packet to the destination. This packet contains a sequence number s. The destination receives the packet and returns a SYN/ACK packet containing the acknowledgment number $s + 1$ and a second sequence number t. The source receives this packet and replies with the acknowledgment number $t + 1$. Figure 21–2 illustrates this exchange, called a *three-way handshake*.

The Land attack arises from an ambiguity of the TCP specification [459]. When the source and destination differ, or the TCP port numbers of the source and destination differ, the two sequence numbers s and t are from different processes. But what happens if the source and destination addresses and ports are the same? The TCP specification is ambiguous.

Consider what happens in the three-way handshake in this case. The target host receives a SYN packet with sequence number s. It responds with a SYN/ACK packet containing sequence number t and acknowledgment number $s + 1$. At this point, the internal state of the connection in that host is that the next acknowledgment number will be $t + 1$. Because the source and destination addresses and ports are the same, the packet returns to the host. The host checks the packet and finds that the acknowledgment number $(s + 1)$ is incorrect. At this point, the TCP specification suggests two different ways to handle the situation.

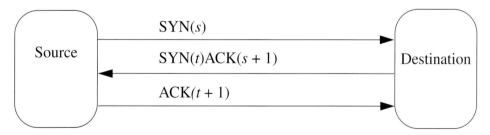

Figure 21–2   The TCP three-way handshake. The SYN packet is a TCP packet with sequence number *s* (or *t*) and the SYN flag set. Likewise, the ACK packet is a TCP packet with acknowledgment number *s* + 1 (or *t* + 1) and the ACK flag set. The middle message is a single TCP packet with both SYN and ACK flags set.

According to one part of the specification,[1] the connection should send a reset (RST). If this is done, it terminates the connection and the attack fails.

According to a different part of the specification,[2] the host should reply with an empty packet with the current sequence number and the expected acknowledgment number. Hence, the host sends a packet with sequence number $t + 1$ and acknowledgment number $s + 1$. Naturally, it receives that packet. It checks that the acknowledgment number is correct, and—again—it is not. Repeating the sequence causes the same packet to be generated, resulting in an infinite loop. If the host has disabled interrupts during this part, the system hangs. Otherwise, it runs very slowly, servicing interrupts but doing little else. The denial of service attack is now successful.

Detecting this attack requires that the initial Land packet be detected. The characteristic of this packet is that the source and destination addresses and port numbers are the same. So, the logging requirement is to record that information. The audit requirement is to report any packets for which the following condition holds.

```
source address = destination address and
          source port number = destination port number
```

21.5   Auditing Mechanisms

Different systems approach logging in different ways. Most systems log all events by default and allow the system administrator to disable the logging of specific events. This leads to bloated logs.

In this section, we present examples of information that systems record and give some details of the auditing mechanisms.

21.5.1   Secure Systems

Systems designed with security in mind have auditing mechanisms integrated with the system design and implementation. Typically, these systems provide a language or interface that allows system managers to configure the system to report specific events or to monitor accesses by a particular subject or to a particular object. This is controlled at the audit subsystem so that irrelevant actions or accesses are not recorded.

EXAMPLE: The VAX VMM system is designed to meet the requirements of the A1 classification of the TCSEC [257]. This classification requires that impending security violations be detected, actions be taken to protect the system, auditing based on

---

[1] See p. 36 of the TCP specification [459].
[2] See p. 69 of the TCP specification [459].

user or object be allowed, and extensive administrative support be provided. Because the VAX VMM was intended to be a production system, the audit mechanism could have only minimal impact on system performance and had to be highly reliable [807].

The system is designed as a layered kernel, and so the logging mechanisms are not unified. Logging occurs at each place in the hierarchy where events of interest occur. Each layer also audits accesses to the objects it controls. In essence, the auditing mechanisms are distributed throughout the layers.

After each layer has audited its information, the logs and results of the audit are passed to the audit subsystem for future use. The audit subsystem manages the system log and has a single entry point (called *AUD$audit*). The parameters are event identification, status (the result), auxiliary data (which depends on the event), and the caller's name. The audit subsystem records the event if the event affects a subject or object listed in an audit table and if the severity of the event (derived from the status code) exceeds that associated with the entity in the audit table. The audit subsystem then adds the date and time, the subject's name and type, and other data to the log entry, dumps the entry into a buffer, and signals the audit logging process, which writes the log event to the log.

Two types of events are always logged. The first results from the caller's setting a special flag and is under the programmers' control. The second is an attempt to violate policy and is required by the criteria used to certify systems. Protection violations and login failures are recorded when the event occurs repeatedly. Use of covert channels is also flagged.

When the log reaches 75% of its capacity, the kernel notifies the audit process to archive the log contents. This resets the log. This follows the philosophy that the kernel never runs without auditing. Should archiving be impossible (as a result of full disks, for example), the system stops.

Audit reduction is based on time (before or after a particular date and time), security or integrity level (at or above a given level), and severity.

EXAMPLE: The Compartmented Mode Workstation [225] auditing subsystem's interface [721] illustrates how the auditing mechanisms interact with users, processes, and the kernel. The auditing subsystem maintains a table of auditable events for the system. Each entry indicates whether or not logging is turned on and what type of logging to use. At the user level, the command *chaud* allows the system manager to turn auditing on or off, to indicate what events and objects are to be audited, and to find out which events and objects are being logged. If the auditor changes the entities being audited, the log is not interrupted.

At the process level, the system call *audit_on* turns on logging for an event and identifies the log file in which to place records. The call *audit_off* turns off logging for that event. The *audit_write* system call takes a pointer to a log entry, validates the putative ID number, and writes it out if logging is turned on for that event. This allows processes to write their own log entries. Finally, the calls *audit_suspend* and *audit_resume* allow the process to turn off system logging for that process. Any calls to *audit_write* are honored.

Some processes, such as the window manager, perform their own auditing. The problem is that low-level auditing, at the system call level, does not map easily into more abstract, high-level events. By disabling low-level auditing and writing its own records, the window manager can maintain a high level of abstraction for its logged events.

Once the process makes a system call, the interface checks that the process is to be audited and that the *audit_suspend* is not in effect. The first three system call arguments are recorded, but if any of them is a pointer, the pointer is not resolved.

At the kernel level, the *audit_write* routine determines what to do with the record. If there is room in the log, it writes the record out. If not, it can halt the system, discard the record, or disable the events that will cause logging. This last technique is unusual, but its goal is to impact system functionality as little as possible while ensuring that auditing will record all events of interest.

The logged events are analyzed using a tool called *redux*. This tool converts records into a printable format and prints events that satisfy conditions based on users, objects, security levels, and events.

21.5.2   Nonsecure Systems

Auditing subsystems for systems not designed with security in mind are generally for purposes of accounting. Although these subsystems can be used to check for egregious security violations, they rarely record the level of detail or the types of events that enable security officers to determine if security has been violated. The level of detail needed is typically provided by an added subsystem.

EXAMPLE: The Basic Security Module (BSM) [887] is an enhancement of SunOS system security. Each log consists of files, and each file is composed of individual records. A record is made up of a sequence of tokens. The record size is not fixed; there is a begin token and an end token. Each record refers to an auditable event. These events are defined either at the system level ("kernel event"), such as a system call, or through library function calls from an application ("application event"), such as a failure to authenticate successfully to the login program. Finally, BSM groups records into audit event classes. These classes are based on the event triggering the generation of the record and can be created either before an audit log is created (in which case the event classes that are defined tell the system which events to generate records for) or after the log is created (in which case the classes that are defined control which records are given to the analysis tools). The latter is an example of log reduction, and the program *auditreduce* allows analysts to define the classes of events about which records are to be extracted.

BSM defines a token as an identification field followed by a series of information fields. These tokens encapsulate user identity (process, which includes a real, effective, and original UID and effective group ID as well as process ID), group list, file system information (pathname and attributes), IPC usage (IPC token, IPC attributes), networking (IP port number, IP address), and process and system call information (return value, arguments) as well as more general information (text, data, opaque). This enables an analyst to tie tokens and records to events of interest and to extract enough information to determine what was done, who did it, and (if applicable) what the outcome was.

An example BSM log record might look like this:

```
header,35,AUE_EXIT,Wed Sep 18 11:35:28 1991, + 570000 msec,
process,bishop,root,root,daemon,1234,
return,Error 0,5
trailer,35
```

The information is stored in a binary format to minimize log size. A program called *praudit* formats and prints records when a human-readable form is needed.

The determination of what to log and what to audit is left to the system managers. This allows BSM to be used in multiple environments and under different policies. This is consistent with BSM being an add-on security module. It provides other security mechanisms as well.

21.6   Examples: Auditing File Systems

The difference between designing a logging and auditing mechanism for an existing file system protocol and designing a logging and auditing mechanism for a new file system protocol illuminates the differences between a priori and a posteriori audit design. This section compares and contrasts the design of an audit mechanism for NFS and the design of a new file system intended to provide logging and auditing.

A bit of background first. Many sites allow computers and users to share file systems, so that one computer (called a *client host*) requests access to the file system of another computer (a *server host*). The server host responds by *exporting* a directory of its file system; the client host *imports* this information and arranges its own file system so that the imported directory (called the *server host's mount point*) appears as a directory in the client host's file system (this directory is called the *client host's mount point*).

21.6.1   Audit Analysis of the NFS Version 2 Protocol[3]

Consider a site connected to the Internet. It runs a local area network (LAN) with several UNIX systems sharing file systems using the Network File System [886] protocol. What should be logged?

---

[3] This analysis was done with Jeremy Frank and Christopher Wee.

We first review the NFS protocol. When a client host wishes to mount a server's file system, its kernel contacts the server host's MOUNT server with the request. The MOUNT server first checks that the client is authorized to mount the requested file system and how the client will mount the requested system. If the client is authorized to mount the file system, the MOUNT server returns a *file handle* naming the mount point of the server's file system. The client kernel then creates an entry in its file system corresponding to the server's mount point. In addition, either the client host or the server host may restrict the type of accesses to the networked file system. If the server host sets the restrictions, the programs on the server host that implement NFS will enforce the restrictions. If the client host sets the restrictions, the client kernel will enforce the restrictions and the server programs will be unaware that any restrictions have been set.

When a client process wishes to access a file, it attempts to open the file as though the file were on a local file system. When the client kernel reaches the client host's mount point in the path, the client kernel sends the file handle of the server host's mount point (which it obtained during the mount) to resolve the next component (name) of the path to the server host's NFS server using a LOOKUP request. If the resolution succeeds, this server returns the requested file handle. The client kernel then requests attributes of the component (a GETATTR request), and the NFS server supplies them. If the file is a directory, the client kernel iterates (passing the directory's file handle and the next component of the path in a LOOKUP request and using the obtained file handle to get the attributes in a GETATTR request) until it obtains a file handle corresponding to the desired file object. The kernel returns control to the calling process, which can then manipulate the file by name or descriptor; the kernel translates these manipulations into NFS requests, which are sent to the server host's NFS server.

Because NFS is a stateless protocol, the NFS servers do not keep track of which files are in use. The file handle is a capability. Furthermore, many versions of NFS require the kernel to present the requests,[4] although some accept requests from any user. In all cases, the server programs can identify the user making the request by examining the contents of the underlying messages.

The site policy drives the logging and auditing requirements because we are capturing events relevant to violations of that policy. In our example, the site wishes to regulate sharing of file systems among all systems on its LAN (with individual restrictions enforced through the NFS mechanism). All imported file systems are supposed to be as secure as the local file systems. Therefore, the policy is as follows.

P1. NFS servers will respond only to authorized clients.
> The site authorizes only local hosts to act as clients. Under this policy, the site administrators could allow hosts not on the LAN to become clients, and so the policy could be less restrictive than the statement above suggests.

---

[4] Validation is from the originating port number; the NFS implementations assume that only the superuser (operator) can send requests from ports with numbers less than 1024.

P2. The UNIX access controls regulate access to the server's exported file system.

Once a client has imported a server host's file system, the client host's processes may access that file system as if it were local. In particular, accessing a file requires search permission on all the ancestor directories (both local and imported).

An important ramification is the effect of the UNIX policy on file type. Only the local superuser can create device (block and character special) files locally, so users should not be able to create device files on any imported file system (or change an existing file's attributes to make it a device file). However, this policy does not restrict a client host from importing a file system that has device files.

P3. No client host can access a nonexported file system.

This means that exporting a file system allows clients to access files at or below the server host's mount point. Exporting a file system does not mean that a client host can access any file on the server host; the client can access only exported files.

These policies produce several constraints.

C1. File access granted $\Rightarrow$ client is authorized to import file system, user can search all parent directories and can access file as requested, and file is descendant of server host's file system mount point.

C2. Device file created or file type changed to device $\Rightarrow$ user has UID of 0.

C3. Possession of a file handle $\Rightarrow$ file handle issued to that user.

Because the MOUNT and NFS server processes issue file handles when a user successfully accesses a file, possession of a file handle implies that the user could access the file. If another user acquires the file handle without accessing either server, that user might access files without authorization.

C4. Operation succeeds $\Rightarrow$ a similar operation local to the client would succeed.

This follows from the second policy rule. Because an ordinary user cannot mount a file system locally, the MOUNT operation should fail if the requesting user is not a superuser.

These constraints follow immediately from the three policy rules.

A transition from a secure to a nonsecure state can occur only when an NFS-related command is issued. Figure 21–3 lists the NFS commands that a client may issue. One set takes no arguments and performs no actions; these commands do not affect the security state of the system. A second set takes file handles as arguments (as well as other arguments) and returns data (including status information). The third set also takes file handles as arguments and returns file handles as results.

Those operations that take file handles as arguments require that the auditor validate the constraint. When a server issues a file handle, the file handle, the user to whom it is issued, and the client to which it is sent must be recorded.

Request	*Arguments*	*Action*
No arguments		
NULL	None	No action
WRITECACHE	None	*Unused*
Returns nonfile handle		
GETATTR	fh	Get attributes of the file
SETATTR	fh, attrib	Set attributes of the file
READ	fh, off, ct	Get ct bytes at position off from file
WRITE	fh, off, ct, data	Write ct bytes of data at position off to file
REMOVE	dh, fn	Delete named file in directory
RENAME	dh1, dh2, fn1, fn2	Rename file
LINK	fh, dh, fn	Create link named fn for file in directory
SYMLINK	dh, fn1, fn2, attrib	Create slink named fn1 for fn2 in directory
READLINK	fh	Get file name that symbolic link refers to
RMDIR	dh, fn	Delete named directory in directory
READDIR	dh, off, ct	Read ct bytes at position off from directory
STATFS	dh	Get file system information
Returns file handle		
ROOT	none	Get root file handle (*obsolete*)
CREATE	dh, fn, attrib	Create file fn in directory with attributes
MKDIR	dh, fn, attrib	Create directory fn in directory with attributes
LOOKUP	dh, fn	Get file handle of named file in directory

Figure 21–3   NFS operations. In the Arguments and Action columns, "fh" is "file handle," "fn" is "file name," "dh" is "directory handle" (effectively, a file handle), "attrib" is "file attributes," "off" is "offset" (which need not be a byte count; it is positioning information), "ct" is "count," "link" is "direct alias," and "slink" is "indirect alias."

L1. When a file handle is issued, the server must record the file handle, the user (UID and GID) to whom it is issued, and the client host making the request.

The semantics of the UNIX file system say that access using a path name requires that the user be able to search each directory. However, once a file has been opened, access to the file requires the file descriptor and is not affected by the search permissions of parent directories. From the operation arguments, file handles seem to refer to open objects. For example, SYMLINK creates a symbolic link, which is effectively a write to a directory object; the argument to SYMLINK is the directory's handle. Hence, file handles resemble descriptors more than path names, so the auditor need not verify access permission whenever a user supplies a file handle. The only issue is whether the server issued the file handle to the user performing the operation.

L2. When a file handle is supplied as an argument, the server must record the file handle and the user (UID and GID).

A file handle allows its possessor to access the file to which the handle refers. Any operation that generates a file handle must record the user and relevant permissions for the object in question. For example, on a LOOKUP, recording the search permissions of the containing directory enables the auditor to determine if the user should have had access to the named file. On a CREATE, recording the write permissions of the containing directory indicates whether the use could legitimately write to the containing directory.

L3. When a file handle is issued, the server must record the relevant attributes of any containing object.

Finally, whether the operation succeeds or fails, the system must record the operation's status so that the auditor can verify the result.

L4. Record the results of each operation.

Because each operation performs a different function, we consider the audit criteria of each operation separately. We illustrate the process for *mount* and *lookup* and leave the rest as an exercise for the reader.

Constraints C1 and C4 define the audit criteria for MOUNT.

A1. Check that the MOUNT server denies all requests by unauthorized client hosts or users to import a file system that the server host exports.

("Unauthorized users" refers specifically to those users who could not perform the operation locally.) This means that the MOUNT server must record L3 and L4. Constraints C1 and C3 give the audit criteria for LOOKUP.

A2. Check that the file handle comes from a client host and a user to which it was issued.

A3. Check that the directory has the file system mount point as an ancestor and that the user has search permission on the directory.

The check for the client being authorized to import the file system (in C1) is implicit in A3 because if the client host is not authorized to import the file system, the client host will not obtain the file handle for the server host's mount point. Performing this audit requires logging of L2, L3 (the relevant attributes being owner, group, type, and permission), and L4. Audit criterion A3 requires recording of the name of the file being looked up; from this and the file handle, the auditor can reconstruct the ancestors of the file.

L5. Record the name of the file argument in the LOOKUP operation.

Given the logs and the auditing checks, an analyst can easily determine if the policy has been violated. This is a transition-based mechanism because checks are performed during the actions and not during an evaluation of the current state of the system.

21.6.2   The Logging and Auditing File System (LAFS)

LAFS [932] takes a different approach. LAFS is a file system that records user level actions taken on files. A policy language allows an auditor to automate checks for violations of policy.

The LAFS file system is implemented as an extension of an existing file system, NFS, in the prototype. A user creates a directory using the *lmkdir* command and then attaches it to LAFS with the *lattach* command. For example, if the file *policy* contains a policy for LAFS, the commands

```
lmkdir /usr/home/xyzzy/project policy
lattach /usr/home/xyzzy/project /lafs/xyzzy/project
```

attach the directory and its contents to LAFS. All references to the files through LAFS will be logged.

LAFS consists of three main components, along with a name server and a file manager. The *configuration assistant*, which interacts with the name server and protection mechanisms of the underlying file system, sets up the required protection modes. This part is invoked when a file hierarchy is placed under LAFS (using *lattach*) and by the LAFS name server. The *audit logger* logs accesses to the file. The LAFS file manager invokes it whenever a process accesses the file. This allows LAFS to log accesses by LAFS-unaware applications. It in turn invokes the file manager of the underlying file system. At no point does the LAFS file manager perform access checking; that is left to the underlying file system. The *policy checker* validates policies and checks that logs conform to the policy.

A goal of LAFS is to avoid modifying applications to enable the logging. This allows users to use existing applications rather than having to develop new ones. The interface is therefore a set of three "virtual" files associated with each file in the LAFS hierarchy. The file *src.c* is a regular file. The file *src.c%log* contains a log of all accesses to *src.c*. The file *src.c%policy* contains a description of the access control policy for the file *src.c*. Accessing the virtual file *src.c%audit* triggers an audit in which the accesses of *src.c* are compared with the policy for the file. Any accesses not conforming to the policy are listed. The virtual files do not appear in file listings; the LAFS interface recognizes the extensions and provides the required access.

The policy language is simple yet powerful. It consists of a sequence of lines in the *%policy* files of the form

```
action:date&time:file:user:application:operation:status
```

For example, the following line says that users may not play the game *wumpus* from 9 A.M. to 5 P.M. The status field is omitted, because the policy checker is to report any attempts to play *wumpus* whether they succeed or not.

```
prohibit:0900-1700:*:*:wumpus:exec
```

The following lines describe a policy for controlling accesses to source code files in a project under development.

```
allow:*:Makefile:*:make:read
allow:*:Makefile:Owner:makedepend:write
allow:*:*.o,*.out:Owner,Group:gcc,ld:write
allow:-010929:*.c,*.h:Owner:emacs,vi,ed:write
allow:010930-:RCS/:librarian:rcs,co,ci:write
```

The first line allows the *make* program to read the Makefile on behalf of any user on the system. The second line allows the owner of the Makefile (indicated by the distinguished user "Owner") to change the Makefile by running the command *makedepend* (which adds dependencies among source code). The owner, or anyone in the group, of an object file can re-create the object file. Line 4 allows the owner of the source code to modify the source files using the *emacs* editor, the *vi* editor, or the *ed* editor, provided that the modification occurs before September 29, 2001. The last line allows the user "librarian" to write into the directory RCS using the *rcs*, *co*, and *ci* commands on any date from September 30, 2001, on. The purpose of this line is to allow the librarian to commit source code changes. The preceding line requires that all such changes be made before September 30, so (presumably) the project code is to be frozen on September 30, 2001.

As users access files, LAFS logs the accesses in a human-readable format, and when the user accesses the appropriate *%audit* file, the audit reports all violations of the relevant policy.

21.6.3   Comparison

The NFS auditing mechanism and the LAFS have important similarities. In both cases, a security policy controls access, and the goal of both mechanisms is to detect and report attempted violations of the policy. Both have auditing mechanisms built into the file system.

The differences are also crucial. LAFS is "stacked" on top of NFS, so if a file is not bound to LAFS, no accesses to it are logged or audited. With the modifications of NFS, an attacker could avoid being audited only by not using NFS. (This is a typical problem with security mechanisms layered on top of existing protocols or other mechanisms.) The auditing mechanisms in NFS are at a lower layer than those in LAFS (because of the stacking). However, LAFS allows users to specify policies for sets of files and to perform audits. The analysis of NFS above is not as flexible. There, a site sets the policy for NFS. Users cannot define their own policies. Thus, the NFS auditing mechanism will examine all file accesses, whereas LAFS may not. This affects not only auditing but also performance because if only a few files need to be audited, much of the effort by the NFS mechanisms is unnecessary. Finally, modifying NFS for auditing requires changes in several privileged daemons, whereas adding LAFS requires no modifications to existing system daemons and a kernel.

Which scheme to use depends on several factors, such as the ability to modify the NFS daemons. The NFS auditing modifications and LAFS can work together, the NFS modifications being for the low-level system checking and LAFS for user level auditing.

21.7   Audit Browsing

In addition to running audit mechanisms to analyze log files, auditors sometimes look through the log files themselves. The audit mechanisms may miss information or irregularities in the log that a knowledgeable auditor can detect. Furthermore, the audit mechanisms may be unsophisticated. By examining the logs directly, the auditors may uncover evidence of previously unknown patterns of misuse and attack. Finally, few systems provide a fully integrated suite of logs. Most have several different log files, each for a different set of applications or kernel events. The logs are usually ordered by timestamp and do not show relations other than the time of day and the program (process) creating the entry. For example, a log typically does not indicate two different programs making a sequence of accesses to a particular file.

The goal of an audit browsing tool is to present log information in a form that is easy for the analyst to understand and use. Specifically, the tool must indicate associations between log entries that are of interest to the analyst. Hoagland, Wee, and Levitt [424] identify six basic browsing techniques.

1. *Text display* shows the logs in a textual format. The format may be fixed, or it may be defined by the analyst through postprocessing. The auditor may search for events based on name, time, or some other attribute; however, the attribute must be recorded in the log file. This method does not indicate relationships among events, entries, and entities.

2. *Hypertext display* shows the logs as a set of hypertext documents with associated log entries linked by hypertext constructs. This allows the auditor to follow relationships between entries and entities by following the links. The browser can include additional information about entities as well. The disadvantage is that the view of the log information is local because the browser does not highlight global relationships in a manner that is clear and easy to understand.

3. *Relational database browsing* requires that the logs be stored in a relational database. The auditor then issues queries to the database, and the database performs the correlations and associations before it replies to the query. The advantage of this method is that the database performs the correlations and can do so after the logs have been preprocessed. That is, the auditor need not know in advance what associations are of interest. The disadvantage is that the representation of the output to the query is usually textual. Furthermore, some preprocessing is required because the elements of the logs must be separated to provide the information for the database. The expected queries imply how this is to be done. This may limit the associations between entities and events that the database can exhibit.

4. *Replay* presents the events of interest in temporal order. It highlights temporal relationships. For example, if three logs are replayed on a single screen, the temporal order of the events in the log will be intermingled and

the order of occurrence across the logs will clearly indicate the order of the events in a way that the analyst can see.

5. *Graphing* provides a visual representation of the contents of logs. Typically, nodes represent entities such as processes and files, and edges represent associations. The associations indicate relationships between various entities. For example, processes may have incoming edges from their parents and outgoing edges to their children. The process hierarchy then becomes clear. One problem with this technique is the size of the drawing. If the area in which the graph is drawn is too small, the information may be unreadable. Reducing the logs to eliminate some information ameliorates this problem. The graph may also represent high-level entities (such as groups of processes or file systems) and their relationships, and the auditor can expand the high-level entities in order to examine relationships within the components of those entities.

6. *Slicing* obtains a minimum set of log events and objects that affect a given object. This comes from the traditional notion of slicing [933], a program debugging technique that extracts a minimum set of statements that affect a given variable. Its advantage is that it focuses attention on the sequence of events, and related objects, that affect some entity. Its disadvantage, like that of hypertext browsing, is the locality of the technique.

Audit browsing tools emphasize associations that are of interest to the auditor. Hence, their configurations depend on the goals of the audit.

EXAMPLE: The Visual Audit Browser tool kit [424] was designed for general-purpose audit browsing. It consists of four tools. Each tool takes BSM logs as input. The *frame visualizer* generates a graphical representation of the logs. The *movie maker* generates a sequence of graphs corresponding to the logs. Each successive audit event generates a new graph with a new node and edge(s) corresponding to the audit event. The *hypertext generator* produces one page for each user in the log, one page for each file modified in the log, a page summarizing the audit records, and an index page. The pages are in HTML, so any Web browser can view them. The *focused audit browser* combines slicing and graphing. The auditor enters the name of a node, and the browser displays that node, the node's incoming and outgoing edges, and the nodes at the ends of those edges.

Suppose a file is changed. The auditor uses the *focused audit browser*, with the file as the initial focus. The edges show which processes have altered the file and how. The auditor determines which process(es) may have caused the unexpected change, focuses on one of the suspect processes, and iterates until it is determined how the attacker gained access to the system (through a login, through a network daemon, and so on). At this point, the auditor needs to determine whether a masquerade is occurring. From the processes seen earlier, the auditor knows the audit UID of the attacker. She uses the *hypertext generator* to access the page with all audit records involving that audit UID and examines all entries on that page for irregular activity. She can also use the *frame visualizer* to graph the sequence of process creations.

Once the auditor has found the entry point, she can probably uncover the vulnerability and then work forward to construct the actions that the attacker took. Finally, the *movie maker* can generate a small movie showing the actions that the attacker took. This will be a compelling visual record for law enforcement authorities and may aid the auditor during presentations to nontechnical people.

EXAMPLE: MieLog [892] computes counts of single words and word pairs in logs. It allows the auditor to define a threshold count. Words and word pairs with counts higher than the threshold are colored to make them stand out. The display of MieLog consists of four fields. The *tag appearance frequency area* has a colored tile indicating the frequency of appearance (red meaning rare). The *time information area* contains a bar graph indicating the number of log entries in that period of time. Clicking on the bar brings up the log entries for that time period. The *outline of message area* shows the outline of the log messages, colored to match the frequency in the *tag appearance frequency area*. The fourth field, the *message in text area*, displays the log entry under study and its surrounding areas. The words and word pairs are colored to reflect their frequencies.

    As an example, an administrator examining a log file notices an unusual gap in the *time information area*. There are no log messages recorded during the period of time in the gap. The system administrator focuses on the log entries just before and just after the gap, to determine why the logging turned off and then turned back on. The color of the words in those log entries will aid the auditor in looking for unusual log entries, words, or phrases indicating an attack.

    Developing a visual interface to logs is as much an art as a science. The science lies in determining what to display; the art lies in the graphics used to express the desired relationships and entities. The human should be able to grasp the relevant parts of the log quickly and to pursue lines of inquiry quickly and easily.

21.8   Summary

Logging is the collection of information; auditing is its analysis. Auditing consists of analysis, which is the study of information gleaned from the log entries, and notification, which is the reporting of the results of the study (and possibly the taking of appropriate actions).

    Designing an audit system requires that the goals of the audit be well formed. Typically, the security policy defines these goals. The audit mechanism reports attempts to violate the constraints imposed by the security policy, such as a subject's attempt to write to a lower-level object. Several considerations affect the auditing. For example, names in the logs must be resolvable to an object. The logs must be well structured to allow unambiguous and consistent parsing. They may need to be sanitized before or after analysis. Application logs reflect actions of the application; system logs reflect events within the operating system.

Auditing mechanisms should be designed into the system. These mechanisms may also be added after the system is completed. In this case, the mechanism may report violations of a defined security policy or may report actions that are considered to be security threats (whether a security policy is defined precisely or not).

A mechanism enabling auditors to browse the logs aids in the analysis. Such a browser helps auditors locate problems that they have not thought of and may speed the analysis of problems that other audit mechanisms have reported.

21.9   Further Reading

Papers about systems designed with security in mind discuss the auditing mechanism and the rationale behind it, usually pointing to the relevant requirements. Sibert [827] discusses auditing in the SunOS MLS system. Rao [743] discusses auditing in an avionics system. Banning and her colleagues [56] discuss auditing of distributed systems. Shieh and Gligor [820] discuss auditing of covert channels.

Interfaces to the logging mechanism control how data can be logged and, once logged, accessed. The POSIX group has defined an interface for UNIX-like systems [726]. The Clio logging service [318] provides an interface that mimics append-only files. The S4 service [883] uses journaling techniques to secure logs even if the system has been compromised.

Various techniques based on artificial intelligence have been used to analyze logs [420, 564, 837, 897]. Data mining techniques show great promise [407]. Jajodia, Gadia, Bhargava, and Sibley [466] discuss a database model that makes past and current log records available for analysis.

Holley and Millar [431] discuss approaches to auditing an online real-time computer system. Markantonakis [591] discusses the application of smart card logs, and Markantonakis and Xenitellis [592] present an implementation.

Fisch, White, and Pooch [319] discuss sanitization of network traffic logs.

Sajaniemi [770] discusses a technique for visualizing an audit of a spreadsheet. Takada and Koike [891] present a visual interface for logs used to detect intruders. Shneiderman [824] discusses human-computer interfaces in general.

21.10   Exercises

1. Extend the example of deriving required logging information to the full Bell-LaPadula Model with both security levels and compartments.

2. In the example of deriving required logging information for the Chinese Wall model, it is stated that the time must be logged. Why? Can something else be logged to achieve the same purpose?

3. The Windows NT logger allows the system administrator to define events to be entered into the security log. In the example, the system administrator configured the logger to record process execution and termination. What other events might the system administrator wish to record?

4. Suppose a notifier sends e-mail to the system administrator when a successful compromise of that system is detected. What are the drawbacks of this approach? How would you notify the appropriate user?

5. Why is adherence to the principle of complete mediation (see Section 12.2.4) a necessity for logging of file accesses?

6. A network monitor records the following information while recording a network connection.

   a. System prompts that name neither the user nor the system
   b. System control files such as the password file
   c. A file containing a list of dictionary words
   d. A user's start-up file
   e. A system banner
   f. A source code file
   g. A Web page downloaded from a remote site

   Which type of information should the monitor check to see if it must sanitize the data to conceal the names of the users and the names and addresses of the computers involved?

7. Fisch, White, and Pooch [319] define four levels of log sanitization.

   a. Simple sanitization, in which all information except the commands issued by an intruder are deleted
   b. Information-tracking sanitization, in which sensitive information is entered into a symbol table as it is encountered, a unique identifier is assigned, and whenever that information is encountered it is replaced with the associated identifier
   c. Format sanitization, in which compressed or encoded data is transformed into its original form, the original form is sanitized using information-tracking sanitization, and the resulting data is returned to its transformed format
   d. Comprehensive sanitization, in which all data is analyzed and sanitized as in information-tracking and format sanitization

Discuss the level of anonymity of each level of sanitization. Which level could be automated, and to what degree would human oversight be required?

8. Suppose a remote host begins the TCP three-way handshake with the local host but never sends the final ACK. This is called a *half-open connection*. The local host waits for some short time and then purges the information from its network tables. If a remote host makes so many half-open connections that the local host cannot accept connections from other hosts, the remote host has launched a *syn flood attack* (See Section 23.4 for more details.) Derive logging and auditing requirements to detect such an attack.

9. What are the logging and auditing requirements for the NFS operations MKDIR and WRITE?

10. In the LAFS file system, what does the following policy line say?

```
prohibit:0800-1700:*:root:solitaire:exec:ok
```

What is the effect of specifying the status field?

Chapter 22
Intrusion Detection

HIPPOLYTA: How chance Moonshine is gone before
Thisbe comes back and finds her lover?
THESEUS: She will find him by starlight. Here
she comes; and her passion ends the play.
—*A Midsummer Night's Dream*, V, i, 320–323.

System managers must protect computer systems from attack. The mechanisms and techniques discussed throughout this book help protect systems, data, and resources. However, nothing is perfect. Even the best protected systems must be monitored to detect successful (and unsuccessful) attempts to breach security. This chapter discusses automated systems for detecting intrusions and looks at responses to attacks.

22.1   Principles

Computer systems that are not under attack exhibit several characteristics.

1. The actions of users and processes generally conform to a statistically predictable pattern. A user who does only word processing when using the computer is unlikely to perform a system maintenance function.
2. The actions of users and processes do not include sequences of commands to subvert the security policy of the system. In theory, any such sequence is excluded; in practice, only sequences known to subvert the system can be detected.
3. The actions of processes conform to a set of specifications describing actions that the processes are allowed to do (or not allowed to do).

Denning [243] hypothesized that systems under attack fail to meet at least one of these characteristics.

EXAMPLE: If the goal is to put in a back door, the intruder may modify a system configuration file or program. If the attacker enters the system as a nonprivileged user, he or she must acquire system privileges to change the files. The nonprivileged user may not be a user who normally acquires system privileges (characteristic 1). The techniques used to acquire those privileges may involve sequences of commands designed to violate the security policy of the system (characteristic 2). If they do not, the alterations in the system files may introduce elements that cause processes to act in ways that violate specifications (characteristic 3).

  If the attacker modifies a user file, processes executing on behalf of that user can now behave in abnormal ways, such as allowing network connections from sites not able to connect earlier, or by executing commands that the user did not execute before (characteristic 1). The commands may subvert the security policy, thereby gaining system privileges for the user—and the attacker (characteristic 2).

EXAMPLE: Cliff Stoll noticed an anomaly in one of the systems he was administering: a 79¢ discrepancy in the output of an accounting log [878]. On investigation, he realized that an intruder was breaking in to search for classified information. This caused the discrepancy. As a result, authorities broke up an espionage ring [880].

22.2   Basic Intrusion Detection

The characteristics listed above guide the detection of intrusions. Once the province of the technologically sophisticated, attacks against systems have been automated. So a sophisticated attack need not be the work of a sophisticated attacker.

> **Definition 22–1.** An *attack tool* is an automated script designed to violate a security policy.

EXAMPLE: The attack tool *rootkit* [699] exists for many versions of the UNIX operating system. It is designed to sniff passwords from the network and to conceal its presence. It assumes that the installer has acquired *root* privileges.

  Rootkit[1] comes with tools to automate the installation procedure. In addition to the network sniffing program, it comes with modified versions of system utilities. The modified version of *netstat,* which lists network connections, uses a control file to determine which network connections to conceal. The modified version of *ps,* which lists executing processes, uses another control file to determine which processes to conceal, such as the sniffer process. The modified versions of *ls* and *du,* which list files and disk space used, use a control file to determine which files to conceal. The network configuration program *ifconfig,* which reports network device con-

---

[1] Rootkit continues to evolve both in doctored programs and in sophistication. At the time of publication, some versions used dynamically loadable kernel modules.

figuration, claims that the network device is not in promiscuous mode, as it must be to sniff the network. Finally, the *login* program accepts a "magic password" as authenticating any user. This enables attackers to return to obtain the sniffed passwords. All the replacement programs are modified so that they and the originals will produce the same checksum, as computed by a simple checksumming program.

    Rootkit contains several other programs for concealing the attacker. The program *zapper* deletes the user's entry from the *utmp* file. This means that the user will not show up when logged in. *Fixer* installs the programs and adjusts their permissions to match those of the replaced programs.

    Attack tools do not change the nature of intrusion detection fundamentally. They do eliminate many errors arising from incorrect installation and perform routine steps to clean up detritus of the attack, but they cannot eliminate *all* traces.

EXAMPLE: Consider an attack involving *rootkit*. If the configuration files controlling *netstat*, *ps*, *ls*, and *du* are set up correctly, these programs will not report any network connections, files, or processes associated with *rootkit*. The files and processes will still be present, and other programs that perform the same functions as *netstat*, *ps*, *ls*, and *du* will report the presence of *rootkit*-related files. For example, *du* prints the number of blocks used by a set of files, and *df* reports the number of free blocks on a file system. Their sum should be approximately the size of the file system (less some space for disk management blocks). The number of files in directories should agree with *ls*'s count. Other programs, such as a locally written directory listing program, can check this. The load average should be consistent with the running processes. Programs other than *ps*, such as local process listers, can list processes. The point is that *rootkit* does not conceal the files, connections, and processes by altering kernel or file structures.[2] It alters the programs that interpret the data in those structures. So, if *rootkit* fails to alter any program that retrieves the data, that program will reveal the correct data. This inconsistency indicates an anomaly, which—by characteristic 1—indicates an attack.

    Denning [243] suggests automation of the intrusion detection process. Her specific hypothesis is that exploiting vulnerabilities requires an abnormal use of normal commands or instructions, so security violations can be detected by looking for abnormalities. Her model is very general and includes abnormalities such as deviation from usual actions (anomaly detection), execution of actions that lead to break-ins (misuse detection), and actions inconsistent with the specifications of privileged programs (specification-based detection).

    Systems that do this are called *intrusion detection systems* (IDS). Their goals are fourfold[3]:

---

[2] If a kernel module is involved, any program using this interface will also return bogus information. Programs that read directly from memory or the disk will not.

[3] Intrusion detection systems may simply log traffic for later analysis. In this case, they are logging engines rather than intrusion detection mechanisms (see Section 21.2.1).

1. Detect a wide variety of intrusions. Intrusions from within the site, as well as those from outside the site, are of interest. Furthermore, both known and previously unknown attacks should be detected. This suggests a mechanism for learning or adapting to new types of attacks or to changes in normal user activity.

2. Detect intrusions in a timely fashion. "Timely" here need not be in real time. Often, it suffices to discover an intrusion within a short period of time. Real-time intrusion detection raises issues of responsiveness. If every command and action must be analyzed before it can be executed, only a very simple analysis can be done before the computer (or network) being monitored becomes unusable. On the other hand, in all but a few rare cases, determining that an intrusion took place a year ago is probably useless.

3. Present the analysis in a simple, easy-to-understand format. Ideally, this should be a light that glows green for no detected intrusions and that changes to red when an attack is detected. Unfortunately, intrusions are rarely this clear-cut, so intrusion detection mechanisms must present more complex data to a site security officer. The security officer determines what action (if any) to take. Because intrusion detection mechanisms may monitor many systems (not just one), the user interface is of critical importance. This leads to the next requirement.

4. Be accurate. A *false positive* occurs when an intrusion detection system reports an attack, but no attack is underway. False positives reduce confidence in the correctness of the results as well as increase the amount of work involved. However, *false negatives* (occurring when an intrusion detection system fails to report an onging attack) are worse, because the purpose of an intrusion detection system is to report attacks. The goal of an intrusion detection system is to minimize both types of errors.

Formalizing this type of analysis provides a statistical and analytical basis for monitoring a system for intrusions. Three types of analyses—anomaly detection, misuse (or signature) detection, and specification detection—look for violations of the three characteristics in Section 22.1. Before discussing these types of analyses, let us consider a model of an intrusion detection system.

22.3   Models

Intrusion detection systems determine if actions constitute intrusions on the basis of one or more models of intrusion. A model classifies a sequence of states or actions, or a characterization of states or actions, as "good" (no intrusions) or "bad" (possible intrusions). Anomaly models use a statistical characterization, and actions or states that are statistically unusual are classified as "bad." Misuse models compare actions or states with sequences known to indicate intrusions, or sequences believed to indicate intrusions, and classify those sequences as "bad." Specification-based models classify states that violate the specifications as "bad." The models may be *adaptive* models that alter their behavior on the basis of system states and actions, or they may be *static* models that are initialized from collected data and do not change as the system runs.

In this section we examine representative models of each class. In practice, models are often combined, and intrusion detection systems use a mixture of two or three different types of models.

22.3.1   Anomaly Modeling

Anomaly detection uses the assumption that unexpected behavior is evidence of an intrusion. Implicit is the belief that some set of metrics can characterize the expected behavior of a user or a process. Each metric relates a subject and an object.

> **Definition 22–2.** *Anomaly detection* analyzes a set of characteristics of the system and compares their behavior with a set of expected values. It reports when the computed statistics do not match the expected measurements.

Denning identifies three different statistical models.

The first model uses a threshold metric. A minimum of m and a maximum of n events are expected to occur (for some event and some values m and n). If, over a specific period of time, fewer than m or more than n events occur, the behavior is deemed anomalous.

EXAMPLE: Microsoft Windows NT 4.0 allows the system to lock a user out after some number n of failed login attempts [479]. This is an intrusion detection system using the threshold metric with the lower limit 0 and the upper limit n. The attempted logins are deemed anomalous after n failed attempts to log in.

Determining the threshold complicates use of this model. The threshold must take into account differing levels of sophistication and characteristics of the users. For example, if n were set to 3 in the example above for a system in France, and the primary users of that system were in the United States, the difference in the keyboards would result in a large number of false alarms. But if the system were located in the United States, setting n to 3 would be more reasonable. One approach is to combine this approach with the other two models to adapt the thresholds to observed or predicted behavior.

The second model uses statistical moments. The analyzer knows the mean and standard deviation (first two moments) and possibly other measures of correlation (higher moments). If values fall outside the expected interval for that moment, the behavior that the values represent is deemed anomalous. Because the *profile*, or description of the system, may evolve over time, anomaly-based intrusion detection systems take these changes into account by aging (or weighting) data or altering the statistical rule base on which they make decisions.

EXAMPLE: The Intrusion Detection Expert System (IDES) [582] was developed at SRI International based on Denning's original model. It used anomaly detection, among other techniques. It represents subjects, which can include a user, a login session, applications, routers, and so on, as an ordered sequence of statistics $<q_{0,j}, ..., q_{n,j}>$, where $q_{i,j}$ is the ith statistic on day j. The metrics are counts or time intervals, as discussed in a preceding example. The profile for each subject is updated every day on the basis of observed behavior.

IDES weights its statistics to favor recent behavior over past behavior. Let $A_{k,l}$ be the summation of counts making up the metric for the kth statistic on day l. Then the statistic $q_{k,l+1} = A_{k,l+1} - A_{k,l} + 2^{-rt}q_{k,l}$, where t is the number of log entries or the total time elapsed since time 0, and r is a half-life determined through experience. This is an exponential decay of previous values and is quite sensitive to changes in behavior over a short period of time.

The statistical moments model provides more flexibility than the threshold model. Administrators can tune it to discriminate better than the threshold model. But with flexibility comes complexity. In particular, an explicit assumption is that the behavior of processes, and users, can be statistically modeled. If this behavior matches a statistical distribution (such as a Gaussian or normal distribution), determining the parameters requires experimental data that can be obtained from the system. But if not, the analysts must use other techniques, such as clustering, to determine the characteristics, the moments, and the values that indicate abnormal behavior. An additional problem is the difficulty of computing these moments in real time.

Denning's third model is a Markov model. Examine a system at some particular point in time. Events preceding that time have put the system into a particular state. When the next event occurs, the system transitions into a new state. Over time, a set of probabilities of transition can be developed. When an event occurs that causes a transition that has a low probability, the event is deemed anomalous. This model suggests that a notion of "state," or past history, can be used to detect anomalies. The anomalies are now no longer based on statistics of the occurrence of individual events, but on sequences of events. This approach heralded misuse detection and was used to develop effective anomaly detection mechanisms.

Teng, Chen, and Lu used this approach in Digital Equipment Corporation's TIM research system [897]. Their scheme used an artificial intelligence technique called *time-based inductive learning*. The system is given a type of event to be predicted. It develops a set of temporally related conditions that predict the time that the event will occur with respect to the set.

EXAMPLE: Consider the sequence of events *abcdedeabcabc*. The goal is to predict these events. The following rules are examples that TIM might derive.

$$R_1: ab \rightarrow c \ (1) \quad R_2: c \rightarrow d \ (0.5) \quad R_3: c \rightarrow e \ (0.5)$$
$$R_4: d \rightarrow e \ (1) \quad R_5: e \rightarrow a \ (0.5) \quad R_6: e \rightarrow d \ (0.5)$$

The left side of each rule is the antecedent, and the right side is the event being predicted. The number in parentheses is the probability that the antecedent event(s) is (are) followed by the event on the right side of the rule. Rules R_1 and R_4 are good indicators of expected behavior. The other rules are not particularly good, and will either be dropped (should the probability decrease over time) or become better (should the probability increase over time).

Anomalies are detected when a sequence of events matches the left side of a rule but the succeeding event differs from the expected right side. Using the rules above, if the sequence *abd* occurs, an alert will be triggered because *c* should always come after *ab*. But the sequence *acf* will not cause an alert, because multiple events may follow *c*. This sequence could cause a new rule to be added, namely, $R_7: c \rightarrow f$ (0.33...)—and the probabilities for rules R_2 and R_3 would change to 0.33.

The effectiveness of Markov-based models depends on the adequacy of the data used to establish the model. This data (called *training data*) is obtained experimentally, usually from populations that are believed to be normal (not anomalous). For example, TIM could obtain data by monitoring a corporate system to establish the relevant events and their sequence. Hofmeyr, Forrest, and Somayaji obtained traces of system calls from processes running in a normal environment. If this training data accurately reflects the environment in which the intrusion detection system is to run, the model will work well, but if the training data does not correspond to the environment, the Markov model will produce false alarms and miss abnormal behaviors. In particular, unless the training data covers all possible normal uses of the system in the environment, the intrusion detection mechanism will issue false reports of abnormalities.

22.3.2   Misuse Modeling

In some contexts, the term "misuse" refers to an attack by an insider or authorized user. In the context of intrusion detection systems, it means "rule-based detection."

Definition 22–3. *Misuse detection* determines whether a sequence of instructions being executed is known to violate the site security policy being executed. If so, it reports a potential intrusion.

Modeling of misuse requires a knowledge of system vulnerabilities or potential vulnerabilities that attackers attempt to exploit. The intrusion detection system incorporates this knowledge into a *rule set*. When data is passed to the intrusion detection system, it applies the rule set to the data to determine if any sequences of data match any of the rules. If so, it reports that a possible intrusion is underway.

Misuse-based intrusion detection systems often use expert systems to analyze the data and apply the rule set. These systems cannot detect attacks that are unknown to the developers of the rule set. Previously unknown attacks, or even variations of known attacks, can be difficult to detect. Later intrusion detection systems used adaptive methods involving neural networks and Petri nets to improve their detection abilities.

One system, IDIOT [538], monitors audit logs looking for a sequence of events that correspond to an attack. An alternative point of view, used by the STAT system [456], is to ignore the actual states and focus on the commands that change them. Researchers at the University of California at Santa Barbara have built several systems that analyze the results of commands to breach a security policy.

One important feature for intrusion detection systems is an interface into which new users and/or maintainers can add new rules or data. Ranum's Network Flight Recorder is a classic example of how this can be done well.

EXAMPLE: The intrusion detection tool Network Flight Recorder (NFR) has three components [742]. A *packet sucker* reads packets off the network. The packets are passed to a *decision engine*, which uses filters written in a language called *N-code* to extract information. (When needed, packets will also be checked against a state table to enable reassembly of fragmented packets.) These filters are bound to events such as packet arrivals. The *backend* writes the data generated by the filters to disk; the packet itself is discarded. A *query backend* allows administrators to extract both raw and postprocessed data from the disk file. Query backends can compute a variety of statistics over the data (such as interpacket arrival time for a particular server) and present the data in a variety of forms, including raw data, histograms, and pie charts. The separation of the query mechanism (output) from the input stream of packets enables administrators to query NFR without impacting its ability to handle incoming packets.

Although some filters are supplied, users can write their own filters using the N-code language. This language is a stack-oriented language with an interpretive engine built into NFR. It includes all usual high-level language features (loops, conditionals, and so forth), as well as a set of data types for counters and IP addresses. Packets are considered structures, and the fields are build into the language. For example, to have the filter ignore all traffic that is not intended for a set of Web servers:

```
# list of my web servers
my_web_servers = [ 10.237.100.189 10.237.55.93 ] ;
# we assume all HTTP traffic is on port 80
filter watch tcp ( client, dport:80 )
{
        if (ip.dest != my_web_servers)
                    return;
```

```
# now process the packet; we just write out packet info
        record system.time, ip.src, ip.dest to www._list;
}
www_list = recorder("log")
```

The greatest strength of NFR is its clean design and its adaptability to the needs of the users. Paradoxically, this is also its greatest weakness, because one must know what to look for.

22.3.3   Specification Modeling

Anomaly detection has been called the art of looking for unusual states. Misuse detection, similarly, is the art of looking for states known to be bad. Specification detection takes the opposite approach; it looks for states known not to be good, and when the system enters such a state, it reports a possible intrusion.

> **Definition 22–4.** *Specification-based detection* determines whether or not a sequence of instructions violates a specification of how a program, or system, should execute. If so, it reports a potential intrusion.

For security purposes, only those programs that in some way change the protection state of the system need to be specified and checked. For example, because the policy editor in Windows NT changes security-related settings, it needs to have an associated specification.

EXAMPLE: Ko, Ruschitzka, and Levitt [519] developed a specification-based intrusion detection system for the UNIX environment. They specified 15 security-related programs. The specifications constrained object access, sequencing of operations, synchronization, and race conditions. The researchers applied this to monitoring of the program *rdist*.

The UNIX program *rdist* (for *remote dist*ribution) updates programs on remote systems. It first creates a temporary file */tmp/rdistxxxxx*. It then copies the contents of the new file into the temporary file, changes the protection mask as required, and copies the temporary file over the file to be replaced. The problem is that *rdist* modifies protection modes by acting on the file name, so if an attacker can replace the file by a symbolic link, he can force *rdist* to modify the protection modes of any file in the system. For example, he can turn on the setuid bit for the program */bin/sh*, which would give him superuser privileges instantly.

A specification in the PE-grammar language describes the accepted behavior of *rdist*. It defines the set of subjects (events) to which the rule should be applied (namely, any process on the host *nobhill* created from the program *rdist* regardless of which user executes it), the environment of execution, and constraints for execution. The latter name the operations of interest and describes when they are valid. For example, if a file is opened and the file is not world-readable, one constraint says that *rdist* must have created it. Similarly, if a *chmod* is applied to a file, the constraint requires that *rdist* have created the file.

The distributed program execution monitor (DPEM) has a set of agents for generating traces from audit logs, and a director for collecting the traces, comparing them with the specifications, and analyzing the results. In the experiments, specifications for all network daemons (including copies of *rdist* and *sendmail* known to have vulnerabilities) were developed, and several attacks were launched. On the average, detecting an attack from *rdist* took 0.06 second. Similarly, a race condition involving two editing sessions of a password file took 0.05 second to detect.

Specification-based intrusion detection is in its infancy. Among its appealing qualities are the formalization (at a relatively low level) of what *should* happen. This means that intrusions using unknown attacks will be detected. Balanced against this desirable feature is the extra effort needed to locate and analyze the programs that may cause security problems. The subtlety of this last point is brought home when one realizes that *any* program is a potential security threat when executed by a privileged user.

22.3.4   Summary

Reflecting on the differences between the three basic types of intrusion detection will clarify the nature of each type.

Some observations on misuse detection will provide a basis for what follows. Definition 22–3 characterizes misuse detection as detection of violations of a policy. The policy may be known (explicit) or implicit. In the former case, one uses the techniques described in Section 21.4.1 to develop the rules for the misuse detection system. In the latter case, one must describe the policy in terms of actions or states that are known to violate the policy, which calls on the techniques described in Section 21.4.2 to develop the relevant rules. This distinction, although subtle, is crucial. In the first case, the rules database is sufficient to detect all violations of policy because the policy itself was used to populate the rule set. In the second case, the rule set contains descriptions of states and/or actions that are known to violate the policy, *but not all such states or actions*. This kind of misuse detection system will not detect all violations of system policy.

Now consider the difference between misuse detection and anomaly detection. The former detects violations of a policy. The latter detects violations of expectation, which may (or may not) violate the policy. For example, TIM uses rules that it derives from logs to construct its Markov model. If the training data contain attacks, the Markov model will accept those attacks as normal. Hence, it is an anomaly detection mechanism. By way of contrast, IDIOT does not construct models from data on the fly. It contains a rule base of sequences that describe known attacks. Hence, it is a misuse detection mechanism.

The distinction between specification-based detection and misuse detection is also worth consideration. The former detects violations of per-program specifications, and makes an implicit assumption that if all programs adhere to their specifications, the site policy cannot be violated. The latter makes no such assumption, focusing instead on the overall site policy. Suppose an attacker could attack a system in such a way that no program violated its specifications but the combined effect of the execution of the programs during the attack did violate the site policy. Misuse intrusion detection might detect the attack (depending on the completeness of the rule set). Anomaly intrusion detection might also detect the attack (depending on the characterization of expected behavior). However, specification-based intrusion detection would not detect this attack. In essence, if the specification of a program is its "security policy," specification-based detection is a local (per-program) form of misuse detection.

22.4   Architecture

An intrusion detection system is also an automated auditing mechanism. Like auditing systems, it consists of three parts (see Section 21.2). The *agent* corresponds to the logger. It acquires information from a target (such as a computer system). The *director* corresponds to the analyzer. It analyzes the data from the agents as required (usually to determine if an attack is in progress or has occurred). The director then passes this information to the *notifier*, which determines whether, and how, to notify the requisite entity. The notifier may communicate with the agents to adjust the logging if appropriate. Figure 22–1 illustrates this.

22.4.1   Agent

An agent obtains information from a data source (or set of data sources). The source may be a log file, another process, or a network. The information, once acquired, may be sent directly to the director. Usually, however, it is preprocessed into a specific format to save the director from having to do this. Also, the agent may discard information that it deems irrelevant.

EXAMPLE: If the agent is to transmit the time and location of a failed login attempt, it will scan the appropriate log file, discard any records of successful logins, and send the remainder to the director.

The director may determine that it needs more information from a particular information source. In that case, the director can instruct the agent to collect additional data, or to process the data it collects differently. The director can use this to

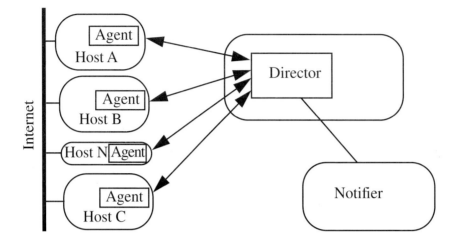

Figure 22–1   Architecture of an intrusion detection system. Hosts A, B, and C are general-purpose computers, and the agents monitor activity on them. Host N is designed for network monitoring, and its agent reports data gleaned from the Net to the director.

cut down on the amount of processing it must do, but can increase the level of information it receives when an attack is suspected.

EXAMPLE: When the director determines that an attack on some other system is underway, it might direct all agents to report all login attempts involving the suspect accounts, whether successful or not.

An agent can obtain information from a single host, from a set of hosts (in which case it may also function as a director; see Section 22.4.2), or from a network. Let us consider the types of information that are available from each, and how they might be gathered.

22.4.1.1   Host-Based Information Gathering

Host-based agents usually use system and application logs to obtain records of events, and analyze them to determine what to pass to the director. The events to look for, and to analyze, are determined by the goals of the intrusion detection mechanism. The logs may be security-related logs (such as BSM and the Windows NT logs discussed in Chapter 21, "Auditing,") or other logs such as accounting logs. Crosbie and Spafford [223] point out that the logs may even be virtual logs if the agent is put directly in the kernel. The agent then simply copies records that the kernel puts into the logs. This eliminates the need to convert from one log format to an internal representation. It also means that the agents are not portable among heterogeneous computers. There is also a drawback involving the granularity of information obtained, which we will discuss in Section 22.4.1.3.

A variant of host-based information gathering occurs when the agent generates its own information. Policy checkers do this. They analyze the state of the system, or of some objects in the system, and treat the results as a log (to reduce and forward). However, these agents are usually somewhat complex, and a fundamental rule of secure design is to keep software simple, usually by restricting its function to one task. This arrangement violates that rule. So, the policy checker usually logs its output, and the agent simply analyzes that log just as it would analyze any other log.

22.4.1.2   Network-Based Information Gathering

Network-based agents use a variety of devices and software to monitor network traffic. This technique provides information of a different flavor than host-based monitoring provides. It can detect network-oriented attacks, such as a denial of service attack introduced by flooding a network. It can monitor traffic for a large number of hosts. It can also examine the contents of the traffic itself (called *content monitoring*).

Network-based agents may use network sniffing to read the network traffic. In this case, a system provides the agent with access to all network traffic passing that host. If the medium is point-to-point (such as a token ring network), the agents must be distributed to obtain a complete view of the network messages. If the medium is a broadcast medium (such as Ethernet), typically only one computer needs to have the monitoring agent. Arranging the monitoring agents so as to minimize the number required to provide complete network coverage is a difficult problem. In general, the policy will focus on intruders entering the network rather than on insiders. In this case, if the network has a limited number of points of access, the agents need to monitor only the traffic through those points. If the computers controlling those entry points do extensive logging on the network traffic that they receive, the network-based information gathering is in effect reduced to host-based information gathering.

Monitoring of network traffic raises several significant issues. The critical issue is that the analysis software must ensure that the view of the network traffic is *exactly* the same as at *all* hosts for which the traffic is intended. Furthermore, if the traffic is end-to-end enciphered, monitoring the contents from the network is not possible.

22.4.1.3   Combining Sources

The goal of an agent is to provide the director with information so that the director can report possible violations of the security policy (intrusions). An aggregate of information is needed. However, the information can be viewed at several levels.

EXAMPLE: Consider a FreeBSD UNIX system with two sources of information. The first is the application level log. Whenever a user changes privileges by executing the program *su*, a log entry is written into that log. The second is the system call log that the (nonstandard, instrumented) kernel generates.

The application level log presents a very high-level view of actions:

```
Feb 12 14:29:53 nob su: root to bishop on /dev/ttyp5
```

The system call level log generates a very different view of this action. Omitting the blocks of data that are read and written, the log contains 401 entries for the single command. A few such entries from the middle of the process give the flavor of the entire log. The entries that follow correspond to obtaining the user's effective UID, opening the password file, and obtaining the password of the user with that effective UID.

```
13285 su        CALL   geteuid
13285 su        RET    geteuid 0
13285 su        CALL   stat(0x28114179,0xbfbfd138)
13285 su        NAMI   "/etc/spwd.db"
13285 su        RET    stat 0
13285 su        CALL   open(0x28114179,0,0)
13285 su        NAMI   "/etc/spwd.db"
13285 su        RET    open 3
13285 su        CALL   fcntl(0x3,0x2,0x1)
13285 su        RET    fcntl 0
13285 su        CALL   read(0x3,0x804e000,0x104)
13285 su        GIO    fd 3 read 260 bytes
13285 su        RET    read 260/0x104
13285 su        CALL   lseek(0x3,0,0x4000,0,0)
13285 su        RET    lseek 16384/0x4000
13285 su        CALL   read(0x3,0x8051000,0x1000)
13285 su        GIO    fd 3 read 4096 bytes
13285 su        RET    read 4096/0x1000
13285 su        CALL   close(0x3)
13285 su        RET    close 0
```

If one views the issue at the application level, the single-line log entry is sufficient, but from a system level view, it is not, because it obscures the many system calls actually made. Similarly, from an application level view, the system level view is inadequate, because the sequence of system calls does not make clear what their combined function is (specifically, to log in a user).

The difference between application and system views (which is, essentially, a problem of layers of abstraction) affects what the agent can report to the director and what the director can conclude from analyzing the information. The agent, or the director, must either obtain information at the level of abstraction at which it looks for security problems or be able to map the information into an appropriate level.

22.4.2   Director

The director itself *reduces* the incoming log entries to eliminate unnecessary and redundant records. It then uses an *analysis engine* to determine if an attack (or the precursor to an attack) is underway. The analysis engine may use any of, or a mixture of, several techniques to perform its analysis.

Because the functioning of the director is critical to the effectiveness of the intrusion detection system, it is usually run on a separate system. This allows the system to be dedicated to the director's activity. It has the side effect of keeping the specific rules and profiles unavailable to ordinary users. Then attackers lack the knowledge needed to evade the intrusion detection system by conforming to known profiles or using only techniques that the rules do not include.

The director must correlate information from multiple logs.

EXAMPLE: A particular user logs in during the day to perform system maintenance functions. Occasionally she logs in during the late evening to write reports. One day, she apparently logs in during the late evening and begins altering the kernel (a system maintenance procedure). Agents provide information from both the log of login times and the log of commands executed. Neither set of data by itself will give an indication of a security problem. However, if the director correlates the two sets of data, the anomaly will be apparent.

Many types of directors alter the set of rules that they use to make decisions. These *adaptive directors* alter the profiles, add (or delete) rules, and otherwise adapt to changes in the systems being monitored. Typical adaptive directors use aspects of machine learning or planning to determine how to alter their behavior.

EXAMPLE: Debar, Becker, and Siboni [237] proposed the use of a neural network to analyze logs. Their goal was to reduce the complexity of analyzing the data from the agent. They constructed a neural network that adapted to the users' behavior over time, enabling them to discard data and simplify the analysis. This also enabled them to use several learning techniques to improve the classification of events as anomalous, thereby reducing the number of false alarms.

Directors rarely use only one analysis technique, because different techniques highlight different aspects of intrusions. The results of each are combined, analyzed and reduced, and then used.

22.4.3   Notifier

The notifier accepts information from the director and takes the appropriate action. In some cases, this is simply a notification to the system security officer that an attack is believed to be underway. In other cases, the notifier may take some action to respond to the attack.

Many intrusion detection systems use graphical interfaces. A well-designed graphics display allows the intrusion detection system to convey information in an easy-to-grasp image or set of images. It must allow users to determine what attacks are underway (ideally, with some notion of how likely it is that this is not a false alarm). This requires that the GUI be designed with a lack of clutter and unnecessary information.

EXAMPLE: The Graphical Intrusion Detection System (GrIDS) [868] uses a graph-oriented user interface to show the progress of attacks across multiple systems. The hosts are represented as nodes, and as an attack from one system to another is identified, the nodes are connected with edges labeled to show the progress of the attack. Figure 22–2 is an example of one of the user displays of GrIDS. It shows the progress of a worm attack as it progresses through a network.

The notifier may send electronic mail to the appropriate person or make entries into the appropriate log files.

EXAMPLE: SATAN was an administrative tool used to analyze UNIX-based systems for network vulnerabilities. The tool *courtney* detected uses of SATAN by analyzing network traffic. When it detected a series of probes consonant with the probes SATAN uses, it invoked a system logging routine to enter the warning into a system log, to notify an administrator of the probe (by electronic mail or messaging), or both. It also may initiate recovery procedures—for example, restoring protection modes of certain files in a system or blocking suspect network traffic.

EXAMPLE: The Intrusion Detection and Isolation Protocol (IDIP) [795] provides a basis for coordinating intrusion detection systems residing on firewalls to block attacks over a network. Figure 22–3 shows a site with three firewalls monitoring traffic from the Internet. If intrusion detection systems on hosts A and B detect a coordinated attack, they can inform host C, which can then reject packets from the source(s) of the attack.

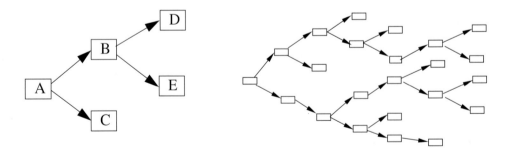

Figure 22–2   An example of GrIDS output showing the spread of a worm. The left figure shows the graph shortly after the spread has begun. The right figure shows the graph after further spread.

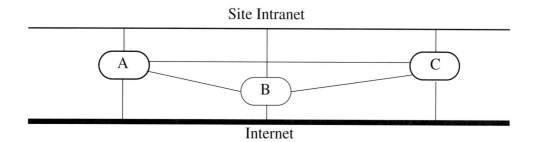

Figure 22–3 Site with three firewalls, each of which has an intrusion detection system running the IDIP protocol.

Incident response is a type of notification. In addition to any human-intelligible notifications, the intrusion detection system communicates with other entities to counteract the attack. Responses include disconnecting from the network, filtering packets from attacking hosts, increasing the level of logging, and instructing agents to forward information from additional sources.

22.5   Organization of Intrusion Detection Systems

An intrusion detection system can be organized in several ways. This section explores three such paradigms using research intrusion detection systems. The first system examined network traffic only. The second explored how to combine network and host sources. The third system distributed the director among multiple systems to enhance security and reliability.

22.5.1   Monitoring Network Traffic for Intrusions: NSM

The Network Security Monitor (NSM) [410] develops a profile of expected usage of a network and compares current usage with that profile. It also allows the definition of a set of *signatures* to look for specific sequences of network traffic that indicate attacks. It runs on a local area network and assumes a broadcast medium. The monitor measures network utilization and other characteristics and can be instructed to look at activity based on a user, a group of users, or a service. It reports anomalous behavior.

The NSM monitors the source, destination, and service of network traffic. It assigns a unique *connection ID* to each connection. The source, destination, and service are used as axes for a matrix. Each element of the matrix contains the number of packets sent over that connection for a specified period of time, and the sum of the data of those packets. NSM also generates expected connection data from the network. The data in the array is "masked" by the expected connection data, and any data not within the expected range is reported as an anomaly.

The developers of the NSM quickly found that too much data was being generated during the network analysis. To reduce the overhead, they constructed a hierarchy of elements of the matrix and generated expected connection data for those elements. If any group in the hierarchy showed anomalous data, the system security officer could ask the NSM to break it down into the underlying elements. The groups were constructed by folding axes of the matrix. For example, one group would be the set of traffic between two hosts for each service. It would have the elements { (A, B, SMTP), (A, B, FTP), ... }, where A and B were host names. The next group would collapse the service names and simply group all traffic into source-destination pairs. At the highest level, traffic would be grouped into its source. The NSM would analyze the data at the source level. If it flagged an anomaly, the system security officer could have the NSM examine each component of the underlying group and determine which specific source-destination pair had the anomaly. From there, it could be broken into the specific service or services involved.

The NSM's use of a matrix allowed a simple signature-based scheme to look for known patterns of misuse. For example, repeated telnet connections that lasted only as long as the normal setup time would indicate a failed login attempt. A specific rule could look in the matrix for this occurrence (although, as the designers point out, these patterns can be hidden as one moves up the hierarchy).

The implementation of the NSM also allowed the analyst to write specific rules against which to compare network traffic. The rules initially used were to check for excessive logins, a single host communicating with 15 or more hosts, or any attempt to communicate with a nonexistent host.

The NSM provided a graphical user display to enable the system security officer to see at a glance the state of the network. Furthermore, the display manager was independent of the NSM matrix analyzer, so the latter could devote full time to the analysis of the data. The prototype system, deployed at the University of California at Davis, detected many attacks. As with all intrusion detection systems, it also reported false positives, such as alumni logging into accounts that had laid dormant for some time. But its capabilities revealed the need for and feasibility of monitoring the network as well as individual hosts.

The NSM is important for two reasons. First, it served as the basis for a large number of intrusion detection systems. Indeed, 11 years after its creation, it was still in use at many sites (although with an augmented set of signatures). Second, it proved that performing intrusion detection on networks was practical. As network traffic becomes enciphered, the ability to analyze the contents of the packets diminishes, but NSM did not look at the *contents* of the traffic. It performed traffic analysis. Hence, its methodology will continue to be effective even after widespread deployment of network encryption.

22.5.2 Combining Host and Network Monitoring: DIDS

The Distributed Intrusion Detection System (DIDS) [846] combined the abilities of the NSM with intrusion detection monitoring of individual hosts. It sprang from the observation that neither network-based monitoring nor host-based monitoring was sufficient. An intruder attempting to log into a system through an account without a password would not be detected as malicious by a network monitor. Subsequent actions, however, might make a host-based monitor report that an intruder is present. Similarly, if an attacker tries to telnet to a system a few times, using a different login name each time, the host-based intrusion detection mechanism would not report a problem, but the network-based monitor could detect repeated failed login attempts.

DIDS used a centralized analysis engine (the *DIDS director*) and required that agents be placed on the systems being monitored as well as in a place to monitor the network traffic. The agents scanned logs for events of interest and reported them to the DIDS director. The DIDS director invoked an expert system that performed the analysis of the data. The expert system was a rule-based system that could make inferences about individual hosts and about the entire system (hosts and networks). It would then pass results to the user interface, which displayed them in a simple, easy-to-grasp manner for the system security officer.

One problem is the changing of identity as an intruder moves from host to host. An intruder might gain access to the first system as user *alice*, and then to the second system as user *bob*. The host-based mechanisms cannot know that *alice* and *bob* are the same user, so they cannot correlate the actions of those two user names. But the DIDS director would note that *alice* connected to the remote host and that *bob* logged in through that connection. The expert system would infer that they were the same user. To enable this type of correlation, each user was identified by a *network identification number* (NID). In the example above, because *alice* and *bob* are the same user, both would share a common NID.

The host agents and network agent provide insight into the problems distributed intrusion detection faces. The host logs are analyzed to extract entries of interest. In some cases, simple reduction is performed to determine if the records should be forwarded; for example, the host agents monitor the system for attacks using signatures. Summaries of these results go to the director. Other events are forwarded directly. To capture this, the DIDS model has host agents report *events*, which are the information contained in the log entries, and an *action* and *domain* (see Figure 22–4). Subjects (such as active processes) perform actions; domains characterize passive entities. Note that a process can be either a subject (as when it changes the protection mode of a file) or an object (as when it is terminated). An object is

session_start	create	tagged	sys_info
session_end	delete	authentication	user_info
read	move	audit	utility
write	change_rights	network	owned
execute	change_user_id	system	not_owned
terminate			

Figure 22–4   DIDS actions and domains. The two left columns name the types of action; the right two, the types of domains. The domains are listed in order of priority, from top to bottom.

assigned to the highest-priority domain to which it belongs. For example, a file may be tagged as important. If the file contains authentication data and also is tagged, it will be reported as a tagged object. A hand-built table dictates which events are sent to the DIDS director based on the actions and domains associated with the events. Events associated with the NID are those with *session_start* actions, and execute actions with network domains. These actions are forwarded so that the DIDS director can update its system view accordingly.

The network agent is a simplified version of the NSM. It provides the information described above.

The expert system, a component of the DIDS director, derives high-level intrusion information from the low-level data sent to it. The rule base comes from a hierarchical model of intrusion detection. That model supplies six layers in the reduction procedure.

1. At this lowest layer, the log records are all visible. They come from the host and the network agent, and from any other sources the DIDS director has.

2. Here, the events abstract relevant information from the log entries.

3. This layer defines a subject that captures all events associated with a single user. The NID is assigned to this subject. This layer defines the boundary between machine-dependent information and the abstraction of a user (subject) and associated events.

4. This layer adds contextual information. Specifically, temporal data such as wall clock time, and spacial data such as proximity to other events, are taken into account. If the user tries to log in at a time when that user has never tried to log in before, or if a series of failed logins follows commands to see who is using a system, the context makes the events suspicious.

5. This layer deals with network threats, which are combinations of events in context. A threat is *abuse* if the protection state of the system is changed (for example, making a protected file world-writable). A threat is *misuse* if it violates policy but does not change the state of the system (for example, copying a world-readable homework file, which is a clear violation of policy at most universities). A threat is a *suspicious act* if it does not violate policy but is of interest (for example, a *finger* probe may be a prelude to an attack).

6. This layer assigns a score, from 1 to 100, representing the security state of the network. This score is derived from the threats to the system developed in layer 5. This is a user convenience, because it enables the system security officer to notice problems quickly. Because the raw data (and intermediate data) used to derive the figure is present, the specifics can be provided quickly.

Within the expert system, each rule has an associated *rule value*. This value is used to calculate the score. The system security officer gives feedback to the expert system, and if false alarms occur, the expert system lowers the value associated with the rules leading to the false alarm.

A later system, GrIDS, extended DIDS to wide area networks. In addition to monitoring hosts and network traffic, the GrIDS directors could obtain data from network infrastructure systems (such as DNS servers). As mentioned earlier (see Figure 22–2), GrIDS deployed a hierarchy of directors, each one reducing data from its children (agents or other directors) and passing the information to its parent. GrIDS directors can be in different organizations. This leads to the ability to analyze incidents occurring over a wide area, and to coordinate responses.

22.5.3   Autonomous Agents: AAFID

In 1995, Crosbie and Spafford examined intrusion detection systems in light of fault tolerance [223]. They noted that an intrusion detection system that obtains information by monitoring systems and networks is a single point of failure. If the director fails, the IDS will not function. Their suggestion was to partition the intrusion detection system into multiple components that function independently of one another, yet communicate to correlate information.

> **Definition 22–5.** An *autonomous agent* is a process that can act independently of the system of which it is a part.

Crosbie and Spafford suggested developing autonomous agents each of which performed one particular monitoring function. Each agent would have its own internal model, and when the agent detected a deviation from expected behavior, a match with a particular rule, or a violation of a specification, it would notify other agents. The agents would jointly determine whether the set of notifications were sufficient to constitute a reportable intrusion.

The beauty of this organization lies in the cooperation of the agents. No longer is there a single point of failure. If one agent is compromised, the others can continue to function. Furthermore, if an attacker compromises one agent, she has learned nothing about the other agents in the system or monitoring the network. Moreover, the director itself is distributed among the agents, so it cannot be attacked in the same way that an intrusion detection system with a director on a single host can be. Other advantages include the specialization of each agent. The agent can be crafted to monitor one resource, making the agent small and simple (and meeting the principle of economy of mechanism; see Section 12.2.3). The agents could also migrate through the local network and process data on multiple systems. Finally, this approach appears to be scalable to larger networks because of the distributed nature of the director.

The drawbacks of autonomous agents lie in the overhead of the communications needed. As the functionality of each agent is reduced, more agents are needed to monitor the system, with an attendant increase in communications overhead. Furthermore, the communications must be secured, as must the distributed computations.

EXAMPLE: The Autonomous Agents for Intrusion Detection (AAFID) system [52, 863] implements these ideas. Each host has a set of agents and a *transceiver,* which controls the execution of the agents, collates the information, and forwards it to a *monitor* (director). If the transceiver's host does not have a monitor, the transceiver simply transmits the information to a monitor on another host.

In theory, each agent obtains its own data. This approach causes unnecessary duplication of work and leads to agents that are highly system-dependent. To avoid this problem, AAFID uses *filters* to provide access to monitored resources in a system-independent way. An agent subscribes to a filter by specifying which records it needs. The filter collects the data, transforms it into a system-independent form, and sends each agent the requested records. Multiple agents may subscribe to a single filter.

Transceivers collect data from the local agents, process it, and forward it to other agents or to monitors as appropriate. A transceiver also tracks the agents on its host, and can initiate them or terminate them. For example, if a system begins to accept TCP connections, the transceiver can initiate the SMTP monitoring agent. When TCP networking is shut down, the transceiver can then terminate that agent.

Monitors are the distributed components of the AAFID director. They accept information from transceivers and can communicate with the transceivers and other monitors. They perform high-level correlations for one or more hosts. Multiple monitors may receive data from, and transmit commands to, a single transceiver. In such cases, the AAFID system must ensure that the transceiver receives consistent information and commands.

Finally, the user interface plays one of the roles of a notifier. This interface interacts with the monitors. It may be graphical (for human interaction) or textual (for command scripts).

The implemented AAFID prototype runs on Linux and Solaris systems. It focused on testing the ideas and architecture outlined above. It was implemented in the Perl language [930] for ease of programming, portability, and modification. Because the prototype was a proof of concept and not a production system, the loss of performance was considered acceptable. The prototype validated the architecture and demonstrated that autonomous agents were a practical method for intrusion detection systems.

22.6   Intrusion Response

Once an intrusion is detected, how can the system be protected? The field of *intrusion response* deals with this problem. Its goal is to handle the (attempted) attack in such a way that damage is minimized (as determined by the security policy). Some intrusion detection mechanisms may be augmented to thwart intrusions. Otherwise, the security officers must respond to the attack and attempt to repair any damage.

22.6.1   Incident Prevention

Ideally, intrusion attempts will be detected and stopped before they succeed. This typically involves closely monitoring the system (usually with an intrusion detection mechanism) and taking action to defeat the attack.

In the context of response, prevention requires that the attack be identified *before* it completes. The defenders then take measures to prevent the attack from completing. This may be done manually or automatically.

EXAMPLE: *Jailing* of attackers is an approach that allows the attackers to think that their attacks have succeeded, but places them in a confined area in which their behavior can be controlled and, if necessary, manipulated. Cheswick [171] used this approach to examine an attack. His system recorded a break-in attempt using the SMTP server. After several attempts to break in had failed, Cheswick created a highly restrictive account and monitored the intruder's actions, including which machines were attacked. (None of the attempts succeeded; Cheswick notified the administrators of those systems.) The jail had a file system that closely resembled a real UNIX file system (but without some programs that would reveal system information, and the deception), and access times to certain critical files were also masked. The attacker returned numerous times. Cheswick finally shut down the jail at the request of his management.

Amoroso [21] points out that multilevel secure systems are excellent places to implement jails, because they provide much greater degrees of confinement than do ordinary systems. The attacker is placed into a security compartment isolated from other compartments. The built-in security mechanisms are designed to limit the access of the subjects in the compartment, thereby confining the attacker.

More sophisticated host-based approaches may be integrated with intrusion detection mechanisms. Signature-based methods enable one to monitor transitions for potential attacks. Anomaly-based methods enable one to monitor relevant system characteristics for anomalies and to react when anomalies are detected in real time.

22.6.2   Intrusion Handling

When an intrusion occurs, the security policy of the site has been violated. Handling the intrusion means restoring the system to comply with the site security policy and taking any actions against the attacker that the policy specifies. Intrusion handling consists of six phases [694].

1. *Preparation* for an attack. This step occurs *before* any attacks are detected. It establishes procedures and mechanisms for detecting and responding to attacks.
2. *Identification* of an attack. This triggers the remaining phases.
3. *Containment* (confinement) of the attack. This step limits the damage as much as possible.
4. *Eradication* of the attack. This step stops the attack and blocks further similar attacks.

5. *Recovery* from the attack. This step restores the system to a secure state (with respect to the site security policy).

6. *Follow-up* to the attack. This step involves taking action against the attacker, identifying problems in the handling of the incident, and recording lessons learned (or lessons not learned that should be learned).

In the following discussions, we focus on the containment, eradication, and follow-up phases.

22.6.2.1   Containment Phase

Containing or confining an attack means limiting the access of the attacker to system resources. The protection domain of the attacker is reduced as much as possible. There are two approaches: passively monitoring the attack, and constraining access to prevent further damage to the system. In this context, "damage" refers to any action that causes the system to deviate from a "secure" state as defined by the site security policy.

Passive monitoring simply records the attacker's actions for later use. The monitors do not interfere with the attack in any way. This technique is marginally useful. It will reveal information about the attack and, possibly, the goals of the attacker. However, not only is the intruded system vulnerable throughout, the attacker could attack other systems.

EXAMPLE: It may be helpful to know the type of operating system from which the intruder is entering. A passive monitor can examine settings of the TCP and IP headers of incoming connections to generate a signature. For example, some systems change the window size field more often, and in different ways, than others. This signature can be compared with known signatures of operating systems, and the analyst may be able to draw some conclusions about the type of the remote system from which the packets have been generated [434].

The other approach, in which steps are taken to constrain the actions of the attacker, is considerably more difficult. The goal is to minimize the protection domain of the attacker while preventing the attacker from achieving her goal. But the system defenders may not know what the goal of the attacker is, and thus may misdirect the confinement so that the data or resources that the attacker seeks lie within the minimal protection domain of the attacker.

EXAMPLE: Stoll [880] detected an attacker in a computer system at the Lawrence Berkeley Laboratory. After a period of monitoring, Stoll concluded that the attacker was looking for documents related to nuclear weaponry. He arranged for a trace over network and telephone lines, but the tracing ended at the attacker's point of entry into the United States. The foreign authorities reported that they would need a longer connection to trace the attacker to his point of origin in Europe. Stoll created a very large file containing some of the keywords for which the attacker had been searching. When the attacker next entered, he found the file and began to upload it. The time required for the upload was more than ample for the trace to be completed, and the attacker was identified and subsequently arrested.

The document that Stoll wrote is an example of a *honeypot*. The file was carefully designed to entice the attacker to upload it but in fact contained false and meaningless information. This technique can be extended to systems and networks. Honeypots, sometimes called *decoy servers*, are servers that offer many targets for attackers. The *targets* are designed to entice attackers to take actions that indicate their goals. Honeypots are also instrumented and closely monitored. When a system detects an attack, it takes actions to shift the attacker onto a honeypot system. The defenders can then analyze the attack without disrupting legitimate work or systems. Two good examples are the Deception Tool Kit and the Honeynet Project.

EXAMPLE: Cohen's Deception Tool Kit (DTK) [185] creates a false network interface that allows the user of the tool kit to present any desired configuration to incoming connections. When an attacker probes the putative network, the DTK returns a wide range of vulnerabilities. The attacker may then choose some subset of the presented network addresses to attack. The defender can configure illusionary systems and servers, and monitor the attacks, so while the attacker is probing nonexistent systems the defender can analyze the attacks to determine the goals and abilities of the attacker. Based on experiments using the DTK, Cohen concluded that this technique of deception was an effective response to keep attackers from targeting real systems.

EXAMPLE: The Honeynet Project was created to learn about the "black hat" (attacker) community. The organizers were interested in the motives, techniques, and tools of the attackers. The honeypot work was split into two phases. The first was to identify common threats against specific operating systems and configurations. The second was to develop a honeypot network that was "easier to deploy, harder to detect, and more efficient in collecting data." The group has written several papers about the attacks and the attackers [433, 435, 436, 438, 439], and about the design of the honeynet [437].

22.6.2.2   Eradication Phase

Eradicating an attack means stopping the attack. The usual approach is to deny access to the system completely (such as by terminating the network connection) or to terminate the processes involved in the attack. An important aspect of eradication is to ensure that the attack does not immediately resume. This requires that attacks be blocked.

A common method for implementing blocking is to place wrappers around suspected targets. The wrappers implement various forms of access control. Wrappers can control access locally on systems or control network access.

EXAMPLE: Wrappers that control local access to resources are usually embedded in the kernel to make them difficult to bypass. In an experiment that used wrappers to improve the security of commercial off-the-shelf programs, Fraser, Badger, and Feldman [337] used loadable kernel modules to place wrappers in the kernels of UNIX systems. When the wrappers were invoked, they waited for some specified event (such as a system call, possibly with particular privilege settings or arguments). When the event occurred, the wrapper would take control of the process and perform a specified action. The action could be to log the call, to deny access (by returning a failure code to the caller), or to generate and process auxiliary data such as system call counts. The wrappers were specified using an extension of the C programming language. The performance impact of using the wrappers was less than 7%.

The researchers noted that the wrappers' uses were varied, ranging from access control and auditing to intrusion detection and response. Others [518] focused on the latter, designing wrappers that would detect intrusions. Their mechanism accepted notifications from multiple wrappers. In one experiment, when two wrappers notified a wrapper monitoring program execution that a process appeared to be launching an attack, the monitoring wrapper terminated the process.

EXAMPLE: Wrappers can also control access from the network. Bina, McCool, Jones, and Winslett [93] describe an application in which a Web server accepts requests for database records and returns the desired records if so authorized. Access to the records is determined by the role of the requester. To determine this, the Web server obtains information from the client (including a public key for authentication) and passes the data to a script that assigns the appropriate role to the request. The role and request are given to the database engine, which returns an appropriate response. The script is a wrapper around the database. It mediates access to the database.

Firewalls (see Section 23.3.1) are systems that sit between an organization's internal network and some other external network (such as the Internet). The firewall controls access from the external network to the internal network and vice versa. The advantage of firewalls is that they can filter network traffic *before* it reaches the target host. They can also redirect network connections as appropriate, or throttle traffic to limit the amount of traffic that flows into (or out of) the internal network.

EXAMPLE: Because Java applets come from (usually) untrusted sources, many organizations want to block the applets from entering their internal networks. A simple method of doing this is to block the applets at a firewall [595]. When an HTTP connection is made through the firewall, the firewall creates a small application (called a *proxy*) to reassemble the packets and determine if they contain a Java applet. The proxy then may use one of three approaches to block the applet.

First, it can rewrite the HTML tag to something other than "<applet>". When the page is delivered to the browser, the browser will not recognize the applet and will not run it. This method requires the firewall to determine that the connection is indeed an HTTP connection and to parse the HTML in that connection. Both are nontrivial tasks.

The second approach is to look for incoming files with the hexadecimal sequence CA FE BA BE. All Java class files must contain this four-byte signature in order to be properly recognized and interpreted. If this sequence is found, the file is immediately discarded. The danger here is a false positive. Because ActiveX and Javascript code are different, this approach cannot block those types of applets.

The third approach is to block based on file name, but this is far more problematic because the names do not necessarily represent the contents of the file. Many browsers require Java class files to end in ".class". The firewall can block these applets. However, more recent browsers allow Java class files to be combined into archives. The names of these archives often end in ".zip". This is a popular format among users of MS-DOS and Windows, so it is not realistic to block all such files.

Martin, Rajagopalan, and Rubin [595] conclude that the situation is rather bleak for stopping Java applets at the firewall.

An organization may have several firewalls on its perimeter, or several organizations may wish to coordinate their responses. The Intruder Detection and Isolation Protocol [795] provides a protocol for coordinated responses to attacks.

The IDIP protocol runs on a set of computer systems. A *boundary controller* is a system that can block connections from entering a perimeter. Typically, boundary controllers are firewalls or routers. A boundary controller and another system are *neighbors* if they are directly connected. If they send messages to one another, the messages go directly to their destination without traversing any other system. If two systems are not boundary controllers and can send messages to each other without the messages passing through a boundary controller, they are said to be in the same *IDIP domain*. This means that the boundary controllers form a perimeter for an IDIP domain.

When a connection passes through a member of an IDIP domain, the system monitors the connection for intrusion attempts. If one occurs, the system reports the attempt to its neighbors. The neighbors propagate information about the attack and proceed to trace the connection or datagrams to the appropriate boundary controllers. The boundary controllers can then coordinate their responses, usually by blocking the attack and notifying other boundary controllers to block the relevant communications.

EXAMPLE: Kahn and Zurko [481] discuss the use of IDIP to handle network flooding attacks, in which one or more sources spew large numbers of packets to a target. This effectively prevents legitimate traffic from being processed, either because the target is overwhelmed with processing the flooding packets or because the legitimate traffic cannot reach the destination (target).

Consider Figure 22–5. Suppose host f launches a flooding attack against host A along the path f, Z, Y, X, W, a, A. The flood effectively stops all traffic along that path. Host a detects the flood and begins blocking traffic for host A. It also notifies its neighbor W, a boundary controller. W detects traffic targeting A, suppresses it, and notifies its neighbor X. X detects the traffic targeting A, suppresses it, and notifies its neighbors Y and C. W then notices the traffic for A has stopped, and it eliminates its

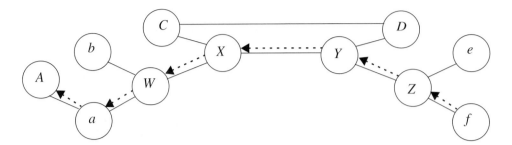

Figure 22–5 Example of IDIP. *C, D, W, X, Y*, and *Z* are boundary controllers. Host *a* runs the IDIP protocol but is not a boundary controller. The flooding attack follows the dashed arrows from *f* to *A*.

suppression. At this point, *A, a, W,* and *b* can again communicate freely, because the traffic formerly saturating the links has been eliminated by *X. C* detects no traffic for *A* and so does nothing. *Y* does detect the traffic, and suppresses it. *X* detects that the traffic going through it for *A* has stopped, and *X* eliminates its suppression. *Y* then communicates with *Z,* and *Z* detects and suppresses the traffic. *Y* also communicates with *D,* which detects no relevant traffic. This process continues until all traffic from *f* to *A* is suppressed.

The IDIP protocol is flexible, because if multiple sources attempt to flood a host, the boundary controllers will block the traffic along each path that the sources use. Of course, if any path has no IDIP controllers, the traffic can flow freely along that path. Kahn and Zurko suggest that IDIP, or a similar protocol, should be widely deployed throughout the Internet to handle flooding attacks. They argue that economic and other incentives will encourage Internet Service Providers and other network providers to cooperate in suppressing distributed flooding attacks.

22.6.2.3   Follow-Up Phase

In the follow-up phase, the systems take some action external to the system against the attacker. The most common follow-up is to pursue some form of legal action, either criminal or civil. The requirements of the law vary among communities, and indeed vary within communities over time.

Counterattacking, or attacking the attacker, takes two forms. The first form involves legal mechanisms, such as filing criminal complaints. This requires protecting a "chain of evidence" so that legal authorities can establish that the attack was real (in other words, that the attacked site did not invent evidence) and that the evidence can be used in court. The precise requirements of the law change over time and jurisdictions, so this first form of counterattacking lies outside the scope of this discussion. The second form is a technical attack, in which the goal is to damage the attacker seriously enough to stop the current attack and discourage future attacks. This approach has several important consequences that must be considered.

1. The counterattack may harm an innocent party. The attacker may be impersonating another site. In this case, the counterattack could damage a completely innocent party, putting the counterattackers in the same position as the original attackers. Alternately, the attackers may have broken into the site from which the attack was launched. Attacking that host does not solve the problem. It merely eliminates one base from which future attacks might be launched.

2. The counterattack may have side effects. For example, if the counterattack consists of flooding a specific target, the flood could block portions of the network that other parties need to transit, which would damage them.

3. The counterattack is antithetical to the shared use of a network. Networks exist to share data and resources and provide communication paths. By attacking, *regardless* of the reason, the attackers make networks less usable because they absorb resources and make threats more immediate. Hence, sites must protect themselves by limiting the sharing and communication on the network beyond what is needed for their safe operation.

4. The counterattack may be legally actionable. If an attacker can be prosecuted or sued, it seems reasonable to assume that one who responds to the attack by counterattacking can also be prosecuted or sued, especially if other innocent parties are damaged by the counterattack.

Under exceptional circumstances, counterattacking may be appropriate. In general, it should be avoided, and legal avenues of prosecution (either civil or criminal) should be pursued. Improving defenses will also hinder attacks. The efforts used to develop and launch counterattacks could be spent far more effectively in that way.

EXAMPLE: Recall the example of the two versions of the *animal* game (see page 364). In that case, the new version of *animal* targeted a specific, older version written by the same authors, and it was unlikely that any organization depended on the existence of that game. Consider moving this example into the world of distributed systems and networks. Imagine a computer worm that enters systems through a widely used network server. The worm spreads rapidly, and despite attempts to eradicate it, systems continue to be reinfected. One company designs a "counterworm." Whenever a break-in comes from a remote site, the "counterworm" detects the break-in, deletes the connection, and uses the same infection technique as that of the original worm to enter the attacking host. On that host, it deletes all worm processes (except its own). It then waits until that system is attacked, and the cycle repeats.

This response raises several questions. First, how can the "counterworm" be set to ensure that it deletes *only* those processes belonging to the original worm? Second, what if the invaded machine is gathering data for research or countermeasures? Third, how can the originators of the "counterworm" ensure that it does no damage to *any* system it is sent to? Fourth, can they be held legally liable for any problems that a site encounters if that site is sent the "counterworm"? The answers to these questions are complex, and illustrate clearly why one needs informed, full consent of a remote site before sending an automated response.

22.7   Summary

Intrusion detection is a form of auditing that looks for break-ins and attacks. Automated methods aid in this process, although it can be done manually. There are three basic models of intrusion detection.

Anomaly detection looks for unexpected behavior. A baseline of expected actions or characteristics of processes, users, or groups of users is developed. Whenever something deviates from that baseline, it is reported as a possible intrusion. In some cases, the profiles are changed over time. In this way, the expected behavior of users is updated as their actual behavior changes over time.

Misuse detection looks for sequences of events known to indicate attacks. A rule set (or database) of attacks provides the requisite information. Ideally, an expert system will use the rule set to detect previously unknown attacks (but efforts of this type have been singularly unsuccessful). Both state-based and transition-based techniques capture the sequence of events in attacks.

Specification-based detection looks for actions outside the specifications of key programs. Each program has a set of rules specifying what actions it is allowed to take. If the program tries to take any other action, the intrusion detection mechanism reports a probable intrusion. This method requires that specifications for programs be written.

Intrusion detection systems are auditing engines, so models of auditing systems can describe their architecture. The director, or analysis engine, may be centralized or distributed, and may be hierarchical or fragmented. Each organization has advantages and disadvantages, but for wide area networks, a distributed director provides the greatest flexibility and power. Information may be gathered from hosts, from the network, from both, or from other directors.

When an intrusion occurs, some response is appropriate. If the intrusion attempt is detected before the attack is successful, the system can take action to prevent the attack from succeeding. Otherwise, the intrusion must be handled. Among the steps involved are confinement of the attack to limit its effectiveness, eradication to eliminate the attacking processes or connections, and follow-up to take action against the attacker as well as learn from the attack.

22.8   Further Reading

Several books describe intrusion detection in detail. Bace [48] provides a wonderful overview with much historical information. Amoroso [21] presents a technical introduction. Northcutt [695] gives a practitioner's overview. Cooper, Northcutt, Fearnow, and Frederick [208] discuss intrusion detection and analysis, again from a practitioner's viewpoint. Proctor [734] presents both managerial and technical information.

Helman and Liepins [417] discuss the statistical foundations of intrusion detection. Immunological approaches to intrusion detection distinguish between normal and abnormal program behavior [263, 331, 332, 333, 429, 854]. Other approaches abound [237, 549, 555, 629]. Sekar, Bowen, and Segal [810] discuss the use of specification-based detection for automated response at the system call level. Badger discusses the relationship among wrappers, reference monitors, and trusted systems [49].

Haystack [840] considered behavior anomalous based on values larger than or smaller than certain limits. Lankewicz and Benard [550] considered the use of statistical models that do not assume any *a priori* distribution of events. Frank demonstrated how feature selection can aid detection of potential problems [334].

Several papers have been written about testing of intrusion detection systems [283, 342, 573, 574, 605, 736]. Axelsson [45] discusses the relationship between false positives and false negatives. Ptacek and Newsham [735] discuss how attackers might evade detection. Securing of mobile agents arises in many contexts [378, 911].

Techniques for response are varied. Some are technical [93, 308, 853, 961], whereas others are procedural and legal and involve special response teams [15, 322, 347, 455, 910]. Some discuss tracing message paths [236, 276, 411, 788, 869].

Sobirey, Fischer-Hübner, and Rannenberg raise the issue of privacy in an intrusion detection context [851]. Others have analyzed this problem and suggested approaches [113, 581].

22.9   Exercises

1. You have been hired as the security officer for Compute Computers, Inc. Your boss asks you to determine the number of erroneous login attempts that should be allowed before a user's account is locked. She is concerned that too many employees are being locked out of their accounts unnecessarily, but is equally concerned that attackers may be able to guess passwords. How would you determine an appropriate value for the threshhold?

2. Why should the administrator (or the superuser) account never be locked regardless of how many incorrect login attempts are made? What should be done instead to alert the staff to the attempted intrusion, and how could the chances of such an attack succeeding be minimized?

3. One view of intrusion detection systems is that they should be of value to an analyst trying to *disprove* that an intrusion has taken place. Insurance companies and lawyers, for example, would find such evidence invaluable in assessing liability. Consider the following scenario. A system has both

classified and unclassified documents in it. Someone is accused of using a word processing program to save an unclassified copy of a classified document. Discuss if, and how, each of the three forms of intrusion detection mechanisms could be used to disprove this accusation.

4. GrIDS uses a hierarchy of directors to analyze data. Each director performs some checks, then creates a higher-level abstraction of the data to pass to the next director in the hierarchy. AAFID distributes the directors over multiple agents. Discuss how the distributed director architecture of AAFID could be combined with the hierarchical structure of the directors of GrIDS. What advantages would there be in distributing the hierarchical directors? What disadvantages would there be?

5. As encryption conceals the contents of network messages, the ability of intrusion detection systems to read those packets decreases. Some have speculated that *all* intrusion detection will become host-based once all network packets have been encrypted. Do you agree? Justify your answer. In particular, if you agree, explain why no information of value can be gleaned from the network; if you disagree, describe the information of interest.

6. Consider the "counterworm" in the example on that begins on page 483.

   a. Pretend you are a technical expert called as a witness in a lawsuit between the sender of the "counterworm" and the target. What arguments could you make for and against the sending of the worm?
   b. How might the arguments for a company providing "worms" to fix security problems in their software differ from those for providing a "counterworm"? How would they be the same?

Chapter 23
Network Security

JOHN OF GAUNT: This fortress built by Nature for herself
Against infection and the hand of war,
This happy breed of men, this little world,
This precious stone set in the silver sea,
Which serves it in the office of a wall,
Or as a moat defensive to a house,
Against the envy of less happier lands;
—*The Tragedy of King Richard the Second*, II, i, 43–49.

The goals of an installation, and its security policy, dictate the functionality required of the site. The distribution of functionality throughout the site's network is critical to improving the security of the site. The functionality of each part of the network controls the nature and configuration of each host on the network. This chapter applies some of the principles and concepts of computer security to a particular situation.

23.1 Introduction

The Dribble Corporation builds and sells dribbles, an electronic item popularly seen as the successor to the Pet Rock. The Drib (the popular name for the corporation) has decided to develop a network infrastructure that would enable it to connect to the Internet, to provide a Web and electronic mail presence that consumers, suppliers, and other partners could access, and to protect its proprietary information. Because of its need to add meaningless but entertaining information gleaned from various Internet Web sites, the Drib developers must have access to the Internet, but external users cannot be allowed to access the development sites. Finally, because dribbles look like their main competitor, gibbles (from the Gibble Gabble Gobble Git Company), the Drib has many lawyers working to defend its patents on dribbles, and its corporate officers are preparing to fight a hostile takeover from GGGGC. Hence, the corporate officers and lawyers also need access to developer data, but the developers are not to have access to the corporation's private or legal information.

The goals of the Drib's security policy are to be as follows.

1. Data related to company plans is to be kept secret. In particular, sensitive corporate data, such as data involved in developing potential products, is to be available only to those who need to know.
2. When a customer provides data (such as a credit card number) to the Drib as part of a purchase, the data, and all information about the customer, are to be available only to those who fill the order. Company analysts may obtain statistics about a number of orders for plannning purposes.
3. Releasing sensitive data requires the consent of the company's officials and lawyers.

Our goal is to design a network infrastructure that will meet these requirements. We begin by analyzing the goals of the policy so that we can make them precise.

23.2   Policy Development

The Drib requires a policy that minimizes the threat of data being leaked to unauthorized entities. However, it is unclear what "unauthorized" should mean. The Drib's internal structure suggests one answer.

The Drib has three main internal organizations. The first is the Customer Service Group (CSG), which handles all dealings with customers. This group maintains all customer data and serves as the interface between the other groups and the clients of the Drib. The second group is the Development Group (DG), which develops, modifies, and maintains products. Members of the DG rely on the CSG for descriptions of customer complaints, suggestions, and ideas; at no time do they talk directly with customers. This prevents them from accidentally revealing confidential information or from learning confidential information such as credit card numbers. The Corporate Group (CG) handles the Drib's debentures, lawsuits, patents, and other corporate-level work.

The policy describes the way information is to flow among these groups.

When one looks at the actual functions of the three groups, how they restrict information, and how they share information, a pattern emerges. Specifications of current products, as well as marketing and sales literature, are publicly available. However, other information about current products, such as problems (especially those that are the subjects of lawsuits), patent applications, and budgets, is not public. The CG and DG groups share this information for planning, budgeting, and development purposes, but beyond this sharing, each group keeps its own private information. The CG keeps corporate information private so that it can be protected by attorney privilege and so that it can comply with government stock regulations.

The DG plans and prototypes future products. The DG waits until it is convinced that production is feasible before it proposes a new product to the CG. The CSG keeps track of customer credit card information and specific clients' ordering information for its own purposes, and it does not share this information (except in the aggregate) with either the CG or the DG. This forms the basis for the policy.

23.2.1   Data Classes

We classify information into five classes that reflect the divisions outlined above. The classification reflects the principle of least privilege[1] by separating the data in such a way that the ability to view one class of data does not imply the ability to view another class of data. Also, the policy and all its rules are not secret, reflecting the principle of open design.[2] Note that "open design" does *not* mean that this information is available to the public. It simply means that anyone within the Drib who is affected by the policy, or who wants to know what the policy is and why it was designed that way, can find out.

1. *Public data (PD)* is available to anyone. It includes product specifications, price information, marketing literature, and any other data that will help the Drib sell dribbles without compromising its secrets.
2. *Development data for existing products (DDEP)* is available only internally. Because of pending lawsuits, it must be available to the company lawyers and officers as well as to the developers. It is kept secret from all others.
3. *Development data for future products (DDFP)* is available to the developers only. The specifications may change, as may various aspects of development, but the Drib never announces information about products under development, and does not intend to change this style of operation.
4. *Corporate data (CpD)* includes legal information that is privileged and information about corporate actions that is not to become known publicly (such as actions that may affect stock values). The corporate officials and lawyers need access to this information; no one else does.
5. *Customer data (CuD)* is data that customers supply, such as credit card information. The Drib protects this data as strongly as it protects its own data.

Data may change from the DDFP class to the DDEP class as products become implemented; from the DDEP class to the PD class when deemed advantageous to publicize some development details; and from the CpD class to the PD class as privileged information becomes publicly known through mergers, lawsuit filings, or the ordinary course of business. There is no provision for revealing CuD directly; this protects the privacy of the Drib's customers.

---

[1] See Section 12.2.1, "Principle of Least Privilege."
[2] See Section 12.2.5, "Principle of Open Design."

23.2.2　User Classes

Four classes of people may access data. The user classes are based on the same principles as the classes of data: separation of privilege[3] and least privilege.[4] Some users may be placed in multiple classes. If so, an underlying assumption of the model is that they will not bypass the restrictions by copying data from one class to another without using the mechanisms provided for that purpose.

1. *Outsiders* (members of the public) get access to some of the Drib's data such as prices, product descriptions, and public corporate information. The public can also order merchandise, download new drivers for their dribbles, and send electronic mail to the company.

2. *Developers* get access to both classes of development data. They cannot alter development data for existing products because that data describes how to manufacture the product. It also provides a historical record for use in developing new products. Developers can modify development data for future products, however.

3. *Corporation executives* (corporation counsel, members of the board of directors, and other executives) get access to corporate data. They can see development data for both existing and future products but may not alter it. They may read customer data (for legal purposes or analysis). Under specific conditions (described below), they may make sensitive data public.

4. *Employees* get access to customer data only.

The following table summarizes the access that each class of users has to each class of data. This table is an access control matrix[5] and defines the access control pol-

	Outsiders	Developers	Corporation executives	Employees
Public data	read	read	read	read
Development data for existing products		read	read	
Development data for future products		read, write	read	
Corporate data			read, write	
Customer data	write		read	read, write

---

[3] See Section 12.2.6, "Principle of Separation of Privilege."
[4] See Section 12.2.1, "Principle of Least Privilege."
[5] See Chapter 2, "Access Control Matrix."

icy. It reflects a mandatory access control policy[6]; the discretionary component is fixed at "allow always." This matrix combines elements of confidentiality[7] and integrity.[8] Left as an implementation detail is the security officer who puts people and data into the appropriate classes (see Exercise 1).

Specific classes of people can move data from one class to another, as indicated above. The specific transformation rules are as follows.

- The developers must propose that a proposed future product be realized. Corporation executives must determine if the proposed action is wise, from both legal and economic standpoints. Hence, both developers and corporation executives must agree to reclassify data from the DDFP class to the DDEP class.

- The employees may identify certain development data as important for answering technical questions from outsiders, or for market literature. In these cases, the employees notify the corporation executives, who then decide whether or not to make the information public. Both employees and corporation executives must agree to reclassify data from the DDEP class to the PD class.

- Corporation executives may reveal corporate data in filings or when revealing that the data will not harm the company. Thus, they can reclassify data from CpD to PD. However, at least two members must agree to do the reclassification.

The principle of separation of privilege[9] dictates that moving data from one class to another requires approval of more than one user. In the first two cases, the users must come from separate classes because the data involved may reveal internal information that would be of use to a competitor. (Two users in different classes may be the same user in two different roles.[10] Hence, the requirement for two different users.) The third case involves corporate business, usually in legal matters (such as lawsuits or stock filings). In this case, the Drib lawyers (all of whom are in the "corporate executive" user class) have the expertise to determine what must be revealed, and because the consequences may involve criminal charges, the lawyers and corporate executives must make the decisions. Because the Drib is a well-run company, they will obtain the appropriate information and recommendations from people in the other user classes as required. However, the requirement that the two members be in the corporate executive class is an acknowledgment of the responsibility of the corporate executives.

---

[6] See Section 4.4, "Types of Access Control."
[7] See Chapter 5, "Confidentiality Policies."
[8] See Chapter 6, "Integrity Policies."
[9] See Section 12.2.6, "Principle of Separation of Privilege."
[10] See Section 13.4, "Groups and Roles."

23.2.3   Availability

The Drib is a world-wide, multinational corporation and does business on all seven continents (although its Antarctic operation is quite small). Orders come from all over the world. Thus, the corporate officers want employees and the public to be able to contact the Drib at any time. In practice, this means that the Drib's systems must be available 99% of the time, the remaining 1% being used for planned maintenance and unexpected downtimes.

23.2.4   Consistency Check

The policy described above should meet the goals of the Drib. Otherwise, it is not an appropriate policy. We will now review the goals of the policy and discuss consistency.

The first goal is to keep sensitive information confidential, on a "need to know" basis. Public data is, by definition, not confidential, and is available to all. Developers clearly need access to both current and future development data, but not to customer data or corporate information (because they do not decide which products to market). They can alter development data as they investigate possibilities and test ideas. Corporate executives need access to corporate data to plan business actions. Some of these actions may be based on development data for existing products; for example, should the Drib invest in a company developing faster CPUs for the Drib's products? Hence, corporate executives also need access to development data for existing products. They can alter corporate data, but not development data. So, the first goal of the policy is met.

The second goal requires that only employees who handle purchases can access customer data, and only they and the customers themselves can alter the customer data. The policy above provides this restriction.

The third goal is met by the rules for changing security classes. Moving data from the DDFP class to the DDEP class requires consent of both a developer and a corporate executive. Moving data from the DDEP class to the PD class requires the consent of an employee and a corporate executive. Finally, moving data from the corporate class to the public class requires consent of a corporate executive. In all cases, a corporate executive can prevent the release of company information. Furthermore, because no other class of users can write public class data, *only* the corporate executives can release the information.

Thus, the policy is valid, because it meets the security requirements of the Drib.[11]

We next verify the consistency of the policy, to show that it is not self-contradictory. We construct the transitive closure of all paths along which information can flow among the classes. From this closure, it is clear that the *only* way information can flow into the public class is when a corporate executive moves it

---

[11] See Section 17.1.2, "The Role of Requirements in Assurance."

there. Hence, the key point of trust is in the corporate executive class. Without an executive acting, information simply cannot become public. Furthermore, by the rules for moving data out of the DDEP and DDFP classes, some other entity beyond the corporate executives must consent to the release of the information. This satisfies the principle of separation of privilege as well as the corporate goals. Because there is no contradiction among the rules in the policy, the policy is self-consistent.

We have now (informally) both validated and verified the policy. Validation and verification are basic aspects of information assurance[12] and provide a basis for asserting that the policy is correct.

We have now defined the confidentiality, integrity, and availability aspects of the Drib's basic security policy. We will now expand this into a simple network architecture.

23.3   Network Organization

The policy discussed above suggests that the network be partitioned into several parts, with guards between parts to prevent information from leaking. Each type of data resides in one of the parts (we combine both types of development data into one type, DD). The resulting partition is shown in Figure 23–1. This is a fairly standard corporate network, with one part available to the public and a second part available only internally.

> **Definition 23–1.** The *DMZ*[13] is a portion of a network that separates a purely internal network from an external network.

When information moves from the Internet to the internal network, confidentiality is not at issue. However, integrity is. The guards[14] between the Internet and the DMZ, and between the DMZ and the internal network, must not accept messages that will cause servers to work incorrectly or to crash. When information moves from the internal network to the Internet, confidentiality and integrity are both at issue. The firewalls must ensure that no confidential information goes to the Internet and that the information that reaches the Internet is correct.[15] The latter issue requires simply that information not be altered in transit from the internal network to the Internet. For simplicity, we make the assumption that the systems as deployed will not change any information in transit (except delivery information, such as packet headers). If such changes are made, then the system has been compromised by an

---

[12] See Chapter 17, "Introduction to Assurance."

[13] "DMZ" stands for "demilitarized zone."

[14] For example, see the Secure Mail Guard (Section 15.4.2). The guards discussed here are called "firewalls" (see Section 23.3.1).

[15] See Chapter 15, "Information Flow."

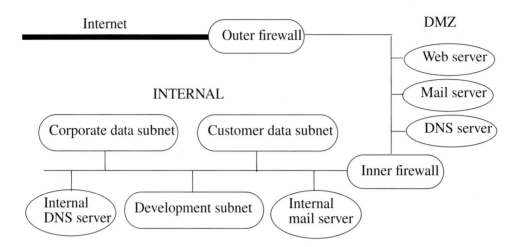

Figure 23–1   The network designed for the Dribble Corporation. The "outer firewall" sits between the Internet and the company network. The subnet labeled "DMZ" provides limited public access to various servers. The "inner firewall" sits between the DMZ and the subnets that are not to be accessed by the public. These subnets share common mail and DNS servers that, like the other hosts, are not publicly accessible.

attacker. This would require the attacker to gain access to the system. This is equivalent to the problem of disallowing certain types of information (namely, attack mechanisms) from entering the internal or DMZ subnets from the Internet—in other words, ensuring the integrity of this information.[16]

The arrangement and configuration of the firewalls provide the supporting access control mechanisms used to implement the policy.[17]

23.3.1   Firewalls and Proxies

The "guards" mentioned above perform access control in both directions,[18] to and from the Drib's network.

> **Definition 23–2.** A *firewall* is a host that mediates access to a network, allowing and disallowing certain types of access on the basis of a configured security policy.

---

[16] See Chapter 20, "Vulnerability Analysis."
[17] See Chapter 15, "Information Flow."
[18] See Chapter 14, "Access Control Mechanisms."

EXAMPLE: A company wishes to prevent any implementations of Back Orifice from allowing outsiders to control their systems. Back Orifice is an attack tool that acts as a remote system administration server, usually illicitly. It requires commands to be sent to a particular port (the exact port number is a configuration parameter; for our purposes, suppose it is 25345). The company can install a firewall that will not allow any messages with destination port number 25345 to pass from the Internet into the corporate network. This prevents messages from accessing any installed copies of Back Orifice. (Of course, if Back Orifice were configured to use port 22222, this particular firewall would not block such messages.)

This firewall accepts or rejects messages on the basis of external information, such as destination addresses or ports, rather than on the basis of the contents of the message.

Definition 23–3. A *filtering firewall* performs access control on the basis of attributes of the packet headers, such as destination addresses, source addresses, and options.

Routers and other infrastructure systems are typical examples of filtering firewalls. They allow connections through the firewall, usually on the basis of source and destination addresses and ports. Access control lists provide a natural mechanism for representing these policies.[19]

This contrasts with the second type of firewall, which never allows such a direct connection. Instead, special agents called *proxies* control the flow of information through the firewall.

Definition 23–4. A *proxy* is an intermediate agent or server that acts on behalf of an endpoint without allowing a direct connection between the two endpoints.

Definition 23–5. A *proxy* (or *applications level*) *firewall* uses proxies to perform access control. A proxy firewall can base access control on the contents of packets and messages, as well as on attributes of the packet headers.

A proxy firewall adds to a filtering firewall the ability to base access on content, either at the packet level or at a higher level of abstraction.

EXAMPLE: A company wishes to check all incoming electronic mail for computer viruses. It implements a mail proxy at the firewall between the Internet and the company intranet. The proxy has a virus scanning program (see Section 19.6.4, on pages 382–383). When mail arrives at the firewall, the proxy mail daemon accepts the mail. It then runs the virus scanner. If the scanner reports that there are no viruses in the

---

[19] See Section 14.1, "Access Control Lists."

mail or in any associated attachments, the proxy forwards the mail to the desired recipient. If the virus scanner reports that the mail or an attachment contains a virus, the mail is discarded (or some other appropriate action is taken). The fact that the electronic mail message is reassembled at the firewall by a mail agent acting on behalf of the mail agent at the ultimate destination makes this a proxy firewall.

A different point of view is to see the firewall as an audit mechanism.[20] It analyzes the packets that enter. Firewalls can then base actions on this analysis, leading to traffic shaping (in which percentages of bandwidth are reserved for specific types of traffic), intrusion response,[21] and other controls.

With these definitions in mind, the reason for this structure of the network falls into place.

23.3.2   Analysis of the Network Infrastructure

The benefits of this design flow from the security policy and the principle of least privilege. The security policy distinguishes "public" entities from those internal to the corporation, but recognizes that some corporate resources must be available to the public. The network layout described above provides this functionality. The public entities may enter the corporate perimeter (bounded by the "outer firewall") but are confined to the DMZ area (bounded inside by the "inner firewall"). The next few paragraphs give an overview of the technical details of this arrangement. We then expand on the configurations of the infrastructure systems.

The key decision is to limit the flow of information from the internal network to the DMZ. The public cannot communicate directly with *any* system in the internal network, nor can any system in the internal network communicate directly with other systems on the Internet (beyond the "outer firewall"). The systems in the DMZ serve as mediators, with the firewalls providing the guards. This setup is derived from the notion of the "pump" (see page 304 in Section 16.3.2). The firewalls and the DMZ systems make up the pump, because they control all access to and from the Internet and filter all traffic in both directions.

The first step is to conceal the addresses of the internal network. In general, the internal network addresses can be any IP addresses (the families of addresses specifically allocated to private networks are $10.x.y.z$, $172.a.x.y$ (where $16 \leq a \leq 31$), and $192.168.x.y$[22] [749]), and the inner firewall can use a protocol such as the Network Address Translation protocol [864] to map these internal host addresses to the firewall's Internet address. A more common method is to assign each host an address but not allow those addresses to leave the corporate network. This is particularly

---

[20] See Chapter 21, "Auditing."
[21] See Section 22.6, "Intrusion Response."
[22] In classless IP terminology, 10.0.0.0/8, 172.16.0.0/12, and 192.168.0.0/16.

simple, because all services are implemented as proxies in the outer firewall. However, electronic mail presents a special problem.

The DMZ mail server must know an address in order for the internal mail server to pass mail back and forth. This need not be the actual address of the internal mail server. It could be a distinguished address that the inner firewall will recognize as representing the internal mail server. Similarly, the internal mail server must know an address for the DMZ mail server. These addresses can be fixed (in which case the DMZ DNS server is unnecessary). For flexibility, we will assume that the Drib has decided to use a DNS server on both the internal and DMZ subnets. As a backup, each system in the DMZ has the network addresses of both firewalls stored locally, so if the DNS system is unavailable, the other servers can function.

The Web server lies in the DMZ for the same reasons that a mail server lies in the DMZ. External connections to the Web server go into the DMZ and no farther. If any information is to be transmitted from the Web server to the internal network (for example, the customer data subnet), the transmission is made separately, and not as part of a Web transaction.

This network organization reflects several of Saltzer and Schroeder's design principles [773]. The containment of internal addresses reflects the principle of least privilege[23] as well as the Drib's solution to the confinement problem.[24] The inner firewall mediates every access involving the DMZ and the internal networks, meeting the principle of complete mediation.[25] Going out of the inner network to the Internet requires that several criteria be met, to implement the principle of separation of privilege.[26] The firewalls are distinct computers, as are the DMZ servers, leading to a duplication rather than a sharing of network services. If the mail server stops working, for example, the WWW server is not affected. The principle of least common mechanism[27] suggests this design. The shared DNS server in the DMZ violates this principle, because multiple systems are affected if it is corrupted or unavailable. The reason for the local, fixed addresses of the two firewalls is to handle the case of unavailability, mitigating this threat. Finally, the applications of confinement, access control,[28] and information flow control[29] have been discussed earlier.

We now examine each component in more detail.

23.3.2.1   Outer Firewall Configuration

The goals of the outer firewall are to restrict public access to the Drib's corporate network and to restrict the Drib's access to the Internet. This arises from the duality of information flow.[30] In the Bell-LaPadula Model,[31] for example, one cannot read

---

[23] See Section 12.2.1, "Principle of Least Privilege."
[24] See Definition 15-1.
[25] See Section 12.2.4, "Principle of Complete Mediation."
[26] See Section 12.2.6, "Principle of Separation of Privilege."
[27] See Section 12.2.7, "Principle of Least Common Mechanism."
[28] See Chapter 14, "Access Control Mechanisms."
[29] See Chapter 15, "Information Flow."
[30] See Chapter 15, "Information Flow."
[31] See Section 5.2, "The Bell-LaPadula Model."

information from a higher level (here, by restricting public access to the Drib's network), but one cannot write information to a lower level, either (here, by restricting the Drib's employees' access to the Internet). Certain sanitized exchanges, however, are allowed. To implement the required access control, the firewall uses an access control list,[32] which binds source addresses and ports and destination addresses and ports to access rights.

The public needs to be able to access the Web server and mail server, and no other services. The firewall therefore presents an interface that allows connections to the WWW services (HTTP and HTTPS) and to electronic mail (SMTP). Sites on the Internet see the addresses of the Web and mail servers as the same—that of the firewall. No other services are provided to sites on the Internet.

The firewall is a proxy-based firewall. When an electronic mail connection is initiated, the SMTP proxy on the firewall collects the mail. It then analyzes it for computer viruses and other forms of malicious logic. If none is found, it forwards the mail to the DMZ mail server. When a Web connection (or datagram) arrives, the firewall scans the message for any suspicious components (such as extraordinarily long lines or other evidence of attacks) and, if none is found, forwards it to the DMZ Web server. These two DMZ servers have different addresses, neither of which is the address of the firewall.

Attackers trying to penetrate the firewall have three methods of entry. The first is to enter through the Web server ports. The unsecured (HTTP) port proxy checks for invalid or illegal HTTP requests and rejects them. The second is to enter through the SMTP port. The mail proxy will detect and reject such attempts. The third is to attempt to bypass the low-level firewall checks by exploiting vulnerabilities in the firewall itself.

The discussion of vulnerabilities in Chapter 20, "Vulnerability Analysis," implies that there is no way to ensure that the firewall software and hardware cannot be breached. Designing the firewall mechanisms to be as simple as possible, in accordance with the principle of economy of mechanism,[33] using assurance techniques minimizes, but does not eliminate, this possibility. So we apply the principle of separation of privilege[34] in the form of a technique called "defense in depth." In order to attack a system in the DMZ by bypassing the firewall checks, the attacker must know something about the internal addresses of the DMZ. If, for example, the attacker knows that the internal address of the DMZ mail server is 10.34.231.19, the attacker may be able to use that information to piggyback packets to that host.[35] But if the attacker has no idea of the internal DMZ mail server's address, even if the

---

[32] See Section 14.1, "Access Control Lists."

[33] See Section 12.2.3, "Principle of Economy of Mechanism."

[34] See Section 12.2.6, "Principle of Separation of Privilege."

[35] The description here is vague out of necessity. Whether or not such a method exists, and how to exploit it, are properties of individual hosts, software, and vendors. The curious reader is invited to use the Flaw Hypothesis Methodology (see Section 20.2.4) to analyze his or her organization's firewall *after* obtaining written permission from the responsible officials.

attacker is able to bypass the firewall checks, he or she will not know where to have the packets sent.

23.3.2.2   Inner Firewall Configuration

The internal network is where the Drib's most sensitive data resides. It may contain data, such as proprietary information, that the Drib does not want outsiders to see. For this reason, the inner firewall will block all traffic except for that specifically authorized to enter (the principle of fail-safe defaults[36]). All such information will come from the DMZ, and never directly from the Internet.

EXAMPLE: The Drib uses the Network File System (NFS) protocol to share files among its systems. The NFS protocol (see Section 21.6.1) sends the contents of files around a network. Were any of these packets containing sensitive information to leak to the Internet, the Drib would be compromised. The outer firewall is configured to disallow NFS packets from leaking to the Internet. However, the principle of least privilege says that, unless hosts in the DMZ require access to the internal NFS information, the packets should not even reach the DMZ. Furthermore, the principle of separation of privilege says that multiple mechanisms should prevent NFS packets from leaking to the Internet. If one mechanism fails, the others will still prevent the leak. Hence, the inner firewall should also disallow NFS packets from going to the DMZ.

Like the outer firewall, the inner firewall allows a limited set of traffic through (using the same type of access control mechanism as does the outer firewall). It allows SMTP connections using proxies, but all electronic mail is sent to the DMZ mail server for disposition. It allows limited transfer of information to the DNS server in the DMZ. It also allows system administrators to access the systems in the DMZ from a trusted administrative server. All other traffic, including Web access, is blocked.

The administrator's connection uses the Secure Shell (SSH) protocol and differs from the other protocols in that a direct connection through the SSH port is allowed (that is, no SSH proxies). This allows the address of the administrative server to leave the internal network. However, the firewall filter ensures that the SSH connection can go only to one of the DMZ servers. This use of cryptography provides message secrecy and integrity as well as strong (cryptographic) authentication of the endpoints.[37] Because the requisite public keys are embedded into the system when SSH is configured, the issue of an infrastructure for public key distribution[38] is finessed.

The access allowed to system administrators violates the principle of least privilege,[39] because the connection allows the administrators full control over the DMZ systems. Several precautions ameliorate this violation. First, if the connection

---

[36] See Section 12.2.2, "Principle of Fail-Safe Defaults."

[37] See Chapter 8, " Basic Cryptography," and Chapter 10, "Cipher Techniques."

[38] See Section 9.3, "Cryptographic Key Infrastructures."

[39] See Section 12.2.1, "Principle of Least Privilege."

to the systems in the DMZ does not originate from a special system in the internal network (dubbed the "administrative server"), the firewall will disallow the connection. Second, the Drib trusts its system administrators, so only trusted users will be allowed unrestricted access to the DMZ servers. Third, the administrators can use the SSH protocol only to connect to the DMZ servers, and all administrative traffic is protected using SSH. This means that an attacker would not only have to spoof the internal network host addresses, but also find the correct set of cryptographic keys. Although not perfect, these precautions reduce the risk of compromise.

23.3.3   In the DMZ

Four servers reside in the DMZ. They are the mail, WWW, DNS, and log servers. We will discuss these servers separately.

23.3.3.1   DMZ Mail Server

The mail server in the DMZ performs address and content checking on all electronic mail messages. The goal is to hide internal information from the outside while being transparent to the inside. When the mail server receives a letter from the Internet, it performs the following steps.

1. The mail proxy reassembles the message into a set of headers, a letter, and any attachments. The attachments are assembled into their native form (not the form used to transmit them through electronic mail). This allows the mail server to work on the original mail, as opposed to a packetized form of the letter. It simplifies the checking.

2. The mail proxy scans the letter and attachments, looking for any "bad" content. "Bad" content here is defined as a computer virus or known malicious logic. The attachments are then restored to the form used to transmit them through electronic mail. The headers, the letter, and the attachments are rescanned for any violation of the SMTP specification. This is the basic content checking. Any binary data (which might indicate a buffer overflow or other attack) is weeded out, as are excessively long lines.[40] Although address lines are limited in length to 1,000 characters, the mail proxy will split them as needed to keep lines less than 80 characters long. The scanning also detects and eliminates known malicious logic (computer viruses and worms, logic bombs, and so forth). The analysis of content for malicious logic uses standard techniques.[41]

---

[40] See Chapter 20, "Vulnerability Analysis."
[41] See Section 19.6.4, "Malicious Logic Altering Files."

3. The mail proxy scans the recipient address lines. The addresses that directed the mail to the Drib are rewritten to direct the mail to the internal mail server. The DMZ mail server then forwards the mail to the internal mail server. This step forwards the mail to the Drib's internal network, on which it will be delivered. Identification is by host name and not user name,[42] because the mail server determines the identity of the correct host to forward the mail to on the basis of host name, not user name.

The procedure for sending mail out of the Drib is similar. All outgoing mail comes from the internal mail server. Steps 1 and 2 are the same (although the content checking in step 2 may be enhanced to detect keywords such as "proprietary"). But the sanitization for step 3 is different.

3′. The mail proxy scans the header lines. All lines that mention internal hosts are rewritten to identify the host as "drib.org," the name of the outside firewall. *All* header lines must be checked. In addition to the source address lines, any "Received" lines are to be removed, and any destinations that name the Drib must also be changed. Following this sanitization, the letter is forwarded to the firewall for delivery. This step forwards the mail to the Internet after hiding all details of the Drib's networks. This idea comes from the principle of least privilege,[43] because those who do not need to know about the internals of the Drib's network do not get that information.

The primary goals of the mail server are to handle mail and to perform all needed checks and sanitization. This way, the firewalls only need to perform rudimentary checks (such as checks on line length and character type) and leave the detailed checking to the mail servers.

The DMZ mail server also runs an SSH server. This server is configured to accept connections only from the trusted administrative host in the internal network. This allows the system administrators to configure and maintain the DMZ mail host remotely (a great convenience) without unnecessarily exposing that host to compromise.

23.3.3.2   DMZ WWW Server

The Web server accepts and services requests from the Internet. It does not contact any servers or information sources within the internal network. This means that if the Web server is compromised, the compromise cannot affect internal hosts. Although the Web server runs CGI scripts, the scripts have been checked for potential attacks and hardened to prevent their success.[44] The server itself contains no confidential data.

---

[42] See Section 13.6.1, "Host Identity."

[43] See Section 12.2.1, "Principle of Least Privilege."

[44] See Chapter 20, "Vulnerability Analysis," and Chapter 26, "Program Security."

The Web server also identifies itself as "www.drib.org" and uses the IP address of the outside firewall. This hides part of the DMZ configuration in accordance with the principle of least privilege[45] (because people outside the network need not know the address), and forces external entities to send Web traffic to the firewall.

A system in the internal network known as the "WWW-clone" is used to update the DMZ Web server. People authorized to update the Drib's Web page can access this system. Periodically (or on request), an administrator will copy the contents of the WWW-clone to the DMZ Web server (see Section 24.7.1). This follows from the principle of separation of privilege,[46] because any unauthorized changes in the Web server are mitigated by the updates. Like the mail server, the WWW server also runs an SSH server for maintenance and updating. The server provides the cryptographic support necessary to ensure confidentiality and data and origin integrity.[47]

The Drib accepts orders for its merchandise through the Web. The data entered by the consumer is saved to a file. After the user confirms an order, the Web server invokes a simple program that checks the format and contents of the file and creates an enciphered version of the file using the public key of a system on the internal customer subnet. This file resides in a spooling area that is *not* accessible to the Web server (see Exercise 3). The program deletes the original file. This way, even if the attacker can obtain the file, the attacker cannot determine the order information or credit card numbers associated with customers. Indeed, because the customer names are in the enciphered files, the attacker cannot even determine the names. Formally, not keeping valuable information online and in the clear follows from the principle of least privilege,[48] because the users of that machine are not authorized to read the data, and from the principle of separation of privilege,[49] because the cryptographic key is needed to read the data. Using public key cryptography means that only a public key need be on the DMZ Web server. This prevents an attacker from deciphering the data on that system should it be compromised, which is an application of the principle of fail-safe defaults.[50]

The internal trusted administrative server periodically connects to the Web server using the SSH protocol, uploads the enciphered order files, and transmits them to the appropriate system on the internal customer subnet. The SSH server on the Web server is configured to reject connections from any host other than the trusted internal administrative server, so an attacker cannot connect from outside (assuming the attacker is able to penetrate the outer firewall). The principle of denying unknown connections, rather than allowing them and then authenticating them, follows the principle of fail-safe defaults.[51]

---

[45] See Section 12.2.1, "Principle of Least Privilege."
[46] See Section 12.2.6, "Principle of Separation of Privilege."
[47] See Chapter 8, "Basic Cryptography," and Chapter 10, "Cipher Techniques."
[48] See Section 12.2.1, "Principle of Least Privilege."
[49] See Section 12.2.6, "Principle of Separation of Privilege."
[50] See Section 12.2.2, "Principle of Fail-Safe Defaults."
[51] See Section 12.2.2, "Principle of Fail-Safe Defaults."

23.3.3.3 DMZ DNS Server

The DMZ DNS host contains directory name service information about those hosts that the DMZ servers must know. It contains entries for the following.

- DMZ mail, Web, and log hosts
- Internal trusted administrative host
- Outer firewall
- Inner firewall

Note that the DNS server does not know the addresses of the internal mail server. The inner firewall will forward mail to that server. The DMZ mail server need only know the addresses of the two firewalls (for mail transfers), and the trusted administrative server. If the mail server knows the address of the DNS server, it can obtain these three addresses. This gives the internal network the flexibility to rearrange its host addressing. The DMZ DNS server must be updated only if the address of the internal trusted administrative host is changed.

The limited information in the DNS server reflects the principle of least privilege,[52] because those entries are sufficient for the systems in the DMZ.

23.3.3.4 DMZ Log Server

The log server performs an administrative function. All DMZ machines have logging turned on. In the event of a compromise (or an attempted compromise), these logs will be invaluable in assessing the method of attack, the damage (or potential damage), and the best response. However, attackers can delete logs, so if the logs were on the attacked machines, they might be tampered with or erased.

The Drib has located a fourth server in the DMZ. All other servers log messages by writing them to a local file and then to the log server. The log server also writes them to a file and then to write-once media, which is a precaution in case some attacker is able to overwrite log files on both the target server and the log server. It is also an application of the principle of separation of privilege.[53]

The log system is placed in the DMZ to confine its activity.[54] It never initiates transfer to the inner network. Only the trusted administrative host does that, and then only if the administrators choose not to read logs by reading the media on which the logs reside.

Like the other servers, the log server accepts connections from the internal trusted administrative host. Administrators can view the logs directly, or they can replace the write-once media with another instance of the media and read the extracted media directly. The use of write-once media is an example of applying the

---

[52] See Section 12.2.1, "Principle of Least Privilege."
[53] See Section 12.2.6, "Principle of Separation of Privilege."
[54] See Chapter 16, "Confinement Problem."

principle of least privilege[55] and fail-safe defaults,[56] because the media cannot be altered; they can only be destroyed, and then only if the attacker has physical access to the system.

23.3.3.5   Summary

Each server has the minimum knowledge of the network necessary to perform its task. This follows the principle of least privilege. Compromise of the servers on these systems will restrict the transfer of information, but will not lead to compromise of the systems on the internal network.

Ideally, the operating systems of the server computers should be very small kernels that provide only the system support services necessary to run the appropriate servers. In practice, the operating systems are trusted operating systems (developed using assurance techniques,[57] or—more commonly—commercial operating systems in which all unnecessary features and services have been disabled. This minimizes the operations that a server can perform on behalf of a remote process. Hence, even if the server is compromised, the attacker cannot use it to compromise other hosts such as the inner firewall.

The use of proxies on the firewalls prevents direct connections across the firewalls. Moreover, the data passing through the firewalls can be checked and, based on the content, filtered or blocked. The only exception is the SSH connection from the internal network to the DMZ. The inner firewall checks the origination of the connection, to ensure that it comes from the internal administrative host, and the destination, to ensure that it goes to one of the servers.

23.3.4   In the Internal Network

The internal network may be organized in several ways. Each of the subnets may have its own firewall and its own server, and may filter traffic just as the inner firewall does. The subnets may share servers. If the primary goal is to guard the Drib's internal data from being stolen by an outside attacker, what goes on behind the inner firewall is irrelevant.

The Drib's policy imposes the opposite requirement. The subnets must guard against unauthorized access to information as dictated by the policy. For these purposes, "read" corresponds to fetching or retrieving a file, and "write" corresponds to putting or depositing a file. For the moment, we ignore electronic mail, updating of Web pages on the DMZ, and the internal administrative host.

The constraints on information flow[58] dictate the arrangement of the network. The firewalls impose the confinement[59] required at the interfaces.

---

[55] See Section 12.2.1, "Principle of Least Privilege."
[56] See Section 12.2.2, "Principle of Fail-Safe Defaults."
[57] See Chapter 17, "Introduction to Assurance."
[58] See Chapter 15, "Information Flow."
[59] See Chapter 16, "Confinement Problem."

The data and users are distributed among the three subnets of the internal network in the obvious way. The firewall on the developer network allows read access from the corporate network but blocks write access to all other subnets. The firewall on the corporate network does not allow read or write access from the other networks. The firewall for the customer subnet allows read access from the corporate network. It also allows write access for information placed by the public onto the DMZ Web server. However, the write access is constrained to be mediated only by the DMZ Web server and the inner firewall, so the public does not have unrestricted access. These firewalls may be proxy firewalls or filtering firewalls.

The internal mail server must be free to communicate with hosts behind each of the subnet firewalls. Either the subnet may have its own mail server, or the internal mail server can deliver mail directly to each host on the subnets. The former has the advantage of flexibility, because the internal DNS server need only know the addresses of the subnet firewalls and (possibly) the mail servers. Thus, other host addresses can be changed freely within each subnet. The latter requires the internal DNS to have the addresses of all hosts on the internal network, but is simpler to configure and maintain. Either arrangement will satisfy the Drib's policy.

In addition to the mail server, an internal Web server provides a staging area for the Drib's Web pages. All internal firewalls allow both read and write access to this server. (The server itself controls the specific access that individuals have to each Web page.) The DMZ Web server's pages are synchronized with the Web pages on this server by using the trusted internal administrative host. This provides a test bed for changes in the pages, so corporate and other internal personnel can review and approve changes before they are made visible to the public. Furthermore, if the DMZ Web server is ever compromised, the Web pages can be restored very quickly.

Finally, the trusted internal administrative server has strict access rules: only system administrators authorized to administer the DMZ systems have access to it. All connections to the DMZ through the inner firewall must use this server, except for the mail server and (possibly) the DNS server. The server itself uses SSH to access systems in the DMZ, and the DMZ servers recognize it as the only host authorized to access their SSH daemons. This prevents a user on the internal network from sending SSH commands from a local workstation to DMZ servers.

With respect to the internal network, the DMZ servers know only about the inner firewall's address and the trusted administrative host's address, by the principle of least privilege.[60] The DMZ servers never communicate directly with the internal servers. They instead send information to the firewall, which routes the messages appropriately. DMZ servers accept only incoming SSH connections from the trusted administrative host. These connections use public key authentication to establish identity,[61] so an attacker cannot forge addresses.

This arrangement is layered with checks. A single action affecting a host on the DMZ requires that several tests be passed (implementing the principle of separation of mechanism). Only a few administrators can alter or update systems on the

---

[60] See Section 12.2.1, "Principle of Least Privilege."

[61] See Section 8.3, "Public Key Cryptography," and Section 13.6.1, "Host Identity."

DMZ. In general, the only data in the DMZ that nonadministrators can alter is the data in the Web pages. However, the alterations occur on a copy on the internal network. An administrator must invoke special functions to move the updated pages to the Web server on the DMZ.

The only data that is written from the DMZ to the internal network comes from customer orders, but the data so received has been checked for potential errors (or deliberately corrupt data), is enciphered, and is transferred to an internal machine in such a way that it cannot be executed. This applies the analysis techniques for analyzing existing systems[62] and developing systems with some level of assurance.[63] This again limits the ability of an attacker to use this data to attack systems on the internal network.

23.3.5   General Comment on Assurance

All of the defenses discussed above depend on software that has been written defensively. This is particularly true of software on the firewalls. Although the amount of software running on the firewalls is minimized, and the software is written to perform only necessary functions and has been extensively audited and tested, the Drib defensive mechanisms all trust that the software is correct and cannot be compromised. If this trust is misplaced, the defensive mechanisms can be breached. This is another reason why the configuration of servers and firewalls is based extensively on the principle of separation of mechanism. If one mechanism fails, another may prevent the attacker from exploiting that failure.

A similar remark applies to hardware. Suppose the network interface card connected to the Internet never cleared its buffer. An attacker could craft a packet that contained data of the form of a legal packet addressed to an interior system. The containing packet would be validated as allowed to go to the interior network and then would be passed to the interior network. The next packet would be short enough to overwrite the contents of the buffer from the beginning up to the data in the form of the valid packet. If the card then flushed the contents of its buffer to the inside network, the legal but unvalidated packet would be sent on, too. (See Exercise 2.) The separation of mechanism inherent in a proxy firewall hinders attacks based on failures in single network cards, but other types of malfunctions may allow other attacks.

Assurance at all levels is important. Here, the informal policy model of the Drib (see Section 23.2) guides the design of the network architecture as well as the analysis of the software and hardware configurations. Infrastructure, software, and hardware all provide the basis for claims that the network actually enforces the policy model correctly.

---

[62] See Chapter 20, "Vulnerability Analysis."
[63] See See Chapter 17, "Introduction to Assurance."

23.4   Availability and Network Flooding

The availability component of the Drib's policy requires that the systems must be available to the public and to Drib personnel. This means that access over the Internet must be unimpeded. We consider this in the context of flooding attacks, in which attackers attempt to overwhelm system resources.

The SYN flood is the most common type of flooding attack. It occurs when incoming connections repeatedly refuse to execute the third part of the TCP three-way handshake (see page 437). This is a denial of service attack. If the packets come from multiple sources but have the same destination, this is an example of a distributed denial of service attack. The source address of these SYN packets is typically set to some unreachable host. This prevents the third part of the handshake from being executed, and prevents the attacked systems from determining the attacker by reading the source address from the SYN packet.

In what follows, the term "legitimate handshake" refers to a connection attempt that is not part of a SYN flood. If the client in a legitimate handshake receives the SYN/ACK packet from the server, it will respond with the appropriate ACK to complete the handshake and begin the connection. The term "attack handshake," on the other hand, refers to a connection attempt that is part of a SYN flood. The client in an attack handshake will never send an ACK packet to complete the handshake. A critical observation is that the server cannot distinguish between a legitimate handshake and an attack handshake. Both follow the same steps. The only difference lies in whether the third part of the handshake is sent (and received).

There are two aspects of SYN flooding. The first is the consumption of bandwidth. If the flooding is more than the capacity of the physical network medium, or of intermediate nodes, legitimate handshakes may be unable to reach the target. The second is the use of resources—specifically, memory space—on the target. If the flooding absorbs all the memory allocated for half-open connections, then the target will discard the SYN packets from legitimate handshake attempts.

We focus on the second aspect, because the first involves infrastructure elements not under the control of the Drib. First, we consider defenses that do not involve the target system. Then we examine the target system.

23.4.1   Intermediate Hosts

This approach tries to reduce the consumption of resources on the target by using routers to divert or eliminate illegitimate traffic. The key observation here is that the SYN flood is handled *before* it reaches the firewall, at the infrastructure level. The goal is to have only legitimate handshakes reach the firewall.

EXAMPLE: Cisco routers can use "TCP intercept mode" to implement this approach [414]. When the router sees a SYN packet coming from the Internet, it does not forward the packet to its destination. Instead, the router responds, and tries to establish the connection. If the SYN packet is part of a legitimate handshake and a connection is established, the router establishes a connection with the intended destination and "merges" the two connections. If the SYN packet is part of an attack handshake, the router never sees a following ACK packet, and times the pending connection out without ever contacting the putative destination. The router uses short time-outs to ensure it does not run out of space for pending connections. The TCP intercept feature may be set either on a per-host basis or for all hosts on the Internet.

An alternative is to have a system monitor the network traffic and track the state of the three-way handshake.

EXAMPLE: Synkill [801] is an active monitor that analyzes packets being sent to some set of systems to be protected. It classifies IP addresses as never seen (*null*), not flooding (*good*), flooding (*bad*), or unknown (*new*). Initially, a set of IP addresses may be put into these classes. As synkill monitors the network, it adds addresses to each class.

When synkill sees an SYN packet, it checks the IP address. If that address is *bad*, synkill immediately sends an RST to the destination. This terminates the pending connection. If the IP address is *good*, synkill ignores the packet. If the IP address has not yet been seen, it is classified as *new*. A subsequent ACK or RST packet from the new address will cause the address to be added to the list of *good* addresses, because its behavior is correct, but if no such packet is seen for a specified *expiry* period of time, the *new* address is assumed to be attempting a SYN flood and is moved into the *bad* set of IP addresses, and an RST is sent to the destination.

If no traffic from a good address is observed during a different time interval, called the *staleness time*, the address is deleted from the list of *good* addresses.

Experiments showed that the effects of using synkill enabled legitimate connections to be completed. Delays grew as the rate of SYN packets from different IP addresses grew, but the developers concluded that the delays were acceptable given a powerful enough computer running synkill.

The problem with these techniques is that they simply push the focus of the attack back from the firewall onto infrastructure systems on the outside of the Drib's network. They do not solve the problem, but they may ameliorate it sufficiently to allow some legitimate connections to reach their destinations.

23.4.2   TCP State and Memory Allocations

This approach springs from the way in which most TCP servers are implemented. When a SYN packet is received, the server creates an entry in a data structure of pending connections and then sends the SYN/ACK packet. The entry remains until either a corresponding ACK is received or a time-out occurs. In the former case, the connection is completed; in the latter case, a new entry for the next SYN packet is created. Under a SYN flood, the data structure is kept full of entries that never move to the connected state. All will be timed out, and new SYNs create new entries to continue the cycle.

The data structure contains the state of the pending connection. This information typically includes the source IP address, a sequence number, and other (internal) information. When the client replies with an ACK packet to complete the handshake, the server uses this information to verify that the ACK packet corresponds to the initial SYN packet. The SYN flood succeeds because the space allocated to hold this state information is filled *before* any three-way handshakes are completed. Legitimate handshakes cannot obtain space in the data structure. However, if legitimate handshakes can be assured space, to some level of probability, then legitimate handshakes have a probability of successfully completing even in the face of a denial of service attack.

Two techniques are used to make availability of space more likely. The first is to push the tracking of state to the client. For example, if the state can be encoded in the initial sequence number of the ACK, the server can rederive the information from information in the client's ACK packet. Then no state needs to be kept on the server system. This approach is called the *SYN cookie* approach.

EXAMPLE: The Linux 2.4.9 kernel can be configured to use the SYN cookie approach [655] when the table of pending connections is full. Linux uses the SYN cookie formula developed by Bernstein and Schenk [82]:

$$h(s_1, s_A, s_P, d_A, d_P, s_1) + n + 2^{24}t + [h(s_2, s_A, s_P, d_A, d_P, t, s_2) \textbf{ mod } 2^{24}]$$

where h is a hash function (either MD-5 or SHA-1), s_1 and s_2 are randomly generated secrets, s_A and s_P are the source address and port, d_A and d_P are the destination address and port, t is a counter incremented every minute, and n is the sequence number of the received SYN packet. When the ACK is received, the SYN cookie is checked by recomputing each part of the SYN cookie anew and subtracting that value from the received SYN cookie [94].

The SYN cookie formula minimizes the threat of an attacker guessing a SYN cookie value and sending an ACK to which there has been no corresponding SYN or SYN/ACK. The t parameter causes successive values of the second hash function to vary unpredictably, so an attacker cannot predict the next value given a set of prior values. The $2^{24}t$ value causes the SYN cookies to increase more rapidly than the standard sequence number n. This makes guessing of SYN cookie values more difficult than guessing of sequence numbers.

If the table of pending connections is full, no state is stored until the ACK from the remote host is received. At this point, the connection is opened, so the state is stored in a different table than the table of pending connections.

The second technique assumes that there is a fixed amount of space for the state of pending connections. A SYN flood causes attack handshakes to fill this space. After some constant amount of time (usually 75 seconds), the server deletes the state information associated with the attack handshake. This is called the "time-out" of the pending connection. This approach simply varies the times before the time-outs depending on the amount of space available for new pending connections. As the amount of available space decreases, so does the amount of time before the system begins to time out connections. This approach is called *adaptive time-out*.

EXAMPLE: Freedman [338] modified the kernel of a SunOS system to provide adaptive time-outs of pending connections. First, he shortened the time-out period for pending connections from 75 to 15 seconds. He then modified the formula for queuing pending connections. Suppose a process allows up to b pending connections on a given port. Let a be the number of completed connections that the process has not begun using.[64] Let p be the number of pending connections. Let c be a tunable parameter. When

$$a + p > cb$$

the current SYN message is dropped.

Both of these techniques improve the resilience of systems in the face of flooding attacks. The first technique changes the allocation of space for pending connections by trading the space used to store the state information of pending connections for extra computations to validate the states of incoming ACKs. The second method times out pending connections quickly to make more space available for the incoming handshakes.

23.5   Anticipating Attacks

In spite of the measures outlined above, the Drib security officers realize that their network and systems might be compromised through unanticipated means. They have taken steps to prepare for, and handle, such attacks.

The extensive logging described above is one step. The DMZ log server contains an intrusion detection mechanism that scans through the logs looking for evidence of known attacks and of anomalous behavior. The reasons, and settings, are bound in the Drib's philosophy of defense.

The Drib security officers are aware of the multitude of attacks that can be launched against networks and systems. They expect these attacks to come from the

---

[64] Specifically, the number of connections that have completed the TCP three-way handshake but are awaiting an *accept* system call from the process.

Internet against the outer firewall. If the attacks are stopped by the firewall, they are logged and ignored. For example, should someone attempt a known buffer overflow attack against the SMTP mail proxy, the proxy will reject the attack, log the attempt, and continue to function. The security officers will not pursue the attacker, and are interested in the attack only as a statistic they can use when higher management asks them to justify their budget, or when they are training new system administrators in security procedures and techniques.

However, should the SMTP proxy be attacked successfully, the Drib's security officers will be very interested. At that point, the SMTP mail proxy will cease to function as a mail proxy. Instead, it will start nonstandard programs (such as a command interpreter or some other program that gives the attacker access to, or information about, the system). At this point, the anomaly detection component of the intrusion detection mechanism will detect the unusual behavior and report a potential problem. The Drib's security staff monitors the intrusion detection system around the clock, so they can act quickly on such reports.

The Drib's security officers are very interested in attempted attacks within the DMZ. Unlike the Internet, where attack tools are commonplace, use of the DMZ is restricted only to those who have access to the internal administrative trusted host or who are using a small set of services. If a known attack occurs on this network, someone who has obtained access to the network has launched it. This means that some trusted administrator should not have been trusted (entry through the administrative trusted host), that one of the servers on the firewall has been compromised (entry through the outer firewall), or that the software on the DMZ systems either is corrupted (already in the DMZ) or does not restrict actions sufficiently tightly (entry through the DMZ Web or mail server). Hence, network traffic is monitored using both anomaly and misuse detection methods, and all attempted compromises are reported.

The philosophy of ignoring attacks that fail seems dangerous, because when an attacker succeeds in compromising the system, the attacker probably has tried—and failed—numerous times before. Although this is true, the Drib's answer is, "So what? We do not have the personnel to handle the false alarms and the failed attacks. Instead, we focus on what we are most concerned about: successful attacks, and failed attacks in areas where attacks ought not to be launched. A failed attack within the DMZ tells us that someone or something is acting in a forbidden way and that some compromise has occurred. But a failed attack from the Internet tells us that someone may have found a new attack script and used us as the target. We put our efforts where we can obtain useful results."

Finally, the Drib security officers analyzed many commercial intrusion detection systems to find one that met their needs. All reported many false positives. Some even failed to detect attacks launched by the security officers. The Drib therefore purchased an intrusion detection system that allowed them to add signatures of known attacks and to tune parameters to control reporting of events. After considerable experimentation, they found a group of settings that seemed to work well. To verify this, every month the Drib security officers select two 1-hour periods at random and analyze the logs for attacks, probes, and other nefarious events. The results of the analysis are compared with the reported events. If they match, the current set of settings is accepted; if not, the settings are retuned.

23.6   Summary

This chapter demonstrated how to develop a network infrastructure from security requirements. The security goals led directly to the development of a security policy, which in turn suggested the form of the network. One firewall limits the types of traffic to public servers; the other firewall blocks all external traffic from reaching the inner-most portions of the corporate network. The servers available to the public are dedicated systems that provide only one service. The firewalls are application level firewalls, so they can check the contents of any connection. Finally, meeting the availability policy requirements led to a discussion of defenses against attackers using SYN floods to prevent legitimate connections accessing the publicly available servers.

23.7   Further Reading

Many books and papers describe firewalls and the design of network infrastructures that use them. Lodin and Schuba [578] describe the basic use of firewalls. Frantzen, Kerschbaum, Schultz, and Fahmy [335] discuss the structure of a firewall in order to shed light on possible vulnerabilities. Bellovin and Cheswick [71], and Zwicky, Cooper, and Chapman [967], discuss the principles of firewalls. Ranum and Avolio [741] have created an early applications layer firewall. Chapman [161] describes an early packet filtering firewall. Schuba and Spafford [802] have created a reference model for firewalls. Epstein, Thomas, and Monteith suggest using wrappers to prevent attackers from exploiting security holes in proxies on firewalls [302]. Mayer, Wool, and Ziskind [600] have developed a tool for examining the policy enforced by a firewall.

Virtual Private Networks (VPNs) build virtual infrastructures on existing infrastructures. They are ideal for corporations with geographically distributed offices, or when telecommuting is used. Several books discuss their creation and management [529, 715, 804]. Caronni, Kumar, Schuba, and Scott present a layering approach to VPNs that hides the existing infrastructure [155].

Web commerce and security uses principles and practices that are common to other systems in which security is desired. Several authors [348, 764, 871] have described the issues and approaches specifically in terms of the Web and electronic commerce.

23.8   Exercises

1. Suppose a new class of users, the *system security officers* (SSOs), were to be added to the access control matrix discussed in Section 23.2.2. Augment the matrix with the *change* right. This right allows the user to alter the classes of other users in that category. For example, if user Amy had change rights over the class "developers," she could change the class of user Tom, who is currently in the "developers" class, to any of the other four classes.

    a. Let Alice be a member of the SSO class, and let her have change rights over the "developers" and "employees" classes. Let Bob be a member of the SSO class, with change rights over "outsiders" and "employees." Redraw the matrix for this situation and write rules describing the allowed transformations of the matrix.

    b. Describe any problems that might occur if Alice and Bob were not careful about the changes of classes they made. Could information leak in undesired ways? If so, give an example. If not, show why not.

    c. Should members of the SSO class be allowed to apply the change right to members of that class? Justify your answer. In particular, state what damage could occur if this were allowed, and if it were not allowed.

2. Assume that an attacker has found a technique for sending packets through the outer firewall to the DMZ without the packets being checked. (The attacker does not know the internal addresses of hosts in the DMZ.) Using this technique, how can the attacker arrange for a packet to be sent to the WWW server in the DMZ without the firewall checking the packet?

3. Consider the scheme used to allow customers to submit their credit card and order information. Section 23.3.3.2 states that the enciphered version of the data is stored in a spooling area that the Web server cannot access.

    a. Why is the file kept inaccessible to the Web server?

    b. Because the file is inaccessible to the Web server, and no other services are available to an attacker from the Internet, the encipherment may seem unnecessary. Discuss this issue, but assume that the attacker is on the internal network.

4. The organization of the network provides a DMZ to which the public has controlled access. This follows the principle of least privilege, as noted in Section 23.3.3.5. For each of Saltzer and Schroeder's other design principles [773] (see Chapter 12), explain how the principle is relevant to the creation of the DMZ. Justify your answer.

5. A security analyst wishes to deploy intrusion detection monitors to determine if any attackers penetrate the Drib's network.

   a. Where should the intrusion detection monitors be placed in the network's topology, and why?
   b. If the analyst wished to monitor insider attacks (that is, attacks by people with access to the Drib's internal network), how would your answer to part (a) change (if at all)? Justify your changes (or lack of changes).

6. The Drib has hired the computer security firm of Dewey, Cheatham, and Howe to audit their networks. The analyst from DC&H arrives and produces a floppy disk. She states that the disk is to be loaded onto a system on the internal network. She will then run the program. It will scan the Drib's networks and send the information to DC&H's headquarters in Upper Bottom. There, DC&H analysts will determine whether the Drib's security is acceptable, and will recommend changes.

   a. The analyst informs the Drib that the program works by sending the data to DC&H's headquarters over the Internet using a proprietary protocol. She requests that the firewalls be opened to allow communications to remote hosts with destination port 80. The audit department manager, who was told to hire DC&H by the Drib's CEO, is nervous. Should his security expert recommend that the communication be allowed, or not? Why?
   b. The analyst is asked exactly what the program does. She assures the Drib that it does nothing harmful. Given that she is so vague, the Drib security officers want to find out more information. Suggest four or five questions that they should ask to obtain the information they seek.
   c. The analyst admits that her answers are based on what the DC&H auditors have told her. When asked for the source code of the program on the floppy, she states that it is proprietary and cannot be released. What could the Drib's officers do to assure themselves that the program is not harmful?
   d. Based on the actions of the analyst, and assuming that finances are not a consideration, would you hire DC&H to analyze your network security? Why or why not?

7. This exercise asks you to compare an SMTP server such as *sendmail* with an SMTP proxy for an application level firewall. Your answers should assume that the questions refer to the Drib's network.

   a. The SMTP server must be able to parse electronic mail addresses. It may have to change the destination address (so the mail can be delivered correctly) and/or the source address (so the recipient can reply). Would an SMTP proxy on the outer firewall need to rewrite addresses of mail moving from the Internet to the DMZ? From the DMZ's mail server to the Internet? If not, explain why not. If so, explain which addresses would need to be rewritten, and how.

b. The SMTP server must be able to deliver mail locally. Does the SMTP proxy server need to deliver mail locally (that is, on the outer firewall)? Why or why not?

c. Considering your answers to the previous two parts, how does the complexity of the SMTP proxy compare with the complexity of the SMTP server? From the point of view of security, is this important? Justify your answer.

8. Suppose the Drib wished to allow employes to telecommute. In order to protect the network, they require all remote connections (other than those for the Web and mail servers) to use SSH.

a. Discuss the required changes in the network infrastructure. In particular, should the outer firewall provide an SSH proxy or a packet filter to incoming SSH connections? Why?

b. The destination of an SSH connection from the Internet might be the address of any host on the internal network. Such addresses, however, are not broadcast to the Internet and in fact may be addresses that routers on the Internet should not pass (such as 10.x.x.x). Devise a method or protocol that will continue to conceal the addresses of the hosts on the internal network but still allow SSH connections from the Internet to arrive at the proper destinations. What supporting infrastructure must the Drib add to its network?

c. The inner firewall will pass SSH connections, provided that one endpoint is the trusted administration server on the internal network. With the above-mentioned change, the destination of the incoming SSH connection may be any host on the internal network. For this question, assume that the addresses of the hosts on the internal network are kept within the internal network—in other words, that the method or protocol in part (b) is implemented. What are the security implications of allowing SSH connections to *any* internal host through the inner firewall? Should such connections be restricted (for example, by requiring users to register the hosts from which they will be connecting)?

d. An alternative to allowing the SSH connections through the firewall is to provide a specific host (the "SSH host") on the internal network that is also connected to the Internet. Telecommuters could use SSH to log into this system, and from it reach systems on the internal network. (The difference between this method and allowing connections through the firewall is that the user must log into the intermediate host, and from there move to the internal system. The firewall approach makes the intermediate system transparent.) Identify the *minimum* number of services that this system should run in order to fulfill its function. Why must these services be run? As part of your answer, identify any other systems (such as DNS servers, mail servers, and so on) that this SSH host would have to trust.

e. From the point of view of Saltzer and Schroeder's design principles [773] (see Chapter 13), is the solution suggested in part (d) better than, worse than, or the same as the solutions involving access through the firewall? Justify your answer.

9. Consider the first example in Section 23.4.1.

a. Why does the router not save time by opening a connection to the destination host before the pending connection completes its three-way handshake?

b. The router is protecting a target from being flooded. Is the router itself vulnerable to a flooding attack? If not, why not, and why won't the same property make the target immune? If the router is vulnerable, does the attack on the router differ from the attack on the target? How?

10. The Linux system uses the SYN cookie approach discussed in the first example in Section 23.4.2, with one modification. The maximum segment size (MSS) is sent as part of the initial SYN. This value must be encoded in the sequence number so that the state can be properly reconstructed when the ACK arrives. The MSS used is three bits. The Linux system simply adds it to the SYN cookie shown in the example. How does the system recover the MSS from the ACK's sequence number?

Chapter 24
System Security

IMOGEN: To your protection I commend me, gods.
From fairies and the tempters of the night
Guard me, beseech ye.
—*Cymbeline*, II, ii, 8–10.

System configuration and administration relies on many principles of security and assurance. This chapter begins with a policy for the DMZ Web server system and for a development system in the internal network. It explores the configuration and maintenance of several system components in light of the policy and in light of principles of computer security. This illuminates how the practice of computer security is guided by the fundamental principles discussed throughout this book.

24.1   Introduction

Among the many functions of system administration is the security of the system and the data it contains. This chapter considers how the administration of security affects the system.

For our purposes, we consider the security policy of the Web server within the DMZ and a user system in the development subnet. This will contrast the manner in which an administrator secures a system that many users use for development of software with the methods used to secure a system that is likely to be attacked and that is not intended for the use of nonadministrative users.

Section 23.3.3.2 discusses the Web server's function in relation to the rest of the Drib's network infrastructure. Briefly, the Web server system provides access to untrusted users through a Web server, and access to trusted users through SSH. Untrusted users can come from any system on the Internet. Trusted users are those users who have access to the trusted administrative host on the internal network. For the purposes of our policy, we assume that any user in that system has been correctly authenticated to that system and is "trusted" as we use the term.

The development system is a standard UNIX or UNIX-like system. A set of developers are allowed to use the system.

24.2   Policy

Policy is at the heart of *every* decision involving security. The DMZ Web server has a policy very different from that of the development system. This section discusses portions of the policies in order to provide a foundation for the remainder of this chapter. We then compare and contrast the policy elements.

24.2.1   The Web Server System in the DMZ

Section 23.3.3.2, "DMZ WWW Server," discusses the basic security policy of the Web server. Some of the consequences of the policy are as follows.

1. All incoming Web connections come through the outer firewall, and all replies are sent through the outer firewall.
2. All users log in from an internal trusted server running SSH. Web pages are never updated locally. New Web pages are downloaded through the SSH tunnel.
3. Log messages are transmitted to the DMZ log server only.
4. The Web server may query the DMZ DNS system for IP addresses.
5. Other than those expressly mentioned here, no network services are provided.
6. The Web server runs CGI scripts. One of these scripts will write enciphered information (transaction data) to a spooling area. The enciphered file will be retrieved from the trusted internal administrative host using the SSH tunnel.
7. The Web server must implement its services correctly, and must restrict access to those services as much as possible.
8. The public key of the principal who will decipher and process the transaction data must reside on the DMZ Web server.

From these implications, several constraints emerge. The Web server consequences (WCs) of interest are as follows.

WC1. Policy consequence 1 requires that no unrequested network connections except those from the outer firewall over the HTTP and HTTPS ports, and those from the internal trusted administrative server over SSH, should be accepted. Replies to DNS queries should be accepted provided that they come from the DMZ DNS server. If other network clients are to be run, only replies to messages originating from the DMZ Web server should be accepted.

WC2. Policy consequence 2 states that user access to the system is to be limited to those users on the internal trusted administrative server. Furthermore, the number of users who need access to the Web server should be as small as possible, with only those privileges needed to perform their tasks. All actions must be attributable to an individual, as opposed to a role, user.

WC3. Policy consequences 4 and 5 suggest that the Web server should be configured to provide minimal access to the system. This prevents an attacker who compromises the Web server from accessing other parts of the system. This requirement leads to one unexpected, interesting consideration. If an attacker gains access to the system through the Web server, she can delete all uncollected transaction files. This denial of service attack would blemish the Drib's reputation. Some other mechanism should capture the transaction files and copy them to an area that the Web server cannot reach. Then, if an attacker compromises the Web server, that attacker cannot reach the transaction files.

WC4. Policy consequences 5, 6, and 8 imply that all software must have a very high assurance of functioning correctly (as specified by its documentation). In practice, this means that the software must be either developed or checked very carefully. It also requires that extensive logging occur, to verify that the software is functioning correctly even when under attack. In essence, we view attacks as situations in which software functions correctly (and the attack fails) or incorrectly (and the attack succeeds).

WC5. Policy consequence 7 states that the Web server must contain as few programs, and as little software, configuration information, and other data, as possible. If the system is compromised, this will minimize the effects of the attack.

24.2.2   The Development System

The development system lies in the internal network, on the development subnet (called the "devnet"). It must provide an environment in which developers can produce code for dribbles. Because users will be active on the system, its policy is considerably different than that of the Web server system.

The devnet has both infrastructure and user systems. The infrastructure systems are the devnet firewall (which separates it from other internal subnets), a DNS server, a logging host (which provides a central repository for logs), one or more file servers, and one or more systems containing user information common to the workstations (the UINFO servers). There is also an isolated system used to build a "base system configuration" (system files, configuration files, company-approved software, and so on) and to burn CD-ROMs. The policy that follows does not apply to these systems. They are under much tighter controls. The components of the security policy relevant to our discussion are as follows.

1. Only authorized users are allowed to use the devnet systems. They may work on any devnet workstation. All actions and system accesses must be tied to an individual user, rather than to a role account.

2. Workstation system administrators must be able to access the workstations at all times, unless the particular workstation has crashed. The set of devnet workstation administrators differs from the set of devnet central server administrators.

3. Within the devnet itself, users are trusted not to attack devnet systems. Users not on the devnet are *not* trusted. They are not allowed to access devnet resources except as permitted by the network security policy (for internal Drib users). Furthermore, devnet users are not allowed to access systems not on the devnet except as permitted by the network policy.

4. All network communications, except electronic mail, are to be confidential and are to be checked to ensure that the messages are not altered in transit.

5. The base standard configuration for each devnet system cannot be changed on that system. There is to be a local area in each system in which developers may install programs that are nonstandard. Before doing this, they must obtain approval from the security officers and system administrators. Should the software prove useful, it may be integrated into the standard configuration.

6. Backups shall enable system administrators to restore any devnet system with the loss of at most one day's changes in user and local files.

7. Security officers shall perform both periodic and ongoing audits of devnet systems. Compromised systems shall be removed from the devnet until they have been restored to an uncompromised state.

These components have several consequences, two of which affect the infrastructure and configuration of workstations. Policy component 3 leads to the use of a firewall at the boundary of the devnet and the other subnets to enforce the network security policy. This allows the network security administrators to enforce changes in the network policy without having to alter each system on the devnet. Any changes need only be made at the firewall. Also, the systems on the devnet need not be so tightly configured as must the firewalls. The firewalls enforce the policy that hosts outside the devnet see; the hosts inside the devnet enforce the policy specific to the developers and their hosts (the policy outlined above).

Policy component 3 also bars direct access between the Internet and devnet systems. This decision was based on a risk analysis. The security officers and management of the Drib realized that the Drib would benefit from allowing telecommuting and access to remote Web sites. However, the dangers of opening up an avenue of attack from Internet hosts to internal hosts, and allowing unsuspecting Drib employees to download untrusted, and possibly malicious, code, outweighed the perceived benefits. This portion of the policy is under review, and the Drib is considering changes to allow telecommuting (see Exercise 8 in Chapter 23).

Some developers need access to the Internet to determine what equipment to obtain as they plan new mechanisms and devices to enhance the value of the Drib's products. These developers are given separate workstations connected to a commercial Internet Service Provider (ISP) outside the Drib's perimeter. These "ISP workstations" are physically separated from the internal network, and the ISP workstation cannot easily be connected with the devnet workstation. These procedural mechanisms enforce the desired separation.

Other consequences of the policy apply to the devnet workstations. The development system consequences (DCs) of interest are as follows.

DC1. Policy components 1 and 4 imply the need for authenticated, enciphered, integrity-checked communications. These policy components also imply a consistent naming scheme across systems, so that a user name refers to the same user on all devnet systems.

DC2. Policy component 2 requires that each workstation have one or more local privileged accounts to administer the system locally. Policy components 1 and 2 imply that multiple local administrative accounts may be used to limit access to particular administrative functions. This division of power into roles allows the administrators to designate special system accounts, such as *mail*, as being limited in their power. Policy requirement 2 also requires that the workstation be able to run without any network connections.

DC3. Policy component 1 also requires that there be a notion of a "login" or "audit" user (see Section 24.4). This identity must be recorded in logs, to tie individuals to actions. Furthermore, users should not be able to log directly into role accounts such as *root,* because this would eliminate the ability to tie an individual to an action. Instead, they must log into an individual account and change to the role account, or add a new role, to their individual account.

DC4. If a developer wants to install a program from the outside onto his devnet workstation, he must first obtain approval from the security officers. Once approved, he installs it in an area separate from the base system configuration (see policy component 5). Adding a program to the base system configuration requires that it be added to the isolated system first. This requires testing and analysis of the program to ensure (to an appropriate level of integrity) that the software is not malicious and will not accidentally damage the system on which it runs.

DC5. Policy component 5 requires that each workstation protect the base system configuration, as installed, from being altered. One approach is to mount the disks containing that configuration as read-only disks. A far simpler and more effective approach is to use read-only media. This meets policy requirements and ensures that all devnet workstations are up to date. A writable hard drive provides space for local files such as spool and temporary files.

DC6. Policy component 1 requires that an employee's files be available to her continuously. This requires that the files be stored on systems other than the workstations, in case a workstation goes down. As a corollary, the file controls should enforce the same sets of permissions regardless of the workstations from which they are accessed.

DC7. Policy component 6 requires regular backups. As explained in Section 24.7.2, the development workstations store only transient files on writable media. Hence, they need not be backed up. Restoration involves rebooting and remounting of file systems from the file servers, which are regularly backed up.

DC8. Policy component 7 requires several security precautions. The primary one is a logging system to which all systems send log messages. Furthermore, security officers need access to both devnet systems and the devnet network. They conduct periodic (and irregular) sweeps of the network, looking for unauthorized servers. They also conduct periodic (and irregular) sweeps of each system looking for dangerous settings in user accounts and the local areas.

Two points about this policy, and its implications, are apparent. First, the system security policy relies on the outer and inner firewalls to prevent Internet users from reaching the system. If one firewall fails, the other will still block such accesses.[1] Also, the firewall at the perimeter of the developer's subnet enforces the access restrictions among the users of the other two subnets and the systems on the developer's subnet.[2] So the system policy assumes that those who can connect to the system are authorized to access developer systems.

The security policy also requires procedural enforcement mechanisms.

EXAMPLE: Consider a system administrator for the development network who has both an ISP workstation and a devnet workstation on her desk. She could download a program to her ISP workstation, copy it onto a floppy disk, and move the floppy disk to the devnet workstation. This clearly would violate policy, but there is no reasonable technical means of preventing it. (See Exercise 1.)

Here, the Drib must rely on procedural mechanisms to enforce the policy. In this case, the procedures should specify both the prohibition and the consequences of violating it. This puts all employees on notice that the prohibition will be enforced, and encourages them to use the allowed methods to obtain approval.

24.2.3   Comparison

The differences between the policies of the DMZ WWW system and the devnet developer system arise from their different roles. The DMZ WWW server is not a general-use system. It exists only to serve Web pages and accept Web orders. The devnet developer system is a general-use computer. It must allow compilation, editing, and other functions that programmers and software engineers need to design, implement, and test software.

---

[1] See Section 12.2.6, "Principle of Separation of Privilege."
[2] See Section 12.2.4, "Principle of Complete Mediation."

The DMZ Web server system's security policy focuses on the single purpose of the server: to run the Web server. Two sets of users can access the server: the system administrators, who maintain the security and the Web pages; and the users from the Internet, who must go through the outer firewall and can access only the Web server. The developer system's security policy focuses on more complex purposes. These purposes include software creation, testing, and maintenance. The developer system requires more supporting software than does the DMZ Web server system. The user population is different and provides an environment more amenable for attackers than does the DMZ Web server system, because the users may not be as security-conscious as the security officers comprising the user population of the DMZ Web server system.

That the system administrators of the DMZ Web server system are trained in security (hence, the term "security officers") should be expected. The developer systems are more numerous and require more administrative effort to maintain. More system administrators are required. The administrators will also have different skills and abilities; some may be very senior and experienced, whereas others will be junior and inexperienced. Hence, the system administrators for the developer systems may not be trained in security. So the system security officers may not be administrators. This leads to situations in which system administrators and security officers disagree on what actions are appropriate. The policy must have some mechanism for resolving these disputes. The mechanism typically involves a person, or a group of people, performing a cost-benefit analysis of each option and selecting the option that provides the greatest benefit at the least cost. This type of analysis was briefly discussed in Section 1.6.1.

24.2.4   Conclusion

We now examine several areas of system administration in light of these security requirements. Our goal is to install, and manage, as secure a system as possible. Our approach is to compare and contrast these two systems. What follows is organized into areas, and each system is examined with respect to the mechanisms used to enforce the policy. We then compare the two systems.

24.3   Networks

Both the DMZ Web server system and the devnet user system are connected to the network. Although the firewalls provide some measure of protection, the principle of separation of privilege says that access should be limited even when the firewalls fail.[3] So we consider how the administrators should set network configurations and services to protect the systems in the case that the firewalls fail.

---

[3] See Section 12.2.6, "Principle of Separation of Privilege."

24.3.1   The Web Server System in the DMZ

Item WC1 limits network access to the Web server.[4] External users can reach the system only by using Web services and connecting through the outer firewall. Internal users can reach the system by using SSH from the trusted administrative system, through the inner firewall. A security mechanism must block any other types of connections, or any connections from sources other than the outer firewall or the trusted administrative server.[5] Moreover, item WC4 requires that *all* attempts to connect be monitored[6] to validate that the security mechanism functions according to this policy (or to detect failures).[7]

Consider the Web server first. Although requests can come from any IP address on the Internet, all such requests go to the outer firewall's Web proxy. That firewall forwards well-formed requests to the DMZ Web server. Hence, the Web server's access control mechanism can discard any requests from sites other than the outer firewall. Whether to accept requests from the inner firewall depends on several policy factors. The current policy for the Drib is not to allow the Web server to accept these requests.[8] However, the policymakers have realized that some situations may require internal users to access the Web server directly (these situations typically will involve debugging or checking for errors). Should this be necessary, the security officers will reconfigure the inner firewall to run a Web proxy identical to the one on the outer firewall. Thus, the DMZ Web server is configured to accept requests from the inner firewall as well as the outer firewall. The server will *not* accept requests from other DMZ systems, because they are not to be used for accessing the Web server.

EXAMPLE: The Apache Web server can control access to specific parts of the Web pages based on IP address. The configuration file controls which addresses are allowed access and which ones are denied access. By default, all accesses are allowed.

In the Apache configuration file, the system administrator sets

```
order allow,deny
```

to evaluate all the "allow" lines before the "deny" lines. If a host is not listed in either line, the Web server disallows access. Then the lines

```
allow from outer_firewall
allow from inner_firewall
deny from all
```

---

[4] See Section 12.2.1, "Principle of Least Privilege."
[5] See Section 15.4, "Example Information Flow Controls."
[6] See Chapter 21, "Auditing."
[7] See Chapter 22, "Intrusion Detection."
[8] See Section 12.2.2, "Principle of Fail-Safe Defaults."

allow access from the inner and outer firewalls but from nowhere else [127]. (Here, *inner_firewall* and *outer_firewall* are the addresses of those hosts.)

Item WC1 requires the DMZ Web server to allow administrative access from the trusted administrative Web server. This allows system administrators to update Web pages, reconfigure and modify software, and perform other administrative tasks. The Web server runs an SSH server. This server provides enciphered, authenticated access to the Web server system using cryptographic mechanisms to provide those security services. Of interest here is that the server requires *both* the host and the user to be authenticated.[9] This allows the system administrators to restrict access to users connecting from the trusted administrative server only.

EXAMPLE: The SSH server controls remote access using a configuration file. The configuration file allows the sysadmin to list a set of hosts from which it may accept connections. Any connection from any other host is refused. The lines

```
allow trusted_admin_server
deny all
```

restrict access to users from the trusted administrative server. Similar keywords allow control over users.

Section 24.4.1 discusses users, and authentication of both hosts and users, on the Web server system.

To maximize availability, the Web server system wraps each server with a small script. If the server terminates, the script starts a new instance of the server.

EXAMPLE: The Web server and the SSH server are started at boot time. Both are wrapped so that, should either fail, a new copy will be run. For example, the Web server *webd* is run from the following shell script.

```
#! /bin/sh
echo $$ > /mnt/users/servers/webdwrapper.pid
while true
do
        /usr/local/bin/webd
        sleep 30
done
```

Now, if the Web server terminates, the script will automatically start a new Web server process after a wait of 30 seconds.

---

[9] See Section 12.2.6, "Principle of Separation of Privilege."

By virtue of item WC3, the Web server system should run a minimum of network servers. Because access is to be given only to Web requests and administrative logins, no network servers other than the Web server and the SSH server are needed.[10]

The Web server runs several network clients, however. Because the Web server system must request IP addresses and host names, it must make requests of, and receive replies from, a DMZ DNS server. At any time, multiple requests may be outstanding. By virtue of item WC1, this satisfies the policy. However, several types of attacks on DNS clients [800] involve "piggybacking" of multiple host name and address associations onto a reply to a request for a single such association.[11] The Web server system's DNS client will use only the requested data. It will discard any additional data as well as any logs that such data has been received.[12] Furthermore, if the client receives a response that provides information that was not requested, or if two responses provide different answers to the same query, both are logged and discarded, and the client acts as though the DNS request has timed out.

The Web server system also runs a logging client to send log messages to the log server. Programs use an internal message delivery system to send messages to the logging client, which then delivers them to the appropriate hosts and files. The delivery addresses lie in a configuration file. Each log message is timestamped and has the name of the process and (Web server) system attached.

The system is configured to log any attempts to connect to network ports on which no servers are listening. The three reasons for doing this follow from item WC4. First, it serves as a check that the outer firewall is intercepting all probes from the Internet to the Drib's Web server. Second, it detects probes from the internal network to the DMZ Web server. Because the inner firewall has one port that is filtered rather than proxied (the SSH port), such probing is possible if the filter does not check the destination port number. This should never happen, of course, unless the inner firewall is misconfigured or compromised. Thus, in order for an attack on the firewall to be undetectable, two failures must occur (the firewall fails to block, and the DMZ Web server fails to log).[13] Third, probes to other ports from within the DMZ indicate unauthorized activities on the DMZ systems, meaning that one of them has been compromised. This requires immediate investigation.

24.3.2   The Development System

Item DC1 requires that the development system accept user connections only when they are authenticated and encrypted. Like the DMZ Web server, the development systems run SSH servers to provide such access. Both hosts and users use public key authentication.[14]

---

[10] See Section 12.2.2, "Principle of Fail-Safe Defaults."

[11] See Section 13.6.1.2, "Security Issues with the Domain Name Service."

[12] See Section 12.2.1, "Principle of Least Privilege."

[13] See Section 12.2.6, "Principle of Separation of Privilege."

[14] See Section 8.3, "Public Key Cryptography."

Unlike the DMZ Web server system, the development system runs several other servers. It runs a line printer spooler to send print requests to a print server. It runs a logging server to accept log messages and dispose of them properly. It also runs servers to support access to both the file server and the user information database system. These servers are necessary in order for the developers to be productive on that system.

The development system does not have the ftp or Web services. Instead, special ftp and Web server systems mount directories from the central file servers. The workstations run an SMTP server as a convenience to users,[15] but all mail is forwarded to a central mail server and is *never* delivered locally. (This allows workstation SMTP servers to be very simple programs.[16]) Users can access mail on any workstation, because the mail spooling directory resides on the central file server. Similarly, users can make files available for ftp and Web access by placing them into user-specific directories on the central file server. The corresponding servers mount these directories for remote access. They cannot access other parts of the file systems on the file servers.

Placing the mail, ftp, and Web services on systems other than the development workstations has two advantages that satisfy item DC2. First, it minimizes the set of network servers that each workstation has to run. Second, it minimizes the number of systems that provide the services.[17] This enables the firewall to be configured to allow traffic for these services through to a small set of systems, and the security administrators can configure those systems to handle access control appropriately.

The development system uses access control wrappers to support access controls. The firewall provides this control for systems not on the devnet, but the workstation's access control wrappers provide this control for other devnet workstations, as well as duplicating the firewall's control rules. If the firewall's access controls fail (for example, as a result of a configuration error), the workstation will still honor the network security policy.[18] Furthermore, the development system logs all attempts to access servers. These logs provide both evidence of intrusions and verification of the correct functioning of the security mechanisms, as required by item DC8.

EXAMPLE: *TCP wrappers* [912] host-based wrappers that intercept requests (connections or datagrams) to some set of servers. The wrapper determines the origin of the request from the packet. If the wrapper is configured to allow the connection, it then spawns the appropriate server and passes the open port to the server. Otherwise, the request is ignored. In either case, the wrapper logs the request and its origin.

TCP wrappers determine if access is allowed by looking in configuration files. *PortSentry* [175], another wrapper tool, is designed to examine network requests from a wide variety of ports. If the ports indicate illicit activity (as configured by the system manager), PortSentry can add appropriate commands to the configuration files to block network access for the responsible hosts.

---

[15] See Section 12.2.8, "Principle of Psychological Acceptability."

[16] See Section 12.2.3, "Principle of Economy of Mechanism."

[17] See Section 12.2.3, "Principle of Economy of Mechanism."

[18] See Section 12.2.6, "Principle of Separation of Privilege."

Item DC8 requires checking of the security of the development workstations. To ensure that they remain at the desired level of security, the system security officers occasionally scan each system. Their scanner probes each port and records those that are open. The results are compared with the list of ports that are expected to be open. Any discrepencies are reported to the security officers. Moreover, the scanners record the address of each system on the network. Any unauthorized system is reported immediately, as are any unexpected changes in addresses. The security officers make these scans periodically. To prevent an attacker from determining the schedule, the security officers launch additional scans at irregular intervals as well.[19]

Finally, the security officers occasionally attack devnet systems to determine how well they withstand attacks.[20] These operations are sustained and take some time, but the information gleaned from them has proven invaluable. When flaws are discovered, the security officers determine whether they are attributable to the initial configuration or to user changes in the system. In the former case, the security officers develop a patch or modification of the standard configuration. In the latter case, they assess the situation in more detail, and act on the basis of that analysis.

24.3.3   Comparison

The difference between approaches to network services and accesses springs from the use of, and the locations of, the systems.

The DMZ Web server system is dedicated to two specific tasks—serving Web pages and accepting commercial transactions. Only those functions and processes required to support this specific task are allowed. Any other programs, such as those required for general use, are simply not present in the system. It need not provide access to a line printer, or handle remote file systems from central servers. Everything is present in the system itself. No extraneous services are provided or used.[21]

The development system performs many tasks, all designed to achieve the goal of providing an environment in which the developers can be productive.[22] It has general-purpose tools ranging from compilers and text editors to electronic mail reading programs. It shares user files with other workstations using a central file server, and user information with a central user information system. Users can run processes freely.

The environment plays a role in configuration. Both systems use a "defense in depth" strategy of providing access controls that duplicate some of the firewall controls.[23] The DMZ Web server system does not depend on the firewall to filter or block Web client requests. Even if the inner firewall allowed messages to flow through it with no control, the DMZ Web server system would function as required by policy. How-

---

[19] See Chapter 21, "Auditing."

[20] See Section 20.2, "Penetration Studies."

[21] See Section 12.2.7, "Principle of Least Common Mechanism."

[22] See Section 12.2.8, "Principle of Psychological Acceptability."

[23] See Section 12.2.6, "Principle of Separation of Privilege."

ever, access to the development systems depends on the devnet firewall's filtering abilities. If a user from another internal subnet tries to access a development system, the devnet firewall will determine whether or not access to the devnet is allowed. If it is, then the developer system determines whether or not to accept the connection. This allows the Drib network administrators to control access among the three subnets and the DMZ independently of the system administrators within the subnets (who do not control the firewalls). It also allows the developer workstations to support developers on other subnets—if the Drib policy allows it.

24.4 Users

Our first step is to determine the accounts needed to run the systems. The user accounts, as distinguished from the system administration accounts (system administrators), require enough privileges to use the computer to perform their jobs, but as few others as possible.[24] Creating, configuring, and maintaining their accounts are crucial to the successful use of the computer. For brevity, we refer to a user account as a "user" and a system administration account as a "sysadmin" in this section.

24.4.1 The Web Server System in the DMZ

Items WC2 and WC3 suggest that the number of user accounts on the system be minimal. The Web server requires at most two users and a sysadmin. The first user is a user with enough privileges to read (and serve) Web pages and to write to the Web server transaction area. The second user is a user who can move files from the Web transaction area to the commerce transaction spooling area. The reason the Web server has minimal privileges lies in the assumption that the Web server, which interacts with other systems on the Internet, may be compromised. A compromised Web server running with sysadmin privileges could allow the attacker to control the system, but if the Web server had only enough priviliges to read Web pages, then compromising it would be less likely to compromise the system. The commerce server and the Web server should be different users in order to prevent an attacker from compromising the Web server and then deleting files from the commerce server's area. Access control mechanisms[25] can inhibit this, but defense should not depend on one control only.[26] If the Web server and commerce server are different users, and the Web server is compromised, the attacker must then compromise either the sysadmin or the commerce server user.

---

[24] See Section 12.2.1, "Principle of Least Privilege."
[25] See Chapter 14, "Access Control Mechanisms."
[26] See Section 12.2.6, "Principle of Separation of Privilege."

EXAMPLE: Let the Web server account's name be *webbie*, and let the commerce server's account be *ecommie*. The Web server's CGI script would create the transaction file, with an ACL allowing *ecommie* to read and delete the file. The commerce server then could simply copy the contents of the file into a file in the spooling area, set the ACL to allow the administrator to read and delete the file, and delete the original file. Note that with the given ACL, *webbie* can no longer read the file. This protects transactions against attack if the Web server is attacked.

Some systems (such as many UNIX systems) use a simplified mechanism that does not allow individual users to be placed in an access control list.[27] However, group mechanisms achieve the same end.

EXAMPLE: The Web server's transaction directory is group-owned by the group *trans*. That group contains two members, *webbie* and *ecommie*. The CGI script writes a transaction file group-owned by *trans* and group-readable. The commerce server can read the file and, because the directory is group-writable,[28] delete the file.

There is a tension between the desire to minimize the number of accounts (item WC2) and the desire to minimize the privileges of these accounts (item WC3). Most computer systems allow the assignment of privilege to accounts independently of name. This means that there can be multiple sysadmin accounts. Each person designated as a system administrator could have a separate sysadmin account or could use a single, role account.[29] The reason for having separate sysadmin accounts is to tie each action to a *particular* user. Whether or not this can be done depends to some extent on the implementation of the Web server system.

EXAMPLE: Most UNIX systems represent accounts by UIDs. The particular UID determines the level of privilege, with 0 being the sysadmin. Having separate system administration accounts would require the account names to be different, but the account UIDs to be the same (0). Hence, the only benefit is to be able to track who logged in as a system administrator. All logged actions would show up as having been executed by the user with UID 0.

Some UNIX systems support an audit, or a login, UID.[30] This UID is assigned at login and is not changed throughout the lifetime of the process. Furthermore, all children of the process inherit that audit UID. Assigning each system administrator a unique user account (each with a unique UID) associates that UID with every action that account takes. This includes acquiring administrator privileges.

---

[27] See Section 14.1.1, "Abbreviations of Access Control Lists."

[28] Some UNIX variants allow the group owner of a file to delete it only if the directory *and the file itself* are group-writable. In this case, the transaction file must be group-writable as well.

[29] See Section 13.3, "Users," and Section 13.4, "Groups and Roles."

[30] See Section 13.3, "Users."

EXAMPLE: Solaris 2.8 supports an audit UID. When the Web server system is set up, each system administrator is assigned a separate, unprivileged account. After the system administrator logs in as the ordinary user, she switches to the sysadmin role. Each action will have three associated UIDs: the real, effective, and audit UIDs. Any action that the sysadmin takes will be tied to the individual account of the particular system administrator who takes it.

Because item WC4 requires strict user accountability, the Web server system is set up to disallow direct logins from system administrators. Each user must log into the system from the trusted administrative server. As stated in Section 24.3.1, this requires the use of SSH, so the user must be an authorized user of the Web server system.[31] The set of allowed users is enumerated in the SSH configuration file in the Web server system. Once logged in, the user may switch to a role account. To do so, the user supplies a password. The program checks that the user has self-authenticated correctly, and then that the user is authorized to access the requested role account. If so, the user is switched into this role.

Direct login to a sysadmin account is allowed in one situation only. The Web server system allows logins to role accounts (such as *root*) from the system console. Although the system cannot identify the individual logging into the role, the console itself is in a locked room to which only a few highly trusted individuals have access. At least three people are in that room at all times, including one security officer. The officer can identify by sight the set of people authorized to enter the room.[32] So, if someone walks up to the console and logs into a role account, the security officer will log that individual's use of the console.[33] Thus, should the SSH server become unexpectedly unavailable, a system administrator could fix it.

24.4.2 The Development System

Unlike the DMZ WWW server system, the development system requires at least one user account per developer (items DC1, DC3, and DC6). It also requires administrative accounts, as well as groups corresponding to projects (items DC2 and DC3). Furthermore, an account on different development systems must refer to the same individual, role, or project (item DC1). Otherwise, inconsistent use of identifiers may allow access rights that exceed the level authorized by the security policy.

EXAMPLE: The *r*-protocols [493] define a set of protocols that implement a trusted host relationship. The host *stokes* names host *navier* in the file */etc/hosts.equiv*. Then, if the user Abby has an account *abby* on *navier*, and there is an account *abby* on *stokes*, then Abby can log into *abby* on *stokes* without supplying a password. The system administrator configures the *hosts.equiv* file.

---

[31] See Section 12.2.6, "Principle of Separation of Privilege."
[32] See Section 12.2.6, "Principle of Separation of Privilege."
[33] See Section 12.2.4, "Principle of Complete Mediation."

Suppose the Drib had two different users named Abraham and Abigail, both of whom use the nickname "Abby." Abraham's account on *navier* is *abby*, and Abigail's account on *stokes* is *abby*. If *navier* trusts *stokes* as described above, then Abraham can log into Abigail's account on *stokes*. This violates the security policy requirement of being able to tie actions to individual users (item DC3).

Shared files increase the risk of accidental or deliberate damage.[34] The NFS protocol for sharing files bases access on the UID of the user requesting access. If *abby* has UID 8924 on *navier*, and *sioban* has UID 8924 on *stokes*, both have access to files owned by the user with UID 8924 on the NFS file server. This violates the security policy requirement of users being able to control access to their files from any development system (item DC6).

To meet the requirement for consistency of naming, the Drib developers have decided to use a central repository to define users and accounts, the UINFO system. They use the NIS protocol [874] to allow distribution of user information. All systems on the developer subnet, except the firewall, use the NIS server to obtain information about users and accounts. Any new account must be instantiated on the databases of this server. No user accounts are created on the developer workstations themselves, and all system accounts have entries in the server databases.

The developers benefit from this arrangement. Because their files are kept on NFS file servers, a developer can access them at any devnet workstation, as required by item DC6. If one workstation cannot function, the developer can walk to another workstation and continue development. The system and network administrators can then repair the malfunctioning workstation with minimal loss of developer time.

To satisfy item DC2, each developer workstation has a local *root* account and one local account for each system administrator.[35] This account gives administrators access should the workstation be unable to contact the NIS server. Because there are both primary and secondary NIS servers, and backups for each, the only reason that this situation might arise would be either a network problem or a workstation problem. Using the local *root* account, the administrator could access the workstation, diagnose the problem, and (if possible) correct the problem at the client.

As allowed by item DC2, the Drib administrators have set up several accounts to perform system functions. Examples are the *mail* account, which allows the user to manipulate mail queues and configuration files, and the *daemon* user, under which most network daemons run. These accounts do not have *root* privileges. This is an application of the principle of least privilege,[36] because few functions require the powers of the *root* account.

EXAMPLE: Backups require access to the raw disk device. Rather than require *root* to do the backups, the Drib administrators have created the *operator* user. This user is in the group *devices*. All files corresponding to raw disk devices are in that group

---

[34] See Section 12.2.7, "Principle of Least Common Mechanism."
[35] See Section 12.2.7, "Principle of Least Common Mechanism."
[36] See Section 12.2.1, "Principle of Least Privilege."

and are group-readable. The operator user can therefore dump the contents of the disk using a backup program.

To enforce the individual accountability of item DC3, the operator account does not allow password authentication. To access the account, the user must log in to her normal account, and then change to the *operator* account.[37] The version of the UNIX operating system that is used here has a login UID, so when the user changes to the *operator* account, the new process inherits the login UID. This is logged (along with the real and effective UIDs), so each action taken as operator can be tied to a particular user's UID.

The NIS mechanism uses cleartext messages to transmit user information. This violates requirement DC1, because the messages are not integrity-checked. They are susceptible to network-based attack, because an attacker can inject responses to queries. However, a quick analysis demonstrates why this is not a problem in the particular environment of the Drib.

The development system is not accessible to users from the Internet. The outer firewall, inner firewall, and devnet firewall prevent any direct connections from the Internet. The threat comes from insiders, people with access to the Drib's internal network. The security analysts classified these threats into two distinct sets.

The first set involves nonadministrative information. This data is sent enciphered and integrity-checked, using mechanisms that the analysts trust. Compromising this data could lead to corruption of user-specific data, and the analysts felt that the other mechanisms provided sufficient protection to deter this.

The second set involves administrative information—specifically, the NIS user records. These records are not encrypted. However, none of these records include administrative accounts, so only ordinary users can be compromised.[38] The security analysts configured each workstation so that only *root* could inject false information that either the clients or the server would accept as legitimate.[39] They then physically secured the network to prevent unauthorized personnel from connecting workstations to the Drib's network. Fake NIS replies can be put on the network only from the outside (such replies would have to go through the devnet firewall) or from a host on the network (such replies would require *root* access). In the first case, the devnet firewall would reject the packets before they entered the devnet network. In the second case, *root* could access that user's account by running the *su* command on the system under attack, making unnecessary the injection of false NIS packets to obtain access to a user's account.

Given this analysis, the Drib's policy managers agreed with the system developers, administrators, and security officers that the violation of item DC1 was acceptable. However, if there is evidence of a problem, the policy managers reserved the right to require that some other scheme be developed with security the foremost consideration.

---

[37] See Section 13.4, "Groups and Roles."

[38] See Section 12.2.7, "Principle of Least Common Mechanism."

[39] See Section 12.2.1, "Principle of Least Privilege."

24.4.3   Comparison

The difference between selecting users for the DMZ Web server system and selecting users for the development system reflects the differences between the security policies of the two systems. The root lies in the intended use of each system.

The DMZ Web server system is in an area that is accessible to untrusted users (specifically, from the Internet). Although access is controlled, the controls may have vulnerabilities. Limiting the number of users on the system, and ensuring that untrusted users access servers running with minimal privileges, increase the difficulty of an attacker obtaining unauthorized access to the system.[40] Except for the superuser, users can perform only restricted actions. Finally, the user information is kept on the system, so attackers cannot inject false information (such as information on other users) into the system's accesses to a user information database.[41]

The development system allows general user access, so it has many more accounts. Furthermore, the development system shares its user population with other systems on the same subnet, so it accesses a centralized database containing the information. This keeps the user and file information consistent across platforms. The features of the NIS system (notably, the "+" and "–") [874] allow each devnet system administrator to control authorization to use that particular system. System accounts other than that of the superuser allow the system administrators to control administrative actions to a fairly high degree of granularity. The trade-off is that these administrative accounts can access files on the file server, whereas the superuser can access only public files.

Finally, the difference in means of access reflects the differences in the environments and uses of the two systems. The DMZ Web server system allows access only through a small set of tightly controlled access points: the Web server (from the outer firewall), the SSH server (from the inner firewall), and a login server bound to the physical console of the system. This reflects the classes of users who are authorized to use the system, as well as the ways in which they are authorized to use it.[42] External users can access only the Web server; internal users, only the SSH server. However, the devnet system is in the internal network. Hence, users can come from a wide variety of systems and can access any server. The only controls on access are that the accesses must come from within the devnet, unless *explicitly* stated otherwise, and that the users must have accounts on the devnet centralized database system.

24.5   Authentication

Authentication binds the identity of the user to processes. Incorrect or compromised authentication leads to security problems. In this section, we consider the authentication techniques used in the two systems.

---

[40] See Section 12.2.1, "Principle of Least Privilege."
[41] See Section 12.2.7, "Principle of Least Common Mechanism."
[42] See Section 12.2.1, "Principle of Least Privilege."

24.5.1   The Web Server System in the DMZ

As required by WC1 and WC2, the SSH server uses cryptographic authentication to ensure that the source of the connection is the trusted administrative host. If the connection is from any other host, the SSH server is configured to reject the connection. Furthermore, SSH uses a cryptographic method of authentication rather than relying on IP addresses.[43]

When a user connects to the SSH server, that server attempts to perform cryptographic authentication. If that attempt fails, that server requests a password from the user. Were this likely to remain unchanged, the administrator would configure the authentication routines directly in the SSH daemon. However, the Drib is experimenting with one smart card system and plans to try two more. Because such a system would require changes in the authentication methods, the system administrator has elected to use PAM to avoid having to modify the source to the SSH server, recompile, and reinstall.[44]

The UNIX system used for the Web server system allows the use of an MD-5-based password hashing mechanism. The advantage of this scheme over the standard UNIX scheme is that the passwords may be of arbitrary length. The password changing program on the Web server system is set to require passwords to have a mixture of letters, numbers, and punctuation (including white space) characters. When a password is changed, the password changing program runs the proposed password through a series of checks to determine if it is too easy to guess.[45] If not, the change is allowed.

The system administrator has disabled password aging. Password aging is suitable when reusable passwords may be tried repeatedly until guessed, or if the hashed passwords can be obtained and cracked.[46] Here, all user connections come from the trusted administrative host, so only users who are authorized to use that system can get to the Web server system's SSH server. These users are trusted. The purpose of password aging is to limit the danger of passwords being guessed. Because the only users who could guess passwords are trusted not to do so, password aging is unnecessary.

24.5.2   Development Network System

The development system supports several users. It is in a physically secure area, accessible only to Drib employees. However, employees other than developers (such as custodians and managers) have access to the restricted area, so authentication controls are required.[47]

---

[43] See Section 8.3, "Public Key Cryptography."
[44] See Section 11.5, "Multiple Methods."
[45] See Section 11.2.2.3, "User Selection of Passwords."
[46] See Section 11.2.3, "Password Aging."
[47] See Section 12.2.6, "Principle of Separation of Privilege."

Item DC1 means that each user must self-authenticate at login. Although the Drib is moving toward a smart card system, each user currently has a reusable password. Because the users are not administrators (and therefore have no superuser privileges), cracking of passwords would gain them additional privileges. Hence, password aging is in effect. The mechanism uses the time-based approach. Once changed, a password may not be changed again for 3 days. Because the Drib has administrators present at all times, if a user suspects a compromise, the system administrator can reset the password. The Drib computed that guessing passwords in 180 days would require more computing power than was conveniently available on site, so the system administrators require users to change their passwords every 90 days. One week before a user's password expires, the user is warned at login that the password is about to expire. Once the password expires, the user may begin logging in but will be asked for a new password before the login can be completed. The user is also given the option of terminating the login at that point rather than supplying a new password.[48]

Each proposed password is checked to ensure that it is not easy to guess.[49] The criteria include a mixture of case, character type, length, and testing against various word lists and transformations of those lists. Like the Web server system, the development system uses a password hashing scheme based on MD-5.

Although the Drib does not expect to upgrade the methods of authentication on the development system, that system uses PAM to provide a uniform, consistent interface for authentication. The system maintainers found that providing consistency and simplicity, as the interface to PAM does, eases the burden of administration.

To allow developers to access the system from anywhere within the Drib's offices, the development system runs an SSH server. This is configured to accept connections from any system within the internal network. It validates host identities using public key encryption and validates users using public key authentication, smart card authentication, and (if needed) password authentication.[50] However, to meet item DC3, *root* access is blocked. A system administrator must log in as an ordinary user and then change to *root*. To enforce this, the server's configuration file disallows *root* logins, and the system is set to disallow *root* logins on all terminals (network terminals and console). Other role accounts simply have a password hash that cannot be produced when any password is entered. Thus, users cannot log into them. To gain access, administrators must use a special program on the workstation that validates their identities, and then checks their authorization to access the desired role account.[51]

---

[48] See Section 11.2.3, "Password Aging."
[49] See Section 11.2.2, "Countering Password Guessing."
[50] See Section 13.6.1, "Host Identity."
[51] See Section 13.4, "Groups and Roles."

EXAMPLE: The programs *lsu* [104] and *sudo* both implement role-based access control for a variety of UNIX systems. These programs require that the user enter his or her password and then, if the password is validated, determine whether or not the user is authorized to assume the requested role.

24.5.3   Comparison

Both the DMZ Web server system and the devnet system use strong authentication measures to ensure that users and hosts are correctly authenticated. The SSH server requires cryptographic authentication of not only the user but also the host from which the user is connecting, and the server responds only to known hosts. Host and user identities are established using the RSA public key cryptosystem. The certificates are initialized by trusted system administrators, so systems that are set up by unauthorized personnel will not be able to connect over SSH to any Drib system.

　　　Both systems also allow reusable passwords. However, the DMZ Web server system uses an MD-5-based hash, whereas the development system uses the traditional UNIX DES-based hash, because it is the version supported by NIS. An undesirable side effect is that reusable passwords on the development system are restricted to a maximum of eight characters, whereas those on the DMZ Web server system may be of arbitrary length. This also explains why the development system uses password aging but the DMZ Web server system does not. Because the users of the Web server system have chosen very long passwords, attackers are expected to take much longer to guess them than if they were only eight characters long, as they are on the development system—assuming that attackers can even get to the SSH server on the DMZ Web server system.

24.6   Processes

A system runs a collection of processes to perform specific tasks. Each process is a potential vulnerability. This section examines the processes run on both systems.

24.6.1   The Web Server System in the DMZ

As required by WC5, the Web server runs a minimum set of processes[52] because its function is only to serve Web pages and batch transactions for off-line processing. The required services are as follows.

---

[52] See Section 12.2.1, "Principle of Least Privilege."

- Web server
- Commerce server
- SSH server
- Login server, if there is a physical terminal or console
- Any essential operating system services (such as pagers)

Items WC2 and WC3 require each server to run with a minimum of privileges. The SSH and login servers need enough privileges to change to the user logging in. The Web and commerce servers run with minimal privileges, because they only need to access public data. Neither the login nor the commerce server accepts network connections.[53] The former is tied to specific, hard-wired terminals (such as a console); the latter simply responds to interprocess communication from the Web server.

EXAMPLE: A typical UNIX system will have the following daemons running.

- *init*, the login server
- *sshd*, the SSH server
- *webd*, the Web server
- *commerced*, the commerce server
- Various servers for the operating system

For example, a Solaris system running with minimal services will include a scheduling process, a paging process, a file system flushing process, and a process for recording logins and logouts. Enabling of accounting creates one more process, but the information gleaned may provide guidance for optimizing the performance of the system.

Consider the level of privilege that the servers need.[54] The SSH server must run with sysadmin privileges to support the remote access and tunnelling facilities. The login server (if present) must run with this level of privilege also. The Web server requires enough privileges to read Web pages and invoke subordinate CGI scripts. The Web pages can be world-readable, so the Web server simply needs minimal privileges. The CGI scripts manipulate Web pages or generate transaction data, and with appropriate settings of file permissions can write into the Web server's area. The commerce server needs enough privileges to copy transaction files from the Web server area to the transaction spooling area. However, it should not have enough privileges to alter Web pages. Other required servers run with appropriate privileges.

---

[53] See Section 12.2.2, "Principle of Fail-Safe Defaults."
[54] See Section 12.2.1, "Principle of Least Privilege."

EXAMPLE: A program may require extra privileges when it begins. Most UNIX systems require that only *root* programs be able to access network ports with numbers of 1023 or lower. These UNIX systems do not enforce the principle of complete mediation, because access is checked only when the port is opened. This allows two approaches to minimizing of privileges.

The Web server can run with *root* privileges. As soon as it opens the network port, it discards those privileges. So it runs as the user *webbie*. This requires special code in the Web server to drop the privileges. If the Web server does not do this, a second approach is to write a wrapper program that runs as *root*, opens the port, spawns the Web server (as the user *webbie*), and passes the file descriptor corresponding to the port to that process. The wrapper then terminates.

File access is an important issue. File system access control lists[55] provide one defense. We can adapt another defense from capabilities.[56] Recall that in a pure capability system, the capability names the object; if the subject does not possess the capability, it cannot even identify an object. An access control-based system does not work this way. However, if we can change the meaning of a file system name, then we can confine all references to a particular part of the file system. The Web server, for example, needs to reference only programs and files within the hierarchy of Web pages (and CGI scripts). The commerce server needs access only to the transaction spooling area and the area where the Web server's CGI script places transactions.

EXAMPLE: Most UNIX systems provide a system call *chroot* that changes the process' notion of the root of the file hierarchy. For example, suppose a process wishes to open the file */usr/web/pages/index.html*.The appropriate system call would be

```
if ((fd = open("/usr/web/pages/index.html",
        O_RDONLY)) < 0)
        perror("open /usr/web/pages/index.html for reading
            failed");
```

But the system call chroot("/usr/web") changes the process' notion of root to *usr/web* rather than */*. After this, the system call that would open the same file as above is

```
if ((fd = open("/pages/index.html", O_RDONLY)) < 0)
        perror("open /usr/web/pages/index.html for reading
            failed");
```

because the kernel maps the first / in */pages/index.html* to the directory */usr/web*. Every full path name that the process refers to uses */usr/web* as its beginning. The process could not directly refer to the file */usr/trans/1*.

---

[55] See Section 14.1, "Access Control Lists."
[56] See Section 14.2, "Capabilities."

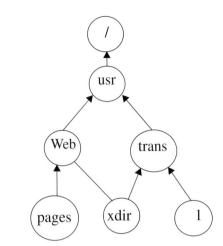

Figure 24–1 A UNIX file system. The directed edges indicate the parents of each directory. A hard link to "xdir" lies in "Web."

Depending on the nature of the hierarchy, the process may be able to refer indirectly to the file */usr/trans/1*. Some variants of the UNIX system allow the superuser to make links to a directory. Consider the hierarchy shown in Figure 24–1. The directory *xdir* is a child of *trans*, so the entry .. in *xdir* refers to *trans*. The superuser has created a hard link in *web* that refers to *xdir*. Now suppose a process executes the call chroot("/usr/web"). The process can no longer access */usr/ trans/1* by that name, but it *can* access it as *xdir/../1* because the change in root does not affect the interpretation of the path name.

This shows that, in addition to the chroot, the file hierarchy in which the process is rooted must not have any hard links extending to directories not in that file hierarchy.

Finally comes interprocess communication. Processes should be able to communicate only through known, well-defined communication channels.[57] The issue here is how the Web server communicates with the commerce server to tell it that transaction files are present, and the names of those files.

The simplest method of communication is to use the directory that both the Web server and commerce server share. The commerce server periodically checks for files with names consisting of *trns* followed by a set of digits. When a transaction begins, the CGI script creates a temporary transaction file. It builds the transaction data and enciphers it using the appropriate public key. It then renames the temporary file with a name consisting of *trns* followed by the integer representation of the date and time, followed by one or more digits. (See Exercise 5.) When the commerce server checks the directory, it moves any files with that type of name to the spooling area.

If the Web server and commerce server run with the same real or effective UID, or either runs with superuser privileges,[58] then they can communicate using the UNIX signaling (asynchronous interrupt) mechanism. If an attacker acquires access through the Web server, and can signal the commerce server, then the attacker can damage the Drib with a denial of service attack. Hence, the Web server and the commerce server should run as distinct users, with different privileges.

---

[57] See Chapter 16, "Confinement Problem."
[58] See Section 13.3, "Users."

24.6.2   The Development System

Unlike the DMZ Web server system, the development workstation serves developers who will compile, test, debug, and manage software. They will also write reports and analyses, communicate with other developers on different systems in the devnet, and send and receive electronic mail over the Internet. The system must support all these functions.

Consider servers and clients first. The devnet workstations may run servers to provide administrative information (such as who is currently logged into the system). These servers require administrative users. As discussed in Section 24.4.2, item DC2 requires these users to be local. Item DC1 requires that users be named (and numbered) consistently. The NIS protocol provides user information to clients, ensuring this consistency. Hence, the devnet workstation runs NIS clients. Similarly, the workstation runs NFS clients to satisfy item DC6. Servers run with the fewest privileges necessary to perform their tasks. In many cases, servers begin with *root* privileges to open privileged ports. They then drop privileges to a more restricted user.[59]

EXAMPLE: Consider a mail server on the devnet mail server system. It must listen for connections on port 25. That port (and all ports with numbers less than 1024) can be opened only by *root* processes, but the mail server itself need not run as *root* to perform other functions. It can forward mail to the central mail server as an ordinary user. Thus, two alternatives arise.

Some mail servers allow the system administrator to specify an execution UID. The mail server begins execution as *root* (either by being setuid to *root* or, more commonly, by being started at boot time), opens port 25, and then switches to the execution UID. The disadvantage of this approach is that the saved UID is *root*. If an attacker can trick the server into executing a system call to set the UID to *root*, the mail server can do so. This means that the mail server must be carefully programmed, as discussed in Chapter 26, "Program Security."

The second approach is to use a wrapper. The wrapper runs as *root*. It opens port 25, redirects standard input and output to that port, drops privileges, and then spawns the mail server. For this to work, the mail server must be able to read messages from the standard input and write messages to the standard output.

The abilities of the mail server dictate which approach to use.

Server processes on the development machine run with as few privileges as necessary, as required by item DC2. Whenever possible, they run with the *nobody* UID and the *nogroup* GID to ensure that the clients can obtain only information that the developers deem public (that is, available to others within the confines of the Drib's internal network).[60] When access to privileged ports is required, one of two methods is used. In the first, the *inetd* daemon (which runs with *root* privileges)

---

[59] See Section 12.2.1, "Principle of Least Privilege."
[60] See Section 12.2.1, "Principle of Least Privilege."

listens for messages at the port. When a message is received, *inetd* spawns the server with the limited privileges. In the second method, the server starts with *root* privileges, opens the ports and other files accessible only to *root*, and drops to a lesser privilege level. This minimizes the actions that the process takes when it has unlimited privilege.[61] It also allows the operating system to enforce normal file system access checks.[62] As with the WWW server system, the servers run in a subtree of the file system whenever possible.

To satisfy item DC3, the development system has a logging mechanism that can record any operating system call, its parameters, and the result.[63] Logged information is recorded locally and sent to a central logging server. The security officers monitor the logs from that server using an intrusion detection system.[64] If an attack is suspected, the central logging server can instruct the kernel to begin (or cease) recording data to augment the current set of data. Initially, the system logs process initiation and termination, along with the audit UID and effective UID of the user executing the command.

In addition to requiring the use of file servers, item DC6 requires that the workstations have sufficient disk space available for local users' work. To meet this goal, every night, or when disk space reaches 95% of capacity, a program scans the file system and deletes auxiliary files such as editor backup files and files in temporary directories that are not in current use (defined as not having been accessed within the last 3 days).

As required by item DC1, the devnet workstations allow remote access using SSH. This allows devnet users to test software using multiple workstations, which is useful when the software involves network connections or concurrency. It also allows system administrators to log in remotely to perform maintenance activities.

24.6.3   Comparison

The DMZ Web server system uses a minimalist approach: only those processes necessary for the Web server, remote administration, and the operating system are present. All other processes are eliminated. This requires that any new software be compiled on other systems and that all development be done elsewhere. Only those programs essential to the serving of Web pages, to remote administration, and to the operating system are available. The number of processes active at any time on this system is small.[65] By way of contrast, the devnet system must provide an environment in which developers can be productive. This requires that more programs be available, and that more processes be active, than on the DMZ Web server system.

---

[61] See Section 12.2.1, "Principle of Least Privilege."
[62] See Section 12.2.4, "Principle of Complete Mediation."
[63] See Section 21.3, "Designing an Auditing System," and Section 21.4, "A Posteriori Design."
[64] See Chapter 22, "Intrusion Detection."
[65] See Section 12.2.1, "Principle of Least Privilege."

Compilers, scripting languages, Web servers, and other tools help the developers carry out their tasks.

Both systems run servers with the minimum level of privilege needed. This includes not only minimizing user privileges but also restricting the environment in which the process runs.[66] The difference between the systems is that the "minimum environment" for the DMZ Web server system is different from the minimum environment for the Web servers on the devnet systems. In the latter, users wish to share data, so users must be able to place data into areas in which the devnet system's Web server can make it available to other users on the development network. The DMZ Web server system has no such requirement.[67] The *root* user installs all new Web pages. So the Web server needs to serve data only from a part of the file system to which the *root* user can write. No other user needs access, except for the commerce user—and that user has tightly restricted access.

Both systems have processes that log information, but the types of the logging processes differ. The devnet system has a log server that accepts messages from other programs, timestamps and formats them, and writes them to locations specified in a control file. This conforms to the way most UNIX-like systems handle logging and allows devnet systems to use off-the-shelf software. The DMZ Web server system has no such daemon. Each program writes log entries to a local log and to a remote daemon on the log server.[68] This minimizes the number of servers on the DMZ Web server system.

24.7 Files

The setting of protection modes, and the contents of files, affect the protection domains of users and so are critical to a system satisfying a security policy. Again, consider each system separately.

24.7.1 The Web Server System in the DMZ

The Web server system's goal is to serve the Web pages. The system programs and configuration files will not change; only the Web pages, log files, and spooling area for the electronic commerce transactions will change. To preserve their integrity, as required by item WC4, all system programs and files are on a CD-ROM. When the system boots, it boots from the CD-ROM. The CD-ROM is mounted as a file system, so even if attackers can break into the Web server, they cannot alter system files or

---

[66] See Section 12.2.1, "Principle of Least Privilege."

[67] See Section 12.2.7, "Principle of Least Common Mechanism."

[68] See Section 12.2.6, "Principle of Separation of Privilege."

configuration files.[69] A hard drive provides space for temporary and spooled files, for the home directories of authorized users, and for portions of the Web pages.

Because the Web pages change often, it is not feasible to burn them onto a CD-ROM. However, the CGI programs change very infrequently, and are to be protected from any attacker who might gain access to the system, as required by item WC4. Hence, the Web page root directory, and the subdirectory containing the CGI programs, are on the CD-ROM. In the Web page root directory is a subdirectory called *pages* that serves as a mount point for a file system on the hard drive. That file system contains the Web pages. In other words, an attacker can alter Web pages, but cannot alter the CGI programs or the internal public key, which is also kept in a directory under the Web page root directory on the CD-ROM. (See Exercise 10.)

When the system boots, one of its start-up actions is to mount two directories from the hard drive onto mount points on the CD-ROM. The hard drive file system containing the Web pages is mounted onto the mount point in the Web page root directory. A separate area, containing user home directories for the system administrators, a temporary file area, and spooling directories for transactions, is also mounted on the root file system.

As dictated by item WC3, the Web server runs confined to the Web page root directory and its subdirectories.[70] An attacker who compromises the Web server cannot alter the CGI programs, nor add new ones, but can only damage the Web pages on the server.

The commerce server has access to the Web page directory and the spooling area. When a CGI program has processed a request for an electronic transaction, it names the transaction file appropriately (see Section 24.6.1). The commerce server copies the data to the spooling area and deletes the original data. Because the Web server is confined to the Web page partition, an attacker who seizes control of the Web server will be unable to control the commerce server. Moreover, because the CGI programs (and the containing directory) cannot be altered, an attacker could not alter the programs to send raw data to the attacker. Because the CGI programs encipher all data using a public key system before writing the data to disk, the attacker cannot read the raw data there.[71] The corresponding private key is on the internal network, not the DMZ system, so the attacker cannot decipher the data without breaking the public key system.[72]

The system administrator partition provides a home directory area when an administrator logs in. It is small and intended for emergency use only.

EXAMPLE: Suppose the Web server system is a UNIX system and the Web server runs as the user *webbie*. This user has access to all world-readable files, but to no others. Moreover, the Web server changes its notion of the root directory to the root of the Web page directory—on this system */mnt/www*. The CGI programs are owned by

---

[69] See Section 12.2.1, "Principle of Least Privilege."

[70] See Section 16.2, "Isolation."

[71] See Section 12.2.7, "Principle of Least Common Mechanism."

[72] See Section 8.3, "Public Key Cryptography."

root and are located in a separate directory, */mnt/www/cgi-bin*, on the CD-ROM. The public key used by the CGI program to encipher the data is in the directory */mnt/www/keys*. All three of these directories are owned by *root* and are not writable by anyone else. The CGI program places all transaction data into the directory */mnt/www/pages/trans*. Because the executing process runs as the user *webbie*, this directory is writable by a group containing the users *webbie* and *ecommie*.

The commerce server, running as the user *ecommie*, periodically checks the directory */mnt/www/pages/trans* for transaction files. When a transaction is completed, the CGI program names it appropriately. The commerce server then copies the contents of the named file into the transaction directory spool */home/com/transact* area.

Both the commerce server and the Web server log to the log server.

Finally, WC5 also specifies that the number of programs on the system be minimal.[73] Fortunately, the system itself requires few programs. No compilers or software development tools are available. Because all executables are statically linked, the dynamic loader is not present (see Exercise 3). The only programs that are available allow the users to log in and out; run commands (command interpreters); monitor the system; copy, create, edit, or delete files; and stop and start servers. Programs such as mail readers, news readers, batching systems (the *at* and *cron* commands), and Web browsers are not present. This minimizes what an attacker can compromise.

WC4 suggests that the integrity of the system should be checked. Periodically, or whenever there is a question about the integrity of the system, the Web server is stopped, transaction files are transferred, the system is rebooted from the CD-ROM, the hard drive is reformatted, and the contents of the user and Web page areas are reloaded from the internal Web server system clone mirroring the DMZ system (see Section 23.3.3.2). This restores the Web pages and user directories to a known, safe state. If an attacker has left any back doors or other processes to gather information, the reformatting of the hard drive eliminates them.

24.7.2   The Development System

The development system's goal is to provide the resources that developers need to develop new software for the Drib's products and (if necessary) infrastructure and systems. This requires a variety of software. A site can take two approaches.

The first approach is to allow each developer to configure his or her own workstation. The Drib rejected this approach because it would create too many different systems for the system administrators to manage. Furthermore, tools available on one workstation might not be available on another, violating the interchangeability required by item DC6. Meeting item DC5 would also be infeasible because read-only media

---

[73] See Section 12.2.1, "Principle of Least Privilege."

would have to be created for each workstation separately—an effort that was deemed unacceptable.[74]

The second approach is to develop a standard configuration that provides developers and system administrators with needed software tools and configuration settings. To create such a configuration, the Drib policy managers gathered developers, system administrators, security officers, and all other users of the development workstations. The group developed a configuration that met the Drib's policies and that was acceptable to as many people as possible, and ensured that all members of the group were willing and able to use systems with that configuration.[75] The system administrators then installed and configured a base system on an isolated workstation system and created a bootable CD-ROM. This CD-ROM was copied and given to all developers. The developers use this CD-ROM to boot their workstations, ensuring that the resulting configuration is the standard one. All updates and upgrades are made to that isolated workstation system and tested, and a new CD-ROM is created. The CD-ROM is copied and distributed to the developers. This eliminates the problem of inconsistent patching or upgrading of workstations.[76] It also ensures that files are available on all workstations (through mounting of the central file server's file systems) and that the naming scheme is consistent (through use of the same user database system), satisfying items DC1 and DC5. Finally, the local system configurations of all workstations are identical, so all have the same administrative accounts.

Some members of the group pointed out the need for local writable storage. In the event that no file servers are available, the local administrators may need to create files (for example, to save output from a program for analysis). Furthermore, spool files require space, and many programs use temporary storage. Hence, each workstation has a hard drive with several file systems. When the computer boots from the CD-ROM, the root file system is located on the CD-ROM itself. All system programs and configuration files lie on the CD-ROM, as indicated above. During the boot, the workstation mounts the file systems on the hard drive at mount points in the CD-ROM file system. This provides the workstation with appropriate writable storage, satisfying item DC5.

This approach also prevents developers from adding new system programs to the workstations. Programs can of course be added to the writable file systems, but adding a program to the configuration requires that it be added to the isolated system and that new CD-ROMs be burned.[77] This satisfies part of item DC4. Procedural mechanisms (ranging from warnings to firings) enforce the requirement that programs be inspected before they are added to the writable file system. The organization of the various file systems allows the writable media to be wiped during the boot procedure, eliminating any and all programs added to the workstation. This is part of the recommended boot procedure, but it can be skipped if spool files are queued.

---

[74] See Section 12.2.8, "Principle of Psychological Acceptability."

[75] See Section 12.2.5, "Principle of Open Design."

[76] See Section 12.2.7, "Principle of Least Common Mechanism."

[77] See Section 12.2.6, "Principle of Separation of Privilege."

Wiping the writable disks deletes some local log files. However, the logging server also forwards log messages to an infrastructure system that records messages from all workstations. Security analysts examine these logs using various analysis tools, including host-based and network-based intrusion detection tools, to detect misuse and attacks. To validate that the analysis tools are working as expected and are configured correctly, every day the analysts select 30 minutes' worth of log entries and examine them to determine if the analysis tools correctly analyzed those entries. The analysis either validates the security mechanisms and procedures as effective, or reports (or finds) problems. This serves two purposes: validation of the current configuration and software (item DC4)[78] and detection of security incidents (item DC8).[79]

The use of read-only media eliminates the need for integrity checking of the development system binaries and configuration files. Scans of the writable media locate files that match patterns of intrusions. When such files are found, the security officer merely reboots the system, wiping the writable hard drive. This cleans up the workstation. An extensive check of the file servers follows.

EXAMPLE: The UNIX file scanning program *binaudit* [98, 103] allows the system administrator to describe the names and attributes of files. If files do not match the attributes, an alarm is raised. Other programs such as Tiger [768], COPS [309], and TITAN [308] report files with names that match suspicious patterns. The Drib's developers developed their own tool to perform both of these functions.

24.7.3   Comparison

Both the Web server system and the development system rely on physical protection of media to prevent unauthorized alteration of system programs and configuration files. Both boot from the CD-ROM and use the CD-ROM's file system as the main file system. Because some files on both systems must change (for example, transaction files on the Web server system and spooled files on the development system), both have file systems on writable media that are mounted on the main file system.[80]

When the Web server system must be reloaded (because the integrity of the system may have been violated), the spooled transaction files are removed from the system, the system is booted, and the writable medium is reformatted. Then the Web pages and user directories are reloaded from a clone kept in a state known to be safe. The development system does not require this, because any nontransient files are kept on a centralized file server that is itself regularly checked. The only local files are temporary files that the users can reinstantiate when they log back in, so the

---

[78] See Section 17.1.3, "Assurance Throughout the Life Cycle."
[79] See Chapter 22, "Intrusion Detection."
[80] See Section 12.2.1, "Principle of Least Privilege."

system is simply rebooted and the media reformatted. Because the main file system is on a CD-ROM, its integrity is ensured.

The differences between the approaches used in developing the two CD-ROMs spring from the question of attack from within the company. The developers are all trusted not to attack the workstation, because at any time a developer may have to use any workstation. However, the developers may be used as "vectors of attack" if they should (accidentally or deliberately) make errors in programming or bring in software from untrusted sources.[81] This led to the consensus-based development of the workstation CD-ROM. The developers had great influence, because they would be using the workstations. Security was a consideration, but it was weighted against productivity and morale. The outer, inner, and devnet firewalls were to provide the bulwark of the security for the development network systems.[82]

The set of users trusted to work on the DMZ Web server system was much smaller. Thus, the DMZ Web server system was designed to withstand attack from both the Internet and the internal network. For example, the Web server originally was intended to handle transactions; the security people vetoed this as allowing too many potential attacks, and instead suggested the staging approach, in which the DMZ Web server acts as a proxy for the transaction processing systems on the customer data subnet (see Figure 23–1). The construction of the CD-ROM began with the security officers devising the most secure, minimal Web server system they could construct and then adding those features necessary for the Drib's special needs.[83] They monitor activities on the Web server, and several vulnerability tracking lists and news services, to ensure that they are up to date on all potential problems.

The DMZ Web server system is self-contained in that all files are local. None are served remotely.[84] If an attacker alters files, a reboot and a reload restore the files to their original state. No other system depends on those files. However, the development workstation relies on file servers. This removes user file integrity from the purview of the development workstation's security. Integrity of the configuration becomes critical, to ensure that the right servers are used, but the CD-ROM ensures that the configuration file data is correct. However, the security of the development systems depends more on the security of the infrastructure of the development network than the security of the DMZ Web server system depends on the security of the infrastructure of the DMZ network.

---

[81] See Section 19.6, "Defenses."

[82] This approach violates the principle of fail-safe defaults, but it was deemed necessary to allow the developers to be as productive and effective as possible. This illustrates a tension between the principle of fail-safe defaults and the principle of psychological acceptability (see Exercise 11).

[83] See Section 12.2.2, "Principle of Fail-Safe Defaults."

[84] See Section 12.2.7, "Principle of Least Common Mechanism."

24.8   Retrospective

This section briefly reviews the basics of the security of the systems.

24.8.1   The Web Server System in the DMZ

The Web server on the DMZ Web server system runs a minimal set of services. It keeps everything possible on unalterable media.[85] Except for the Web server process, the system accepts only enciphered, authenticated connections from a known, trusted host by known, trusted users.[86]

The Web server process must accept connections from any host on the Internet. However, all such connections go through an outer firewall that can (if desired) be configured to reject requests.[87] This means that denial of service attacks could be handled at the outer firewall and not by the DMZ Web server.

The Web server and commerce server run with minimal privileges. Neither may communicate with the other except through a shared directory used to transfer transaction requests from the public Web server area to a private spooling area from which they can be retrieved through the enciphered link.[88] The transaction files themselves are enciphered using a public key algorithm, so an attacker who compromises the Web server cannot alter the transaction files, but can only delete them. To minimize this risk, the commerce server moves the transaction files as quickly as possible to an area that is inaccessible to the Web server.

Access to the administrative account requires that the user access a trusted host (the internal trusted administrative host) and then authenticate to the DMZ Web server using a public key protocol. Automated processes will authenticate on the basis of the host from which they are run, which is the internal trusted administrative host. The SSH server ignores connections from other hosts, and host identity is determined using public key authentication, not IP addresses.

Other servers and programs are simply deleted from the system, so they cannot be run even by accident.[89] This simplifies system maintenance. It also deprives any attackers of available tools should they penetrate the Web server system.

---

[85] See Section 12.2.1, "Principle of Least Privilege."

[86] See Section 12.2.4, "Principle of Complete Mediation."

[87] See Section 12.2.6, "Principle of Separation of Privilege."

[88] See Section 16.2, "Isolation."

[89] See Section 12.2.2, "Principle of Fail-Safe Defaults."

24.8.2 The Development System

The development system also runs a minimal set of programs and services.[90] The notion of "minimal" is different for the development system than for the DMZ Web server system, because the systems must serve many functions. Users compile and debug programs. They test programs, and they integrate different programs into a single software system. They may use ancillary hardware (such as embedded systems) to support the development. The development systems must support this functionality.

Given this, security plays a prominent but not dominant role. Hidden behind three firewalls, each development workstation has sufficient security mechanisms to hinder attackers, and to allow quick recovery if an attack does occur,[91] but these systems rely more on the infrastructure than does the DMZ Web server system.

The development system allows a large number of users access from any development network system and (possibly) from systems in other subnets of the internal network. User information resides in a centralized repository to maintain consistency across all development systems. Reusable passwords are supported, and password aging is not enforced. However, passwords are tested for strength before they are accepted, and the security officers periodically try to guess passwords. Other password schemes are also supported.

Backups occur daily. Because each workstation has a local writable area, users may keep files in that area rather than place them on the file servers. These areas are backed up. The dumps are typically small, because most users work on directories mounted from the file servers. The main reason for these backups is to preserve the log files should an investigation require them.

24.9 Summary

This chapter refined parts of a security policy to derive requirements for mechanisms on systems to implement the policy. The mechanisms rely in part on infrastructure systems and the environment in which those systems function. The server in the DMZ is based on assumptions under which a small set of users is trusted, and everyone else is distrusted. This leads to a system that provides minimal services. System files are kept on protected media so that they cannot be physically altered. Other files, such as those containing transactions, are protected using cryptographic mechanisms so that alterations will be detected, and sanity checks are performed on their contents both before encryption and after delivery and decryption. By way of contrast, the development workstations are general-purpose workstations designed to support a development environment. They support many more functions, and more

---

[90] See Section 12.2.1, "Principle of Least Privilege."
[91] See Section 22.6.2, "Intrusion Handling."

open access, than the DMZ server. Furthermore, their user population is trusted to a greater degree than that of the DMZ Web server. This leads to differences in infrastructure support and workstation configuration.

24.10   Further Reading

Many books discuss system administration and security for UNIX and UNIX-like systems [30, 341, 347, 380, 685], Windows systems [450, 479, 609, 946], and Macintosh systems [744].

As sites grow in complexity and number of systems, automated system administration tools are becoming more important. Several authors [142, 143, 214, 317, 387] discuss systems for administering sites.

The role of policy is increasingly driving work in systems administration. The balance between centralized system administration and distributed system administration is delicate [430, 792], as is the balance between security and convenience [474, 747]. Others [391, 444, 968] focus on case studies of system administration and policy. Burgess [144] discusses some theory to evaluate system administration policies. Sloman [839] and Lupu and Sloman [584] discuss policy and framework in the context of distributed systems. Kubicki [536] adapts the Capabilities Maturity Model to the examination of quality control in system administration.

24.11   Exercises

1. A system administrator on a development network workstation wants to execute a program stored on a floppy disk. What steps could the Drib take to configure the workstation to prevent the system administrator from mounting the floppy and executing the program?

2. Suppose a user has physical access to computer hardware (specifically, the box containing the CPU and a hard drive). The user does not have an account on the computer. How can the user force the computer to shut down? To reboot?

3. Some systems support dynamic loading, in which system library routines are not loaded until they have been referenced. A library can be updated independently of any programs that use the library. If the program loads the library routines dynamically, the updated routines will be used. If the program does not load the library routines dynamically, the program will use the versions of the routines that were in the library at link time. This exercise examines this property from the viewpoint of security.

  a. From the point of view of assurance, what problems might dynamic loading introduce? (*Hint:* Think about the assumptions the programmer made when writing the code that calls the library functions.)

  b. Does dynamic loading violate any of Saltzer and Schroeder's principles of secure design [773]? (See Chapter 12.) Justify your answer.

  c. If an attacker wanted to implant a Trojan horse into as many processes as possible, how would dynamic loading lower the amount of work that the attacker would need to do?

4. Suppose there is no system dedicated to the bootable CD-ROM discussed in Section 24.7.2. How would you go about constructing such a CD-ROM? Discuss procedures, and justify them. What is the problem with updating a running system and burning a CD-ROM of the changes only?

5. The Web server on the DMZ Web server system renames temporary files used to record transactions. The name has the form *trns* followed by the integer representation of the date and time, followed by one or more digits. Why are the extra digits necessary?

6. Consider a developer who has both an ISP workstation and a devnet workstation on his desk, and who wants to move a program from the ISP workstation to the devnet workstation.

  a. Assume that the user is not allowed to mount media such as the floppy disk. Thus, he would not be able to access the data on the disk as though it were a file system. Would he be able to access the data in some other way? (*Hint:* Must data on all media be accessed as though it were a file system, or can it be read in some other way?)

  b. Assume that the *root* user is asked to mount the floppy for the user, so he can access data on it. What precautions should *root* take before making the data available to the user?

  c. Suppose the ISP workstation were removed. How could the Drib prevent the developer from bringing a floppy into his office?

  d. Suppose the floppy reader were removed from the development network workstation. Would this solve the problem? Why or why not? Discuss the advantages and disadvantages of this approach.

7. The second line of the Web server starting script puts the process ID number of the Web server wrapper into a file. Why? (*Hint:* Think of how to terminate the process automatically.)

8. This exercise reconsiders the use of NIS to distribute user information such as password hashes.

    a. In general, why might an administration want to use encryption techniques to protect the transmission of NIS records over a network?

    b. Why is secrecy of the NIS records not important to the system administrators?

    c. Assume the devnet firewall (and the inner and outer firewalls) did not prevent outside users from monitoring the development network. How important would secrecy of the NIS records be then? Why?

    d. The NIS client accepts the first response to its query that it receives from *any* NIS server. Why is physical control of the development network critical to the decision not to use cryptography to protect the NIS network traffic?

9. The system administrators on the development network believe that any password can be guessed in 180 days of continuous trial and error. They set the lifetime of each password at a maximum of 90 days. After 90 days, a password must be changed. Why did they use 90 days rather than 180 days?

10. Section 24.7.1 discusses CGI scripts on the DMZ Web server system. It points out that Web pages change too frequently to be placed on a CD-ROM, but that the CGI scripts are changed infrequently enough to allow them to be placed on the CD-ROM.

    a. In light of the fact that the CGI scripts do not contain data, why is their alteration a concern?

    b. CGI scripts can generate Web pages from data stored on the server. Discuss the integrity issues arising from storing of the data that those scripts use on writable media but storing of the scripts themselves on read-only media. In particular, how trustworthy are the pages resulting from the script's use of stored data? (*Hint:* See Section 6.2.)

    c. Assume that the CGI scripts are to be changed frequently. Devise a method that allows such changes and also keeps the interface to those scripts on read-only media. Where would you store the actual scripts, and what are the benefits and drawbacks of such a scheme?

11. Brian Reid has noted that "[p]rogrammer convenience is the antithesis of security" [747]. Discuss how the Drib's trade-off between security and convenience exemplifies the conflict between users (programmers) and security. In particular, when should the principle of psychological acceptability (see Section 12.2.8) override other principles of secure design?

12. Computer viruses and worms are often transmitted as attachments to electronic mail. The Drib's development network infrastructure directs all

electronic mail to a mail server. Consider an alteration of the development network infrastructure whereby workstations download user mail rather than mounting the file system containing the mailboxes.

 a. The Drib has purchased a tool that scans mail as it is being received. The tool looks for known computer worms and viruses in the contents of attachments, and deletes them. Should this antivirus software be installed on the mail server, on the desktop, or on both? Justify your answer.

 b. What other actions should the Drib take to limit incoming computer worms and viruses in attachments? Specifically, what *attributes* should cause the Drib to flag attachments as suspicious, even when the antivirus software reports that the attachment does not contain any known virus?

 c. What procedural mechanisms (such as warnings) should be in place to hinder the execution of computer worms and viruses that are not caught by the antivirus filters? Specifically, what should users be advised to do when asked to execute a set of instructions to (for example) print a pretty picture?

Chapter 25
User Security

> COMINIUS: Away! the tribunes do attend you: arm yourself
> To answer mildly; for they are prepar'd
> With accusations, as I hear, more strong
> Than are upon you yet.
> —*Coriolanus*, III, ii, 138–141.

Although computer systems provide security mechanisms and policies that can protect users to a great degree, users must also take security precautions for a variety of reasons. First, although system controls limit the access of unauthorized users to the system, such controls often are flawed and may not prevent *all* such access. Second, someone with access to the system may want to attack an authorized user—for example, by reading confidential or private data or by altering files. The success of such attacks may depend on the victim's failure to take certain precautions. Finally, users may notice problems with their accounts, causing them to suspect compromises. The system administrator can then investigate thoroughly.

This chapter considers a user of a workstation on the development network at the Drib. The user's primary job is to develop products or support for the Drib. It is not to secure her system. We explore the precautions, settings, and procedures that such a user can use to limit the effect of attacks on her account.

25.1 Policy

Most users have informal policies in mind when they decide on security measures to protect their accounts, data, and programs. Few analyze the policies or even write them down. However, as with the development of a network infrastructure, and of the configuration and operation of a system, users' security policies are central to the actions and settings that protect them.

The components of users' policies that we focus on are as follows.

U1. Only users have access to their accounts.

U2. No other user can read or change a file without the owner's permission.

U3. Users shall protect the integrity, confidentiality, and availability of their files.

U4. Users shall be aware of all commands that they enter, or that are entered on their behalf.

25.2   Access

Component U1 requires that users protect access to their accounts. Consider the ways in which users gain access to their accounts. These points of entry are ideal places for attackers to attempt to masquerade as users. Hence, they form the first locus of users' defenses.

25.2.1   Passwords

Section 11.2.2, "Countering Password Guessing," discussed the theory behind good password selection. Ideally, passwords should be chosen randomly.[1] In practice, such passwords are difficult to remember. So, either passwords are not assigned randomly, or they require that some information be written down.

Writing down passwords is popularly considered to be dangerous. In reality, the degree of danger depends on the environment in which the system is accessed and on the manner in which the password is recorded.

EXAMPLE: Consider the isolated system that the development network administrators use to create the CD-ROM from which other workstations boot (see Section 24.7.2). This system is kept in a locked room, and only the authorized users of the system have keys. The system is not connected to networks or telephone lines and can be accessed only from within that room. The password for the role account used to construct the CD-ROM is written on a whiteboard in the room. Given that all users of the isolated system are authorized to know that password, and that anyone else entering the room is under observation, this arrangement meets policy component U1. (But see Exercise 1.)

Users with accounts on many systems will choose the same password for each system, choose passwords that follow a pattern, or write passwords down.[2] On the

---

[1] See Section 11.2.2.1, "Random Selection of Passwords."
[2] See Section 11.2.2.3, "User Selection of Passwords."

development network, the first of these is a result of centralizing the user database. Even there, users (especially system administrators) may have multiple accounts, including some on infrastructure systems that do not use the centralized user database. These users must take precautions to protect their passwords.

EXAMPLE: The development network has 10 infrastructure systems (mail, file, Web, and other servers). Anne and Paul are the lead system administrators for the infrastructure systems. They must have privileged access to all those systems. To make the *root* and *Administrator* passwords as difficult as possible to guess, those passwords are chosen randomly. But Paul and Anne cannot remember 10 random passwords. Instead, each has decided on a transformation algorithm.[3] Anne's is "Change the third letter's case, and delete the last character." Paul's is "Add 2 mod 10 to the first digit, and delete the first letter." The following table summarizes the actual passwords and what Paul and Anne have written on small pieces of paper that they carry with them.

Actual password	Anne's version	Paul's version
C04cEJxX	C04ceJxX5	RC84cEJxX
4VX9q3GA	4VX9Q3GA2	a2VX9q3GA
8798Qqdt	8798QqDt$	67f98Qqdt
3WXYwgnw	3WXYwgnwS	Z1WXYwgnw
feOioC4f	feoioC4f9	YfeOioC2f
VRd0Hj9E	VRD0Hj9Eq	pVRd8Hj9E
e7Bukcba	e7BUkcbaX	Xe5Bukcba
ywyj5cVw	ywYj5cVw*	rywyj3cVw
5iUikLB4	5iUIkLB4m	3JiUikLB4
af4hC2kg	af4HC2kg+	daf2hC2kg

If someone obtains either Anne's or Paul's list, the thief will not be able to determine the correct password before Anne or Paul notices that the list is missing and takes appropriate action.

The users of development network workstations can choose their own passwords, but a proactive password checking program checks the proposed password before accepting it.[4] The proactive password checker rejects proposed passwords

---

[3] See Section 11.2.2.1, "Random Selection of Passwords."
[4] See Section 11.2.2.3, "User Selection of Passwords."

that are deemed too easy to guess.[5] Most users choose verses of poetry or sayings, and use them to generate their passwords.

EXAMPLE: The third verse of the nonsense poem *Jabberwocky* [156] is

> He took his vorpal sword in hand:
> Long time the manxome foe he sought—
> So rested he by the Tumtum tree,
> And stood awhile in thought.

Marilyn, a developer at the Drib, chose her password by taking the first letter of the second and fourth words from each line and putting an "&" between them. Her password is "ttrs&vmbi."

If a user chooses a password that is easy to guess, it may cause a violation of policy component U1.

25.2.2   The Login Procedure

To log in, the user must supply her login name and authentication information. First, the user obtains a prompt at which she can enter the information. She then logs in.

The first potential attack arises from the lack of mutual authentication on most systems. An attacker may place a program at the access point that emulates the login prompt sequence. Then, if the user has a reusable password, the name and password are captured. Crude versions of this Trojan horse[6] save the name and password to a file and then terminate by spawning a legitimate login session. The user will be reprompted for the information. Most users simply assume that they have mistyped some part of the password (which, after all, is usually not printed) and proceed to repeat the login procedure. A more sophisticated version saves the name and password to a file and then spawns the login process and feeds it the name and password. The program terminates, giving control of the access point to the login process.

EXAMPLE: Students at many university sites in the 1970s tried this attack in public terminal rooms. They had varying degrees of success. An early version of one operating system had a feature that defeated the crude versions of this attack. If a user mistyped his name or password, the login program would reprompt him for this information. However, the prompt for the user name would change from "Login:" to "Name:". If a user saw the prompt "Login:" twice in a row, he had reason to believe that a spoof was underway.

---

[5] An example set of criteria begins on p. 178.
[6] See Section 19.2, "Trojan Horses."

EXAMPLE: Secure Xenix [361] had an alternative approach that is common to systems that desire high assurance authentication of users. When a user wished to log in, he struck a particular combination of keys that created a trusted path to the kernel. No application program could disable this feature; no application program could read or alter the information given to the kernel over that path. The kernel then performed the identification and authentication processing and granted or denied the user access.

The second potential attack arises from an attacker reading the password as it is entered. At a later date, the attacker can reuse the password. This differs from the first attack in that it succeeds even when the user and system mutually authenticate each other. The problem is that the password is no longer confidential.

EXAMPLE: "Shoulder surfing" is a technique in which an attacker watches the target enter the password. Variations on this attack include reading of the characters from kernel variables, which requires that the attacker have access to those structures (usually as a result of a system configuration error[7]), and passive wiretapping of an unenciphered connection.

The latter opportunity for reading the password is important. Many protocols, such as *ftp* and *telnet*, do not encipher messages. If a user name and password are sent over such a connection, they are visible at every intermediate node and network. Other protocols, such as SSH and SSL, provide enciphered "tunnels" through which other protocols can be sent.[8] This provides the user with confidentiality even when the protocols themselves do not. In some environments, this is unnecessary. For example, the Drib firewalls block any traffic to the Internet, and hosts and networks within the Drib are trusted not to capture network traffic. In other environments, *especially when messages are sent over untrusted links*, enciphering of all messages is prudent.

As part of the login procedure, many systems print useful information. If the date, time, and location of the last successful login are shown, the user can verify that no one has used her account since she last did. If the access point is shown, the user can determine if some program is intercepting and rerouting her communications.

EXAMPLE: Suppose a user logs in from the console. After the login, the system prints a message indicating that she last successfully logged in on the previous Tuesday and was currently using a network terminal. The time of login happens to be correct, but the terminal is not, and the user should contact the system administrator. One possible explanation is that a Trojan horse is capturing all commands, saving them in a file, and then passing the commands back to the normal system login process over a network connection.

---

[7] See Section 24.4.2, "The Development System."
[8] See the examples in Section 10.4, "Example Protocols."

Policy component U1 suggests that the user should be alert when logging in. If something suspicious occurs, or the link to the system is not physically or cryptographically protected, an unauthorized user may acquire access to the system.

25.2.2.1 Trusted Hosts

The notion of "trusted hosts" comes from the belief that if two hosts are under the same administrative control, each can rely on the other to authenticate a user. It allows certain mechanisms, such as backups, to be automated without placing passwords or cryptographic keys on the system.

EXAMPLE: The Drib uses a remote backup scheme run from a backup system. It logs into each system as the user "backup" and executes a backup program. The backup program sends the data to be backed up over the network connection. If logging in required a password, then an administrator password would have to be present on the backup system. The Drib development network administrators considered this to be an unacceptable risk. Instead, they made all systems trust the backup host. Then the backup user could simply log in without a password.

The trusted host mechanism requires accurate identification of the connecting host. The primary identification token of a host is its IP address,[9] but the authentication mechanism can be either the IP address itself [493] or a challenge-response exchange[10] based on cryptography [959]. The Drib uses the latter. This prevents IP spoofing.

The development network workstations use the cryptographically based trusted host mechanism. The implementation provides enciphered and integrity-checked connections. Because all development network workstations use the same user information database, a developer need only log into one using a password. She can then access any workstation on that subnet.

Hence, the development network provides an infrastructure that supports this aspect of policy component U1.

25.2.3 Leaving the System

The Drib has many physical and procedural controls that limit access to its facility, but some people not authorized to use the systems have access to the rooms in which those systems reside. For example, custodians clean the rooms. If lights or air conditioning units need to be repaired, maintenance workers need entry. Hence, physical security is not sufficient to control access to the systems.

Users must authenticate themselves to begin a session. However, once authenticated, the user must also control access to the session. A common problem is that users will leave their sessions unattended—for example, by walking away from their

---

[9] See Section 13.6.1, "Host Identity."
[10] See Section 11.3, "Challenge-Response."

monitors to go to the bathroom. If a custodian came into the room, she would see that the monitor was logged in and could enter commands, thereby obtaining access to the system even though she was not authorized to do so.

When a user of a system leaves a session unattended, he must restrict physical access to the endpoint of the session.[11] When that endpoint is a monitor or terminal, a screen locking program provides an approriate defense against this threat.

EXAMPLE: The X window system provides a program called *xlock*. When run, *xlock* blocks access to the monitor until the user's password is entered. Only the user or the system administrator can terminate the program without the password by sending an appropriate termination signal to it from another session.

Screen locking programs may have security holes. The most common is a "master password" that unlocks the terminal if the user forgets the password used to lock it.[12]

EXAMPLE: In one version of the UNIX operating system, the *lock* program prompted the user for a password and then locked access to the terminal until the password was entered. If the user forgot the password, the master password "Hasta la vista!" would unlock the terminal. (See Exercise 2.)

A modem bank provides similar opportunities for open sessions. When a modem detects *carrier drop* (that is, when the remote user hangs up), it terminates the session. However, two problems arise. The first and simpler one is that the detection of carrier drop is configurable. Some modems have a physical switch that must be set properly to detect the termination of a telephone call.[13]

EXAMPLE: The author once accessed a UNIX system through a modem to make some changes in his role as a system administrator. Unfortunately, the configuration of the system had changed so that he was unable to acquire superuser privileges. One not only needed the password but also had to be a member of the group *wheel*.[14] The author logged out and hung up. When he accessed the system 20 minutes later, through the same modem bank, the modem connected him to an ongoing session. This session, left when a previous user had hung up without logging out, had superuser privileges. The author made the required changes, sent electronic mail to warn everyone to log out before disconnecting, and then logged out and hung up the telephone. The next day, he checked the modem configurations and reset the switch that detected carrier drop. (It had been bumped accidentally when someone was adding two new modems to the rack of modems.)

---

[11] See Section 12.2.1, "Principle of Least Privilege."

[12] Section 1.4, "Assumptions and Trust," discusses the role of beliefs underlying security mechanisms such as a screen locking program. Section 17.1.3, "Assurance Throughout the Life Cycle," discusses the role of assurance in developing software.

[13] See Section 12.2.2, "Principle of Fail-Safe Defaults."

[14] See Section 12.2.6, "Principle of Separation of Privilege."

The second problem is similar but more subtle. Some older telephone systems mishandle the propagation of call terminations. The result is a race condition,[15] in which a new connection arrives at the switch and is forwarded before the termination signal arrives at the modem. The effect is exactly the same as in the example above: the modem never sees the carrier drop. If the session is terminated, the modem initiates a new session and the race condition does not affect the system's accessibility, but if the session is unterminated, the new connection will have access to the session.

The Drib's solution to these problems is a mixture of physical and technical means. All workstations have display locking programs that do not accept a master password. They use the user's login password as the key to unlocking the display. If the user is unable to supply that password (for example, if the user forgets it or becomes ill and cannot communicate it), the system administrators can remotely log into the workstation and terminate the process. The procedural mechanisms involve disciplinary action against developers who fail to lock displays, or fail to lock the doors of their offices when they leave. As far as modems go, the Drib does not allow modems to be connected to the development network.

25.3   Files and Devices

Users keep information and programs in files. This makes file protection a security mechanism that users can manipulate to refine the protection afforded their data. Similarly, users manipulate the system through devices of various types. Their protection is to some degree under the user's control. This section explores both.

25.3.1   Files

Users must protect confidentiality and integrity of the files to satisfy policy component U2. To this end, they use the protection capabilities of the system to constrain access. Complicating the situation are the interpretation of permissions on the containing directories.

EXAMPLE: Peter is using a UNIX-based system. He wants to allow Deborah to read the file *design* but prevent other users from doing so. He can use the abbreviated ACL mechanism of standard UNIX systems[16] to do this in three ways.

If Deborah and Peter are the only members of a group, Peter can make the file owned by that group and readable by that group but not readable by others.

---

[15] See Section 20.4.5.1, "The *xterm* Log File Flaw," and Section 26.5.3.3, "Race Conditions in File Accesses," for other examples of race conditions.

[16] See Section 14.1.1, "Abbreviations of Access Control Lists."

If Deborah is the only member of a group and the UNIX system semantics allow the owner of a file to give the file to a group of which the owner is not a member, Peter can give group ownership of the file to Deborah's group and then set the group ownership privileges as described above.

An alternative approach is to set permissions on the containing directory. Peter can set the permissions of the directory to allow search access only to himself and to the group of which Deborah is the only member by turning on read and execute permission for the group owner of the directory. Then the protections of the file can allow anyone to read the file. Because only Peter and Deborah can search the directory (the execute permission), only they can reach the file.

This example illustrates the cumbersome nature of abbreviated ACLs (see Exercise 3; Exercise 4 explores an approach to the situation in which Peter and Deborah are the only members in common to two groups). Ordinary ACLs make the task considerably simpler.

EXAMPLE: The Windows NT access control lists[17] allow Peter to give Deborah access directly. Peter creates an ACL for *design* with two entries:

```
(Peter, full control) (Deborah, read)
```

The semantics of Windows NT disallow access to any user or group omitted from the ACL. Hence, only Peter and Deborah can access the file.

Users can control several aspects of file protection. The remainder of this section explores some of these aspects.

25.3.1.1 File Permissions on Creation

Many systems allow users to specify a template of permissions to be given to a file when it is created. The owner can then modify this set as required.

EXAMPLE: When Roger creates a directory on Windows NT, it inherits the ACL of its parent directory.

UNIX-like systems take an alternative approach. A user can identify specific permissions to be *denied* on creation.

The variable *umask* contains a set of permissions to be disabled. It uses the nine-bit format of the standard UNIX protection mask, in which the first set of three bits corresponds to the owner, the second set corresponds to the group, and the third set corresponds to others (everyone except the owner and members of the group). The first bit in each triplet controls read access, the second bit controls write access, and the

---

[17] See Section 14.1.4, "Example: Windows NT Access Control Lists."

third bit controls execute access. So, if a user sets her *umask* to 022, then, when she creates a file, group and other write permissions are turned off, *regardless* of the permissions she requested. If she wants the group members to have write access, she can use a command such as *chmod* to enable that access. (See Exercise 5.)

25.3.1.2   Group Access

Group access provides a selected set of users with the same access rights.[18] The problem is that the membership of the group is not under the control of the owner of the file. This has an advantage and a disadvantage.

The advantage arises when the group is used as a role.[19] Then, as users are allowed to assume the role, their access to the file is altered. Because the owner of the file is concerned only with controlling access of those role users, reconfiguration of the access to the role reconfigures user access to the file, which is what the user wants.

EXAMPLE: Tom is working on a project to develop the next generation of widgets, called Widget-NG. All members of the Widget-NG design team are in the group *widgetngd*. The files that contain the design are group-owned by *widgetngd*, and the members of that group can read from and write to the file.

Even when the membership of the group changes, the function of the group does not. Hence, the new users are given access to the Widget-NG information. The group ownership mechanism provides that access.

The disadvantage arises when a group is used as a shorthand for a set of specific users. If the membership of the group changes, unauthorized users may obtain access to the file, or authorized users may be denied access to the file.

EXAMPLE: Maria wants her friends Anne and Joan to have access to the file *movies*. She has the system administrator create a group called *maj*, which contains those three users, and makes the file group-owned, readable, and writable by the group *maj*.

The system administrator is later asked to create a group containing Maria, Anne, Joan, and Lorraine. He notices that the group *maj* contains three of those four users, and he simply adds Lorraine to the group. Now Lorraine can read and alter the file *movies*, even though Maria never intended for her to do so.

In general, users should limit access as much as possible when creating new files. So ACLs and C-Lists should include as few entries as possible, and permissions for each entry should be as restrictive as possible. Constructs such as the *umask* should be set to deny permissions to as many users as possible (in the specific case of

---

[18] See Section 13.4, "Groups and Roles."
[19] See Section 13.4, "Groups and Roles."

UNIX systems, *umask* should deny all permissions to all but the owner, unless there are specific reasons to set it differently).

25.3.1.3   File Deletion

A user deletes a file. Either the file data or the file name is discarded. The effects of these differ widely.

Computer systems store files on disk. The *file attribute table* contains information about the file. The *file mapping table* contains information that allows the operating system to locate the disk blocks that compose the file. Systems represent a file being in a directory in a variety of ways. All involve an entry in the directory for that file, but the entry may contain attribute information (such as permissions and file type) or may merely point to an entry in the file attribute table.

> **Definition 25–1.** A *direct alias* is a directory entry that points to (names) the file. An *indirect alias* is a directory entry that points to a special file containing the name of the target file. The operating system interprets the indirect alias by substituting the contents of the special file for the name of the indirect alias file.

All direct aliases that name the same file are equal. Each direct alias is an alternative name for the same file.[20]

The representation of containment in a directory affects security. If each direct alias can have different permissions, the owner of a file must change the access modes of each alias in order to control access. To avoid this, most systems associate the file attribute information with the actual data, and directory entries consist of a pointer to the file attribute table.

When a user deletes a file, the directory entry is removed. The system tracks the number of directory entries for each file, and when that number becomes 0, the data blocks and table entries for that file are released. This means that deleting a file does *not* ensure that the file is unavailable; it merely deletes the directory entry.

EXAMPLE: Anna uses a UNIX-based system. She has a program *runasanna* that is setuid to herself.[21] She wishes to delete it so that no one can use it. However, if she executes the command

```
rm runasanna
```

she will delete the directory entry for that file. If no one else has a direct alias (or, in UNIX terminology, a *hard link*) to the file, it will be removed from the system.

---

[20] See Section 13.2, "Files and Objects."
[21] See Section 13.3, "Users."

Sandra, however, has made a direct alias to the file. Anna has deleted the file, but there is still a directory entry (Sandra's direct alias) corresponding to the file, so the file has not been deleted. Sandra can still execute the program. Because it is still setuid to Anna, the program runs with Anna's, not Sandra's, permissions.

On UNIX systems, Anna can delete the file from Sandra's directory only if Sandra has given Anna write permission to the directory. To prevent anyone from using the program, Anna must change the permissions of the program to disable it. She can then delete her direct alias. The first line turns off *all* access permissions to the file, including the setuid permission.

```
chmod 000 runasanna
rm runasanna
```

Sandra will retain her alias, and the program will still reside on disk, but it will be useless.

The second issue affecting file deletion is persistence. When a file is deleted, its disk blocks are returned to the pool of unused disk blocks, and they may be reused. However, the data on them remains, and if an attacker can read those blocks, he may read information that was intended to be confidential. When sensitive files are deleted, the contents should be erased before deletion.[22]

EXAMPLE: Many Windows and Macintosh system utilities programs have mechanisms for "wiping" files before they are deleted. These mechanisms overwrite the contents of the file with a bit pattern. The patterns used, and the number of times the contents of the file are overwritten, are configurable. Some versions of the *rm* (file deletion) command on UNIX systems have a similar option.

The third issue lies in the difference between direct and indirect aliases. When a command that affects a file is executed, it may have different effects depending on whether the file is a direct alias or an indirect alias. This may mislead a user into believing that certain information has been protected or deleted when in fact the protection or deletion applied only to the indirect alias and not to the file itself.

EXAMPLE: Suppose Angie executes a command to add read permission to a file for Lucy. If the file is a direct alias, Lucy will be able to read the contents of the file, but if it is an indirect alias, does Lucy have permission to read the file or the indirect alias file? The answer depends entirely on the semantics of the system. The semantics may not be consistent. For example, on Red Hat Linux 7.1, the *chmod* command changes the permissions of the file named by the indirect alias, whereas the *rm* command deletes the indirect alias file itself.

---

[22] See, for example, Section 18.2.1.1, "TCSEC Functional Requirements," and Section 18.4.3, "CC Security Functional Requirements."

25.3.2   Devices

Users communicate with the system through devices. The devices may be virtual, such as network ports, or physical, such as terminals. Policy components U1 and U4 require that these devices be protected so that the user can control what commands are sent to the system in her name and so that others are prevented from seeing her interactions.

25.3.2.1   Writable Devices

Devices that allow any user to write to them can pose serious security problems. Unless necessary for the correct functioning of the system, devices should restrict write access as much as possible.[23] Two examples will demonstrate why.

EXAMPLE: Many systems have tape drives set so that anyone can write to them. When a process begins writing, the ACL of the device changes so that only that process (or the user executing the process) can write to the device. However, between the mounting of the media and the execution of the process is an interval during which another user's process can access the tape drive and read, or overwrite, the tape. For this reason, users should always write-protect mounted media unless they are to be altered.[24] If possible, processes should be attached to such devices, or the devices should be locked to prevent anyone except the user from accessing them, *before* the media are mounted.

EXAMPLE: If any user can write to another user's terminal, an attacker can erase the terminal screen by writing an appropriate control sequence to it. On some early UNIX systems, such a denial of service attack could terminate sessions because the attacker could set the communications speed of the terminal line to 0. The terminal session would immediately terminate [96].

The development network users have a default configuration that denies write privileges to everyone except the user of a terminal.

25.3.2.2   Smart Terminals

A *smart terminal* provides built-in mechanisms for performing special functions. Most importantly, a smart terminal can perform a *block send*. Using this mode, a process can instruct a terminal to send a set of characters that are printed on the screen. The instructions are simply a sequence of characters that the process sends to the terminal. This can be used to implant a Trojan horse.[25]

---

[23] See Section 12.2.1, "Principle of Least Privilege."
[24] See Section 12.2.2, "Principle of Fail-Safe Defaults."
[25] See Section 19.2, "Trojan Horses."

EXAMPLE: Robert wants to trick Craig into executing the command

```
chmod 666 .profile
```

so that Robert can add commands to Craig's startup file. Robert carefully crafts a letter that contains the following.

```
Dear Craig,
Please be careful. Someone may ask you to execute
chmod 666 .profile
You shouldn't do it!
Your friend,
Robert
<BLOCK SEND (-2,18), (-2,18)><BLOCK SEND
(-3,0),(3,18)><CLEAR>
```

(The sequence

```
<BLOCK SEND (a,b), (c,d)>
```

sends all characters from screen position (a,b) to position (c,d) to the system, as though the user had typed them. On Craig's terminal, a newline is stored as an invisible character at the end of each line. The sequence

```
<CLEAR>
```

clears the terminal screen.) When Craig reads this letter, the command

```
!chmod 666 .profile
```

will be sent to the system as though the user had typed it. In this particular mail reading program, the "!" causes the mail program to send the rest of the line to a command interpreter. That interpreter promptly executes the forbidden command and clears the screen to hide the visible traces of the command.

    The difference between a smart terminal and a writable terminal is subtle. Only the user of the terminal need have write access to the smart terminal, whereas the earlier attacks required the attacker as well as the user of the terminal to be able to write to the terminal. An attacker must therefore trick the user into reading data in order to spring the smart terminal attack. This requires malicious logic (or, in this context, malicious data).[26]

---

[26] See Chapter 19, "Malicious Logic."

25.3.2.3   Monitors and Window Systems

Window systems provide a graphical user interface to a system. Typically, a process called the *window manager* controls what is displayed on the monitor and accepts input from input devices. Other processes, called *clients*, register with the window manager. They can then receive input from the window manager and send output to the window manager. The window manager draws the output on the monitor screen if appropriate. The window manager is also responsible for routing input to the correct client.

The obvious question is how the window manager determines which clients it may talk to. If an attacker is able to register a client with the window manager, the attacker can intercept input and send bogus output to the monitor.

EXAMPLE: In some versions of the X window system [347], it was possible for an attacker to overlay an invisible window the size of the monitor screen. The attacker could then record all mouse motions and keystrokes from that monitor and then transmit them to the appropriate window on the screen. The effect was to record everything, including passwords and cryptographic keys.

Window systems can use any of the access control mechanisms described in Chapter 15 to control access to the window manager. The granularity of the access control mechanism varies among different window systems.

EXAMPLE: The X window system controls access on the basis of host name or possession of a token [132]. If access is granted to the window manager, the client may control the display. The window manager cannot control which parts of the display, or which clients, the new client communicates with. The X window system offers two modes of control. Neither provides any confidentiality.

The first mode, called the *xhost* method, determines the name of the host from which the client is trying to connect.[27] The window manager then checks a list of hosts from which processes are authorized to connect. If the process comes from one of those hosts, access is granted. Otherwise, access is denied.

The second mode, called the *xauth* method, requires that a process be able to supply a fixed random number (called a *magic cookie*).[28] When the X window manager starts, it creates (or is given) a magic cookie. This cookie is stored in the file *.Xauthority* in the user's home directory. Any client that attempts to connect to the window manager for that user's display must supply that magic cookie. If the process is local and is run by the user, it can obtain the magic cookie directly from the *.Xauthority* file. If the process is to be run on a remote host, the user must ensure that the process has the magic cookie before it connects to the window manager (this is usually done by copying the *.Xauthority* file to the remote system).

---

[27] See Section 13.6.1, "Host Identity."
[28] See Section 13.6.2, "State and Cookies."

25.4   Processes

Processes manipulate objects, including files. Policy component U3 requires the user to be aware of how processes manipulate files. This section examines several aspects of this requirement.

25.4.1   Copying and Moving Files

Copying a file duplicates its contents. The semantics of the copy command determine if the file attributes are also copied. If the attributes are not copied, the user may need to take steps to preserve the integrity and confidentiality of the file.

EXAMPLE: Suppose Mona Anne wants to copy the file *xyzzy* on a UNIX system. She gives the following command.

```
cp xyzzy plugh
```

If the file *plugh* does not exist, this command creates it and copies the contents of *xyzzy* into it. The permissions will be the same as for *xyzzy*, except that the setuid and setgid attributes will be discarded (see Section 25.4.5).

If the file *plugh* exists, the command copies the contents of *xyzzy* into it. It does not alter the permissions of *plugh*. This is a security problem, because if *xyzzy* is not readable by everyone but *plugh* is, the contents of *xyzzy* will no longer be confidential because anyone reading *plugh* will learn them.

Similarly, sometimes the semantics of moving files involve copying a file and deleting the original copy. In this case, the file attributes of the move command follow those of the copy command. Otherwise, the move command may preserve the attributes of the original command.

EXAMPLE: Now Mona Anne decides to move the file *plugh* to another directory. She gives the command

```
mv plugh /usr/monaanne/advent
```

If the directory resides in the same file system, the direct alias is deleted from the current directory and placed in the directory */usr/monaanne/advent*. Otherwise, the *mv* command executes:

```
cp plugh /usr/monaanne/advent/plugh
rm plugh
```

In the first case, the permissions of *plugh* are preserved. In the second, those permissions may be changed, as noted above.

The semantics of the commands, and how well the user knows those semantics and can take steps to handle potential security problems, affect their ability to satisfy policy component U3.

25.4.2   Accidentally Overwriting Files

Part of policy component U3 is to protect users from themselves.[29] Sometimes people make mistakes when they enter commands. These mistakes can have unpleasant consequences.

EXAMPLE: Scout wants to delete all the files in her directory whose names end in the characters ".o". She uses the pattern "*.o" to match these file names. The "*" is a wildcard that matches 0 or more characters, so the pattern is read as "all file names that end in .o". Unfortunately, she mistypes the command, putting a space between the "*" and the ".o" accidentally:

```
rm * .o
```

This command says to delete all files in the current directory, and the file ".o". Scout will discover this when the command prints the error message

```
.o: No such file or directory
```

after all the files have been deleted.

Many programs that delete or overwrite files have an interactive mode. Before any file is deleted or overwritten, the program requests confirmation that the user intends for this to happen.[30] Policy component U3 strongly suggests that these modes be used. In fact, the development workstations have these modes set in user start-up files. The users can disable the modes, but generally do not.

25.4.3   Encryption, Cryptographic Keys, and Passwords

The basis for encryption is trust. Cryptographic considerations aside, if the encryption and decryption are done on a multiuser system, the cryptographic keys are potentially visible to anyone who can read memory and, possibly, swap space. Anyone who can alter the programs used to encipher and decipher the files, or any of the supporting tools (such as the operating system), can also obtain the cryptographic keys or the cleartext data itself. For this reason, unless users trust the privileged

---

[29] See Section 12.2.2, "Principle of Fail-Safe Defaults."
[30] See Section 12.2.8, "Principle of Psychological Acceptability."

users,[31] and trust that other users cannot acquire the privileges needed to read memory, swap space, or alter the relevant programs, the sensitive data should never be on the system in cleartext.[32]

EXAMPLE: PGP protects a user's private key by enciphering it with a pass-phrase. Mary Ann receives a letter that the sender has enciphered for confidentiality using PGP. She enters her pass-phrase to allow the PGP deciphering program to obtain her private key. It uses her key to decipher the data encryption key, and then the message. Unknown to Mary Ann, Eve has broken into her system and has implanted a keystroke recording module. When Eve retrieves the log of the session, she will have the pass-phrase, from which she can obtain Mary Ann's private key, and thus her identity (as far as Mary Ann's PGP recipients are concerned).

The saving of passwords on a multiuser system suffers from the same problem. In addition, some programs that allow users to put passwords into a file do not rely on enciphering the passwords; they simply require the user to set file permissions so that only the owner can read the file.

EXAMPLE: An implementation of the *ftp* client under some versions of the UNIX system allows users to keep account names, host names, and passwords in a file called *.netrc*. Kathy uses the remote host *gleep* to store files, so she often connects using *ftp*. Her *.netrc* file looks like this:

```
machine gleep
login kathy
password oi4ety98
```

The security risks of keeping her information in this file were brought home when one day *ftp* ignored the file. On investigation, Kathy determined that the *.netrc* file was readable by all users on the system. By looking at her previously typed commands, Kathy realized that she had mistyped one of them. The unfortunate effect of that command was to make the *.netrc* file readable.

The circumstances under which a password should reside in a system are few.[33] Unless unavoidable, no password should reside unenciphered in a system, either on disk or in memory. The Drib has modified its *ftp* programs to ignore *.netrc* files. This discourages their use. Furthermore, system administrators have embedded a check for such files in their audit tools that check the systems.

---

[31] Here, "privileged users" means those who can read memory, swap space, or alter system programs.

[32] See Section 12.2.1, "Principle of Least Privilege."

[33] See Section 12.2.2, "Principle of Fail-Safe Defaults."

25.4.4   Start-up Settings

Many programs, such as text editors and command interpreters, use start-up information. These variables and files contain commands that are executed when the program begins but before any input is accepted from the user. The set of start-up files, and the order in which they are accessed, affect the execution of the program.

EXAMPLE: When a user logs in to a FreeBSD 4.4 system, her login shell *sh* initializes itself by accessing start-up information in the following order.

1. The contents of the start-up file */etc/profile*
2. The contents of the start-up file *.profile* in the user's home directory
3. The contents of the start-up file named in the environment variable **ENV**

If any of these files do not exist, the step is skipped.

The security threat lies in the program's trust of the start-up information. For example, if the environment variable **ENV** were to name a file that an untrusted user could alter, then that user could insert commands to delete files or give the attacker privileges to perform actions that violate policy. This Trojan horse can be difficult to detect, especially because it can erase itself after execution but before the shell allows interaction.

25.4.5   Limiting Privileges

Users should know which of their programs grant additional privileges to others. They should also understand the implications of granting such privileges.

EXAMPLE: Part of Toni's job as a secretary to the manager of the Drib Development Group is to read mail sent to her boss, Fran. Because Fran knew about the dangers of sharing passwords, she copied the UNIX command interpreter into a file that she owned, and turned on the setuid permission.[34] This allowed Toni to read Fran's mail.

Toni quickly discovered that the command interpreter allowed her to do anything as Fran. She suggested to Fran that perhaps some other approach could be found.[35] After some discussion, the two decided to forward to Toni a copy of every letter that Fran received. This enabled Toni to process Fran's mail without having access to her account.

The two had considered an alternative approach—to make a copy of the mail reading program setuid to Fran. Unfortunately, the mail program had an escape mechanism that allowed the user to pass commands to a command interpreter—and that had the same effect as giving Toni the shell.

---

[34] See Section 13.3, "Users."
[35] See Section 12.2.1, "Principle of Least Privilege."

25.4.6   Malicious Logic

Section 24.2.2 discusses mechanisms for preventing users from bringing malicious software from outside the development network. However, insiders can write malicious programs in order to gain additional privileges or to sabotage others' work. Also, if an attacker breaks in, he may not acquire the desired privileges and may leave traps for authorized users to spring. Hence, users need to take precautions.

> **Definition 25–2.** A *search path* is a sequence of directories that a system uses to locate an object (program, library, or file).

Because programs rely on search paths, users must take care to set theirs appropriately.

EXAMPLE: Johannes' coworker wants to see Johannes' confidential designs. The coworker has created a small program called *ls* that will copy the designs to a public area, from which the coworker can retrieve them. She has placed copies of *ls* in various publicly writable directories, including */tmp*. Johannes changed to that directory to clean up files he had left there. Johannes' program search path was

```
. /bin /usr/bin /usr/local/bin
```

where "." means the current directory. Johannes executed the *ls* program. The command interpreter first looked in the current directory for an executable named *ls*, found it, and executed it. The coworker got the desired files.

Some systems have many types of search paths. In addition to searching for executables, a common search path contains directories that are used to search for libraries when the system supports dynamic loading. In this case, an attacker can create a new library that the unsuspecting victim will load, much as Johannes executed the wrong program in the example above.[36]

Part of policy component U4 requires that the users have only trusted directories in their search paths. Here, "trusted" means that only trusted users can alter the contents of the directory. The default start-up files for all the development workstation users have search paths set in this way.[37]

---

[36] See Section 20.2.8, "Example: Penetrating a UNIX System."
[37] See Section 12.2.2, "Principle pf Fail-Safe Defaults."

25.5   Electronic Communications

Electronic communications deserves discussion to emphasize the importance of users understanding basic security precautions. Electronic mail may pass through firewalls (as the Drib policy allows; see Section 23.3.3.1). Although it can be checked for malicious content, such checking cannot detect all forms of such content.[38] Finally, users may unintentionally send out more material than they realize. Hence, users must understand the threats and follow the procedures that are appropriate to the site policy.

25.5.1   Automated Electronic Mail Processing

Some users automate the processing of electronic mail. When mail arrives, a program determines how to handle it. The mail may be stored for the user, or it may be interpreted as a sequence of commands causing execution of either programs already on the system or part of the content of the message, or both. The danger is that the execution may have unintended side effects.

EXAMPLE: The NIMDA worm [204] used several methods to propagate itself. One method involved the use of e-mail. The worm would mail itself to a user on the target system, encapsulated as an attachment to a letter. When the user opened the letter, the default configuration of the mail programs involved would pass the attachment to another program to be displayed. The other program would execute the code comprising the worm, thereby infecting the system.

Electronic mail comes from untrusted sources. Hence, in general, the contents of e-mail messages are not trustworthy. Mail programs should be configured not to execute attachments, or indeed any component of the letter.[39] The trust in the result of such execution is the same as the trust the reader puts in the data contained in the mail message.

25.5.2   Failure to Check Certificates

Electronic signatures can be misleading. In particular, a certificate may validate a signature, but the certificate itself may be compromised, invalid, or expired. Mail reading programs must notify the user of these problems, as well as provide a mechanism for allowing the user to validate certificates.

---

[38] See Section 19.6, "Theory of Malicious Logic."
[39] See Section 19.6.1, "Malicious Logic Acting as Both Data and Instructions."

EXAMPLE: Someone pretending to be a Microsoft employee obtained two certificates that could be used to sign programs under the name of Microsoft Corporation [203].[40] The issuer (*not* Microsoft Corporation) immediately revoked both certificates and placed them on the Certificate Revocation List,[41] but sites that had not received the revocation notice would accept the certificates as valid and could execute malicious logic that the attackers had signed. Although the mechanism involved used Web pages, the generalization to electronic mail is obvious.

The Drib has enhanced all mail reading programs that use certificates to validate the certificates as far as possible. The programs then display the certificates that could not be validated, to allow users to determine how to proceed.

25.5.3   Sending Unexpected Content

Attachments to electronic mail may contain data of which the sender is not aware. When these files are sent, the recipient may see more than the sender intended.

EXAMPLE: A sales director once sent her sales team a chart showing the effects of a proposed reorganization. Unfortunately, she did not realize that the spreadsheet in which she had created the chart also contained confidential information such as names and addresses, salaries, and personal comments about each employee. The information disrupted the efficiency of the sales force [43].

Some programs perform "rapid saves," in which data is appended to the file and pointers are updated. When the program rereads the file, the document appears as it was last saved, and the extraneous data is ignored. However, if the file is sent to a different system, or if other programs are used to access the file, the "deleted" contents will be accessible.

The users of the development workstations are periodically warned about this risk. Furthermore, all programs with "rapid saves" have them disabled by default.[42]

25.6   Summary

This chapter covered only a few aspects of how users can protect the data and programs with which they work. The security policy of the site and the desires of the user combine to provide a personalized, if unwritten, security policy.

---

[40] See Section 13.5, "Naming and Certificates."
[41] See Section 9.4.2, "Key Revocation."
[42] See Section 12.2.8, "Principle of Psychological Acceptability."

Well-chosen reusable passwords, or (even better) one-time passwords, inhibit unauthorized access. Other authentication mechanisms allow users to control access to some degree on the basis of the host of origin and cryptographic keys (although in some cases the system administrator can override these access controls). Users can prevent interference with their sessions by using enciphered, integrity-checked sessions and by physically securing the monitors or terminals they use to interact with the system (as well as the system of origin, if they are working remotely).

Basic file permission mechanisms help protect the confidentiality and integrity of data and programs. The user can check programs for an "interactive" mode that will require verification of any request to delete or overwrite files. Other aspects of file handling, such as erasing files before deleting them, and verifying that deletion of a file does not delete only an alias and leave the file accessible, also affect file security.

Equally important are the controls on devices. The sophistication of most modern equipment allows devices to be programmed from the computer to which they are connected. Hence, devices should be configured to refuse unexpected or untrusted connections. Ideally, access control mechanisms will provide sufficient granularity to allow access based on users or processes.

Processes act on the user's behalf, and can perform any action that the user requests. Malicious logic, or corrupt input, can cause the process to act in ways that the user does not want. Users can minimize this risk by setting up their environments carefully and by not executing untrusted programs or giving untrusted data to trusted programs.

25.7   Further Reading

Discussions of user level mechanisms in various systems abound. Books on the security of various systems (such as Braun [132], Garfinkel and Spafford [347], and McLean [609]) focus on the system administration aspects of security but also describe user level mechanisms. Books on how to use the systems (such as Crawford [219] and Glass [359]) cover the material more effectively for ordinary users.

Zurko and Simon discuss the notion of user-centered security as fundamental to secure systems [966]. Whitten and Tygar examine PGP from a usability point of view [939].

25.8   Exercises

1. Consider the isolated system described in the first example in Section 25.2.1. If custodians and other people not authorized to use the isolated system were allowed into the room without observation, would that violate policy component U1? Justify your answer.

2. Reconsider the *lock* program discussed in Section 25.2.3.

   a. The program requires a user to choose a password (rather than using her login password) to lock the screen. Does this violate the principle of psychological acceptability (see Section 12.2.8)? Justify your answer.

   b. If a user forgets her password, how might she terminate the program *without* using the master password? (*Hint:* Although she cannot use that terminal, she can use another terminal to access the system.)

   c. How might a user determine the master password? Discuss steps that the implementer could take to prevent such a discovery. In particular, could a per-system master password be implemented (rather than a single master password for the program)? How?

3. The example of Peter and Deborah on the UNIX system in Section 25.3.1 assumes that Deborah is the only member, or that Deborah and Peter are the only members, of a group. If this is not so, can Peter give *only* himself and Deborah access to the file by using the abbreviated ACL? Explain either how he can or why he cannot.

4. Suppose that Deborah, Peter, and Kathy are the only members of the group *proj* and that Deborah, Peter, and Elizabeth are the only members of the group *exeter*. Show how Peter can restrict access to the file *design* to himself and Deborah using *only* abbreviated ACLs. (*Hint:* Consider both *design* and its containing directory.)

5. The UNIX *umask* disables access by default. The Windows scheme enables it. Discuss the implications of enabling access by default and of disabling access by default with respect to security. In particular, which of Saltzer and Schroeder's design principles [773] (see Chapter 12, "Design Principles") is violated by either enabling or disabling access by default?

6. Many UNIX security experts say that the *umask* should be set to 077 (that is, to allow access only to the owner). Why? What problems might this cause?

Chapter 26
Program Security

CLOWN: What is he that builds stronger than either
the mason, the shipwright, or the carpenter?
OTHER CLOWN: The gallows-maker; for that frame outlives
a thousand tenants.
—*Hamlet*, V, i, 42–45.

The software on systems implements many mechanisms that support security. Some of these mechanisms reside in the operating system, whereas others reside in application and system programs. This chapter discusses the design and implementation of a system program. It also presents common programming errors that create security problems, and offers suggestions for avoiding those problems. Finally, testing and distribution are discussed.

This chapter shows the development of the program from requirements to implementation, testing, and distribution.

26.1 Introduction

This section considers a specific problem on the Drib's development network infrastructure systems. Numerous system administrators must assume certain roles, such as *bin* (the installers of software), *mail* (the manager of electronic mail), and *root* (the system administrator). Each of these roles is implemented as a separate account, called a *role account*. Unfortunately, this raises the problem of password management. To avoid this problem, as well as to control when access is allowed, the Drib will implement a program that verifies a user's identity, determines if the requested change of account is allowed, and, if so, places the user in the desired role.

26.2   Requirements and Policy

The problem of sharing a password arises when a system implements administrative roles as separate user accounts.

EXAMPLE: Linux systems implement the administrator role as the account *root* (and several other accounts that have more limited functionality).[1] All individuals who share access to the account know the account's password. If the password is changed, all must be notified. All these individuals must remember to notify the other individuals should they change the password.

An alternative to using passwords is to constrain access on the basis of identity and other attributes. With this scheme, a user would execute a special program that would check the user's identity and any ancillary conditions. If all these conditions were satisfied, the user would be given access to the role account.

26.2.1   Requirements

The first requirement comes directly from the description of the alternative scheme above. The system administrators choose to constrain access through known paths (locations) and at times of day when the user is expected to access the role account.

Requirement 26.2.1. Access to a role account is based on user, location, and time of request.

Users often tailor their environments to fit their needs. This is also true of role accounts. For example, a role account may use special programs kept in a subdirectory of the role account's home directory. This new directory must be on the role account's search path. A question is whether the user's environment should be discarded and replaced by the role account's environment, or whether the two environments should be merged. The requirement chosen for this program is as follows.

Requirement 26.2.2. The settings of the role account's environment shall replace the corresponding settings of the user's environment, but the remainder of the user's environment shall be preserved.

The set of role accounts chosen for access using this scheme is critical. If unrestricted access is given (essentially, a full command interpreter), then any user in the role that maintains the access control information can change that information

---

[1] See Section 12.2.1, "Principle of Least Privilege," for an explanation of how the existence of the *root* account violates the principle of least privilege.

and acquire unrestricted access to the system. Presumably, if the access control information is kept accessible only to *root*, then the users who can alter the information—all of whom have access to *root*—are trusted. Thus:

> **Requirement 26.2.3.** Only *root* can alter the access control information for access to a role account.

In most cases, a user assuming a particular role will perform specific actions while in that role. For example, someone who enters the role of *oper* may perform backups but may not use other commands. This restricts the danger of commands interacting with the system to produce undesirable effects (such as security violations) and follows from the principle of least privilege.[2] This form of access is called "restricted access."

> **Requirement 26.2.4.** The mechanism shall allow both restricted access and unrestricted access to a role account. For unrestricted access, the user shall have access to a standard command interpreter. For restricted access, the user shall be able to execute only a specified set of commands.

Requirement 26.2.4 implicitly requires that access to the role account be granted to authorized users meeting the conditions in Requirement 26.2.1. Finally, the role account itself must be protected from unauthorized changes.

> **Requirement 26.2.5.** Access to the files, directories, and objects owned by any account administered by use of this mechanism shall be restricted to those authorized to use the role account, to users trusted to install system programs, and to *root*.

We next check that these requirements are complete.

26.2.2   Threats

The threats against this mechanism fall into distinct classes. We enumerate the classes and discuss the requirements that handle each threat.

26.2.2.1   Group 1: Unauthorized Users Accessing Role Accounts

There are four threats that involve attackers trying to acquire access to role accounts using this mechanism.

> **Threat 26.2.1.** An unauthorized user may obtain access to a role account as though she were an authorized user.

---

[2] See Section 12.2.1, "Principle of Least Privilege."

Threat 26.2.2. An authorized user may use a nonsecure channel to obtain access to a role account, thereby revealing her authentication information to unauthorized individuals.

Threat 26.2.3. An unauthorized user may alter the access control information to grant access to the role account.

Threat 26.2.4. An authorized user may execute a Trojan horse (or other form of malicious logic),[3] giving an unauthorized user access to the role account.

Requirements 26.2.1 and 26.2.5 handle Threat 26.2.1 by restricting the set of users who can access a role account and protecting the access control data. Requirement 26.2.1 also handles Threat 26.2.2 by restricting the locations from which the user can request access. For example, if the set of locations contains only those on trusted or confidential networks, a passive wiretapper cannot discover the authorized user's password or hijack a session begun by an authorized user. Similarly, if an authorized user connects from an untrusted system, Requirement 26.2.1 allows the system administrator to configure the mechanism so that the user's request is rejected.

The access control information that Requirement 26.2.1 specifies can be changed. Requirement 26.2.3 acknowledges this but restricts changes to trusted users (defined as those with access to the *root* account). This answers Threat 26.2.3.

Threat 26.2.4 is more complex. This threat arises from an untrusted user, without authorization, planting a Trojan horse at some location at which an authorized user might execute it. If the attacker can write into a directory in the role account's search path, this attack is feasible. Requirement 26.2.2 states that the role account's search path may be selected from two other search paths: the default search path for the role account, and the user's search path altered to include those components of the role account's search path that are not present. This leads to Requirement 26.2.5 which states that, regardless of how the search path is derived, the final search path may contain only directories (and may access only programs) that trusted users or the role account itself can manipulate. In this case, the attacker cannot place a Trojan horse where someone using the role account may execute it.

Finally, if a user is authorized to use the role account but is a novice and may change the search path, Requirement 26.2.4 allows the administrators to restrict the set of commands that the user may execute in that role.

26.2.2.2   Group 2: Authorized Users Accessing Role Accounts

Because access is allowed here, the threats relate to an authorized user changing access permissions or executing unauthorized commands.

---

[3] See Chapter 19, "Malicious Logic."

Threat 26.2.5. An authorized user may obtain access to a role account and perform unauthorized commands.

Threat 26.2.6. An authorized user may execute a command that performs functions that the user is not authorized to perform.

Threat 26.2.7. An authorized user may change the restrictions on the user's ability to obtain access to the account.

The difference between Threats 26.2.5 and 26.2.6 is subtle but important. In the former, the user deliberately executes commands that violate the site security policy. In the latter, the user executes authorized commands that perform covert, unauthorized actions as well as overt, authorized actions—the classic Trojan horse. Threat 26.2.6 differs from Threat 26.2.4 because the action may not give access to authorized users; it may simply damage or destroy the system.

Requirement 26.2.4 handles Threat 26.2.5. If the user accessing the role account should execute only a specific set of commands, then the access controls must be configured to restrict the user's access to executing only those commands.

Requirements 26.2.2 and 26.2.5 handle Threat 26.2.6 by preventing the introduction of a Trojan horse, as discussed in the preceding section.

Requirement 26.2.3 answers Threat 26.2.7. Because all users who have access to *root* are trusted by definition, then the only way for an authorized user to change the restrictions on obtaining access to the role account is to implant a back door (which is equivalent to a Trojan horse) or to modify the access control information. But the requirement holds that only trusted users can do that, so the authorized user cannot change the information unless he is trusted—in which case, by definition, the threat is handled.

26.2.2.3   Summary

Because the requirements handle the threats, and because all requirements are used, the set of requirements is both necessary and sufficient. We now proceed with the design.

26.3   Design

To create this program, we build modules that fit together to supply security services that satisfy the requirements. First, we create a general framework to guide the development of each interface. Then we examine each requirement separately, and design a component for each requirement.

26.3.1   Framework

The framework begins with the user interface and then breaks down the internals of the program into modules that implement the various requirements.

26.3.1.1   User Interface

The user can run the program in two ways. The first is to request unrestricted access to the account. The second is to request that a specific program be run from the role account. Any interface must be able to handle both.

The simplest interface is a command line. Other interfaces, such as graphical user interfaces, are possible and may make the program easier to use. However, these GUIs will be built in such a way that they construct and execute a command line version of the program.

The interface chosen is

```
role role_account [ command ]
```

where *role_account* is the name of the role account and *command* is the (optional) command to execute under that account. If the user wants unrestricted access to the role account, he omits *command*. Otherwise, the user is given restricted access and *command* is executed with the privileges of the role account.

The user need not specify the time of day using the interface, because the program can obtain such information from the system. It can also obtain the location from which the user requests access, although the method used presents potential problems (see Section 26.4.3.1). The individual modules handle the remainder of the issues.

26.3.1.2   High-Level Design

The basic algorithm is as follows.

1. Obtain the role account, command, user, location, and time of day. If the command is omitted, the user requests unrestricted access to the role account.
2. Check that the user is allowed to access the role account

    a. at the specified location;

    b. at the specified time; and

    c. for the specified command (or without restriction).

    If the user is not, log the attempt and quit.
3. Obtain the user and group information for the role account. Change the privileges of the process to those of the role account.

4. If the user has requested that a specific command be run, overlay the child process with a command interpreter that spawns the named command.

5. If the user has requested unrestricted access, overlay the child process with a command interpreter.

This algorithm points out an important ambiguity in the requirements. Requirements 26.2.1 and 26.2.4 do not indicate whether the ability of the user to execute a command in the given role account requires that the user work from a particular location or access the account at a particular time. This design uses the interpretation that a user's ability to run a command in a role account is conditioned on location and time.

The alternative interpretation, that *access only* is controlled by location and time, and that commands are restricted by role and user, is equally valid. But sometimes the ability to run commands may require that users work at particular times. For example, an operator may create the daily backups at 1 A.M. The operator is not to do backups at other times because of the load on the system. The interpretation of the design allows this. The alternative interpretation requires the backup program, or some other mechanism, to enforce this restriction. Furthermore, the design interpretation includes the alternative interpretation, because any control expressed in the alternative interpretation can be expressed in the design interpretation.

Requirement 26.2.4 can now be clarified. The addition is in italics.

Requirement 26.3.1. The mechanism shall allow both restricted access and unrestricted access to a role account. For unrestricted access, the user shall have access to a standard command interpreter. For restricted access, the user shall be able to execute only a specified set of commands. *The level of access (restricted or unrestricted) shall depend on the user, the role, the time, and the location.*

Thus, the design phase feeds back into the requirements phase, here clarifying the meaning of the requirements. It is left as an exercise for the reader to verify that the new form of this requirement counters the appropriate threats (see Exercise 2).

26.3.2   Access to Roles and Commands

The user attempting access, the location (host or terminal), the time of day, and the type of access (restricted or unrestricted) control access to the role account. The access checking module returns a value indicating success (meaning that access is allowed) or failure (meaning that access is not allowed). By the principle of fail-safe defaults, an error causes a denial of access.

We consider two aspects of the design of this module. The interface controls how information is passed to the module from its caller, and how the module returns success or failure. The internal structure of the module includes how it handles errors. This leads to a discussion of how the access control data is stored. We consider these issues separately to emphasize that the interface provides an entry point into the module, and that the entry point will remain fixed even if the internal design of the module is completely changed. The internal design and structures are hidden from the caller.

26.3.2.1   Interface

Following the practice of hiding information among modules,[4] we minimize the amount of information to be passed to the access checking module. The module requires the user requesting access, the role to which access is requested, the location, the time, and the command (if any). The return value must indicate success or failure. The question is how this information is to be obtained.

The command (or request for unrestricted access) must come from the caller, because the caller provides the interface for the processing of that command. The command is supplied externally, so the principles of layering require it to pass through the program to the module.

The caller could also pass the other information to the module. This would allow the module to provide an access control result without obtaining the information directly. The advantage is that a different program could use this module to determine whether or not access *had been* or *would be* granted at some past or future point in time, or from some other location. The disadvantage is a lack of portability, because the interface is tied to a particular representation of the data. Also, if the caller of the module is untrusted but the module is trusted, the module might make trusted decisions based on untrusted data, violating a principle of integrity.[5] Either approach is reasonable. In this design, we choose to have the module determine all of the data.

This suggests the following interface.

```
boolean accessok(role rname, command cmd);
```

where *rname* is the name of the requested role and *cmd* is the command to be executed (or is empty if unrestricted access is desired). The routine returns *true* if access is to be granted, and *false* otherwise.

26.3.2.2   Internals

This module has three parts. The first part gathers the data on which access is to be based. The second part retrieves the access control information. The third part determines whether or not the data and the access control information require access to be granted.

The module queries the operating system to determine the needed data. The real user identification data is obtained through a system call, as is the current time of day. The location consists of two components: the entry point (terminal or network

---

[4] This is one aspect of the principle of least common mechanism (see Section 12.2.7).
[5] This follows from Biba's integrity model (see Section 6.2).

connection) and the remote host from which the user is accessing the local system. The latter component may indicate that the entry point is directly connected to the system, rather than using a remote host.

Part I: Obtain user ID, time of day, entry point, and remote host.

Next, the module must access the access control information. The access control information resides in a file. The file contains a sequence of records of the following form.

```
role account
user names
locations from which the role account can be accessed
times when the role account can be accessed
command and arguments
```

If the "command and arguments" line is omitted, the user is granted unrestricted access. Multiple command lines may be listed in a single record.

Part II: Obtain a handle (or descriptor) to the access control information. The programmer will use this handle to read the access control records from the access control information.

Finally, the program iterates through the access control information. If the role in the current record does not match the requested role, it is ignored. Otherwise, the user name, location, time, and command are compared with the appropriate fields of the record. If they all match, the module releases the handle and returns success.[6] If any of them does not match, the module continues on to the next record. If the module reaches the end of the access control information, the handle is released and the module returns failure. Note that records never deny access, but only grant it. The default action is to deny. Granting access requires an explicit record.

If any record is invalid (for example, if there is a syntax error in one of the fields or if the user field contains a nonexistent user name), the module logs the error and ignores the record. This again follows the principle of fail-safe defaults, in which the system falls into a secure state when there is an error.

Part III: Iterate through the records until one matches the data or there are no more records. In the first case, return success; in the second case, return failure.

26.3.2.3   Storage of the Access Control Data

The system administrators of the local system are to control access to privileged accounts. To keep maintenance of this information simple, the administrators store the access control information in a file. Then they need only edit the file to change a user's ability to access the privileged account. The file consists of a set of records,

---

[6] If the time interval during which access is allowed expires after the access control check but before the access is granted, Requirement 26.2.1 is met (as it refers to the time of *request*). This eliminates a possible race condition.

each containing the components listed above. This raises the issue of expression. How should each part of the record be written?

For example, must each entry point be listed, or are wildcards acceptable? Strictly speaking, the principle of fail-safe defaults[7] says that we should list explicitly those locations from which access may be obtained. In practice, this is too cumbersome. Suppose a particular user was trusted to assume a role from any system on the Internet. Requiring the administrators to list all hosts would be time-consuming as well as infeasible. Worse, if the user were not allowed to access the role account from one system, the administrators would need to check the list to see which system was missing. This would violate the principle of psychological acceptability.[8] Given the dynamic nature of the Internet, this requirement would be absurd. Instead, we allow the following special host names, all of which are illegal [644].

> ***any*** (a wildcard matching any system)
> ***local*** (matches the local host name)

In BNF form, the language used to express location is

> *location* ::= '(' *location* ')' | 'not' *location* | *location* 'or' *location* | *basic*
> *basic* ::= '*any*' | '*local*' | '.' *domain* | *host*

where *domain* and *host* are domain names and host names, respectively. The strings in single quotation marks are literals. The parentheses are grouping operators, the 'not' complements the associated locations, and the 'or' allows either location.

EXAMPLE: A user is allowed to assume a role only when logged into the local system, the system "control.fixit.com", and the domain "watchu.edu". The appropriate entry would be

> `*local* | control.fixit.com | .watchu.edu`

A similar question arises for times. Ignoring how times are expressed, how do we indicate when users may access the role account? Considerations similar to those above lead us to the following language, in which the keyword

> ***any*** (allow access at any time)

allows access at any time. In BNF form, the language used to express time is

> *time* ::= '(' *time* ')' | 'not' *time* | *time* 'or' *time* | *time time* | *time* '-' *time* | *basic*
> *basic* ::= *day_of_year day_of_week time_of_day* | '*any*' |

---

[7] See Section 12.2.2.
[8] See Section 12.2.8.

> *day_of_year* ::= *month* [*day*] [',' *year*] | *nmonth* '/' [*day* '/'] *year* | *empty*
> *day_of_week* ::= 'Sunday' | ... | 'Saturday' | 'Weekend' | 'Weekday' | *empty*
> *time_of_day* ::= *hour* [':' *min*] [':' *sec*] ['AM' | 'PM'] | *special* | *empty*
> *special* ::= 'noon' | 'midnight' | 'morning' | 'afternoon' | 'evening'
> *empty* ::= ''

where *month* is a string naming the month, *nmonth* is an integer naming the month, *day* is an integer naming the day of the month, and *year* is an integer specifying the year. Similarly, *hour*, *min*, and *sec* are integers specifying the hour, minute, and second. If *basic* is empty, it is treated as not allowing access.[9]

EXAMPLE: A user is allowed to assume a role between the hours of 9 o'clock in the morning and 5 o'clock in the evening on Monday through Thursday. An appropriate entry would be

>   Monday–Thursday 9 AM–5 PM

This is different than saying

>   Monday 9 AM–Thursday 5 PM

because the latter allows access on Monday at 10 PM, whereas the former does not.

Finally, the users field of the record has a similar structure.

any (match any user)

In BNF form, the language used to express the set of users who may access a role is

> *userlist* ::= '(' *userlist* ')' | 'not' *userlist* | *userlist* ',' *userlist* | *user*

where *user* is the name of a user on the system.

These "little languages" are straightforward and simple (but incomplete; see Exercise 4). Various implementation details, such as allowing abbreviations for day and month names, can be added, as can an option to change the American expression of days of the year to an international one. These points must be considered in light of where the program is to be used. Whatever changes are made, the administrators must be able to configure times and places quickly and easily, and in a manner that a reader of the access control file can understand quickly.[10]

The listing of commands requires some thought about how to represent arguments. If no arguments are listed, is the command to be run without arguments, or

---

[9] By the principle of fail-safe defaults (see Section 12.2.2).

[10] See Section 12.2.8, "Principle of Psychological Acceptability."

should it allow any set of arguments? Conversely, if arguments are listed, should the command be run only with those arguments? Our approach is to force the administrator to indicate how arguments are to be treated.

Each command line contains a command followed by zero or more arguments. If the first word after the command is an asterisk ("*"), then the command may be run with any arguments. Otherwise, the command must be run with the exact arguments provided.

EXAMPLE: Charles is allowed to run the *install* command when he accesses the *bin* role. He may supply any arguments. The line in the access control file is

```
/bin/install *
```

He may also copy the file *log* from the current working directory to the directory */var/install*. The line for this is

```
/bin/cp log /var/install/log
```

Finally, he may run the *id* command to ensure that he is working as *bin*. He may not supply other arguments to the command, however. This would be expressed by

```
/usr/bin/id
```

The user must type the command as given in the access control file. The full path names are present to prevent the user from accidentally executing the command *id* with *bin* privileges when *id* is a command in the local directory, rather than the system *id* command.[11]

26.4   Refinement and Implementation

This section focuses on the access control module of the program. We refine the high-level design presented in the preceding section until we produce a routine in a programming language.

26.4.1   First-Level Refinement

Rather than use any particular programming language, we first implement the module in pseudocode. This requires two decisions. First, the implementation language will be block-structured, like C or Modula, rather than functional, like Scheme or

---

[11] See Chapter 19, "Malicious Logic."

ML. Second, the environment in which the program will function will be a UNIX-like system such as FreeBSD or Linux.

The basic structure of the security module is

```
boolean accessok(role rname, command cmd);
    stat ← false
    user ← obtain user ID
    timeday ← obtain time of day
    entry ← obtain entry point (terminal line, remote host)
    open access control file
    repeat
            rec ← get next record from file; EOF if nonw
            if rec ≠ EOF then
                        stat ← match(rec, rname, cmd,
                        user, timeday, entry)
    until rec = EOF or stat = true
    close sccess control file
return stat
```

We now verify that this sketch matches the design. Clearly, the interface is unchanged. The variable *stat* will contain the status of the access control file check, becoming true when a match is found. Initially, it is set to false (deny access) because of the principle of fail-safe defaults. If *stat* were not set, and the access control file were empty, *stat* would never be set and the returned value would be undefined.

The next three lines obtain the user ID, the current time of day, and the system entry point. The following line opens the access control file.

The routine then iterates through the records of that file. The iteration has two requirements—that if any record allows access, the routine is to return *true*, and that if no record grants access, the routine is to return *false*. From the structure of the file, one cannot create a record to deny access. By default, access is denied. Entries explicitly grant access. So, iterating over the records of the file either produces a record that grants access (in which case the *match* routine returns true, terminating the loop and causing *accessok* to return with a value of *true*) or produces no such record. In that case, *stat* is false, and *rec* is set to EOF when the records in the access control file are exhausted. The loop then terminates, and the routine returns the value of *stat*, which is false. Hence, this pseudocode matches the design and, transitively, the requirements.

26.4.2   Second-Level Refinement

Now we will focus on mapping the pseudocode above to a particular language and system. The C programming language is widely available and provides a convenient interface to UNIX-like systems. Given that our target system is a UNIX-like system, C is a reasonable choice. As for the operating system, there are many variants of the

UNIX operating system. However, they all have fundamental similarities. The Linux operating system will provide the interfaces discussed below, and they work on a wide variety of UNIX systems.

On these systems, roles are represented as normal user accounts. The *root* account is really a role account,[12] for example. Each user account has two distinct representations of identity:[13] an internal user type *uid_t*,[14] and a string (name). When a user specifies a role, either representation may be used. For our purposes, we will assume that the caller of the *accessok* routine provides the *uid_t* representation of the role identity. Two reasons make this representation preferable. First, the target systems are unable to address privilege in terms of names, because, within the kernel, process identity is *always* represented by a *uid_t*. So the routines will need to do the conversion anyway. The second reason is more complex. Roles in the access control file can be represented by numbers or names. The routine for reading the access control file records will convert the roles to *uid_t*s to ensure consistency of representation. This also allows the input routine to check the records for consistency with the system environment. Specifically, if the role name refers to a nonexistent account, the routine can ignore the record. So any comparisons would require the role from the interface to be converted to a *uid_t*.

This leads to a design decision: *represent all user and role IDs as integers internally.* Fortunately, none of the design decisions discussed so far depend on the representation of identity, so we need not review or change our design.

Next, consider the command. On the target system, a command consists of a program name followed by a sequence of words, which are the *command line arguments* to the command. The command representation is an array of strings, in which the first string is the program name and the other strings are the command line arguments.

Putting this all together, the resulting interface is

```
int accessok(uid_t rname, char *cmd[])
```

Next comes obtaining the user ID. Processes in the target system have several identities, but the key ones are the *real UID* (which identifies the user running the process) and the *effective UID* (which identifies the privileges with which the process runs).[15] The effective UID of this program must have *root* privileges (see Exercise 3), regardless of who runs the process. Hence, it is useless for this purpose. Only the real UID identifies the user running the program. So, to obtain the user ID of the user running the program:

```
userid = getuid();
```

---

[12] See Section 13.4, "Groups and Roles."
[13] See Section 13.3, "Users."
[14] On Linux systems, and on most UNIX-like systems, this is an integer.
[15] See Section 13.3, "Users."

The time of day is obtained from the system and expressed in internal format. The internal representation can be given in seconds since a specific date and time (the *epoch*)[16] or in microseconds since that time. It is unlikely that times will need to be specified in microseconds in the access control file, so for both simplicity of code and simplicity of the access control data,[17] the internal format of seconds will be used. So, to obtain the current time:

```
timeday = time(NULL);
```

Finally, we need to obtain the location. There is no simple method for obtaining this information, so we defer it until later by encapsulating it in a function. This also localizes any changes should we move this program to a different system (for example, the methods used on a Linux system may differ from those used on a FreeBSD system).

```
entry = getlocation();
```

Opening the access control file for reading is straightforward:

```
if ((fp = fopen(acfile, "r")) == NULL{
    logerror(errno, acfile);
    return(stat);
}
```

Notice first the error checking, and the logging of information on an error. The variable *errno* is set to a code indicating the nature of the error. The variable *acfile* points to the access control file name.

The processing of the access control records follows:

```
do {
    acrec = getnextacrec(fp);
    if (acrec != NULL)
            stat = match(rec, rname, cmd, user, timeday, entry);
} until (acrec == NULL || stat == 1);
```

Here, we read in the record—assuming that any records remain—and check the record to see if it allows permission. This looping continues until either some record indicates that permission is to be given or all records are checked. The exact internal record format is not yet specified; hence, the use of functions.

---

[16] On Linux and most other UNIX-like systems, the epoch is midnight on January 1, 1970 (GMT).

[17] See Section 12.2.3, "Principle of Economy of Mechanism," and Section 12.2.8, "Principle of Psychological Acceptability."

The routine concludes by closing the access control file and returning status:

```
(void) fclose(fp);
return(stat);
```

26.4.3   Functions

Three functions remain: the function for obtaining location, the function for getting an access control record, and the function for checking the access control record against the information of the current process. Each raises security issues.

26.4.3.1   Obtaining Location

UNIX and Linux systems write the user's account name, the name of the terminal on which the login takes place, the time of login, and the name of the remote host (if any) to the *utmp* file. Any process may read this file. As each new process runs, it may have an associated terminal. To determine the *utmp* record associated with the process, a routine may obtain the associated terminal name, open the *utmp* file, and scan through the record to find the one with the corresponding terminal name. That record contains the name of the host from which the user is working.

This approach, although clumsy, works on most UNIX and Linux systems. It suffers from two problems related to security.

1. If any process can alter the *utmp* file, its contents cannot be trusted. Several security holes have occurred because any process could alter the *utmp* file [189].

2. A process may have no associated terminal. Such a *detached* process must be mapped into the corresponding *utmp* record through other means. However, if the *utmp* record contains only the information described above, this is not possible because the user may be logged into multiple terminals. The issue does not arise if the process has an associated terminal, because only one user at a time may be logged into a terminal.

In the first case, we make a design decision that if the data in the *utmp* file cannot be trusted because any process can alter that file, we return a meaningless location. Then, unless the location specifier of the record allows access from any location, the record will not match the current process information and will not grant access. A similar approach works if the process does not have an associated terminal. The outline of this routine is

```
hostname getlocation()
        myterm ← name of terminal associated with process
        obtain utmp file access control list
```

```
if any user other than root can alter it then
return "*nowhere*"
open utmp file
repeat
term ← get next record from utmp file; EOF if none
if term ≠ EOF and myterm = term then
            stat ← true
        else
            stat ← false
until term = EOF or stat = true
if host field in utmp record = empty
        host = "localhost"
else
        host = host field of utmp record
close utmp file
return host
```

We omit the implementation due to space limitations.

26.4.3.2   The Access Control Record

The format of the records in the access control file affects both the reading of the file and the comparison with the process information, so we design it here.

Our approach is to consider the match routine first. Four items must be checked: the user name, the location, the time, and the command. Consider these items separately.

The user name is represented as an integer. Thus, the internal format of the user field of the access control record must contain either integers or names that the match routine can convert to integers. If a match occurs before all user names have been checked, then the program needs to convert no more names to integers. So, we adopt the strategy of representing the user field as a string read directly from the file. The match routine will parse the line and will use lazy evaluation to check whether or not the user ID is listed.

A similar strategy can be applied to the location and the set of commands in the record.

The time is somewhat different, because in the previous two cases, the process user ID and the location had to match one of the record entries exactly. However, the time does not have to do so. Time in the access control record is (almost always) a range. For example, the entry "May 30" means any time on the date of May 30. The day begins at midnight and ends at midnight, 24 hours later. So, the range would be from May 30 at midnight to May 31 at midnight, or in internal time (for example) between 1022742000 and 1022828400. In those rare cases in which a user may assume a role only at a precise second, the range can be treated as having the same beginning and ending points. Given this view of time as ranges, checking that the current time falls into an acceptable range suggests having the match routine parse the times and checking whether or not the internal system time falls in each range as it is constructed.

This means that the routine for reading the record may simply load the record as a sequence of strings and let the match routine do the interpretation. This yields the following structure.

```
record
        role rname
        string userlist
        string location
        string timeofday
        string commands[]
        integer numcommands
end record;
```

The *commands* field is an array of strings, each command and argument being one string, and *numcommands* containing the number of commands.

Given this information, the function used to read the access control records, and the function used to match them with the current process information, are not hard to write, but error handling does deserve some mention.

26.4.3.3   Error Handling in the Reading and Matching Routines

Assume that there is a syntax error in the access control file. Perhaps a record specifies a time incorrectly (for example, "Thurxday"), or a record divider is garbled. How should the routines handle this?

The first observation is that they cannot ignore the error. To do so violates basic principles of security (specifically, the principle of psychological acceptability[18]). It also defeats the purpose of the program, because access will be denied to users who need it.[19] So, the program must produce an indication of error. If it is printed, then the user will see it and should notify the system administrator maintaining the access control file. Should the user forget, the administrator will not know of the error. Hence, the error must be logged. Whether or not the user should be told *why* the error has occurred is another question. One school of thought holds that the more information users have, the more helpful they will be. Another school holds that information should be denied unless the user needs to know it, and in the case of an error in the access control file, the user only needs to know that access will be denied.

Hence, the routines must log information about errors. The logged information must enable the system administrator to locate the error in the file. The error message should include the access control file name and line or record number. This

---

[18] See Section 12.2.8, "Principle of Psychological Acceptability."

[19] Note that a record with a syntax error will never grant access (see Exercise 5).

suggests that *both* routines need access to that information. Hence, the record counts, line numbers, and file name must be shared. For reasons of modularity, this implies that these two routines should be in a submodule of the access checking routine. If they are placed in their own module, no other parts of the routine can access the line or record numbers (and none need to, given the design described here). If the module is placed under the access control routine, no external functions can read records from the access control file or check data against that file's contents.

26.4.4 Summary

This section has examined the development of a program for performing a security-critical function. Beginning with a requirements analysis, the design and parts of the implementation demonstrate the need for repeated analysis to ensure that the design meets the requirements and that design decisions are documented. From the point at which the derivation stopped, the implementation is simple.

We will now discuss some common security-related programming problems. Then we will discuss testing, installation, and maintenance.

26.5 Common Security-Related Programming Problems

Unfortunately, programmers are not perfect. They make mistakes. These errors can have disastrous consequences in programs that change the protection domains. Attackers who exploit these errors may acquire extra privileges (such as access to a system account such as *root* or *Administrator*). They may disrupt the normal functioning of the system by deleting or altering services over which they should have no control. They may simply be able to read files to which they should have no access.[20] So the problem of avoiding these errors, or security holes, is a necessary issue to ensure that the programs and system function as required.

We present both management rules (installation, configuration, and maintenance) and programming rules together. Although there is some benefit in separating them, doing so creates an artificial distinction by implying that they can be considered separately. In fact, the limits on installation, configuration, and maintenance affect the implementation, just as the limits of implementation affect the installation, configuration, and maintenance procedures.

Researchers have developed several models for analyzing systems for these security holes.[21] These models provide a framework for characterizing the problems.

---

[20] See Chapter 20, "Vulnerability Analysis."
[21] See Section 20.4, "Frameworks."

The goal of the characterization guides the selection of the model. Because we are interested in technical modeling and not in the reason or time of introduction, many of the categories of the NRL model[22] are inappropriate for our needs. We also wish to analyze the multiple components of vulnerabilities rather than force each vulnerability into a particular point of view, as Aslam's model[23] does. So either the PA model[24] or the RISOS model[25] is appropriate. We have chosen the PA model for our analysis.

We examine each of the categories and subcategories separately. We consider first the general rules that we can draw from the vulnerability class, and then we focus on applying those rules to the program under discussion.

26.5.1   Improper Choice of Initial Protection Domain

Flaws involving improper choice of initial protection domain arise from incorrect setting of permissions or privileges. There are three objects for which permissions need to be set properly: the file containing the program, the access control file, and the memory space of the process. We will consider them separately.

26.5.1.1   Process Privileges

The principle of least privilege[26] dictates that no process have more privileges than it needs to complete its task, but the process must have enough privileges to complete its task successfully.

Ideally, one set of privileges should meet both criteria. In practice, different portions of the process will need different sets of privileges. For example, a process may need special privileges to access a resource (such as a log file) at the beginning and end of its task, but may not need those privileges at other times. The process structure and initial protection domain should reflect this.

> **Implementation Rule 26.5.1.** Structure the process so that all sections requiring extra privileges are modules. The modules should be as small as possible and should perform only those tasks that require those privileges.

The basis for this rule lies in the reference monitor.[27] The reference monitor is verifiable, complete (it is always invoked to access the resource it protects), and tamperproof (it cannot be compromised). Here, the modules are kept small and

---

[22] See Section 20.4.3, "The NRL Taxonomy."

[23] See Section 20.4.4, "Aslam's Model."

[24] See Section 20.4.2, "Protection Analysis Model."

[25] See Section 20.4.1, "The RISOS Study."

[26] See Section 12.2.1, "Principle of Least Privilege."

[27] See Section 17.3, "Building Security In or Adding Security Later." Programs implemented following this rule are *not* reference monitors.

simple (verifiable), access to the privileged resource requires the process to invoke these modules (complete), and the use of separate modules with well-defined interfaces minimizes the chances of other parts of the program corrupting the module (tamperproof).

Management Rule 26.5.1. Check that the process privileges are set properly.

Insufficient privileges could cause a denial of service. Excessive privileges could enable an attacker to exploit vulnerabilities in the program. To avoid these problems, the privileges of the process, and the times at which the process has these privileges, must be chosen and managed carefully.

One of the requirements of this program is availability (Requirements 26.2.1 and 26.2.4). On Linux and UNIX systems, the program must change the effective identity of the user from the user's account to the role account. This requires special (setuid) privileges of either the role account or the superuser.[28] The principle of least privilege[29] says that the former is better than the latter, but if one of the role accounts is *root*, then having multiple copies of the program with limited privileges is irrelevant, because the program with privileges to access the *root* role account is the logical target of attack. After all, if one can compromise a less privileged account through this program, the same attack will probably work against the *root* account. Because the Drib plans to control access to *root* in some cases, the program requires setuid to *root* privileges.

If the program does not have *root* privileges initially, the UNIX protection model does not allow the process to acquire them; the permissions on the program file corresponding to the program must be changed. The process must log enough information for the system administrator to identify the problem,[30] and should notify users of the problem so that the users can notify the system administrator. An alternative is to develop a server that will periodically check the permissions on the program file and reset them if needed, or a server that the program can notify should it have insufficient privileges. The designers felt that the benefits of these servers were not sufficient to warrant their development. In particular, they were concerned that the system administrators investigate any unexpected change in file permissions, and an automated server that changed the permissions back would provide insufficient incentive for an analysis of the problem.

As a result, the developers required that the program acquire *root* permission at start-up. The access control module is executed. Within that module, the privileges are reset to the user's once the log file and access control file have been opened.[31] Superuser privileges are needed only once more—to change the privileges to those of the role account should access be granted. This routine, also in a separate module,

---

[28] See Section 13.3, "Users."
[29] See Section 12.2.1, "Principle of Least Privilege."
[30] See Section 21.3, "Designing an Auditing System."
[31] Section 12.2.4, "Principle of Complete Mediation," provides detail on why this works.

supplies the granularity required to provide the needed functionality while minimizing the time spent executing with *root* privileges.

26.5.1.2   Access Control File Permissions

Biba's models[32] emphasize that the integrity of the process relies on both the integrity of the program and the integrity of the access control file. The former requires that the program be properly protected so that only authorized personnel can alter it. The system managers must determine who the "authorized personnel" are. Among the considerations here are the principle of separation of duty[33] and the principle of least privilege.[34]

Verifying the integrity of the access control file is critical, because that file controls the access to role accounts. Some external mechanism, such as a file integrity checking tool, can provide some degree of assurance that the file has not changed. However, these checks are usually periodic, and the file might change *after* the check. So the program itself should check the integrity of the file when the program is run.

> **Management Rule 26.5.2.** The program that is executed to create the process, and all associated control files, must be protected from unauthorized use and modification. Any such modification must be detected.

In many cases, the process will rely on the settings of other files or on some other external resources. Whenever possible, the program should check these dependencies to ensure that they are valid. The dependencies must be documented so that installers and maintainers will understand what else must be maintained in order to ensure that the program works correctly.

> **Implementation Rule 26.5.2.** Ensure that any assumptions in the program are validated. If this is not possible, document them for the installers and maintainers, so they know the assumptions that attackers will try to invalidate.

The permissions of the program, and its containing directory, are to be set so only *root* can alter or move the program. According to Requirement 26.2.2, only *root* can alter the access control file. Hence, the file must be owned by *root,* and only *root* can write to it. The program should check the ownership and permissions of this file, and the containing directories, to validate that only *root* can alter it.

EXAMPLE: The naive way to check that only *root* can write to the file is to check that the owner is *root* and that the file permissions allow only the owner to write to it. But consider the group permissions. If *root* is the only member of the group, then the

---

[32] See Section 6.2, "Biba Integrity Model."
[33] See Section 6.1, "Goals."
[34] See Section 12.2.1, "Principle of Least Privilege."

group permissions may allow members of the group to write to the file. The problem is that checking group membership is more complicated than looking up the members of the group. A user may belong to a group without being listed as a member, because the GID of the user is assigned from the password file, and group membership lists are contained in a different file.[35] Either the password file and the group membership list must both be checked, or the program should simply report an error if anyone other than the user can write to the file. For simplicity,[36] the designers chose the second approach.

26.5.1.3   Memory Protection

As the program runs, it depends on the values of variables and other objects in memory. This includes the executable instructions themselves. Thus, protecting memory against unauthorized or unexpected alteration is critical.

Consider sharing memory. If two subjects can alter the contents of memory, then one could change data on which the second relies. Unless such sharing is required (for example, by concurrent processes), it poses a security problem because the modifying process can alter variables that control the action of the other process. Thus, each process should have a protected, unshared memory space.

If the memory is represented by an object that processes can alter, it should be protected so that only trusted processes can access it. Access here includes not only modification but also reading, because passwords reside in memory after they are types. Multiple abstractions are discussed in more detail in the next section.

> **Implementation Rule 26.5.3.** Ensure that the program does not share objects in memory with any other program, and that other programs cannot access the memory of a privileged process.

Interaction with other processes cannot be eliminated. If the running process obtains input or data from other processes, then that interface provides a point through which other processes can reach the memory. The most common version of this attack is the buffer overflow.

Buffer overflows involve either altering of data or injecting of instructions that can be executed later. There are a wide variety of techniques for this [13].[37] Several remedies exist. For example, if buffers reside in sections of memory that are not executable, injecting of instructions will not work. Similarly, if some data is to remain unaltered, the data can be stored in read-only memory.

---

[35] Specifically, if the group field of the password file entry for *matt* is 30, and the group file lists the members of group 30 as *root*, the user *matt* is still in group 30, but a query to the group file (the standard way to determine group membership) will show that only *root* is a member.

[36] See Section 12.2.3, "Principle of Economy of Mechanism."

[37] However, alternative techniques involving corrupting data, causing the flow of control to change improperly, do work. See Section 26.5.6, "Improper Validation."

Management Rule 26.5.3. Configure memory to enforce the principle of least privilege. If a section of memory is not to contain executable instructions, turn execute permission off for that section of memory. If the contents of a section of memory are not to be altered, make that section read-only.

These rules appear in three ways in our program. First, the implementers use the language constructs to flag unchanging data as constant (in the C programming language, this is the keyword *const*). This will cause compile-time errors if the variables are assigned to, or runtime errors if instructions try to alter those constants.

The other two ways involve program loading. The system's loader places data in three areas: the *data* (initialized data) segment, the *stack* (used for function calls and variables local to the functions), and the *heap* (used for dynamically allocated storage). A common attack is to trick a program into executing instructions injected into three areas. The vector of injection can be a buffer overflow,[38] for example. The characteristic under discussion does not stop such alteration, but it should prevent the data from being executed by making the segments or pages of all three areas nonexecutable. This suffices for the data and stack segments and follows Management Rule 26.5.3.

If the program uses dynamic loading to load functions at runtime, the system on which the program runs will load those functions into the heap. Thus, if the segments or pages of the heap are not executable, the program cannot use dynamic loading or it will not execute properly. One solution is to compile the program in such a way that it does not use dynamic loading. Thus, the heap segment or pages can also be made nonexecutable, meeting Management Rule 26.5.3. It also prevents the program from loading a module at runtime that may be missing. This could occur if a second process deleted the appropriate library. So disabling of dynamic loading also follows Implementation Rule 26.5.3.[39]

Finally, some UNIX-like systems (including the one on which this program is being developed) allow execution permission to be turned off for the stack. The boot file sets the kernel flag to enforce this.

26.5.1.4   Trust in the System

This analysis overlooks several system components. For example, the program relies on the system authentication mechanisms to authenticate the user, and on the user information database to map users and roles into their corresponding UIDs (and, therefore, privileges). It also relies on the inability of ordinary users to alter the system clock. If any of this supporting infrastructure can be compromised, the program will not work correctly. The best that can be done is to identify these points of trust in the installation and operation documentation so that the system administrators are aware of the dependencies of the program on the system.

---

[38] Buffer overflows can also alter data. See Section 26.5.3.1, "Memory," for an example.

[39] Other considerations contributed. See Section 26.5.4, "Improper Naming."

Management Rule 26.5.4. Identify all system components on which the program depends. Check for errors whenever possible, and identify those components for which error checking will not work.

For this program, the implementers should identify the system databases and information on which the program depends, and should prepare a list of these dependencies. They should discuss these dependencies with system managers to determine if the program can check for errors. When this is not possible, or when the program cannot identify all errors, they should describe the possible consequences of the errors. This document should be distributed with the program so that system administrators can check their systems before installing the program.

26.5.2   Improper Isolation of Implementation Detail

The problem of improper isolation of implementation detail arises when an abstraction is improperly mapped into an implementation detail. Consider how abstractions are mapped into implementations. Typically, some function (such as a database query) occurs, or the abstraction corresponds to an object in the system. What happens if the function produces an error or fails in some other way, or if the object can be manipulated without reference to the abstraction?

The first rule is to catch errors and failures of the mappings. This requires an analysis of the functions and a knowledge of their implementation. The action to take on failure also requires thought. In general, if the cause cannot be determined, the program should fail by returning the relevant parts of the system to the states they were in when the program began.[40]

Implementation Rule 26.5.4. The error status of every function must be checked. Do not try to recover unless the cause of the error, and its effects, do not affect any security considerations. The program should restore the state of the system to the state before the process began, and then terminate.

The abstractions in this program are the notion of a user and a role, the access control information, and the creation of a process with the rights of the role. We will examine these abstractions separately.

26.5.2.1   Resource Exhaustion and User Identifiers

The notion of a user and a role is an abstraction because the program can work with role names and the operating system uses integers (UIDs). The question is how those user and role names are mapped to UIDs. Typically, this is done with a user information database that contains the requisite mapping, but the program must detect any failures of the query and respond appropriately.

---

[40] See Section 12.2.2, "Principle of Fail-Safe Defaults."

EXAMPLE: A mail server allowed users to forward mail by creating a forwarding file [194]. The forwarding file could specify files to which the mail should be appended. In this case, the mail server would deliver the letter with the privileges of the owner of the forwarding file (represented on the system as an integer UID). In some cases, the mail server would queue the message for later delivery. When it did so, it would write the name (*not* the UID) of the user into a control file. The system queried a database, supplying the UID, and obtaining the corresponding name. If the query failed, the mail server used a default name specified by the system administrator.

Attackers discovered how to make the queries fail. As a result, the user was set to a default user, usually a system-level user (such as *daemon*). This enabled the attackers to have the mail server append mail to any file to which the default user could write. They used this to implant Trojan horses into system programs. These Trojan horses gave them extra privileges, compromising the system.

The designers and implementers decided to have the program fail if, for any reason, the query failed. This application of the principle of fail-safe defaults[41] ensured that in case of error, the users would not get access to the role account.

26.5.2.2   Validating the Access Control Entries

The access control information implements the access control policy (an abstraction). The expression of the access control information is therefore the result of mapping an abstraction to an implementation. The question is whether or not the given access control information correctly implements the policy. Answering this question requires someone to examine the implementation expression of the policy.

The programmers developed a second program that used the same routines as the role-assuming program to analyze the access control entries. This program prints the access control information in an easily readable format. It allows the system managers to check that the access control information is correct. A specific procedure requires that this information be checked periodically, and always after the file or the program is altered.

26.5.2.3   Restricting the Protection Domain of the Role Process

Creating a role process is the third abstraction. There are two approaches. Under UNIX-like systems, the program can spawn a second, *child*, process. It can also simply start up a second program in such a way that the parent process is replaced by the new process. This technique, called *overlaying*, is intrinsically simpler than creating a child process and exiting. It allows the process to replace its own protection domain with the (possibly) more limited one corresponding to the role. The programmers elected to use this method. The new process inherits the protection domain of the original one. Before the overlaying, the original process must reset its protection

---

[41] See Section 12.2.2, "Principle of Fail-Safe Defaults."

domain to that of the role. The programmers do so by closing all files that the original process opened, and changing its privileges to those of the role.

EXAMPLE: The effective UIDs and GIDs[42] control privileges. Hence, the programmers reset the effective GID first, and then the effective UID (if resetting were done in the opposite order, the change to GIDs would fail because such changes require *root* privileges). However, if the UNIX-like system supports saved UIDs, an authorized user may be able to acquire *root* privileges even if the role account is not *root*. The problem is that resetting the effective UID sets the saved UID to the previous UID—namely, *root*. A process may then reacquire the rights of its saved UID. To avoid this problem, the programmers used the *setuid* system call to reset *all* of the real, effective, and saved UIDs to the UID of the role. Thus, all traces of the *root* UID are eliminated and the user cannot reacquire those privileges.

Similarly, UNIX-like systems check access permissions only when the file is opened. If a *root* process opens a privileged file and then the process drops *root* privileges, it can still read (or write to) the file.

The components of the protection domain that the process must reset before the overlay are the open files (except for standard input, output, and error), which must be closed, the signal handlers, which must be reset to their default values, and any user-specific information, which must be cleared.

26.5.3   Improper Change

This category describes data and instructions that change over time. The danger is that the changed values may be inconsistent with the previous values. The previous values dictate the flow of control of the process. The changed values cause the program to take incorrect or nonsecure actions on that path of control.

The data and instructions can reside in shared memory, in nonshared memory, or on disk. The last includes file attribute information such as ownership and access control list.

26.5.3.1   Memory

First comes the data in shared memory. Any process that can access shared memory can manipulate data in that memory. Unless all processes that can access the shared memory implement a concurrent protocol for managing changes, one process can change data on which a second process relies. As stated above, this could cause the second process to violate the security policy.

---

[42] See Section 13.3, "Users."

EXAMPLE: Two processes share memory. One process reads authentication data and writes it into the shared memory space. The second process performs the authentication, and writes a boolean *true* back into the shared memory space if the authentication succeeds, and *false* if it fails. Unless the two processes use concurrent constructs to synchronize their reading and writing, the first process may read the result before the second process has completed the computation for the current data. This could allow access when it should be denied, or vice versa.

> **Implementation Rule 26.5.5.** If a process interacts with other processes, the interactions should be synchronized. In particular, all possible sequences of interactions must be known and, for all such interactions, the process must enforce the required security policy.

A variant of this situation is the asynchronous exception handler. If the handler alters variables and then returns to the previous point in the program, the changes in the variables could cause problems similar to the problem of concurrent processes. For this reason, if the exception handler alters any variables on which other portions of the code depend, the programmer must understand the possible effects of such changes. This is just like the earlier situation in which a concurrent process changes another's variables in a shared memory space.

> **Implementation Rule 26.5.6.** Asynchronous exception handlers should not alter any variables except those that are local to the exception handling module. An exception handler should block all other exceptions when begun, and should not release the block until the handler completes execution, unless the handler has been designed to handle exceptions within itself (or calls an uninvoked exception handler).

A second approach applies whether the memory is shared or not. A user feeds bogus information to the program, and the program accepts it. The bogus data overflows its buffer, changing other data, or inserting instructions that can be executed later.

EXAMPLE: The buffer overflow attack on *fingerd* described in Section 20.4.5.2 illustrates this approach. The return address is pushed onto the stack when the input routine is called. That address is not expected to change between its being pushed onto the stack and its being popped from the stack, but the buffer overflow changes it. When the input function returns, the address popped from the stack is that of the input buffer. Execution resumes at that point, and the input instructions are used.

This suggests an approach to detecting such transformations (the *stack guard approach*) [216]. Immediately after the return address is pushed onto the stack, push a random number onto the stack (the *canary*). Assume that the input overflows the buffer on the stack and alters the return address on the stack. If the canary is n bits long and has been chosen randomly, the probability of the attacker not changing that cookie is 2^{-n}. When the input procedure returns, the canary is popped and compared with the value that was pushed onto the stack. If the two differ, there has been an overflow.[43]

In terms of trust, the return address (a trusted datum) can be affected by untrusted data (from the input). This lowers the trustworthiness of the return address to that of input data. One need not supply instructions to breach security.

EXAMPLE: One version of a UNIX login program allocated two adjacent arrays. The first held the user's cleartext password and was 80 characters long, and the second held the password hash[44] and was 13 characters long. The program's logic loaded the password hash into the second array as soon as the user's name was determined. It then read the user's cleartext password and stored it in the first array. If the contents of the first array hashed to the contents of the second array, the user was authenticated. An attacker simply selected a random password (for example, "password") and generated a valid hash for it (here, "12CsGd8FRcMSM"). The attacker then identified herself as *root*. When asked for a password, the attacker entered "password," typed 72 spaces, and then typed "12CsGd8FRcMSM." The system hashed "password," got "12CsGd8FRcMSM," and logged the user in as *root*.

A technique in which canaries protect data, not only the return address, would work, but raises many implementation problems (see Exercise 6).

Implementation Rule 26.5.7. Whenever possible, data that the process trusts and data that it receives from untrusted sources (such as input) should be kept in separate areas of memory. If data from a trusted source is overwritten with data from an untrusted source, a memory error will occur.

In more formal terms, the principle of least common mechanism[45] indicates that memory should not be shared in this way.

These rules apply to our program in several ways. First, the program does not interact with any other program except through exception handling.[46] So Implementation Rule 26.5.5 does not apply. Exception handling consists of calling a procedure that disables further exception handling, logs the exception, and immediately terminates the program.

Illicit alteration of data in memory is the second potential problem. If the user-supplied data is read into memory that overlaps with other program data, it could

---

[43] If the goal is to alter data on the stack other than the return address, the canary will not be altered. This technique will not detect the change. (See Exercise 6.)

[44] See Section 11.2, "Passwords."

[45] See Section 12.2.7, "Principle of Least Common Mechanism."

[46] If the access control information or the authentication information came from servers, then there would be interaction with other programs (the servers). The method of communication would need to be considered, as discussed above.

erase or alter that data. To satisfy Implementation Rule 26.5.7, the programmers did not reuse variables into which users could input data. They also ensured that each access to a buffer did not overlap with other buffers.

The problem of buffer overflow is solved by checking all array and pointer references within the code. Any reference that is out of bounds causes the program to fail after logging an error message to help the programmers track down the error.

26.5.3.2   Changes in File Contents

File contents may change improperly. In most cases, this means that the file permissions are set incorrectly or that multiple processes are accessing the file, which is similar to the problem of concurrent processes accessing shared memory. Management Rule 26.5.2 and Implementation Rule 26.5.5 cover these two cases.

A nonobvious corollary is to be careful of dynamic loading. Dynamic load libraries are not part of this program's executable. They are loaded, as needed, when the program runs. Suppose one of the libraries is changed, and the change causes a side effect. The program may cease to function or, even worse, work incorrectly.

If the dynamic load modules cannot be altered, then this concern is minimal, but if they can be upgraded or otherwise altered, it is important. Because one of the reasons for using dynamic load libraries is to allow upgrades without having to recompile programs that depend on the library, security-related programs using dynamic load libraries are at risk.

> **Implementation Rule 26.5.8.** Do not use components that may change between the time the program is created and the time it is run.

This is another reason that the developers decided not to use dynamic loading.

26.5.3.3   Race Conditions in File Accesses

A race condition in this context is the *time-of-check-to-time-of-use* problem. As with memory accesses, the file being used is changed after validation but before access.[47] To thwart it, either the file must be protected so that no untrusted user can alter it, or the process must validate the file and use it indivisibly. The former requires appropriate settings of permission, so Management Rule 26.5.2 applies. Section 26.5.7, "Improper Indivisibility," discusses the latter.

This program validates that the owner and access control permissions for the access control file are correct (the check). It then opens the file (the use). If an attacker can change the file after the validation but before the opening, so that the file checked is not the file opened, then the attacker can have the program obtain access control information from a file other than the legitimate access control file. Presumably, the attacker would supply a set of access control entries allowing unauthorized accesses.

---

[47] Section 20.3.1, "Two Security Flaws," discusses this problem in detail.

EXAMPLE: The UNIX operating system allows programs to refer to files in two ways: by name and by file descriptor.[48] Once a file descriptor is bound to a file, the referent of the descriptor does not change. Each access through the file descriptor *always* refers to the bound file (until the descriptor is closed). However, the kernel reprocesses the file name at each reference, so two references to the same file name may refer to two *different* files. An attacker who is able to alter the file system in such a way that this occurs is exploiting a race condition. So any checks made to the file corresponding to the first use of the name may not apply to the file corresponding to the second use of the name. This can result in a process making unwarranted assumptions about the trustworthiness of the file and the data it contains.

In the *xterm* example[49] the program can be fixed by opening the file and then using the file descriptor (handle) to obtain the owner and access permissions.[50] Those permissions belong to the opened file, because they were obtained using the file descriptor. The validation is now ensured to be that of the access control file.

The program does exactly this. It opens the access control file and uses the file descriptor, which references the file attribute information directly to obtain the owner, group, and access control permissions. Those permissions are checked. If they are correct, the program uses the file descriptor to read the file. Otherwise, the file is closed and the program reports a failure.

26.5.4 Improper Naming

Improper naming refers to an ambiguity in identifying an object. Most commonly, two different objects have the same name.[51] The programmer intends the name to refer to one of the objects, but an attacker manipulates the environment and the process so that the name refers to a different object. Avoiding this flaw requires that every object be unambiguously identified. This is both a management concern and an implementation concern.

Objects must be uniquely identifiable or completely interchangeable. Managing these objects means identifying those that are interchangeable and those that are not. The former objects need a controller (or set of controllers) that, when given a name, selects one of the objects. The latter objects need unique names. The managers of the objects must supply those names.

Management Rule 26.5.5. Unique objects require unique names. Interchangeable objects may share a name.

---

[48] See Section 13.2, "Files and Objects."

[49] See Section 20.3.1, "Two Security Flaws."

[50] The system call used would be *fstat*(2).

[51] See the example on page 363 in Section 19.1.

A name is interpreted within a context. At the implementation level, the process must force its own context into the interpretation, to ensure that the object referred to is the intended object. The context includes information about the character sets, process and file hierarchies, network domains, and any accessible variables such as the search path.

EXAMPLE: Stage 3 in Section 20.2.8 discussed an attack in which a privileged program called *loadmodule* executed a second program named *ld.so*. The attack exploited *loadmodule*'s failure to specify the context in which *ld.so* was named. *Loadmodule* used the context of the user invoking the program. Normally, this caused the correct *ld.so* to be invoked. In the example, the attacker changed the context so that another version of *ld.so* was executed. This version had a Trojan horse that would grant privileged access. When the attacker executed *loadmodule*, the Trojan horse was triggered and maximum privileges were acquired.

> **Implementation Rule 26.5.9.** The process must ensure that the context in which an object is named identifies the correct object.

This program uses names for external objects in four places: the name of the access control file, the names of the users and roles, the names of the hosts, and the name of the command interpreter (the *shell*) that the program uses to execute commands in the role account.

The two file names (access control file and command interpreter) must identify specific files. Absolute path names specify the location of the object with respect to a distinguished directory called / or the "root directory." However, a privileged process can redefine / to be any directory.[52] This program does not do so. Furthermore, if the root directory is anything other than the root directory of the system, a trusted process has executed it. No untrusted user could have done so. Thus, as long as absolute path names are specified, the files are unambiguously named.

The name provided may be interpreted in light of other aspects of the environment. For example, differences in the encoding of characters can transform file names. Whether characters are made up of 16 bits, 8 bits, or 7 bits can change the interpretation, and therefore the referent, of a file name. Other environment variables can change the interpretation of the path name. This program simply creates a new, known, safe environment for execution of the commands.[53]

This has two advantages over sanitization of the existing context. First, it avoids having the program analyze the environment in detail. The meaning of each aspect of the environment need not be analyzed and examined. The environment is simply replaced. Second, it allows the system to evolve without compromising the security of the program. For example, if a new environment variable is assigned a

---

[52] Specifically, the system call *chroot*(2) resets / to mean the named directory. All absolute path names are interpreted with respect to that directory. Only the superuser, *root*, may execute this system call.

[53] The principle of fail-safe defaults (see Section 12.2.2) supports this approach.

meaning that affects how programs are executed, the variable will not affect how the program executes its commands because that variable will not appear in the command's environment. So this program closes all file descriptors, resets signal handlers, and passes a new set of environment variables for the command.

These actions satisfy Implementation Rule 26.5.9.

The developers assumed that the system was properly maintained, so that the names of the users and roles would map into the correct UIDs. (Section 26.5.2.1 discusses this.) This applies to Management Rule 26.5.5.

The host names are the final set of names. These may be specified by names or IP addresses. If the former, they must be fully qualified domain names to avoid ambiguity. To see this, suppose an access control entry allows user *matt* to access the role *wheel* when logging in from the system *amelia*. Does this mean that the system names *amelia* in the local domain, or any system named *amelia* from any domain? Either interpretation is valid. The former is more reasonable,[54] and applying this interpretation resolves the ambiguity. (The program implicitly maps names to fully qualified domain names using the former interpretation. Thus, *amelia* in the access control entry would match a host named *amelia* in the local domain, and not a host named *amelia* in another domain.) This implements Implementation Rule 26.5.9.[55]

As a side note, if the local network is mismanaged or compromised, the name *amelia* may refer to a system other than the one intended. For example, the real host *amelia* may crash or go offline. An attacker can then reset the address of his host to correspond to *amelia*. This program will not detect the impersonation.

26.5.5   Improper Deallocation or Deletion

Failing to delete sensitive information raises the possibility of another process seeing that data at a later time. In particular, cryptographic keywords, passwords, and other authentication information should be discarded once they have been used. Similarly, once a process has finished with a resource, that resource should be deallocated. This allows other processes to use that resource, inhibiting denial of service attacks.

A consequence of not deleting sensitive information is that dumps of memory, which may occur if the program receives an exception or crashes for some other reason, contain the sensitive data. If the process fails to release sensitive resources before spawning unprivileged subprocesses, those unprivileged subprocesses may have access to the resource.

Implementation Rule 26.5.10. When the process finishes using a sensitive object (one that contains confidential information or one that should not be

---

[54] According to the principle of least privilege (see Section 12.2.1).

[55] As discussed in Section 13.6.1, "Host Identity," host names can be spoofed. For reasons discussed in the preceding chapters, the Drib management and security officers are not concerned with this threat on the Drib's internal network.

altered), the object should be erased, then deallocated or deleted. Any resources not needed should also be released.

Our program uses three pieces of sensitive information. The first is the cleartext password, which authenticates the user. The password is hashed, and the hash is compared with the stored hash. Once the hash of the entered password has been computed, the process must delete the cleartext password. So it overwrites the array holding the password with random bytes.

The second piece of sensitive information is the access control information. Suppose an attacker wanted to gain access to a role account. The access control entries would tell the attacker which users could access that account using this program. To prevent the attacker from gaining this information, the developers decided to keep the contents of the access control file confidential. The program accesses this file using a file descriptor. File descriptors remain open when a new program overlays a process. Hence, the program closes the file descriptor corresponding to the access control file once the request has been validated (or has failed to be validated).

The third piece of sensitive information is the log file. The program alters this file. If an unprivileged program such as one run by this program were to inherit the file descriptor, it could flood the log. Were the log to fill up, the program could no longer log failures. So the program also closes the log file before spawning the role's command.

26.5.6   Improper Validation

The problem of improper validation arises when data is not checked for consistency and correctness. Ideally, a process would validate the data against the more abstract policies to ensure correctness. In practice, the process can check correctness only by looking for error codes (indicating failure of functions and procedures) or by looking for patently incorrect values (such as negative numbers when positive ones are required).

As the program is designed, the developers should determine what conditions must hold at each interface and each block of code. They should then validate that these conditions hold.

What follows is a set of validations that are commonly overlooked. Each program requires its own analysis, and other types of validation may be critical to the correct, secure functioning of the program, so this list is by no means complete.

26.5.6.1   Bounds Checking

Errors of validation often occur when data is supposed to lie within bounds. For example, a buffer may contain entries numbered from 0 to 99. If the index used to access the buffer elements takes on a value less than 0 or greater than 99, it is an invalid operand because it accesses a nonexistent entry. The variable used to access the element may not be an integer (for example, it may be a set element or pointer), but in any case it must reference an existing element.

Implementation Rule 26.5.11. Ensure that all array references access existing elements of the array. If a function that manipulates arrays cannot ensure that only valid elements are referenced, do not use that function. Find one that does, write a new version, or create a wrapper.

In this program, all loops involving arrays compare the value of the variable referencing the array against the indexes (or addresses) of both the first and last elements of the array. The loop terminates if the variable's value is outside those two values. This covers all loops within the program, but it does not cover the loops in the library functions.

For loops in the library functions, bounds checking requires an analysis of the functions used to manipulate arrays. The most common type of array for which library functions are used is the character string, which is a sequence of characters (bytes) terminating with a 0 byte. Because the length of the string is not encoded as part of the string, functions cannot determine the size of the array containing the string. They simply operate on all bytes until a 0 byte is found.

EXAMPLE: The program sometimes must copy character strings (defined in C as arrays of character data terminating with a byte containing 0). The canonical function for copying strings does no bounds checking. This function, *strcpy(x, y)*, copies the string from the array *y* to the array *x*, even if the string is too long for *x*. A different function, *strncpy(x, y, n)*, copies at most *n* characters from array *y* to array *x*. However, unlike *strcpy*, *strncpy* may not copy the terminating 0 byte.[56] The program must take two actions when *strncpy* is called. First, it must insert a 0 byte at the end of the *x* array. This ensures that the contents of *x* meet the definition of a string in C. Second, the process must check that both *x* and *y* are arrays of characters, and that *n* is a positive integer.

The programmers use only those functions that bound the sizes of arrays. In particular, the function *fgets* is used to read input, because it allows the programmer to specify that a maximum number of characters are to be read. (This solves the problem that plagued *fingerd*.[57])

26.5.6.2 Type Checking

Failure to check types is another common validation problem. If a function parameter is an integer, but the actual argument passed is a floating point number, the function will interpret the bit pattern of the floating point number as an integer and will produce an incorrect result.

---

[56] If the string in *y* is longer than *n* characters, *strncpy* will not add a 0 byte to the characters copied into *x*.

[57] See Section 20.4.5.2, "fingerd Buffer Overflow."

Implementation Rule 26.5.12. Check the types of functions and parameters.

A good compiler and well-written code will handle this particular problem. All functions should be declared before they are used. Most programming languages allow the programmer to specify the number and types of arguments, as well as the type of the return value (if any). The compiler can then check the types of the declarations against the types of the actual arguments and return values.

Management Rule 26.5.6. When compiling programs, ensure that the compiler flags report inconsistencies in types. Investigate all such warnings and either fix the problem or document the warning and why it is spurious.

26.5.6.3   Error Checking

A third common problem involving improper validation is failure to check return values of functions. For example, suppose a program needs to determine ownership of a file. It calls a system function that returns a record containing information from the file attribute table. The program obtains the owner of the file from the appropriate field of the record. If the function fails, the information in the record is meaningless. So, if the function's return status is not checked, the program may act erroneously.

Implementation Rule 26.5.13. Check all function and procedure executions for errors.

This program makes extensive use of system and library functions, as well as its own internal functions (such as the access control module). Every function returns a value, and the value is checked for an error before the results of the function are used. For example, the function that obtains the ownership and access permissions of the access control file would return meaningless information should the function fail. So the function's return value is checked first for an error; if no error has occurred, then the file attribute information is used.

As another example, the program opens a log file. If the open fails, and the program tries to write to the (invalid) file descriptor obtained from the function that failed, the program will terminate as a result of an exception. Hence, the program checks the result of opening the log file.

26.5.6.4   Checking for Valid, not Invalid, Data

Validation should apply the principle of fail-safe defaults.[58] This principle requires that valid values be known, and that all other values be rejected. Unfortunately, programmers often check for *in*valid data and assume that the rest is valid.

---

[58] See Section 12.2.2, "Principle of Fail-Safe Defaults."

EXAMPLE: A *metacharacter* is a character that is interpreted as something other than itself. For example, to the UNIX shells, the character "?" is a metacharacter that represents all single character files. A vendor upgraded its version of the command interpreter for its UNIX system. The new command interpreter (shell) treated the character "`" (back quote) as a delimiter for a command (and hence a metacharacter). The old shell treated the back quote as an ordinary character. Included in the distribution was a program for executing commands on remote systems. The set of allowed commands was restricted. This program carefully checked that the command was allowed, and that it contained no metacharacters, before sending it to a shell on the remote system. Unfortunately, the program checked a list of metacharacters to be rejected, rather than checking a list of characters that were allowed in the commands. As a result, one could embed a disallowed command within a valid command request, because the list of metacharacters was not updated to include the back quote.

Implementation Rule 26.5.14. Check that a variable's values are valid.

This program checks that the command to be executed matches one of the authorized commands. It does not have a set of commands that are to be denied. The program will detect an invalid command as one that is not listed in the set of authorized commands for that user accessing that role at the time and place allowed.

As discussed in Section 26.3.2.3, it is possible to allow all users *except some specific users* access to a role by an appropriate access control entry (using the keyword *not*). The developers debated whether having this ability was appropriate because its use could lead to violations of the principle of fail-safe defaults. On one key system, however, the only authorized users were system administrators and one or two trainees. The administrators wanted the ability to shut the trainees out of certain roles. So the developers added the keyword and recommended against its use except in that single specific situation.

Management Rule 26.5.7. If a trade-off between security and other factors results in a mechanism or procedure that can weaken security, document the reasons for the decision, the possible effects, and the situations in which the compromise method should be used. This informs others of the trade-off and the attendant risks.

26.5.6.5 Checking Input

All data from untrusted sources must be checked. Users are untrusted sources. The checking done depends on the way the data is received: into an input buffer (bounds checking) or read in as an integer (checking the magnitude and sign of the input).

Implementation Rule 26.5.15. Check all user input for both form and content. In particular, check integers for values that are too big or too small, and check character data for length and valid characters.

The program determines what to do on the basis of at least two pieces of data that the user provides: the role name and the command (which, if omitted, means unrestricted access).[59] Users must also authenticate themselves appropriately. The program must first validate that the supplied password is correct. It then checks the access control information to determine whether the user is allowed access to the role at that time and from that location.

The length of the input password must be no longer than the buffer in which it is placed. Similarly, the lines of the access control file must not overflow the buffer allocated for it. The contents of the lines of the access control file must make up a valid access control entry. This is most easily done by constraining the format of the contents of the file, as discussed in the next section.

An excellent example of the need to constrain user input comes from formatted print statements in C.

EXAMPLE: The *printf* function's first parameter is a character string that indicates how *printf* is to format output data. The following parameters contain the data. For example,

```
printf("%d %d\n", i, j);
```

prints the values of *i* and *j*. Some versions of this library function allow the user to store the number of characters printed at any point in the string. For example, if *i* contains 2, *j* contains 21, and *m* and *n* are integer variables,

```
printf("%d %d%n %d\n%n", i, j, &m, i, &n);
```

prints

```
2 21 2
```

and stores 4 in *m* and 7 in *n*, because four characters are printed before the first "%n" and seven before the second "%n" (the sequence "\n" is interpreted as a single character, the newline). Now, suppose the user is asked for a file name. This input is stored in the array *str*. The program then prints the file name with

```
printf(str);
```

If the user enters the file name "log%n", the function will overwrite some memory location with the integer 3. The exact location depends on the contents of the program stack, and with some experimentation it is possible to cause the program to change the return address stored on the stack. This leads to the buffer overflow attack described earlier.

---

[59] See Section 12.2.6, "Principle of Separation of Privilege."

26.5.6.6   Designing for Validation

Sometimes data cannot be validated completely. For example, in the C programming language, a programmer can test for a NULL pointer (meaning that the pointer does not hold the address of any object), but if the pointer is not NULL, checking the validity of the pointer may be very difficult (or impossible). Using a language with strong type checking is another example.

The consequence of the need for validation requires that data structures and functions be designed and implemented in such a way that they can be validated. For example, because C pointers cannot be properly validated, programmers should not pass pointers or use them in situations in which they must be validated. Methods of data hiding, type checking, and object-oriented programming often provide mechanisms for doing this.

> **Implementation Rule 26.5.16.** Create data structures and functions in such a way that they can be validated.

An example will show the level of detail necessary for validation. The entries in the access control file are designed to allow the program to detect obvious errors. Each access control entry consists of a block of information in the following format.

```
role name
    users comma-separated list of users
    location comma-separated list of locations
    time comma-separated list of times
    command command and arguments
    ...
    command command and arguments
endrole
```

This defines each component of the entry. (The lines need not be in any particular order.) The syntax is well-defined, and the access control module in the program checks for syntax errors. The module also performs other checks, such as searching for invalid user names in the **users** field and requiring that the full path names of all commands be specified. Finally, note that the module computes the number of commands for the module's internal record. This eliminates a possible source of error—namely, that the user may miscount the number of commands.

In case of any error, the process logs the error, if possible, and terminates. It does not allow the user to access the role.

26.5.7   Improper Indivisibility

Improper indivisibility[60] arises when an operation is considered as one unit (indivisible) in the abstract but is implemented as two units (divisible). The race conditions

---

[60] This is often called "atomicity."

discussed in Section 26.5.3.3 provide one example. The checking of the access control file attributes and the opening of that file are to be executed as one operation. Unfortunately, they may be implemented as two separate operations, and an attacker who can alter the file after the first but before the second operation can obtain access illicitly. Another example arises in exception handling. Often, program statements and system calls are considered as single units or operations when the implementation uses many operations. An exception divides those operations into two sets: the set before the exception, and the set after the exception. If the system calls or statements rely on data not changing during their execution, exception handlers must not alter the data.

Section 26.5.3 discusses handling of these situations when the operations cannot be made indivisible. Approaches to making them indivisible include disabling interrupts and having the kernel perform operations. The latter assumes that the operation is indivisible when performed by the kernel, which may be an incorrect assumption.

> **Implementation Rule 26.5.17.** If two operations must be performed sequentially without an intervening operation, use a mechanism to ensure that the two cannot be divided.

In UNIX systems, the problem of divisibility arises with *root* processes such as the program under consideration. UNIX-like systems do not enforce the principle of complete mediation.[61] For *root*, access permissions are not checked. Recall the *xterm* example in Section 20.4.5.1. A user needed to log information from the execution of *xterm*, and specified a log file. Before appending to that file, *xterm* needed to ensure that the real UID could write to the log file. This required an extra system call. As a result, operations that should have been indivisible (the access check followed by the opening of the file) were actually divisible. One way to make these operations indivisible on UNIX-like systems is to drop privileges to those of the real UID, then open the file. The access checking is done in the kernel as part of the open.

Improper indivisibility arises in our program when the access control module validates and then opens the access control file. This should be a single operation, but because of the semantics of UNIX-like systems, it must be performed as two distinct operations. It is not possible to ensure the indivisibility of the two operations. However, it *is* possible to ensure that the target of the operations does not change, as discussed in Section 26.5.3, and this suffices for our purposes.

26.5.8   Improper Sequencing

Improper sequencing means that operations are performed in an incorrect order. For example, a process may create a lock file and then write to a log file. A second process may also write to the log file, and then check to see if the lock file exists. The

---

[61] See Section 12.2.4, "Principle of Complete Mediation."

first program uses the correct sequence of calls; the second does not (because that sequence allows multiple writers to access the log file simultaneously).

> **Implementation Rule 26.5.18.** Describe the legal sequences of operations on a resource or object. Check that all possible sequences of the program(s) involved match one (or more) legal sequences.

In our program, the sequence of operations in the design shown in Section 26.3.1.2 follow a proper order. The user is first authenticated. Then the program uses the access control information to determine if the requested access is valid. If it is, the appropriate command is executed using a new, safe environment.

A second sequence of operations occurs when privileges to the role are dropped. First, group privileges are changed to those of the role. Then all user identification numbers are changed to those of the role. A common error is to switch the user identification numbers first, followed by the change in group privileges. Because changing group privileges requires *root* privileges, the change will fail. Hence, the programmers used the stated ordering.

26.5.9 Improper Choice of Operand or Operation

Preventing errors of choosing the wrong operand or operation requires that the algorithms be thought through carefully (to ensure that they are appropriate). At the implementation level, this requires that operands be of an appropriate type and value, and that operations be selected to perform the desired functions. The difference between this type of error and improper validation lies in the program. Improper implementation refers to a validation failure. The operands may be appropriate, but no checking is done. In this category, even though the operands may have been checked, they may still be inappropriate.

EXAMPLE: The UNIX program *su* allows a user to substitute another user's identity, obtaining the second user's privileges. According to an apocryphal story, one version of this program granted the user *root* privileges if the user information database did not exist (see Exercise 10 in Chapter 12). If the program could not open the user information database file, it assumed that the database did not exist. This was an inappropriate choice of operation because one could block access to the file even when the database existed.

Assurance techniques[62] help detect these problems. The programmer documents the purpose of each function and then checks (or, preferably, others check) that the algorithms in the function work properly and that the code correctly implements the algorithms.

---

[62] See Chapter 17, "Introduction to Assurance," and Chapter 18, "Evaluating Systems."

Management Rule 26.5.8. Use software engineering and assurance techniques (such as documentation, design reviews, and code reviews) to ensure that operations and operands are appropriate.

Within our program, many operands and operations control the granting (and denying) of access, the changing to the role, and the execution of the command. We first focus on the access part of the program, and afterwards we consider two other issues.

First, a user is granted access only when an access control entry matches *all* characteristics of the current session. The relevant characteristics are the role name, the user's UID, the role's name (or UID), the location, the time, and the command. We begin by checking that if the characteristics match, the access control module returns true (allowing access). We also check that the caller grants access when the module returns *true* and denies access when the module returns *false*.

Next, we consider the user's UID. That object is of type *uid_t*. If the interface to the system database returns an object of a different type, conversion becomes an issue. Specifically, many interfaces treat the UID as an integer. The difference between the types *int* and *uid_t* may cause problems. On the systems involved, *uid_t* is an unsigned integer. Since we are comparing signed and unsigned integers, C simply converts the signed integers to unsigned integers, and the comparison succeeds. Hence, the choice of operation (comparison, here) is proper.

Checking location requires the program to derive the user's location, as discussed above, and pass it to the validator. The validator takes a string and determines whether it matches the pattern in the location field of the access control entry. If the string matches, the module should continue; otherwise, it should terminate and return *false*.

Unlike the location, a variable of type *time_t* contains the current time. The time checking portion of the module processes the string representing the allowed times and determines if the current time falls in the range of allowed times. Checking time is different than checking location because legal times are ranges, except in one specific situation: when an allowed time is specified to the exact second. A specification of an exact time is useless, because the program may not obtain the time at the exact second required. This would lead to a denial of service, violating Requirement 26.2.4. Also, allowing exact times leads to ambiguity.

EXAMPLE: The system administrator specifies that user *matt* is allowed access to the role *mail* at 9 AM on Tuesdays. Should this be interpreted as *exactly* 9 AM (that is, 9:00:00 AM) or as *sometime during* the 9 AM hour (that is, from 9:00:00 to 9:59:59 AM)? The latter interprets the specification as a range rather than an exact time, so the access control module uses that interpretation.

The use of signal handlers provides a second situation in which an improper choice of operation could occur. A signal indicates either an error in the program or a request from the user to terminate, so a signal should cause the program to terminate. If the program continues to run, and then grants the user access to the role account, either the program has continued in the face of an error or it has overridden the user's attempt to terminate the program.

26.5.10   Summary

This type of top-down analysis differs from the more usual approach of taking a checklist of common vulnerabilities and using it to examine code. There is a place for each of these approaches. The top-down approach presented here is a design approach, and should be applied at each level of design and implementation. It emphasizes documentation, analysis, and understanding of the program, its interfaces, and the environment in which it executes. A security analysis document should describe the analysis and the reasons for each security-related decision. This document will help other analysts examine the program and, more importantly, will provide future developers and maintainers of the program with insight into potential problems they may encounter in porting the program to a different environment, adding new features, or changing existing features.

Once the appropriate phase of the program has been completed, the developers should use a checklist to validate that the design or implementation has no common errors. Given the complexity of security design and implementation, such checklists provide valuable confirmation that the developers have taken common security problems into account. The following lists summarize the implementation and management rules above.

List of Implementation Rules

Implementation Rule 26.5.1. Structure the process so that all sections requiring extra privileges are modules. The modules should be as small as possible and should perform only those tasks that require those privileges.

Implementation Rule 26.5.2. Ensure that any assumptions in the program are validated. If this is not possible, document them for the installers and maintainers, so they know the assumptions that attackers will try to invalidate.

Implementation Rule 26.5.3. Ensure that the program does not share objects in memory with any other program, and that other programs cannot access the memory of a privileged process.

Implementation Rule 26.5.4. The error status of every function must be checked. Do not try to recover unless the cause of the error, and its effects, do not affect any security considerations. The program should restore the state of the system to the state before the process began, and then terminate.

Implementation Rule 26.5.5. If a process interacts with other processes, the interactions should be synchronized. In particular, all possible sequences of interactions must be known and, for all such interactions, the process must enforce the required security policy.

List of Implementation Rules (Continued)

Implementation Rule 26.5.6. Asynchronous exception handlers should not alter any variables except those that are local to the exception handling module. An exception handler should block all other exceptions when begun, and should not release the block until the handler completes execution, unless the handler has been designed to handle exceptions within itself (or calls an uninvoked exception handler).

Implementation Rule 26.5.7. Whenever possible, data that the process trusts and data that it receives from untrusted sources (such as input) should be kept in separate areas of memory. If data from a trusted source is overwritten with data from an untrusted source, a memory error will occur.

Implementation Rule 26.5.8. Do not use components that may change between the time the program is created and the time it is run.

Implementation Rule 26.5.9. The process must ensure that the context in which an object is named identifies the correct object.

Implementation Rule 26.5.10. When the process finishes using a sensitive object (one that contains confidential information or one that should not be altered), the object should be erased, then deallocated or deleted. Any resources not needed should also be released.

Implementation Rule 26.5.11. Ensure that all array references access existing elements of the array. If a function that manipulates arrays cannot ensure that only valid elements are referenced, do not use that function. Find one that does, write a new version, or create a wrapper.

Implementation Rule 26.5.12. Check the types of functions and parameters.

Implementation Rule 26.5.13. Check all function and procedure executions for errors.

Implementation Rule 26.5.14. Check that a variable's values are valid.

Implementation Rule 26.5.15. Check that a variable's values are valid.

Implementation Rule 26.5.16. Create data structures and functions in such a way that they can be validated.

Implementation Rule 26.5.17. If two operations must be performed sequentially without an intervening operation, use a mechanism to ensure that the two cannot be divided.

Implementation Rule 26.5.18. Describe the legal sequences of operations on a resource or object. Check that all possible sequences of the program(s) involved match one (or more) legal sequences.

List of Management Rules

Management Rule 26.5.1. Check that the process privileges are set properly.

Management Rule 26.5.2. The program that is executed to create the process, and all associated control files, must be protected from unauthorized use and modification. Any such modification must be detected.

Management Rule 26.5.3. Configure memory to enforce the principle of least privilege. If a section of memory is not to contain executable instructions, turn execute permission off for that section of memory. If the contents of a section of memory are not to be altered, make that section read-only.

Management Rule 26.5.4. Identify all system components on which the program depends. Check for errors whenever possible, and identify those components for which error checking will not work.

Management Rule 26.5.5. Unique objects require unique names. Interchangeable objects may share a name.

Management Rule 26.5.6. When compiling programs, ensure that the compiler flags report inconsistencies in types. Investigate all such warnings and either fix the problem or document the warning and why it is spurious.

Management Rule 26.5.7. If a trade-off between security and other factors results in a mechanism or procedure that can weaken security, document the reasons for the decision, the possible effects, and the situations in which the compromise method should be used. This informs others of the trade-off and the attendant risks.

Management Rule 26.5.8. Use software engineering and assurance techniques (such as documentation, design reviews, and code reviews) to ensure that operations and operands are appropriate.

26.6   Testing, Maintenance, and Operation

Testing provides an informal validation of the design and implementation of the program. The goal of testing is to show that the program meets the stated requirements. When design and implementation are driven by the requirements, as in the method used to create the program under discussion, testing is likely to uncover only minor problems, but if the developers do not have well-articulated requirements, or if the requirements are changed during development, testing may uncover major problems, requiring changes up to a complete redesign and reimplementation of a program. The worst mistake managers and developers can make is to take a program that does not meet the security requirements and add features to it to meet those requirements. The problem is that the basic design does not meet the security requirements. Adding security features will not ameliorate this fundamental flaw.

Once the program has been written and tested, it must be installed. The installation procedure must ensure that when a user starts the process, the environment in which the process is created matches the assumptions embodied in the design. This constrains the configuration of the program parameters as well as the manner in which the system is configured to protect the program. Finally, the installers must enable trusted users to modify and upgrade the program and the configuration files and parameters.

26.6.1   Testing

The results of testing a program are most useful if the tests are conducted in the environment in which the program will be used (the *production environment*). So, the first step in testing a program is to construct an environment that matches the production environment. This requires the testers to know the intended production environment. If there are a range of environments, the testers must test the programs in all of them. Often there is overlap between the environments, so this task is not so daunting as it might appear.

The production environment should correspond to the environment for which the program was developed. A symptom of discrepancies between the two environments is repeated failures resulting from erroneous assumptions. This indicates that the developers have implicity embedded information from the development environment that is inconsistent with the testing environment. This discrepancy must be reconciled.

The testing process begins with the requirements. Are they appropriate? Do they solve the problem? This analysis may be moot (if the task is to write a program meeting the given requirements), but if the task is phrased in terms of a *problem* to be solved, the problem drives the requirements. Because the requirements drive the design of the program, the requirements must be validated *before* designing begins.

As many of the software life cycle models indicate, this step may be revisited many times during the development of the program. Requirements may prove to be impossible to meet, or may produce problems that cannot be solved without changing the requirements. If the requirements are changed, they must be reanalyzed and verified to solve the problem.

Then comes the design. Section 26.4 discusses the stepwise refinement of the program. The decomposition of the program into modules allows us to test the program as it is being implemented. Then, once it has been completed, the testing of the entire program should demonstrate that the program meets its requirements in the given environment.

The general philosophy of testing is to execute all possible paths of control and compare the results with the expected results. In practice, the paths of control are too numerous to test exhaustively. Instead, the paths are analyzed and ordered. Test data is generated for each path, and the testers compare the results obtained from the actual data with the expected results. This continues until as many paths as possible have been tested.

For security testing, the testers must test not only the most commonly used paths but also the *least commonly used* paths. The latter often create security problems that attackers can exploit. Because they are relatively unused, traditional testing places them at a lower priority than that of other paths. Hence, they are not as well scrutinized, and vulnerabilities are missed.

The ordering of the paths relies on the requirements. Those paths that perform multiple security checks are more critical than those that perform single (or no) security checks because they introduce interfaces that affect security requirements. The other paths affect security, of course, but there are no interfaces.

First, we examine a module that calls no other module. Then we examine the program as a composition of modules. We conclude by testing the installation, configuration, and use instructions.

26.6.1.1   Testing the Module

The module may invoke one or more functions. The functions return results to the caller, either directly (through return values or parameter lists) or indirectly (by manipulation of the environment). The goal of this testing is to ensure that the module exhibits correct behavior regardless of what the functions returns.

The first step is to define "correct behavior." During the design of the program, the refinement process led to the specification of the module and the module's interface. This specification defines "correct behavior," and testing will require us to check that the specification holds.

We begin by listing all interfaces to the module. We will then use this list to execute four different types of tests. The types of test are as follows.

1. *Normal data tests*. These tests provide unexceptional data. The data should be chosen to exercise as many paths of control through the module as possible.

2. *Boundary data tests*. These tests provide data that tests any limits to the interfaces. For example, if the module expects a string of up to 256 characters to be passed in, these tests invoke the module and pass in arrays of 255, 256, and 257 characters. Longer strings should also be used in an effort to overflow internal buffers. The testers can examine the source code to determine what to try. Limits here do not apply simply to arrays or strings. In the program under discussion, the lowest allowed UID is 0, for *root*. A good test would be to try a UID of –1 to see what happens. The module should report an error.

EXAMPLE: One UNIX system had UIDs of 16 bits. The system used a file server that would not allow a client's *root* user to access any files. Instead, it remapped *root*'s UID to the public UID of –2. Because that UID was not assigned to any user, the remapped *root* could access only those files that were available to all users. The limit problem arose because one user, named Mike, had the UID 65534. Because 65534 = –2 in twos' complement 16-bit arithmetic, the remote *root* user could access all of Mike's files—even those that were not publicly available.

3. *Exception tests.* These tests determine how the program handles interrupts and traps. For example, many systems allow the user to send a signal that causes the program to trap to a signal handler, or to take a default action such as dumping the contents of memory to a core file. These tests determine if the module leaves the system in a nonsecure state—for example, by leaving sensitive information in the memory dump. They also analyze what the process does if ordinary actions (such as writing to a file) fail.

EXAMPLE: An FTP server ran on a system that kept its authentication information confidential. An attacker found that she could cause the system to crash by sending an unexpected sequence of commands, causing multiple signals to be generated before the first signal could be handled. The crash resulted in a core dump. Because the server would be restarted automatically, the attacker simply connected again and downloaded the core dump. From that dump, she extracted the authentication information and used a dictionary attack[63] to obtain the passwords of several users.

4. *Random data tests.* These tests supply inputs generated at random and observe how the module reacts. They should not corrupt the state of the system. If the module fails, it should restore the system to a safe state.[64]

EXAMPLE: In a study of UNIX utilities [636], approximately 30% crashed when given random inputs. In one case, an unprivileged program caused the system to crash.

Throughout the testing, the testers should keep track of the paths taken. This allows them to determine how complete the testing is. Because these tests are highly informal, the assurance they provide is not as convincing as the techniques used to develop high assurance systems. However, it is more than random tests, or no tests, would provide.

26.6.2 Testing Composed Modules

Now consider a module that calls other modules. Each of the invoked modules has a specification describing its actions. So, in addition to the tests discussed in the preceding section, one other type of test should be performed.

5. *Error handling tests.* These tests assume that the called modules violate their specifications in some way. The goal of these tests is to determine how robust the caller is. If it fails gracefully, and restores the system to a safe state, then the module passes the test. Otherwise, it fails and must be rewritten.

---

[63] See Section 11.2.1, "Attacking a Password System."
[64] See Section 13.2.2, "Principle of Fail-Safe Defaults."

EXAMPLE: Assume that a security-related program, running with *root* privileges, logs all network connections to a UNIX system. It also sends mail to the network administrator with the name of the connecting host on the subject line. To do this, it executes a command such as

```
mail -s hostname netadmin
```

where *hostname* is the name of the connecting host. This module obtains *hostname* from a different module that is passed the connecting host's IP address and uses the Domain Name Service to find the corresponding host name. A serious problem arose because the DNS did not verify that the *hostname* was composed of legal characters. The effects were discovered when one attacker changed the name of his host to

```
hi nobody; rm -rf *; true
```

causing the security-related program to delete critical files. Had the calling module expected failure, and checked for it, the error would have been caught before any damage was done.

26.6.3   Testing the Program

Once the testers have assembled the program and its documentation, the final phase of testing begins. The testers have someone follow the installation and configuration instructions. This person should *not* be a member of the testing team, because the testing team has been working with the program and is familiar with it. The goal of this test is to determine if the installation and configuration instructions are correct and easy to understand. The principle of psychological acceptability[65] requires that the tool be as easy to install and use as possible. Because most installers and users will not have experience with the program, the testers need to evaluate how they will understand the documentation and whether or not they can install the program correctly by following the instructions. An incorrectly installed security tool does not provide security; it may well detract from it. Worse, it gives people a false sense of security.

26.7   Distribution

Once the program has been completed, it must be distributed. Distribution involves placing the program in a repository where it cannot be altered except by authorized

---

[65] See Section 12.2.8, "Principle of Psychological Acceptability."

people, and from which it can be retrieved and sent to the intended recipients. This requires a policy for distribution. Specific factors to be considered are as follows.

1. *Who can use the program?* If the program is licensed to a specific organization, or to a specific host, then each copy of the program that is distributed must be tied to that organization or host so it cannot be redistributed or pirated. This is an originator controlled policy.[66] One approach is to provide the licensee with a secret key and encipher the software with the same key. This prevents redistribution without the licensee's consent, unless the attacker breaks the cryptosystem or steals the licensee's key.[67]

2. *How can the integrity of the master copy be protected?* If an attacker can alter the master copy, from which distribution copies are made, then the attacker can compromise all who use the program.

EXAMPLE: The program *tcp_wrappers*[68] provides host-level access control for network servers. It is one of the most widely used programs in the UNIX community. In 1996, attackers broke into the site from which that program could be obtained [199]. They altered the program to allow all connections to succeed. More than 50 groups obtained the program before the break-in was detected.

> Part of the problem is credibility. If an attacker can pose as the vendor, then all who obtain the program from the attacker will be vulnerable to attack. This tactic undermines trust in the program and can be surprisingly hard to counter. It is analogous to generating a cryptographic checksum for a progam infected with a computer virus.[69] When an uninfected program is obtained, the integrity checker complains because the checksum is wrong. In our example, when the real vendor contacts the duped customer, the customer usually reacts with disbelief, or is unwilling to concede that his system has been compromised.

3. *How can the availability of the program be ensured?* If the program is sent through a physical medium, such as a CD-ROM, availability is equivalent to the availability of mail or messenger services between the vendor and the buyer. If the program is distributed through electronic means, however, the distributor must take precautions to ensure that the distribution site is available. Denial of service attacks such as SYN flooding[70] may hamper the availability.

---

[66] See Section 7.3, "Originator Controlled Access Control."
[67] See Section 12.2.5, "Principle of Open Design."
[68] See Section 24.3.2, "The Development System."
[69] See Section 19.6.4, "Malicious Logic Altering Files."
[70] See Section 23.4, "Availability and Network Flooding."

Like a program, the distribution is controlled by a policy. All considerations that affect a security policy affect the distribution policy as well.

26.8   Conclusion

The purpose of this chapter was to provide a glimpse of techniques that provide better than ordinary assurance that a program's design and implementation satisfy its requirements. This chapter is not a manual on applying high-assurance techniques. In terms of the techniques discussed in Part 6, "Assurance," this chapter describes low-assurance techniques.

However, given the current state of programming and software development, these low-assurance techniques enable programmers to produce significantly better, more robust, and more usable code than they could produce without these techniques. So, using a methodology similar to the one outlined in this chapter will reduce vulnerabilities and improve both the quality and the security of code.

26.9   Summary

This chapter discussed informal techniques for writing programs that enforce security policies. The process began with a requirements analysis and continued with a threat analysis to show that the requirements countered the threats. The design process came next, and it fed back into the requirements to clarify an ambiguity. Once the high-level design was accepted, we used a stepwise refinement process to break the design down into modules and a caller. The categories of flaws in the program analysis vulnerability helped find potential implementation problems. Finally, issues of testing and distribution ensured that the program did what was required.

26.10   Further Reading

All too little has been written about robust programming—the art of writing programs that work correctly and handle errors gracefully. Kernighan and Plauger's book [505] describes the principles and ideas underlying good programming style. Stavely's book [870] combines formalisms with informal steps. Maguire's book [585] is much more informal, and is a collection of tips on how to write robust programs. Koenig [525] focuses on the C programming language.

Viega and McGraw's book [914] is somewhat general, with many examples focusing on UNIX and Linux systems. Its design principles give good advice.

Although they are dated, Wood and Kochan's book [955] and Bishop's paper [100] cover principles and techniques that are still valid. Braun [132] also provides a good overview, as do Garfinkel and Spafford [347]. The latter book has a wonderful section on trust, which is must reading for anyone interested in security-related programming. Wheeler [937] also provides valuable information and insight.

Several books discuss aspects of secure programming in a Windows environment. Howard and LeBlanc's book [443] illuminates many of the problems that programmers must be aware of. It is good reading even for those who work in non-Windows environments. Other books [162, 442] discuss security in relation to various aspects of the Windows environment.

26.11   Exercises

1. Consider the two interpretations of a time field that specifies "1 AM" One interpretation says that this means *exactly* 1:00 AM and no other time. The other says that this means any time during the 1 AM hour.

   a. How would you express the time of *exactly* 1 AM in the second interpretation?

   b. How would you express "any time during the 1 AM hour" in the first interpretation?

   c. Which is more powerful? If they are equally powerful, which do you think is more psychologically acceptable? Why?

2. Verify that the modified version of Requirement 26.2.4 shown as Requirement 26.3.1 on page 585 counters the appropriate threats.

3. Currently, the program described in this chapter is to have setuid-to-*root* privileges. Someone observed that it could be equally well-implemented as a server, in which case the program would authenticate the user, connect to the server, send the command and role, and then let the server execute the command.

   a. What are the advantages of using the server approach rather than the single program approach?

   b. If the server responds only to clients on the local machine, using interprocess communication mechanisms on the local system, which approach would you use? Why?

   c. If the server were listening for commands from the network, would that change your answer to part (b)? Why or why not?

   d. If the client sent the password to the server, and the server authenticated, would your answers to any of the three previous parts change? Why or why not?

4. The little languages presented in Section 26.3.2.3 have ambiguous semantics. For example, in the location language, does "not host1 or host2" mean "not at host1 and not at host2" or "not at host1, or at host2"?

    a. Rewrite the BNF of the location language to make the semantics reflect the second meaning (that is, the precedence of "not" is higher than that of "or"). Are the semantics unambiguous now? Why or why not?

    b. Rewrite the BNF of the time language to make the semantics reflect the second meaning (that is, the precedence of "not" is higher than that of "or"). Are the semantics unambiguous now? Why or why not?

5. Suppose an access control record is malformed (for example, it has a syntax error). Show that the access control module would deny access.

6. The canary for StackGuard simply detects overflow that might change the return address. This exercise asks you to extend the notion of a canary to detection of buffer overflow.

    a. Assume that the canary is placed directly after the array, and that after every array, access is checked to see if it has changed. Would this detect a buffer overflow? If so, why do you think this is not suitable for use in practice? If not, describe an attack that could change a number beyond the buffer without affecting the canary.

    b. Now suppose that the canary was placed directly after the buffer but—like the canary for StackGuard—was only checked just before a function return. How effective do you think this method would be?

Chapter 27
Lattices

A lattice is a mathematical construction built on the notion of a group. First, we review some basic terms. Then we discuss lattices.

27.1 Basics

For a set S, a relation R is any subset of $S \times S$. For convenience, if $(a, b) \in R$, we write aRb.

EXAMPLE: Let $S = \{ 1, 2, 3 \}$. Then the relation *less than or equal to* (written $\leq$) is defined by the set $R = \{ (1, 1), (1, 2), (1, 3), (2, 2), (2, 3), (3, 3) \}$. We write $1 \leq 1$ and $2 \leq 3$ for convenience, because $(1, 2) \in R$ and $(2, 3) \in R$, but not $3 \leq 2$, because $(3, 2) \notin R$.

The following definitions describe properties of relations.

Definition 27–1. A relation R defined over a set S is *reflexive* if aRa for all $a \in S$.

Definition 27–2. A relation R defined over a set S is *antisymmetric* if aRb and bRa imply $a = b$ for all $a, b \in S$.

Definition 27–3. A relation R defined over a set S is *transitive* if aRb and bRc imply aRc for all $a, b, c \in S$.

EXAMPLE: Consider the set of complex numbers C. For any $a \in C$, define a_R as the real component and a_I as the imaginary component (that is, $a = a_R + a_I i$). Let $a \leq b$ if and only if $a_R \leq b_R$ and $a_I \leq b_I$. This relation is reflexive, antisymmetric, and transitive.

A *partial ordering* occurs when a relation orders some, but not all, elements of a set. Such a set and relation are often called a *poset*. If the relation imposes an ordering among all elements, it is a *total ordering*.

EXAMPLE: The relation *less than or equal to*, as defined in the usual sense, imposes a total ordering on the set of integers, because, given any two integers, one will be less than or equal to the other. However, the relation in the preceding example imposes a partial ordering on the set C. Specifically, the numbers $1 + 4i$ and $2 + 3i$ are not related under that relation (because $1 \leq 2$ but $4 \leq 3$).

Under a partial ordering (and a total ordering), we define the "upper bound" of two elements to be any element that follows both in the relation.

Definition 27–4. For two elements $a, b \in S$, if there exists a $u \in S$ such that aRu and bRu, then u is an *upper bound* of a and b.

A pair of elements may have many upper bounds. The one "closest" to the two elements is the least upper bound.

Definition 27–5. Let U be the set of upper bounds of a and b. Let $u \in U$ be an element such that there is no $t \in U$ for which tRu. Then u is the *least upper bound* of a and b (written $lub(a, b)$ or $a \otimes b$).

Lower bounds, and greatest lower bounds, are defined similarly.

Definition 27–6. For two elements $a, b \in S$, if there exists an $l \in S$ such that lRa and lRb, then l is a *lower bound* of a and b.

Definition 27–7. Let L be the set of lower bounds of a and b. Let $l \in L$ be an element such that there is no $m \in L$ for which lRm. Then l is the *greatest lower bound* of a and b (written $glb(a, b)$ or $a \oplus b$).

EXAMPLE: Consider the subset of the set of complex numbers for which the real and imaginary parts are integers from 0 to 10, inclusive, and the relation defined in the second example in this chapter. The set of upper bounds for $1 + 9i$ and $9 + 3i$ is $\{ 9 + 9i, 9 + 10i, 10 + 9i, 10 + 10i \}$. The least upper bound of $1 + 9i$ and $9 + 3i$ is $9 + 9i$. The set of lower bounds is $\{ 1 + 1i, 1 + 0i, 0 + 0i \}$. The greatest lower bound is $1 + 1i$.

27.2   Lattices

A *lattice* is the combination of a set of elements S and a relation R meeting the following criteria.

1. R is reflexive, antisymmetric, and transitive on the elements of S.
2. For every $s, t \in S$, there exists a greatest lower bound.
3. For every $s, t \in S$, there exists a least upper bound.

EXAMPLE: The set $\{0, 1, 2\}$ forms a lattice under the relation "less than or equal to" ($\leq$). By the laws of arithmetic, the relation is reflexive, antisymmetric, and transitive. The greatest lower bound of any two integers is the smaller, and the least upper bound is the larger.

EXAMPLE: Consider the subset C' of the set of complex numbers for which the real and imaginary parts are integers from 0 to 10, inclusive. For any $a \in C'$, define a_R as the real component and a_I as the imaginary component (that is, $a = a_R + a_I i$). Let $a \leq b$ if and only if $a_R \leq b_R$ and $a_I \leq b_I$. This set and relation define a lattice, because the relation is reflexive, antisymmetric, and transitive (see the second example of this chapter) and any pair of elements a, b have a least upper bound and a greatest lower bound.

27.3   Exercises

1. Determine the least upper bound and greatest lower bound for the pair of complex integers a and b in the subset C' used in the examples.
2. Prove that the set of all subsets of a given set S (called the *power set* of S) forms a lattice under the relation "subset" ($\subseteq$).
3. Consider a set with elements that are totally ordered by a relation. Does the set form a lattice under that relation? If so, show that it does. If not, give a counterexample.

Chapter 28
The Extended Euclidean Algorithm

The Extended Euclidean Algorithm is a staple of number theory and is used to solve equations of the form $ax \bmod n = b$. This chapter reviews this algorithm and its applications. We begin with the classical algorithm and then extend it to solve simple equations.

28.1   The Euclidean Algorithm

Euclid's algorithm determines the greatest common divisor of two integers. The algorithm is based on the observation that, if x divides both a and b, then x divides their difference $a - b$. The trick is to find the largest such x.

Assume (without loss of generality) that $a > b$. If x divides $a - b$, then it also divides $a - qb$, where q is an integer. Let $r = a - qb$. If $n \neq 0$, and x divides $a - qb$, then x divides r. We have now reduced the problem of finding the largest x such that x divides a and b to the problem of finding the largest x such that x divides b and r. (To see this, realize that if x divides b and r, then x divides $qb + r$, or a.) We iterate until r is 0. Then x is the greatest common divisor of a and b.

If we take q to be the integer portion of a/b, these operations can form a simple table, as follows.

EXAMPLE: Find the greatest common divisor of 15 and 12.

Take $a = 15$ and $b = 12$. Then:

a	b	q	r
15	12	1	3
12	3	4	0

The greatest common divisor of 15 and 12 is 3.

EXAMPLE: Find the greatest common divisor of 35,731 and 24,689.

Take $a = 35{,}731$ and $b = 24{,}689$. Then:

a	b	q	r
35,731	24,689	1	11,042
24,689	11,042	2	2,605
11,042	2,605	4	622
2,605	622	4	117
622	117	5	37
117	37	3	6
37	6	6	1
6	1	6	0

The numbers 35,731 and 24,689 have 1 as the greatest (and only) common factor.

The algorithm (in pseudocode) is as follows.

```
function gcd(a : integer, b : integer) : integer;
var r : integer;
    rprev: integer;
begin
rprev := r := 1;
while r <> 0 do begin
    rprev := r;
    r := a mod b;
    write 'a = ', a, 'b =', b, 'quotient = ', a div b,
        'remainder = ', r, endline;
    a := b;
    b := r;
end;
gcd := rprev;
end.
```

The "write" corresponds to the lines in the tables in the examples above.

28.2   The Extended Euclidean Algorithm

The Extended Euclidean Algorithm determines two integers x and y such that

$$xa + yb = 1$$

In order for these integers to exist and be unique, the greatest common divisor of a and b must be 1. The following algorithm (in pseudocode) returns x and y.

```
    proc eeuclid(a : integer, b : integer,
                    var x : integer, var y : integer) : integer;
    var q, u: integer;
            xprev, yprev, uprev: integer;
            xtmp, ytmp, utmp: integer;
    begin
            uprev := a; u := b;
            xprev := 0; x := 1; yprev := 1; y := 0;
            write 'u = ', uprev, 'x = ', xprev, 'y = ', yprev,
                    endline;
            write 'u = ', u, 'x = ', x, 'y = ', y;
            while u <> 0 do begin
                    q := uprev div u;
                    write 'q = ', q, endline;
                    utmp := uprev - u * q; uprev := u; u := utmp;
                    xtmp := xprev - x * q; xprev := x; x := xtmp;
                    ytmp := yprev - y * q; yprev := y; y := ytmp;
                    write 'u = ', u, 'x = ', x, 'y = ', y;
            end;
            write endline;
            x := xprev; y := yprev;
    end.
```

The "write" corresponds to the lines in the tables in the examples below. The variable u contains $xa + yb$ at each step.

EXAMPLE: Find x and y such that $51x + 100y = 1$.

u	x	y	q
100	0	1	
51	1	0	$100/51 = 1$
49	-1	1	$51/49 = 1$
2	2	-1	$49/2 = 24$
1	-49	25	$2/1 = 2$
0	100	-51	

So, $51 \times (-49) + 100 \times 25 = 1$.

EXAMPLE: Find x and y such that $24{,}689x + 35{,}731y = 1$.

u	r	y	q
35,731	0	1	
24,689	1	0	35,731/24,689 = 1
11,042	−1	1	24,689/11,042 = 2
2,605	3	−2	11,042/2,605 = 4
622	−13	9	2,605/622 = 4
117	55	−38	622/117 = 5
37	−288	199	117/37 = 3
6	919	−635	37/6 = 6
1	−5,802	4,009	
0	35,731	−24,689	

So $24{,}689 \times (-5{,}802) + 35{,}731 \times 4{,}009 = 1$.

28.3   Solving *ax* mod *n* = 1

Recall that if $ax \bmod n = 1$, then there exists an integer k such that $ax = 1 + kn$. Rewriting this, $ax - kn = 1$. Define $j = -k$, to yield $ax + jn = 1$. So, to find x and j, use the Extended Euclidean Algorithm. As before, a and n must be relatively prime.

EXAMPLE: Find x such that $51x \bmod 100 = 1$.
Because $51 \times (-49) + 100 \times 25 = 1$ from the first example in Section 31.2, $x = -49 \bmod 100 = 51$. Checking, $51 \times 51 \bmod 100 = 2{,}601 \bmod 100 = 1$.

EXAMPLE: Find x such that $24{,}689x \bmod 35{,}731 = 1$.
Because $24{,}689 \times (-5{,}802) + 35{,}731 \times 4{,}009 = 1$ from the last example in Section 31.2, $x = -5{,}802 \bmod 35{,}731 = 29{,}929$. Checking, $24{,}689 \times 29{,}929 \bmod 35{,}731 = 738{,}917{,}081 \bmod 35{,}731 = 1$.

28.4   Solving *ax* mod *n* = *b*

From the fundamental laws of modular arithmetic,

$$xy \bmod n = (x \bmod n)(y \bmod n)$$

Thus, if x solves the equation $ax \bmod n = 1$, we can multiply both sides by b to get

$$b(ax \bmod n) = a(bx) \bmod n = b \times 1 = b$$

So, we first solve $ax \bmod n = 1$ for x and then compute $bx \bmod n$.

EXAMPLE: Find x such that $51x \bmod 100 = 10$.
 Solving $51y \bmod 100 = 1$, $y = -49 \bmod 100 = 51$. Then, $x = by \bmod n = 10 \times 51 \bmod 100 = 510 \bmod 100 = 10$.

EXAMPLE: Find x such that $24{,}689x \bmod 35{,}731 = 1{,}753$.
 Solving $24{,}689y \bmod 35{,}731 = 1$, $y = -5{,}802 \bmod 35{,}731 = 29{,}929$. Then, $x = by \bmod n = 1{,}753 \times 29{,}929 \bmod 35{,}731 = 52{,}465{,}537 \bmod 35{,}731 = 12{,}429$.

28.5   Exercises

1. Find the greatest common divisor of 234 and 124.
2. Find r and s such that $8{,}092r + 1{,}111s = 1$.
3. Find a counterexample to the claim that if the greatest common divisor of a and b is not 1, there exists a unique r and a unique s such that $ra + sb = 1$.
4. Solve for x: $324x \bmod 121 = 1$.
5. Solve for x: $99{,}997x \bmod 8{,}888 = 1{,}234$.

Chapter 29
Virtual Machines

Virtual memory provides the illusion of physical memory. The abstraction allows a process to assume that its memory space both is contiguous and begins at location 0. This simplifies the process' view of memory and hides the underlying physical locations of the process' memory. The physical memory corresponding to the virtual memory need not be contiguous. Indeed, some of the locations in virtual memory may have no corresponding physical addresses until the process references them.

Like virtual memory, a virtual machine provides the illusion of a physical machine. The abstraction allows operating systems to assume that they are running directly on the hardware. This allows one to run the operating system, and allows the operating system to run processes, with no changes in either the operating system or the programs. A second, lower "virtual machine monitor" runs directly on the hardware and provides the illusion of hardware to the operating systems run above it. The physical machine may support many virtual machines, each running its own operating system.

This chapter reviews the structure of a virtual machine.

29.1   Virtual Machine Structure

A virtual machine runs on a virtual machine monitor. That monitor virtualizes the resources of the underlying system and presents to each virtual machine the illusion that it and it alone is using the hardware.

EXAMPLE: IBM's VM/370 and its successors provide each user with the illusion that she has complete access to the resources of a single IBM mainframe system. Many users will use the same physical machine, but each one is isolated from the others. (See Figure 29–1.)

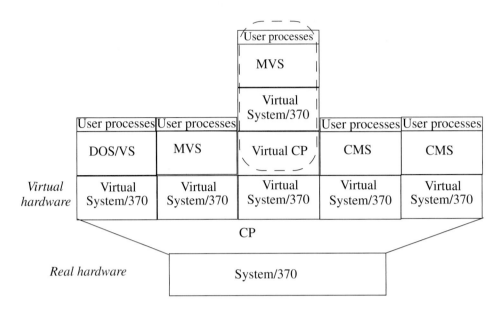

Figure 29–1   A virtual machine environment, with five virtual machines each running a different operating system. The control program (CP) manages their interactions with the physical resources. The middle virtual machine is running a virtual system within a virtual system. (Adapted from [266], pages 606 and 607.)

29.2   Virtual Machine Monitor

The virtual machine monitor runs at the highest level of privilege. It keeps track of the state of each virtual machine just as an ordinary operating system keeps track of the states of its processes. When a privileged instruction is executed, the hardware causes a trap to the virtual machine monitor. The monitor services the interrupt and restores the state of the caller.

EXAMPLE: Suppose the virtual machine monitor VMM is running the operating system OS. Process p running under OS makes a system call to read data from a disk. The system call causes a trap. The VMM is invoked and detects that the trap occurred from within OS. It updates the state of OS to make it appear that the hardware on which OS is running (the virtual machine) invoked OS. OS then tries to read from the disk to service the interrupt. This causes another trap, and the VMM is again invoked. It services the trap by carrying out the read and placing the results in the locations that OS indicates. It then returns control to OS, which updates the appropriate parts of process p (such as the return value of the system call). OS then performs a context switch to return control to *p*. This is a privileged instruction, so VMM is again invoked. It updates the virtual machine on which OS runs to make it appear that OS performed the context switch, and then performs the context switch itself. The process *p* now resumes execution.

29.2.1   Privilege and Virtual Machines

The Digital Equipment Corporation VAX/VMM project examined the issues of privilege in virtual machines [498]. Consider the requirements for a computer architecture to be virtualizable [723].

> **Definition 29–1.** A *sensitive instruction* is an instruction that discloses or alters the state of privilege of the processor. A *sensitive data structure* is a data structure that contains information about the state of privilege of the system.

EXAMPLE: The VAX architecture has four levels of privilege: user, supervisor, executive, and kernel. On the VAX architecture, the CHMK instruction is privileged because it changes the privilege level (to kernel mode), and the MOVPSL instruction copies the processor status longword (PSL) to a memory location. The former instruction is a sensitive instruction because it alters the state of privilege (moving it to kernel mode). The latter is also sensitive because it reveals information about the current level of privilege (the level of privilege is encoded in two bits in the PSL).

Page table entries are sensitive data structures because they contain information about the protection state of the processor (notably, they can contain a copy of the PSL for the process).

A computer architecture is virtualizable if it meets the following requirements.

1. All sensitive instructions cause traps when executed by processes at lower levels of privilege.
2. All references to sensitive data structures cause traps when executed by processes at lower levels of privilege.

EXAMPLE: The CHMK instruction meets requirement 1, because it causes a trap unless it is executed in kernel mode. The MOVPSL instruction meets neither requirement, because it does not cause a trap regardless of the level of privilege of the process executing it. User level processes can alter page table entries, so references to those data structures also fail to meet the second requirement (but see Exercise 1).

If the hardware supports *n* levels of privilege, each virtual machine must appear to support *n* levels of privilege. However, only the virtual machine monitor can run at the highest level of privilege. This makes *n* − 1 levels of privilege available to each virtual machine. The virtual machine monitor virtualizes the levels of privilege. This technique is called *ring compression*.

EXAMPLE: Recall that the VAX system has four levels of privilege: user, supervisor, executive, and kernel. The VMM monitor must emulate all of these levels for each virtual machine that it runs. However, it cannot allow the operating system of any of those virtual machines to enter kernel mode, because then that operating system could access the physical resources directly, bypassing the virtual machine monitor. Yet to run the VAX standard operating system, VAX/VMS, the virtual machine must appear to provide all four levels.

The solution is to virtualize the executive and kernel privilege levels. The executive and kernel levels of the virtual machine (called *VM executive* and *VM kernel* levels, respectively) are mapped into the physical executive mode. The architects of VAX/VMM added three extensions to the VAX hardware to support this compression.

First, a *virtual machine* bit was added to the PSL. If this bit is set, the current process is running on a virtual machine. Second, a special register, the VMPSL register, records the PSL of the running virtual machine. Third, all sensitive instructions that could reveal the level of privilege either obtain their information from the VMPSL or cause a trap to the virtual machine monitor. In the latter case, the virtual machine monitor emulates the instruction.

One interesting approach to privilege is to divide users into different classes and control access to the system by limiting the access of each class.

EXAMPLE: The IBM VM/370 uses this approach to associate various CP commands with users [266]. Each CP command is associated with one or more *user privilege classes*. For example, class G is the "general user" class. Members of that class can start a virtual machine. Class A is the "primary system operator" class. Members of that class can control system accounting, the availability of virtual machines, and other system resources. Members of class "Any" can gain access to, or surrender access to, a virtual machine.

29.2.2   Physical Resources and Virtual Machines

The virtual machine monitor manages the physical resources by distributing them among the virtual machines as appropriate. Each virtual machine therefore appears to have a reduced amount of resources. For example, if the control program is to allocate space on a single disk for ten virtual machines, it will divide the disk into ten *minidisks*. Each virtual machine will have access to a different portion of the physical disk. The size of each minidisk is less than the size of the actual disk (although the sizes of the ten minidisks may differ). The virtual machine monitor handles the mapping from the minidisk address (presented to it by the virtual machine) and the physical disk.

EXAMPLE: When a virtual machine's operating system tries to write to a disk, the I/O instruction is privileged and causes a trap to the virtual machine monitor. The virtual machine monitor translates the addresses to be accessed (read from or written to), verifies that the I/O references disk space allocated to that virtual machine, and services the request. It returns control to the virtual machine when the request is satisfied (completed for synchronous I/O, begun for asynchronous I/O).

29.2.3   Paging and Virtual Machines

On an ordinary machine, paging occurs at the highest level of privilege. When a virtual machine attempts to page, it does so from the virtual machine's level of privilege. The attempt to read from, or write to, the disk causes a trap to the virtual machine monitor. At that point, the request is handled as any other request for I/O. However, two problems unique to virtual machines arise.

First, because of the way some operating systems are designed, some pages may be accessible only to processes running at the highest level of privilege, but the virtual machine operating systems run at a lower level of privilege. The virtual machine must change the protection level of these pages to the appropriate level of privilege.

EXAMPLE: On the VAX/VMS system, only kernel level processes can read some pages. Hence, the virtual machine monitor on the VAX/VMM system must ensure that executive level processes on a virtual machine cannot read the pages for kernel level processes on that virtual machine. This is necessary because the kernel level processes on the virtual machine are actually running at the VM kernel level, which is in the physical executive level of privilege.

In theory, reducing the level of protection for these pages poses a security risk (because processes at the VM executive level could then access the pages). In practice, the VMS system allows processes in executive mode to change to kernel mode freely. Hence, there is no loss of security. But if the process running at the VM executive level should attempt to access one of these pages, the access would be allowed. Were the VAX/VMS system running directly on the hardware and not under a virtual machine, the access would be denied. Hence, there is a loss of reliability.

The second problem is performance. The virtual machine monitor paging its own data or instructions is transparent to the virtual machines. If the virtual machines attempt to page, the virtual machine monitor must handle the request as described above. If the virtual machine operating system pages heavily, this indirection may cause significant delays.

EXAMPLE: IBM's VM/370 provides support for several different operating systems. OS/MFT and OS/MVT are designed to access storage on disk. If the jobs being run under those systems depend on timings, the delays caused by the virtual machine may affect the success of the jobs. With a system that supports virtual storage, such as MVS, either MVS or CP (the virtual machine monitor) may cause paging. Again, if timings are important, the delays could cause failure of a process that would not fail were there no intermediate CP.

29.3   Exercises

1. The second example in Section 29.2.1 states that "user level processes can alter page table entries, so references to those data structures also fail to meet the second requirement." How can an operating system prevent a user level process from altering its page table entries?

2. Suppose a virtual machine monitor (call it VMM-1) is running another virtual machine monitor (VMM-2), which in turn is running a version of the Linux operating system. The user running the Linux system is editing a file. The user requests that the editor write the file to disk.

    a. Is the instruction RFT (Return From Trap) sensitive? Why or why not?

    b. Trace the flow of control among VMM-1, VMM-2, Linux, and the editor.

    c. How many RFT instructions will be executed? Justify your answer.

Bibliography

1. M. Abadi, "Explicit Communication Revisited: Two New Attacks on Authentication Protocols," *IEEE Transactions on Software Engineering* **23** (3), pp. 185–186 (Mar. 1997).

2. M. Abadi and R. Needham, "Prudent Engineering Practice for Cryptographic Protocols," *Proceedings of the 1994 IEEE Symposium on Research in Security and Privacy*, pp. 122–136 (May 1994).

3. R. Abbott, J. Chin, J. Donnelley, W. Konigsford, S. Tokubo, and D. Webb, "Security Analysis and Enhancements of Computer Operating Systems," Technical Report NBSIR 76–1041, ICET, National Bureau of Standards, Washington, DC 20234 (Apr. 1976).

4. M. Abrams and D. Bailey, "Abstraction and Refinement of Layered Security Policy," in *Information Security: An Integrated Collection of Essays* [6], pp. 126–136.

5. M. Abrams and P. Brusil, "Application of the Common Criteria to a System: A Real-World Example," *Computer Security Journal* **16** (2), pp. 11–21 (Spring 2000).

6. M. Abrams, S. Jajodia, and H. Podell (eds.), *Information Security: An Integrated Collection of Essays*, IEEE Computer Society Press, Los Alamitos, CA (1975).

7. C. Adams and S. Lloyd, *Understanding the Public-Key Infrastructure*, Macmillan, New York, NY (1999).

8. E. Adams and S. Muchnick, "Dbxtool: A Window-Based Symbolic Debugger for Sun Workstations," *Software—Practice and Experience* **16** (7), pp. 653–669 (July 1986).

9. L. Adleman, "An Abstract Theory of Computer Viruses," *Advances in Cryptology—Proceedings of CRYPTO '88* (1988).

10. L. Adleman, C. Pomerance, and R. Rumley, "On Distinguishing Prime Numbers from Composite Numbers," *Annals of Mathematics* **117** (1), pp. 173–206 (1983).

11. Adobe Systems, Inc., *PostScript Language Reference*, 3rd Edition, Addison-Wesley, Reading, MA (1999).

12. G. Agnew, "Random Sources for Cryptographic Systems," *Advances in Cryptology—Proceedings of EUROCRYPT '87*, pp. 77–81 (1988).

13. Aleph One, "Smashing the Stack," *PHRACK* **7** (49), File 14 (1998).

14. S. Alexander and R. Droms, *DHCP Options and BOOTP Vendor Extensions*, RFC 2132 (Mar. 1997).

15. J. Allen, *The CERT® Guide to System and Network Security Practices*, Addison-Wesley, Boston, MA (2001).

16. J. Alves-Foss, D. Frincke, and G. Saghi, "Applying the TCSEC Guidelines to a Real-Time Embedded System Environment," *Proceedings of the 19th National Information Systems Security Conference*, pp. 89–97 (Oct. 1996).

17. P. Ammann and P. Black, "A Specification-Based Coverage Metric to Evaluate Test Sets," *Proceedings of the 4th IEEE International Symposium on High-Assurance Systems Engineering*, pp. 239–248 (Nov. 1999).

18. P. Ammann and R. Sandhu, "Expressive Power of the Schematic Protection Model (Extended Abstract)," *Proceedings of the Computer Security Foundations Workshop*, MITRE Technical Report M88-37, MITRE Corporation, Bedford, MA, pp. 188–193 (June 1988).

19. P. Ammann and R. Sandhu, "The Extended Schematic Protection Model," *Journal of Computer Security* **1** (3, 4), pp. 335–385 (1992).

20. P. Ammann, R. Sandhu, and R. Lipton, "The Expressive Power of Multi-Parent Creation in Monotonic Access Control Models," *Journal of Computer Security* **4** (2, 3), pp. 149–166 (Dec. 1996).

21. E. Amoroso, *Intrusion Detection*, Intrusion.net Books, Sparta, NJ (1999).

22. E. Amoroso, T. Nguyen, J. Weiss, J. Watson, P. Lapiska, and T. Starr, "Towards an Approach to Measuring Software Trust," *Proceedings of the 1991 IEEE Symposium on Research in Security and Privacy*, pp. 198–218 (May 1991).

23. R. Anand, N. Islam, T. Jaeger, and J. Rao, "A Flexible Security Model for Using Internet Content," *Proceedings of the 16th Symposium on Reliable Distributed Systems*, pp. 89–96 (Oct. 1997).

24. J. Anderson, "Information Security in a Multi-User Computer Environment," in Morris Rubinoff (ed.), *Advances in Computers* **12**, Academic Press, New York, NY (1972).

25. J. Anderson, "Computer Security Technology Planning Study," Technical Report ESD-TR-73–51, Electronic Systems Division, Hanscom Air Force Base, Hanscom, MA (1974).

26. J. Anderson, "Computer Security Threat Monitoring and Surveillance," James P. Anderson Co., Fort Washington, PA (1980).

27. J. Anderson, "On the Feasibility of Connecting RECON to an External Network," James P. Anderson Co., Fort Washington, PA (1981).

28. R. Anderson, "UEPS—A Second Generation Electronic Wallet," *Proceedings of the 2nd European Symposium on Research in Computer Security,* pp. 411–418 (Nov. 1992).

29. R. Anderson, "A Security Policy Model for Clinical Information Systems," *Proceedings of the 1996 IEEE Symposium on Security and Privacy,* pp. 34–48 (May 1996).

30. R. Anderson and A. Johnston, *UNIX® Unleashed*, 4th Edition, SAMS Publishing, Indianapolis, IN (2002).

31. R. Anderson and R. Needham, "Robustness Principles for Public Key Protocols," *Advances in Cryptology—Proceedings of CRYPTO '95,* pp. 236–247 (1995).

32. N. Andrews, "A Standard for Assuring/Monitoring Telephony Switching Real Time Performance," *Proceedings of the 1990 IEEE Global Telecommunications Conference and Exhibition*, pp. 237–240 (Dec. 1990).

33. G. Andrews and R. Reitman, "An Axiomatic Approach to Information Flow in Parallel Programs," *ACM Transactions on Programming Languages* **2** (1), pp. 56–76 (Jan. 1980).

34. A. Appel and A. Felty, "A Semantic Model of Types and Machine Instructions for Proof-Carrying Code," *Proceedings of the 27th ACM SIGPLAN-SIGACT Symposium on Principles of Programming Languages,* pp. 243–253 (Jan. 2000).

35. J. Arnold, "Analysis Requirements for Low Assurance Evaluations," *Proceedings of the 18th National Information Systems Security Conference*, pp. 356–365 (Oct. 1995).

36. N. Arnold, *UNIX Security: A Practical Tutorial*, McGraw-Hill, New York, NY (1993).

37. A. Arsenault and R. Housley, "Protection Profiles for Certificate Issuing and Management Systems," *Proceedings of the 22nd National Information Systems Security Conference*, pp. 189–199 (Oct. 1999).

38. J. Ashworth, *The Naming of Hosts*, RFC 2100 (Apr. 1997).

39. T. Aslam, "A Taxonomy of Security Faults in the UNIX Operating System," Master's Thesis, Department of Computer Sciences, Purdue University, West Lafayette, IN (1995).

40. T. Aslam, I. Krsul, and E. H. Spafford, "Use of a Taxonomy of Security Faults," *Proceedings of the 19th National Information Systems Security Conference*, pp. 551–560 (Oct. 1996).

41. C. Asmuth and J. Bloom, "A Modular Approach to Key Safeguarding," *IEEE Transactions on Information Theory* **29** (2), pp. 208–210 (Mar. 1983).

42. V. Atluri, E. Betino, and S. Jajodia, "Achieving Stricter Correctness Requirements in Multilevel Secure Databases," *Proceedings of the 1993 Symposium on Research in Security and Privacy*, pp. 135–147 (May 1993).

43. C. Augier, "Excel-lent Leaks," *Risks Digest* **21** (39) (May 2001).

44. A. Avižienis, "The N-Version Approach to Fault-Tolerant Software," *IEEE Transactions on Software Engineering* **11** (12), pp. 1491–1501 (Dec. 1985).

45. S. Axelsson, "The Base-Rate Fallacy and the Difficulty of Intrusion Detection," *ACM Transactions on Information and System Security* **3** (3), pp. 186–205 (Aug. 2000).

46. A. Bacard, *The Computer Privacy Handbook*, Peachpit Press, Berkeley, CA (1995).

47. A. Bacard, "Anonymous Remailer FAQ" (Nov. 1999); available at http://www.andrebacard.com/remail.html.

48. R. Bace, *Intrusion Detection*, Macmillan Technical Publishing, Indianapolis, IN (2000).

49. L. Badger, "Information Security: From Reference Monitors to Wrappers," *IEEE Aerospace and Electronic Systems Magazine* **13** (3), pp. 32–34 (Mar. 1998).

50. L. Badger, D. Sterne, D. Sherman, and K. Walker, "A Domain and Type Enforcement UNIX Prototype," *Computing Systems* **9** (1), pp. 47–83 (Winter 1996).

51. D. Bailey, "A Philosophy of Security Management," in *Information Security: An Integrated Collection of Essays* [6], pp. 98–110.

52. J. Balasubramaniyan, J. Garcia-Fernandez, D. Isacoff, E. Spafford, and D. Zamboni, "An Architecture for Intrusion Detection Using Autonomous Agents," *Proceedings of the 14th Annual Computer Security Applications Conference*, pp. 13–24 (Dec. 1998).

53. D. Balenson and T. Markham, "ISAKMP Key Recovery Extensions," *Computers and Security* **19** (1), pp. 91–99 (Jan./Feb. 2000).

54. D. Balfanz and D. Simon, "WindowBox: A Simple Security Model for the Connected Desktop," *Proceedings of the 4th USENIX Windows Systems Symposium* (Aug. 2000).

55. M. Banks, *Web Psychos, Stalkers, and Pranksters: How to Protect Yourself in Cyberspace*, The Coriolis Group (1997).

56. D. Banning, G. Ellingwood, C. Franklin, C. Muckenhirn, and D. Price, "Auditing of Distributed Systems," *Proceedings of the 14th National Computer Security Conference*, pp. 59–68 (Oct. 1991).

57. D. Barrett, *Bandits on the Information Superhighway (What You Need to Know)*, O'Reilly and Associates (1996).

58. J. Bartlett, *Familiar Quotations*, Little, Brown and Co., Boston, MA (1901).

59. B. Bayh, "Unclassified Summary: Involvement of NSA in the Development of the Data Encryption Standard (United States Senate Select Committee on Intelligence)," *IEEE Communications Society Magazine* **16** (6), pp. 53–55 (1978).

60. D. Bell, "Concerning 'Modeling' of Computer Security," *Proceedings of the 1988 IEEE Symposium on Security and Privacy*, pp. 8–13 (Apr. 1988).

61. P. Barker and S. Kille, *The COSINE and Internet X.500 Schema*, RFC 1274 (Nov. 1991).

62. H. Beker and F. Piper, *Cipher Systems: The Protection of Communications*, Northwood Books, London, UK (1982).

63. D. Bell and L. LaPadula, "Secure Computer Systems: Mathematical Foundations," Technical Report MTR-2547, Vol. I, MITRE Corporation, Bedford, MA (Mar. 1973).

64. D. Bell and L. LaPadula, "Secure Computer System: Unified Exposition and Multics Interpretation," Technical Report MTR-2997 Rev. 1, MITRE Corporation, Bedford, MA (Mar. 1975).

65. M. Bellare, R. Canetti, and H. Krawczyk, "Keyed Hash Functions and Message Authentication," *Advances in Cryptology—Proceedings of CRYPTO '96*, pp. 1–15 (1996).

66. M. Bellare and S. Micali, "Non-Interactive Oblivious Transfer and Applications," *Advances in Cryptology—Proceedings of CRYPTO '89*, pp. 547–559 (1989).

67. M. Bellare and R. Rivest, "Translucent Cryptography—An Alternative to Key Escrow, and Its Implementation via Fractional Oblivious Transfer," *Journal of Cryptology* **12** (2), pp. 117–139 (Spring 1999).

68. S. Bellovin, "Security Problems in the TCP/IP Protocol Suite," *Computer Communication Review* **19** (2), pp. 32–48 (Apr. 1989).

69. S. Bellovin, "Using the Domain Name System for System Break-Ins," *Proceedings of the 5th USENIX UNIX Security Symposium*, pp. 199–208 (June 1995).

70. S. Bellovin, "Probable Plaintext Cryptanalysis of the IP Security Protocols," *Proceedings of the 1997 Symposium on Network and Distributed System Security*, pp. 52–59 (Feb. 1997).

71. S. Bellovin and W. Cheswick, *Firewalls and Internet Security: Repelling the Wily Hacker*, Addison-Wesley, Reading, MA (1994).

72. S. Bellovin and M. Merritt, "Limitations of the Kerberos Protocol," *Proceedings of the 1991 Winter USENIX Conference*, pp. 253–267 (Jan. 1991).

73. S. Bellovin and M. Merritt, "Encrypted Key Exchange: Password-Based Protocols Secure Against Dictionary Attacks," *Proceedings of the 1992 IEEE Symposium on Research in Security and Privacy*, pp. 74–82 (May 1992).

74. F. Belvin, D. Bodeau, and S. Razvi, "Design Analysis in Evaluations Against the TCSEC C2 Criteria," *Proceedings of the 19th National Information Systems Security Conference*, pp. 67–75 (Oct. 1996).

75. J. Bennett, "Analysis of the Encryption in Word Perfect," *Cryptologia* **11** (4), pp. 206–210 (Oct. 1987).

76. F. Bergadano, B. Crispo, and G. Ruffo, "Proactive Password Checking with Decision Trees," *Proceedings of the 4th ACM Conference on Computer and Communications Security*, pp. 67–77 (Nov. 1998).

77. F. Bergadano, B. Crispo, and G. Ruffo, "High Dictionary Compression for Proactive Password Checking," *ACM Transactions on Information and System Security* **1** (1), pp. 3–25 (Apr. 1997).

78. H. Bergen and W. Caelli, "File Security in WordPerfect 5.0," *Cryptologia* **15** (1), pp. 57–66 (Jan. 1991).

79. A. Bernstein, "Analysis of Programs for Parallel Processing," *IEEE Transactions on Computers* **15** (5), pp. 757–762 (Oct. 1966).

80. C. Bernstein and B. Woodward, *All the President's Men*, Simon and Schuster, New York, NY (1974).

81. C. Bernstein and B. Woodward, *The Final Days*, Simon and Schuster, New York, NY (1976).

82. D. Bernstein and E. Schenk, "Syncookies Mailing List Archive" (Oct. 1996); available at http://cr.yp.to/syncookies.html.

83. B. Bershad and C. Pinkerton, "Watchdogs: Extending the UNIX File System," *Proceedings of the 1988 Winter USENIX Conference*, pp. 267–276 (Feb. 1988).

84. B. Bershad, S. Savage, P. Pardyak, E. Sirer, D. Becker, M. Fiuczynski, C. Chambers, and S. Eggers, "Extensibility, Safety, and Performance in the SPIN Operating System," *Proceedings of the 15th Symposium on Operating Systems Principles*, pp. 267–284 (Dec. 1995).

85. V. Berzins, *Software Engineering with Abstractions*, Addison-Wesley, Reading, MA (1991).

86. T. Beth, H.-J. Knobloch, M. Otten, G. Simmons, and P. Wichmann, "Towards Acceptable Key Escrow Systems," *Proceedings of the 2nd ACM Conference on Computer and Communications Security*, pp. 51–58 (Nov. 1994).

87. R. Bharadwaj and C. Heitmeyer, "Developing High Assurance Avionics Systems with the SCR Requirements Method," *Proceedings of the 19th Digital Avionics Systems Conference*, pp. 1D1/1–8 (Oct. 2000).

88. K. Biba, "Integrity Considerations for Secure Computer Systems," Technical Report MTR-3153, MITRE Corporation, Bedford, MA (Apr. 1977).

89. E. Biham and A. Shamir, "Differential Cryptanalysis of Snefru, Khafre, REDOC-II, LOKI, and Lucifer," *Advances in Cryptology—Proceedings of CRYPTO '91*, pp. 156–171 (Aug. 1991).

90. E. Biham and A. Shamir, "Differential Cryptanalysis of DES-Like Cryptosystems," *Journal of Cryptology* **4** (1), pp. 3–72 (1991).

91. E. Biham and A. Shamir, "Differential Cryptanalysis of the Full 16-Round DES," *Advances in Cryptology—Proceedings of CRYPTO '92*, pp. 487–496 (1992).

92. E. Biham and A. Shamir, *Differential Cryptanalysis of the Data Encryption Standard*, Springer-Verlag, New York, NY (1993).

93. E. Bina, R. McCool, V. Jones, and M. Winslett, "Secure Access to Data Over the Internet," *Proceedings of the 3rd International Conference on Parallel and Distributed Information Systems*, pp. 99–102 (Sep. 1984).

94. R. Biro, F. van Kempen, M. Evans, C. Minyard, F. La Roche, C. Hedrick, L. Torvalds, A. Cox, M. Dillon, A. Gulbrandsen, and J. Cwik, *Linux Kernel 2.4.9 Networking Source Code*, directory linux/net/ipv4 (Aug. 2001).

95. R. Bisbey II and D. Hollingworth, "Protection Analysis: Final Report," Technical Report ISI/SR-78–13, University of Southern California Information Sciences Institute, Marina Del Rey, CA (May 1978).

96. M. Bishop, "Security Problems with the UNIX Operating System" (unpublished) (Jan. 1981).

97. M. Bishop, "Sendmail Wizardry," Research Memo 86.3, Research Institute for Advanced Computer Science, NASA Ames Research Center, Moffett Field, CA (Jan. 1986).

98. M. Bishop, "The RIACS Intelligent Auditing and Checking System," Technical Report 86.3, Research Institute for Advanced Computer Science, NASA Ames Research Center, Moffett Field, CA (June 1986).

99. M. Bishop, "Analyzing the Security of an Existing Computer System," *Proceedings of the 1986 Fall Joint Computer Conference*, pp. 1115–1119 (Nov. 1986).

100. M. Bishop, "How to Write a Setuid Program," *;login:* **12** (1), pp. 5–11 (Jan. 1987).

101. M. Bishop, "Profiling Under UNIX by Patching," *Software—Practice and Experience* **17** (10), pp. 729–739 (Oct. 1987).

102. M. Bishop, "An Application of a Fast Data Encryption Standard Implementation," *Computing Systems* **1** (3), pp. 221–254 (Summer 1988).

103. M. Bishop, "Auditing Files on a Network of UNIX Machines," *Proceedings of the USENIX UNIX Security Workshop*, pp. 51–52 (Aug. 1988).

104. M. Bishop, "Collaboration Using Roles," *Software—Practice and Experience* **20** (5), pp. 485–497 (May 1990).

105. M. Bishop, "A Security Analysis of the NTP Protocol Version 2," *Proceedings of the 6th Annual Computer Security Applications Conference*, pp. 20–29 (Dec. 1990).

106. M. Bishop, "Password Management," *Proceedings of COMPCON '91*, pp. 167–169 (Feb. 1991).

107. M. Bishop, "A Proactive Password Checker," in *Information Security*, D. T. Lindsay and W. L. Price (eds.), North-Holland, New York, NY, pp. 169–180 (May 1991).

108. M. Bishop, "Anatomy of a Proactive Password Changer," *Proceedings of the 3rd USENIX Security Symposium*, pp. 171–184 (Sep. 1992).

109. M. Bishop and D. Bailey, "A Critical Analysis of Vulnerability Taxonomies," Technical Report CSE-96–11, Department of Computer Science, University of California, Davis, CA (Sep. 1996).

110. M. Bishop and M. Dilger, "Checking for Race Conditions in File Accesses," *Computing Systems* **9** (2), pp. 131–152 (Spring 1996).

111. M. Bishop and D. Klein, "Improving System Security via Proactive Password Checking," *Computers and Security* **14** (3), pp. 233–249 (Apr. 1995).

112. J. Biskup, "Some Variants of the Take-Grant Protection Model," *Information Processing Letters* **19** (3), pp. 151–156 (Mar. 1984).

113. J. Biskup and U. Flegel, "Transaction-Based Pseudonyms in Audit Data for Privacy Respecting Intrusion Detection," *Proceedings of the 3rd International Workshop on Recent Advances in Intrusion Detection*, pp. 28–48 (Oct. 2000).

114. G. Blakley, "Safeguarding Cryptographic Keys," *1979 National Computer Conference, AFIPS Conference Proceedings* **48**, pp. 313–317 (Nov. 1979).

115. G. Blakley, "One-Time Pads are Key Safeguarding Schemes, Not Cryptosystems: Fast Key Safeguarding Schemes (Threshold Schemes) Exist," *Proceedings of the 1980 IEEE Symposium on Security and Privacy*, pp. 108–113 (Apr. 1980).

116. M. Blaze, "Protocol Failure in the Escrowed Encryption Standard," *Proceedings of the 2nd ACM Conference on Computer and Communications Security*, pp. 59–67 (Nov. 1994).

117. W. Boebert, "On the Inability of an Unmodified Capability Machine to Enforce the *-Property," *Proceedings of the 7th DOD/NBS Computer Security Conference*, pp. 291–293 (Sep. 1984).

118. W. Boebert and C. Ferguson, "A Partial Solution to the Discretionary Trojan Horse Problem," *Proceedings of the 8th National Computer Security Conference*, pp. 245–253 (Sep. 1985).

119. W. Boebert and R. Kain, "A Practical Alternative to Hierarchical Integrity Policies," *Proceedings of the 8th National Computer Security Conference*, p. 18 (Oct. 1985).

120. W. Boebert, W. Young, R. Kain, and S. Hansohn, "Secure Ada Target: Issues, System Design, and Verification," *Proceedings of the 1985 IEEE Symposium on Security and Privacy*, pp. 176–183 (Apr. 1985).

121. D. Bolignano, D. Le Metayer, and C. Loiseaux, "Formal Methods in Context: Security and Java Card," *Proceedings of the 1st International Workshop on Java on Smart Cards: Programming and Security*, pp. 1–5 (Sep. 2000).

122. J.-P. Boly, A. Bosselaers, R. Cramer, R. Michelsen, S. Mjølsnes, F. Muller, T. Pedersen, B. Pfitzmann, P. De Rooji, B. Schoenmakers, M. Schunter, L. Vallee, and M. Waidner, "The ESPRIT Project CAFE—High Security Digital Payment Systems," *Proceedings of the 3rd European Symposium on Research in Computer Security*, pp. 217–229 (Nov. 1994).

123. A. Bomberger, A. Frantz, W. Frantz, A. Hardy, N. Hardy, C. Landau, and J. Shapiro, "The KeyKOS Nanokernel Architecture," *Proceedings of the USENIX Workshop on Micro-Kernels and Other Kernel Architectures*, pp. 95–112 (Apr. 1992).

124. D. Bonyun, "The Role of a Well-Defined Auditing Process in the Enforcement of Privacy Policy and Data Security," *Proceedings of the 1981 IEEE Symposium on Security and Privacy*, pp. 19–26 (1981).

125. D. Bonyun, "The Use of Architectural Principles in the Design of Certifiably Secure Systems," *Computers and Security* **2** (2), pp. 153–162 (June 1983).

126. A. Borrett, "A Perspective of Evaluation in the UK Versus the US," *Proceedings of the 18th National Information Systems Security Conference*, pp. 322–334 (Oct. 1995).

127. R. Bowen, K. Coar, and M. Marlowe, *Apache Server Unleashed*, SAMS Publishing, Indianapolis, IN (2000).

128. J. Boyer, "Inferring Sequences Produced by Pseudo-Random Number Generators," *Journal of the ACM* **36** (1), pp. 129–141 (Jan. 1989).

129. J. Boyer, "Inferring Sequences Produced by a Linear Congruential Generator Missing Low-Order Bits," *Journal of Cryptology* **1** (3), pp. 177–184 (1989).

130. K. Brady, "Integrating B2 Security into a UNIX System," *Proceedings of the 14th National Computer Security Conference*, pp. 338–346 (Oct. 1991).

131. S. Brands, "Electronic Cash on the Internet," *Proceedings of the 1995 Symposium on Network and Distributed System Security*, pp. 64–84 (Feb. 1995).

132. C. Braun, *UNIX™ System Security Essentials*, Addison-Wesley, Reading, MA (1995).

133. D. Brewer and M. Nash, "The Chinese Wall Security Policy," *Proceedings of the 1989 IEEE Symposium on Security and Privacy*, pp. 206–214 (May 1989).

134. E. Brickell and D. Stinson, "The Detection of Cheaters in Threshold Schemes," *Advances in Cryptology—Proceedings of CRYPTO '88* pp. 564–577 (Aug. 1988).

135. P. Brinch Hansen, *Operating System Principles*, Prentice-Hall, Englewood Cliffs, NJ (1973).

136. F. Brooks, *The Mythical Man-Month: Essays on Software Engineering*, Anniversary Edition, Addison-Wesley, Reading, MA (1995).

137. L. Brown, J. Pieprzyk, and J. Seberry, "LOKI: A Cryptographic Primitive for Authentication and Secrecy Applications," *Advances in Cryptology—Proceedings of AUSCRYPT '90*, pp. 229–236 (Jan. 1990).

138. L. Brown, M. Kwan, J. Pieprzyk, and J. Seberry, "Improving Resistance to Differential Cryptanalysis and the Redesign of LOKI," *Advances in Cryptology—Proceedings of ASIACRYPT '91*, pp. 36–50 (1991).

139. M. Brown and S. Rodgers, "User Identification via Keystroke Characteristics of Typed Names Using Neural Networks," *International Journal of Man-Machine Studies* **39** (6), pp. 999–1014 (1993).

140. R. Browne, "Mode Security: An Infrastructure for Covert Channel Suppression," *Proceedings of the 1994 Symposium on Research In Privacy and Security*, pp. 39–45 (May 1994).

141. T. Budd, "Safety in Grammatical Protection Systems," *International Journal of Computer and Information Sciences* **12** (6), pp. 413–431 (1983).

142. M. Burgess, "A Site Configuration Engine," *Computing Systems* **8** (1), pp. 309–324 (Winter 1995).

143. M. Burgess, "Automated System Administration with Feedback Regulation," *Software—Practice and Experience* **28** (14), pp. 1519–1530 (Dec. 1998).

144. M. Burgess, "Theoretical System Administration," *Proceedings of the 14th Systems Administration Conference (LISA 2000)*, pp. 1–13 (Dec. 2000).

145. M. Burmester, Y. Desmedt, and J. Seberry, "Equitable Key Escrow with Limited Time Span (Or, How to Enforce Time Expiration Cryptographically)," *Advances in Cryptology—Proceedings of ASIACRYPT '98*, pp. 380–391 (Oct. 1998).

146. M. Burrows, M. Abadi, and R. Needham, "A Logic of Authentication," *ACM Transactions on Computer Systems* **8** (1), pp. 18–36 (Feb. 1990).

147. J. Burton, *The Pentagon Wars: Reformers Challenge the Old Guard*, Naval Institute Press, Annapolis, MD (1993).

148. W. Caelli and A. Rhodes, "An Evaluation of HP-UX (UNIX) for Database Protection Using the European ITSEC," *Computers and Security* **11** (5), pp. 463–479 (Sep. 1992).

149. B. Callaghan, B. Pawlowski, and P. Staubach, *NFS Version 3 Protocol Specification*, RFC 1813 (June 1995).

150. J. Callas, L. Donnerhacke, H. Finney, and R. Thayer, *OpenPGP Message Format*, RFC 2440 (Nov. 1998).

151. J. Campbell, Jr., "Speaker Recognition: A Tutorial," *Proceedings of the IEEE* **85** (9), pp. 1437–1462 (Sep. 1997).

152. M. Campione, K. Walrath, A. Huml, and the Tutorial Team, *The Java™ Tutorial Continued: The Rest of the JDK ™*, Addison-Wesley, Reading, MA (1999).

153. Canadian System Security Centre, *The Canadian Trusted Computer Product Evaluation Criteria*, Version 3.0e (Jan. 1993).

154. J. Canoles, "Quality Assurance in the ATC System," *Proceedings of the 44th Annual Air Traffic Control Association Conference*, pp. 151–153 (Sep. 1999).

155. G. Caronni, S. Kumar, C. Schuba, and G. Scott, "Virtual Enterprise Networks: the Next Generation of Secure Enterprise Networking," *Proceedings of the 16th Annual Computer Security Applications Conference*, pp. 42–51 (Dec. 2000).

156. L. Carroll, *The Annotated Alice*, New American Library, New York, NY (1960).

157. L. Chalmers, "An Analysis of the Differences Between the Computer Security Practices in the Military and Private Sector," *Proceedings of the 1986 IEEE Symposium on Privacy and Security*, pp. 71–74 (Apr. 1986).

158. R. Chandramouli, "Implementation of Multiple Access Control Policies Within a CORBASEC Framework," *Proceedings of the 22nd National Information Systems Security Conference*, pp. 112–130 (Oct. 1999).

159. K. Chandy and L. Lamport, "Distributed Snapshots: Determining Global States of Distributed Systems," *ACM Transactions on Computer Systems* **3** (1), pp. 63–75 (Feb. 1985).

160. F. Chang, A. Itzkovitz, and V. Karamcheti, "User-Level Resource-Constrained Sandboxing," *Proceedings of the 4th USENIX Windows Systems Symposium*, pp. 25–35 (Aug. 2000).

161. D. Chapman, "Network (In)security Through IP Packet Filtering," *Proceedings of the 3rd USENIX UNIX Security Symposium*, pp. 63–76 (Sep. 1992).

162. D. Chapman, *Developing Secure Applications with Visual Basic*, Microsoft Press, Redmond, WA (2000).

163. E. Charles, D. Diodati, and W. Mozdzierz, "Trusted Systems: Applying the Theory in a Commercial Firm," *Proceedings of the 13th National Computer Security Conference*, pp. 283–291 (Sep. 1993).

164. D. Chaum, "Untraceable Electronic Mail, Return Addresses, and Digital Pseudonyms," *Communications of the ACM* **24** (2), pp. 84–88 (Feb. 1981).

165. D. Chaum, "Security Without Identification: Transaction Systems to Make Big Brother Obsolete," *Communications of the ACM* **28** (10), pp. 1030–1044 (Oct. 1985).

166. D. Chaum, "The Dining Cryptographers Problem: Unconditional Sender and Receiver Untraceability," *Journal of Cryptology* **1** (1), pp. 65–75 (1988).

167. D. Chaum, "Online Cash Checks," *Advances in Cryptology—Proceedings of EUROCRYPT '89*, pp. 288–293 (Aug. 1989).

168. D. Chaum, "Numbers Can Be a Better Form of Cash than Paper," *Selected Papers from the 2nd International Smart Card 2000 Conference*, pp. 151–156 (Oct. 1989).

169. D. Chaum, B. den Boer, E. van Heyst, S. Mjølsnes, and A. Steenbeek, "Efficient Offline Electronic Checks," *Advances in Cryptology—Proceedings of EUROCRYPT '89*, pp. 294–301 (Aug. 1989).

170. D. Chaum and T. Pedersen, "Wallet Databases with Observers," *Advances in Cryptology—Proceedings of CRYPTO '92*, pp. 89–105 (Aug. 1992).

171. W. Cheswick, "An Evening with Berferd, in Which a Cracker Is Lured, Endured, and Studied," *Proceedings of the 1992 Winter USENIX Conference*, pp. 163–173 (Jan. 1992).

172. S. Chokhani, "Trusted Products Evaluation," *Communications of the ACM* **35** (7), pp. 64–76 (July 1992).

173. L. Cholvy and F. Cuppens, "Analyzing Consistency of Security Policies," *Proceedings of the 1997 IEEE Symposium on Security and Privacy*, pp. 103–112 (May 1997).

174. S. Christey, D. Baker, W. Hill, and D. Mann, "The Development of a Common Vulnerabilities and Exposures List," *Proceedings of the 2nd International Workshop on Recent Advances in Intrusion Detection* (Sep. 1999).

175. A. Cinelli, "Using PortSentry and LogCheck," *SysAdmin* **10** (3), pp. 29–31 (Mar. 2001).

176. A. Clark, "Key Recovery—Why, How, Who?" *Computers and Security* **16** (8), pp. 669–674 (Dec. 1997).

177. D. Clark and D. Wilson, "A Comparison of Commercial and Military Security Policies," *Proceedings of the 1987 IEEE Symposium on Security and Privacy*, pp. 184–194 (Apr. 1987).

178. T. Coe and T. Peter, "It Takes Six Ones to Reach a Flaw (Pentium Processor)," *Proceedings of the 12th Symposium on Computer Arithmetic*, pp. 140–146 (July 1995).

179. E. Cohen and D. Jefferson, "Protection in the HYDRA Operating System," *Proceedings of the 5th Symposium on Operating System Principles*, pp. 141–160 (Nov. 1975).

180. F. Cohen, "Computer Viruses: Theory and Experiments," *Proceedings of the 7th DOD/NBS Computer Security Conference*, pp. 240–263 (Sep. 1984).

181. F. Cohen, "Computer Viruses: Theory and Experiments," *Computers and Security* **6** (1), pp. 22–35 (Feb. 1987).

182. F. Cohen, "Practical Defenses Against Computer Viruses," *Computers and Security* **8** (2), pp. 149–160 (Apr. 1989).

183. F. Cohen, "Computational Aspects of Computer Viruses," *Computers and Security* **8** (4), pp. 325–344 (Nov. 1989).

184. F. Cohen, *A Short Course on Computer Viruses*, 2nd Edition, John Wiley and Sons, New York, NY (1994).

185. F. Cohen, "A Note on the Role of Deception in Information Protection," *Computers and Security* **17** (6), pp. 483–506 (Nov. 1998).

186. Commission of the European Communities, *Information Technology Security Evaluation Criteria*, Version 1.2 (1991).

187. "Common Criteria Web Site," http://www.commoncriteria.org.

188. Computer Emergency Response Team, *SunOS SPARC Integer4 Division Vulnerability*, CERT Advisory CA-91.16 (Sep. 1991).

189. Computer Emergency Response Team, *Writable /etc/utmp Vulnerability*, CERT Advisory CA-94.06 (Mar. 1994).

190. Computer Emergency Response Team, *Sendmail v5 Vulnerability*, CERT Advisory CA-95.08 (Aug. 1995).

191. Computer Emergency Response Team, *Ghostscript Vulnerability*, CERT Advisory CA-95.10 (Aug. 1995).

192. Computer Emergency Response Team, *Sun 4.1.X Loadmodule Vulnerability*, CERT Advisory CA-95.12 (Oct. 1995).

193. Computer Emergency Response Team, *rpc.ypupdated Vulnerability*, CERT Advisory CA-95.17 (Dec. 1995).

194. Computer Emergency Response Team, *Sendmail Vulnerabilities*, CERT Advisory CA-96.20 (Sep. 1996).

195. Computer Emergency Response Team, *Sendmail Daemon Mode Vulnerability*, CERT Advisory CA-96.24 (Nov. 1996).

196. Computer Emergency Response Team, *Sendmail Group Permissions Vulnerability*, CERT Advisory CA-96.25 (Dec. 1996).

197. Computer Emergency Response Team, *MIME Conversion Buffer Overflow in Sendmail Versions 8.8.3 and 8.8.4*, CERT Advisory CA-97.05 (Jan. 1997).

198. Computer Emergency Response Team, *IP Denial-of-Service Attacks*, CERT Advisory CA-97.28 (Dec. 1997; revised May 1998).

199. Computer Emergency Response Team, *Trojan Horse Version of TCP Wrappers*, CERT Advisory CA-99.01 (Jan. 1999).

200. Computer Emergency Response Team, *Buffer Overflows in SSH Daemon and RSAREF2 Library*, CERT Advisory CA-99.15 (Dec. 1999).

201. Computer Emergency Response Team, *Multiple Buffer Overflows in Kerberos Authenticated Services*, CERT Advisory CA-2000.06 (May 2000).

202. Computer Emergency Response Team, *Input Validation Problem in rpc.statd*, CERT Advisory CA-2000.17 (Aug. 2000).

203. Computer Emergency Response Team, *Unauthentic "Microsoft Corporation" Certificates*, CERT Advisory CA-2001.04 (Mar. 2001).

204. Computer Emergency Response Team, *Nimda Worm*, CERT Advisory CA-2001.17 (Sep. 2001).

205. R. Conway, W. Maxwell, and H. Morgan, "On the Implementation of Security Measures in Information Systems," *Communications of the ACM* **15** (4), pp. 211–220 (Apr. 1972).

206. C. Coombs, R. Dawes, and A. Tversky, *Mathematical Psychology: An Elementary Introduction*, Mathesis Press, Ann Arbor, MI (1981).

207. D. Cooper, "A Model of Certificate Revocation," *Proceedings of the 15th Annual Computer Security Applications Conference*, pp. 256–264 (Dec. 1999).

208. M. Cooper, S. Northcutt, M. Fearnow, and K. Frederick, *Intrusion Signatures and Analysis*, New Riders Publishing, Indianapolis, IN 46290 (2001).

209. D. Coppersmith, "The Data Encryption Standard (DES) and Its Strength Against Attacks," *IBM Journal of Research and Development* **38** (3), pp. 243–250 (May 1994)

210. F. Corbató and V. Vyssotsky, "Introduction and Overview of the Multics System," *Proceedings of the 1965 Fall Joint Computer Conference*, pp. 185–196 (Fall 1965).

211. O. Costich and I. Moskowitz, "Analysis of a Storage Channel in the Two Phase Commit Protocol," *Proceedings of the Foundations of Computer Security Workshop IV*, pp. 201–208 (June 1991).

212. L. Cottrell, "Frequently Asked Questions About Mixmaster Remailers," Obscura Information Security, La Mesa, CA (July 1996); available at http://www.obscura.com/~loki/remailer/mixmaster-faq.html.

213. L. Cottrell, "Mixmaster and Remailer Attacks," Obscura Information Security, La Mesa, CA (1996); available at http://www.obscura.com/~loki/remailer/remailer-essay.html.

214. A. Couch and M. Gilfix, "It's Elementary, Dear Watson: Applying Logic Programming to Convergent System Management Processes," *Proceedings of the 13th Systems Administration Conference (LISA 1999)*, pp. 123–137 (1999).

215. S. Coutinho, *The Mathematics of Ciphers: Number Theory and RSA Cryptography*, A. K. Peters Publishing Co., Natick, MA (1999).

216. C. Cowan, C. Pu, D. Maier, H. Hinton, J. Walpole, P. Bakke, S. Beattie, A. Grier, P. Wagle, and Q. Zhang, "StackGuard: Automatic Adaptive Detection and Prevention of Buffer-Overflow Attacks," *Proceedings of the 7th USENIX Security Symposium*, pp. 63–77 (Jan. 1998).

217. C. Cowan, S. Beattie, G. Kroah-Hartman, C. Pu, P. Wagle, and V. Gligor, "SubDomain: Parsimonious Server Security," *Proceedings of the 14th LISA Conference*, pp. 355–367 (Dec. 2000).

218. M. Crabb, "Password Security in a Large Distributed Environment," *Proceedings of the 2nd USENIX UNIX Security Workshop*, pp. 17–30 (Aug. 1990).

219. S. Crawford, *Windows 2000 Pro: The Missing Manual*, O'Reilly and Associates, Sebastopol, CA (2000).

220. Cray Research, Inc., *UNICOS® Security Administration Reference Manual*, Document Number SR-2062A, Cray Research, Inc., Mendota Heights, MN (1989).

221. D. Crocker, *Standard for the Format of ARPA Internet Text Messages*, RFC 822 (Aug. 1982).

222. S. Crocker and M. Pozzo, "A Proposal for a Verification-Based Virus Filter," *Proceedings of the 1989 IEEE Symposium on Security and Privacy*, pp. 319–324 (May 1989).

223. M. Crosbie and E. Spafford, "Defending a Computer System Using Autonomous Agents," *Proceedings of the 18th National Information Systems Security Conference*, pp. 549–558 (Oct. 1995).

224. J. Cugini, R. Dobry, V. Gligor, and T. Mayfield, "Functional Security Criteria for Distributed Systems," *Proceedings of the 18th National Information Systems Security Conference*, pp. 310–321 (Oct. 1995).

225. P. Cummings, D. Fullam, M. Goldstein, M. Gosselin, J. Picciotto, J. Woodward, and J. Wynn, "Compartmented Mode Workstation: Results Through Prototyping," *Proceedings of the 1987 IEEE Symposium on Security and Privacy*, pp. 2–12 (Apr. 1987).

226. T. Cusdick and M. Wood, "The REDOC-II Cryptosystem," *Advances in Cryptology—Proceedings of CRYPTO '90*, pp. 1–16 (Aug. 1990).

227. K. Cutler and F. Jones, *Commercial International Security Requirements*, draft (Jan. 1991).

228. J. Daemen and V. Rijmen, *The Design of Rijndael*, Springer-Verlag, New York, NY (2002).

229. T. Daniels and E. Spafford, "Identification of Host Audit Data to Detect Attacks on Low-Level IP Vulnerabilities," *Journal of Computer Security* **7** (1), pp. 3–35 (1999).

230. Data General Corporation, *Managing Security on the DG/UX® System*, Manual 093-701138-04, Westboro, MA (Nov. 1996).

231. J. Daughman, "High Confidence Visual Recognition of Persons by a Test of Statistical Independence," *IEEE Transactions on Pattern Analysis and Machine Intelligence*, **15** (11), pp. 1148–1161 (Nov. 1993).

232. G. Davida and B. Matt, "UNIX Guardians: Delegating Security to the User," *Proceedings of the UNIX Security Workshop*, pp. 14–23 (Aug. 1988).

233. G. Davida, Y. Desmedt, and B. Matt, "Defending Systems Against Viruses Through Cryptographic Authentication," *Proceedings of the 1989 Symposium on Security and Privacy*, pp. 312–318 (May 1989).

234. D. Davis, R. Ihaka, and P. Fenstermacher, "Cryptographic Randomness from Air Turbulence in Disk Drives," *Advances in Cryptology—Proceedings of CRYPTO '94*, pp. 114–120 (Aug. 1994).

235. D. Dean, E. Felten, and D. Wallach, "Java Security: From HotJava to Netscape and Beyond," *Proceedings of the 1996 IEEE Symposium on Security and Privacy*, pp. 190–200 (May 1996).

236. D. Dean, M. Franklin, and A. Stubblefield, "An Algebraic Approach to IP Traceback," *Proceedings of the 2000 Symposium on Network and Distributed System Security* (Feb. 2001).

237. H. Debar, M. Becker, and D. Siboni, "A Neural Network Component for an Intrusion Detection System," *Proceedings of the 1992 IEEE Symposium on Research in Security and Privacy*, pp. 240–250 (May 1992).

238. R. Demillo, D. Dobkin, A. Jones, and R.Lipton (eds.), *Foundations of Secure Computing*, Academic Press, New York, NY (1978).

239. D. Denning, "Secure Information Flow in Computer Systems," Ph.D. thesis, Dept. of Computer Sciences, Purdue University, West Lafayette, IN (May 1975); cited in *Cryptography and Data Security* [242].

240. D. Denning, "A Lattice Model of Secure Information Flow," *Communications of the ACM* **19** (5), pp. 236–243 (May 1976).

241. D. Denning, "Secure Personal Computing in an Insecure Network," *Communications of the ACM* **22** (8), pp. 476–482 (Aug. 1979).

242. D. Denning, *Cryptography and Data Security*, Addison-Wesley, Reading, MA (1982).

243. D. Denning, "An Intrusion-Detection Model," *IEEE Transactions on Software Engineering* **13** (2), pp. 222–232 (Feb. 1987).

244. D. Denning, *Information Warfare and Security*, Addison-Wesley, Reading, MA (1999).

245. D. Denning, S. Akl, M. Heckman, T. Lunt, M. Morgenstern, P. Neumann, and R. Schell, "Views for Multilevel Database Security," *IEEE Transactions on Software Engineering* **13** (2), pp. 129–140 (Feb. 1987).

246. D. Denning and D. Branstad, "A Taxonomy for Key Escrow Encryption Systems," *Communications of the ACM* **39** (3), pp. 34–40 (Mar. 1996).

247. D. Denning and P. Denning, "Certification of Programs for Secure Information Flow," *Communications of the ACM* **20** (7), pp. 504–513 (July 1977).

248. D. Denning, T. Lunt, R. Schell, W. Shockley, and M. Heckman,"The Sea View Security Model," *Proceedings of the 1988 Symposium on Security and Privacy*, pp. 218–233 (May 1988).

249. D. Denning and P. MacDoran, "Location-Based Authentication: Grounding Cyberspace for Better Security," *Computer Fraud and Security*, pp. 12–16 (Feb. 1996).

250. D. Denning and G. Sacco, "Timestamps in Key Distribution Protocols," *Communications of the CACM* **24** (8), pp. 533–536 (Aug. 1981).

251. D. Denning and M. Smid, "Key Escrowing Today," *IEEE Communications Magazine* **32** (9), pp. 58–68 (Sep. 1994).

252. P. Denning, "Third Generation Computer Systems," *Computing Surveys* **3** (4), pp. 175–216 (Dec. 1971).

253. P. Denning, "The Science of Computing: Computer Viruses," *American Scientist* **76** (3), pp. 236–238 (May 1988).

254. P. Denning, *Computers Under Attack: Intruders, Worms, and Viruses*, Addison-Wesley, Reading, MA (1990).

255. J. Dennis and E. Van Horn, "Programming Semantics for Multiprogrammed Computations," *Communications of the ACM* **9** (3), pp. 143–155 (Mar. 1966).

256. Department of Defense, *Password Management Guideline*, CSC-STD-002-85 (Apr. 1985).

257. Department of Defense, *Trusted Computer System Evaluation Criteria*, DOD 5200.28-STD (Dec. 1985).

258. Department of Defense, *Trusted Network Interpretation of the Trusted System Evaluation Criteria*, NCSC-TG-005 (July 1987).

259. Department of Defense, *A Guide to Understanding Audit in Trusted Systems*, NCSC-TG-001 Version 2 (June 1988).

260. Department of Defense, *Trusted Database Management System Interpretation of the Trusted Computer System Evaluation Criteria*, NCSC-TG-021 Version 1 (Apr. 1991).

261. Department of Defense, *A Guide to Understanding Covert Channel Analysis of Trusted Systems*, NCSC-TG-030 (Nov. 1993).

262. A. Dewdeny, "Computer Recreations: A Core War Bestiary of Viruses, Worms, and Other Threats to Computer Memories," *Scientific American* **252** (3), pp. 14–23 (Mar. 1985).

263. P. D'Haeseleer, S. Forrest, and P. Helman, "An Immunological Approach to Change Detection: Algorithms, Analysis, and Implications," *Proceedings of the 1996 IEEE Symposium on Security and Privacy*, pp. 110–119 (May 1996).

264. U. Dieckmann, P. Plankensteiner, and T. Wagner, "SESAM: a Biometric Person Identification System Using Sensor Fusion," *Pattern Recognition Letters* **18** (9), pp. 827–833 (Sep. 1997).

265. T. Dierks and C. Allen, *The TLS Protocol Version 1.0*, RFC 2246 (Jan. 1999).

266. H. Dietel, *An Introduction to Operating Systems* (Revised 1st Edition), Addison-Wesley, Reading, MA (1984).

267. W. Diffie and M. Hellman, "New Directions in Cryptography," *IEEE Transactions on Information Theory* **22** (6), pp. 644–654 (Nov. 1976).

268. W. Diffie and M. Hellman, "Exhaustive Cryptanalysis of the NBS Data Encryption Standard," *IEEE Computer* **10** (6), pp. 74–84 (June 1977).

269. Digital Equipment Corporation, *PDP-11 Architecture Handbook*, Maynard, MA (1983).

270. E. Dijkstra, "The Structure of the 'THE'-Multiprogramming System," *Communications of the ACM* **11** (5), pp. 341–346 (May 1968).

271. L. Dion, "A Complete Protection Model," *Proceedings of the 1981 IEEE Symposium on Security and Privacy*, pp. 49–55 (Apr. 1981).

272. B. Di Vito, P. Palmquist, E. Anderson, and M. Johnston, "Specification and Verification of the ASOS Kernel," *Proceedings of the 1990 Symposium on Research in Security and Privacy*, pp. 61–74 (May 1990).

273. H. Dobbertin, "The Status of MD5 After a Recent Attack," *CryptoBytes* **2** (2), pp. 1ff. (Summer 1996).

274. H. Dobbertin, "Cryptanalysis of MD4," *Journal of Cryptology* **11** (4), pp. 253–271 (1998).

275. D. Dobkin, A. Jones, and R. Lipton, "Secure Databases: Protection Against User Inference," *ACM Transactions on Database Systems* **4** (1), pp. 97–106 (Mar. 1979).

276. T. Doeppner, P. Klein, and A. Koyfman, "Using Router Stamping to Identify the Source of IP Packets," *Proceedings of the 7th ACM Conference on Computer and Communications Security*, pp. 184–189 (Nov. 2000).

277. B. Dole, S. Lodin, and E. Spafford, "Misplaced Trust: Kerberos 4 Session Keys," *Proceedings of the 1997 Symposium on Network and Distributed System Security*, pp. 60–70 (Mar. 1997).

278. F. Donner, *The Un-Americans*, Ballantine Books, New York, NY (1961).

279. N. Doraswamy and D. Harkins, *IPSEC: The New Security Standard for the Internet, Intranets, and Virtual Private Networks*, Prentice Hall, Upper Saddle River, NJ (1999).

280. D. Downs, J. Rub, K. Kung, and C. Jordan, "Issues in Discretionary Access Control," *Proceedings of the 1984 IEEE Symposium on Security and Privacy*, pp. 208–218 (Apr. 1984).

281. B. Duc, E. Bigun, J. Bigun, G. Maire, and S. Fischer, "Fusion of Audio and Video Information for Multi-Model Person Authentication," *Pattern Recognition Letters* **18** (9), pp. 835–843 (Sep. 1997).

282. T. Duff, "Experiences with Viruses on UNIX Systems," *Computing Systems* **2** (2), pp. 155–172 (Spring 1989).

283. R. Durst, T. Champion, B. Witten, E. Miller, and L. Spagnuolo, "Testing and Evaluating Computer Intrusion Detection Systems," *Communications of the ACM* **42** (7), pp. 53–61 (July 1999).

284. D. Eastlake, *Domain Name System Security Extensions*, RFC 2535 (Mar. 1999).

285. D. Eastlake, *DSA KEYs and SIGs in the Domain Name System (DNS)*, RFC 2536 (Mar. 1999).

286. D. Eastlake, *RSA/MD5 KEYs and SIGs in the Domain Name System (DNS)*, RFC 2537 (Mar. 1999).

287. D. Eastlake, *Storage of Diffie-Hellman Keys in the Domain Name System (DNS)*, RFC 2539 (Mar. 1999).

288. D. Eastlake and O. Gudmundsson, *Storing Certificates in the Domain Name System (DNS)*, RFC 2538 (Mar. 1999).

289. D. Eastlake, S. Crocker, and J. Schiller, *Randomness Recommendations for Security*, RFC 1750 (Dec. 1994).

290. S. Eckmann, "Eliminating Formal Flows in Automated Information Flow Analysis," *Proceedings of the 1994 IEEE Symposium on Research in Security and Privacy*, pp. 30–38 (May 1994).

291. W. Ehrsam, S. Matyas, C. Meyer, and W. Tuchman, "A Cryptographic Key Management Scheme for Implementing the Data Encryption Standard," *IBM Systems Journal* **17** (2), pp. 106–125 (1978).

292. M. Eichin and J. Rochlis, "With Microscope and Tweezers: An Analysis of the Internet Virus of November 1988," *Proceedings of the 1989 IEEE Symposium on Security and Privacy*, pp. 326–343 (May 1989).

293. T. Eisenberg, D. Gries, J. Hartmanis, D. Holcomb, M. Lynn, and T. Santoro, *The Computer Worm: A Report to the Provost of Cornell University on an Investigation Conducted by the Commission of Preliminary Enquiry*, Cornell University, Ithaca, NY (Feb. 1989).

294. T. El Gamal, "A Public Key Cryptosystem and Signature Scheme Based on Discrete Logarithms," *IEEE Transactions in Information Theory* **31** (4), pp. 469–472 (July 1985).

295. J. Eller, M. Mastrorocco, and B. Stauffer, "The Department of Defense Information Technology Security Certification and Accreditation Process

(DITSCAP)," *Proceedings of the 19th National Information Systems Security Conference*, pp. 46–53 (Oct. 1996).

296. B. Elliott, "A High-Level Debugger for PL/1, FORTRAN and BASIC," *Software—Practice and Experience* **12** (4), pp. 331–340 (April 1982).

297. C. Ellison, "Establishing Identity Without Certification Authorities," *Proceedings of the 6th USENIX Security Symposium*, pp. 67–76 (July 1996).

298. C. Ellison, "Naming and Certificates," *CFP '00, Proceedings of the 10th Conference on Computers, Freedom and Privacy: Challenging the Assumptions*, pp. 213–217 (Apr. 2000).

299. E. Engeler, *Introduction to the Theory of Computation*, Academic Press, New York, NY (1973).

300. A. Engelfriet, "Anonymity and Privacy on the Internet" (Jan. 1997); available at http://www.stack.nl/~galactus/remailers/index.html.

301. J. Epstein, J. McHugh, H. Orman, R. Pascale, A. Marmor-Squires, B. Danner, C. Martin, M. Branstad, G. Benson, and D. Rothnie, "A High Assurance Window System Prototype," *Journal of Computer Security* **2** (2, 3), pp. 159–190 (1993).

302. J. Epstein, L. Thomas, and E. Monteith, "Using Operating System Wrappers to Increase the Resiliency of Commercial Firewalls," *Proceedings of the 16th Annual Computer Security Applications Conference*, pp. 236–245 (Dec. 2000).

303. Ernst & Whinney, *Audit, Control, and Security Issues in RACF Environments*, Technical Reference Series No. 37052, The EDP Auditors Foundation, Inc., Carol Stream, IL (1992).

304. K. Eswaran and D. Chamberlin, "Functional Specifications of Subsystem for Database Integrity," *Proceedings of the International Conference on Very Large Data Bases*, pp. 48–68 (Sep. 1975).

305. S. Evans, S. Bush, and J. Hershey, "Information Assurance Through Kolmogorov Complexity," *Proceedings of the DARPA Information Survivability Conference and Exposition II*, pp. 322–331 (June 2001).

306. R. Fabry, "Capability-Based Addressing," *Communications of the ACM* **17** (7), pp. 403–412 (July 1974).

307. R. Fairfield, R. Mortenson, and K. Joulthart, "An LSI Random Number Generator (RNG)," *Advances in Cryptology—Proceedings of CRYPTO '84*, pp. 115–143 (Aug. 1984).

308. D. Farmer and B. Powell, "TITAN," *Proceedings of the 12th Systems Administration Conference (LISA '98)*, pp. 1–10 (Dec. 1998).

309. D. Farmer and E. Spafford, "The Cops Security Checker System," *Proceedings of the 1990 Summer USENIX Conference*, pp. 165–170 (June 1990).

310. R. Feiertag, K. Levitt, and L. Robinson, "Proving Multilevel Security of a System Design," *Proceedings of the 6th Symposium on Operating System Principles*, pp. 57–65 (Dec. 1977).

311. H. Feistel, "Cryptography and Computer Privacy," *Scientific American* **228** (5), pp. 15–23 (May 1973).

312. D. Feldmeier and P. Karn, "UNIX Password Security—Ten Years Later," *Advances in Cryptology—Proceedings of CRYPTO '89*, pp. 44–63 (Aug. 1989).

313. J. Fenton, "Memoryless Subsystems," *Computer Journal* **17** (2), pp. 143–147 (Feb. 1974).

314. D. Ferbrache, *A Pathology of Computer Viruses*, Springer-Verlag, New York, NY (1991).

315. K. Ferraiolo, L. Gallagher, and V. Thompson, "Building a Case for Assurance from Process," *Proceedings of the 21st National Information Systems Security Conference*, pp. 49–61 (Oct. 1998).

316. K. Ferraiolo, "Tutorial: The Systems Security Engineering Capability Maturity Model," *Proceedings of the 21st National Information Systems Security Conference*, pp. 719–729 (Oct. 1998).

317. R. Finkel and B. Sturgill, "Tools for System Administration in a Heterogeneous Environment," *Proceedings of the 3rd Large Installation Systems Administration Workshop (LISA 1989)*, pp. 15–30 (1989).

318. R. Finlayson and D. Cheriton, "Log Files: An Extended File Service Exploiting Write-Once Storage," *Proceedings of the 11th Symposium on Operating Systems Principles*, pp. 139–148 (Nov. 1987).

319. E. Fisch, G. White, and U. Pooch, "The Design of an Audit Trail Analysis Tool," *Proceedings of the 10th Annual Computer Security Applications Conference*, pp. 126–132 (Dec. 1994).

320. J. Fisch and L. Hoffman, "The Cascade Problem: Graph Theory Can Help," *Proceedings of the 14th National Computer Security Conference*, pp. 88–100 (Oct. 1991).

321. P. Fites, P. Johnston, and M. Kratz, *The Computer Virus Crisis*, Van Nostrand Reinhold, New York, NY (1988).

322. K. Fithen and B. Fraser, "CERT Incident Response and the Internet," *Communications of the ACM* **37** (8), pp. 108–113 (Aug. 1994).

323. C. Flack and M. Atallah, "Better Logging Through Formality: Applying Formal Specification Techniques to Improve Audit Logs and Log Consumers," *Proceedings of the 3rd International Workshop on Recent Advances in Intrusion Detection*, pp. 1–16 (Oct. 2000).

324. E. Flahavin and R. Snouffer, "The Certification of the Interim Key Escrow System," *Proceedings of the 19th National Information Systems Security Conference*, pp. 26–33 (Oct. 1996).

325. C. Flink II and J. Weiss, "System V/MLS Labeling and Mandatory Policy Alternatives," *Proceedings of the 1989 Winter USENIX Conference*, pp. 413–427 (Jan. 1989).

326. S. Fluhrer and D. McGrew, "Statistical Analysis of the Alleged RC4 Keystream Generator," *Proceedings of the 7th International Workshop on Fast Software Encryption*, pp. 19–39 (Apr. 2000).

327. S. Foley, "A Model for Secure Information Flow," *Proceedings of the 1989 IEEE Symposium on Research in Security and Privacy*, pp. 248–258 (May 1989).

328. S. Foley, "Separation of Duty Using High Water Marks," *Proceedings of the Computer Security Foundations Workshop IV*, pp. 79–88 (June 1991).

329. S. Foley and J. Jacob, "Specifying Security for CSCW Systems," *Proceedings of the 8th IEEE Computer Security Foundations Workshop*, pp. 136–145 (June 1995).

330. W. Ford and M. Baum, *Secure Electronic Commerce: Building the Infrastructure for Digital Signatures and Encryption*, Prentice-Hall, Upper Saddle River, NJ (1997).

331. S. Forrest, S. Hofmeyr, and A. Somayaji, "Computer Immunology," *Communications of the ACM* **40** (10), pp. 88–96 (Oct. 1997).

332. S. Forrest, S. Hofmeyr, A. Somayaji, and T. Longstaff, "A Sense of Self for UNIX Processes," *Proceedings of the 1996 IEEE Symposium on Security and Privacy*, pp. 120–128 (May 1996).

333. S. Forrest, A. Perelson, L. Allen, and R. Cherukuri, "Self-Nonself Discrimination," *Proceedings of the 1994 IEEE Symposium on Security and Privacy*, pp. 202–212 (May 1994).

334. J. Frank, "Artificial Intelligence and Intrusion Detection: Current and Future Directions," *Proceedings of the 17th National Computer Security Conference*, pp. 21–33 (Oct. 1994).

335. M. Frantzen, F. Kerschbaum, E. Schultz, and S. Fahmy, "A Framework for Understanding Vulnerabilities in Firewalls Using a Dataflow Model of Firewall Internals," *Computers and Security* **20** (3), pp. 263–270 (May 2001).

336. T. Fraser and L. Badger, "Ensuring Continuity During Dynamic Security Policy Reconfiguration in DTE," *Proceedings of the 1998 IEEE Symposium on Security and Privacy*, pp. 15–26 (May 1998).

337. T. Fraser, L. Badger, and M. Feldman, "Hardening COTS Software with Generic Software Wrappers," *Proceedings of the 1999 IEEE Symposium on Security and Privacy*, pp. 2–16 (May 1999).

338. A. Freedman, "How to Make BSD (SunOS) Kernels SYN-Attack Resistant" (Sep. 1996); available at http://www.netaxs.com/~freedman/syn/.

339. D. Freedman and C. Mann, *At Large: The Strange Case of the World's Biggest Internet Invasion*, Simon and Schuster, New York, NY (1997).

340. A. Freier, P. Kariton, and P. Kocher, *The SSL Protocol: Version 3.0*, Netscape Communications, Inc., Mountain View, CA (Mar. 1996).

341. A.E. Frisch, *Essential System Administration*, O'Reilly and Associates, Sebastopol, CA (1991).

342. J. Gaffney and J. Ulvila, "Evaluation of Intrusion Detectors: A Decision Theory Approach," *Proceedings of the 2001 IEEE Symposium on Security and Privacy*, pp. 50–61 (May 2001).

343. H. Gaines, *Cryptanalysis: A Study of Ciphers and Their Solution*, Dover, New York, NY (1956).

344. D. Gambel, "Security Modeling for Public Safety Communication Specifications," *Proceedings of the 20th National Information Systems Security Conference*, pp. 514–521 (Oct. 1997).

345. R. Ganesan and C. Davies, "A New Attack on Pronounceable Password Generators," *Proceedings of the 17th National Computer Security Conference*, pp. 184–197 (Oct. 1994).

346. R. Ganesan, "The Yaksha Security System," *Communications of the ACM* **39** (3), pp. 55–60 (Mar. 1996).

347. S. Garfinkel and E. Spafford, *Practical UNIX and Internet Security*, 2nd Edition, O'Reilly and Associates, Sebastopol, CA (1996).

348. S. Garfinkel and E. Spafford, *Web Security & Commerce*, O'Reilly and Associates, Sebastopol, CA (1996).

349. P. Garnett, "Selective Disassembly: A First Step Towards Developing a Virus Filter," *Proceedings of the 4th Aerospace Computer Security Conference*, pp. 2–6 (Dec. 1988).

350. M. Gasser, "A Random Word Generator for Pronounceable Passwords," Technical Report ESD-TR-75-97, Electronic Systems Division, Hanscom Air Force Base, Bedford, MA (Nov. 1975).

351. M. Gendler-Fishman and E. Gudes, "Compile-Time Flow Analysis of Transactions and Methods in Object-Oriented Databases," *Proceedings of the IFIP TC11 WG11.3 11th International Conference on Database Security*, pp. 110–133 (Aug. 1997).

352. T. George, "A Touch of Magex," *Banking Technology* **16** (6), p. 54 (July-Aug. 1999).

353. A. Ghosh, *E-Commerce Security: Weak Links, Best Defenses*, John Wiley and Sons, New York, NY (1998).

354. A. Ghosh, T. O'Connor, and G. McGraw, "An Automated Approach for Identifying Potential Vulnerabilities in Software," *Proceedings of the 1998 IEEE Symposium on Security and Privacy*, pp. 104–114 (May 1998).

355. A. Ghosh, V. Rana, B. Johnson, and J. Profeta III, "A Distributed Safety-Critical System for Real-Time Train Control," *Proceedings of the 21st IEEE International Conference on Industrial Electronics, Control, and Instrumentation*, pp. 760–767 (Nov. 1995).

356. D. Gifford, "Cryptographic Sealing for Information Secrecy and Authentication," *Communications of the ACM* **25** (4), pp. 274–286 (Apr. 1982).

357. H. Gilbert and G. Chase, "A Statistical Attack on the Feal-8 Cryptosystem," *Advances in Cryptology—Proceedings of CRYPTO '90*, pp. 22–33 (Aug. 1990).

358. J. Gilmore, *Cracking the DES*, O'Reilly and Associates, Sebastopol, CA (1998).

359. G. Glass, *UNIX® for Programmers and Users*, Prentice-Hall, Englewood Cliffs, NJ (1993).

360. V. Gligor, "Guidelines for Trusted Facility Management and Audit," University of Maryland, College Park, MD (1985); cited in *A Guide to Understanding Audit in Trusted Systems* [259].

361. V. Gligor, C. Chandersekaran, R. Chapman, L. Dotterer, M. Hecht, W.-D. Jiang, A. Johri, G. Luckenbaugh, and N. Vasudevan, "Design and Implementation of Secure Xenix," *IEEE Transactions on Software Engineering* **13** (2), pp. 208–221 (Feb. 1987).

362. B. Gold, R. Linde, and P. Cudney, "KVM/370 in Retrospect," *Proceedings of the 1984 Symposium on Security and Privacy*, pp. 13–24 (Apr. 1984).

363. B. Gold, R. Linde, R. Peeler, M. Schaefer, J. Scheid, and P. Ward, "A Security Retrofit of VM/370," *Proceedings of the National Computer Conference* **48**, pp. 335–344 (June 1979).

364. I. Goldberg, D. Wagner, R. Thomas, and E. Brewer, "A Secure Environment for Untrusted Helper Applications: Confining the Wily Hacker," *Proceedings of the 6th USENIX Security Symposium*, pp. 1–13 (July 1996).

365. O. Goldreich, *Modern Cryptography, Probabilistic Proofs, and Pseudorandomness*, Springer-Verlag, New York, NY (1999).

366. J. Golic, "Linear Statistical Weakness of Alleged RC4 Keystream Generator," *Advances in Cryptology—Proceedings of EUROCRYPT '97*, pp. 226–238 (May 1997).

367. L. Gong, "A Secure Identity-Based Capability System," *Proceedings of the 1989 IEEE Symposium on Security and Privacy*, pp. 56–63 (May 1989).

368. L. Gong, "A Security Risk of Depending on Synchronized Clocks," *Operating Systems Review* **26** (1), pp. 49–53 (Jan. 1992).

369. L. Gong, M. Mueller, H. Prafullchandra, and R. Schemers, "Going Beyond the Sandbox: An Overview of the New Security Architecture in the Java™ Development Kit 1.2," *Proceedings of the USENIX Symposium on Internet Technologies and Systems*, pp. 103–112 (Dec. 1997).

370. G. Graham and P. Denning, "Protection—Principles and Practice," *Spring Joint Computer Conference, AFIPS Conference Proceedings* **40**, pp. 417–429 (1972).

371. F. Grampp and R. Morris, "UNIX Operating System Security," *AT&T Bell Laboratories Technical Journal* **63** (8), pp. 1649–1672 (Oct. 1984).

372. G. Grant, *Understanding Digital Signatures*, McGraw-Hill, New York, NY (1998).

373. L. Grant, "DES Key Crunching for Safer Cipher Keys," *ACM Special Interest Group Security Audit and Control Review* **5** (3), pp. 9–16 (Summer 1987).

374. R. Graubart, "The Integrity-Lock Approach to Secure Database Management," *Proceedings of the 1990 Symposium on Security and Privacy*, pp. 62–74 (Apr. 1990).

375. R. Graubert, "On the Need for a Third Form of Access Control," *Proceedings of the 12th National Computer Security Conference*, pp. 296–304 (Oct. 1989).

376. J. Gray III, "On Introducing Noise into the Bus-Contention Channel," *Proceedings of the 1993 IEEE Symposium on Research in Security and Privacy*, pp. 90–98 (May 1993).

377. J. Green and P. Sisson, "The 'Father Christmas' Worm," *Proceedings of the 12th National Computer Security Conference*, pp. 359–368 (Oct. 1989).

378. M. Greenberg, L. Byington, and D. Harper, "Mobile Agents and Security," *IEEE Communications Magazine* **36** (7), pp. 76–85 (July 1998).

379. M. Greenwald, S. Singh, J. Stone, and D. Cheriton, "Designing an Academic Firewall: Policy, Practice, and Experience," *Proceedings of the 1996 Symposium on Network and Distributed Systems Security*, pp. 79–92 (Feb. 1996).

380. P. Gregory, *Solaris™ Security*, Prentice-Hall, Upper Saddle River, NJ (2000).

381. P. Griffiths and B. Wade, "An Authorization Mechanism for a Relational Database System," *ACM Transactions on Database Systems* **1** (3), pp. 242–255 (Sep. 1976).

382. C. Gülcü and G. Tsudik, "Mixing Email with BABEL," *Proceedings of the 1996 Symposium on Network and Distributed System Security*, pp. 1–15 (Feb. 1996).

383. S. Gupta and V. Gligor, "Towards a Theory of Penetration-Resistant Systems and Its Applications," *Proceedings of the Computer Security Foundations Workshop IV*, pp. 62–78 (June 1991).

384. S. Gupta and V. Gligor, "Experience with a Penetration Analysis Method and Tool," *Proceedings of the 15th National Computer Security Conference*, pp. 165–183 (Oct. 1992).

385. J. Guttman, "Information Flow and Invariance," *Proceedings of the 1987 IEEE Symposium on Security and Privacy*, pp. 67–73 (Apr. 1987).

386. K. Hafner and J. Markoff, *Cyberpunk: Outlaws and Hackers on the Computer Frontier*, Simon and Schuster, New York, NY (1991).

387. B. Hagemark and K. Zadeck, "Site: A Language and System for Configuring Many Computers as One Computer Site," *Proceedings of the 3rd Large Installation Systems Administration Workshop (LISA 1989),* pp. 1–15 (1989).

388. J. Haigh and W. Young, "Extending the Non-Interference Version of MLS for SAT," *Proceedings of the 1986 IEEE Symposium on Security and Privacy,* pp. 232–239 (Apr. 1986).

389. J. Haigh, R. Kemmerer, J. McHugh, and W. Young, "An Experience Using Two Covert Channel Analysis Techniques on a Real System Design," *IEEE Transactions on Software Engineering* **13** (2), (Feb. 1987).

390. N. Haller, "The S/Key™ One-Time Password System," *Proceedings of the 1994 Symposium on Network and Distributed System Security,* pp. 151–157 (Feb. 1994).

391. S. Hambridge and J. Sedayao, "Horses and Barn Doors: Evolution of Corporate Guidelines for Internet Usage," *Proceedings of the 7th Systems Administration Conference (LISA 1993),* pp. 9–16 (Nov. 1993).

392. A. Hamilton, J. Madison, and J. Jay, *The Federalist Papers* (C. Rossiter, ed.), New American Library, New York, NY (1961).

393. D. Hanson, "A Machine-Independent Debugger—Revisited," *Software—Practice and Experience* **29** (10), pp. 849–862 (Oct. 1999).

394. S. Hansen and E. Atkins, "Centralized System Monitoring with Swatch," *Proceedings of the 3rd USENIX UNIX Security Symposium,* pp. 105–117 (Sep. 1992).

395. S. Hansen and E. Atkins, "Automated System Monitoring and Notification with Swatch," *Proceedings of the 7th Systems Administration Conference (LISA 1993),* pp. 145–155 (Nov. 1993).

396. S. Hardcastle-Kille, *Encoding Network Addresses to Support Operation over Non-OSI Lower Layers,* RFC 1277 (Nov. 1991).

397. S. Hardcastle-Kille, *A String Encoding of Presentation Address,* RFC 1278 (Nov. 1991).

398. N. Hardy, "KeyKOS Architecture," *Operating Systems Review* **19** (4), pp. 8–25 (Oct. 1985).

399. A. Harmon, "Hackers May 'Net' Good PR for Studio," *Los Angeles Times,* p. D1 (Aug. 12, 1995).

400. B. Harris and R. Hunt, "Firewall Certification," *Computers and Security* **18** (2), pp. 165–177 (Mar./Apr. 1999).

401. M. Harrison, W. Ruzzo, and J. Ullman, "Protection in Operating Systems," *Communications of the ACM* **19** (8), pp. 461–471 (Aug. 1976).

402. M. Harrison and W. Ruzzo, "Monotonic Protection Systems," in *Foundations of Secure Computing* [238], pp. 337–363 (Oct. 1977).

403. H. Härtig, O. Kowalski, and W. Kühnhauser, "The BirliX Security Architecture," *Journal of Computer Security* **2** (1), pp. 5–21 (1993).

404. H. Hartson and D. Hsiao, "Full Protection Specifications in the Semantic Model for Database Protection Languages," *Proceedings of the 1976 ACM Annual Conference*, pp. 90–95 (Oct. 1976).

405. J. Haskett, "Pass-Algorithms: A User Validation Scheme Based on Knowledge of Secret Algorithms," *Communications of the ACM* **27** (8), pp. 777–781 (Aug. 1984).

406. J. Haugh II, "Shadow Password Suite," *Proceedings of the 3rd USENIX UNIX Security Symposium*, pp. 133–144 (Sep. 1992).

407. S. Heatley and J. Otto, "Data Mining Computer Audit Logs to Detect Computer Misuse," *International Journal of Intelligent Systems in Accounting, Finance and Management* **7** (3), pp. 125–134 (Sep. 1998).

408. B. Hebbard, P. Grosso, T. Baldridge, C. Chan, D. Fishman, P. Goshgarian, T. Hilton, J. Hoshen, K. Hoult, G. Huntley, M. Stolarchuk, and L. Warner, "A Penetration Analysis of the Michigan Terminal System," *Operating Systems Review* **14** (1), pp. 7–20 (Jan. 1980).

409. L. Heberlein and M. Bishop, "Attack Class: Address Spoofing," *Proceedings of the 19th National Information Systems Security Conference*, pp. 371–377 (Oct. 1996).

410. L. Heberlein, G. Dias, K. Levitt, B. Mukherjee, J. Wood, and D. Wolber, "A Network Security Monitor," *Proceedings of the 1990 IEEE Symposium on Research in Security and Privacy*, pp. 296–304 (May 1990).

411. L. Heberlein, K. Levitt, and B. Mukherjee, "Internetwork Security Monitor: An Intrusion-Detection System for Large-Scale Networks," *Proceedings of the 15th National Information Systems Security Conference*, pp. 262–271 (Oct. 1992).

412. R. Hefner, "Lessons Learned with the Systems Security Engineering Capability Maturity Model," *Proceedings of the 1997 International Conference on Software Engineering*, pp. 566–567 (May 1997).

413. R. Hefner, "A Process Standard for System Security Engineering: Development Experiences and Pilot Results," *Proceedings of the IEEE International Symposium on Software Engineering Standards*, pp. 217–221 (June 1997).

414. G. Held and K. Hundley, *Cisco® Access Lists Field Guide*, McGraw-Hill, New York, NY (1999).

415. H. Hellman, *Great Feuds in Science: Ten of the Liveliest Disputes Ever*, John Wiley and Sons, New York, NY (1998).

416. M. Hellman, "A Cryptanalytic Time-Memory Tradeoff," *IEEE Transactions on Information Theory* **26** (4), pp. 401–406 (July 1980).

417. P. Helman and G. Liepins, "Statistical Foundations of Audit Trail Analysis for the Detection of Computer Misuse," *IEEE Transactions on Software Engineering* **19** (9), pp. 886–901 (Sep. 1993).

418. J. Helsingius, *Press Release: Johan Helsingius Closes His Internet Remailer*, Oy Penetic Ab (Aug. 1996).

419. Hewlett-Packard Co., *Sendmail Release 8.8.6 Causes Denial of Service Failures*, Security Bulletin #00097 (Apr. 1999).

420. F. Hickman, "An 'Intelligent' Approach to Audit Trail Analysis," *Proceedings of the 2nd International Meeting on Expert Systems Applications*, pp. 51–63 (1992).

421. H. Highland, "Random Bits and Bytes: Case History of a Virus Attack," *Computers and Security* **7** (1), pp. 3–5 (Feb. 1988).

422. H. Highland, *Computer Virus Handbook*, Elsevier Advanced Technology, Oxford, UK (1990).

423. H. Highland, "Random Bits and Bytes: Testing a Password System," *Computers and Security* **11** (2), pp. 110–113 (Apr. 1992).

424. J. Hoagland, C. Wee, and K. Levitt, "Audit Log Analysis Using the Visual Audit Browser Toolkit," Technical Report CSE-95-11, Department of Computer Science, University of California, Davis, CA (Sep. 1995).

425. L. Hoffman, "The Formulary Model for Flexible Privacy and Access Control," *Proceedings of the 1971 Fall Joint Computer Conference*, pp. 587–601 (1971).

426. L. Hoffman, *Modern Methods for Computer Security and Privacy*, Prentice-Hall, Englewood Cliffs, NJ 07632 (1977).

427. L. Hoffman, *Rogue Programs: Viruses, Worms, and Trojan Horses*, Van Nostrand Reinhold, New York, NY (1990).

428. L. Hoffman and R. Davis, "Security Pipeline Interface (SPI)," *Proceedings of the 6th Annual Computer Security Applications Conference*, pp. 349–355 (Dec. 1990).

429. S. Hofmeyr, S. Forrest, and A. Somayaji, "Intrusion Detection Using Sequences of System Calls," *Journal of Computer Security* **6** (3), pp. 151–180 (1988).

430. C. Hogan, A. Cox, and T. Hunter, "Decentralizing Distributed System Administration," *Proceedings of the 9th Systems Administration Conference (LISA 1995)*, pp. 139–147 (Sep. 1995).

431. C. Holley and F. Millar, "Auditing the On-Line, Real-Time Computer System," *Journal of Systems Management* **34** (1), pp. 14–19 (Jan. 1983).

432. Homer, *The Odyssey* (translated by E. V. Rieu), Penguin Books, New York, NY (1946).

433. The Honeypot Project, "Know Your Enemy: III" (March 2000); available at http://project.honeynet.org/papers/enemy3.

434. The Honeypot Project, "Know Your Enemy: Passive Fingerprinting" (May 2000); available at http://project.honeynet.org/papers/finger.

435. The Honeypot Project, "Know Your Enemy: A Forensic Analysis" (May 2000); available at http://project.honeynet.org/papers/forensics.

436. The Honeypot Project, "Know Your Enemy" (July 2000); available at http://project.honeynet.org/papers/enemy.

437. The Honeypot Project, "Know Your Enemy: Honeynets" (Apr. 2001); available at http://project.honeynet.org/papers/honeynet.

438. The Honeypot Project, "Know Your Enemy: II" (June 2001); available at http://project.honeynet.org/papers/enemy2.

439. The Honeypot Project, "Know Your Enemy: Statistics" (July 2001); available at http://project.honeynet.org/papers/stats.

440. J. Horton, R. Cooper, W. Hyslop, B. Nickerson, O. Ward, R. Harland, E. Ashby, and W. Stewart, "The Cascade Vulnerability Problem," *Journal of Computer Security* **2** (4), pp. 279–290 (1993).

441. J. Horton, R. Harland, E. Ashby, R. Cooper, W. Hyslop, B. Nickerson, W. Stewart, and O. Ward, "The Cascade Vulnerability Problem," *Proceedings of the 1993 IEEE Symposium on Research in Security and Privacy*, pp. 110–116 (May 1993).

442. M. Howard, *Designing Secure Web-Based Applications for Microsoft® Windows® 2000*, Microsoft Press, Redmond, WA (2000).

443. M. Howard and D. LeBlanc, *Writing Secure Code*, Microsoft Press, Redmond, WA (2001).

444. B. Howell and B. Satdeva, "We Have Met the Enemy, an Informal Survey of Policy Practices in the Internetworked Community," *Proceedings of the 5th Large Installation Systems Administration Conference (LISA 1991)*, pp. 159–170 (Sep./Oct. 1991).

445. J. Hruska, *Computer Viruses and Anti-Virus Warfare*, Ellis Horwood, New York, NY (1992).

446. W. Hsieh, M. Fiuczynski, C. Garrett, S. Savage, D. Becker, and B. Bershad, "Language Support for Extensible Operating Systems," *Proceedings of the Inaugural Workshop on Compiler Support for Systems Software*, pp. 127–133 (Feb. 1996).

447. N. Htoo-Mosher, R. Nasser, N. Zunic, and J. Straw, "E4 ITSEC Evaluation of PR/SM on ES/9000 Processors," *Proceedings of the 19th National Information Systems Security Conference*, pp. 1–11 (Oct. 1996).

448. W.-M. Hu, "Reducing Timing Channels with Fuzzy Time," *Proceedings of the 1991 IEEE Symposium on Research in Security and Privacy*, pp. 52–61 (May 1991).

449. W.-M. Hu, "Lattice Scheduling and Covert Channels," *Proceedings of the 1992 IEEE Symposium on Research in Security and Privacy*, pp. 8–20 (May 1992).

450. R. Hudson, *Windows NT Administration and Security*, Prentice-Hall, Upper Saddle River, NJ (2001)

451. J. Hughes, "Certificate Inter-Operability White Paper," *Computers and Security* **18** (3), pp. 221–250 (May 1999).

452. J. Hughes, "The Realities of PKI Inter-Operability," *Proceedings of Secure Networking—CQRE [Secure] '99 International Exhibition and Congress*, pp. 127–132 (Nov. 1999).

453. G. Iachello and K. Rannenberg, "Protection Profiles for Remailer Mixes," *Proceedings of the International Workshop on Design Issues in Anonymity and Unobservability*, pp. 181–225 (July 2000).

454. C. I'Anson and C. Mitchell, "Security Defects in CCITT Recommendation X.509—the Directory Authentication Framework," *Computer Communication Review* **20** (2), pp. 30–34 (Apr. 1990).

455. D. Icove, "Collaring the Cybercrook: An Investigator's View," *IEEE Spectrum* **34** (6), pp. 31–36 (June 1997).

456. K. Ilgun, R. Kemmerer, and P. Porras, "State Transition Analysis: A Rule-Based Intrusion Detection Approach," *IEEE Transactions on Software Engineering* **21** (3), pp. 181–199 (Mar. 1995).

457. J. Iliffe and J. Jodeit, "A Dynamic Storage Allocation System," *Computer Journal* **5**, pp. 200–209 (1962); cited in *Cryptography and Data Security* [242].

458. J. Iliffe, *Basic Machine Principles*, 2nd Edition, Elsevier MacDonald Publishing Co., New York, NY (1972); cited in *Cryptography and Data Security* [242].

459. Information Sciences Institute, *Transmission Control Protocol DARPA Internet Program Protocol Specification*, RFC 793 (Sep. 1981).

460. International Telecommunications Union, *Recommendation X.509—the Directory Authentication Framework* (1993).

461. C. Irvine and D. Volpano, "A Practical Tool for Developing Trusted Applications," *Proceedings of the 11th Annual Computer Security Applications Conference*, pp. 190–195 (Dec. 1995).

462. H. Isa, W. Shockley, and C. Irvine, "A Multi-threading Architecture for Multilevel Secure Transaction Processing," *Proceedings of the 1999 IEEE Symposium on Security and Privacy*, pp. 166–180 (May 1999).

463. D. Isenor and S. Zaky, "Fingerprint Identification Using Graph Matching," *Pattern Recognition* **19** (2), pp. 113–122 (1986).

464. H. Israel, "Computer Viruses: Myth or Reality?" *Proceedings of the 10th National Computer Security Conference*, pp. 226–230 (Sep. 1987).

465. N. Itoi and P. Honeyman, "Pluggable Authentication Modules for Windows NT," *Proceedings of the 2nd USENIX Windows NT Symposium*, pp. 97–108 (Aug. 1998).

466. S. Jajodia, S. Gadia, G. Bhargava, and E. Sibley, "Audit Trail Organization in Relational Databases," *Results of the IFIP WG 11.3 Workshop on Database Security, III: Status and Prospects*, pp. 269–281 (Sep. 1989).

467. S. Jajodia, P. Samarati, and V. Subrahamanian, "A Logical Language for Expressing Authorizations," *Proceedings of the 1997 IEEE Symposium on Security and Privacy*, pp. 31–42 (May 1997).

468. S. Jajodia and R. Sandhu, "Towards a Multilevel Secure Relational Data Model," *Proceedings of the ACM-SIGMOD Conference*, pp. 50–59 (May 1991).

469. K. Jensen and N. Wirth, *PASCAL: User Manual and Report*, 2nd Edition, Springer-Verlag, New York, NY (1974).

470. I. Jermyn, A. Mayer, F. Monrose, M. Reiter, and A. Rubin, "The Design and Analysis of Graphical Passwords," *Proceedings of the 8th USENIX Security Symposium*, pp. 1–14 (Aug. 1999).

471. H. Johnson and M. De Vilbiss, "Use of the Trusted Computer System Evaluation Criteria (TCSEC) for Complex, Evolving, Multipolicy Systems," *Proceedings of the 16th National Computer Security Conference*, pp. 137–145 (Sep. 1993).

472. A. Jones and R. Lipton, "The Enforcement of Security Policies for Computation," *Proceedings of the 5th Symposium on Operating System Principles*, pp. 197–206 (Nov. 1975).

473. A. Jones, R. Lipton, and L. Snyder, "A Linear-Time Algorithm for Deciding Security," *Proceedings of the 17th Symposium on the Foundations of Computer Science*, pp. 33–41 (Oct. 1976).

474. V. Jones and D. Schrodel, "Balancing Security and Convenience," *Proceedings of the Large Installation Systems Administration Workshop*, pp. 5–6 (Apr. 1987).

475. M. Joseph, "Towards the Elimination of the Effects of Malicious Logic: Fault Tolerance Approaches," *Proceedings of the 10th National Computer Security Conference*, pp. 238–244 (Sep. 1987).

476. M. Joseph and A. Avižienis, "A Fault Tolerant Approach to Computer Viruses," *Proceedings of the 1988 IEEE Symposium on Security and Privacy*, pp. 52–58 (Apr. 1988).

477. R. Joyce and G. Gupta, "Identity Authentication Based on Keystroke Latencies," *Communications of the ACM* **33** (2), pp. 168–176 (Feb. 1990).

478. J. Juni and R. Ponto, "Computer-Virus Infection of a Medical Diagnostic Computer," *New England Journal of Medicine* **320** (12), pp. 811–812 (Mar. 12, 1989).

479. J. Jumes, N. Cooper, P. Chamoun, and T. Feinman, *Microsoft® Windows NT® 4.0 Security, Audit, and Control*, Microsoft Press, Redmond, WA (1999).

480. F. Kafka, *The Trial*, Alfred Knopf, New York, NY (1992).

481. C. Kahn and M. Zurko, "Incentives to Help Stop Floods," *Proceedings of the 2000 New Security Paradigms Workshop*, pp. 127–132 (Sep. 2000).

482. D. Kahn, *The Codebreakers: The Story of Secret Writing* (revised edition), Macmillan Publishing Co., New York, NY (1967).

483. D. Kahn, *Seizing the Enigma: The Race to Break the German U-Boat Codes, 1939–1943*, Houghton Mifflin Co., Boston, MA (1991).

484. D. Kahn, *Codebreaking and the Battle of the Atlantic*, US Air Force Academy, Colorado Springs, CO (1994).

485. D. Kahn, *The Codebreakers; The Story of Secret Writing* (revised edition), Scribner, New York, NY (1996).

486. R. Kahn, W. Corwin, T. Dennis, H. D'Hooge, D. Hubka, L. Hutcchins, J. Montague, F. Pollack, and M. Gifkins, "iMAX: A Multiprocessor Operating System for an Object-Based Computer," *Proceedings of the 8th Symposium on Operating Systems Principles*, pp. 117–121 (Dec. 1979).

487. R. Kain, *Advanced Computer Architecture: A Systems Design Approach*, Prentice-Hall, Englewood Cliffs, NJ 07632 (1996).

488. R. Kain and C. Landwehr, "On Access Checking in Capability-Based Systems," *Proceedings of the 1986 IEEE Symposium on Security and Privacy*, pp. 95–100 (May 1986).

489. B. Kaliski, *The MD2 Message Digest Algorithm*, RFC 1319 (Apr. 1992).

490. M. Kang and I. Moskowitz, "A Pump for Rapid, Reliable, Secure Communication," *Proceedings of the 1st ACM Conference on Computer and Communication Security*, pp. 119–129 (Nov. 1993).

491. M. Kang, I. Moskowitz, and D. Lee, "A Network Version of the Pump," *Proceedings of the 1995 IEEE Symposium on Security and Privacy*, pp.144–154 (May 1995).

492. M. Kang, I. Moskowitz, and D. Lee, "A Network Pump," *IEEE Transactions on Software Engineering* **22** (5), pp. 329–338 (May 1996).

493. B. Kantor, *BSD Rlogin*, RFC 1282 (Dec. 1991).

494. P. Karger, "Limiting the Damage Potential of Discretionary Trojan Horses," *Proceedings of the 1987 IEEE Symposium on Security and Privacy*, pp. 32–37 (Apr. 1987).

495. P. Karger and A. Herbert, "An Augmented Capability Architecture to Support Lattice Security and Traceability of Access," *Proceedings of the 1984 IEEE Symposium on Security and Privacy*, pp. 2–12 (Apr. 1984).

496. P. Karger and R. Schell, "MULTICS Security Evaluation, Volume II: Vulnerability Analysis," ESD-TR-74-193, Vol. II, Electronic Systems Division, Air Force Systems Command, Hanscom Field, Bedford, MA (June 1974).

497. P. Karger and J. Wray, "Covert Storage Channels in Disk Arm Optimization," *Proceedings of the 1991 Symposium on Research in Security and Privacy*, pp. 52–61 (May 1991).

498. P. Karger, M. Zurko, D. Bonin, A. Mason, and C. Kahn, "A VMM Security Kernel for the VAX Architecture," *Proceedings of the 1990 Symposium on Research in Security and Privacy*, pp. 2–19 (May 1990).

499. G. Kedem and Y. Ishihara, "Brute Force Attack on UNIX Passwords with SIMD Computer," *Proceedings of the 8th USENIX Security Symposium*, pp. 93–98 (Aug. 1999).

500. R. Kemmerer, "A Practical Approach to Identifying Storage and Timing Channels," *Proceedings of the 1982 IEEE Symposium on Security and Privacy*, pp. 66–73 (Apr. 1982).

501. R. Kemmerer, "Shared Resource Matrix Methodology: An Approach to Identifying Storage and Timing Channels," *ACM Transactions on Computer Systems*, **1** (3), pp. 256–277 (Aug. 1983).

502. S. Kent, "Encryption-Based Protection Protocols for Interactive User-Computer Communication," Technical Report MIT/LCS/TR-162, Laboratory for Computer Science, Massachusetts Institute of Technology, Cambridge, MA (May 1976); cited in *Cryptography and Data Security* [242].

503. S. Kent, "Comments on 'Security Problems in the TCP/IP Protocol Suite'," *Computer Communications Review* **19** (3), pp. 10–19 (July 1989).

504. S. Kent, *Privacy Enhancement for Internet Electronic Mail: Part II: Certificate-Based Key Management*, RFC 1422 (Feb. 1993).

505. B. Kernighan and P. Plauger, *The Elements of Programming Style*, McGraw-Hill Book Co., Reading, MA (1974).

506. B. Kernighan and P. Plauger, *Software Tools*, Addison-Wesley, Reading, MA (1976).

507. K. Keus, W. Kirth, and D. Loevenich, "Quality Assurance in the ITSEC-Evaluation Environment in Germany," *Proceedings of the 16th National Information Systems Security Conference*, pp. 324–333 (Sep. 1993).

508. K. Keus and K.-W. Schröder, "Measuring Correctness and Effectiveness: A New Approach Using Process Evaluation," *Proceedings of the 18th National Information Systems Security Conference*, pp. 366–373 (Oct. 1995).

509. G. Kim and E. Spafford, "Experiences with Tripwire: Using Integrity Checkers for Intrusion Detection," *Proceedings of SANS III*, pp. 89–102 (Apr. 1994).

510. G. Kim and E. Spafford, "The Design and Implementation of Tripwire: A File System Integrity Checker," *Proceedings of the 2nd ACM Conference on Computer and Communications Security* (Nov. 1994).

511. D. Klein, "A Capability Based Protection Mechanism Under Unix," *Proceedings of the 1985 Winter USENIX Conference*, pp. 152–159 (Jan. 1995).

512. D. Klein, "Foiling the Cracker: A Survey of, and Improvements to, Password Security," *Proceedings of the 2nd USENIX UNIX Security Workshop*, pp. 5–14 (Aug. 1990).

513. J. Knight and N. Leveson, "An Experimental Evaluation of the Assumption of Independence in Multi-Version Programming," *IEEE Transactions on Software Engineering* **12** (1), pp. 96–109 (Jan. 1986).

514. J. Knight and N. Leveson, "On N-version Programming," *Software Engineering Notes* **15**(1), pp. 24–35 (Jan. 1990).

515. Knightmare, *Secrets of a Super Hacker*, Loompanics Unlimited (1994).

516. L. Knudsen, "Cryptanalysis of LOKI91," *Advances in Cryptology—AUSCRYPT '92 Proceedings*, pp. 196–208 (1992).

517. L. Kohnfelder, "A Method for Certification," Laboratory for Computer Science, Massachusetts Institute of Technology, Cambridge, MA (May 1978); cited in *Cryptography and Data Security* [242].

518. C. Ko, T. Fraser, L. Badger, and D. Kilpatrick, "Detecting and Countering System Intrusions Using Software Wrappers," *Proceedings of the 9th USENIX Security Symposium*, pp. 145–156 (Aug. 2000).

519. C. Ko, M. Ruschitzka, and K. Levitt, "Execution Monitoring of Security-Critical Programs in Distributed Systems: A Specification-Based Approach," *Proceedings of the 1997 IEEE Symposium on Security and Privacy*, pp. 175–187 (May 1997).

520. H.-P. Ko, "Security Properties of Ring Brackets," *Proceedings of the Computer Security Foundations Workshop II*, pp. 41–46 (June 1989).

521. N. Koblitz, *A Course in Number Theory and Cryptography*, Springer-Verlag, New York, NY (1994).

522. C. Kocher, "Connecting Classified Nets to the Outside World: Costs and Benefits," *Proceedings of the 20th National Information Systems Security Conference*, pp. 534–542 (Oct. 1997).

523. P. Kocher, "Timing Attacks on Implementations of Diffie-Hellman, RSA, DSS, and Other Systems," *Advances in Cryptology—Proceedings of CRYPTO '96*, pp. 104–113 (Aug. 1996).

524. P. Kocher, J. Jaffe, and B. Jun, "Differential Power Analysis," *Advances in Cryptology—Proceedings of CRYPTO '99*, pp. 388–397 (Aug. 1999).

525. A. Koenig, *C Traps and Pitfalls*, Addison-Wesley, Reading, MA (1989).

526. J. Kohl and C. Neuman, *The Kerberos Network Authentication Service (V5)*, RFC 1510 (Sep. 1993).

527. A. Konheim, *Cryptography: A Primer*, John Wiley and Sons, New York, NY (1981).

528. C. Kormos, L. Gallagher, N. Givans, and N. Bartol, "Using Security Metrics to Assess Risk Management Capabilities," *Proceedings of the 22nd National Information Systems Security Conference*, pp. 370–388 (Oct. 1999).

529. D. Kosiur, *Building and Managing Virtual Private Networks*, John Wiley and Sons, New York, NY (1998).

530. S. Kramer, "On Incorporating Access Control Lists into the UNIX Operating System," *Proceedings of the USENIX UNIX Security Workshop*, pp. 38–48 (Aug. 1988).

531. H. Krawczyk, M. Bellare, and R. Canetti, *HMAC: Keyed-Hashing for Message Authentication*, RFC 2104 (Feb. 1997).

532. H. Krawczyk, "How to Predict Congruential Generators," *Journal of Algorithms* **13** (4), pp. 527–545 (Dec. 1992).

533. W. Kremer, H. Saraidaridis, and A. Sripad, "The D5 Digital Terminal System: A Case Study of a Comprehensive Quality and Reliability Program," *IEEE Journal on Selected Areas in Communications* **4** (7), pp. 1099–1103 (Oct. 1986).

534. D. Kristol and L. Montulli, *HTTP State Management Mechanism*, RFC 2109 (Feb. 1997).

535. I. Krsul and E. Spafford, "Authorship Analysis: Identifying the Author of a Program," *Proceedings of the 18th National Information Systems Security Conference*, pp. 514–524 (Oct. 1995).

536. C. Kubicki, "The System Administration Maturity Model—SAMM," *Proceedings of the 7th Systems Administration Conference (LISA 1993)*, pp. 213–225 (Nov. 1993).

537. R. Kuhn, "Mutual Exclusion of Roles as a Means of Implementing Separation of Duty in Role-Based Access Control Systems," *Proceedings of the 2nd ACM Workshop on Role-Based Access Control*, pp. 23–30 (Nov. 1997).

538. S. Kumar and E. Spafford, "A Pattern Matching Model for Misuse Intrusion Detection," *Proceedings of the 17th National Computer Security Conference*, pp. 11–21 (Oct. 1994).

539. J. Lacy, D. Mitchell, and W. Schell, "CrptoLib: Cryptography in Software," *Proceedings of the 4th USENIX UNIX Security Symposium*, pp. 1–17 (June 1993).

540. N. Lai and T. Gray, "Strengthening Discretionary Access Controls to Inhibit Trojan Horses and Computer Viruses," *Proceedings of the 1988 Summer USENIX Conference*, pp. 275–286 (June 1988).

541. X. Lai, J. Massey, and S. Murphy, "Markov Ciphers and Differential Cryptanalysis," *Advances in Cryptology—Proceedings of EUROCRYPT '91*, pp. 17–38 (1991).

542. L. Lamport, "Password Authentication with Insecure Communication," *Communications of the ACM* **24** (11), pp. 770–771 (Nov. 1981).

543. B. Lampson, "Protection," *Proceedings of the Fifth Princeton Symposium of Information Science and Systems*, pp. 437–443 (Mar. 1971); reprinted in *Operating Systems Review* **8** (1), pp. 18–24 (Jan. 1974).

544. B. Lampson, "A Note on the Confinement Problem," *Communications of the ACM* **16** (10), pp. 613–615 (Oct. 1973).

545. C. Landwehr, "Formal Models for Computer Security," *Computing Surveys* **13** (3), pp. 247–278 (Sep. 1981).

546. C. Landwehr, A. Bull, J. McDermott, and W. Choi, "A Taxonomy of Computer Program Security Flaws," *Computing Surveys* **26** (3), pp. 211–254 (Sep. 1994).

547. C. Landwehr and D. Goldschlag, "Security Issues in Networks with Internet Access," *Proceedings of the IEEE* **85** (12), pp. 2034–2051 (Dec. 1997).

548. C. Landwehr, C. Heitmeyer, and J. McLean, "A Security Model for Military Message Systems," *ACM Transactions on Computer Systems* **2** (2), pp. 198–222 (Aug. 1984).

549. T. Lane and C. Brodley, "Temporal Sequence Learning and Data Reduction for Anomaly Detection," *ACM Transactions on Information and System Security* **2** (3), pp. 295–332 (Aug. 1999).

550. L. Lankewicz and M. Benard, "Real-Time Anomaly Detection Using a Nonparametric Pattern Recognition Approach," *Proceedings of the 7th Annual Computer Security Applications Conference*, pp. 80–89 (Dec. 1991).

551. L. LaPadula, "The 'Basic Security Theorem' of Bell and LaPadula Revisited," handout from *Computer Security Foundations Workshop* (April 18, 1988).

552. L. Laudan, *The Book of Risks: Fascinating Facts About the Chances We Take Every Day*, John Wiley and Sons, New York, NY 10158 (1994).

553. G. Lawton, "Biometrics: A New Era in Security," *IEEE Computer* **31** (8), pp. 16–18 (Aug. 1998).

554. T. Lee, "Using Mandatory Integrity to Enforce 'Commercial' Security," *Proceedings of the 1988 IEEE Symposium on Security and Privacy*, pp. 140–146 (Apr. 1988).

555. W. Lee, "A Data Mining Framework for Building Intrusion Detection Models," *Proceedings of the 1999 IEEE Symposium on Security and Privacy*, pp. 120–132 (May 1999).

556. P. Leong and C. Tham, "UNIX Password Encryption Considered Insecure," *Proceedings of the 1991 Winter USENIX Technical Conference*, pp. 269–280 (Jan. 1991).

557. N. Leveson, *Safeware: System Safety and Computers*, Addison-Wesley, Reading, MA (1995).

558. A. Levi and M. Caglayan, "An Efficient, Dynamic, and Trust Preserving Public Key Infrastructure," *Proceedings of the 2000 IEEE Symposium on Security and Privacy*, pp. 203–214 (May 2000).

559. R. Levin, *The Computer Virus Handbook*, Osborne McGraw-Hill, Berkeley, CA (1990).

560. W. Ley, *Watchers of the Skies: An Informal History of Astronomy from Babylon to the Space Age*, Viking Press, New York, NY (1966).

561. Q. Li and B.-H. Juang, "Speaker Verification Using Verbal Information Verification for Automatic Enrollment," *Proceedings of the 1998 IEEE International Conference on Acoustics, Speech, and Signal Processing*, pp. 133–136 (May 1998).

562. Q. Li, B.-H. Juang, and C.-H. Lee, "Automatic Verbal Information Verification for User Authentication," *IEEE Transactions on Speech and Audio Processing* **8** (5), pp. 585–596 (Sep. 2000).

563. Q. Li, B.-H. Juang, C.-H. Lee, Q. Zhou, and F. K. Soong, "Recent Advancements in Automatic Speaker Authentication," *IEEE Robotics and Automation Magazine* **6** (1), pp. 24–34 (Mar. 1999).

564. A. Liebenberg and J. Eloff, "MASS—Model for an Auditing Security System," *Proceedings of SEC 2000: Information Security*, pp. 141–150 (Aug. 2000).

565. H.-Y. Lin and L. Harn, "A Generalized Secret Sharing Scheme with Cheater Detection," *Advances in Cryptology—Proceedings of ASIACRYPT '91*, pp. 149–158 (1991).

566. T. Lin, "Chinese Wall Security Policy—An Aggressive Model," *Proceedings of the 5th Annual Computer Security Conference*, pp. 282–289 (Dec. 1989).

567. R. Linde, "Operating Systems Penetration," *1978 National Computer Conference, AFIPS Conference Proceedings* **44**, pp. 361–368 (Nov. 1975).

568. R. Linde, C. Weissman, and C. Fox, "The ADEPT-50 Time-Sharing System," *Proceedings of the 1969 Fall Joint Computer Conference*, pp. 39–50 (Nov. 1969).

569. J. Linn, *Privacy Enhancement for Internet Electronic Mail: Part I: Message Encryption and Authentication Procedures*, RFC 1421 (Feb. 1993).

570. S. Lipner, "A Comment on the Confinement Problem," *Proceedings of the 5th Symposium on Operating Systems Principles*, pp. 192–196 (Nov. 1975).

571. S. Lipner, "Non-Discretionary Controls for Commercial Applications," *Proceedings of the 1982 Symposium on Privacy and Security*, pp. 2–10 (Apr. 1982).

572. S. Lipner, "Twenty Years of Evaluation Criteria and Commercial Technology," *Proceedings of the 1999 IEEE Symposium on Security and Privacy*, pp. 111–112 (May 1999).

573. R. Lippmann, D. Fried, I. Graf, J. Haines, K. Kendall, D. McClung, D. Weber, S. Webster, D. Wyschogrod, R. Cunningham, and M. Zissman, "Evaluating Intrusion Detection Systems: The 1998 DARPA Off-Line Intrusion Detection Evaluation," *Proceedings of the DARPA Information Survivability Conference and Exposition*, **2**, pp. 12–26 (Jan. 2000).

574. R. Lippmann, J. Haines, D. Fired, J. Korba, and K. Das, "Analysis and Results of the 1999 DARPA Off-Line Intrusion Detection Evaluation," *Proceedings of the 3rd International Workshop on Recent Advances in Intrusion Detection*, pp. 162–182 (Oct. 2000).

575. R. Lipton and T. Budd, "On Classes of Protection Systems," in *Foundations of Secure Computing* [238], pp. 281–291.

576. R. Lipton and L. Snyder, "A Linear Time Algorithm for Deciding Subject Security," *Journal of the ACM* **24** (3), pp. 455–464 (July 1977).

577. J. Littman, *The Watchman: The Twisted Life and Crimes of Serial Hacker Kevin Poulsen*, Little, Brown, & Co., Boston, MA (1997).

578. S. Lodin and C. Schuba, "Firewalls Fend Off Invasions from the Net," *IEEE Spectrum* **35** (2), pp. 26–34 (Feb. 1998).

579. L. Lopez and J. Carracedo, "Hierarchical Organization of Certification Authorities for Secure Environments," *Proceedings of the 1997 Symposium on Network and Distributed System Security*, pp. 112–121 (Feb. 1997).

580. M. Ludwig, *The Giant Black Book of Computer Viruses*, American Eagle Publishers, Phoenix, AZ (1998).

581. E. Lundin and E. Jonsson, "Anomaly-Based Intrusion Detection: Privacy Concerns and Other Problems," *Computer Networks* **34** (4), pp. 623–640 (Oct. 2000).

582. T. Lunt and R. Jagannathan, "A Prototype Real-Time Intrusion-Detection Expert System," *Proceedings of the 1988 IEEE Symposium on Security and Privacy*, pp. 2–10 (Apr. 1988).

583. T. Lunt, R. Schell, W. Shockley, M. Heckman, and D. Warren, " A Near-Term Design for the SeaView Multilevel Database System," *Proceedings of the 1988 IEEE Symposium on Security and Privacy*, pp. 234–244 (Apr. 1988).

584. E. Lupu and M. Sloman, "Towards a Role-Based Framework for Distributed Systems Management," *Journal of Network and Systems Management* **5** (1), pp. 5–30 (Mar. 1997).

585. S. Maguire, *Writing Solid Code: Microsoft's Techniques for Developing Bug-Free C Programs*, Microsoft Press, Redmond, WA (1993).

586. Her Majesty's Stationery Office, *Securities and Investment Board Rules, Chapter III, Part 5:08*, London, UK; cited in "The Chinese Wall Policy" [133].

587. Her Majesty's Stationery Office, *Financial Services Act 1986*, §48(2)(h), London, UK (1986); cited in "The Chinese Wall Policy" [133].

588. D. Malkhi, M. Reiter, and A. Rubin, "Secure Execution of Java Applets Using a Remote Playground," *Proceedings of the 1998 IEEE Symposium on Security and Privacy*, pp. 40–51 (May 1998).

589. U. Manber, "A Simple Scheme to Make Passwords Based on One-Way Functions Much Harder to Crack," *Computers and Security* **15** (2), pp. 171–176 (Mar. 1996).

590. D. Mann and S. Christey, "Towards a Common Enumeration of Vulnerabilities," *Proceedings of the 2nd Workshop on Research with Security Vulnerability Databases* (Jan. 1999).

591. C. Markantonakis, "Secure Log File Download Mechanisms for Smart Cards," *Proceedings of the 3rd International Conference on Smart Card Research and Applications*, pp. 285–304 (Sep. 1998).

592. C. Markantonakis and S. Xenitellis, "Implementing a Secure Log File Download Manager for the Java Card," *Proceedings of the Conference on Communications and Multi-Media Security*, pp. 143–159 (Sep. 1999).

593. T. Markham and C. Williams, "Key Recovery Header for IPSEC," *Computers and Security* **19** (1), pp. 86–90 (Jan./Feb. 2000).

594. M. Marrinan, "In the Chips (Smart Card Applications)," *Bank Systems and Technology* **32** (5), pp. 46–48 (May 1995).

595. D. Martin, S. Rajagopalan, and A. Rubin, "Blocking Java Applets at the Firewall," *Proceedings of the 1997 Symposium on Network and Distributed System Security*, pp. 16–26 (Feb. 1997).

596. M. Matsui, "Linear Cryptanalysis Method for DES Cipher," *Advances in Cryptology—Proceedings of EUROCRYPT '93*, pp. 386–397 (May 1993).

597. M. Matsumoto, S. Shimagaki, D. Watanabe, and K. Mori, "Assurance Technologies for Autonomous Train On-Board Computer System," *Proceedings of the 8th IEEE Workshop on Future Trends of Distributed Computing Systems*, pp. 170–175 (Oct. 2001).

598. S. Matyas and C. Meyer, "Generation, Distribution, and Installation of Cryptographic Keys," *IBM Systems Journal* **17** (2), pp. 126–137 (1978).

599. D. Maughan, M. Schertler, M. Schneider, and J. Turner, *Internet Security Association and Key Management Protocol (ISAKMP)*, RFC 2408 (Nov. 1998).

600. A. Mayer, A. Wool, and E. Ziskind, "Fang: a Firewall Analysis Engine," *Proceedings of the 2000 IEEE Symposium on Security and Privacy*, pp. 177–187 (May 2000).

601. D. Mazières and M. Kaashoek, "The Design, Implementation, and Operation of an Email Pseudonym Server," *Proceedings of the 5th ACM Conference on Computer and Communications Security*, pp. 27–36 (Nov. 1998).

602. S. McCanne and V. Jacobson, "The BSD Packet Filter: A New Architecture for User-Level Packet Capture," *Proceedings of the 1993 Winter USENIX Conference*, pp. 259–269 (Jan. 1993).

603. C. McCollum, J. Messing, and L. Notargiacomo, "Beyond the Pale of MAC and DAC—Defining New Forms of Access Control," *Proceedings of the 1990 IEEE Computer Society Symposium on Research in Security and Privacy*, pp. 190–200 (May 1990).

604. D. McCullagh, "DVD Lawyers Make Secret Public," *Wired News* (Jan. 26, 2000); available at http://www.wired.com/news/politics/ 0,1283,33922,00.html.

605. J. McHugh, "The 1998 Lincoln Laboratory IDS Evaluation: A Critique," *Proceedings of the 3rd International Workshop on Recent Advances in Intrusion Detection*, pp. 145–161 (Oct. 2000).

606. J. McHugh and D. Good, "An Information Flow Tool for Gypsy," *Proceedings of the 1985 IEEE Symposium on Security and Privacy*, pp. 46–48 (Apr. 1985).

607. M. McIlroy, "Virology 101," *Computing Systems* **2** (2), pp. 173–181 (Spring 1989).

608. M. McKusick, K. Bostic, M. Karels, and J. Quarterman, *The Design and Implementation of the 4.4BSD Operating System*, Addison-Wesley Publishing Co., Reading, MA (1996).

609. I. McLean, *Windows 2000 Security*, The Coriolis Group, LLC, Scottsdale, AZ (2000).

610. J. McLean, "A Comment on the 'Basic Security Theorem' of Bell and LaPadula," *Information Processing Letters* **20** (2), pp. 67–70 (Feb. 1985).

611. J. McLean, "Reasoning About Security Models," *Proceedings of the 1987 IEEE Symposium on Security and Privacy*, pp. 123–131 (Apr. 1987).

612. J. McLean, "Proving Noninterference and Functional Correctness Using Traces," *Journal of Computer Security* **1** (1), pp. 37–57 (1992).

613. J. McLean, "Is the Trusted Computing Base Concept Fundamentally Flawed?" *Proceedings of the 1997 IEEE Symposium on Security and Privacy*, p. 2 (May 1997).

614. D. McNutt, "Role-Based System Administration or Who, What, Where, and How," *Proceedings of the 7th System Administration Conference (LISA '93)*, pp. 107–112 (Nov. 1993).

615. C. Meadows, "The Integrity Lock Architecture and Its Application to Message Systems: Reducing Covert Channels," *Proceedings of the 1987 IEEE Symposium on Security and Privacy*, pp. 212–218 (Apr. 1987).

616. C. Meadows, "Extending the Brewer-Nash Model to a Multilevel Context," *Proceedings of the 1990 IEEE Symposium on Research in Security and Privacy*, pp. 95–102 (May 1990).

617. G. Medvinsky and B. Neuman, "NetCash: A Design for Practical Electronic Currency on the Internet," *Proceedings of the 1st ACM Conference on Computer and Communications Security*, pp. 102–106 (Oct. 1993).

618. N. Mehta and K. Sollins, "Expanding and Extending the Security Features of Java," *Proceedings of the 7th USENIX Security Symposium*, pp. 159–172 (Jan. 1998).

619. A. Menezes, P. Van Oorschot, and S. Vanstone, *Handbook of Applied Cryptography*, CRC Press, Boca Raton, FL (1997).

620. C. Menk III, "System Security Engineering Capability Maturity Model and Evaluations: Partners Within the Assurance Framework," *Proceedings of the 19th National Information Systems Security Conference*, pp. 76–88 (Oct. 1996).

621. R. Merkle, "Protocols for Public Key Cryptosystems," *Proceedings of the 1980 Symposium on Privacy and Security*, pp. 122–133 (Apr. 1980).

622. R. Merkle, "A Fast Software One-Way Hash Function," *Journal of Cryptology* **3** (1), pp. 43–58 (1990).

623. R. Merkle, "Fast Software Encryption Functions," *Advances in Cryptology—Proceedings of CRYPTO '90*, pp. 476–501 (Aug. 1990).

624. R. Merkle and M. Hellman, "On the Security of Multiple Encryption," *Communications of the ACM* **24** (7), pp. 465–467 (July 1981).

625. C. Meyer, "Ciphertext/Plaintext and Ciphertext/Key Dependence vs. Number of Rounds for the Data Encryption Standard," *1978 National Computer Conference, AFIPS Conference Proceedings* **47**, pp. 1119–1126 (June 1978).

626. C. Meyer and S. Matyas, *Cryptography: A New Dimension in Computer Data Security: A Guide for the Design and Implementation of Secure Systems*, John Wiley and Sons, New York, NY (1982).

627. G. Meyer, *The PPP Encryption Control Protocol (ECP)*, RFC 1968 (June 1996).

628. S. Mhlaba, "The Efficacy of International Regulation of Transborder Data Flows: The Case for the Clipper Chip," *Government Information Quarterly* **12** (4), pp. 353–366 (1995).

629. C. Michael and A. Ghosh, "Two State-Based Approaches to Program-Based Anomaly Detection," *Proceedings of the 16th Annual Computer Security Applications Conference*, pp. 21–30 (Dec. 2000).

630. G. Michaelson and M. Prior, *Naming Guidelines for the AARNet X.500 Directory Service*, RFC 1562 (Dec. 1993).

631. J. Millen, "The Cascading Problem for Interconnected Networks," *Proceedings of the 4th Aerospace Computer Security Applications Conference*, pp. 269–274 (Dec. 1988).

632. J. Millen, "Covert Channel Capacity," *Proceedings of the 1993 IEEE Symposium on Research in Security and Privacy*, pp. 60–65 (May 1993).

633. J. Millen, "Unwinding Forward Correctability," *Journal of Computer Security* **3** (1), pp. 35–54 (1994/1995).

634. J. Millen, "20 Years of Covert Channel Modeling and Analysis," *Proceedings of the 1999 IEEE Symposium on Security and Privacy*, pp. 113–114 (May 1999).

635. B. Miller, "Vital Signs of Identity," *IEEE Spectrum* **31** (2), pp. 22–30 (Jan. 1994).

636. B. Miller, L. Fredriksen, and B. So, "An Empirical Study of the Reliability of UNIX Utilities," *Communications of the ACM* **33** (12), pp. 32–44 (Dec. 1990).

637. D. Miller and R. Baldwin, "Access Control by Boolean Expression Evaluation," *Proceedings of the 5th Annual Computer Security Applications Conference*, pp. 131–139 (Dec. 1990).

638. T. Miller and T. De Raadt, "strlcpy and strlcat—Consistent, Safe, String Copy and Concatenation," *Proceedings of the FREENIX Track of the 1999 USENIX Conference*, pp. 175–178 (June 1999).

639. N. Minsky, "Selective and Locally Controlled Transport of Privileges," *ACM Transactions on Programming Languages and Systems* **6** (4), pp. 573–602 (Oct. 1984).

640. S. Mister and S. Tavares, "Cryptanalysis of RC4-Like Ciphers," *Proceedings of the 5th Annual International Workshop on Selected Areas in Cryptography*, pp. 131–143 (Aug. 1998).

641. J. Mitchell, V. Shmatikov, and U. Stern, "Finite-State Analysis of SSL 3.0," *Proceedings of the 7th USENIX Security Symposium*, pp. 201–215 (Jan. 1998).

642. S. Miyaguchi, "The FEAL Cipher Family," *Advances in Cryptology— Proceedings of EUROCRYPT '90*, pp. 627–638 (1991).

643. P. Mockapetris, *Domain Names Concepts and Facilities*, RFC 1034 (Nov. 1987).

644. P. Mockapetris, *Domain Names Implementation and Specification*, RFC 1035 (Nov. 1987).

645. J. Mogul, R. Rashid, and M. Accetta, "The Packet Filter: An Efficient Mechanism for User-Level Network Code," *Proceedings of the 11th Symposium on Operating Systems Principles*, pp. 39–51 (Nov. 1987).

646. V. Molak (ed.), *Fundamentals of Risk Analysis and Risk Management*, CRC Press, Boca Raton, FL (1996).

647. F. Monrose, "Biometrics for Automatic Identity Verification," Technical Report 722, Department of Computer Science, New York University, New York, NY (1998).

648. F. Monrose and A. Rubin, "Authentication via Keystroke Dynamics," *Proceedings of the 4th ACM Conference on Computer and Communications Security*, pp. 48–56 (Nov. 1997).

649. J. Moore, "Protocol Failures in Cryptosystems," *Proceedings of the IEEE* **76** (5), pp. 594–602 (May 1988).

650. M. Moriconi, X. Qian, R. Riemenschneider, and L. Gong, "Secure Software Architectures," *Proceedings of the 1997 IEEE Symposium on Security and Privacy*, pp. 84–93 (May 1997).

651. R. Morris and K. Thompson, "Password Security: A Case History," *Communications of the ACM* **22** (11), pp. 594–597 (Nov. 1979).

652. I. Moskowitz, "Variable Noise Effects upon a Simple Timing Channel," *Proceedings of the 1991 IEEE Symposium on Research in Security and Privacy*, pp. 362–372 (May 1991).

653. I. Moskowitz and A. Miller, "The Influence of Delay upon an Idealized Channel's Bandwidth," *Proceedings of the 1992 IEEE Symposium on Security and Privacy*, pp. 62–67 (May 1992).

654. I. Moskowitz, S. Greenwald, and M. Kang, "An Analysis of the Timed Z-Channel," *Proceedings of the 1996 IEEE Symposium on Security and Privacy*, pp. 2–9 (May 1996).

655. G. Mourani, *Securing and Optimizing Linux: Red Hat Edition—A Hands-On Guide*, OpenDocs, LLC, Salem, OR (Aug. 2000).

656. A. Muffett, "crack" (unpublished) (1992).

657. A. Muffett, "WAN-Hacking with *AutoHack*: Auditing Security *Behind* the Firewall," *Proceedings of the 5th USENIX UNIX Security Symposium*, pp. 21–34 (June 1995).

658. S. Murphy, "The Cryptanalysis of FEAL-4 with 20 Chosen Plaintexts," *Journal of Cryptology* **2** (3), pp. 145–154 (1990).

659. W. Murray, "The Application of Epidemiology to Computer Viruses," *Computers and Security* **7** (1), pp. 139–150 (Feb. 1988).

660. A. Myers and B. Liskov, "Complete, Safe Information Flow with Decentralized Labels," *Proceedings of the 1998 IEEE Computer Society Symposium on Security and Privacy*, pp. 186–197 (May 1998).

661. M. Nash and K. Poland, "Some Conundrums Concerning Separation of Duty," *Proceedings of the 1990 IEEE Computer Society Symposium on Research in Security and Privacy*, pp. 201–207 (May 1990).

662. National Bureau of Standards, *Data Encryption Standard*, FIPS PUB 46 (Jan. 1977).

663. National Bureau of Standards, *DES Modes of Operation*, FIPS PUB 81 (Dec. 1980).

664. National Institute of Standards and Technology, *Secure Hash Standard*, FIPS PUB 180 (May 1993).

665. National Institute of Standards and Technology, *Escrowed Encryption Standard (EES)*, FIPS PUB 185 (Feb. 1994).

666. National Institute of Standards and Technology, *Digital Signature Standard*, FIPS PUB 187 (May 1994).

667. National Institute of Standards and Technology, "SKIPJACK and KEA Algorithm Specifications," Version 2.0 (May 1998); available at http://csrc.nist.gov/encryption/skipjack.pdf.

668. National Institute of Standards and Technology, *Common Criteria for Information Technology Security Evaluation, Part 1: Introduction and General Model*, Version 2.1, CCIMB-99-031 (Aug. 1999).

669. National Institute of Standards and Technology, *Common Criteria for Information Technology Security Evaluation, Part 2: Security Function Requirements*, Version 2.1, CCIMB-99-031 (Aug. 1999).

670. National Institute of Standards and Technology, *Common Criteria for Information Technology Security Evaluation, Part 3: Security Assurance Requirements*, Version 2.1, CCIMB-99-031 (Aug. 1999).

671. National Institute of Standards and Technology, *Security Requirements for Cryptographic Modules*, FIPS PUB 140-2 (May 2001).

672. National Institute of Standards and Technology, *Advanced Encryption Standard (AES)*, FIPS PUB 197 (Nov. 2001).

673. National Institute of Standards and Technology, "National Information Assurance Partnership: Common Criteria Evaluation and Validation Scheme Web Site," http://niap.nist.gov/cc-scheme (Apr. 2002).

674. National Institute of Standards and Technology, "Cryptographic Module Validation (CMV) Program Web Site," http://csrc.nist.gov/cryptval (May 2002).

675. National Institute of Standards and Technology and National Security Agency, *Federal Criteria for Information Technology Security*, Version 1.0 (1992).

676. National Security Agency, *Cryptolog Interface Programmers Guide for the Fortezza Crypto Card, Revision 1.52*, Ft. George Meade, MD (Nov. 1995).

677. National Security Agency, *Fortezza Message Security Protocol Software Interface Control Document, Version 3.01*, Ft. George Meade, MD (Nov. 1995).

678. National Security Agency, *Press Release: NSA Releases Fortezza Algorithms*, Ft. George Meade, MD (June 1998).

679. National Security Telecommunications and Information Systems Security Committee, *National Information Systems Security (INFOSEC) Glossary*, NSTISSI No. 4009 (Sep. 2000).

680. G. Necula, "Proof-Carrying Code," *Proceedings of the 24th ACM SIGPLAN-SIGACT Symposium on Principles of Programming Languages*, pp. 106–119 (Jan. 1997).

681. G. Necula and P. Lee, "Safe Kernel Extensions Without Run-Time Checking," *Proceedings of the 2nd Symposium on Operating Systems Design and Implementation*, pp. 229–243 (Oct. 1996).

682. R. Needham and M. Schroeder, "Using Encryption for Authentication in Large Networks of Computers," *Communications of the ACM* **21** (12), pp. 993–999 (Dec. 1978).

683. R. Needham and M. Schroeder, "Authentication Revisited," *Operating Systems Review* **21** (1), p. 7 (Jan. 1987).

684. R. Needham and R. Walker, "The Cambridge CAP Computer and Its Protection System," *Proceedings of the 5th Symposium on Operating System Principles*, pp. 1–10 (Nov. 1975).

685. E. Nemeth, G. Snyder, S. Seebass, and T. Hein, *UNIX System Administration Handbook*, Prentice-Hall, Upper Saddle River, NJ (2000).

686. B. Neuman and S. Stubblebine, "A Note on the Use of Timestamps as Nonces," *Operating Systems Review* **27** (2), pp. 10–14 (Apr. 1993).

687. P. Neumann, "Rainbows and Arrows: How the Security Criteria Address Computer Misuse," *Proceedings of the 13th National Computer Security Conference*, pp. 414–422 (Oct. 1990).

688. P. Neumann, *Computer-Related Risks*, Addison-Wesley, Reading, MA (1995).

689. P. Neumann, L. Robinson, K. Levitt, R. Boyer, and A. Saxena, "A Provably Secure Operating System: The System, Its Applications, and Proofs," Technical Report, SRI International, Menlo Park, CA (June 1975).

690. J. Newman, *The World of Mathematics: A Small Library of the Literature of Mathematics from A'h-mosé the Scribe to Albert Einstein*, Simon and Schuster, New York, NY (1956).

691. J. Newman and S. Wander, "The Knowledge Path to Mission Success: Overview of the NASA PBMA-KMS," *Proceedings of the 2002 Annual Reliability and Maintainability Symposium*, pp. 601–606 (Jan. 2002).

692. J. Nieh and O. Leonard, "Examining VMware," *Dr. Dobb's Journal* **25** (8), pp. 70–76 (Aug. 2000).

693. L. Nizer, *The Jury Returns*, Doubleday, Garden City, NY (1966).

694. S. Northcutt, *Computer Security Incident Handling: Step by Step*, Version 1.5, The SANS Institute, Bethesda, MD (May 1998).

695. S. Northcutt, *Network Intrusion Detection: An Analyst's Handbook*, 2nd Edition, New Riders Publishing, Indianapolis, IN (2000).

696. L. Notargiacomo, B. Blaustein, and C. McCollum, "Merging Models: Integrity, Dynamic Separation of Duty, and Trusted Data Management," *Journal of Computer Security* **3** (2, 3), pp. 207–230 (1994/1995).

697. M. Nyanchama and S. Osborn, "Role-Based Security, Object Oriented Databases and Separation of Duty," *SIGMOD Record* **22** (4), pp. 45–51 (Dec. 1993).

698. C. Oakes, "DVD Hackers Hit with Lawsuit," *Wired News* (Dec. 28, 1999); available at http://www.wired.com/news/business/0,1367,33303,00.html.

699. D. O'Brien, "Recognizing and Recovering from Rootkit Attacks," *SysAdmin* **5** (11), pp. 8–20 (Nov. 1996).

700. R. O'Brien and C. Rogers, "Developing Applications on LOCK," *Proceedings of the 14th National Computer Security Conference*, pp. 147–156 (Oct. 1991).

701. T. Okamoto and K. Ohta, "Universal Electronic Cash," *Advances in Cryptology—Proceedings of CRYPTO '91*, pp. 324–337 (Aug. 1992).

702. R. Oppliger, "Security at the Internet Layer," *IEEE Computer* **31** (9), pp. 43–47 (Sep. 1998).

703. E. Organick, *The MULTICS System: An Examination of Its Structure*, The MIT Press, Cambridge, MA (1972).

704. E. Organick, *Computer System Organization: The B5700/6700 Series*, Academic Press, New York, NY (1973).

705. H. Orman, *The OAKLEY Key Determination Protocol*, RFC 2412 (Nov. 1998).

706. D. Otway and O. Rees, "Efficient and Timely Mutual Authentication," *Operating Systems Review* **21** (1), pp. 8–10 (Jan. 1987).

707. J. Page, "An Assured Pipeline Integrity Scheme for Virus Protection," *Proceedings of the 12th National Computer Security Conference*, pp. 369–377 (Oct. 1989).

708. R. Pandey and B. Hashii, "Providing Fine-Grained Access Control for Java Programs," *Proceedings of the 13th European Conference on Object-Oriented Programming*, pp. 449–473 (June 1999).

709. J. Park, B. Montrose, and J. Froscher, "Tools for Information Security Assurance Arguments," *Proceedings of the DARPA Information Survivability Conference and Exposition II*, pp. 287–296 (June 2001).

710. J. Park and R. Sandhu, "Smart Certificates: Extending X.509 for Secure Attribute Services on the Web," *Proceedings of the 22nd National Information Systems Security Conference*, pp. 337–348 (Oct. 1999).

711. S. Park and K. Miller, "Random Number Generators: Good Ones Are Hard to Find," *Communications of the ACM* **31** (10), pp. 1192–1201 (Oct. 1988).

712. D. Parker, "Cease and DeCSS: DVD's Encryption Code Cracked," *eMedia Industry News* (Nov. 4, 1999); available at http://www.emediapro.net/news99/news111.html.

713. D. Parker, *Crime by Computer*, Macmillan Publishing Co., New York, NY (1978).

714. R. Perlman, "An Overview of PKI Trust Models," *IEEE Network* **13** (6), pp. 38–43 (Nov. 1999).

715. B. Perlmutter and J. Zarkower, *Virtual Private Networking*, Prentice-Hall, Upper Saddle River, NJ (2000).

716. J. Perry and J. Carney, "Human Face Recognition Using a Multilayer Perceptron," *International Conference on Neural Networks* **2**, p. 413 (1990); cited in "Biometrics for Automated Identity Verification" [647].

717. I. Peterson, *Fatal Defects: Chasing Killer Computer Bugs*, Vintage Books, New York, NY 10022 (1996).

718. J. Peterson and A. Silberschatz, *Operating Systems Concepts* (6th Edition), John Wiley and Sons, New York, NY (2002).

719. C. Pfleeger, "Comparison of Trusted Systems Evaluation Criteria," *Proceedings of the 5th Annual Conference on Computer Assurance*, *Systems Integrity, Software Safety and Process Security*, pp. 135–143 (June 1990).

720. S. Pfleeger, *Software Engineering: The Production of Quality Software*, 2nd Edition, Macmillan Publishing Co., New York, NY (1991).

721. J. Picciotto, "The Design of an Effective Auditing Subsystem," *Proceedings of the 1987 IEEE Symposium on Security and Privacy*, pp. 13–22 (1987).

722. W. Polk, "Approximating Clark-Wilson 'Access Triples' with Basic UNIX Controls," *Proceedings of the 4th USENIX UNIX Security Symposium*, pp. 145–154 (Oct. 1993).

723. G. Popek and R. Goldberg, "Formal Requirements for Virtualizable Third Generation Architectures," *Communications of the ACM* **17** (7), pp. 412–421 (July 1974).

724. G. Popek and B. Walker, *The LOCUS Distributed System Architecture*, The MIT Press, Cambridge, MA (1985).

725. P. Porras and R. Kemmerer, "Covert Flow Trees: A Technique for Identifying and Analyzing Covert Storage Channels," *Proceedings of the 1991 IEEE Symposium on Security and Privacy*, pp. 36–51 (May 1991).

726. POSIX, *Standard for Information Technology Portable Operating System Interface (POSIX) Part I: System Application Program Interface* (API), Report 1003.1e (Apr. 1994).

727. J. Postel, *Simple Mail Transfer Protocol*, RFC 821 (Aug. 1982).

728. J. Postel and J. Reynolds, *File Transfer Protocol*, RFC 959 (Oct. 1985).

729. E. Powanda and J. Genovese, "Configuring a Trusted System Using the TNI," *Proceedings of the 4th Aerospace Computer Security Applications Conference*, pp. 256–261 (Dec. 1988).

730. M. Pozzo and T. Gray, "A Model for the Containment of Computer Viruses," *Proceedings of the AIAA/ASIS/DODCI 2nd Aerospace Computer Security Conference*, pp. 11–18 (Dec. 1986).

731. M. Pozzo and T. Gray, "An Approach to Containing Computer Viruses," *Computers and Security* **6** (4), pp. 321–331 (Aug. 1987).

732. D. Price, "Pentium FDIV Flaw—Lessons Learned," *IEEE Micro* **15** (2), pp. 86–88 (Apr. 1995).

733. N. Proctor, "The Restricted Access Processor: An Example of Formal Verification," *Proceedings of the 1985 IEEE Symposium on Security and Privacy*, pp. 49–53 (Apr. 1985).

734. P. Proctor, *The Practical Intrusion Detection Handbook*, Prentice-Hall, Upper Saddle River, NJ (2001).

735. T. Ptacek and T. Newsham, *Insertion, Evasion, and Denial of Service: Eluding Network Intrusion Detection*, Technical Report, Secure Networks, Inc., Calgary, Alberta, Canada (Jan. 1998).

736. N. Puketza, M. Chung, R. Olsson, and B. Mukherjee, "A Software Platform for Testing Intrusion Detection Systems," *IEEE Software* **14** (5), pp. 43–51 (Sep. 1997).

737. L. Quarantiello, *Cyber Crime: How to Protect Yourself from Computer Criminals*, Tiare Publications, Lake George, WI (1996).

738. M. Rabin, "Probabilistic Algorithms for Primality Testing," *Journal of Number Theory* **12** (1), pp. 128–138 (Feb. 1980).

739. S. Rajunas, N. Hardy, A. Bomberger, W. Frantz, and C. Landau, "Security in KeyKOS," *Proceedings of the 1986 IEEE Symposium on Security and Privacy*, pp. 78–85 (Apr. 1986).

740. The RAND Corporation, *A Million Random Digits with 100,000 Normal Deviates*, Free Press Publishers, Glencoe, IL (1955).

741. M. Ranum and F. Avolio, "A Toolkit and Methods for Internet Firewalls," *Proceedings of the Summer 1994 USENIX Conference*, pp. 37–44 (June 1994).

742. M. Ranum, K. Landfield, M. Stolarchuk, M. Sienkiewicz, A. Lambeth, and E. Wall, "Implementing a Generalized Tool for Network Monitoring," *Proceedings of the 11th Systems Administration Conference (LISA 1997)*, pp. 26–31 (Dec. 1997).

743. K. Rao, "Security Audit for Embedded Avionics Systems," *Proceedings of the 5th Annual Computer Security Applications Conference*, pp. 78–84 (Dec. 1989).

744. J. Ray and W. Ray, *Mac OS X Unleashed*, SAMS Publishing, Indianapolis, IN (2001).

745. D. Redell and R. Fabry, "Selective Revocation and Capabilities," *Proceedings of the International Workshop on Protection in Operating Systems*, pp. 197–209 (Aug. 1974).

746. J. Reeds, "Cracking a Random Number Generator," *Cryptologia* **1** (1), pp. 20–26 (Jan. 1977); cited in *Applied Cryptography* [796].

747. B. Reid, "Reflections on Some Recent Widespread Computer Break-Ins," *Communications of the ACM* **30** (2), pp. 103–105 (Feb. 1987).

748. R. Reitman, "A Mechanism for Information Control in Parallel Programs," *Proceedings of the 7th Symposium on Operating Systems Principles*, pp. 55–62 (Dec. 1979).

749. Y. Rekhter, B. Moscowitz, D. Karrenberg, G. de Groot, and E. Lear, *Address Allocation for Private Internets*, RFC 1918 (Feb. 1996).

750. T. Riechmann and F. Hauck, "Meta Objects for Access Control: Extending Capability-Based Security," *Proceedings of the 1997 New Security Paradigms Workshop*, pp. 17–22 (Sep. 1997).

751. D. Ritchie, "Joy of Reproduction," *net.lang.c* (Nov. 4, 1982).

752. D. Ritchie, "On the Security of UNIX," *UNIX System Manager's Manual*, pp. SM17: 1–3 (1979).

753. R. Rivest, *The MD4 Message Digest Algorithm*, RFC 1320 (Apr. 1992).

754. R. Rivest, *The MD5 Message Digest Algorithm*, RFC 1321 (Apr. 1992).

755. R. Rivest, M. Hellman, J. Anderson, and J. Lyons, "Responses to NIST's Proposal," *Communications of the ACM* **35** (7), pp. 41–54 (July 1992).

756. R. Rivest, A. Shamir, and L. Adleman, "A Method for Obtaining Digital Signatures and Public-Key Cryptosystems," *Communications of the ACM* **21** (2), pp. 120–126 (Feb. 1978).

757. J. Rochlis and M. Eichin, "The Internet Worm, with Microscope and Tweezers: the Worm from MIT's Perspective," *Communications of the ACM* **32** (6), pp. 689–698 (June 1989).

758. G. Rodney, "Assuring Safety and Mission Success for Space Station Freedom," *Proceedings of the 1990 International Symposium on Reliability and Maintainability*, pp. 7–12 (June 1990).

759. E. Rodríguez and J. Piquer, "The Persistent Hacker: An Intruder Attacks a New Internet Host," *Proceedings of the 4th USENIX UNIX Security Symposium*, pp. 131–138 (Oct. 1993).

760. W. Royce, "Managing the Development of Large Software Systems," *1970 WESTCON Technical Papers* **14**, p. 8 (Aug. 1970).

761. M. Rubia, J. Cruellas, and M. Medina, "The DEDICA Project: The Solution to the Interoperability Problems Between the X.509 and EDIFACT Public Key Infrastructures," *Proceedings of Secure Networking—CQRE [Secure] '99 International Exhibition and Congress*, pp. 242–250 (Nov. 1999).

762. L. Romano, A. Mazzeo, and N. Mazzocca, "SECURE: A Simulation Tool for PKI Design," *Proceedings of Secure Networking—CQRE [Secure] '99 International Exhibition and Congress*, pp. 17–29 (Nov. 1999).

763. A. Rubin, "Independent One-Time Passwords," *Computing Systems* **9** (1), pp. 15–27 (Winter 1996).

764. A. Rubin and M. Ranum, *Web Security Sourcebook*, John Wiley and Sons, New York, NY (1997).

765. C. Rubin, "UNIX System V with B2 Security," *Proceedings of the 13th National Computer Security Conference*, pp. 1–9 (Oct. 1990).

766. R. Rueppel, "Stream Ciphers," in *Contemporary Cryptology: The Science of Information Integrity* [834], pp. 65–134.

767. C. Rutstein, *Windows NT Security: A Practical Guide to Securing Windows NT Servers and Workstations*, McGraw-Hill, New York, NY (1997).

768. D. Safford, D. Schales, and D. Hess, "The TAMU Security Package: An Ongoing Response to Internet Intruders in an Academic Environment," *Proceedings of the 4th USENIX UNIX Security Symposium*, pp. 91–118 (Oct. 1993).

769. M. St. Johns, *Identification Protocol*, RFC 1413 (Feb. 1993).

770. J. Sajaniemi, "Modeling Spreadsheet Audit: A Rigorous Approach to Automatic Visualization," *Journal of Visual Languages and Computing* **11** (1), pp. 49–82 (Feb. 2000).

771. R. Saltman, "Accuracy, Integrity and Security in Computerized Vote-Tallying," *Communications of the ACM* **31** (10), pp. 1184–1191 (Oct. 1988).

772. J. Saltzer, "Protection and the Control of Information Sharing in Multics," *Communications of the ACM* **17** (7), pp. 388–402 (July 1974).

773. J. Saltzer and M. Schroeder, "The Protection of Information in Computer Systems," *Proceedings of the IEEE* **63** (9), pp. 1278–1308 (Sep. 1975).

774. J. Saltzer, *On the Naming and Binding of Network Destinations*, RFC 1498 (Aug. 1993).

775. A. Samal and P. Iyengar, "Automatic Recognition and Analysis of Human Faces and Facial Expressions: A Survey," *Pattern Recognition* **25**, pp. 65–77 (1992); cited in "Biometrics for Automatic Identity Verification" [647].

776. V. Samar, "Unified Login with Pluggable Authentication Modules (PAM)," *Proceedings of the 3rd ACM Conference on Computer and Communications Security*, pp. 1–10 (Mar. 1996).

777. R. Sandhu, "Analysis of Acyclic Attenuating Systems for the SSR Protection Model," *Proceedings of the 1985 IEEE Symposium on Security and Privacy*, pp. 197–206 (Apr. 1985).

778. R. Sandhu, "The Schematic Protection Model: Its Definition and Analysis for Acyclic Attenuating Schemes," *Journal of the ACM* **35** (2), pp. 404–432 (Apr. 1988).

779. R. Sandhu, "The Demand Operation in the Schematic Protection Model," *Information Processing Letters* **32** (4), pp. 213–219 (Apr. 1989).

780. R. Sandhu, "Expressive Power of the Schematic Protection Model," *Journal of Computer Security* **1** (1), pp. 59–98 (1992).

781. R. Sandhu, "Transformation of Access Rights," *Proceedings of the 1989 IEEE Symposium on Security and Privacy*, pp. 259–268 (May 1989).

782. R. Sandhu, "Non-Monotonic Transformation of Access Rights," *Proceedings of the 1992 IEEE Symposium on Research in Security and Privacy*, pp. 148–161 (Apr. 1992).

783. R. Sandhu, "The Typed Access Matrix Model," *Proceedings of the 1992 IEEE Symposium on Security and Privacy*, pp. 122–136 (Apr. 1992).

784. R. Sandhu and G.-J. Ahn, "Decentralized Group Hierarchies in UNIX: An Experiment and Lessons Learned," *Proceedings of the 21st National Information Systems Security Conference*, pp. 486–502 (Oct. 1998).

785. R. Sandhu and S. Ganta, "On Testing for the Absence of Rights in Access Control Models," *Proceedings of the Computer Security Foundations Workshop IV*, pp. 109–118 (June 1993).

786. R. Sandhu and S. Ganta, "On the Minimality of Testing for Rights in Transformation Models," *Proceedings of the 1994 IEEE Symposium on Research in Security and Privacy*, pp. 230–241 (Apr. 1994).

787. P. Sands, "Building an FTP Guard," *Proceedings of the 21st National Information Systems Security Conference*, pp. 432–442 (Oct. 1998).

788. S. Savage, D. Wetherall, A. Karlin, and T. Anderson, "Practical Network Support for IP Traceback," *Computer Communication Review* **30** (4) pp. 295–306 (Aug. 2000).

789. O. Saydjari, J. Beckman, and J. Leaman, "Locking Computers Securely," *Proceedings of the 10th National Computer Security Conference*, pp. 129–141 (Sep. 1987).

790. O. Saydjari, J. Beckman, and J. Leaman, "LOCK Trek: Navigating Uncharted Space," *Proceedings of the 1989 Symposium on Security and Privacy*, pp. 167–175 (May 1989).

791. M. Schaefer, B. Gold, R. Linde, and J. Scheid, "Program Confinement in KVM/370," *Proceedings of the 1977 ACM Annual Conference*, pp. 404–410 (Oct. 1977).

792. P. Schafer, "Is Centralized System Administration the Answer?" *Proceedings of the 6th Systems Administration Conference (LISA 1992)*, pp. 55–61 (Oct. 1992).

793. R. Shell, T. Tao, and M. Heckman, "Designing the GEMSOS Security Kernel for Security and Performance," *Proceedings of the 8th National Computer Security Conference*, pp. 108–119 (Oct. 1985).

794. K. Scheurer, "The Clipper Chip: Cryptography, Technology and the Constitution—the Government's Answer to Encryption 'Chips' Away at Constitutional Rights," *Rutgers Computer and Technology Law Journal* **21** (1), pp. 263–292 (1995).

795. D. Schnackenberg, K. Djahandari, and D. Sterne, "Infrastructure for Intrusion Detection and Response," *Proceedings of the DARPA Information Survivability Conference and Exposition* **2**, pp. 3–11 (Jan. 2000).

796. B. Schneier, *Applied Cryptography*, 2nd Edition, John Wiley and Sons, New York, NY (1996).

797. J. Schoch and J. Hupp, "The 'Worm' Programs—Early Experiences with a Distributed Computation," *Communications of the ACM* **25** (3), pp. 172–180 (Mar. 1982).

798. T. Schoriak, "SSL/TLS Protocol Enablement for Key Recovery," *Computers and Security* **19** (1), pp. 100–104 (Jan./Feb. 2000).

799. K. Schroeder and J. Ledger, *Life and Death on the Internet*, Supple Publishing, Menosha, WI (1998).

800. C. Schuba, "Addressing Weaknesses in the Domain Name System Protocol," Master's thesis, Department of Computer Sciences, Purdue University, West Lafayette, IN (Aug. 1993).

801. C. Schuba, I. Krsul, M. Kuhn, E. Spafford, A. Sundaram, and D. Zamboni, "Analysis of a Denial of Service Attack on TCP," *Proceedings of the 1997 IEEE Symposium on Security and Privacy*, pp. 208–223 (May 1997).

802. C. Schuba and E. Spafford, "A Reference Model for Firewall Technology," *Proceedings of the 13th Annual Computer Security Applications Conference*, pp. 133–145 (Dec. 1997).

803. R. Scott, "Wide Open Encryption Design Offers Flexible Implementations," *Cryptologia* **9** (1), pp. 75–90 (Jan. 1985).

804. C. Scott, P. Wolfe, and M. Erwin, *Virtual Private Networks*, O'Reilly & Associates, Sebastopol, CA (1998).

805. J. Seberry and J. Pieprzyk, *Cryptography: An Introduction to Computer Security*, Prentice-Hall, Englewood Cliffs, NJ (1989).

806. SSE-CMM Support Organization, "Secure Software Engineering Capability Maturity Model Web Page," http://www.sse-cmm.org (2001).

807. K. Seiden and J. Melanson, "The Auditing Facility for a VMM Security Kernel," *Proceedings of the 1990 IEEE Symposium on Research in Security and Privacy*, pp. 262–277 (1990).

808. D. Seeley, "Password Cracking: A Game of Wits," *Communications of the ACM* **32** (6), pp. 700–703 (June 1989).

809. D. Seeley, "A Tour of the Worm," *Proceedings of the 1989 Winter USENIX Conference*, pp. 287–304 (Jan. 1989).

810. R. Sekar, T. Bowen, and M. Segal, "On Preventing Intrusions by Process Behavior Monitoring," *Proceedings of the Workshop on Intrusion Detection and Network Monitoring*, pp. 29–40 (Apr. 1999).

811. G. Serrao, "Rating Network Components," *Proceedings of the 18th National Information Systems Security Conference*, pp. 344–355 (Oct. 1995).

812. SET Secure Electronic Transaction LLC, *SET Secure Electronic Transaction Specification, Book 1: Business Description*, Version 1.0 (May 1997).

813. SET Secure Electronic Transaction LLC, *SET Secure Electronic Transaction Specification, Book 2: Programmers' Guide*, Version 1.0 (May 1997).

814. SET Secure Electronic Transaction LLC, *SET Secure Electronic Transaction Specification, Book 3: Formal Protocol Definition*, Version 1.0 (May 1997).

815. A. Shamir, "How to Share a Secret," *Communication of the ACM* **22** (11), pp. 612–613 (Nov. 1979).

816. J. Shapiro and N. Hardy, "EROS: A Principle-Driven Operating System from the Ground Up," *IEEE Software* **19** (1), pp. 26–33 (Jan./Feb. 2002).

817. J. Shapiro, J. Smith, and D. Farber, "EROS: A Fast Capability System," *Proceedings of the 17th ACM Symposium on Operating Systems Principles*, pp. 170–185 (Dec. 1999).

818. J. Shapiro and S. Weber, "Verifying the EROS Confinement Mechanism," *Proceedings of the 2000 IEEE Symposium on Security and Privacy*, pp. 166–176 (May 2000).

819. R. Shell, T. Tao, and M. Heckman, "Designing the GEMSOS Security Kernel for Security and Performance," *Proceedings of the 8th National Computer Security Conference*, pp. 108–119 (Oct. 1985).

820. S.-P. Shieh and V. Gligor, "Detecting Illicit Leakage of Information in Operating Systems," *Journal of Computer Security* **4** (2, 3), pp. 123–148 (Dec. 1996).

821. T. Shimomura and J. Markoff, *Takedown: The Pursuit and Capture of Kevin Mitnick, America's Most Wanted Computer Outlaw—By the Man Who Did It*, Hyperion Books, New York, NY (1996).

822. A. Shimizu and S. Miyaguchi, "Fast Data Encipherment Algorithm FEAL," *Advances in Cryptology—Proceedings of EUROCRYPT '87*, pp. 267–278 (1987).

823. R. Shirey, *Security Architecture for Internet Protocols: A Guide for Protocol Designs and Standards*, Internet Draft: draft-irtf-psrg-secarch-sect1-00.txt (Nov. 1994).

824. B. Shneiderman, *Designing the User Interface: Strategies for Effective Human-Computer-Interaction*, 3rd Edition, Addison Wesley Longman, Reading, MA (1998).

825. J. Shoch, "Inter-Network Naming, Addressing, and Routing," *Proceedings of COMPCON '78*, pp. 72–79 (1978).

826. R. Shore, "IGOR: The Intelligence Guard for ONI Replication," *Proceedings of the 19th National Computer Security Conference*, pp. 607–619 (Oct. 1996).

827. W. Sibert, "Auditing in a Distributed System: Secure SunOS Audit Trails," *Proceedings of the 11th National Computer Security Conference*, pp. 81–91 (Oct. 1988).

828. D. Sidhu and M. Gasser, "A Multilevel Secure Local Area Network," *Proceedings of the 1982 IEEE Symposium on Privacy and Security*, pp. 137–143 (Apr. 1982).

829. Silicon Graphics, Inc., *sendmail 8.9.3 for IRIX 6.5.7*, SGI Security Advisory 20000302-01-P3865 (Mar. 2000).

830. G. Simmons, "Forward Search as a Cryptanalytic Tool Against a Public Key Privacy Channel," *Proceedings of the 1982 IEEE Symposium on Security and Privacy*, pp. 117–128 (Apr. 1982).

831. G. Simmons, "How to (Really) Share a Secret," *Advances in Cryptology—Proceedings of CRYPTO '88*, pp. 390–448 (Aug. 1988).

832. G. Simmons, "Prepositioned Secret Sharing Schemes and/or Shared Control Schemes," *Advances in Cryptology—Proceedings of EUROCRYPT '89*, pp. 436–467 (Apr. 1989).

833. G. Simmons, "Geometric Shared Secret and/or Shared Control Schemes," *Advances in Cryptology—Proceedings of CRYPTO '90*, pp. 216–241 (1990).

834. G. Simmons, *Contemporary Cryptology: The Science of Information Integrity*, IEEE Press, Piscataway, NJ (1992).

835. R. Simon and M. Zurko, "Separation of Duty in Role-Based Environments," *Proceedings of the Computer Security Foundations Workshop*, MITRE Technical Report M88-37, MITRE Corporation, Bedford, MA, pp. 183–194 (June 1997).

836. A. Sinkov, *Elementary Cryptanalysis: A Mathematical Approach*, Random House, New York, NY (1968).

837. B. Skingle, S. Valentine, M. Grisoni, A. McLachlan, and J. Fenn, "Trailer—an Inspection and Audit Tool for System-Usage Logs," *Proceedings of the 2nd European Conference*, pp. 151–161 (June 1988).

838. M. Slatalla and J. Quittner, *Masters of Deception: The Gang That Ruled Cyberspace*, Harperperennial Library, New York, NY (1996).

839. M. Sloman, "Policy Driven Management for Distributed Systems," *Journal of Network and Systems Management* **2** (4), pp. 333–360 (Dec. 1994).

840. S. Smaha, "Haystack: An Intrusion Detection System," *Proceedings of the 4th Aerospace Computer Security Applications Conference*, pp. 37–44 (Dec. 1988).

841. C. Small, "Misfit: A Tool for Constructing Safe Extensible C++ Systems," *Proceedings of the 3rd USENIX Conference on Object-Oriented Technologies*, pp. 38–48 (June 1997).

842. G. Smith and D. Volpano, "Secure Information Flow in a Multi-Threaded Imperative Language," *Proceedings of the 25th ACM SIGPLAN-SIGACT Symposium on Principles of Programming Languages*, pp. 355–364 (Jan. 1998).

843. K. Smith and M. Winslett, "Entity Modelling in the MLS Relational Model," *Proceedings of the 18th International Conference on Very Large Data Bases*, pp. 199–210 (Aug. 1992).

844. R. Smith, "Constructing a High Assurance Mail Guard," *Proceedings of the 17th National Computer Security Conference*, pp. 247–253 (Oct. 1994).

845. T. Smith, "User Definable Domains as a Mechanism for Implementing the Least Privilege Principle," *Proceedings of the 9th National Computer Security Conference*, pp. 143–148 (Sep. 1986).

846. S. Snapp, J. Brentano, G. Dias, T. Goan, L. Heberlein, C. Ho, K. Levitt, B. Mukherjee, S. Smaha, T. Grance, D. Teal, and D. Mansur, "DIDS (Distributed Intrusion Detection System): Motivation, Architecture, and an Early Prototype," *Proceedings of the 14th National Computer Security Conference*, pp. 167–176 (Oct. 1991).

847. B. Snow, "The Future Is Not Assured—But It Should Be," *Proceedings of the 1999 IEEE Symposium on Security and Privacy*, pp. 240–241 (May 1999).

848. L. Snyder, "On the Synthesis and Analysis of Protection Systems," *Proceedings of the Sixth Symposium on Operating Systems Principles*, pp. 141–150 (Nov. 1977).

849. L. Snyder, "Formal Models of Capability-Based Protection Systems," *IEEE Transactions on Computers* **30** (3), pp. 172–181 (Mar. 1981).

850. L. Snyder, "Theft and Conspiracy in the Take-Grant Protection Model," *Journal of Computer and System Science* **23** (3), pp. 333–347 (Dec. 1981).

851. M. Sobirey, S. Fischer-Hübner, and K. Rannenberg, "Pseudonymous Audit for Privacy Enhanced Intrusion Detection," *Information Security in Research and Business—Proceedings of the IFIP TC11 13th International Conference on Information Security*, pp. 151–163 (May 1997).

852. S. von Solms and D. Naccache, "On Blind Signatures and Perfect Crimes," *Computers and Security* **11** (6), pp. 581–583 (Oct. 1992).

853. A. Somayaji and S. Forrest, "Automated Response Using System-Call Delays," *Proceedings of the 9th USENIX Security Symposium*, pp. 185–197 (Aug. 2000).

854. A. Somayaji, S. Hofmeyr, and S. Forrest, "Principles of a Computer Immune System," *Proceedings of the 1997 New Security Paradigms Workshop*, pp. 75–82 (Sep. 1997).

855. I. Sommerville, *Software Engineering*, 6th Edition, Addison-Wesley, Boston, MA (2001).

856. S. Son, C. Chaney, and N. Thomlinson, "Partial Security Policies to Support Timeliness in Secure Real-Time Databases," *Proceedings of the 1998 IEEE Symposium on Security and Privacy*, pp. 136–147 (May 1998).

857. E. Spafford, "The Internet Worm Program: An Analysis," *Computer Communications Review* **19** (1), pp. 17–57 (Jan. 1989).

858. E. Spafford, "Crisis and Aftermath," *Communications of the ACM* **32** (6), pp. 678–687 (June 1989).

859. E. Spafford, "Observing Reusable Password Choices," *Proceedings of the 3rd UNIX Security Symposium*, pp. 299–312 (Sep. 1992).

860. E. Spafford, "OPUS: Preventing Weak Password Choices," *Computers and Security* **11** (3), pp. 273–278 (June 1992).

861. E. Spafford, K. Heaphy, and D. Ferbrache, *Computer Viruses: Dealing with Electronic Vandalism and Programmed Threats*, ADAPSO, Arlington, VA (1989).

862. E. Spafford and S. Weeber, "Software Forensics: Can We Track Code to Its Authors?" *Proceedings of the 15th National Information Systems Security Conference*, pp. 641–650 (Oct. 1992).

863. E. Spafford and D. Zamboni, "Intrusion Detection Using Autonomous Agents," *Computer Networks* **34** (4), pp. 547–570 (Oct. 2000).

864. P. Srisuresh and K. Egevang, *Traditional IP Network Address Translator (Traditional NAT)*, RFC 3022 (Jan. 2001).

865. W. Stallings, *Network Security Essentials: Applications and Standards*, Prentice-Hall, Upper Saddle River, NJ (2000).

866. R. Stallman, "The Right to Read," *Communications of the ACM* **40** (2), pp. 85–87 (Dec. 1997).

867. R. Stallman and R. Pesch, "Debugging with GDB: The GNU Source-Level Debugger," www.Iuniverse.com, New York, NY (Dec. 2000).

868. S. Staniford-Chen, S. Cheung, R. Crawford, M. Dilger, J. Frank, J. Hoagland, K. Levitt, C. Wee, R. Yip, and D. Zerkle, "GrIDS—A Graph-Based Intrusion Detection System for Large Networks," *Proceedings of the 19th National Information Systems Security Conference*, pp. 361–370 (Oct. 1996).

869. S. Staniford-Chen and L. Heberlein, "Holding Intruders Accountable on the Internet," *Proceedings of the 1995 IEEE Symposium on Security and Privacy*, pp. 39–49 (May 1995).

870. A. Stavely, *Toward Zero-Defect Programming*, Addison-Wesley, Reading, MA (1998).

871. L. Stein, *Web Security: A Step-by-Step Reference Guide*, Addison-Wesley, Reading, MA (1998).

872. J. Steiner, C. Neuman, and J. Schiller, "Kerberos: An Authentication Service for Open Network Systems," *Proceedings of the 1988 Winter USENIX Conference*, pp. 191–202 (Feb. 1988).

873. B. Sterling, *The Hacker Crackdown: Law and Disorder on the Electronic Frontier*, Bantam Books, New York, NY (1993).

874. H. Stern, M. Eisler, and R. Labiaga, *Managing NFS and NIS*, 2nd Edition, O'Reilly and Associates, Sebastopol, CA (2001).

875. D. Sterne, "On the Buzzword 'Security Policy'," *Proceedings of the 1991 IEEE Symposium on Security and Privacy*, pp. 219–230 (May 1991).

876. F. Stevenson, "Cryptanalysis of Contents Scrambling System" (Nov. 8, 1999); available at http://www.lemuria.org/DeCSS/crypto.gq.nu/.

877. H. Stiegler, "A Structure for Access Control Lists," *Software—Practice and Experience* **9** (10), pp. 813–819 (Oct. 1979).

878. C. Stoll, "Stalking the Wily Hacker," *Communications of the ACM* **31** (5), pp. 484–497 (May 1988).

879. C. Stoll, "An Epidemiology of Viruses and Network Worms," *Proceedings of the 12th National Computer Security Conference*, pp. 369–377 (Oct. 1989).

880. C. Stoll, *The Cuckoo's Egg: Tracking a Spy Through the Maze of Computer Espionage*, Pocket Books, New York, NY (1995).

881. J. Straw, "The Draft Federal Criteria and the ITSEC: Progress Towards Alignment," *Proceedings of the 16th National Computer Security Conference*, pp. 311–323 (Sep. 1993).

882. E. Strother, "Denial of Service Protection—The Nozzle," *Proceedings of the 16th Annual Computer Security Applications Conference*, pp. 32–41 (Dec. 2000).

883. J. Strunk, G. Goodson, M. Scheinholtz, C. Soules, and G. Ganger, "Self-Securing Storage: Protecting Data in Compromised Systems," *Proceedings of the 4th Symposium on Operating Systems Design and Implementation*, pp. 165–179 (Oct. 2000).

884. P. Su and M. Bishop, "How to Encrypt /usr/dict/words in About a Second," Technical Report PCS-TR92-182, Department of Mathematics and Computer Science, Dartmouth College, Hanover, NH (Jan. 1992).

885. J. Sugerman, G. Venkitachalam, and B.-H. Lim, "Virtualizing I/O Devices on VMware Workstation's Hosted Virtual Machine Monitor," *Proceedings of the 2001 USENIX Annual Technical Conference*, pp. 1–14 (June 2001).

886. Sun Microsystems, Inc., *NFS: Network File System Protocol Specification*, RFC 1094 (Mar. 1989).

887. Sun Microsystems, Inc., *Installing, Administering, and Using the Basic Security Module*, Sun Microsystems, Inc., Mountain View, CA (April 1992).

888. Sun Microsystems, Inc., *Version 8.8.8 Sendmail for SunOS™ 5.6 and 5.5.1*, Security Bulletin #00187 (June 1999).

889. Systems Security Engineering Capability Maturity Model Project, *Systems Security Engineering Capability Maturity Model*, Version 2.0 (Apr. 1999).

890. P. Syverson, "Limitations on Design Principles for Public Key Protocols," *Proceedings of the 1996 Symposium on Privacy and Security*, pp. 62–72 (May 1996).

891. T. Takada and H. Koike, "Tudumi: Log Information Visualization System for Intrusion Detection," Technical Report UEC-IS-TR-2000-08, Graduate School of Information Systems, University of Electro-Communications, Chofu, Tokyo, Japan (Sep. 2000).

892. T. Takada and H. Koike, "MieLog: Visual Log Information Browsing System With their Characteristics," *Transactions of the Information Processing Society of Japan*, **41** (12), pp. 3265–3275 (Dec. 2000).

893. A. Tanenbaum, *Modern Operating Systems*, Prentice-Hall, Englewood Cliffs, NJ (1992).

894. A. Tanenbaum, *Computer Networks*, 3rd Edition, Prentice-Hall, Upper Saddle River, NJ (1996).

895. J. Tardo and K. Alagappan, "SPX: Global Authentication Using Public Key Certificates," *Proceedings of the 1991 IEEE Symposium on Research in Security and Privacy*, pp. 232–244 (May 1991).

896. T. Taylor, "Comparison Paper Between the Bell and LaPadula Model and the SRI Model," *Proceedings of the 1984 Symposium on Security and Privacy*, pp. 195–202 (Apr. 1984).

897. H. Teng, K. Chen, and S. Lu, "Adaptive Real-Time Anomaly Detection Using Inductively Generated Sequential Patterns," *Proceedings of the 1990 IEEE Symposium on Research in Security and Privacy*, pp. 278–284 (May 1990).

898. C. Testa, B. Wilner, and V. Gligor, "Trusted RUBIX Architecture and Policy Model Interpretation," *Proceedings of the 8th Annual Computer Security Applications Conference*, pp. 97–110 (Nov./Dec. 1992).

899. K. Thompson, "Reflections on Trusting Trust," *Communications of the ACM* **27** (8), pp. 761–763 (Aug. 1984).

900. D. Thomsen, "Sidewinder: Combining Type Enforcement and UNIX," *Proceedings of the 11th Annual Computer Security Applications Conference*, pp. 14–20 (Dec. 1995).

901. M. Tompa and H. Woll, "How to Share a Secret with Cheaters," *Journal of Cryptology* **1** (2), pp. 133–138 (1988).

902. W. Trapp and L. Washington, *Introduction to Cryptography with Coding Theory*, Prentice-Hall, Upper Saddle River, NJ (2002).

903. J. Trostle, "Modelling a Fuzzy Time System," *Proceedings of the 1993 IEEE Symposium on Research in Security and Privacy*, pp. 82–89 (May 1993).

904. Trusted Information Systems, *A Proposed Interpretation of the TCSEC for Virtual Machine Monitor Architectures*, Trusted Information Systems, Glenwood, MD (May 1990).

905. C.-R. Tsai, V. Gligor, and C. Chandersekaran, "A Formal Method for the Identification of Covert Storage Channels in Source Code," *Proceedings of the 1987 Symposium on Security and Privacy*, pp. 108–121 (Apr. 1987).

906. C.-R. Tsai and V. Gligor, "A Bandwidth Computation Model for Covert Storage Channels and Its Applications," *Proceedings of the 1988 Symposium on Security and Privacy*, pp. 74–86 (Apr. 1988).

907. W. Tuchman, "Hellman Presents No Shortcut Solutions to DES," *IEEE Spectrum* **16** (7), pp. 40–41 (July 1979).

908. W. L. Tuchman and C. Meyer, "Efficacy of the Data Encryption Standard in Data Processing," *Proceedings of Compcon '78*, pp. 340–347 (Sep. 1978).

909. P. Tyner, *iAPX 432 General Data Processor Architecture Reference Manual*, Intel Corporation, Aloha, OR (1981).

910. K. van Wyk and R. Forno, *Incident Response*, O'Reilly and Associates, Inc., Sebastopol, CA 95472 (Aug. 2001).

911. V. Varadharajan, "Security Enhanced Mobile Agents," *Proceedings of the 7th ACM Conference on Computer and Communications Security*, pp. 200–209 (Nov. 2000).

912. W. Venema, "TCP Wrapper: Network Monitoring, Access Control, and Booby Traps," *Proceedings of the 3rd USENIX UNIX Security Symposium*, pp. 85–92 (Sep. 1992).

913. B. Venkatraman and R. Newman-Wolfe, "Capacity Estimation and Auditability of Network Covert Channels," *Proceedings of the 1995 Symposium on Security and Privacy*, pp. 186–198 (May 1995).

914. J. Viega and G. McGraw, *Building Secure Software: How to Avoid Security Problems the Right Way*, Addison-Wesley, Boston, MA (2002).

915. D. Vincenzetti, S. Taino, and F. Bolognesi, "STEL: Secure TELnet," *Proceedings of the 5th USENIX UNIX Security Symposium*, pp. 75–83 (June 1995).

916. Virgil, *The Aeneid* (translated by R. Fitzgerald), Vintage Books, New York, NY (1983).

917. P. Vixie, "DNS and BIND Security Issues," *Proceedings of the 5th USENIX UNIX Security Symposium*, pp. 209–216 (June 1995).

918. J. Voas, A. Ghosh, G. McGraw, P. Charron, and K. Miller, "Defining an Adaptive Software Security Metric from a Dynamic Software Failure

Tolerance Measure," *Proceedings of the 11th Annual Conference on Computer Assurance*, pp. 250–263 (June 1996).

919. C. Vogt, "PUMA: A Capability-Based Architecture to Support Security and Fault Tolerance," *Proceedings of the International Workshop on Computer Architectures to Support Security and Persistence of Information*, pp. 217–228 (May 1990).

920. D. Volpano, C. Irvine, and G. Smith, "A Sound Type System for Secure Flow Analysis," *Journal of Computer Security* **4** (2, 3), pp. 167–187 (1996).

921. V. Voydock and S. Kent, "Security Mechanisms in High-Level Network Protocols," *Computing Surveys* **15** (2), pp. 135–171 (June 1983).

922. J. Wack and L. Carnahan, *Computer Viruses and Related Threats: A Management Guide*, NIST Special Publication 500–166, National Institute of Standards and Technology, Washington, DC (Aug. 1989).

923. D. Wagner, J. Foster, E. Brewer, and A. Aiken, "A First Step Towards Automated Detection of Buffer Overrun Vulnerabilities," *Proceedings of the 2000 Symposium on Network and Distributed System Security*, pp. 1–15 (Feb. 2000).

924. D. Wagner and B. Schneier, "Analysis of the SSL 3.0 Protocol," *Proceedings of the 2nd USENIX Workshop on Electronic Commerce*, pp. 29–40 (Nov. 1996).

925. R. Wahbe, S. Lucco, T. Anderson, and S. Graham, "Efficient Software-Based Fault Isolation," *Proceedings of the 14th Symposium on Operating Systems Principles*, pp. 202–216 (Dec. 1993).

926. M. Wahl, S. Kille, and T. Howes, *Lightweight Directory Access Protocol (v3): UTF-8 String Representation of Distinguished Names*, RFC 2253 (Dec. 1997).

927. M. Waidner and B. Pfitzmann, "The Dining Cryptographers in the Disco: Unconditional Sender and Recipient Untraceability with Computationally Secure Serviceability," *Advances in Cryptology—Proceedings of EUROCRYPT '89*, pp. 690 (Apr. 1989).

928. K. Walker, L. Badger, M. Petkac, D. Sterne, K. Oostendorp, and D. Sherman, "Confining Root Programs with Domain and Type Enforcement (DTE)," *Proceedings of the 6th USENIX Security Symposium*, pp. 21–36 (1996).

929. S. Walker, S. Lipner, C. Ellison, and D. Balenson, "Commercial Key Recovery," *Communications of the ACM* **39** (3), pp. 41–47 (Mar. 1996).

930. L. Wall, T. Christensen, and R. Schwartz, *Programming Perl*, 2nd Edition, O'Reilly and Associates, Sebastopol, CA (Sep. 1996).

931. S. Warren and L. Brandeis, "The Right to Privacy," *Harvard Law Review* **4**, pp. 193ff. (1890).

932. C. Wee, "LAFS: A Logging and Auditing File System," *Proceedings of the 11th Annual Computer Security Applications Conference*, pp. 231–240 (Dec. 1995).

933. M. Weiser, "Program Slicing," *IEEE Transactions on Software Engineering*, **10** (4), pp. 352–357 (July 1984).

934. C. Weissman, "Security Controls in the ADEPT-50 Time-Sharing System," *Proceedings of the 1969 Fall Joint Computer Conference*, pp. 119–133 (Nov. 1969).

935. C. Weismann, "Security Penetration Testing Guideline," Chapter 10, *Handbook for the Computer Security Certification of Trusted Systems*, TM 5540:082A, Naval Research Laboratory, Washington, DC (Jan. 1995).

936. C. Weismann, "Penetration Testing," in *Information Security:An Integrated Collection of Essays* [6], pp. 269–296.

937. D. Wheeler, "Secure Programming for Linux and UNIX HOWTO"; available at http://www.dwheeler.com/secure-programs.

938. T. Whiteside, *Computer Capers: Tales of Electronic Thievery, Embezzlement, and Fraud*, Crowell Publishers, New York, NY (1978).

939. A. Whitten and J. Tygar, "Why Johnny Can't Encrypt: A Usability Evaluation of PGP 5.0," *Proceedings of the 8th USENIX Security Symposium* (Aug. 1999).

940. D. Wichers, D. Cook, R. Olsson, J. Corssley, P. Kerchen, K. Levitt, and R. Lo, "PACLs: An Access Control List Approach to Anti-Viral Security," *Proceedings of the 13th National Computer Security Conference*, pp. 340–349 (Oct. 1990).

941. D. Wiemer and M. Murray, "Wiemer-Murray Domain Security Policy Model for International Interoperability," *Proceedings of the 21st National Information Systems Security Conference*, pp. 526–536 (Oct. 1998).

942. R. Wildes and J. Asmuth, "A System for Automatic Iris Recognition," *Pattern Recognition* **27**, pp. 121–128 (1994).

943. M. Wilkes, *Time-Sharing Computing Systems*, 3rd Edition, Elsevier McDonald Publishing Co., New York, NY (1975).

944. A. Wilkinson, D. Anderson, D. Chang, L. Hin, A. Mayo, I. Viney, R. Williams, and W. Wright, "A Penetration Analysis of a Burroughs Large System," *Operating Systems Review* **15** (1), pp. 14–25 (Jan. 1981).

945. J. Williams and K. Ferraiolo, "P/sup 3/I–Protection Profile Process Improvement," *Proceedings of the 22nd National Information Systems Security Conference*, pp. 175–188 (Oct. 1999).

946. W. Willis, D. Watts, and T. Strahan, *Windows 2000 System Administration Handbook*, Prentice-Hall, Upper Saddle River, NJ (2000).

947. I. Winkler, "The Non-Technical Threat to Computing Systems," *Computing Systems* **9** (1), pp. 3–14 (Winter 1996).

948. H. Winkler-Parenty, "SYBASE: The Trusted Subject DBMS," *Proceedings of the 13th National Computer Security Conference*, pp. 589–593 (Oct. 1990).

949. S. Wiseman, "A Secure Capability Computer System," *Proceedings of the 1986 IEEE Symposium on Security and Privacy*, pp. 86–94 (Apr. 1986).

950. S. Wiseman, "Preventing Viruses in Computer Systems," *Computers and Security* **8** (5), pp. 427–432 (Aug. 1989).

951. T. Woo and S. Lam, "Authentication for Distributed Systems," *IEEE Computer* **25** (1), pp. 39–52 (Jan. 1992).

952. C. Wood, "Principles of Secure Information Systems Design," *Computers and Security* **9** (1), pp. 13–24 (Feb. 1990).

953. C. Wood, "Principles of Secure Information Systems Design with Groupware Examples," *Computers and Security* **12** (7), pp. 663–678 (Nov. 1993).

954. C. Wood, *Information Security Policies Made Easy: A Comprehensive Set of Information Security Policies*, Version 4, Baseline Software, Sausalito, CA (1994).

955. P. Wood and S. Kochan, *UNIX System Security*, Hayden Books, Indianapolis, IN (1985).

956. J. Wray, "An Analysis of Covert Timing Channels," *Proceedings of the 1991 IEEE Symposium on Research in Security and Privacy*, pp. 2–6 (May 1991).

957. W. Wulf, E. Cohen, W. Corwin, A. Jones, R. Levin, C. Pierson, and F. Pollack, "HYDRA: The Kernel of a Multiprocessor System," *Communications of the ACM* **17** (6), pp. 337–345 (June 1974).

958. T. Yetiser, "Polymorphic Viruses: Implementation, Detection, and Protection," VDS Advanced Research Group, Baltimore, MD (Jan. 1993).

959. T. Ylönen, "SSH—Secure Login Connections over the Internet," *Proceedings of the 6th Annual USENIX Security Symposium*, pp. 37–42 (June 1996).

960. C. Young, "Taxonomy of Computer Virus Defense Mechanisms," *Proceedings of the 10th National Computer Security Conference*, pp. 220–225 (Sep. 1987).

961. J. Yuill, F. Wu, J. Settle, F. Gong, R. Forno, M. Huang, and J. Asbery, "Intrusion-Detection for Incident-Response, Using a Military Battlefield-Intelligence Process," *Computer Networks* **34** (4), pp. 671–697 (Oct. 2000).

962. A. Yulie, D. Cohen, and P. Halinan, "Feature Extraction Using a Multilayer Perceptron," *Computer Vision and Pattern Recognition*, pp. 104–109 (1989).

963. Y. Zheng, J. Pieprzyk, and J. Seberry, "HAVAL—A One-Way Hashing Algorithm with Variable Length of Output," *Advances in Cryptology— Proceedings of AUSCRYPT '92*, pp. 83–104 (Dec. 1992).

964. D. Zimmerman, *The Finger User Information Protocol*, RFC 1288 (Dec. 1991).

965. P. Zimmermann, *PGP Source Code and Internals*, MIT Press, Boston, MA (1995).

966. M. Zurko and R. Simon, "User-Centered Security," *Proceedings of the 1996 New Security Paradigms Workshop*, pp. 27–33 (Sep. 1996).

967. E. Zwicky, S. Cooper, and D. Chapman, *Building Internet Firewalls*, 2nd Edition, O'Reilly and Associates, Sebastopol, CA (2000).

968. E. Zwicky, S. Simmons, and R. Dalton, "Policy as a System Administration Tool," *Proceedings of the 4th Systems Administration Conference (LISA 1990)*, pp. 115–124 (Oct. 1990).

Index

Wouldn't it be great

if the world's leading technical publishers joined forces to deliver their best tech books in a common digital reference platform?

They have. Introducing
InformIT Online Books
powered by Safari.

■ Specific answers to specific questions.

ormIT Online Books' powerful search engine gives you relevance-
nked results in a matter of seconds.

■ Immediate results.

ith InformIT Online Books, you can select the book you want
d view the chapter or section you need immediately.

■ Cut, paste and annotate.

ste code to save time and eliminate typographical errors.
ake notes on the material you find useful and choose whether
not to share them with your work group.

■ Customized for your enterprise.

stomize a library for you, your department or your entire
ganization. You only pay for what you need.

et your first 14 days **FREE!**

r a limited time, InformIT Online Books is offering its
embers a 10 book subscription risk-free for 14 days. Visit
tp://www.informit.com/onlinebooks for details.

POWERED BY
Safari®
TECH BOOKS ONLINE®

InformIT Online Books

informit.com/onlinebooks

Register
Your Book

at www.awprofessional.com/register

You may be eligible to receive:

- Advance notice of forthcoming editions of the book
- Related book recommendations
- Chapter excerpts and supplements of forthcoming titles
- Information about special contests and promotions throughout the year
- Notices and reminders about author appearances, tradeshows, and online chats with special guests

Contact us

If you are interested in writing a book or reviewing manuscripts prior to publication, please write to us at:

Editorial Department
Addison-Wesley Professional
75 Arlington Street, Suite 300
Boston, MA 02116 USA
Email: AWPro@aw.com

Visit us on the Web: http://www.awprofessional.com